FONDATION HARDT

POUR L'ÉTUDE DE L'ANTIQUITÉ CLASSIQUE

ENTRETIENS

TOME LXII

LA RHÉTORIQUE DU POUVOIR
UNE EXPLORATION DE L'ART ORATOIRE DÉLIBÉRATIF GREC

ENTRETIENS SUR L'ANTIQUITÉ CLASSIQUE

TOME LXII

LA RHÉTORIQUE DU POUVOIR
UNE EXPLORATION DE L'ART ORATOIRE DÉLIBÉRATIF GREC

NEUF EXPOSÉS
SUIVIS DE DISCUSSIONS
par

Michael Edwards, Christos Kremmydas,
Lene Rubinstein, Angelos Chaniotis,
Jean-Louis Ferrary, Daniela Colomo,
Laurent Pernot, Manfred Kraus, Maria Silvana Celentano

Entretiens préparés par Michael Edwards
et présidés par Pierre Ducrey
24-28 août 2015

Volume édité par Pascale Derron

FONDATION HARDT
POUR L'ÉTUDE DE L'ANTIQUITÉ CLASSIQUE
VANDŒUVRES
2016

Illustration de la jaquette : Démosthène, *Troisième Philippique*, édition de Johann Hervagius, Bâle, 1532, avec le sommaire de Libanius.

© Fondation Martin Bodmer, Cologny.

Réalisation de la jaquette et des planches : Alexandre Pointet, Shaolin-Design, Lausanne.

ISSN 0071-0822
ISBN 978-2-600-00762-7

TABLE DES MATIÈRES

Préface par Pierre DUCREY   VII
Introduction par Michael EDWARDS   1

I.   MICHAEL EDWARDS

     Greek political oratory and the canon of ten Attic
     orators   15

     Discussion   35

II.   CHRISTOS KREMMYDAS

     Demosthenes' Philippics *and the art of characterisation*
     for the Assembly   41

     Discussion   71

III.   LENE RUBINSTEIN

     Envoys and ethos*: team speaking by envoys in classical*
     Greece   79

IV.   ANGELOS CHANIOTIS

     History as an argument in Hellenistic oratory:
     The evidence of Hellenistic decrees   129

     Discussion   175

V.   JEAN-LOUIS FERRARY

     Les Grecs devant le Sénat romain   183

     Discussion   202

VI. Daniela Colomo

Interstate relations: The papyrological evidence 209

Discussion 254

VII. Laurent Pernot

La rhétorique délibérative de Dion de Pruse 261

Discussion 292

VIII. Manfred Kraus

Rhetorik und Macht: Theorie und Praxis der deliberativen Rede in der dritten Sophistik – Libanios und Aphthonios 299

Discussion 332

IX. Maria Silvana Celentano

Giovanni Crisostomo, Sulle statue 2*: omelia e/o orazione politica?* 343

Discussion 369

Index 377

Table des Illustrations 403

Illustrations 405

PRÉFACE

Les anciens Grecs étaient-ils de grands bavards ? Les dieux et les héros de l'*Iliade* et de l'*Odyssée* passent plus de temps à s'apostropher, à s'insulter ou à dire leurs passions qu'à se battre, tout cela dans de longs discours. Heureusement, car sans cela on ignorerait tout de leur pensée profonde. Hérodote, Thucydide, Xénophon, Polybe placent dans la bouche des hommes politiques et généraux des discours composés ou recomposés. Les philosophes ne sont pas en reste. Il suffit d'évoquer les dialogues platoniciens pour saisir que le philosophe préfère donner la parole à Socrate et à ses disciples, plutôt que de rédiger des traités. Démosthène est l'incarnation de l'éloquence antique.

Avant Quintilien, Aristote, le premier, a consacré un ouvrage théorique à l'art oratoire, la *Rhétorique*. Le dramaturge français Jean Racine (1639-1699) en possédait un exemplaire en traduction française, qu'il a lu de près. Il a signé son exemplaire du volume en page de couverture et a enrichi le texte de notes. Par un concours de circonstances qui témoigne du génie de son créateur, Martin Bodmer, la Fondation qui porte son nom, à Cologny, est propriétaire de cet ouvrage unique. Grâce à la générosité de la Fondation Martin Bodmer, nous pouvons reproduire ici la page de couverture signée par Racine de ce volume (pl. 0.1).

C'est à Aristote que l'on doit le classement de la rhétorique en trois genres. Et c'est à ce traité que se réfèrent sans cesse les auteurs des communications que l'on découvrira ci-dessous. Mais les participants aux 62e *Entretiens* de la Fondation Hardt sur l'Antiquité classique, consacrés à "La rhétorique du pouvoir. Une exploration de l'art oratoire délibératif grec", ont à la fois restreint et élargi le propos du philosophe et théoricien de l'art oratoire. En effet, des trois catégories aristotéliciennes, ils n'en ont retenu qu'une, celle qui comprend les discours politiques. Mais le thème traité est infiniment vaste, puisqu'il couvre une période allant du Ve siècle av. J.-C. à l'Antiquité tardive, avec Libanius et Jean Chrysostome. Il couvre en outre deux catégories de sources à première vue extérieures s'agissant de discours, les inscriptions sur pierre et les sources papyrologiques.

On trouvera sous la plume de Michael Edwards, qui était chargé de 'préparer' les *Entretiens*, selon le vocable propre à la Fondation, une présentation des participants, une introduction sur la problématique et un résumé analytique des communications. Nous n'y reviendrons donc pas ici. En revanche, il nous tient à cœur de rappeler comment dès 1952 le baron Kurd von Hardt, créateur de la Fondation, avait prévu de réunir une fois l'an un groupe d'environ huit savants, spécialistes dans leur domaine, autour d'un thème choisi. La formule inventée pour les premiers *Entretiens* est demeurée la même depuis lors.

C'est ainsi que du 24 au 28 août 2015, sept professeurs et chercheurs, deux dames et cinq messieurs, ont dormi, pris leurs repas et échangé leurs vues au siège de la Fondation, à Vandœuvres près de Genève. Chacune et chacun présenta une conférence d'une heure, qui fut suivie d'une discussion de même durée (d'où le terme d'*Entretiens*). Les séances étaient présidées par le soussigné. On a déploré l'absence de Lene Rubinstein, retenue par la maladie de son époux. Heureusement, son texte figure dans le présent volume. Pour des raisons découlant de l'absence de l'oratrice, seule exception à la règle, cette communication, qui fut lue par Christos Kremmydas, n'est pas suivie d'une discussion.

La parution du présent volume marque la fin d'un cycle de plusieurs années : présentation du thème aux membres de la Commission scientifique de la Fondation, délibérations, orales et par échanges écrits, désignation d'un responsable, mise sur pied d'un groupe d'intervenants, hommes et femmes, jeunes et moins jeunes, représentant plusieurs bassins linguistiques et culturels, dans l'esprit de la volonté du baron von Hardt, déroulement des *Entretiens* proprement dits, préparation des manuscrits, édition et finalement publication du volume.

La semaine fut agrémentée d'une visite à la Fondation Martin Bodmer, sous la conduite de son directeur, le professeur Jacques Berchtold, et de la découverte de l'exposition "J'aime les panoramas", au Musée Rath, sous la conduite de la commissaire de l'exposition, Mme Laurence Madeline, conservatrice en chef du pôle Beaux-Arts des Musées d'art et d'histoire de la Ville de Genève.

Les *Entretiens* furent organisés par Gary Vachicouras, aujourd'hui secrétaire général de la Fondation Hardt, assisté de Patricia Burdet, secrétaire, et de Heidi dal Lago, gouvernante et chef de cuisine. Les collaborateurs de la Fondation, le personnel de maison et le jardinier-concierge, ont contribué au succès de la 62ᵉ série des *Entretiens*. L'édition du volume a été assurée par Pascale Derron, docteur ès lettres, bibliothécaire de la Fondation. La jaquette et les planches ont été réalisées par Alexandre Pointet, Shaolin-Design, Lausanne.

Que toutes et tous soient chaleureusement remerciés ici.

Pierre DUCREY,
directeur de la Fondation Hardt

INTRODUCTION

Le discours public joua un rôle important dans la vie des Grecs et des Romains tout au long de l'Antiquité, comme le montrent les œuvres littéraires les plus anciennes, l'*Iliade*, et les plus récentes, celles de Libanius au IVᵉ siècle ap. J.-C., ainsi que d'autres, plus tardives encore. Achille fut un "diseur de paroles" tout autant que l'auteur de grands exploits (*Iliade* 9, 443). Aristote, dont la *Rhétorique* a dominé l'approche occidentale des études dans ce domaine, a classé les discours publics en trois genres: délibératif ou politique, forensique ou judiciaire, enfin épidictique ou démonstratif. Mais, alors que de nombreuses œuvres oratoires nous sont conservées dans deux de ses catégories, judiciaire et démonstrative, très peu d'exemples de la première, délibérative ou politique, nous sont parvenus. C'est pourquoi les *Entretiens* 2015 avaient pour premier objectif l'examen des discours politiques en Grèce ancienne dans divers contextes allant de l'époque classique (Vᵉ-IVᵉ siècles av. J.-C.) à la fin de l'Antiquité. Il importait de compléter l'apport des sources littéraires par le recours aux textes transmis par des papyrus ou des pierres. Le but n'était pas une étude totale ou exhaustive, mais une analyse de quelques auteurs ou de périodes-clés de l'histoire dans un domaine ou une activité qui à plus d'un titre définit le monde grec antique.

La succession des communications suivit pour l'essentiel un ordre chronologique. Le soussigné, professeur de *Classics* à l'Université de Roehampton, président de la Société internationale d'histoire de la rhétorique et spécialiste des orateurs attiques, qui avait 'préparé' les *Entretiens*, a ouvert les feux en passant en revue les fragments de discours politiques des orateurs du 'canon' prédémosthénien.

Christos Kremmydas, chercheur et professeur d'origine grecque, aujourd'hui *Senior Lecturer* en histoire grecque à Royal

Holloway, Université de Londres, a dégagé les principales caractéristiques des discours de Démosthène.

Professeur d'histoire ancienne et collègue de C. Kremmydas à Royal Holloway, Lene Rubinstein, Danoise d'origine, est l'une des meilleures spécialistes du droit grec en Grande-Bretagne. Empêchée de participer aux *Entretiens*, elle accepta que sa communication soit lue par C. Kremmydas. Elle y étudie les discours des ambassadeurs tels que rapportés par Hérodote, Thucydide et Xénophon.

Angelos Chaniotis, membre de la Commission scientifique de la Fondation Hardt, professeur à l'Institute for Advanced Study de Princeton, a examiné, à la lumière des sources épigraphiques, qu'il connaît mieux que personne, les discours des ambassadeurs devant les assemblées des cités à l'époque hellénistique.

Jean-Louis Ferrary, directeur d'études à l'École pratique des Hautes Études à Paris, lui aussi membre de la Commission scientifique de la Fondation Hardt et membre de l'Académie des Inscriptions et Belles-Lettres, est le grand spécialiste des relations entre la Grèce et Rome à l'époque républicaine. Excellent connaisseur de Polybe et de Cicéron, épigraphiste confirmé, il s'est penché sur les discours prononcés par les ambassadeurs grecs devant le Sénat de Rome.

Après des études à la Scuola Normale Superiore de Pise, Daniela Colomo s'est concentrée sur la papyrologie. Elle occupe aujourd'hui un poste de chercheuse à l'Université d'Oxford et d'associée de recherches et de conservatrice de la collection des papyrus d'Oxyrhynque. Reconnue comme la meilleure spécialiste des papyrus égyptiens touchant à l'art oratoire et à la rhétorique, elle a présenté une communication sur la place qu'occupe la rhétorique délibérative ou politique dans les relations entre l'Égypte et Rome durant les trois premiers siècles de notre ère.

Laurent Pernot, professeur à l'Université de Strasbourg, membre de l'Académie des Inscriptions et Belles-Lettres et ancien président de la Société internationale d'histoire de la rhétorique, a mis en évidence le rôle central de Dion de Pruse dans toute analyse de la rhétorique politique sous l'Empire romain.

Manfred Kraus enseigne à l'Université de Tübingen. Comme L. Pernot, il est un ancien président de la Société internationale d'histoire de la rhétorique. Expert des *progymnasmata* ou exercices préparatoires de rhétorique, il s'est intéressé à la figure de Libanius comme orateur politique et à son influence dans les cercles les plus haut placés d'Antioche.

Enfin, dernière personne à prendre la parole dans ces *Entretiens*, Maria Silvana Celentano, professeur à l'Université de Chieti-Pescara, ancien membre du Comité de la Société internationale de l'histoire de la rhétorique et présidente du Comité des programmes de la conférence 2015 de la société, s'est arrêtée sur un ensemble de textes de Jean Chrysostome, les homélies, peu étudié jusqu'ici dans le contexte de la rhétorique politique.

Cette réunion de philologues, d'historiens, d'épigraphistes, de papyrologues et de spécialistes de la rhétorique est bien conforme à la tradition des *Entretiens*. Les participants proposent, dans un esprit d'échanges académiques, des approches différentes, mais complémentaires, des textes. Les discussions qui suivirent les exposés témoignent d'une démarche rigoureusement scientifique. Nous en donnons ci-dessous des reflets plus détaillés.

Analyse et résumé des communications

Athènes, à l'époque où elle jouit d'un régime démocratique, est la cité par excellence où s'épanouit l'art oratoire politique. Les textes les mieux conservés proviennent en majorité du corpus des discours de Démosthène, dont tous les composants ne sont d'ailleurs pas authentiques. Un très petit nombre seulement des discours politiques de ses adversaires nous sont parvenus et moins nombreux encore sont les discours conservés du Ve siècle, l'époque de la gloire d'Athènes. Ce phénomène est dû au fait que l'art d'écrire des discours, y compris politiques, et de les publier n'était guère pratiqué à cette époque. La contribution du soussigné aux *Entretiens* consiste à examiner les modestes vestiges et fragments des discours politiques laissés par les membres du 'canon' des dix orateurs attiques avec en arrière-plan la théorie d'Aristote exposée dans sa *Rhétorique*.

Le choix des dix orateurs du canon remonte peut-être à l'Alexandrie de l'époque hellénistique. Il s'agit des représentants les plus notoires de l'art oratoire athénien, toutes catégories confondues. Toutefois, bien que la majorité d'entre les auteurs aient été des politiciens en vue qui ont adressé leurs discours à l'Assemblée (ou les aient rédigés pour qu'ils y soient lus), c'est essentiellement leur œuvre judiciaire qui nous est parvenue. Nous savons cependant qu'ils ont aussi prononcé des discours politiques, aujourd'hui perdus pour toutes sortes de raisons. Et pourtant des choix de discours avaient été faits dans l'Antiquité. Mais ceux-ci sont devenus des 'florilèges' contenant essentiellement des discours judiciaires. Le troisième discours d'Andocide, *Sur la paix avec les Spartiates*, offre un bon exemple de discours politique. En revanche, les fragments préservés des autres orateurs, surtout ceux de la période prédémosthénienne, sont moins caractéristiques.

Pour parler de Démosthène, le choix allait de soi, car il n'est pas de meilleur connaisseur du grand orateur attique, et tout particulièrement de son *Contre Leptine*, que Christos Kremmydas, dont la thèse de doctorat, soutenue en 2005, est consacrée à ce plaidoyer. Kremmydas s'appuie lui aussi sur la *Rhétorique* d'Aristote. Il insiste sur l'importance de la "caractérisation" (*ethos*) dans l'art de la persuasion. Par *ethos*, on entend l'image que l'orateur donne de lui-même dans son discours. Kremmydas examine comment celle de Démosthène évolue de 354 à 341, au fil de ses discours contre Philippe II de Macédoine et ses partisans (*Philippiques*) devant l'Assemblée d'Athènes. La troisième *Olynthienne* et la troisième *Philippique* sont des œuvres-clés dans l'analyse de Kremmydas, ce qui ne l'empêche pas de s'intéresser aussi aux autres. Il montre comment les interventions de l'orateur le présentent de plus en plus sûr de lui et attaquant ses adversaires avec une hostilité sans cesse croissante. L'évolution de son caractère montre à quel point Démosthène reflète ce que Kremmydas appelle à juste titre la "toxicité" de la politique à Athènes à la fin des années 340 et en tire profit.

L'exposé de Kremmydas marque la fin de la partie des *Entretiens* consacrée à l'étude des discours conservés en tout ou en partie dans le 'canon'. Mais la conférence se proposait aussi d'explorer d'autres genres oratoires pour tout ce qu'ils apportent à notre connaissance de la rhétorique politique grecque. L'historiographie ou l'art d'écrire l'histoire est notre seconde source majeure d'information sur le discours public au Vᵉ et au IVᵉ siècle av. J.-C. Nous 'entendons' les discours des grands politiciens athéniens grâce à la plume des historiens, Thémistocle chez Hérodote ou Périclès chez Thucydide. Les paroles de Xénophon chef militaire nous parviennent par l'intermédiaire des œuvres de Xénophon historien, preuve par ailleurs que l'Assemblée n'était pas le seul lieu où se tenait le discours public. L'ambassade, la mission d'ambassadeur offraient d'autres occasions d'exercer son éloquence, occasions où l'*ethos* de l'intéressé, l'image qu'il donnait de sa personne, avait aussi son importance.

Ce type d'allocution fait l'objet de la contribution de Lene Rubinstein, consacrées aux discours d'ambassadeurs et autres envoyés chez Hérodote et Thucydide ou encore dans les traités historiques de Xénophon, l'*Anabase* et les *Helléniques*. L'*ethos* des orateurs y est mis en évidence, mais aussi le travail d'équipe et la répartition des tâches entre les ambassadeurs, tactique notoirement négligée par les missions des Athéniens auprès de Philippe II, qui incluaient deux adversaires acharnés, Démosthène et Eschine. L. Rubinstein analyse les discours d'envoyés en divers lieux, y compris le camp des Dix Mille, où Xénophon reçoit une délégation des Sinopéens. Elle s'arrête à deux épisodes rapportés par les historiens au cours desquels des ambassadeurs ont prononcé leurs discours en style 'direct', l'ambassade des Athéniens à Sparte en 371 et celle des Péloponnésiens à Athènes en 370/369.

Ce n'est pas un hasard si certains des meilleurs discours politiques conservés ont été prononcés en période de crise. Lorsque les Grecs perdent leur indépendance, d'abord par suite de la conquête macédonienne, plus tard de la conquête romaine, le type de discours nationaliste incarné par Démosthène disparaît, mais pas pour autant le discours politique. À l'époque hellénistique, les discours effectivement prononcés cèdent la place dans nos sources à ceux dont rendent compte les traités des historiens, Polybe marchant dans les pas d'Hérodote, de Thucydide et de Xénophon. Pour cette période, les sources épigraphiques sont aussi d'un apport précieux. On pense en particulier aux textes des décrets qui rappellent les décisions prises par de nombreux États du monde hellénistique, principalement pour honorer leurs bienfaiteurs.

Angelos Chaniotis est l'un des meilleurs historiens actuels de l'époque hellénistique. S'appuyant sur Polybe et une série d'inscriptions, il analyse les stratégies oratoires employées par les politiciens et les ambassadeurs devant les assemblées du monde grec. Il s'attache tout particulièrement à mettre en évidence d'une manière très convaincante le recours régulier à une argumentation basée sur le passé historique. Après avoir passé en revue les sources rapportant l'usage de discours 'indirects', il analyse dans le détail une série de textes, littéraires et épigraphiques, utilisant le passé historique dans la perspective d'arguments faisant appel tantôt à la raison, tantôt à l'émotion. À titre d'exemple, le décret proposé par Chrémonidès à Athènes en 267 pour ratifier une alliance entre Athènes, Sparte et d'autres cités grecques, qui conduisit à la Guerre de Chrémonidès ; les discours prononcés en 210 et rapportés par Polybe de l'Étolien Chlénéas, un allié des Romains, et de l'Acarnanien Lykiskos, un allié des Macédoniens, dans le but de convaincre les Spartiates de devenir leurs alliés ; un décret de Milet reprenant les arguments de Peithenous, fils de Tharsagoras, à l'appui de sa proposition de traité entre la cité de Milet et le roi Ptolémée II ;

un document dans lequel le préteur romain M. Valerius Messalla justifie la garantie de l'inviolabilité de Téos en soulignant le rôle de la piété ; enfin le recours au thème de la mémoire culturelle, resté sans effet en 87 av. J.-C., dans un discours des délégués athéniens résumé par Plutarque pour tenter d'obtenir que Sylla lève son siège d'Athènes.

Les *Entretiens* ont bénéficié de la participation d'un second spécialiste distingué de l'époque hellénistique en la personne de Jean-Louis Ferrary. Celui-ci s'appuie sur sa vaste érudition pour présenter une analyse détaillée des tactiques mises en œuvre par les envoyés grecs comparaissant devant le Sénat romain et devant l'empereur Claude. Leurs discours consistent notamment à rappeler leur fidélité envers Rome et les services que leurs cités lui ont rendus dans le passé. J.-L. Ferrary cite pour exemples le discours d'Apollonius Molon, adressé au Sénat en grec ; ou encore, plus d'un siècle plus tard, une inscription découverte à Samothrace, selon laquelle la cité libre et fédérée de Maronée obtint de l'empereur Claude la pleine restitution de ses droits grâce à l'envoi d'une ambassade, qui évoqua devant lui la fidélité dont la cité avait fait preuve pendant la guerre de Mithridate. L'exercice n'était cependant pas sans risques : mentionner les services rendus aux Romains exposait les envoyés au reproche de *superbia*: ainsi, lorsque l'ambassadeur rhodien Archélaos rappela à Cassius la dette de Rome envers Rhodes, et accessoirement qu'il avait été lui-même le professeur d'éloquence du général, les Romains répliquèrent en punissant sévèrement la ville. Enfin, J.-L. Ferrary soulève une question devenue un thème récurrent de ces *Entretiens*, à savoir dans quelle mesure le discours des ambassadeurs (*presbeutikos logos*) trouve place dans les trois catégories aristotéliciennes mentionnées plus haut ou si ces catégories se multiplient dans la théorie rhétorique ultérieure.

Ces deux communications promettent de devenir une référence pour l'étude en pleine expansion de l'art oratoire et de la rhétorique à l'époque hellénistique. Une troisième communication portant sur les relations inter-cités ou inter-États conduit les *Entretiens* plus tard dans la chronologie et plus loin dans la géographie. Avec Daniela Colomo, on s'intéresse au rôle de la rhétorique dans les relations entre l'Égypte et Rome. La validité du classement tripartite d'Aristote est à nouveau mise en question, car les genres judiciaire, politique et épidictique se superposent alors dans les discours des ambassadeurs. D. Colomo se penche principalement sur la tactique adoptée par les ambassades grecques et juives à la lumière des textes de Philon d'Alexandrie et de Flavius Josèphe, avec en complément la collection des textes pseudo-littéraires connue sous le nom d'*Acta Alexandrinorum*. Ce document donne des récits romancés des ambassades alexandrines auprès des empereurs romains, tout en se conformant au modèle des comptes rendus officiels de la cour (*acta*). Ces textes montrent que les envoyés alexandrins ne se distinguaient nullement des autres ambassadeurs. Il faut dire que dès l'origine des relations entre les Romains et les Égyptiens, les Grecs d'Alexandrie se sont efforcés de préserver leur indépendance, alors que les Juifs, au contraire, tendaient à soutenir le point de vue de Rome. Il s'en est suivi que les auditions impériales revêtaient la forme d'une confrontation devant un juge, selon la procédure légale instaurée par Auguste de *cognitio extra ordinem* (juridiction impériale) avec pour conséquence que les Alexandrins furent régulièrement (mais pas toujours) condamnés à mort. D. Colomo s'appuie sur les *Acta Isidori* pour étudier le statut des Juifs d'Alexandrie sous Gaius et Claudius, sur les *Acta Hermaisci,* qui relatent l'audition d'ambassades juives et grecques par Trajan, sur les *Acta Appiani*, pour la confrontation du gymnasiarque Appien et de l'empereur Commode, enfin sur le papyrus *P.Giss.Lit.* 4, 7, qui rapporte comment les Grecs d'Alexandrie sont parvenus dans une audience à se rallier l'empereur Caligula au détriment des Juifs. L'auteur évoque la question de la fiabilité des sources, que ce soient les auteurs mentionnés ci-dessus ou les écrits apologétiques comme ceux de Philon d'Alexandrie ou de Flavius Josèphe.

L'art oratoire grec et la rhétorique sont florissants à l'époque impériale. Les trois dernières communications ont trait aux orateurs actifs aux origines du christianisme. Dion de Pruse, connu aussi sous le nom de Dion Chrysostome, était l'un des plus célèbres rhéteurs de ce que l'on appelle la Seconde Sophistique, dont l'*akmé* se situe au début du IIe siècle ap. J.-C. Le corpus de ses œuvres, qui compte quatre-vingts textes, comprend quatre discours sur le pouvoir adressés à l'empereur Trajan et des discours politiques pour louer ou blâmer des cités et des États. Laurent Pernot choisit de présenter et d'étudier ce riche ensemble de textes. Il souligne l'importance accordée par Dion à la philosophie dans les discours politiques et montre aussi comment l'éloquence délibérative ou politique s'adapte aux nouvelles conditions régnant dans le monde grec sous domination romaine, en l'occurrence dans la province de Bithynie en Asie Mineure. Dion ne manque pas de relever ce changement lorsqu'il s'adresse aux Rhodiens. En conséquence, les trois catégories de discours établies par Aristote dans la *Rhétorique* et énoncées dans le texte contemporain *La Rhétorique à Alexandre* ne conviennent pas aux discours d'un personnage comme Dion. Cela vaut tout particulièrement pour le genre délibératif, ainsi que le remarque Quintilien dans son *Institutio oratoria*. Aussi L. Pernot préfère-t-il le terme "rhétorique du conseil", sous lequel il réunit le dialogue *Sur la délibération* (*Or.* 26) et le *Discours eubéen* (*Or.* 7). Il montre comment, selon Dion, le philosophe doit s'engager en politique et la politique doit être philosophique. Il tente un classement des discours qui contiennent des conseils politiques et philosophiques et dégage quelques caractéristiques de la rhétorique délibérative de Dion. Ce dernier note, contre l'avis des théoriciens, que ses conseils sont accompagnés de reproches. Deux thèmes retiennent une attention spéciale, ceux de l'hellénisme et de l'autorité romaine. L. Pernot conclut comme les intervenants antérieurs en soulignant l'importance de l'*ethos* de l'orateur dans le genre délibératif.

Le prochain grand ensemble de discours politiques grecs appartient au IVe siècle ap. J.-C. et provient d'une ville plus éloignée encore, Antioche. Il s'agit des œuvres de Libanius, dont soixante-quatre se rattachant aux trois catégories d'Aristote. Les liens d'amitié qu'entretenait Libanius avec l'empereur Julien l'Apostat, mais aussi avec des personnages haut placés de son entourage de religion chrétienne illustrent son rôle de conseiller politique. De plus, le fait qu'il occupait ce que nous appellerions aujourd'hui la chaire de rhétorique d'Antioche indique qu'il était un formateur et éducateur reconnu. De son enseignement, nous conservons cinquante et une déclamations commentant les discours de Démosthène (*hypothèses*), ainsi que de nombreux modèles d'exercices écrits (*progymnasmata*). Ces derniers le rapprochent de son ami Aphthonius, dont le manuel *progymnasmata* est l'un des quatre ouvrages analogues qui nous sont parvenus. Ces importants exposés de la théorie et de la pratique des discours délibératifs sont remarquablement analysés par Manfred Kraus, qui se fait l'avocat d'une Troisième Sophistique et affirme que l'art oratoire et la rhétorique de cette période ne devraient pas être considérés comme étant en déclin.

M. Kraus commence par explorer l'origine de ces idées, qui doivent beaucoup aux travaux de Laurent Pernot et s'élève contre leur mise en cause récente. Il passe ensuite à Libanius, incarnation de l'art oratoire délibératif à la fin de l'époque impériale. Il décrit le contexte dans lequel il exerce, l'Empire romain au IVe siècle ap. J.-C. Les circonstances sont bien différentes de celles qui régnaient à Athènes au IVe siècle av. J.-C., réalité dont Libanius lui-même était parfaitement conscient. L'orateur joua un grand rôle comme conseiller des autorités d'Antioche, même si certains de ses discours au contenu particulièrement critique n'étaient peut-être pas destinés à être publiés. M. Kraus s'intéresse au programme de l'école de Libanius. Il observe qu'en dépit de la prééminence du genre oratoire épidictique dans l'Antiquité tardive, les anciennes méthodes de formation dans les genres délibératif et judiciaire restaient en vigueur, à en juger par les exercices d'éloquence (*progymnasmata*). Les thèmes traditionnels continuent à être traités, comme par exemple les attaques contre la tyrannie. En comparant leurs œuvres, M. Kraus relève que l'enseignement d'Aphthonius et de Libanius s'appuyait sur la tradition païenne dans une ville, Antioche, qui à leur époque était à quatre-vingts pour cent peuplée de chrétiens. Il montre que la division aristotélicienne entre les genres judiciaire et délibératif est brouillée chez Libanius en se fondant sur l'analyse d'une série de ses déclamations et de ses discours politiques. Ces derniers sous-entendent qu'une position sociale élevée et un réseau de personnalités susceptibles de vous protéger sont des conditions indispensables pour pouvoir participer activement à la vie politique de l'époque.

Le riche corpus des homélies prononcées par Jean Chrysostome offre un excellent exemple de la manière dont la rhétorique classique, et particulièrement celle de Libanius, était mise en pratique dans l'Antiquité tardive, notamment dans un contexte chrétien. Jean Chrysostome est le sujet de la dernière communication de la série, celle de Maria Silvana Celentano. À l'instar de Libanius, Jean est né à Antioche au milieu du IVe siècle ap. J.-C. Il fut l'élève de Libanius, bien que de foi chrétienne. Alors que ce dernier est resté professeur de rhétorique, Jean est devenu archevêque de Constantinople. M.S. Celentano analyse la seconde homélie de Jean Chysostome, *Sur les statues*, discours politique nourri de la formation de l'auteur à la rhétorique et de son expérience dans cet art. Cette homélie fut prononcée en 387 ap. J.-C. à la suite de l'émeute des statues, au cours de laquelle des statues des membres de la famille impériale furent abattues pour protester contre les impôts nouveaux imposés par l'empereur Théodose Ier. M.S. Celentano s'arrête sur la structure bipartite de l'homélie, la première étant consacrée à la situation critique dans laquelle se trouve la cité, que Jean compare à celle de Job, et la seconde, inspirée par la lecture du jour, l'enseignement de l'apôtre Paul sur la richesse. M.S. Celentano étudie les douze sections de la première partie de l'homélie et les méthodes rhétoriques appliquées par Jean. Selon elle, la méthode consistant à recourir tour à tour aux émotions, aux réprimandes, aux exhortations et à la

raison permet au chercheur moderne d'imaginer la manière
dont l'homélie fut prononcée et l'effet que faisait l'orateur sur
son public.

Comme il est d'usage dans les *Entretiens*, chaque session
comprend deux parties, l'une consacrée à l'exposé, la seconde à
la discussion. Inévitablement, dans une conférence consacrée à
la pratique du modèle le plus noble de l'art oratoire grec, le
genre délibératif ou politique, et à la réflexion théorique sous-
jacente, la figure d'Aristote se profile à l'arrière-plan de toutes
les discussions. L'une des observations ressorties des débats
portait sur l'influence disproportionnée exercée par le Stagirite
sur les aspects théoriques de l'art oratoire, aussi bien dans
l'Antiquité qu'aujourd'hui. Son classement en trois catégories
ou trois genres s'est maintenu jusqu'à celui qui fut peut-être le
plus grand des rhétoriciens, Quintilien, et même jusqu'à la
science moderne. Il reste qu'il est forgé par la situation politique, constitutionnelle et sociale d'Athènes. Or la cité a connu
sa période la plus glorieuse au Ve et au IVe siècle av. J.-C.
À cette époque, elle jouit d'un système démocratique appuyé
sur une assemblée composée de citoyens mâles. De constantes
menaces militaires pèsent cependant sur elle, internes à la Grèce,
en particulier du fait de Sparte, et externes, en provenance de
la Perse, tout au long de la période, puis de la Macédoine qui
grandit en puissance et en influence.

C'est cette situation qui a donné naissance au genre oratoire
délibératif ou politique, dont les spécificités et la force atteintes
alors sont restées inégalées en Grèce ancienne. Les *Philippiques*
de Démosthène ont inspiré Cicéron dans son combat contre la
tyrannie avinée de Marc Antoine et servirent de modèle durant
des siècles dans la lutte pour la liberté. Pour prendre un exemple
dans l'histoire de l'Angleterre, Élizabeth I a étudié les *Philippiques* avec son maître Roger Ascham avant de devenir la souveraine d'une nation qui dut faire face à une invasion conduite
par un autre Philippe, le deuxième, alors roi d'Espagne en
1588. Mais la Grèce ancienne devait connaître encore sept
siècles d'histoire politique, durant lesquels les pratiques de ses

orateurs évolueront profondément. Ils feront face à la demande de multiples manières et recevront une formation très différente de celle qu'avait proposée ou même recommandée Aristote en d'autres temps. Les participants aux *Entretiens* 2015 se sont livrés à une exploration de la rhétorique dans le monde classique, non sans se pencher aussi sur l'évolution qu'elle connut dans les siècles ultérieurs.

Michael EDWARDS
(Traduction Pierre Ducrey)

I

Michael Edwards

GREEK POLITICAL ORATORY AND THE CANON OF
TEN ATTIC ORATORS

My purpose in this paper is to set the scene for the discussion of later Greek deliberative oratory by surveying the largely fragmentary evidence we have of the practice of political speaking during the classical period of the 5th and 4th centuries BC, with a focus on the ten members of the later Canon.[1] The great irony of Athenian political oratory from the period that was to be so influential on later oratorical practice, rhetorical theory, literary criticism and education is, of course, that so little of it survives, even though in rhetorical theory deliberative oratory was often assigned the first place in importance, preceding mention of judicial and epideictic. So Aristotle at the start of the *Rhetoric* (1, 1, 10):

> "It is for this reason that although the method of deliberative and judicial speaking is the same and though deliberative subjects are finer and more important to the state than private transactions ..." (trans. Kennedy)[2]

And again, a little later on (*Rhet.* 1, 3, 2-3):

> "Now it is necessary for the hearer to be either a spectator or a judge, and [in the latter case] a judge of either past or future

---

[1] For a recent survey on the likely date and compiler of the Canon see Roisman / Worthington (2015) 6-9.

[2] διὰ γὰρ τοῦτο τῆς αὐτῆς οὔσης μεθόδου περὶ τὰ δημηγορικὰ καὶ δικανικά, καὶ καλλίονος καὶ πολιτικωτέρας τῆς δημηγορικῆς πραγματείας οὔσης ἢ τῆς περὶ τὰ συναλλάγματα ...

happenings. A member of a democratic assembly is an example of one judging about future happenings, a juryman an example of one judging the past. A spectator is concerned with the ability [of the speaker]. Thus, there would necessarily be three genera of rhetorics; *symbouleutikon* ["deliberative"], *dikanikon* ["judicial"], *epideiktikon* ["demonstrative"]." (trans. Kennedy)[3]

On the other hand, Laurent Pernot, in his excellent survey of *Rhetoric in Antiquity*,[4] details "The Practice of Oratory", and treats the contexts of judicial and political oratory in that order, thereby reflecting the actual state of affairs in what remains of both Athenian oratory and rhetorical theory. Now, it may well be that the standard version of why in practice the judicial predominates is correct. For example, as George Kennedy stated, "(t)he statesmen of the 5th century did not publish their orations and perhaps made little or no use of writing in composing them ... deliberative oratory was not regarded as a literary form".[5] But as Kennedy himself indicates, there is evidence that there were both deliberative speeches which *were* written down during the 5th century, and theoretical works about how to write them. In the latter category Kennedy mentions the *Demegoric prooemia* of Critias (Hermogenes, *Peri Ideon* 2, 11, p. 402 Rabe). Into the former category falls Antiphon, the first in the Canon of Ten Attic Orators.

According to Thucydides (8, 68, 1), Antiphon never willingly spoke in the assembly because of his reputation for cleverness. However,

τοὺς μέντοι ἀγωνιζομένους καὶ ἐν δικαστηρίῳ καὶ ἐν δήμῳ πλεῖστα εἷς ἀνήρ, ὅστις ξυμβουλεύσαιτό τι, δυνάμενος ὠφελεῖν. "(W)hen other people were engaged in lawsuits or had points to make before the assembly, he was the man to give the best and

---

[3] ἀνάγκη δὲ τὸν ἀκροατὴν ἢ θεωρὸν εἶναι ἢ κριτήν, κριτὴν δὲ ἢ τῶν γεγενη-μένων ἢ τῶν μελλόντων. ἔστιν δ' ὁ μὲν περὶ τῶν μελλόντων κρίνων ὁ ἐκκλησια-στής, ὁ δὲ περὶ τῶν γεγενημένων [οἷον] ὁ δικαστής, ὁ δὲ περὶ τῆς δυνάμεως ὁ θεωρός, ὥστ' ἐξ ἀνάγκης ἂν εἴη τρία γένη τῶν λόγων τῶν ῥητορικῶν, συμβου-λευτικόν, δικανικόν, ἐπιδεικτικόν.
[4] PERNOT (2005) 24-26.
[5] KENNEDY (1963) 203.

most helpful advice to those who asked him for it." (trans. Warner)

In my opinion, commentators have paid insufficient attention to the phrase ἐν δήμῳ, which is strengthened by the καὶ ... καὶ ... correspondence. It is dismissed by Simon Hornblower in his *Commentary on Thucydides* as "perhaps something of a tag";[6] and the focus has been on Antiphon's activities as a forensic logographer and whether or not he was the first to publish speeches.[7] But Thucydides' statement, which is later reflected by Hermogenes (*Peri Ideon* 2, 11, p. 400 Rabe),[8] should not be lightly dismissed when we have evidence that Antiphon did indeed compose at least two deliberative speeches, *On the Tribute of the Lindians* and *On the Tribute of the Samothracians*.[9] Hornblower questions whether these speeches were delivered in the assembly or rather before the Council – I do not follow his logic that ἐς ἄλλον ἀγῶνα does not indicate the courts, because "it is agreed that Antiphon appeared in court", and so might mean the Council, when he goes on to say that Thucydides' "formulation (ἑκούσιος, "willingly") in any case allows some degree of participation in both assembly and whatever the 'other arenas' may be" – which therefore, to my mind, "allows some degree of participation" in the courts as well (presumably Antiphon will not "willingly" have stood trial for his role in the revolution of the Four Hundred). Further, while Hornblower may be right to note that the two tribute speeches are assigned to the assembly in the Loeb translation without ancient authority, and hence "(t)he Council is as least as likely", the flow of Thucydides' sentence (καὶ ἐς μὲν δῆμον οὐ παριὼν οὐδ᾽ ἐς ἄλλον ἀγῶνα ἑκούσιος οὐδένα ... τοὺς μέντοι ἀγωνιζομένους καὶ ἐν δικαστηρίῳ καὶ ἐν δήμῳ ...) suggests to me that

---

[6] HORNBLOWER (2008) 956.

[7] See, for example, EDWARDS (2000).

[8] οὗπερ οἱ φονικοὶ φέρονται λόγοι καὶ οἱ δημηγορικοὶ ... ("to whom the speeches about homicide, as well as deliberative speeches ... are attributed") (trans. WOOTEN).

[9] Frgs 25-33 and 49-56 THALHEIM; see MAIDMENT (1941) 290-293.

he is referring chiastically to the same arenas, even if ἄλλον ἀγῶνα ... οὐδένα may also bring in the Council. Either way, Antiphon is composing deliberative speeches for others to deliver.

I have one observation to make at this point on the four fragments that survive of the speech for the Samothracians in later writers. This is, that three of the four could easily derive from a narrative section or sections of the speech.[10] All three, indeed, begin with the particle γάρ, which is a regular indicator of the start of the narrative in the orators, although interestingly none of the narratives in the three surviving judicial speeches of Antiphon have it:[11]

καὶ γὰρ οἱ τὴν ἀρχὴν οἰκίσαντες τὴν νῆσον ἦσαν Σάμιοι, ἐξ ὧν ἡμεῖς ἐγενόμεθα. κατῳκίσθησαν δὲ ἀνάγκῃ, οὐκ ἐπιθυμίᾳ τῆς νήσου· ἐξέπεσον γὰρ ὑπὸ τυράννων ἐκ Σάμου καὶ τύχῃ ἐχρήσαντο ταύτῃ ... καὶ λείαν λαβόντες ἀπὸ τῆς Θρᾴκης ἀφικνοῦνται εἰς τὴν νῆσον. (frg. 49 Thalheim = Suidas, s.v. Σαμοθράκη)
"For those who originally occupied the island were Samians; and from them we are descended. They settled there from force of circumstances, not from any desire for the island; for they were driven from Samos by tyrants and met with the following adventures ... and after a successful raid on Thrace they reached the island." (trans. Maidment)

ἡ <μὲν> γὰρ νῆσος, ἣν ἔχομεν, δήλη μὲν καὶ πόρρωθεν <ὅτι> ἐστὶν ὑψηλὴ καὶ τραχεῖα· καὶ τὰ μὲν χρήσιμα καὶ ἐργάσιμα μικρὰ αὐτῆς ἐστι, τὰ δ' ἀργὰ πολλά, μικρᾶς αὐτῆς οὔσης. (frg. 50 Thalheim = Demetrius, On Style 53)
"For the island we inhabit is mountainous and rocky, as can be seen even from afar. It is but small; yet the productive and cultivable portion is small, and the unproductive large." (trans. Maidment)

---

[10] The other, frg. 51 THALHEIM (= PRISCIAN 18, 280), could also, but is more likely to come from the proofs section: καίτοι οὐκ ἂν τῆς μὲν τῶν ἄλλων πολιτῶν ταλαιπωρίας προὐσκέψαντο, τῆς δὲ σφετέρας αὐτῶν σωτηρίας οὐκ ἐνεθυμήθησαν ("Yet if they were concerned for the sufferings of their fellows, they can hardly have failed to take thought for their own lives") (trans. MAIDMENT).

[11] The narrative of speech 1, Against the Stepmother (14-20) has a tripartite structure, in which the third and main part in § 18 does begin with γάρ. See EDWARDS (2004) 60-61.

ἡρέθησαν γὰρ ἐκλογῆς παρ' ἡμῖν οἷς πλεῖστα ἐδόκει χρήματα εἶναι. (frg. 52 Thalheim, = Harpocration, *s.v.* ἐκλογεῖς) "Those of us were appointed Collectors who were reputed the wealthiest." (trans. Maidment)

This is interesting because, as is well known, Aristotle in the *Rhetoric* (3, 16, 11) begins his very brief discussion of deliberative narrative with the statement that "(n)arrative is least common in deliberative oratory, because no one narrates future events". However, Aristotle goes on to suggest two things, that if there is a narrative of past events it will serve to remind the audience about them and take better counsel for the future; and if something is unbelievable, the speaker should "promise to tell the cause of it immediately and to refer [judgment] to somebody". Both pieces of advice apply here, the first to frg. 50 (not an event, but a geographical feature which should lead to a reduction in tribute), the second to frg. 49, where the perhaps unlikely origins of the Samothracians in Samos are explained (note the second γάρ in the passage, which serves Aristotle's function of promising to tell the cause).

It would be good to know how the speeches and fragments of a man executed for being a traitor to the democracy were preserved, when he suffered *damnatio memoriae*, with his house rased to the ground, and himself and his descendants disfranchised.[12] Their preservation may be due to the activities of one of the oligarchic clubs (ἑταιρεῖαι) of the period, and the same probably applies to the speeches of the second member of the Canon, Andocides, who was also a member of a club[13] and was banished after his unsuccessful peace mission to Sparta in 392/1.[14] With Usher,[15] Andocides was the least esteemed of the ten orators, his reputation being summed up in the infamous

[12] See the decree preserved in Ps.-Plut. *Antiphon* 834a-b.
[13] See the fragment of his speech *To the Members of His Party* (πρὸς τοὺς ἑταίρους), frg. 3 Blass.
[14] Cf. Dem. 19, 277-279; Philoch. *FGrH* 328 F 149a; Ps.-Plut. *Andocides* 835a; Roisman / Worthington (2015) 114-115.
[15] Usher (1999) 42.

statement of Herodes Atticus, "at least I am better than Andocides" (Philostr. *VS* 2, 1, 565).[16] But Andocides has the distinction of being the author of our earliest surviving deliberative speech, *On the Peace with the Spartans*.[17] This speech, despite its failure,[18] is a good example of the deliberative genre, though its opening indicates that discussion of the arrangement (τάξις) of a speech is not a clear-cut, scientific matter.[19] For most commentators, myself included,[20] the speech has no formal proem, in line with Aristotelian theory (*Rhet.* 3, 14, 12, "there is very little need for them"). Aristotle does, however, add the remark that "the subject needs no prooemion except because of the speaker or the opponents". We might, therefore, think alternatively that the speech opens with some general remarks ("That it is better to make a just peace than to make war you all seem to me, Athenians, to understand"), followed by an anticipation of his opponents' arguments ("but that the public speakers accept the name of peace but are opposed to the actions by which peace might be concluded ..."). Nevertheless, this opening is hardly designed to win over the listeners, with its "this you do not at all perceive".[21]

Andocides indicates at the outset his concern that the people, advised by their leaders, will regard peace with Sparta as potentially leading to oligarchy. He attempts to counter this immediately with a set of historical examples (3, 3-12). The use of paradigms would later be recommended by Aristotle as

---

[16] He is discussed last by HERMOG. *De ideis* 2, 11, p. 403 RABE.

[17] I accept, with most scholars, that *On the Peace* is a genuine speech of Andocides. For the view that it was a later rhetorical forgery, see HARRIS (2000). For TODD (2000) 335, n. 1, "it may be a pamphlet rather than a real speech".

[18] It is easy to forget that many of Demosthenes' political and quasi-political legal speeches were also unsuccessful, despite the brilliance of their rhetoric.

[19] For BLASS (²1887) 330, indeed, the whole speech is problematic: "Erstlich das gänzliche Fehlen einer Ordnung und eines Planes". See further ALBINI (1964) 24-26.

[20] EDWARDS (1995) 194. See USHER (1999) 50.

[21] Indeed, the opening (3, 1-12) is for Anna Missiou an indicator of Andocides' 'subversive' attitude towards the Athenian democracy. See MISSIOU (1992) 85.

being "most appropriate to deliberative oratory" (*Rhet*. 3, 17, 5), and the theme of expediency (συμφέρον) runs through the examples employed by Andocides here. Expediency and justice are the key themes also of Thucydides' deliberative speeches, and these recur in Aristotle (*Rhet*. 1, 3, 5):

> "The 'end' of each of these is different, and there are three ends for three [species]: for the deliberative speaker [the end] is the advantageous [*sympheron*] and the harmful (for someone urging something advises it as the better course and one dissuading dissuades on the ground that it is worse), and he includes other factors as incidental: whether it is just or unjust, or honorable or disgraceful." (trans. Kennedy)[22]

Andocides continues by refuting the claim that continuing the war was a necessity imposed by justice (3, 13-16) and arguing that peace will bring advantages (3, 17-23).[23] Alliance with Corinth and Argos, on the other hand, would be disadvantageous (3, 24-32); expediency is to the fore in 3, 28:

> "What I fear the most is this, Athenians, our accustomed error that we always abandon our stronger friends and choose the weaker, and make war for the sake of others when it is possible for our own sakes to live in peace." (trans. Edwards)[24]

This bad habit is illustrated by a second set of historical parallels (3, 28-32), and the speech concludes with a justification of the referral to the assembly of the decision in the matter (3, 33-41, including a third set of historical examples at 37-39). Andocides pointedly fails to indicate the advantages Sparta would gain from the proposed agreement, especially peace with

---

[22] τέλος δὲ ἑκάστοις τούτων ἕτερόν ἐστι, καὶ τρισὶν οὖσι τρία, τῷ μὲν συμβουλεύοντι τὸ συμφέρον καὶ βλαβερόν· ὁ μὲν γὰρ προτρέπων ὡς βέλτιων συμβουλεύει, ὁ δὲ ἀποτρέπων ὡς χείρονος ἀποτρέπει, τὰ δ' ἄλλα πρὸς τοῦτο συμπαραλαμβάνει, ἢ δίκαιον ἢ ἄδικον, ἢ καλὸν ἢ αἰσχρόν.

[23] Included here (3, 17-19) is a highly provocative defence of the Spartans, ending with "(y)et what kind of peace would they have obtained from us, if they had been defeated in one single battle?".

[24] ἐγὼ μὲν οὖν ἐκεῖνο δέδοικα μάλιστα, ὦ Ἀθηναῖοι, τὸ εἰθισμένον κακόν, ὅτι τοὺς κρείττους φίλους ἀφιέντες ἀεὶ τοὺς ἥττους αἱρούμεθα, καὶ πόλεμον ποιού-μεθα δι' ἑτέρους, ἐξὸν δι' ἡμᾶς αὐτοὺς εἰρήνην ἄγειν.

Persia, which would allow Sparta to dominate Greece and at the same time cede control of the Greek cities in Asia Minor to the Persians. His opponents must have played on the expediency of resisting this outcome, and it is perhaps no surprise that Andocides and his fellow-ambassadors were exiled.

Before leaving Andocides, we should note two other speeches of his, one of which survives: the second speech in the corpus, entitled *On his Return*. This speech, whose date is unclear,[25] was delivered by Andocides before the assembly on the private matter of his own recall from exile. It is not, therefore, strictly a deliberative speech,[26] but it is a δημηγορία and so can only fall under the first of Aristotle's three categories. The dramatic narrative (2, 10-16), in which Andocides lists his services to the democracy's army during his exile and the way he was treated by the Four Hundred on his first attempt to return, is an example (however unsuccessful) of creating pathos, of which "[deliberative oratory] does not have many opportunities", according to Aristotle (*Rhet.* 3, 17, 10). Andocides' own past services, and those of his ancestor Leogoras (2, 26), are supplemented by his current services in supplying grain (2, 20-21) and additional 'secret' services which he has revealed only to the Council (2, 19) – the underlying message, it is clear, is of the expediency for the democracy of allowing Andocides to return from exile. Justice also plays a role. Andocides admits his past 'mistake', his involvement in the Herms scandal of 415, but in § 22 he twice says that the favour (χάρις) he is requesting, in return for his secret services, is just.[27] We also have a fragment of a speech *To the Members of his Party* (preserved at Plut. *Them.* 32):

> "The Athenians removed his remains by stealth and scattered them to the winds." (trans. Maidment)[28]

---

[25] Perhaps 409 or 408, but possibly later. See EDWARDS (1995) 89.

[26] See, for example, JEBB (1893) 109, n. 1.

[27] The repeated adjective δικαίαν ... δικαία. Andocides additionally uses the adverb δικαίως five times in the course of the speech (2, 5, 12, 18, 19, 24), though not with reference to the favour he is asking.

[28] φωράσαντας τὰ λείψανα διαρρῖψαι τοὺς Ἀθηναίους.

This is perhaps too short a fragment to allow the inference that it derives from a narrative section of the speech, but Andocides is clearly trying, as Plutarch comments, "to incite the oligarchs against the democracy", that is, to arouse pathos. The six other fragments of Andocides in Blass' 1871 edition may also belong to this speech, and interestingly in the two that are more than a single word there are clearly again attempts to arouse pathos.[29] The second counts, indeed, as a 'diatribe' (personal abuse) against the opponent, which for Aristotle is, once more, rare in deliberative oratory (*Rhet.* 3, 17, 10).[30] It is unclear what the *To the Members of his Party* actually was – Roisman / Worthington, for example, suggest "a literary composition written in the form of a speech",[31] but again by its nature it would appear to fall under the Aristotelian deliberative category. Both the *De Reditu* and the *Pros tous Hetairous*, then, indicate the difficulties which can arise from Aristotle's rather simplistic schematisation.

The practice of speechwriting for politicians is a very familiar one today, with membership bodies such as the "Professional Speechwriters Association".[32] Indeed, one can hardly imagine a

---

[29] μὴ γὰρ ἴδοιμέν ποτε πάλιν ἐκ τῶν ὀρῶν τοὺς ἀνθρακευτὰς καὶ τὰς ἀμάξας εἰς τὸ ἄστυ ἥκοντας, καὶ πρόβατα καὶ βοῦς καὶ γύναια, καὶ πρεσβυτέρους ἄνδρας καὶ ἐργάτας ἐξοπλιζομένους· μηδὲ ἄγρια λάχανα καὶ σκάνδικας ἔτι φάγοιμεν ("May we never again see the charcoal-burners and their waggons arriving in Athens from the mountains, nor sheep and cattle and helpless women, no, nor old men and labourers arming for battle. May we never again eat wild herbs and chervil"); περὶ Ὑπερβόλου λέγειν αἰσχύνομαι, οὗ ὁ μὲν πατὴρ ἐστιγμένος ἔτι καὶ νῦν ἐν τῷ ἀργυροκοπείῳ δουλεύει τῷ δημοσίῳ, αὐτὸς δὲ ξένος ὢν καὶ βάρβαρος λυχνοποιεῖ ("Hyperbolus I blush to mention. His father, a branded slave, still works at the public mint; while he himself, a foreign interloper, makes lamps for a living"). (trans. MAIDMENT)

[30] KENNEDY compares "the general absence of personal invective against his Athenian opponents in Demosthenes' deliberative speeches with his extended invectives in judicial speeches such as *On the Crown*" (1991) 275, n. 239. Andocides' pithy abuse of Hyperbolus compares well with Demosthenes' more extended abuse of Aeschines' parents at 18, 129-131.

[31] ROISMAN / WORTHINGTON (2015) 115.

[32] See, for instance, LANCASTER (2010). Lancaster wrote speeches for the former UK Labour cabinet minister, Alan Johnson.

British politician delivering a speech which had not been prepared for him or her in advance. It is usual to think the opposite of ancient Athenian politicians, and Laurent Pernot sums
up the standard view:

"Les discours judiciaires, dont le contenu était préparé à l'avance,
se sont prêtés de préférence à la mise par écrit, qui d'ailleurs était
nécessaire quand intervenait un logographe. Les discours adressés à l'Assemblée, au contraire, qui faisaient une large place à
l'improvisation en fonction des propositions présentées en séance
et de la tournure prise par les débats, ont été confiés à l'écriture
plus rarement et plus tard."[33]

Generally speaking, Pernot is correct, but we have already seen
evidence in the Antiphontean fragments and Thucydides of the
use of a speechwriter in a political setting. The third member
of the Canon, Lysias, provides further evidence. As a metic,
Lysias cannot have addressed the assembly other than during
the brief period when he was granted citizenship. But Dionysius
of Halicarnassus (*Lysias* 1, cf. 3) says that Lysias "wrote many
speeches for the lawcourts, and for debates in the Council and
the Assembly, each well-adapted to its medium",[34] while the
Pseudo-Plutarchan *Life* (836b, cf. Photius 262, p. 488b) mentions 'deliberative speeches' without subdivision. The only extant
deliberative speech by Lysias is the fragment of the *Against
the Subversion of the Ancestral Constitution of Athens* preserved
by Dionysius (*Lysias* 31-33) and numbered 34 in modern editions. Dionysius himself is not sure that the speech, opposing a
proposal by Phormisius to restrict the franchise to Athenians
who owned land, was actually delivered,[35] and modern scholars
have been sceptical, as Stephen Todd in the introduction to his

---

[33] PERNOT (2000) 46-47. See also TREVETT (2011) 19: "Most speeches to
the Assembly will have been made extemporaneously; almost by definition politicians had to be capable public speakers, who could participate in a debate without being tied to a prepared text".

[34] Trans. USHER (πλείστους δὲ γράψας λόγους εἰς δικαστήριά τε καὶ βουλὰς
καὶ πρὸς ἐκκλησίας εὐθέτους).

[35] Though "at all events it is composed in a suitable style for an actual debate"
(*Lys.* 31).

Texas translation.[36] Todd is inclined to regard the speech as a political pamphlet, but we should note that Dionysius is not in doubt that the speech was written "for one of the prominent politicians".[37] It contains various features of which Aristotle would have approved in a deliberative speech, most notably countering the fears of the listeners (34, 6):

> "Our situation is such that they ask what security there will be for the city if we do not do what the Spartans command. In my view, however, these men should say how the democracy will benefit if we do what they [the Spartans] recommend." (trans. Todd)[38]

Aristotle discusses fear at *Rhetoric* 2, 5, defining it as "a sort of pain or agitation derived from the imagination of a future destructive or painful evil", and since deliberative oratory concerns the future, this is an appropriate topic for the deliberative context. As Usher notes,[39] dispelling the fears of the audience "was a standard task for a deliberative orator", and Lysias supports his defiant attitude with reference to the Spartans' past record of conservatism in their foreign policy. The example of the Mantineans and Argives leads into a recollection of the Athenians' own attitude during their time of empire (34, 7-9).

Todd follows the standard opinion with regard to the written circulation of deliberative oratory as noted above with Pernot. I do not think that Dionysius' doubts over whether speech 34 was delivered or not necessarily warrant the conclusion that he "appears to have had considerable difficulty finding a deliberative

---

[36] TODD (2000) 335, 338. ROISMAN / WORTHINGTON (2015) 133 sit on the fence: "It is possible, then, that he composed it for a speaker in the Assembly or circulated it as a pamphlet".

[37] See further FLORISTÁN IMÍZCOZ (2000) 171: "Los argumentos que pueden inducirnos a sospechar de la pronunciación del discurso son muy débiles. La duda que Dionisio manifesta afecta tan sólo a su propia certeza, y nada hay en el discurso que nos mueva a considerarlo un mero ejercicio de retórica".

[38] εἶτα τοιούτων ἡμῖν ὑπαρχόντων ἐρωτῶσι τίς ἔσται σωτηρία τῇ πόλει, εἰ μὴ ποιήσομεν <ἃ> Λακεδαιμόνιοι κελεύουσιν; ἐγὼ δὲ τούτους εἰπεῖν ἀξιῶ, τίς τῷ πλήθει περιγενήσεται, εἰ ποιήσομεν ἃ ἐκεῖνοι προστάττουσιν;

[39] USHER (1999) 69, with n. 57.

speech" in a corpus of 425 speeches, of which he thought 233 were genuine (Ps.-Plut. 836a) and among which, as we noted, he says there were speeches for the Council as well as the assembly. But there is no doubt that the great majority of Lysias' speeches were forensic, and indeed it is hard for us, at least, to find possible examples of any other deliberative orations. Blass lists only frg. CXI Carey (= CV FI), the Ὑπὲρ Νικίου mentioned by Dionysius (*Lysias* 14) as being a speech delivered by the captive Nicias before the Syracusans whose authenticity was rejected by Theophrastus. Blass' square brackets indicate the general modern opinion too that the speech is spurious.[40] One other possible candidate I might suggest, listed by Blass among the public legal suits as 'Vereinzelt',[41] is the speech Περὶ τῆς εἰσφορᾶς (frg. XLVI Carey, = XLIV FI).

The complex, periodic style of the demegoric discourses of Isocrates, the fourth member of the Canon, reflects the purpose of their composition for use in his school, rather than the assembly.[42] This technically renders them worthless as examples of practical deliberative oratory, but it is useful for the purposes of this survey to note the key themes that they rely on in persuading their readers to adopt a course of action, that is, the regular deliberative topics of justice (δίκαιον), expediency (συμφέρον) and possibility (δυνατόν), and also opportunity (καιρός), which plays such a prominent role in the *Olynthiacs* and *Philippics* of Demosthenes. These topics may be briefly illustrated from Isocrates' most famous discourse, the *Panegyricus*. More than half of the *Panegyricus* is epideictic in nature (4, 21-132),[43] with the theme of justice underpinning an encomium of the Athenians' past achivements, which in turn justify

---

[40] See CAREY (2007) 444: "recte Sauppe hanc orationem exercitationem esse intellexit"; less helpful is FLORISTÁN IMÍZCOZ (2000) 317, n. 100): "No es seguro que el discurso sea espurio, pero tampoco que sea auténtico".

[41] BLASS (²1887) 363.

[42] As was clear to DION. HAL. *Isoc.* 2.

[43] See USHER (1990) 19, 154 and (1999) 299. (In his 1990 commentary Usher takes the epideictic section to end at § 128, followed by a transitional passage §§ 129-132.)

their claims to leadership of Isocrates' proposed Panhellenic expedition against Persia. Forms of δίκαιος occur sixteen times in the discourse, including seven examples of the adverbial form δικαίως; of these, just over half (nine instances, including four of the adverb) fall in this section. Το δίκαιος may be added ἀδικ- cognates, of which there are seven examples, including one of συναδικεῖν (4, 53), and six of these fall in this section of the speech. But it is perhaps significant that only just under half of the δίκαιος cognates (seven instances, including three of the adverb) are found in the deliberative section of the discourse (4, 133-169),[44] where Isocrates proposes the expedition after establishing both its justice and that of the Athenians to lead it – the theme of justice in fact permeates throughout. But the main topics of the deliberative section of the discourse are expediency (4, 133-137) and possibility (4, 138-156). For example (4, 133, 138):[45]

"I believe that anyone coming from abroad and witnessing the present spectacle would pronounce both our sides guilty of utter insanity, as we risk so much over unimportant matters when we could have so much without danger, and we ruin our own land after neglecting to reap the riches of Asia ... Yet there are some who express wonder at the extent of the King's power and say that he is a difficult opponent; and they catalogue the many changes he has caused to Greek fortunes. But in my opinion those who say this are arguing not against the expedition but in favour of hastening it: for if he is going to be difficult to wage war against when we are united and he is in a state of confusion, surely we should greatly dread that time when the barbarians have settled their differences and are of one mind, while we continue in our present hostile attitude to one another." (trans. Usher)[46]

---

[44] As USHER notes (1990) 20, this section deals with the future, after the past has been addressed in the epideictic section.

[45] See USHER (1990) 185-186) and (1999) 301.

[46] Ἡγοῦμαι δ' εἴ τινες ἄλλοθεν ἐπελθόντες θεαταὶ γένοιντο τῶν παρόντων πραγμάτων, πολλὴν ἂν αὐτοὺς καταγνῶναι μανίαν ἀμφοτέρων ἡμῶν, οἵτινες οὕτω περὶ μικρῶν κινδυνεύομεν, ἐξὸν ἀδεῶς πολλὰ κεκτῆσθαι, καὶ τὴν ἡμετέραν αὐτῶν χώραν διαφθείρομεν, ἀμελήσαντες τὴν Ἀσίαν καρποῦσθαι ... Καίτοι τινὲς θαυμάζουσιν τὸ μέγεθος τῶν βασιλέως πραγμάτων καὶ φασὶν αὐτὸν εἶναι

The end of the second passage above touches on the theme of opportunity, which is picked up in § 160:

> "Therefore it seems to me that the factors that should encourage us to start a war against them are very numerous, but the main one is the present opportunity, which we must not let slip." (trans. Usher)[47]

The *Panegyricus* was completed in c. 380, and while its theme of justice is (as we noted earlier) familiar from the deliberative speeches of Thucydides, the emphasis on expediency and possibility foreshadows the order of the advice of Aristotle, that the 'end' of deliberative oratory is *sympheron* (*Rhet.* 1, 3, 5) and that the subjects for deliberation are those which are within our power (*Rhet.* 1, 4, 3).[48]

Pseudo-Plutarch (*Isoc.* 839c) attributes both forensic and political speeches also to Isocrates' adopted son, Aphareus. We only know from elsewhere about his involvement in the defence of his adoptive father concerning his trierarchy (which prompted the *Antidosis*), and scholars have been sceptical.[49] Even more questionable is Pseudo-Plutarch's statement (839f, repeated at Photius 263, p. 490a), as translated by Roisman / Worthington, that Isaeus, the fifth member of the Canon, "was also the first to introduce figures and to specialize in political oratory, in which he was followed above all by Demosthenes" (πρῶτος δὲ καὶ σχηματίζειν ἤρξατο καὶ τρέπειν ἐπὶ τὸ πολιτικὸν τὴν διάνοιαν· ὃ μάλιστα μεμίμηται Δημοσθένης).[50] This sentence

---

δυσπολέμητον, διεξιόντες ὡς πολλὰς τὰς μεταβολὰς τοῖς Ἕλλησιν πεποίηκεν. Ἐγὼ δ' ἡγοῦμαι μὲν τοὺς ταῦτα λέγοντας οὐκ ἀποτρέπειν, ἀλλ' ἐπισπεύδειν τὴν στρατείαν· εἰ γὰρ ἡμῶν ὁμονοησάντων αὐτὸς ἐν ταραχαῖς ὢν χαλεπὸς ἔσται προσπολεμεῖν, ἦ που σφόδρα χρὴ δεδιέναι τὸν καιρὸν ἐκεῖνον ὅταν τὰ μὲν τῶν βαρβάρων καταστῇ καὶ διὰ μιᾶς γένηται γνώμης, ἡμεῖς δὲ πρὸς ἀλλήλους ὥσπερ νῦν πολεμικῶς ἔχωμεν.

[47] ὥστε μοι δοκεῖ πολλὰ λίαν εἶναι τὰ παρακελευόμενα πολεμεῖν αὐτοῖς, μάλιστα δ' ὁ παρὼν καιρός, οὗ σαφέστερον οὐδέν. ὃν οὐκ ἀφετέον.

[48] See further QUINT. 3, 8, 22-25; USHER (1990) 187.

[49] See ROISMAN / WORTHINGTON (2015) 169.

[50] But Isaeus on all the evidence we have (and the ancients had) clearly did not "specialize in political oratory". The Loeb translation by FOWLER (1936)

makes much more (or indeed only makes) sense if, with Blass, we construe τὴν διάνοιαν with σχηματίζειν.[51] The biographer refers to figures of thought (not figures of speech), which Isaeus (he claims) was the first to use in political oratory, a practice in which he was followed above all by Demosthenes. Whatever the truth of the claim, it implies that Isaeus wrote political speeches, probably for others to deliver, since he was in all likelihood a metic from Chalcis.[52] I have argued elsewhere that in addition to the surviving eleven speeches connected with inheritance, plus the fragment on the subject of citizenship quoted by Dionysius that is regularly printed as speech 12, there are numerous fragments and titles of speeches that were more or less certainly concerned with inheritance and citizenship; and also that together with the speeches these fragments and titles account for nearly all the speeches of Isaeus that were known later in antiquity.[53] There is then far less room in the corpus of Isaeus than in that of Lysias for this metic to have been writing political speeches. Only one of the fragments, in my estimation, might have been deliberative: frg. XXVII, entitled *On the Speeches Made in Macedonia* (Περὶ τῶν ἐν Μακεδονίᾳ ῥηθέντων), but no details are preserved in the three entries in Harpocration that mention the speech.[54]

This fragment of Isaeus reminds us that with Isocrates and Isaeus we reach the threshold of the five later orators, who were active during and after the Macedonian conflict and of whom four were leading Athenian politicians. The most notable, of course, is Demosthenes, in whose corpus the first seventeen speeches are of a deliberative nature.[55] I say "of a deliberative

makes little sense: "He was also the first to give artistic form to his speech and to turn his attention to the urbane style of the orator; in which Demosthenes has closely imitated him".

[51] See BLASS (²1892) 498-499, n. 1.

[52] See, e.g., ROISMAN / WORTHINGTON (2015) 170-171.

[53] See EDWARDS (2006) 72-75.

[54] HARP. *s.v.* Ἀλκέτας, Ἐπικράτης, πέπλος. The fragment is listed among the forensic public speeches by BLASS (²1892) 495.

[55] For a succinct survey see TREVETT (2011) 18-22.

nature" advisedly, because Dem. 12, *Letter of Philip*, clearly is not meant to be a speech (nor of course is it by Demosthenes, though it may be by Philip), while Dem. 17, *On the Agreement with Alexander*, may be a later exercise, though MacDowell argues that it was written by a politician other than Demosthenes around 331.[56] It is also the case that at least one of the deliberative speeches (7, *On Halonnesus*) was not written by Demosthenes, in this instance probably Hegesippus.[57] Other speeches whose authenticity has been doubted are 10 (*Fourth Philippic*), 11 (*Response to Philip's Letter*) and 13 (*On Organisation*), but all are defended by MacDowell both in terms of their Demosthenic authorship and as being genuine political speeches.[58]

I shall not examine Demosthenes' speeches in this survey, especially since the next paper in the *Entretiens* by Christos Kremmydas will focus on Demosthenes. My focus here is on the publication of the speeches and also the set of *Proems*, a task which many scholars take to have been carried out by Demosthenes' nephew Demochares at the start of the 3rd century.[59] This would be designed to justify Demosthenes' policies, and would fit the pattern of the preservation of the speeches of Antiphon and Andocides noted above. It may be that Demosthenes was unusual in writing out drafts of his speeches in advance,[60] perhaps through nervousness;[61] and he may have published the speeches himself, presumably to justify his actions and policies.[62] But I tend to agree with Trevett and MacDowell that it is more likely they were published after his death.[63] However, the publishing of political speeches by Demosthenes, whether by himself or by his heir, does tend to obscure the fact

---

[56] MacDowell (2009) 377-381.

[57] See MacDowell (2009) 343-346.

[58] MacDowell (2009) 354-359, 360-366, 223-229.

[59] As Trevett (2011) 19.

[60] Hence his opponents could mock that they "smelled of the lamp" (Plut. *Dem.* 8).

[61] See Aeschin. 2, 34; Plut. *Dem.* 11; MacDowell (2009) 6.

[62] See, e.g., Tuplin (1998).

[63] See Trevett (1996); MacDowell (2009) 7-8.

that we have no examples of deliberative speeches from any
of the other four later members of the Canon. The three
preserved speeches of Aeschines are all technically forensic,
however much they are thinly disguised political attacks on
Demosthenes and his supporters. A fourth speech known to
the ancient critics, *The Delian Oration*, was pronounced spurious by Pseudo-Plutarch (840e, cf. 850a; Photius 264, p. 490a,
266, p. 496a, 61, p. 20a), since Aeschines was replaced on the
embassy to the Amphictyonic Council by Hyperides (see below).
Only one speech of Lycurgus survives, the forensic *Against
Leocrates*, and all of the fourteen fragments of Lycurgus in
Conomis' Teubner text appear to be forensic.[64] As for Hyperides,
recent discoveries mean that eight speeches survive in part, six on
papyrus (including five forensic and one epideictic speech) and
two forensic speeches from the Archimedes Palimpsest.[65] Blass
listed the titles of thirteen speeches as possibly ambassadorial or
demegoric, but the genuineness and classification of a number
of these are doubtful.[66] Six of them would have been delivered
abroad, including the *Delian Oration* mentioned earlier, but
the greatest scepticism has been reserved for the seven that
seem to qualify as speeches delivered to the assembly. Thus,
for Whitehead, the *Plataean Speech* (Plut. *Mor.* 350b = *P.Oxy.*
3360) "cannot be safely classified as demegoric, ambassadorial,
or even, if border disputes had given rise to litigation, forensic"; while Pseudo-Plutarch's passage from which are drawn
the titles *On the Generals*, *On the Triremes* and *In Defence of
Chares on the Mercenary Force at Taenarum* (Ps.-Plut. *Hyperides*
848e) "does indicate that H spoke on these three topics in the
ekklêsia, but not necessarily that those speeches themselves
had ever been published". Finally, Dinarchus was a Corinthian

---

[64] CONOMIS (1970). See further BURTT (1954) 135-157; CONOMIS (1961);
HARRIS (2001) 204-218. The *Suda* (Λ 825) records the titles of fifteen speeches
(cf. PHOT. 268, p. 496b)

[65] For references to texts and translations see ROISMAN / WORTHINGTON (2015)
246.

[66] See BLASS (²1898) 19; WHITEHEAD (2000) 5-7.

metic and so, like Lysias and Isaeus, could not address the
assembly in person.[67] Pseudo-Plutarch, however, states that
Dinarchus made a fortune under Cassander writing speeches
for clients, whose adversaries "were the most eminent orators,
but not in the sense that he came up against them in person in
the Assembly, for he was unable to attend it; but he wrote
speeches for their opponents" (*Dinarchus* 850c). This seems to
imply deliberative speeches, though Dinarchus' surviving three
speeches are forensic.[68] The fragments, too, appear mostly to
be forensic, but I draw attention to one noted by Dionysius
which might have claims to being deliberative, *The Tyrrhenian
Speech* (*Din.* 10), and to several of what Dionysius lists as spurious speeches (*Din.* 11): *The Attic Speech, The Aetolian Speech,
For Diphilus* ("a deliberative speech requesting privileges"), *On
the Refusal to Surrender Harpalus to Alexander* and yet another
Delian Speech.

Such, in brief, is the meagre and problematic evidence for
political oratory at Athens in the late 5th and 4th centuries. The
importance of the Canon of Attic orators for the later development of oratory and rhetoric in Graeco-Roman antiquity can
hardly be overstated, yet frustratingly little remains of what
Aristotle considered to be the highest form of the art. The situation with regard to the preservation and publishing of political speeches seems to have changed very little during the course
of a century or more, Demosthenes' practice of carefully preparing written drafts being wholly exceptional (though equally
the vast majority of the speeches preserved in the Demosthenic
corpus are forensic), and there can be no doubt that the standard view of the necessity for extemporaneous speaking is largely
correct. This does not mean, however, that no other political
speeches were composed in advance and written down, whether

---

[67] For references to texts and translations see ROISMAN / WORTHINGTON
(2015) 262.

[68] See also DION. HAL. *Din.* 2: "Having revealed a natural talent for political
oratory, he began to write speeches when Demosthenes and his party were still
at the height of their power, and gradually acquired a reputation" (trans. USHER).

by individual politicians or indeed by professional logographers, and all ten members of the Canon may, to varying degrees, have participated in this activity.

Works cited

ALBINI, U. (1964), *Andocide. De Pace* (Florence).
BLASS, F. (1871), *Andocidis Orationes* (Leipzig).
—— (²1887), *Die attische Beredsamkeit.* Abt. I (Leipzig).
—— (²1892), *Die attische Beredsamkeit.* Abt. II (Leipzig).
—— (²1898), *Die attische Beredsamkeit.* Abt. III.2 (Leipzig).
BURTT, J.O. (1954), *Minor Attic Orators.* Vol. II (Cambridge, Mass.).
CAREY, C. (2007), *Lysiae Orationes cum Fragmentis* (Oxford).
CONOMIS, N.C. (1961), "Notes on the Fragments of Lycurgus", *Klio* 39, 72-152.
—— (1970), *Lycurgi Oratio in Leocratem cum ceterarum Lycurgi orationum fragmentis* (Leipzig).
EDWARDS, M.J. (1995), *Greek Orators. IV, Andocides* (Warminster).
—— (2000), "Antiphon and the Beginnings of Athenian Literary Oratory", *Rhetorica* 18, 227-242.
—— (2004), "Narrative Levels in Antiphon 1, *Against the Stepmother*", in A. LÓPEZ EIRE / A. RAMOS GUERREIRA (eds.), *Registros Lingüísticos en las lenguas clásicas* (Salamanca), 51-63.
—— (2006), "Isaeus the Rhetorician: A Forgotten Classic", in L. CALBOLI MONTEFUSCO (ed.), *Papers on Rhetoric* VII (Rome), 67-80.
FLORISTÁN IMÍZCOZ, J.M. (2000), *Lisias. Discursos.* Vol. III (Madrid).
FOWLER, H.N. (1936), *Plutarch's Moralia.* Vol. X (Cambridge, Mass. and London).
HARRIS, E.M. (2000), "The Authenticity of Andokides' *De pace*: A Subversive Essay", in P. FLENSTED-JENSEN / T.H. NIELSEN / L. RUBINSTEIN (eds.), *Polis & Politics. Studies in Ancient Greek History Presented to Mogens Herman Hansen on his Sixtieth Birthday* (Copenhagen), 479-505.
—— (2001), see WORTHINGTON / COOPER / HARRIS (2001).
HORNBLOWER, S. (2008), *A Commentary on Thucydides.* Vol. III (Oxford).
JEBB, R.C. (1893), *The Attic Orators from Antiphon to Isaeus.* Vol. I (London).
KENNEDY, G.A. (1963), *The Art of Persuasion in Greece* (Princeton).
—— (1991), *Aristotle* On Rhetoric. *A Theory of Civic Discourse* (Oxford).
LANCASTER, S. (2010), *Speechwriting. The Expert Guide* (London).

34   MICHAEL EDWARDS

MACDOWELL, D.M. (2009), *Demosthenes the Orator* (Oxford).
MAIDMENT, K.J. (1941), *Minor Attic Orators* vol. I (Cambridge, Mass.).
MISSIOU, A. (1992), *The Subversive Oratory of Andokides. Politics, Ideology and Decision-making in Democratic Athens* (Cambridge).
PERNOT, L. (2000), *La rhétorique dans l'Antiquité* (Paris).
—— (2005), *Rhetoric in Antiquity*, trans. W.E. HIGGINS (Washington).
ROISMAN, J. / WORTHINGTON, I. (2015), *Lives of the Attic Orators. Texts from Pseudo-Plutarch, Photius, and the* Suda (Oxford).
TODD, S.C. (2000), *Lysias* (Austin).
TREVETT, J.C. (1996), "Did Demosthenes Publish his Deliberative Speeches?", *Hermes* 124, 425-441.
—— (2011), *Demosthenes. Speeches 1-17* (Austin).
TUPLIN, C. (1998), "Demosthenes' *Olynthiacs* and the Character of the Demegoric Corpus", *Historia* 47, 276-320.
USHER, S. (1974), *Dionysius of Halicarnassus. The Critical Essays.* Vol. I (Cambridge, MA).
—— (1985), *Dionysius of Halicarnassus. The Critical Essays.* Vol. II (Cambridge, MA).
—— (1990), *Greek Orators.* Vol. III, *Isocrates,* Panegyricus *and* To Nicocles (Warminster).
—— (1999), *Greek Oratory. Tradition and Originality* (Oxford).
WARNER, R. (1954), *Thucydides. History of the Peloponnesian War* (Harmondsworth).
WHITEHEAD, D. (2000), *Hypereides. The Forensic Speeches* (Oxford).
WOOTEN, C.W. (1987), *Hermogenes' On Types of Style* (Chapel Hill).
WORTHINGTON, I. / COOPER, C.R. / HARRIS, E.M. (2001), *Dinarchus, Hyperides, & Lycurgus* (Austin).

DISCUSSION

M. Kraus: Vielen Dank für diese ausgezeichnete Bestands-
aufnahme dessen, was wir an deliberativer Rhetorik aus der
Periode der attischen Redner haben. Es ist weniger, als man
erwartet. Es verwundert freilich ein wenig, gerade Aristoteles
als Gewährsmann für das Gewicht der deliberativen Rede in
der frühen Zeit angeführt zu finden, und nicht etwa die praktisch gleichzeitige *Rhetorik an Alexander*, die dafür noch sehr
viel mehr Substanz geboten hätte. Die *Rhetorik an Alexander*
kennt ja nach der korrekten Rekonstruktion des Textes nur zwei
Grundtypen von Reden, ,demegorische' (d.h. an das Volk gerich-
tete) und dikanische (gerichtliche), mit zusammen sieben Unter-
gattungen: Empfehlende, abratende, lobende und tadelnde
Rede gehören zum demegorischen, anklagende, verteidigende
und prüfende Rede zum dikanischen Typus. Nicht nur steht
die Behandlung des demegorischen Typus am Anfang und
erhält weitaus mehr Raum, sondern sie fungiert explizit auch als
Modell für die gerichtlichen Redegattungen, die „analog dazu"
(ὁμοιοτρόπως τούτοις, 4, 1426b22) beschrieben werden sollen.
Dasselbe Grundmuster findet sich wieder in den späten Kapiteln
(*cap.* 29-36), wo wiederum stets die demegorischen Gattungen
(insbesondere die empfehlende Rede) das universelle Paradigma
auch für die dikanischen Gattungen bilden. Bei Aristoteles ist
dieser Schwerpunkt auf der deliberativen Rede zwar ebenfalls
vorhanden, indem auch er erklärt, dass ,demegorische' und
dikanische Reden im Grunde denselben Regeln gehorchen, die
ersteren aber als ethisch hochwertiger und politisch relevanter
einstuft und ältere Theoretiker dafür kritisiert, die demegori-
sche Rede als die komplexere Gattung vernachlässigt zu haben
(*Rhet.* 1, 1, 1354b22-35). Allerdings ist diese Vorrangstellung
bei ihm deutlich schwächer ausgeprägt als in der *Rhetorik an*

Alexander, insofern die Darstellung der gerichtlichen Rede in etwa denselben Umfang zugebilligt erhält wie die der deliberativen und epideiktischen zusammen und sich konzeptuell völlig vom demegorischen Modell löst. Aber auch bei ihm steht die deliberative Rede noch immer an erster Stelle. Erst die hellenistische und vor allem die römische Rhetorik scheinen die Gewichte hier zugunsten eines paradigmatischen Vorrangs der Gerichtsrede ins Gegenteil verkehrt zu haben.

M. Edwards: You are quite right, of course, to draw attention to the absence of the *Rhetoric to Alexander* from my discussion, Manfred. Indeed, I would have been surprised if you had not. This was deliberate on my part, in order to keep the paper focused on a specific rhetorical theory, that of Aristotle, though I recognise that Anaximenes (if he wrote the *Rhetoric to Alexander*) is often very similar in his approach. In addition, my expectation is that Aristotelian rhetorical theory will dominate this *Entretiens*, as it has tended to dominate histories of Greek rhetoric.

L. Pernot: Les traces de publication de discours délibératifs existent, mais sont limitées et parfois douteuses : on peut faire un parallèle entre cette situation et celle de l'*epitaphios logos*. L'*epitaphios logos* est un discours qui, lui aussi, était fréquent et régulier dans la vie publique athénienne, et pour lequel les traces de publication sont rares. C'est que, probablement, la plupart des orateurs ne publiaient pas leurs discours. L'Athènes classique était entre oralité et écriture. Certains auteurs de discours rhétoriques avaient conscience de composer des ouvrages qui constituaient un corpus (Isocrate), d'autres non (Démosthène). L'éloquence délibérative est le plus souvent du côté de la seconde attitude. De même, en philosophie, il y avait une opposition entre Aristote, qui composait un corpus pour construire méthodiquement un système, et Platon, qui faisait recommencer le monde à chaque nouveau dialogue.

M. Edwards: Thank you, Laurent, for your comments, which reflect your deeply informed knowledge of the subject.

You suggest what is a very interesting comparison between deliberative and epideictic rhetoric, and I am sure you are right. It was specifically the forensic genre of oratory whose speeches were in the main published, perhaps because these were what the slowly but surely growing reading public wanted. There is also the question of the logographers, who naturally focused on forensic oratory and published their speeches in order to enhance their future business prospects. You make a comparison between Isocrates and Demosthenes, and Isocrates had additional reasons to compose and publish his discourses, both in terms of his political agenda of a Panhellenic expedition against the Persians, and as materials for his highly successful school. The publication of Demosthenes' speeches has been recently explored by Douglas MacDowell in his *Demosthenes the Orator* (Oxford, 2009), 7-9.

A. Chaniotis: This presentation makes clear that Aristotle's categorisation (*Rhet.* 1, 3, 2-3) does not really work, and a sharp distinction between deliberative and forensic oratory is not possible. The aim of a 'forensic' speech is to convince an audience of jurors, exactly as a deliberative oration (and most epideictic orations and speeches of ambassadors). So, instead of using the reference of a speech to the past (forensic) or the future (deliberative) as a criterion, we should look at whether the speaker is part of the deliberating body that will take a decision or not. For instance, in a forensic speech the orator is not a member of the deciding body; in orations in the assembly some orators (citizens) are members of the body to which their speech is addressed, others (e.g. ambassadors) are not. The problems of categorisation are clear, e.g., in the speeches of Antiphon and Andocides that were commented on by Mike Edwards. Thucydides reflects contemporary mentality, when he uses the general term *agôn*.

My second comment concerns Antiphon's fragments 49 and 50; both fragments share the use of images and language for the arousal of pity. The orator explains the arrival of the Samians to Samothrace as the result of *anankê*, not desire (*epithymia*) of gain. He highlights the poverty of the island (*tracheia, ergasima mikra, arga polla, mikras ousês*) and the status of the immigrants as exiles. Here, references to the past are used in order to justify the orator's request.

M. Edwards: Thank you for those comments. This is a very interesting way of looking at the categorisation of forensic and deliberative oratory. Almost (but not quite: cf. Antiphon 5, delivered by a Mytilenean; Isocrates 19, delivered before a court in Aegina) all of speeches of the corpus of Attic orators were delivered in Athens by Athenians, so I suspect your approach would have been a little too broad for Aristotle's liking.

D. Colomo: With regard to the fact that so little of Athenian political oratory survives, as you say in the first paragraph of your contribution, on the basis of my experience with fragmentary papyri recovered in archaeological excavations, I would like to point out that in any case we have to take into consideration the factor of chance in the survival of material in the process of transmission of texts and information through the centuries.

M. Edwards: The survival of manuscripts and papyri, and the vagaries of chance in that survival, are complex topics, as you know from your papyrological expertise. Isocrates and Demosthenes have their separate, extensive manuscript traditions, while Hyperides' medieval manuscript tradition has only recently been established by the discovery of two fragments in the Archimedes Palimpsest. It seems that the speeches of the other members of the canon were preserved from some point after the survey in the pseudo-Plutarchan *Lives* of the orators in selections (cf. Palatinus Graecus 88 for Lysias) and florilegia, such as the one that has come down to us as the codex Crippsianus (Burney 95 in the British Library) and which contains Antiphon, Andocides, Isaeus, Lycurgus and Dinarchus (also Gorgias, Alcidamas and Lesbonax).

A. Chaniotis: Finally, a question concerning the question why orations that were delivered after the 4th century BC were not included in the canon. Could it be related with developments in performative aspects of oratory?

M. Edwards: Performance is an increasingly important area of study in the orators, but it is not clear to me that this necessarily played a part in the formation of the canon. It is far from clear, indeed, when that formation took place, but it seems that the orators of what became the canon, like members of other canons in classical literature, very quickly acquired a status that was later cemented by the activities of the librarians in Alexandria. There were clearly other contenders, and the canon of ten that we have, and which may be due to Caecilius of Caleacte, was not agreed immediately – Dionysius, who recalls the names of other orators, only writes six essays, with the later addition of Dinarchus, but all seven, it should be noted, are in the Caecilian canon. But there does not seem to have been any appetite to include orators of the post-classical period.

J.-L. Ferrary: Ma question viendra en complément de celles de D. Colomo et de M. Kraus. J'aimerais savoir ce que l'on sait exactement de la collecte et de la transmission des discours délibératifs de l'Athènes classique à l'époque hellénistique. Peut-on exclure que l'importance de la rhétorique judiciaire et de ses développements avec la théorie des états de cause ait contribué à favoriser la préservation des discours judiciaires plutôt que des discours délibératifs ?

M. Edwards: Yes, this is entirely possible, and the transmission processes are entirely unclear. I would note, however, that there is very little evidence that orators were publishing deliberative speeches before the time of Demosthenes, and so while more deliberative speeches might have been preserved under other conditions of transmission, these are unlikely to have come in the main from, for example, the 5th century – Pericles and his contemporaries do not appear to have left any written record.

M. Kraus: Zusätzlich zu bewussten Selektionen und Kanonbildungen der hellenistischen Zeit ist für die Frage der Erhaltung der Reden auch noch mit den Unwägbarkeiten und Zufälligkeiten der handschriftlichen Überlieferung in Spätantike und Mittelalter zu rechnen.

M. Edwards: That is an important observation, Manfred, thank you.

M. Kraus: Verantwortlich für die zähe Langlebigkeit der Aristotelischen Kategorien und Distinktionen trotz ihrer vereinfachenden und im Laufe der Zeit auch zunehmend unpraktischen Rigidität ist neben der Autorität des Namens Aristoteles zweifellos auch der starre Konservatismus der Schulrhetorik, die seit dem Hellenismus das verzweigte rhetorische System über Generationen hin bewahrt und tradiert, wofür etwa das Kompendium Quintilians ein schönes Beispiel gibt.

II

CHRISTOS KREMMYDAS

DEMOSTHENES' *PHILIPPICS* AND THE ART OF CHARACTERISATION FOR THE ASSEMBLY

The projection of the speaker's character (*ethos*) is of paramount importance in oratory. This is acknowledged by Aristotle in the *Rhetoric* where *ethos* is singled out as one of the three 'artistic' means of persuasion (1356a) and key issues regarding the perception of a speaker's character and its role in persuasion are identified:

"[There is persuasion] through character whenever the speech is spoken in such a way as to make the speaker worthy of credence; for we believe fair-minded people to a greater extent and more quickly [than we do others], on all subjects in general and completely so in cases where there is not exact knowledge but room for doubt. And this should result from the speech, not from a previous opinion that the speaker is a certain kind of person; for it is not the case, as some of the handbook writers propose in their treatment of the art, that fair-mindedness [*epieikeia*] on the part of the speaker makes no contribution to persuasiveness; rather, character is almost, so to speak, the most authoritative form of persuasion." (1356a, trans. Kennedy)[1]

---

[1] διὰ μὲν οὖν τοῦ ἤθους, ὅταν οὕτω λεχθῇ ὁ λόγος ὥστε ἀξιόπιστον ποιῆσαι τὸν λέγοντα· τοῖς γὰρ ἐπιεικέσι πιστεύομεν μᾶλλον καὶ θᾶττον, περὶ πάντων μὲν ἁπλῶς, ἐν οἷς δὲ τὸ ἀκριβὲς μὴ ἔστιν ἀλλὰ τὸ ἀμφιδοξεῖν, καὶ παντελῶς. δεῖ δὲ καὶ τοῦτο συμβαίνειν διὰ τοῦ λόγου, ἀλλὰ μὴ διὰ τοῦ προδεδοξάσθαι ποιόν τινα εἶναι τὸν λέγοντα· οὐ γάρ, ὥσπερ ἔνιοι τῶν τεχνολογούντων, <οὐ> τίθεμεν ἐν τῇ τέχνῃ καὶ τὴν ἐπιείκειαν τοῦ λέγοντος, ὡς οὐδὲν συμβαλλομένην πρὸς τὸ πιθανόν, ἀλλὰ σχεδὸν ὡς εἰπεῖν κυριωτάτην ἔχει πίστιν τὸ ἦθος.

Later on in the same work, Aristotle stresses that "there are three reasons that make speakers persuasive ... besides logical argument", and cites two character traits and an emotional response: "practical wisdom and virtue and goodwill" (*Rhet.* 1378a).[2]

Anaximenes, too, is aware of the importance of *ethos*, and whilst he generally avoids theorising in the *Rhetorica ad Alexandrum*,[3] he makes a few practical recommendations on how to project the speaker's *ethos* in the most positive way.[4] However, it is probably fair to say that these theoretical works of the second half of the 4th century BC lend more emphasis to their treatment of emotions and logical arguments[5] than to the projection of character.[6]

A key question remains: To what extent does rhetorical theory reflect oratorical practice? It is doubtful whether Aristotle, in particular, took into account the Attic orations that have come down to us.[7] A similar question has recently been addressed by Christopher Pelling, who compared speeches in Herodotus and Thucydides with the rhetorical treatises of Aristotle and Anaximenes and concluded that despite the methodological difficulties posed by them, 4th-century rhetorical

---

[2] τοῦ μὲν οὖν αὐτοὺς εἶναι πιστοὺς τοὺς λέγοντας τρία ἐστὶ τὰ αἴτια· τοσαῦτα γάρ ἐστι δι' ἃ πιστεύομεν ἔξω τῶν ἀποδείξεων. ἔστι δὲ ταῦτα φρόνησις καὶ ἀρετὴ καὶ εὔνοια.

[3] Note, however, 35, 17-18 (οἱ δὲ λόγοι τῶν ἠθῶν καὶ τῶν τρόπων εἰσὶν οἷον εἰκόνες, "reports are in a way reflections of character and personality", trans. MIRHADY), where he talks about narratives regarding an opponent's life in a forensic setting.

[4] E.g. 35, 18: φυλάττου δὲ καὶ τὰς αἰσχρὰς πράξεις μὴ αἰσχροῖς ὀνόμασι λέγειν, ἵνα μὴ διαβάλῃς τὸ ἦθος, ἀλλὰ τὰ τοιαῦτα αἰνιγματωδῶς ἑρμηνεύειν καὶ ἑτέρων πραγμάτων ὀνόμασι χρώμενος δηλοῦν τὸ πρᾶγμα.

[5] Aristotle explicitly mentions the neglect of enthymemes in contemporary rhetorical treatises (1354a-b).

[6] Anaximenes cites now-lost rhetorical handbooks by himself and Corax, and alludes to the existence of others whose authors he does not name who had also provided "political and forensic precepts" (*Rhet. ad Alex.* Ep. 16-17). It is unknown whether the construction of *ethos* in the Assembly would have received greater attention in those works.

[7] TREVETT (1996) argues that Aristotle does not quote from Athenian deliberative or forensic orations because they did not reflect his pupils' interests and were not widely circulated anyway.

theory can still shed light on speeches embedded in 5th-century historiography.[8]

Modern scholarship has generally sought to identify direct links between theory and oratorical practice (e.g. types of arguments or emotions described in rhetorical theory and also occurring in extant Attic oratory).[9] However, most of the time, the relationships and interplays are far subtler and more complex than one might expect. And whilst techniques of characterisation in Attic oratory have attracted attention with regard to the forensic context,[10] the deliberative context has not been explored in depth.

In this paper I hope to shed some light on characterisation as an integral part of rhetorical strategies in deliberative oratory in the setting of the Assembly. Since the overwhelming majority of our surviving deliberative orations date to the 4th century BC and are found in the *corpus Demosthenicum*, I shall examine Demosthenes' Assembly speeches as evidence for the presentation of character as a means of persuasion. In particular, I shall focus on speeches of the so-called 'Philippic cycle', which date to the heyday of his political career (351-341). First, I shall make some preliminary methodological observations in relation to the portrayal of *ethos* in a deliberative context. I shall then consider how Demosthenes makes his *ethos* central to his endeavour to assert his leadership credentials in the Assembly, and briefly examine the range of rhetorical strategies he employs in order to project his character in his deliberative speeches. I shall explore how some of the techniques of characterisation he uses evolved over time in response to the changing political context and conclude that Demosthenes' *ethos* in the speeches of the Philippic cycle was flexible, adaptable, and carefully crafted in order to persuade the audience of his trustworthiness.

---

[8] PELLING (2012).

[9] A few recent works on *ethos* in Greek rhetoric and oratory: GILL (1984); WISSE (1989); RUSSELL (1990); FORTENBAUGH (1992); CAREY (1994); WOERTHER (2005).

[10] E.g. CAREY (1994) 34-43; DE BRAUW (2002); KREMMYDAS (2013).

The orator's *ethos* and the Assembly

Given the importance of the projection of character in all genres of oratory, it is worth reflecting briefly on its rhetorical constitution. Three questions need to be considered: first, is the *ethos* of an individual speaker essentially the same at any given time, yet what varies is its perception by diverse audiences, whilst different character traits are projected in different rhetorical contexts? This would mean that some members of the audience in an Assembly might perceive certain aspects of a speaker's character through his speech, while others may take in different traits. At the same time, a speaker might choose to focus on a core set of traits (e.g. reliability, experience, knowledge, and foresight) in the context of the Assembly,[11] while promoting his non-litigiousness, his *metriotes*, civic-spiritedness, and unimpeachable public life in the law-courts. The *ethos* of the individual is thus the same and internally consistent, and the projection of different traits reflects the different contextual rhetorical needs of the speaker.

Second, to what extent does prior familiarity with a person's life and character affect the perception of his character in a rhetorical context? And to what extent does the rhetorical construction of a speaker's *ethos* depend on the audience's familiarity with his personality, and his public and private life?

Third, should a distinction be drawn between real and rhetorical *ethos*? Real *ethos* emanates from an individual's life, social interactions, interpersonal relationships, political position and general standing in the community, personal successes and failures. However, is it independent from any rhetorical representations thereof in the public *fora* of the city? Many members of the audience might have already formed a positive or negative view of an individual's *ethos* based on their

---

[11] Cf. the triptych of traits in ARIST. *Rhet.* 1378a (φρόνησις καὶ ἀρετὴ καὶ εὔνοια; see n. 2 above). On foresight (προορᾶν) in political-deliberative contexts see, e.g., DEM. 4, 41; 6, 6, 8; 18, 27.

established public *persona*. The rhetorically skilled speaker (or a logographer employed by a speaker in a forensic setting) may portray his *ethos* in such a way as to maximise the positive and minimise or conceal any negative traits.[12] This rhetorically crafted presentation of *ethos* (rhetorical *ethos*) helps bolster the prior positive views among the audience and seeks to sway those who hold no or negative views. This rhetorical *ethos* is the orator's (or logographer's) 'artistic' creation, but the exact relation it bears to the real *ethos* is subject to negotiation and manipulation. In the *Rhetoric* Aristotle seems to suggest that one can draw a distinction between these two kinds of *ethos*, but a firm distinction cannot be substantiated.[13] There are clearly smaller or larger overlaps between the real and the artistic *ethos*, otherwise the latter ·would not have been either credible or effective as a tool of persuasion; the gulf between the real and the constructed would have been apparent to many in the audience.

Further issues relating to the presentation of the orator's *ethos* in the Assembly should be considered before proceeding to a discussion of techniques of self-presentation: first, since Assembly debates were meant to consider questions of expediency for the polis in terms of future policy,[14] while questions of justice[15] and legal, personal liability of politicians were mostly

[12] E.g. the self-presentation of Nicias and Alcibiades in Thucydides' *Redetrias* (6, 9-23); see further KREMMYDAS (2016a).

[13] *Rhet.* 1356a (contrast ISOC. 15, 278); Aristotle's distinction between *ethos* emanating from and enhanced by people's position and rhetorically constructed *ethos* is too firm.

[14] Anaximenes' *Rhet. ad Alex.* highlights "concord, military forces, money and good supply of revenues, good and plentiful allies" (ὁμόνοια, δυνάμεις πρὸς πόλεμον, χρήματα καὶ προσόδων εὐπορία, συμμάχων ἀρετὴ καὶ πλῆθος; 1, 1) as advantageous for a city (πόλει δὲ συμφέροντα).

[15] Aristotle's *Rhetoric* probably overstresses the dominance of *sympheron*-related themes and arguments in deliberative oratory, while Thucydides' speeches suggest the importance of arguments from justice in Assembly debates: e.g. ARIST. *Rhet.* 1358b22; 1362a18-20; 1365b25; cf., e.g., THUC. 3, 38, 1; 3, 40 (Cleon); note Diodotus' contestation of the blurring of the lines between *sympheron* and *dikaion* in Cleon's speech: 3, 44, 4; 47, 5; cf. 3, 56, 3 (the Plataeans' speech before a 'court' of Spartan judges); 3, 59, 3.

delegated to the *dikasteria* in the second half of the 4th century,[16] one does not encounter strong vituperation in deliberative orations of the kind encountered in forensic speeches where acquittal of the speaker (or of an individual for whom the speaker acted as a *synegoros*) and conviction of an opponent (and a penalty) are at stake.[17] Thus not only the etiquette but also techniques of self-characterisation in the *ekklesia* are different from those used in the courts.[18] And so, the role of the speaker's *ethos* in deliberative oratory is different from the role it performs in a forensic context.[19]

Second, one should not rush into the hasty conclusion that all speakers taking the speakers' *bema* would have been well-known to the Assembly-going public. Hansen's work on the prosopography of 4th-century Athenian politicians has highlighted 373 individuals attested as *rhetores* and *strategoi* for the period 403-322.[20] Athenian proposers of decrees would have delivered shorter or longer speeches to introduce their draft proposals to the assembly (epigraphic formula τάδε εἶπεν), while others would have spoken up to introduce riders to the draft proposal. How important was the perception of their *ethos* by the audience in the Assembly? To what extent did the projection of their *ethos* matter in terms of persuading their audience or did other considerations, such as the political group they belonged to at the time and their association with widely known politicians, weigh more heavily when it came to voting for or against a proposal? Was it a case of *ethos*

---

[16] In the 5th century (and the first-half of the 4th) the Assembly maintained a large role in judging political trials. Cases of *eisangeliai* were still tried in the *ekklesia* until 362. HANSEN (1991) 158-159, and in greater detail HANSEN (1975).

[17] E.g. the different uses of language denoting deception in the Assembly and the law-courts: KREMMYDAS (2013) esp. 52.

[18] Note DEM. 18, 143, which suggests that the Assembly would not tolerate accusations of a personal character.

[19] In this paper, I shall focus primarily on the speaker's self-presentation; I shall consider the way in which the *ethos* of opponents is presented only where it is relevant to the projection of the speaker's own *ethos*.

[20] HANSEN (1989a); (1989b).

by association, i.e. the projection of the character traits of an individual onto a political associate? The benefits for a leading politician in such a case would be obvious, while the risks would be minimised. If this was indeed the case, then an awareness of the politician/speaker's *ethos* would have been central to success in the Assembly.

Third, one should also take into account the rhetorical tactics in the Assembly and the possibility that some speakers representing a political group or advocating a specific position would have put forward specific proposals (thus also assuming the legal responsibility for them), while key political figure(s) might have confined themselves to cameo appearances, lending their ethical and political support to the case made by their associates.[21]

Projecting *ethos* in the Assembly: techniques of self-presentation

Since rhetorical theory is not too helpful in terms of elucidating the construction and projection of rhetorical *ethos* in deliberative oratory, it is worth considering different means through which a speaker could portray his *ethos* in the Assembly in order to project authority and engender trust in the audience. The rhetorical techniques of characterisation highlighted below do not represent an exhaustive checklist,[22] yet they might facilitate the discussion of *ethos* in deliberative oratory as we navigate through the deliberative speeches of the Demosthenic corpus. Some of these techniques shed light on the orator's *ethos* explicitly (nos. 1 and 2), while others (nos. 3-6) do so implicitly.

---

[21] I am considering team-speaking in the Athenian Assembly as well as the possibility of logographic speeches delivered in the Assembly in KREMMYDAS (2017a). See also RUBINSTEIN (2017).

[22] Assembly speakers in Thucydides do not use explicit self-characterisation to the same extent as Demosthenes; e.g. Pericles uses self-referential passages in 2, 60, 1, 5; 61, 2 (in response to personal criticism), Cleon employs meta-rhetorical passages to lament the state of deliberative oratory (3, 38, 2-7); Alcibiades is the most explicit of all speakers in his self-promotion (6, 16, 1, 3-6).

1) **Meta-rhetorical passages:** generic passages regarding the role and failures of rhetoric in deliberation, criticising the tendency to prioritise what is pleasant to the ears over what is expedient (e.g. Dem. 3, 18, 22; 9, 2; *Ex.* 44, 1).

2) **Self-referential passages** and *topoi* (e.g. the speaker's inability to do justice to a topic):[23] while the speaker's *ethos* is important in persuasion, the promotion of his personal rhetorical skills and ethical qualities tends to take place indirectly (see n. 15 above with references to Assembly speakers in Thucydides; cf. Andoc. 4). But is this reticence to engage in direct, explicit self-characterisation simply a feature of oratorical etiquette in the Assembly? Demosthenes states (5, 4) that he does not wish to talk about himself and, although this was a profitable exercise for some, he considers it "vulgar and offensive" (φορτικὸν καὶ ἐπαχθές). Had standards really slipped by Demosthenes' time and speakers simply did not pay attention to oratorical etiquette anymore? How can we account for the growing prominence of direct means of promoting the speaker's *ethos* in the corpus of Demosthenes' deliberative speeches? Can it be attributed to contextual factors (the speaker's age, experience, and responses to specific criticisms)?

What is of greater interest in terms of the projection of a speaker's *ethos* is not the mere rehashing of *topoi* and meta-rhetorical passages that represented stock material of deliberative oratory. Instead, one should examine how such material is combined as part of wider rhetorical strategies and adapted to the different oratorical contexts,[24] what is the likely effect of such adaptations, and what the latter may reveal about the development/change in the projection of the orator's *ethos*.

3) **The use of praise and criticism:** as part of the projection of his *ethos*, the orator *qua* teacher and adviser of the people, may praise the audience for their past successes and criticise

---

[23] This *topos* is attested in *prooemia* of deliberative speeches and forms part of the speaker's *captatio beneuolentiae* (e.g. 3, 1; 5, 1; 15, 32; 16, 2; cf. *Ex.* 4; 8, 2).

[24] On Demosthenes' tailoring of arguments to fit the context, see YUNIS (1996) 237.

their past failures or errors of judgment. He may also wish to castigate the actions and *ethos* of rival politicians, thus implicitly promoting his reliability and integrity. However, both praise and criticism carry potential pitfalls for the orator. Even though one might think that by lavishing praise on the audience the orator can hardly go wrong, the orator has to be cautious lest he come across as sycophantic. Praise of the people (mostly the Athenian ancestors) has to be balanced with the need to criticise the audience without alienating it. Finally, by castigating the decisions or harmful advice given by rival politicians the orator promotes his own wisdom and reliability, although excessive criticism of rivals also risks alienating the audience.

4) **Types of logical argument (especially *gnomai*)**: logical argumentation (*enthymemes*) and especially *gnomai* help project an air of authority and credibility by appealing to a sense of shared presuppositions.[25] Anaximenes offers quite a helpful categorisation of *gnomai* into 'conventional' and 'paradoxical' and provides a few examples (*Rhet. ad Alex.* 11, 1-6), while Aristotle identifies four species (*Rhet.* 1394a-1395b) and stresses the fact that they make a speech 'ethical', i.e. they demonstrate the good character of an individual.

5) **The knowledge and use of past history**: the orator's demonstration of knowledge and his use of past Athenian (and Greek) history help to enhance his authority and, ultimately, reliability in the eyes of the audience.

6) **The speaker's adherence to communal values and ideals**: as in forensic oratory, the speaker in a deliberative context needs to persuade the audience that he espouses the same set of values and ideals and therefore can be trusted.

Since it is not possible to do justice here to all the different ways in which this wide range of techniques is being used, I shall focus my attention in the rest of this paper on nos. 1, 2, and 3.

---

[25] I develop this point further in Kremmydas (2017a).

Demosthenes and the limits of deliberative *ethos*: the early Assembly speeches

Demosthenes' Assembly speeches are central to our appreciation of Demosthenes as an orator and leading Athenian politician.[26] The speeches in which he is dealing with the threat of Philip of Macedon played a significant role in cementing his fame as a politician fighting for Greek freedom. However, before examining the Philippic speeches, it is worth considering the creation of Demosthenes' *ethos* in his early Assembly speeches (354-351). After all, in 354, when he delivered his first recorded deliberative oration *On the Symmories*, he would have been just over thirty.

Although the age limit for attending Assembly proceedings was twenty (*Ath. Pol.* 42, 5),[27] it would have probably taken promising young Athenians a while before they could make their mark on the *bema* of the Assembly (cf. Dem. 4, 1). Demosthenes, of course, did not wait to make his name in the Assembly, as he had already been active in the law-courts since his well-known dispute with his guardians between 364 and 362. Even if one assumes that he had refrained from or had been unsuccessful at making a break into the Assembly, he would have been fairly well-known to the wider public as a logographer and *synegoros*.[28] His first two trierarchies (363, 360/59)[29] and the speeches delivered in connection with trier-archic affairs suggest that he was very much active in the public sphere.[30] The absence of recorded Assembly speeches from the period 362-354 suggests either that he did not deliver any

---

[26] DEM. 1-6, 8-10, 14-16 are genuine; [DEM.] 7 should be attributed to Hegesippus, [DEM.] 13 may be an early Demosthenic speech, but there are some doubts; [DEM.] 17 is probably a rhetorical exercise.

[27] Perhaps since the early 4th century: HANSEN (1991) 89.

[28] Note his participation as logographer or supporting speaker in public suits (*graphai paranomôn* and *nomon mê epitedeion theinai*) between 356 and 354: DEM. 47 (in 356/5), 20, 22 (both dated in 355/4).

[29] Demosthenes' trierarchies: DEM. 51; DEM. 21, 154; AESCHIN. 3, 173.

[30] See also DAVIES (1971) 135-137.

formal speeches or that he did not wish to preserve any of these early specimens of his deliberative oratory. This would make sense, if this eight-year period was seen as a formative period during which Demosthenes was busy networking and preparing for his later political career.[31] In the retrospective on his career, the speech *On the Crown*, Demosthenes chooses to emphasise the fact that he made a late entry into Athenian politics (18, 18, 60). This is roughly consistent with the publication dates of his earliest extant speeches, although Demosthenes fails to specify the exact point of his first intervention in Athenian politics.

One should also bear in mind that the three earliest (genuine) Demosthenic speeches deal with internal Athenian affairs (the organisation of the navy), the situation in mainland Greece (Thebes vs. Sparta) and the possibility of a fall-out with the Persian King. Conversely, in the *Philippics* the focus shifts to Northern Greece and an enemy that had not attracted attention before. This new reality and the growing realisation of the danger posed by Philip may have also affected the tenor of Demosthenes' rhetoric and, ultimately, the way in which he portrayed himself as an adviser of the city.

Demosthenes 14 (*On the Symmories*), his first surviving Assembly oration, sheds some light on the precocity of his rhetorical endeavour. It is a tentative attempt to promote his *ethos* as an orator and politician to a demanding Athenian audience. An attempt to engage with well-known rhetorical *topoi* and other (unidentified) Athenian speakers and thus demonstrate knowledge, good understanding of foreign relations and internal affairs, and foresight helps establish his *ethos* in the Assembly. He commences his speech with a meta-rhetorical *prooemium* criticising rhetorical commonplaces ('the praise of the Athenian ancestors') used by other orators (1). This is indeed a *topos* occurring in extant specimens of deliberative (and epideictic)

---

[31] For a reconstruction of Demosthenes' political connections early in his career, see BURKE (2002) 176-183.

oratory,[32] but the way it is being used demonstrates the failure of the present orators properly to extol the virtues of the ancestors. Demosthenes employs *praeteritio* while seeking to refocus this *topos* and his speech as a whole towards what is useful under the current circumstances (2).

Demosthenes' censure of orators (1) echoes Cleon's castigation of the culture of deliberative debate for pleasure and intellectual stimulation (Thuc. 3, 38, 7) and suggests a continued distortion of the objective of deliberative oratory in the Athenian Assembly in the 4th century.[33] Demosthenes thus seeks to project his *ethos* in contrast to that of other (established?) orators. He downplays his rhetorical skill, while foregrounding his ability to offer advice. He is circumspect: he presents himself as one of potentially many speakers (εἷς ὁστισοῦν) who can benefit the city through their advice (note the use of the hypothetical syllogism εἰ μὲν... εἰ δὲ...):

> "If someone, whoever he may be, who comes up to speak, could teach and persuade you what kind of preparations and what size of force will be required and how it should be paid for, all our present fears would be relieved" (14, 2).[34]

This is capped by the *topos* of the speaker's inability (ὡς ἂν ἄρ' οἷός τ' ὦ), the use of the conative verb (πειράσομαι ...) and the expression ὡς ἔχω γνώμης ("what I think about ...") instead of a more assertive and confident verbal expression.[35]

This apparent reticence or lack of confidence recurs throughout the speech: e.g. at 14 he draws attention away from his rhetorical skill and to his practical proposals for preparation, while later he introduces a suggestion about Athenian finances

---

[32] E.g. 3, 36; 9, 74; 10, 46; 60, 4-5; THUC. 2, 36; LYS. 2, 3, 6, 17.

[33] One cannot help wondering whether this reflected 4th century realities or had become a *topos* in deliberative oratory. Cf. the discussion of meta-rhetorical passages below.

[34] εἰ δὲ παρελθὼν εἰς ὁστισοῦν δύναιτο διδάξαι καὶ πεῖσαι, τίς παρασκευὴ καὶ πόση καὶ πόθεν πορισθεῖσα χρήσιμος ἔσται τῇ πόλει, πᾶς ὁ παρὼν φόβος λελύσεται.

[35] Such as ὑπολαμβάνω or δοκῶ, DEM. 4, 1 (ἂν ... ἐπειρώμην ἃ γιγνώσκω λέγειν ...); 5, 3 (... οἴομαι καὶ πεπεικὼς ἐμαυτὸν ἀνέστηκα); 5, 4 (ἀκριβῶς εἰδώς ...).

(24ff.) and suggests that what he is going to say will come across as a paradox (αἰνίγματι γὰρ ὅμοιον ...: "it is like a riddle ..."). This is followed by a more assertive expression of his foresight (24: "My view is that we do not need to talk about money now ... for this sounds like a riddle").[36] The presentation of his *ethos* is rounded off (it is possible that ring-composition is being employed here) in the conclusion, where he stresses the importance of action over fruitless rhetoric (41).

In *On the Megalopolitans*, which was delivered just one year later, Demosthenes advances his quest to establish his *ethos* in the Assembly as he presents himself as the middle-of-the-road politician who will be attacked by opponents on both sides, those who advocate supporting the Arcadians and those who are in favour of lending a hand to the Spartans (1-3).[37] He thus seeks to create political space for himself as the city's adviser by opposition to those who slander and accuse each other. His *ethos* as an honest adviser is also shaped through the use of an anti-deception *topos* (3).[38] Throughout the speech he presents himself in opposition to other politicians but conforming with what is expedient for the city. The characterisation by means of antithesis to the (unnamed) opponents when the latter are collectively denounced is a useful, indirect means of self-characterisation.

In the third of his early deliberative speeches, *On the Freedom of the Rhodians*, Demosthenes seems to have grown in confidence. One can only speculate on the possible effect that his earlier interventions may have had on the perception of his *ethos* by the public, but his tone in this speech is markedly different. He is prepared to criticise the Athenians right from

---

[36] ἐγώ φημι χρῆναι μὴ λέγειν νυνὶ περὶ χρημάτων ... αἰνίγματι γὰρ ὅμοιον τοῦτό γε.

[37] According to BLASS (Abt. III.i) 308, the language, metaphors, rhetorical devices, and style become more forceful in later speeches whereas in this speech "im allgemeinen der Ton ruhig und gemessen bleibt, wie es dem verständingen Rathgeber zukommt".

[38] οὐ μὴν ἀλλ' αἱρήσομαι μᾶλλον αὐτός, ἂν ἄρα τοῦτο πάθω, δοκεῖν φλυαρεῖν, ἢ παρ' ἃ βέλτιστα νομίζω τῇ πόλει, προέσθαι τισὶν ὑμᾶς ἐξαπατῆσαι (16, 3). On anti-deception *topoi* in Attic Oratory, see KREMMYDAS (2013) 65-80, 87.

the outset for not acting on the decisions they take in the Assembly. His criticism is mild but unambiguous:

"Until now I have never thought it was difficult to teach you what the best policy is, for, to put it simply, I believe you all seem to know what it is, but to persuade you to implement it. For when a decision has been approved and voted on, it is no closer to being implemented than it was before it was approved" (15, 1).[39]

Later in the speech he hints at a growing relationship between Demosthenes as orator and adviser and the Athenian audience; he has advised them in the past to prepare their military to face the Persian King (he stresses that he was the first to take to the speakers' platform) and "his advice was pleasing to them" (15, 6).[40]

His deliberative *ethos* is also enhanced by his emphasis on the constancy and correctness of his advice: he would have said the same thing to the Persian King if he took him on as his adviser (7); what he says is nothing new (9).

A final touch to Demosthenes' Assembly *ethos* in this speech is added through the (apparent) self-contradiction between the *Schadenfreude* (at the deserved suffering of the Rhodians) and the pity (at the suffering of an equal) he expresses at the misfortune of the Rhodians; it is likely that he is trying to address and reconcile the mixed emotional responses of the audience towards the plight of the Rhodians (15, 15).[41] Demosthenes addresses the potentially mixed emotional responses of the audience by reducing the distance between them and the Rhodians; he claims that the Athenians, like the Rhodians, have been deceived by schemers (15, 16).[42]

---

[39] ἐγὼ δ' οὐδεπώποθ' ἡγησάμην χαλεπὸν τὸ διδάξαι τὰ βέλτισθ' ὑμᾶς (ὡς γὰρ εἰπεῖν ἁπλῶς, ἅπαντες ὑπάρχειν ἐγνωκότες μοι δοκεῖτε), ἀλλὰ τὸ πεῖσαι πράττειν ταῦτα· ἐπειδὰν γάρ τι δόξῃ καὶ ψηφισθῇ, τότ' ἴσον τοῦ πραχθῆναι ἀπέχει ὅσονπερ πρὶν δόξαι.

[40] ... καὶ ὑμῖν ἤρεσκε ταῦτα.

[41] But contrast his comments at 15, 21, where he demonstrates a sound understanding of mass psychology and an ability to give moral guidance to the people.

[42] φημὶ δὴ χρῆναι πειρᾶσθαι σώζειν τοὺς ἄνδρας καὶ μὴ μνησικακεῖν, ἐνθυμουμένους ὅτι πολλὰ καὶ ὑμεῖς ὑπὸ τῶν ἐπιβουλευσάντων ἐξηπάτησθε, ὧν οὐδενὸς αὐτοὶ δοῦναι δίκην δίκαιον ἂν εἶναι φήσαιτε (15, 16).

Thus, one notices development and flexibility in the construction of Demosthenes' deliberative *ethos* as the young orator and politician seeks to define his role in Athenian politics. He emerges as a politician who demonstrates confidence in the correctness of his advice, awareness of and careful handling of the audience's emotions, and seeks to carve out his own space as a reliable alternative to Athenian politicians who prioritise their skill in rhetoric over much-needed action.

Demosthenic *ethos* in the *Philippic* cycle: increasing confidence and sophistication in the use of tools of self-characterisation

In this section, I shall argue that Demosthenes' projection of his own *ethos* becomes more direct and assertive in the speeches of the *Philippic* cycle as he uses techniques of self-characterisation more frequently, directly, and in more sophisticated ways. However, one should not attribute this only to his growing experience as a statesman and orator. One should also take into account the changing landscape of political affairs in the Greek world with the emergence of Philip as a direct threat to Athenian interests. The city needed strong leaders to lead it through a crisis that magnified the tensions and led to polarisation among Athenian political groups. One might claim, on the evidence of Demosthenic oratory, that Athenian politics had become increasingly toxic.[43] It is impossible, of course, to gauge levels of toxicity in default of satisfactory evidence, but there are signs of convergence between the deliberative and forensic discourse especially after the Peace of Philocrates in 346.

The newfound confidence exhibited by Demosthenes in *On the freedom of the Rhodians* reappears in the (almost contemporary) *First Philippic* (Dem. 4; date: 351). One might be justified

---

[43] This is not to say that Athenian politics and political discourse were not toxic before this time. One would have to look at forensic speeches originating in the first decade of the 4th century for parallels, but there are no parallels from the Assembly.

in claiming that once Demosthenes had emerged as an important player on the Athenian political scene, his *ethos* had become better known, and although it was still malleable and subject to rhetorical manipulation, it had to be recognisable and credible.

In the introduction to his first speech of the *Philippic* cycle, he suggests that this was going to be the first time he was going to speak first in an Assembly debate; he explains that he is forced to do so due to the fact that the usual speakers have failed to give good advice to the people (1). He thus clearly sets himself apart from other, possibly better-established speakers. This demonstration of confidence appears alongside old (e.g. an ability to make a diagnosis of the problem, familiarity with history, knowledge of the financial affairs of the city, prognosis and proposed cure of the problem at hand) and new techniques of self-presentation of his *ethos*. He now expresses belief in the Athenian people and injects confidence in them at a time when they were dispirited. This demonstrates a deepening relationship of trust between the orator and the people, while playing to the audience's deepest felt emotions and enhancing the possibility of a positive response on the part of the audience.

Demosthenes' confidence in his ability to advise them on what is expedient for the city reaches a peak in the conclusion of the speech. The verbal forms in the text below highlighted in bold typescript underscore his boldness and confidence in full knowledge of possible consequences, while the underlined words stress the centrality of συμφέρον in his peroration:[44]

> "As for me, I have never yet chosen to please you by saying anything that I was not **convinced** would be <u>beneficial</u> to you; and now, **I have said freely** everything that I know **without holding anything back**. However, just as I **know** what is most <u>beneficial</u> for you to hear, I wish that the person who gave the best speech would also <u>benefit</u>. For I should have felt happier, if that were the case. Now, however, because what is going to happen to me as a result of having given this advice is uncertain, I still choose

---

[44] Five attestations in a single section. Note also the contrast between χάριν and τὰ βέλτιστ'.

to speak because I am convinced that what I will say will benefit
you if you also implement it. Whatever is going to benefit all,
may that prevail" (4, 51).[45]

On the face of it, this is a variation of the meta-rhetorical passages relating to the role of rhetoric. Here, however, the meta-
rhetorical passage develops into a self-referential passage asserting
Demosthenes' constancy as an adviser, his confidence, boldness,
and knowledge of what is expedient for the city. And while this
passage rounds off the speech, he goes one step further by
expressing his confidence in the way that events will develop.

But Demosthenes' growing confidence as an adviser is also
evident in his criticism of Athenian passivity in relation to specific failures of foreign policy. Whereas in earlier speeches he had
confined himself to generalising criticisms of Athenian decision-
making and policy (e.g. 14, 15) or brief criticisms in passing
(e.g. 15, 1), here he points to Athenian slowness as a reason for
Philip's success (4, 5-6) and criticises their lethargy and inaction
in the past (4, 10-11), whilst pointing to concrete examples from
recent Athenian history when they managed to overcome it:

> "For you must put the thought in his mind that you may get rid
> of apathy and attack, as you did at Euboea and, as it is reported,
> also at Haliartus and more recently at Thermopylae ..." (4, 17).[46]

However, in this speech he does not confine himself to castigating Athenian passivity, and inaction. His detailed analysis
and logical presentation of the concrete proposals he puts forward serve to enhance his *ethos* as a man of action rather than

---

[45] ἐγὼ μὲν οὖν οὔτ' ἄλλοτε πώποτε πρὸς χάριν εἱλόμην λέγειν ὅ τι ἂν μὴ καὶ
συνοίσειν **πεπεισμένος** ὦ, νῦν τε ἃ **γιγνώσκω** πάνθ' ἁπλῶς, **οὐδὲν ὑποστει-
λάμενος, πεπαρρησίασμαι.** ἐβουλόμην δ' ἄν, ὥσπερ ὅτι ὑμῖν συμφέρει τὰ
βέλτιστ' ἀκούειν **οἶδα,** οὕτως εἰδέναι συνοῖσον καὶ τῷ τὰ βέλτιστ' εἰπόντι·
πολλῷ γὰρ ἂν ἥδιον εἶχον. νῦν δ' ἐπ' ἀδήλοις οὖσι τοῖς ἀπὸ τούτων ἐμαυτῷ
γενησομένοις, ὅμως ἐπὶ τῷ συνοίσειν ὑμῖν, ἂν πράξητε, ταῦτα πεπεῖσθαι λέγειν
αἱροῦμαι. νικώη δ' ὅ τι πᾶσιν μέλλει συνοίσειν.

[46] δεῖ γὰρ ἐκείνῳ τοῦτ' ἐν τῇ γνώμῃ παραστῆσαι, ὡς ὑμεῖς ἐκ τῆς ἀμελείας
ταύτης τῆς ἄγαν, ὥσπερ εἰς Εὔβοιαν καὶ πρότερόν ποτε φασιν εἰς Ἁλίαρτον καὶ
τὰ τελευταῖα πρώην εἰς Πύλας, ἴσως ἂν ὁρμήσαιτε ...

words. This is the only extant speech that probably accompanied a draft proposal by Demosthenes himself.[47] Thus, the *topos* of fruitless deliberation ('fighting with decrees': e.g. 4, 30)[48] is addressed and refuted as he pledges his willingness to take part in the expedition. Demosthenes thus portrays himself as a man of action, not just words.

Demosthenes, Philip, and Athenian politicians: a triptych of *ethe* in the *Olynthiacs*

In the three *Olynthiacs* (delivered in 349/8), *ethos* plays an even more prominent role than in the earlier deliberative speeches. Demosthenes draws on his arsenal of techniques of characterisation in order to promote the *ethos* of three categories of individuals (or groups of politicians/orators), a triptych of *ethe*: his *ethos*, that of other Athenian politicians/orators, and that of Philip. The promotion of his own *ethos* takes place in the *First Olynthiac* through passages of self-characterisation and meta-rhetoric in the middle of the speech (e.g. 1, 14-16), before he makes concrete proposals to address the current crisis (17-20). Note how he combines meta-rhetoric with criticism of the audience and promotion of his boldness as an adviser:

> "Now, someone may say that it is easy to be critical and anyone can do it, but that **to give an opinion regarding what should be done about the current situation is an adviser's task**. As for me, men of Athens, I am aware that many times, when things go against your plans, you are angry not at those responsible but at the orators who happen to have spoken last. **I, however, do not think I should hold back from saying what I think will benefit you out of concern for my own safety**" (1, 16).[49]

---

[47] Cf. criticism by his opponents alluded to by DEM. in 8, 68, 73.
[48] MADER (2006).
[49] τὸ μὲν οὖν ἐπιτιμᾶν ἴσως φήσαι τις ἂν ῥᾴδιον καὶ παντὸς εἶναι, **τὸ δ' ὑπὲρ τῶν παρόντων ὅ τι δεῖ πράττειν ἀποφαίνεσθαι, τοῦτ' εἶναι συμβούλου.** ἐγὼ δ' οὐκ ἀγνοῶ μέν, ὦ ἄνδρες Ἀθηναῖοι, τοῦθ' ὅτι πολλάκις ὑμεῖς οὐ τοὺς αἰτίους, ἀλλὰ τοὺς ὑστάτους περὶ τῶν πραγμάτων εἰπόντας ἐν ὀργῇ ποιεῖσθε, ἂν

The extended presentation of Philip's character dominates the *Second Olynthiac* (2, 5-10, 14-20), familiarises the audience with their great adversary, and implicitly draws a contrast with their collective Athenian *ethos*. Philip represents an antithesis to the democratic Athenian *ethos*, which Demosthenes endorsed and promoted. He reminds the audience that Philip's success is due to the failures (2, 3-4) and inaction (2, 27-30) of the Athenians and pleads with them to take action (2, 30-31). Thus, the promotion of Demosthenes' *ethos* is only implicit and oblique in this speech.

Finally, in the *Third Olynthiac* the orator's role and responsibility take a more central role again: in the *prooemium*, a variation of the *topos* of the speaker's inability to address a topic (ἐγὼ δ' οὐχ ὅ τι χρὴ ... πρὸς ὑμᾶς περὶ αὐτῶν εἰπεῖν) and a *captatio beneuolentiae* are combined with a brief meta-rhetorical passage on how the current state of affairs is due to the fact that orators tend to gratify the audience rather than benefit the city (note the use of verbs expressing knowledge and confidence):

> "Now, the current situation, more than ever before, requires great care and deliberation. I, for one, do not think that the hardest thing is to give advice regarding the current circumstances; I am at a loss, however, men of Athens, as to how I should best speak to you about them. For, I am convinced from what I have seen and heard that we have missed more opportunities because of our reluctance to do our duty rather than because of our failure to understand it. I expect you to bear with me if I speak frankly and to examine whether what I am saying is true, but also for this additional reason, namely, so that things might improve in the future. For you see how our current situation has reached this level of wickedness due to the fact that public speakers seek to please their audience in the Assembly" (3, 3).[50]

τι μὴ κατὰ γνώμην ἐκβῇ. οὐ μὴν οἶμαι δεῖν τὴν ἰδίαν ἀσφάλειαν σκο-
ποῦνθ' ὑποστείλασθαι περὶ ὧν ὑμῖν συμφέρειν ἡγοῦμαι.

[50] ὁ μὲν οὖν παρὼν καιρός, εἴπερ ποτέ, πολλῆς φροντίδος καὶ βουλῆς δεῖται·
ἐγὼ δ' οὐχ ὅ τι χρὴ περὶ τῶν παρόντων συμβουλεῦσαι χαλεπώτατον ἡγοῦμαι,
ἀλλ' ἐκεῖν' ἀπορῶ, τίνα χρὴ τρόπον, ὦ ἄνδρες Ἀθηναῖοι, πρὸς ὑμᾶς περὶ αὐτῶν
εἰπεῖν. πέπεισμαι γὰρ ἐξ ὧν παρὼν καὶ ἀκούων **σύνοιδα**, τὰ πλείω τῶν πραγμάτων ἡμᾶς ἐκπεφευγέναι τῷ μὴ βούλεσθαι τὰ δέοντα ποιεῖν ἢ τῷ μὴ συνιέναι.

A more extended meta-rhetorical passage follows passages containing concrete proposals (3, 10-13), a passage criticising the Athenians once again for their idleness and stressing the importance of action (3, 14-15), and a brief, memorable passage castigating Philip's *ethos* (3, 16: "Is he not our enemy? Does he not possess our lands? Is he not a barbarian? Is any description too bad for him?").[51] Demosthenes comments on the culture of deliberation in the Assembly and stresses the need to choose what is best rather than what is pleasant, thus criticising the Athenians, albeit obliquely (3, 18). Mild censure of the Athenians is expressed in the following couple of sections (3, 19-20) before Demosthenes finally focuses on his *ethos* in what is a masterful, extended passage of self-characterisation (3, 21-27) combining a number of different techniques:

i) an elaborate *captatio beneuolentiae* dealing with the possibility of adverse audience reactions against him. His credentials as a speaker are stressed through a statement of opinion (21: "I believe that it is a mark of a good citizen to consider the city's safety more important than his own popularity as a speaker"),[52] which essentially glosses the recurrent criticism of the Athenians who preferred what was pleasant over what was expedient;

ii) a reference to past history and illustrious examples of orators and politicians (e.g. Nicias, Pericles, Aristides, and Miltiades: 3, 21, 26). The two comparisons with 5th-century Athenian politicians echo moralising passages in forensic oratory,[53] which

ἀξιῶ δ' ὑμᾶς, ἂν μετὰ παρρησίας ποιῶμαι τοὺς λόγους, ὑπομένειν, τοῦτο θεωροῦντας, εἰ τἀληθῆ λέγω, καὶ διὰ τοῦτο, ἵνα τὰ λοιπὰ βελτίω γένηται· ὁρᾶτε γὰρ ὡς ἐκ τοῦ πρὸς χάριν δημηγορεῖν ἐνίους εἰς πᾶν προελήλυθε μοχθηρίας τὰ παρόντα.

[51] οὐκ ἐχθρός; οὐκ ἔχων τὰ ἡμέτερα; οὐ βάρβαρος; οὐχ ὅ τι ἂν εἴποι τις;

[52] ἀλλὰ δικαίου πολίτου κρίνω τὴν τῶν πραγμάτων σωτηρίαν ἀντὶ τῆς ἐν τῷ λέγειν χάριτος αἱρεῖσθαι.

[53] [DEM.] 13, 29 is a close parallel, although the order and contents of the list have been changed. Themistocles and Cimon are mentioned in 3, 24 instead of Miltiades.

stress the simplicity (and exemplary behaviour) of politicians of old;[54]

iii) a contrast to the orators and politicians of the present time (3, 22);

iv) an amplification of the previous contrasts through a reference to the effects that the conduct of politicians of old had on the position of the city in the Greek world and its visible affluence during the days of the Athenian Empire as opposed to the current predicament of the city (3, 24-27).

This sophisticated combination of the different techniques of self-characterisation in an extended passage towards the conclusion of the speech clearly serves to enhance Demosthenes' *ethos* as an orator and politician and impress it on his Athenian audience.

In the three *Olynthiacs*, Demosthenes demonstrates a more sophisticated command of diverse techniques of self-characterisation. His approach in the three speeches is joined-up and sensitive to the needs of the wider political context. It is no coincidence that his *ethos* receives more attention in the third speech and accompanies the presentation of proposals in response to the deteriorating situation in Northern Greece. The stress on his reliability as an adviser is intended to counteract the potentially hostile reaction to the proposal for the transfer of money from the Theoric to the military fund (e.g. 3, 11, 34). At the same time, the comparison between the politicians of an Athenian 'golden age' and contemporary politicians implies that Demosthenes stands out as a politician who can be trusted. Thus, the *Olynthiacs* can be seen as a milestone in the rhetorical portrayal of Demosthenes' *ethos*.

---

[54] Cf. DEM. 23, 209 (Aristides), 196 (Miltiades), 198 (Themistocles and Miltiades compared with 4th-century generals, Iphicrates, Timotheus and Chabrias who are being identified with their military victories), 207.

Demosthenes' *ethos* after 346

Thereafter the presentation of his *ethos* becomes even more assertive in tone. The self-referential passages become longer and more direct. The reasons for this change might be identified in the heated Athenian political context after 346. The discussion of the merits of peace with Philip (Demosthenes recommends the acceptance of the peace)[55] gives Demosthenes an opportunity to talk up his credentials as a reliable adviser with an excellent track record. In the *prooemium* of the speech *On the Peace,* after a variation of the *topos* of the speaker's inability (5, 1) and a passing criticism of the Athenian culture of deliberation (5, 2),[56] Demosthenes launches into an extended presentation of his *ethos* and past successes, and stresses the correctness of his advice (e.g. 5, 9). After all, a successful politician can be trusted to lead the people. Demosthenes uses *praeteritio* to lay even more emphasis on a self-referential excursus (5, 4-12). However, this long self-referential passage reveals that Demosthenes now adopts a radically different strategy of self-presentation. He claims that he is not used to self-promotion, although this practice is expedient for speakers engaging in it (4). Demosthenes was aware of the fact that he was pushing the boundaries of his own deliberative *ethos* and had to account for this departure: he justifies his self-referential excursus by claiming that it would enable the audience to make up their minds about his current speech. There is no doubt that Demosthenes was crafting his public *persona* and cultivating his Assembly *ethos* during the years he hogged the limelight. He even argues

[55] On the problems of accepting the notion that Demosthenes was in favour of the peace when in DEM. 19, 113 it is claimed that only Aeschines had spoken in support of the peace treaty, see BLASS (1893) 342-343, MACDOWELL (2009) 327.

[56] 5, 2: οἱ μὲν γὰρ ἄλλοι πάντες ἄνθρωποι πρὸ τῶν πραγμάτων εἰώθασι χρῆσθαι τῷ βουλεύεσθαι, ὑμεῖς δὲ μετὰ τὰ πράγματα. BLASS (1893) 343-344 argues that this *prooemium* does not belong organically to the rest of the speech. He identifies "ein zweites Prooemium" in 5, 4 and avers that, due to the absence of *pathos*, this speech is closer to the 'not Philippic' speeches.

that his *ethos* was challenging norms of contemporary deliberative oratory:

"Although I am well aware, men of Athens, that it is always very
profitable for a bold speaker to talk to you about himself and his
own speeches, if one is bold enough to do so, I believe it is such
a vulgar and offensive practice that I shrink from it, even though
I see that it is necessary. However, I think that you will be better
placed to make a judgement about what I am going to say, if I
remind you briefly of what I told you before" (5, 4).[57]

And Demosthenes does not only claim to breach the norms
of deliberative *ethos*; at the same time, he also engages in the
agonistic culture of the Assembly. He needs to compare himself with other advisers/politicians and persuade the audience
of the superiority of his advice and judgment. However, even
when drawing such comparisons, he is mindful of the boundaries
of deliberative *ethos* and the pitfalls of boasting and, therefore,
stresses the fact that he does not possess any negative ethical/
intellectual qualities. One of the reasons he identifies is his
good luck (which demonstrates his piety) and the fact that he
does not receive bribes (contrast 5, 5):[58]

"Now, if I have been more successful than others to foresee what
was going to happen, I do not attribute this to my cleverness or
any other charisma I might have, nor do I pretend to have any
special knowledge or understanding, except these two: first, men
of Athens, my good luck, which from what I can see is more

---

[57] ἀκριβῶς δ᾽ εἰδώς, ὦ ἄνδρες Ἀθηναῖοι, τὸ λέγειν περὶ ὧν αὐτὸς εἶπέ τις καὶ
περὶ αὑτοῦ παρ᾽ ὑμῖν ἀεὶ τῶν πάνυ λυσιτελούντων τοῖς τολμῶσιν ὄν, οὕτως
ἡγοῦμαι φορτικὸν καὶ ἐπαχθὲς ὥστ᾽ ἀνάγκην οὖσαν ὁρῶν ὅμως ἀποκνῶ. νομίζω
δ᾽ ἄμεινον ἂν ὑμᾶς περὶ ὧν νῦν ἐρῶ κρῖναι, μικρὰ τῶν πρότερόν ποτε ῥηθέντων
ὑπ᾽ ἐμοῦ μνημονεύσαντας.
[58] This passage looks forward to his disclaimer of bribery in the speech *On the
Crown* (18, 298); bribery was one of the major political offences covered by
the *nomos eisangeltikos*; on venality as a standard accusation against Athenian
politicians/orators, especially after the Peace of Philocrates, see, e.g., DEM. 19,
127; DIN. 4, 1, 3, 13, 29, 103; 6, 6, 22; HYP. 1 (*Dem.*), fr. 8, col. 35, l. 25
(λῆμμα, λήμματα); 1 (*Dem.*) fr. 62, col. 25, l. 25; 1 (*Dem.*) fr. 9, col. 40, l. 1; 3
(*Eux.*) col. 39, l. 25 (δῶρον, δῶρα); DIN. 4, 11, 26, 45, 93, 98; HYP. 1 (*Dem.*) fr. 3,
col. 15, l. 2; fr. 8, col. 34, l. 9; *Epitaph.* col. 5, l. 2 (δωροδοκία, δωροδοκήσας).

powerful than any cleverness or wisdom. [12] Second, I reach my judgements and decisions without receiving gifts and no one can ever show that I have made any profit from my policies and speeches" (5, 11-12).[59]

How can this change of tone and the emphasis on Demosthenes' self-presentation be explained? One possible explanation is that the speech was used as a tool of 'propaganda' to promote Demosthenes' political role in Athens. This would be consistent with the view expressed by Libanius that the speech was prepared but not delivered at the assembly meeting where Aeschines spoke in favour of the peace. Similarly, MacDowell suggests that Demosthenes' speech might have been delivered at a different, subsequent meeting from the one tasked with responding to the Amphictyons.[60] Although these explanations do carry weight, I believe one should attribute the changes in Demosthenes' self-presentation to his different needs in a tense political situation. His closer engagement with active Athenian politics and the deterioration in Athens' relationship with Philip had increased the hostility against him (the theme of anger and hostility against orators appears more frequently now),[61] and this did not leave his position as an Assembly speaker unaffected. And while he could shelter himself from the threat of litigation by using a network of friends and associates in order to pass any concrete proposals and drafts, he felt an increasing need to defend his reputation in the Assembly.

---

[59] ταῦτα τοίνυν ἅπανθ᾽, ὅσα φαίνομαι βέλτιον τῶν ἄλλων προορῶν, οὐδ᾽ εἰς μίαν, ὦ ἄνδρες Ἀθηναῖοι, οὔτε δεινότητ᾽ οὔτ᾽ ἀλαζονείαν ἐπανοίσω, οὐδὲ προσποιήσομαι δι᾽ οὐδὲν ἄλλο γιγνώσκειν καὶ προαισθάνεσθαι πλὴν δι᾽ ἂν ὑμῖν εἴπω, δύο· ἓν μέν, ὦ ἄνδρες Ἀθηναῖοι, δι᾽ εὐτυχίαν, ἣν συμπάσης ἐγὼ τῆς ἐν ἀνθρώποις οὔσης δεινότητος καὶ σοφίας ὁρῶ κρατοῦσαν· [12] ἕτερον δέ, προῖκα τὰ πράγματα κρίνω καὶ λογίζομαι, καὶ οὐδὲν λῆμμ᾽ ἂν οὐδεὶς ἔχοι πρὸς οἷς ἐγὼ πεπολίτευμαι καὶ λέγω δεῖξαι προσηρτημένον.

[60] MacDowell (2009) 327. But even if one were to suppose that Demosthenes did not deliver this speech, it might still have contributed to the enhancement of his public *persona*.

[61] ὀργή, ὀργίζεσθαι, and their cognates occur six times in speeches delivered post-346 (three times in speeches before that).

The *Second Philippic* (Dem. 6) builds on strategies of projecting *ethos* deployed in earlier speeches, especially in the *Olynthiacs* and the speech *On the Peace*. I shall briefly identify a couple of features that create a sense of continuity in terms of the speaker's *ethos*, whilst also developing his strategies of characterisation.

The standard meta-rhetorical passage in the *prooemium* regarding the responsibility of the orators for giving sound advice now involves censure of the Athenian public for their idleness. Demosthenes then joins audience and orators together in a call to reform the culture of deliberation and decision-making (6, 5). He also claims that the fear of stirring enmity in the audience had prevented politicians from making proposals that would actually stop Philip in his tracks (4). Philip's appearance in this speech recalls the dominance of his *ethos* in the *Second Olynthiac*; here, the dangerous villain and arch-enemy of Athens is the figure of authority who praises the Athenian *ethos* (9-11) and even mentions Philip's ancestor Alexander I (11).

The reporting of Demosthenes' speech to the Messenians ('speech in speech': 6, 20-25) is a new device employed in order to enhance authority (cf. 5, 5: his advice proved unpopular, he was isolated and suffered abuse by his venal opponents), an interesting development on the self-referential excursus of the speech *On the Peace* (5, 4-12). If the Messenians thought that he was correct yet in the end chose not to act on his recommendations, the Athenians who are more intelligent ought to listen more carefully and act on his advice.

Demosthenes defends his *ethos* against the calumnies of those who disparaged him from the speakers' platform (30) and his tone now recalls forensic discourse (31-34).[62] The political temperature in Athens had risen significantly by the time of this speech (344/3), and this is also reflected in the way that Demosthenes talks about his *ethos* and that of his unnamed

---

[62] Note the use of nouns and adjectives frequently attested in forensic orations of the Demosthenic corpus: λοιδορία, ὀργή, αἰτίους, αἴσχιστον, ὀργίλους.

political opponents.[63] The polarisation of Athenian political life in response to the deepening crisis in Athens' relations with Philip ultimately helps Demosthenes promote his own role in the city as a standout politician and his *ethos* as a trustworthy adviser.

That the wider political context has affected the tone of political discourse can be seen in the last three speeches of the *Philippic* cycle (Dem. 8, 9, 10), all of which were delivered in the same year (341). Take, for example, the development of the meta-rhetorical passage criticising politicians and orators (Dem. 8, 23; cf. 38). Demosthenes now turns it on its head and he is asking the people (in an *apostrophe*) to instruct him what to say (cf. 10, 11). A little later, another extended meta-rhetorical passage criticises the current culture of deliberation, while offering practical examples from recent history through a hypothetical speech in the Assembly by the Greeks (35-37).

Finally, as he edges towards the end of the speech *On the Chersonese*, he produces an extended passage of masterful characterisation, once again combining different techniques of characterisation (8, 67-76): i) a self-referential passage in response to criticism by political opponents of his reluctance to propose decrees and expose himself to risk (68); ii) criticism of the prevalent litigious culture and extensive overlaps between the forensic and deliberative sphere (69), which favour his opponents; iii) a self-referential passage on his contributions to the city, including his benefactions (69-70); iv) self-referential response to criticism of his reluctance to propose (decrees leading to) action (73); v) the example of Timotheus' proposals in the Athenian Assembly (74-75); v) Demosthenes' own proposals (76).[64]

It is also worth noting the emphasis on the need to punish bribe-receiving politicians and the stirring of hostile emotions

---

[63] Cf. the use of a verb relating to deception in 36: παρεκρούσθητε. For the use of language of deception in deliberative speeches, see KREMMYDAS (2013) 80-82, 88.

[64] Note the rhetorical device of *kyklos* in this passage of self-characterisation.

against them (9, 77; cf. 10, 7). This recalls strategies also attested in forensic oratory and confirms the idea of the toxicity of contemporary political life, which also emerges from the *prooemium* of the *Third Philippic* (cf. also 10, 35-36 before the introduction of the Theoric Fund issue). Demosthenes goes beyond the criticism of political opponents (9, 2) and claims that the Athenians have "banished freedom of speech" (trans. Trevett) from the Assembly as far as giving advice is concerned (9, 3: ὑμεῖς τὴν παρρησίαν ἐκ δὲ τοῦ συμβουλεύειν παντάπασιν ἐξεληλάκατε). He confirms this toxic political context at 9, 7 and 9, 53 (punishment of Philip's fifth column in Athens; cf. 10, 57), while he showcases the *ethos* of Euphraeus of Oreus (9, 59-64) as a moral paradigm that parallels his own role in Athens (implicit characterisation).

The *ethos* of the Athenians also receives coverage (9, 36-37) as it is contrasted with the *ethos* of the ancestors (42-46: the decree of Arthmius of Zelea) and that of citizens in other cities (49-50) who have been taken advantage of by Philip (see also 9, 65).

By contrast, most of the *Fourth Philippic* seems to focus on what the Athenians need to do in the current circumstances.[65] Demosthenes' *ethos* surfaces towards the end of the speech (76), following up on a section criticising rival politicians (10, 70-74). In the middle of that section (71-73), Aristomedes is singled out and seems to embody the harmful tendency of politicians to prioritise their own interests over the interests of the city.[66] Having deplored the practices of rival politicians

---

[65] The *prooemium* combines meta-rhetoric and criticism of the Athenians (1-5); 46-47 comment on the decline of Athens from a position of hegemony in the Greek world. At 68 the *ethos* and actions of Philip's Athenian associates are being castigated.

[66] VINCE (1930) *ad loc.* suggested that this was probably a fictional character, but that does not have to be the case. Conversely, Didymus argued that Aristo-medes was a contemporary politician. Although this name was not uncommon in the 4th century and features on contemporary decrees (see *LGPN* ii.A *s.v.* [3]), it is a speaking name ('the one who has the best plans') and Demosthenes may be being ironical here.

(70-74) and the contemporary culture of deliberation in the city, Demosthenes has one final chance to justify the advice he has offered in the Assembly (76). The contrast between the abusive behaviour, the deceptive words of his opponents and his truth-telling, integrity, and good-will is marked as he brings the speech to a close:

> "That is the whole truth. I have said what is best for the city out of goodwill, not what is harmful in order to flatter you, nor what is full of deceit so that the speaker can make money, while the affairs of the city are handed over to our enemies. Therefore, you must either put a stop to these habits or you will not have anyone else to blame for the terrible state of our city's affairs but yourselves" (10, 76).[67]

Conclusion

It is clear that Demosthenes paid great attention to the creation and projection of his *ethos* in the Athenian assembly between 354 and 341. The close reading of his deliberative speeches suggests that he sought to find his own 'voice' in the din of Athenian politics and to project his unique *ethos*, his own 'brand' of adviser of the people. His early deliberative speeches testify to his experimentation with stock themes and techniques of self-characterisation peculiar to Assembly oratory and to his growing confidence as a politician: self-referential, meta-rhetorical passages and passages praising or blaming the Athenian people are just three of the techniques of projecting *ethos*, which can be traced throughout his assembly speeches. Demosthenes had to rely more on the projection of his *ethos* as he became more established in the personality-driven politics of Athens. He demonstrated flexibility at combining these techniques as he responded to challenges in the contemporary

---

[67] ταῦτ' ἐστὶ τἀληθῆ, μετὰ πάσης παρρησίας, ἁπλῶς εὐνοίᾳ τὰ βέλτιστ' εἰρημένα, οὐ κολακείᾳ βλάβης καὶ ἀπάτης λόγος μεστός, ἀργύριον τῷ λέγοντι ποιήσων, τὰ δὲ πράγματα τῆς πόλεως τοῖς ἐχθροῖς ἐγχειριῶν.

political context. The increasingly personal, direct tone he adopted and the progressively more hostile tone of his criticism of other politicians seems to suggest that the deliberative discourse was not immune from the toxicity of Athenian politics of the late 340's. It should be noted that the projection of his deliberative *ethos* in the forensic sphere (e.g. the review of his career in *On the Crown*) is consistent with his self-presentation in speeches of the *Philippic* cycle, and this suggests the great care with which he moulded and promoted his political *ethos* over time. The study of Demosthenes' *ethos* in the speeches of the *Philippic* cycle demonstrates his skill at projecting a compelling image as an adviser in the Athenian Assembly.

Works cited

BLASS, F. (1893), *Die attische Beredsamkeit.* Abt. III.2, *Demosthenes' Genossen und Gegner* (Hildesheim).

DE BRAUW, M. (2002), "'Listen to the Laws Themselves': Citations of Laws and Portrayal of Character in Attic Oratory", *CJ* 97, 161-176.

BURKE, E.M. (2002), "The Early Political Speeches of Demosthenes: Elite Bias in the Response to Economic Crisis", *ClAnt* 21.2, 165-193.

CAREY, C. (1994), "Rhetorical Means of Persuasion", in I. WORTHINGTON (ed.), *Persuasion. Greek Rhetoric in Action* (London), 26-45.

DAVIES, J.K. (1971), *Athenian Propertied Families: 600-300 B.C.* (Oxford).

FORTENBAUGH, W.W. (1992), "Aristotle on Persuasion through Character", *Rhetorica* 10.3, 207-244.

GILL, C. (1984), "The *ēthos/pathos* Distinction in Rhetorical and Literary Criticism", *CQ* 34.1, 149-166.

HANSEN, M.H. (1975), *Eisangelia. The Sovereignty of the People's Court in the Fourth Century B.C. and the Impeachment of Generals and Politicians* (Odense).

—— (1989a), "*Rhetores* and *Strategoi* in Fourth-century Athens", in M.H. HANSEN, *The Athenian Ecclesia II* (Copenhagen), 25-33.

—— (1989b), "Updated Inventory of *Rhetores* and *Strategoi* (1988)", in M.H. HANSEN, *The Athenian Ecclesia II* (Copenhagen), 34-72.

—— (1991), *The Athenian Democracy in the Age of Demosthenes* (London).

KENNEDY, G.A. (1991), *Aristotle On Rhetoric. A Theory of Civic Discourse*. Newly translated with Introduction, Notes, and Appendices (New York).

KREMMYDAS, C. (2013), "The Discourse of Deception and Characterization in Attic Oratory", *GRBS* 53, 51-89.

—— (2017a, forthcoming), "*Ethos* and Logical Argumentation in Thucydides' Assembly Debates", in S. PAPAIOANNOU / A. SERAFIM / B. DA VELLA (eds.), *A Theatre of Justice. Aspects of Performance in Greco-Roman Oratory and Rhetoric* (Leiden).

—— (2017b, forthcoming), "Reflections on political speechwriting in Athens", in C. KREMMYDAS / L. RUBINSTEIN / J.G.F. POWELL (eds.), *From Antiphon to Autocue. Speechwriting Ancient and Modern* (Stuttgart).

MACDOWELL, D.M. (2009), *Demosthenes the Orator* (Oxford).

MADER, G. (2006), "Fighting Philip with Decrees: Demosthenes and the Syndrome of Symbolic Action", *AJPh* 127.3, 367-386.

—— (2007), "Foresight, Hindsight, and the Rhetoric of Self-Fashioning in Demosthenes' Philippic Cycle", *Rhetorica* 25.4, 339-360.

PELLING, C.B.R. (2012), "Aristotle's *Rhetoric,* the *Rhetorica ad Alexandrum,* and the Speeches in Herodotus and Thucydides", in E. FOSTER / D. LATEINER (eds.), *Thucydides and Herodotus* (Oxford), 281-315.

RUBINSTEIN, L. (2017, forthcoming), "Stage-managing Symbouleutic Speeches", in C. KREMMYDAS / L. RUBINSTEIN / J.G.F. POWELL (eds.), *From Antiphon to Autocue. Speechwriting Ancient and Modern* (Stuttgart).

RUSSELL, D.A. (1990), "*Ēthos* in Oratory and Rhetoric", in C.B.R. PELLING (ed.), *Characterization and Individuality in Greek Literature* (Oxford), 197-212.

TREVETT, J.C. (1996), "Aristotle's Knowledge of Athenian Oratory", *CQ* 46.2, 371-379.

VINCE, J.H. (1930), *Demosthenes.* I, With an English translation (Cambridge, MA).

WISSE, J. (1989), *Ethos and Pathos from Aristotle to Cicero* (Amsterdam).

WOERTHER, F. (2005), "Aux origines de la notion rhétorique d'*èthos*", *REG* 118, 79-116.

WOOTEN, C. (2010), "On the Road to *Philippic* III: The Management of Argument and the Modulation of Emotion in the Deliberative Speeches of Demosthenes", *Rhetorica* 28.1, 1-22.

YUNIS, H. (1996), *Taming Democracy. Models of Political Rhetoric in Classical Athens* (Ithaca).

DISCUSSION

M. Edwards: You did not use term *ethopoiia* in your paper – was there a reason for that?

C. Kremmydas: Thank you for your question, Mike. I intentionally avoided the term because it is a Hellenistic coinage and I felt that its application to 4th-century deliberative oratory would be anachronistic. The term was also used later to denote one particular type of advanced rhetorical exercises (e.g. Theon's *progymnasmata*; cf. the term *prosopopoiia*) whereby students had to create a speech demonstrating a speaker's *ethos*. I prefer to use terminology used by contemporary rhetorical theorists (i.e. Aristotle and Anaximenes) in my analysis of 4th-century oratory.

M. Edwards: Yes, of course. More substantively, I have questions on two different paths, the first of which is to follow up our discussion of this morning: how far does the lack of comparanda make a difference to what we can infer from Demosthenes' deliberative speeches? For example, you very correctly draw attention in your paper to the relative lack of invective against Demosthenes' opponents, at least in the earlier speeches, and in contrast to forensic speeches; but might Aeschines and his followers have nevertheless attacked Demosthenes personally?

C. Kremmydas: This is a valid point. We are very much limited by the absence of other 4th-century deliberative orations. Naturally, it is impossible to rule out that Demosthenes' opponents were a lot more virulent and personal in their attacks on him in the Assembly. However, I do not believe that this would have been the case at least before the mid-340's. First, there is some evidence suggesting that the absence of invective was probably not peculiar to Demosthenic Assembly oratory but was rather a question of rhetorical etiquette that was largely adhered to. Speakers in the Athenian Assembly speeches reported by Thucydides (no matter what one thinks of their historical reliability) also avoid direct personal attacks against their opponents, while the speaker/author of *On the treaty with Sparta* (attributed to Andocides but almost certainly spurious) also eschews personal invective. Second, early on in Demosthenes' public career, when he was still trying to carve out his own place on Athens' political landscape, it is unlikely that he would have represented a target worth attacking personally and directly.

M. Edwards: It is interesting that you think Andocides 3 is very likely spurious. But secondly, again following on from earlier discussion, how far should we be drawing a firm distinction between deliberative and forensic rhetoric in the sphere of *ethos*? See, for example, the concluding paragraph of your paper, where you say 'the projection of his deliberative *ethos* in the forensic sphere ... is consistent with his self-presentation in the Assembly speeches of the *Philippic* cycle'. And additionally, acting as *aduocatus diaboli*, does *ethos* really matter?

C. Kremmydas: I have tried to argue that the requirements in terms of presentation of a speaker's *ethos* are slightly different in a deliberative setting from what they are in a forensic context. Of course, one should allow for a certain degree of plasticity in the construction and projection of a speaker's *ethos* in order to adapt to the rhetorical needs of the different contexts. But Demosthenes' speeches *On the Crown* and *On the Embassy* are interesting cases in so far as he had to demonstrate that his character and track record as advisor of the city had been irreproachable throughout his public career (in the speech *On the Crown*) and in the particular affair debated in Aeschines' and Demosthenes' speeches on the Embassy. Therefore, the recognisability and consistency of his *ethos* was of paramount importance, especially since his opponent was alleging that he was merely an opportunist. And to respond to your concluding question, a well-known political figure could neglect *ethos* at his peril, whether in the Assembly or the Courts.

A. Chaniotis: You have clearly shown both the importance of *ethos* in Demosthenes' orations and the various layers of the subject. Apart from the *ethos* of an individual, the collective *ethos* of a community plays an important part in deliberative oratory, for instance in the speech of the Corinthians in Thucydides (Book 1) and in speeches in Polybius (e.g. 9, 28-39). Unlike reported speeches in historiography, in Athenian oratory we usually only have the speech of one orator, not his opponents' arguments. Of course, even one speech may provide allusions to what the opponent had said or was planning to say, or to street gossip. It is harder to assess what was exchanged during the meeting of the assembly or how the audience responded to the speeches, e.g. by interrupting the speaker or shouting in approval or disagreement. E.g., while an assembly for an *epidosis* was in process in Athens, Phokion's son, Phokos, notorious for having spent his father's fortune, came forward and said: "I am giving a contribution, too". The Athenians allegedly responded in one voice "Yes, to obscenity!" (this anecdote is narrated by Athenaios). We see again the object of the audience's criticism was *ethos*.

With such audience responses in mind but also considering the fact that the opponent of an orator would probably focus on *ethos* (praising his own and castigating that of the opponent), the self-representation of an orator's *ethos* serves a preemptive function as much as it is a persuasion strategy. So, Demosthenes' growing interest in *ethos* may not reflect growing confidence but growing hostility against him.

C. Kremmydas: Thank you for your insightful comments. It is important to bear in mind the role of the collective *ethos* ("national character" as some scholars have called it) which also appears in passing in Demosthenes' deliberative oratory but is most prominent in representations of ambassadorial speeches, as you point out. This *ethos* appears to have a cohesive effect and helps promote a single identity and a single voice when teams of envoys represent a given community. However, even these representations of community *ethos* are not immune from opponents' attacks, as can be seen in Thucydidean speeches.

Your reference to the reception of orators' characters by contemporary Assembly audiences is very instructive. It is indeed unfortunate that we do not have more evidence on this apart from those occasions when orators allege that the Assembly shouted down their opponents (as in the *Embassy* speeches), but this is not always related to the latter's *ethos*.

I totally agree that Demosthenes' changing tactics as time goes by may also reflect his need to respond to the increasing attacks on him, and this is supported by the growing frequency of vocabulary denoting "anger" in post-346 speeches. Giving an impression of growing confidence in his own abilities as advisor and a need to combat hostility are probably two sides of the same coin.

L. Pernot: Les mots φορτικὸν καὶ ἐπαχθές employés dans le passage de Démosthène 5, 4 sont des termes caractéristiques, presque des termes techniques, de l'éloge de soi-même (cf. *REG* 111, 1998, p. 108, n. 22-23). Pourquoi l'éloge de soi-même est-il déplaisant ? Dans le contexte athénien, la réponse à cette question a certainement à voir avec l'idéal démocratique d'égalité et d'appartenance à une collectivité. Le traité de Plutarque *De laude ipsius* analyse ces problèmes, en faisant notamment référence à Démosthène. Le *locus classicus* sur le sujet, chez Démosthène, est le début du discours *Sur la couronne* : le rapprochement avec le présent passage du discours 5 jette un pont entre genre délibératif et genre judiciaire.

C. Kremmydas: Many thanks for your observations and helpful references, Laurent. You are right to question the reasons for considering self-praise counter-normative in the context of a democracy. However, the boundaries of what is acceptable in terms of talking about oneself are not always easily clear and are therefore prone to rhetorical manipulation. As the passage you cite from Demosthenes' *On the Crown* suggests, the key here might be the question of an individual's public conduct in so far as it affects the outcome of a court case on the one hand and decision-making in the Assembly on the other. But the issue of *metron* is also crucial, and Demosthenes in *On the Crown* stresses the fact that he is going to talk about himself *hôs metriôtata* (18, 4: ὡς μετριώτατα). It is therefore the perception of the extent to which a speaker's reference to his own actions and/or life adhere to the *metron* that is going to determine the reactions of an audience, whether in a court or in the Assembly.

L. Pernot: Sur l'*êthos*, Aristote a été prolongé, en un sens, par Théophraste dans les *Caractères*. L'influence de la comédie est également importante.

C. Kremmydas: Thank you for this additional remark. Theophrastus' treatise is certainly valuable, especially since his examination is not restricted to the contrived characters of the court but also covers the wider perception of an individual's character as represented by their conduct in everyday life. Comedy, too, reflects individual character, but also exaggerates and distorts and therefore has to be treated with caution.

M. Kraus: Auch in diesem Zusammenhang ist zu bedauern, dass es uns, worauf Mike Edwards bereits verwiesen hat, für das 5. und 4. Jahrhundert an geeigneten Vergleichstexten für die *Ethos*-Gestaltung des Demosthenes fehlt. Gerade deshalb scheint es notwendig, die Reden im Werk des Thukydides, auch wenn sie vom Autor literarisch nachgestaltet sind, mit heranzuziehen, da sie oft exemplarische und instruktive Beispiele für gelungene (oder misslungene) *Ethos*-Konstitutionen bieten. Es fehlt aber auch an ausreichenden theoretischen Grundlagen. Selbst Aristoteles, der doch in Buch I der *Rhetorik* das *ethos* zunächst eindeutig der Person des Redners zuordnet (*Rhet.* 1, 2, 1356a2), gibt in Buch II dann überraschenderweise lediglich eine – allerdings ausführliche – Typologie des *ethos* der Zuhörerschaft (2, 12-17, 1388b31-1391b6). Erst über den Zwischenschritt der Analyse des Zuhörer-*Ethos* durch den Redner zum Zwecke der entsprechenden Anpassung des eigenen *ethos* gelingt der Übergang zum Redner-*Ethos*. Somit stellt sich aber das Problem des Verhältnisses der artifiziell konstruierten *ethopoiia* zum „echten", quasi naturgegebenen Redner-*Ethos*. In diesem Zusammenhang scheint wichtig, dass die *Rhetorik an Alexander*, falls man den dort verwendeten hochproblematischen Terminus der δόξα τοῦ λέγοντος (14, 1431b9-19) als „Ansehen des Redners" (und nicht als „persönliche Meinung des Redners") und somit als Vorstufe des rednerischen *ethos* deuten darf, diesen tatsächlich noch eindeutig den ‚äusserlichen' oder untechnischen, dem Zugriff des Redners entzogenen *pisteis* zuordnet. Das ist besonders wichtig in unserem Zusammenhang, eben weil die *Rhetorik an Alexander* die deliberative Rede als Muster in den Mittelpunkt stellt. Erst Aristoteles also vollzieht den Schritt zum vom Redner selbst bewusst gestalteten *ethos* als Überzeugungsmittel.

C. Kremmydas: Thank you for your observations, Manfred. It is true that Aristotle is not always satisfactory in his treatment of rhetorical issues. It is indeed surprising that on this specific issue of *ethos* he prefers to focus on the character and the likely emotional responses of the audience members rather than on the ways in which character of the speaker might be shaped rhetorically in order to render it more persuasive. As you say, Anaximenes often offers us helpful insights where Aristotle is not satisfactory and these two rhetorical treatises have to be read in conjunction with each other.

A. Chaniotis: A final remark. Individual *ethos* is the background of speeches in Xenophon's *Hellenika* (e.g. in Book 6), whose significance for the study of oratory is rather understudied.

C. Kremmydas: Thank you. You are certainly right that Xenophon's works represent snippets of contemporary oratory and offer a complementary and profitable avenue of further exploration. In the last decade or so, there has been growing scholarly interest in Xenophon and his rhetoric. When it comes to broad rhetorical strategies, the speeches he records are probably accurate reflections of contemporary oratory. However, with the exception of his own speeches and those of his fellow commanders as recorded in the *Anabasis,* I am not sure whether the speeches are more faithful as records of the real speeches than Thucydides' speeches. But Lene Rubinstein will have more to say on Xenophon.

L. Pernot: Voir *Xénophon et la rhétorique* par Pierre Pontier (Paris, 2014).

C. Kremmydas: Thank you, Laurent, for this bibliographical suggestion.

J.-L. Ferrary: Cette reconstitution très convaincante de l'évolution de l'art de l'auto-caractérisation dans les discours politiques de Démosthène suggère que les discours qui nous ont été transmis reflètent assez exactement les discours prononcés. Nous savons que la réalité est plus complexe dans le cas des discours cicéroniens, non seulement pour les discours judiciaires, bien éloignés d'une sténographie des débats, mais aussi pour un certain nombre au moins des discours politiques : ainsi les discours consulaires de 63, 'édités' en 60 seulement, et partiellement révisés compte tenu d'un contexte politique nouveau (voir P. Moreau, "Cicéron, Clodius et la publication du *Pro Murena*", *REL* 58, 1980, 220-237). Pour les harangues politiques de Démosthène, doit-on supposer des 'éditions' séparées suivant immédiatement les interventions de l'orateur devant l'Assemblée ?

C. Kremmydas: Thank you, Jean-Louis, for raising the important issue of revision and publication of speeches. The revision of Cicero's speeches demonstrates the increasing importance of careful 'impression management' on the part of politicians who used their published speeches in order to advance their political careers and ultimately to leave behind a favourable impression of their careers for posterity. It is likely that such a 'trend' of post-delivery editing and publication of revised versions of speeches had already started well before Demosthenes' time. However, the existing evidence is not at all straightforward. In Demosthenes' case, things are complicated even further by the fact that he is known to have written drafts of Assembly speeches before delivery (as reported by the biographical tradition). Was he unique? Possibly not. We do not have much information on what exactly happened post-delivery. It is very likely that Demosthenes was unusual in writing out draft sections of his Assembly speeches (perhaps only introductory passages, hence the collection of *Prooemia* in the corpus). However, this does not tell us much about what happened after delivery and there is no consensus among scholars as to whether Demosthenes published his deliberative speeches during his lifetime or not. There is some evidence of post-delivery revision of Demosthenes' speech *On the Crown* (and Aeschines' speech *Against Ctesiphon*), although in the trial on the *False Embassy* Demosthenes seems not to have revised his speech after delivery. But even if one were to admit that Demosthenes consistently revised and published his Assembly speeches, this would probably not have involved such systematic and large-scale 'moulding' of his *ethos* across all these speeches. Rather, it might have concerned the interpretation of controversial historical points or might have involved his responses to criticism or to specific arguments used by opponents in the 'real time' Assembly debates. As far as rhetorical strategies of representing the orator's *ethos* are concerned, I doubt we should expect significant divergences between the speech as delivered and the text put together and edited post-delivery with a view to wider circulation.

III

LENE RUBINSTEIN

ENVOYS AND *ETHOS*:
TEAM SPEAKING BY ENVOYS IN CLASSICAL GREECE

I. Introduction: envoys' speeches and the genre of symbouleutic
oratory

There is broad agreement in modern scholarship that envoys'
speeches were not recognised as a specific genre of oratory until
the late classical or early Hellenistic period. The earliest attestations of the terminology *logos presbeutikos* may be traced back
to Apollodoros' *Chronika*, and possibly even as far back as
Douris of Samos, who wrote in the late 4ᵗʰ and early 3ʳᵈ century.[1]
The most famous use of the generic designation *logos presbeutikos*
is found in Polybios' *Histories* (12, 25a3 and 12, 25i3) where,
rather surprisingly, *logoi presbeutikoi* are juxtaposed with
demegoriai and *logoi symbouleutikoi* respectively. But in fact so
little is left of 4ᵗʰ and 3ʳᵈ century literature that it would be
very ill-advised to argue *e silentio* that envoys' speeches were
not recognised as an important category of oratory until the
early Hellenistic period. Nor does the coinage itself necessarily
indicate that envoys' speeches were recognised as a more important part of the diplomatic process in the Hellenistic period than
they had been in the 5ᵗʰ and 4ᵗʰ centuries.[2]
    On the other hand, it is worth noting that the designation
logos presbeutikos is very much at odds with the main generic

---

[1] See BARON (2013) 171 n. 9 for references to the debate.
[2] *Pace* WOOTEN (1973).

distinctions applied by classical rhetoricians, and in particular
with those we find articulated in Aristotle's *Rhetoric*: symbouleutic, dikanic and epideiktic. True, envoys' speeches were
often deliberative in nature, which is reflected by the fact that
both Aischines and Demosthenes quite happily refer to such
symbouleutic speeches as *demegoriai* and to the delivery of
them with the verb δημηγορέω, without any qualification.[3]
However, when an envoy spoke for his *polis* in an interstate
dispute, or when one *polis* sent out representatives to complain
to another *polis* about the latter's conduct or the conduct of
one of its citizens, his speech would most likely have borne a
closer resemblance to the dikanic genre in Aristotelian terms.[4]
Likewise, some envoys' speeches seem to have been mainly epideiktic in nature, such as the one allegedly delivered by Ktesiphon when sent as Athenian envoy to Philip's daughter Kleopatra
to offer condolences upon the death of her husband, Alexander
of Epeiros.[5] Thus, it is unsurprising that the generic terminology attested in Polybios is not used either by classical rhetorical
theorists or by the Attic orators themselves. The classification
of *logoi presbeutikoi* as a separate genre, sitting alongside battle
exhortations and symbouleutic oratory delivered before domestic
audiences, makes excellent sense in a historiographical universe,
but less sense when applied to oratory as it may have been performed in real life.

Nevertheless, it is striking that neither the *Rhetorica ad Alexandrum* nor Aristotle's *Rhetoric* has much advice to offer on the
specific oratorical challenges that envoys had to overcome in
order to persuade their non-domestic audiences. It may have
been taken for granted by both authors that the observations
and recommendations issued for each of the three main genres
would apply also when the speaker was addressing a foreign

---

[3] E.g. AESCHIN. 2, 79 and DEM. 19, 11, 304 (Aischines); AESCHIN. 3, 137
(Demosthenes).
[4] E.g. HDT. 6, 49 (Athenian envoys accusing Aiginetans at Sparta); cf.
THUC. 1, 95, 3; XEN. *Hell.* 3, 1, 8; 7, 4, 39-40.
[5] AESCHIN. 3, 242.

audience, and at one level this makes good sense. The subject matters typically dealt with by attested embassies overlap considerably with those listed by the two treatises as topics characteristic of symbouleutic oratory generally. The *Rhetoric to Alexander* enumerates seven main themes: religious matters, legislation, constitutional framework, alliances and covenants with other *poleis*, war and peace, and revenue.[6] The corresponding list offered by Aristotle numbers five main themes: revenue, war and peace, territorial defence, imports and exports, and legislation.[7] While legislation, constitutional matters and territorial defence undoubtedly had particular relevance in an internal context, envoys sent out by states with hegemonic ambitions and a desire to interfere with the laws and constitutions of other states sometimes found themselves in a situation where these themes were part of their brief, too.[8]

Yet, there are three areas in particular where the position of an envoy would have differed significantly from that of a speaker addressing a domestic audience. The first relates to style. Aristotle himself notes that the choice of style must match the type of speaker – child, adult, and elderly; male and female, Lakonian and Thessalian.[9] The last mentioned is important, in so far as it strongly indicates that oratorical conventions and etiquette may have differed significantly from one Greek community to the next. Yet Aristotle offers no direct observations on how such differences might affect an envoy's ability to engage with his foreign audience, let alone advice on how an envoy might be able to negotiate them in his own oratory. The second area, which largely depends on the envoy's successful handling of the first, concerns the speaker's ability to control the mood of his audience and the listeners' emotional response

---

[6] *Rhet. ad Alex.* 2, 2.

[7] ARIST. *Rhet.* 1359b19-23.

[8] See, e.g., the Athenian envoys who, after the installation of the 400, were instructed to set up oligarchies in the *poleis* still subject to Athens (THUC. 8, 64, 1-2). Cf. HDT. 5, 92.

[9] ARIST. *Rhet.* 1408a25-30.

to his argumentation. The third concerns the speaker's character (ἦθος) as projected in his speech, which may or may not be reinforced by the audience's prior knowledge of the speaker himself and his personal as well as official track-record.

It is this third area of difference that will be the focus of the present paper. After a brief discussion of the differences between the position of an envoy and that of a speaker advising a domestic audience, I shall turn to the question of how the practice of team-speaking, which is well attested for the Athenian courtroom, may provide at least one key to understanding how envoys may have been able to overcome these challenges.

II. Envoys and *Ethos*

Aristotle's emphasis on character projection by the speaker as essential for the persuasiveness of his speech is, of course, well known.[10] He adds that the three personal qualities most essential for a speaker's ability to win the audience's trust are practical wisdom (*phronesis*), virtue (*arete*), and goodwill (*eunoia*).[11] Likewise, the author of the *Rhetoric to Alexander* offers hands-on instructions to speakers in his treatment of *prooimia* to symbouleutic speeches. He provides examples of arguments that may serve to create goodwill towards the speaker, depending on whether the audience is already favourably disposed to him, neutral, or prejudiced against him because of his personal record and past deeds, his age, or his position either as a habitual speaker or as someone who has never before addressed the decision-making body in question.[12] Earlier he has warned against arguments that run counter to the character of the speaker, advocating that the speaker should represent his own deeds and words as being incompatible with what is unjust,

---

[10] ARIST. *Rhet.* 1377b20-31.
[11] ARIST. *Rhet.* 1378a6-9.
[12] *Rhet. ad Alex.* 29, 6-23.

lawless, harmful and generally characteristic of men who are regarded as morally depraved.[13]

This is all sensible advice – so sensible, indeed, as to sound self-evident. After all, a modern audience, too, may judge a speaker's words against what they believe are the speaker's real convictions and moral outlook. If the speaker's words and reasoning appear to be in marked conflict with the latter, the result is that the speaker, and thus the speech itself, may come across as inauthentic and insincere at best and, at worst, as an active attempt to deceive. In the context of ancient Greek political decision-making, oligarchic and democratic alike, this consideration is of paramount importance. Because of the absence of formal party-political structures, and because the idea of representation played only a very limited part in Greek political life (and thought), speakers who attempted to persuade their fellow citizens would take the stage first and foremost *as themselves*. To be sure, each community had its political groupings, and it is important not to underestimate their importance especially at times of crisis. Yet, the idea that a speaker might – like a modern loyal party-politician – be prepared to suppress his own personal convictions and judgement and deliver a speech which promoted a course of action that he himself, in his heart of hearts, did not fully support was anathema. Any suspicion that he did not sincerely believe in the soundness of his own advice, any hint that he was speaking as the mouthpiece of others would undermine the persuasiveness of his speech as a whole. In fact, it might even land him in court on a charge of bribery, subversion or treason, if his perceived insincerity gave rise to the suspicion that he had spoken in the service of a hostile paymaster.

The position of an envoy was different, however. He was not just speaking as himself; he was, above all, speaking as a mouthpiece of the community that sent him out. This does not mean that who he was or how he spoke did not matter –

---

[13] *Rhet. ad Alex.* 10, 1-2.

far from it! The foreign listeners were likely to relate both to the personality that he projected in his speech, and to the perceived character of the community that he represented. As highlighted by Low,[14] the moral vocabulary that was applied to individuals was also applied to communities as collective characters, and so the envoy's task would be to counter not only any prejudice that might relate to his own person, but also the prejudices which the audience might harbour against his community. He had to convince his audience that the advice he offered would benefit the addressees at least as much as his own *polis*; and success depended on his ability to make his audience believe not only the rational case itself and the arguments that underpinned it, but also that both he and his community could be trusted, and that his advice was offered in good faith. Particularly when relations between their communities were strained, the envoy's ability to project personal goodwill (*eunoia*) with sincerity may have been decisive for his audience's willingness to listen to his advice with an open mind.

The persons in the most obvious position to command trust in this respect were undoubtedly those who were known to their audience already, and whose personal track-record was regarded as positive. Precisely this is emphasised in a passage in the *Rhetoric to Alexander* that seems to pertain to a debate on the election of envoys. It is used among a number of examples that illustrate arguments on competence and capability in general:

> "That this man is not capable, but that someone else is capable, along these lines: he himself will be powerless as an envoy on our behalf, whereas this man is a friend of the *polis* of the Lakedaimonians and will be especially able to achieve what you want."[15]

---

[14] Low (2007) 132-151.
[15] *Rhet. ad Alex.* 24, 3: ὅτι δὲ οὗτος μὲν οὐ δύναται, ἕτερος δὲ δύναται, τοιόνδε· αὐτὸς μὲν οὖν ἀδυνάτως ἔχει πρεσβεύειν ὑπὲρ ἡμῶν, οὗτος δὲ φίλος ἐστὶ τῇ πόλει τῶν Σπαρτιατῶν καὶ μάλιστ᾽ ἂν δυνηθείη πρᾶξαι, ἃ βούλεσθε.

It is not unreasonable to expect *proxenoi* to have been especially
well placed as speakers. Their recognised position in the community of the addressees would most likely have placed them
in the category of symbouleutic speakers for whom, if we go by
the advice in the *Rhetorica ad Alexandrum* (29, 6-7), professions of personal *eunoia* would be superfluous.[16] Yet, there
were considerable limits to how far such individuals would be
able to win over their audiences simply on the basis of their
own record. That much is clear, for instance, from Aischines'
enumeration of a succession of Athenian envoys with close personal ties to Thebes, who nevertheless failed to persuade their
Theban audiences on a number of important occasions.[17]

Aischines hints that the envoys' failure on these missions was
due mainly to the Thebans' own intransigence and ambitions.
But there is also a more general point to be made here. From
the perspective of the non-domestic audience, two questions
would have been of paramount importance for their judgement of the speech by a person with a past record of *eunoia*
towards them. The first related to the honesty with which he
professed that his advice would be beneficial to both their communities. Although a *proxenos* may have had an advantage over
envoys who were unknown to their foreign audience, there
was, as recently emphasised by Mack,[18] still an expectation
that, when it came to the crunch, a *proxenos* would put his own
community first. Thus, his standing would not in itself provide
a guarantee against deception.[19] The same would, *a fortiori*,

---

[16] Particularly if the *proxenos* had acquired the title on his own merit, but
there seems also to have been a presumption that the descendants of a *proxenos*
inherited not only his title but also his goodwill and sense of obligation. See,
e.g., MOGGI (1995) 143-144; MITCHELL (1997) 30; MACK (2015) 130-134.

[17] AESCHIN. 3, 138-139.

[18] MACK (2015) 138-142.

[19] Cf. THUC. 2, 85, 5: the Cretan *proxenos* Nikias of Gortyn persuaded the
Athenians to take military action against Kydonia, arguing that this would be in
Athens' interests, but in reality obliging Polichna in order to obtain its allegiance.
On this Nikias, see HORNBLOWER (1991) 366 and PERLMAN (2004) 1182.

have applied to a speaker who was connected with the foreign community by less formal, personal ties.

Even when the audience was entirely persuaded of his sincerity and personal goodwill, they would still be left with an even more important, second question: how much political influence did the speaker actually wield at home? This may have been decisive in regard to their inclination to trust that promises would be kept and commitments fully honoured. Demosthenes asserts (14, 12) that teams of envoys who cannot back their words up with a credible commitment from their community to work in the addressees' interest will be merely "declaiming like rhapsodes" (ῥαψῳδήσουσιν). That applies equally to individual envoys.

Even a speaker known to occupy a position of political influence in his own *polis* nevertheless faced a risk that his very ties with the particular community he was addressing might give rise to suspicion at home. That in turn might limit his powers of persuasion in his own domestic setting when advocating a course of action that would demonstrably benefit the *polis* with which he was connected.[20] He may also, paradoxically, have faced a further difficulty in relation to his non-domestic audience if he tried to counter prejudice by projecting a personal character that he expected would appeal most to his audience. For in doing so, he might inadvertently cause his audience to question his domestic influence further, if his *ethos* was perceived as conflicting with their perceptions of the character of the *polis* he was representing.[21]

---

[20] Demosthenes in *On the Freedom of the Rhodians* (15, 15) emphasises that he is neither their *proxenos*, nor a personal *xenos* of any Rhodian individual; while Aischines attributes Demosthenes' alleged *prodosia* to his being *proxenos* of the Thebans (2, 141). See further MACK (2015) 114-115.

[21] Cf. PLUT. *Apophthegmata Laconica* 221E: "When the envoy from Elis said that his fellow citizens had sent him out precisely because he alone emulated the Spartan way of life, Theopompos asked: 'Elean, which is the better way of life, yours or that of your fellow citizens?' When the envoy answered that it was his own, Theopompos said 'So how can this *polis* be safe, in which only a single man of a large population is good?'". MOSLEY (1973) 44 cites this as an example of

There were thus some very clear limits to the oratorical potential of *proxenoi* and others with comparable ties to the community of the addressees. Moreover, there is considerable scholarly disagreement as to how often such people were in fact deployed as envoys. The attestations of *proxenoi* acting in this capacity are surprisingly few in 5th and 4th century literature,[22] so too in the contemporary epigraphical material. As far as classical Athens is concerned, Mitchell remarks that "[what] is surprising about the trends in ambassadorial appointments in Athens is the small percentage made on the criterion of personal connections".[23] By contrast, Mack regards it as likely that *proxenoi* were frequently deployed as envoys on diplomatic missions to the states with which they were affiliated.[24] But the actual examples he cites are very limited in number as far as the classical period is concerned. A pressing methodological question then is how to interpret this apparent rarity in our sources. One possibility is to take it as an indication that the use of this type of envoy was indeed limited, due to the problems just mentioned. Another is that speakers who were already personally connected with their foreign audiences

how envoys might be selected for their popularity in the state to which they were sent; but the anecdote is more likely a reflection of the problems that might arise because of a perceived discrepancy between the personal *ethos* of the envoy and that of his community.

[22] In addition to Polydamas of Pharsalos (XEN. *Hell.* 6, 1, 4), I have found eight instances of *proxenoi* who acted as envoys: Alexander, King of Makedonia (HDT. 8, 136); Miltiades son of Kimon, *proxenos* of Sparta (ANDOC. 3, 3; or Kimon, THEOPOMP., *FGrH* 115F88); Arthmios of Zeleia, *proxenos* of Athens (AESCHIN. 3, 258); Lichas of Sparta, *proxenos* of the Argives (THUC. 5, 76, 3); Kallias of Athens, *proxenos* of Sparta (XEN. *Hell.* 6, 3, 4); Timesitheos of Trapezous, *proxenos* of the Mossynoikoi (XEN. *Anab.* 5, 4, 1-4); Demosthenes, *proxenos* of Thebes (AESCHIN. 2, 141); Thrason Erchieus, *proxenos* of Thebes (AESCHIN. 3, 138). To these may be added Iason of Pherai, *proxenos* of Sparta, who addresses the Spartan assembly in XEN. *Hell.* 6, 1, 4, but since he, like Polydamas, is an autocratic ruler, he is not 'representing' his community in the same way as an elected envoy. In addition there are some parallel cases which do not concern conventional envoys, such as THUC. 5, 59, 5, where two Argives, of whom one is *proxenos* of Sparta and the other a general, approach Agis, but without authorisation from their home community.

[23] MITCHELL (1997) 94-95.

[24] MACK (2015) 69-70.

were used, but that they may be difficult for us to spot because they would often operate as part of a larger ambassadorial team, without their individual contributions being specifically mentioned in our sources.

III. Ambassadorial teams and rhetorical strategies

That Greek envoys frequently were sent out as teams is well known, and the practice has been much discussed in modern scholarship. Questions surrounding the size of such teams, their appointment, and the political considerations that may have informed their composition have likewise been the focus of considerable attention. It is less clear, however, how such teams operated in practice when they addressed their foreign audiences in councils and assemblies. Various team-based strategies can be envisaged: that one member spoke on behalf of the team as a whole, with the rest standing by his side offering non-verbal support; or that one member of the team set out the position of his community in a long address, while other team members added shorter contributions in support of the main speech. A third possibility is that more than one member of the team (and sometimes all of them) delivered a speech of his own, each speech in itself amounting to a full symbouleutic oration.

It is important to be aware of the possibility that the choice of strategy may have varied according to the composition of the team, the situation to which the embassy was responding, and composition of the audience. In the classical period (as later) most Greek warfare was coalition warfare. This meant that envoys often had to take into account that their audience would comprise representatives from several different communities who had an important stake in the outcome of the decisions. Likewise, several attested ambassadorial teams sent out by hegemonic *poleis* numbered not only representatives of the hegemonic *polis* itself, but also envoys representing other members of the alliance. The role of the latter as speakers is not always easy to discern. But what the evidence does show is that on several occasions such envoys did have a speaking part; thus, their potential importance in terms of the embassy's oratorical strategy as a whole should not be underestimated.[25]

Team-speaking was an important aspect of Greek performance culture. The phenomenon is well attested not only in the context of Athenian courtrooms, but also in the courts of other Greek states, as is clear from the numerous judicial curse tablets that bind co-speakers, *synegoroi* or *syndikoi*, as well as main litigants. It would therefore not be at all surprising if team-speaking was likewise an important aspect of oratory in the context of Greek inter-state relations. As far as Athenian court-practice is concerned, it is often possible to form an impression, on the basis of surviving oratory, of how the members of teams may have coordinated their contributions. Moreover, it is also possible to identify the way in which supporting speeches, *synegoriai*, differed in practice from the advice given in the two contemporary rhetorical treatises, the *Rhetoric to Alexander* and Aristotle's *Rhetoric*, especially in regard to their structure and organisation of material.

Above all, the surviving Athenian forensic speeches show the very diverse strategies such teams could adopt. In some cases, the team appears to have conformed to the model usually assumed by modern scholars to have been the norm in Athenian litigation: the main litigant did all of the speaking, but his performance would be visually backed by supporters who endorsed witness-statements read out by the court attendant. In other cases, the main litigant would deliver a full speech that set out the main features of the case; other members of the team would also address the court, but only with supplementary speeches, demonstrating verbally that the main litigant, and his case, commanded support from fellow citizens (and sometimes others) with a clear personal interest in a positive outcome. Yet another attested strategy is that of assigning only

---

[25] The most famous examples are those reported in XEN. *Hell.* 6, 5, 37-48 and 7, 1, 1-11.

a relatively brief speech, effectively a *prooimion*, to the first speaker who formally was the main party, while leaving the main oratorical performance to one or several other speakers whose voices, visibility and significance in the *agon* itself would have been at least as, and often more important than that of the person who was named as prosecutor or defendant in the case. This diversity in itself suggests that we should be wary of supposing that a single model and strategy was invariably applied in connection with rhetorical teamwork in other contexts, including in diplomatic relations.

It appears from several attested forensic teams in the Athenian courts that the arguments presented by an individual *synegoros* would often be precisely those that would gain in persuasive force through the personal authority of the speaker, either because of his own involvement in the case, or because of his recognised expertise in a particular area, as a general or as a figure of political or religious authority. It does not seem far-fetched to assume that the advantages of such a strategy would be recognised also in the context of oratorical performances before non-domestic audiences. But to prove this assumption right is not altogether an easy thing.

The famous accounts by Demosthenes and Aischines of the Athenian missions to Philip suggest that it was not unusual for several or even all of the members of an ambassadorial team to speak, and also that teams of envoys were expected to coordinate their oratory so as to constitute a unified rhetorical effort.[26] On each occasion the teams numbered ten Athenian envoys and at least one further envoy representing Athens' allies. After their appointment (and apparently *en route*) the envoys allegedly organised their performance as a team, including the decision on the order of their individual presentations. According to Aischines, it was largely because of Demosthenes' refusal to engage with his fellow envoys in devising a shared rhetorical strategy that the missions failed to work optimally.

[26] E.g. AESCHIN. 2, 21-22; 2, 101-107.

Aischines' narrative may be taken to suggest that such team work and coordination were perceived as the ideal, but it is hard to determine to what extent the use of multiple speakers can be regarded as typical. The missions to Makedonia were conducted in a climate of deep political division within Athens itself. This may have meant that the individual envoys who appear to have belonged to different political camps may each have had stronger reasons than usual to demand an active speaking role on the team. Moreover, the context of both Demosthenes' trial against Aischines for *parapresbeia* in 343 and Aischines' trial against Ktesiphon in 330 was one of bitter political rivalry that went far beyond the persons of Aischines and Demosthenes themselves. In both actions the political stakes were extremely high, and since Aischines especially needed to defend his record as an envoy whose competence and integrity were beyond question, the role assigned to individual members of the teams may be exaggerated both in his account and in that of Demosthenes.

Unfortunately, a major methodological problem caused by the nature of our sources hampers any attempt to establish the value of the accounts of the Makedonian episodes as evidence for general oratorical practice in inter-state relations. Although written speeches delivered by envoys in the 5th and 4th centuries are known to have been in circulation in antiquity, none has survived, except for a few fragments. Despite the fact that teams of envoys are frequently mentioned in Attic oratory, especially in the speeches delivered in the second half of the 4th century, there is precious little information on how they operated. In fact, leaving aside Andoc. 3, Aeschin. 2 and 3, and Dem. 18 and 19, there are surprisingly few comments on the type of arguments envoys deployed in order to persuade their audiences, whether foreign envoys in Athens or Athenian envoys in other Greek states.[27]

---

[27] DEM. 1, 8; 2, 12; 6, 19-26; 7, 1, 19, 20-23; 9, 72; 15, 22; 17, 16-17; 17, 19; 20, 73; [50, 5]; DIN. 1, 12-13, 16, 18-20, 28, 80-82; HYP. 1 *Dem.* col. 8; HYP. 3 *Eux.* 24-25.

The inscriptions from the classical period are equally frustrating. Although they normally permit us to establish the existence of ambassadorial teams, they, unlike many comparable inscriptions from the Hellenistic period, normally offer no specific information on the argumentation presented by the teams in their speeches.[28] Thus it goes without saying that they tell us nothing about how the envoys in question had distributed the arguments among themselves.

Any reconstruction of envoys' symbouleutic oratory and the operation of ambassadorial teams therefore depends almost entirely on the evidence of the historiographers. A considerable proportion of the set speeches in the works of Herodotos, Thucydides and Xenophon is given to envoys advising foreign listeners on important matters of policy. However, as sources for real-life oratorical practice these speeches are notoriously problematic. The debate on the extent to which they reflect what was actually said on each occasion is never-ending, with no clear consensus emerging, and it is not my intention to enter that debate here. On the other hand, many scholars, especially recently, have adopted an approach that in some ways gets round the problem of historical accuracy. Although the speeches themselves may be partly or wholly the product of the historiographers' creative imagination, their intended effect of drawing the reader into the narrative by letting him experience debates and arguments as they unfold may well have depended considerably on dramatic realism, *mimesis*. Thus, it may be possible to identify themes and argumentative strategies that were characteristic of this particular type of symbouleutic oratory, on the assumption that what we are listening to, in the company of the internal audiences in the stories, conforms in generic terms to the real-life oratory typically delivered in similar circumstances. A recent attempt to produce

---

[28] Note, however, that although the Hellenistic inscriptions tend to be far more eloquent as evidence for the contents and themes of envoys' speeches, they only rarely throw light on how the speeches delivered by individual envoys on a team may have complemented each other.

a systematic overview of such features is that of Piccirilli (2002), who draws primarily on historiography with supplementary evidence especially from the philosophers and from later biographies. But even this cautious approach is not without its potential pitfalls. The most pressing question is how far we can be confident that the historiographical speeches were in fact plausible and realistic imitations of envoys' speeches as delivered in real life. That question is extremely difficult to answer, because we have so few surviving comparanda, apart from Aischines' and Demosthenes' accounts of the speeches that they themselves delivered to audiences abroad, in the Peloponnese, Makedonia, and Delphi.[29] Even more problematic is the fact that the historiographers only rarely inform us on the composition of individual teams, let alone on the rhetorical strategies adopted by them on each occasion. These, as suggested earlier, may have varied considerably depending on the aims, context and composition of each delegation.

IV. Envoys and *ethos* in the works of Xenophon

For all its limitations as evidence, classical historiography at least confirms that the rhetorical strategies adopted by ambassadorial teams could vary just as much as those of legal teams. The best illustrations of the range can be found in particular in Xenophon's works. Xenophon's interest in exploring *mimesis* and the artistic characterisation of individuals is attested in his *Memorabilia* (3, 10, 1-8), and it is thus not altogether surprising if Xenophon likewise took a particular interest in the characterisation of individual envoys, including how they interacted not only with their audiences but also with other speakers, supporters as well as opponents.

---

[29] E.g. AESCHIN. 2, 25-33, 109-112, 113-117; 3, 119-122.

At one end of the spectrum we find teams of multiple speakers on at least four occasions in Xenophon's *Hellenica*,[30] and I shall return to two of these later in this section. At the other end we find communities making use of a single speaker who acts as the mouthpiece of the collectivity and does not even attempt to back up his words with his own personal authority. This is perhaps most graphically depicted in Xenophon's representation of the messenger sent by the Thebans to Athens after their victory at Leuktra. Through him the Thebans not only announce their victory but also urge the Athenians to join them in following up their success. But despite this clear symbouleutic aspect of the messenger's brief, he remains nameless and faceless. He is merely a conduit for the Thebans' request, expressed with a speaking verb and circumstantial participle in the plural (ἐκέλευον λέγοντες).[31] According to Xenophon, the Athenians cannot even be bothered to issue a reply. Their pointed dismissal of both the messenger and his message may reflect broader concerns about the growth of Theban power, but Xenophon probably also intended the episode as an illustration of Theban arrogance. Athenian support is so taken for granted that they feel able to dispense with any professions of goodwill, and their collective attempt to persuade the Athenians to join them in a new phase of war for the sake of revenge is – apparently – assigned to a man who seems to have had no authority of his own.

More complicated is an episode related by Xenophon in *Anabasis* 5, 5, 7-24. The 10,000 are approached by a team of envoys from Sinope with a request that they stop imposing on the communities that paid tribute to the Sinopeans. Xenophon prefaces the Sinopean address as follows:

> "When they had entered the camp, they began to speak. Hekatonymos, who was regarded as a formidable speaker, spoke as representative (προηγόρει)."

---

[30] XEN. *Hell.* 5, 2, 11-23; 6, 3, 2-19; 6, 5, 33-48; 7, 1, 1-14.
[31] XEN. *Hell.* 6, 4, 19.

The verb προηγόρει may be taken to suggest that the original plan was to let Hekatonymos speak alone on behalf of the entire team. If so, the strategy adopted here resembles one attested for numerous Athenian private legal actions: the main litigant does the speaking, while silent support is provided by witnesses through their physical presence on the litigant's *bema* and confirmation of their written testimony.

The reader is next treated to Hekatonymos' speech in *oratio recta*. It begins with a profession of Sinopean goodwill, stressing their admiration and joy at the army's victories over the barbarians, and emphasising the shared Greek identity of both sides. But it ends with a threat: the Sinopeans intend to form alliances with the Paphlagonians against the 10,000 unless their request is met.

Hekatonymos' speech is followed by a reply delivered by Xenophon, again in *oratio recta*, defending the actions of the army and ending with a warning and a counter-threat, suggesting that the Paphlagonians could just as well be used against the Sinopeans themselves (5, 5, 22-23). In his speech, Xenophon twice resorts to *apostrophe*: he counters the accusations as emanating from Hekatonymos himself (λέγεις, 5, 5, 20); and he holds Hekatonymos personally responsible for the threat (ἠπείλησας, 5, 5, 22), rather than responding to it as a threat issued collectively by the Sinopeans. At this point the rest of the Sinopean team springs into action (5, 5, 24), visibly angry with Hekatonymos for his words. One of them, unnamed, delivers a speech of his own in which he promises, on behalf of his city, to receive the soldiers kindly. After that, cordial relations are established, resulting in the envoys' being invited to offer advice to a council of officers on the following day (5, 6, 1-14). Again Hekatonymos is given a speech to deliver in *oratio recta*, but his persona as projected in this address is strikingly different from that in his oration on the previous day.

In his first oration, Hekatonymos is made to speak exclusively in the first person plural. His own character is entirely suppressed, and he plays the part of the 'walking voice' of Sinope to perfection. But when Xenophon the character exposes his reasoning as flawed (and indeed harmful to his own community) and responds directly to him *as an individual* rather than as the mouthpiece of his *polis*, cracks open up in the Sinopean team itself. The resulting discord between the envoys is not unlike Aischines' description of the conflict within the Athenian teams sent to Makedonia more than half a century later. Perhaps as a direct result of his unmasking by Xenophon the character on the previous day, Hekatonymos' second speech (5, 6, 3-10) is a highly personal one, in the first person singular, except for one instance.[32] He apologises for having made the threat and begins his symbouleutic speech with a solemn oath, emphasising that his personal reputation is at stake. It is peppered with verbs indicating that he is voicing his personal opinion,[33] based on his own considerable expertise.[34] But despite his strenuous efforts, he is unable to generate trust: some in his audience are suspicious that he is in reality motivated by his ties of friendship and *proxenia* with the Paphlagonian king Korylas, while others suspect him of speaking in return for a bribe. Hekatonymos' two *ethe*, as the Sinopean 'walking voice' and as the god-fearing and knowledgeable man, could hardly be more different, but both of them utterly fail to lend persuasive force to his arguments. Had it not been for the (apparently improvised) intervention by other members of his team, the whole mission, at least in Xenophon's representation, looked set to end in disaster.

The projection by Hekatonymos of two different *ethe*, as the Sinopean mouthpiece and as 'himself', is not without literary precedent. A parallel can be found in Herodotos 8, 140, only here it is not two but three characters that are represented, and the representations are combined in a single speech, delivered by Alexander son of Amyntas of Makedonia. Alexander is acting as envoy for Mardonios, and Herodotos has already informed

---

[32] XEN. *Anab.* 5, 6, 5 (ἕξομεν, ἡμᾶς).

[33] οἶδ', γιγνώσκω (5, 6, 5); οἶδα (5, 6, 7); οἶδα (5, 6, 8); οἶμαι (5, 6, 9); νομίζω (5, 6, 10).

[34] ἔμπειρος (5, 6, 6).

us (8, 136) that Mardonios has chosen him because he was the Athenians' *proxenos* and *euergetes*. The first half of his speech is an intricate construction of Chinese boxes: he announces, and then performs, a speech by Mardonios directly to the Athenians, which in turn includes a message from the Persian King to Mardonios. Mardonios' address to the Athenians is in *oratio recta* using the first person singular, as is the King's message to Mardonios, in which the King professes himself willing to forgive the Athenians, offer them autonomy, and rebuild their sanctuaries, if they conclude an agreement with him. Alexander's personality is completely suppressed in this part of the speech; there is, by contrast a very clear projection of the *ethos* of the absent Mardonios, whose retelling of the King's message paves the way for his representation of himself as being compelled to carry out the King's bidding.[35] This in turn lends credibility to his assurance that, as far as he is concerned, the Athenians will be able to preserve their territory and their freedom, if they accept the pact. Thus, the threat inherent in his reference to the size of the Persian invading forces and to those under his own command is not left to stand on its own. A key objective of Mardonios' strategy is to establish trust, which is particularly clear from his assurance that the agreement will be concluded without trickery and deceit. Combined with his self-projection as both loyal servant of the King and a military commander in his own right, Mardonios' demonstration that his words are congruent with the words of the King is an essential part of his strategy.

In the second half of his address, Alexander abandons his impersonation of Mardonios. He delivers in his own voice what is in effect a *synegoria*, which in many ways conforms to the pattern observable in Attic forensic oratory. Initially he asserts his goodwill in the form of a *praeteritio*,[36] a strategy he

---

[35] HDT. 8, 140A2.
[36] HDT. 8, 140B1: ἐγὼ δὲ περὶ μὲν εὐνοίης τῆς πρὸς ὑμέας ἐούσης ἐξ ἐμεῦ οὐδὲν λέξω (οὐ γὰρ ἂν νῦν πρῶτον ἐκμάθοιτε) ...

can adopt only because he is who he is. It is also his pre-existing ties with the Athenians that allow him to appeal to the audience's fear, not by a crude threat, but by asserting that he himself is afraid for the Athenians.[37] His reference to his own direct emotional engagement is an argument that can be voiced with conviction only by a friend, and it adds a tone of earnestness and urgency to his imperative: ἀλλὰ πείθεσθε.

The three characters given a voice by Alexander all depend on each other for the overall persuasive effect of the address. Mardonios' ability to persuade depends partly on the words of the King and partly on his own reputation as a military commander with experience of dealing with the Greeks. The plausibility of the King's message itself depends on Mardonios' commitment to implementing it in practice. On their own, the two of them might have been in a position to persuade the Athenians to come to terms by appealing to the emotion of fear alone. But the trust that would be required for the Athenians to accept their offer of an alliance depended on a sincere and credible expression of goodwill, *eunoia*, which only Alexander himself was in a position to make.[38] And only he could plausibly appeal to both fear and hope when stressing the benefit to the Athenians of winning the Persian King as a friend.[39]

How crucial Alexander's *ethos* is for the persuasiveness of his address is signalled by Herodotos when he lets a delegation of unnamed Spartan envoys unmask him (8, 143), not unlike the way in which Xenophon the character is made to unmask Hekatonymos. The Spartans do not have much to offer the Athenians other than appeals to Athenian pride in their reputation for defending Greek freedom and an assurance that they will provide for the Athenians' dependants for the duration of the war. But their intervention consists of a devastating attack

[37] HDT. 8, 140B3.
[38] Contrast the strategy employed by Kroisos in HDT. 1, 69, 1-3, who sends a group of envoys with presents to the Spartans, *having instructed them on what to say*, and manages to project his own character in the words conveyed by them.
[39] HDT. 8, 140B4.

on Alexander, designed to undermine precisely the sincerity of his address and thus his trustworthiness.[40]

According to Herodotos, the Athenians were perfectly able to see through Alexander's deception unaided, and he seems to suggest that his rhetorical strategy (and that of Mardonios) was doomed to fail from the outset.[41] On the other hand, the strategic distribution of arguments between different characters provides a suggestive parallel to the strategies adopted by other Persians, by Philip II of Makedonia, and by the Greeks themselves in their dealings with each other. Thus, Xenophon relates how the Chians and other *poleis* allied to the Spartans agree to send an embassy to Sparta to complain about the behaviour of the Spartan commander Eteonikos and request he be replaced by Lysandros. On this mission they were joined by envoys sent by Kyros, who appear to have had a speaking role of their own.[42]

As for Philip, a delegation was organised by him, probably in 343,[43] that comprised representatives of his allied states as well as Python of Byzantion, formerly a pupil of Isokrates with strong ties to Athens. From [Dem.] 7, 19-20, it can be inferred that several of them spoke, although it was apparently Python's speech, summarised in 7, 20-23, that made an especially strong impression. It is to this speech in particular that Demosthenes (18, 136) claims that he himself responded, with such spectacular success that even the envoys representing Philip's allies rose to voice their agreement. If we can trust his account, this event bears a striking resemblance to Xenophon's description of the Sinopean episode in terms of the dynamics between the individual members of Philip's ambassadorial team. The difference is that Philip's team most likely had performed as a team *before* the cracks began to show.

---

[40] HDT. 8, 142, 4-5.
[41] Cf. HDT. 8, 141, where he claims that the Athenians delayed Alexander's performance until the arrival of the Spartan ambassadors.
[42] XEN. *Hell.* 2, 1, 6-7.
[43] WANKEL (1976) 739-740.

Despite the obvious risk of open discord arising among the members of an ambassadorial team, the use of multiple speakers may well have been a safer strategy than letting a single speaker carry the entire performance, acting as a spokesman for them all. It might not be too difficult to demolish the character and reasoning of a single speaker in a counter-speech that calls into question his motives, his sincerity, or his power to deliver on his promises. But if the same basic advice and course of action are advocated by a range of different characters, it may have been considerably harder to carry out a demolition job in the way the Spartans undermined the character of Alexander and Xenophon that of Hekatonymos. Additionally, a team performance may have presented further strategic advantages when the envoys were addressing a composite audience that numbered attendants from more than one community.

How this may have worked in practice can be illustrated by one of the most famous historiographical depictions of ambassadorial teamwork: Xenophon's account of the Athenian peace embassy to Sparta in 371 (*Hell.* 6, 3, 2-17). Xenophon's dramatisation of the embassy is one of only two instances in surviving classical historiography where several envoys belonging to the same ambassadorial team are given speeches in *oratio recta*. The other episode is the Peloponnesian mission to Athens in the winter of 370/69, likewise depicted by Xenophon in his *Hellenika* (6, 5, 33-48). Not least because of their rarity, the two representations of team-based ambassadorial oratory have been the focus of intense debate, in particular the one representing the Athenian team in action. This episode also provides the closest parallel to the operations of ambassadorial teams as described by Demosthenes and Aischines.

The narrator prefaces the scene by naming the members of the Athenian team, most of whom are known from other sources to have occupied a prominent standing in Athenian political life.[44]

---

[44] The exact number of envoys selected is disputed, but the team must have numbered at least eight, possibly as many as ten. See DILLERY (1995) 243 with n. 7.

We are also told that their audience at Sparta consists of Spartan *ekkletoi* and representatives sent by Sparta's allies. In the scene itself, only three members of the team are given a voice of their own: Kallias son of Hipponikos; Autokles, introduced as having a reputation for being a particularly earnest orator;[45] and Kallistratos, whom the narrator has already introduced as 'the Orator' (ὁ δημηγορός) in 6, 3, 3. Kallias and Kallistratos are both known from other sources to have had prior dealings with the Spartans,[46] but only Kallias makes explicit reference to his own connections in his speech, the first to be delivered.

The three speakers project very different and distinctive characters, and each employs the first person singular at the beginning of his speech: Kallias extensively (*Hell.* 6, 3, 4-5), Autokles three times (*Hell.* 6, 3, 7), and Kallistratos five times (*Hell.* 6, 3, 10-11). Kallistratos, alone of the three, refers to himself and his own opinion throughout his address.[47] Each uses verbs that serve to demonstrate that he is voicing his own personal opinion, as well as expressing the collective will and views of the Athenians (in the first person plural). Yet, the tone adopted by each speaker and the contents of their speeches differ considerably. Kallias, hereditary *proxenos* of the Spartans, devotes his *prooimion* (a considerable part of his speech) to an exposition of his own and his ancestors' ties with the Spartans. He emphasises his own positive track-record as successful broker of peace between his own *polis* and the Spartans, as well as the fact that he is a man of military standing and highly regarded in his *polis* as a peace-maker. The substance of the rest of his speech relates to the mythical ties between Athens and Sparta, including Demeter's gift of grain to the Peloponnese. Autokles

---

[45] The adjective ἐπιστρεφής, rare in classical prose, is ambiguous. It may mean sharp in tone (as HDT. 1, 30); earnest or vehement (as AESCHIN. 1, 71); or "attentive".

[46] Kallistratos spearheaded the successful prosecution of four Athenian ambassadors on their return from Sparta in 392/1 (PHILOCH., *FGrH* 328 F149a), but in 374 spoke against the Thebans in favour of the renewal of the King's Peace (DIOD. SIC. 15, 38, 3).

[47] ἐλπίζω (6, 3, 11), ἐπιμνησθῶ (6, 3, 14), ἔγωγε ἐπαινῶ, ὁρῶ (6, 3, 16).

adopts a different line, rebuking the Spartans for depriving their allies of *autonomia* and their bullying of the latter, who are obliged to follow the Spartans in war, but whom the Spartans do not consult on questions of alliances and choice of enemies. This is followed by explicit criticism of Sparta's occupation of Thebes, and he ends with the comment that those who are on the verge of concluding an alliance should not expect to receive just treatment from others while they themselves appear to grasp as much they can. Kallistratos' speech is the one that has won most approval from modern commentators. In it, he acknowledges the mistakes committed by the Athenians as well as the Spartans as hegemonic powers and argues that the two states may benefit equally from the mutual support that peace and an alliance will make possible. He ends by stating that, together, both states will enjoy a stronger position within Greece than either of them has ever had before (6, 3, 17).

On the surface the impression is one of discord within the team, or at least of three very different positions in relation to the subject matter and to the audience itself. Precisely this has given rise to very different scholarly interpretations of what it is that Xenophon the author is trying to show us. Until the publication of Gray (1989), there was a fairly wide consensus that Kallias and Autokles are both set up as foils to Kallistratos. He has been regarded as the only 'true diplomat' of the trio, and his speech as the one which alone is responsible for the final positive outcome of the envoys' performance. Kallias' speech has been widely dismissed as empty rhetoric delivered by a conceited man,[48] and that of Autokles as "an extraordinarily undiplomatic, bitterly anti-Spartan speech".[49] However, Gray argued for an entirely different interpretation, insisting that Xenophon meant us to interpret the speeches as representing, in combination,

---

[48] Esp. DALFEN (1976) 66-68, who dismisses Kallias' speech as hot air; see also TUPLIN (1993) 104-108; DILLERY (1995) 243; MARINCOLA (2010) 270.

[49] DAVIES (1971) 161. See DALFEN (1976) 70; also DILLERY (1995) 243-244; MARINCOLA (2010) 272.

different aspects of the Athenian character.[50] Her interpretation of the trilogy as effectively presenting different arguments all leading to the same conclusion is further developed by Tuplin.[51] He notes the very important comment by the narrator that all three speakers were thought to have spoken well (6, 3, 18), and that "the overall effect is one of unanimity",[52] even though Tuplin himself is less than complimentary in his analysis of Kallias' speech in particular.

Other scholars have adopted a more charitable line than Tuplin towards Kallias' contribution. Buckler noted that Kallias' use of mythological examples is well attested in political discourse already in the classical period.[53] He also highlights the importance of Kallias' personal standing as *proxenos* and friend of the Spartans: it is precisely this which allows him to produce a *prooimion* that ticks most of the boxes provided by the two surviving classical rhetorical treatises. Kallias' contribution has been further rehabilitated in a penetrating analysis by Schepens, who observes that his use of myth reflects the fact that myths "were regarded as some kind of quintessential history", and that Kallias' reference to the mythical connection between Athens and Sparta permits him to represent their recent conflicts as "temporary disturbances". This in turn paves the way for Kallistratos' discussion of cooperation in the present in the third speech in the trilogy.[54]

Undoubtedly, Kallias' personal relations with the Spartans lent extra weight to his professions of personal goodwill in his own voice, and his connection with the Eleusinian sanctuary as a *dadouchos* and a member of the *Kerykes* lent particular force to his use of myth. However, despite its clear function as a *captatio beneuolentiae*, Kallias' speech is not quite as anodyne as is commonly assumed. The mythical material that he deploys has a very important significance that places it firmly in the

[50] GRAY (1989) 123-131.
[51] TUPLIN (1993) 101-110.
[52] TUPLIN (1993) 104.
[53] Buckler in BECK / BUCKLER (2008) 158-159.
[54] SCHEPENS (2001) 92-93.

present. His reference to Triptolemos' gift of Demeter's grain to the Peloponnese is followed immediately by the rhetorical question (6, 3, 6), "How can it then be just (δίχαιον) either for you ever to come to destroy the crops of those from whom you received seeds, or for us not to wish for those to whom we gave it to have as much abundance of it as possible?" This, in my reading, is not a casual reference. One of the recent incidents known to have poisoned the relationship between Athens and Sparta and which, according to the narrator, had driven the Athenians to support the Thebans (5, 4, 34), was Sphodrias' invasion of Attica in 379. In 5, 4, 20-21 we have heard how Sphodrias and his troops, when his original design failed, stole livestock and plundered the houses in the Thriasian plain – that is, in the vicinity of Eleusis. Although the raid itself took place in late winter or early spring, green grain would have been vulnerable to trampling during this period, and any grain stored in unprotected houses exposed to looting.[55] Moreover, we are told that at the time of the attack three named Spartan envoys were staying in Kallias' home in the *asty*, enjoying his hospitality as Sparta's *proxenos*. We learn that the envoys were arrested and questioned, and we are told the gist of their defence and how they were judged to have had no knowledge of the affair and acquitted. How far Kallias had been responsible for getting his guests off the hook is not revealed. Even so, it is clear that Kallias himself had been personally affected by Sphodrias' actions, not only because of his role as Spartan *proxenos* but also because of his position in Eleusis, in whose backyard Sphodrias and his army had been on the rampage.

It seems inconceivable that Sphodrias' invasion eight years earlier could have been left to remain as the elephant in the room during any meaningful peace negotiations, and it would no doubt have been possible for any of the members of the delegation to voice the collective Athenian grievance over the matter. But precisely because he was who he was, Kallias was in

---

[55] See, e.g., HANSON (²1998) 38-40.

an especially good position to do so. As a member of the *Kerykes* he could endow the episode with a religious dimension, which would hardly have been lost on the internal audience in the story (or for that matter on Xenophon's intended readership).[56] Most importantly, Kallias was especially well placed for tempering his accusation by a credible display of his own goodwill towards the Spartans.[57] His use of myth can be seen as a diplomatic masterstroke: Athenian grievances are brought out in the open, but so delicately that Kallias' own *ethos* as Sparta's well-meaning friend is not undermined.

Kallias' diplomatic criticism paves the way for the second speech by Autokles. The aggressive tone of the speech given to him has puzzled even those modern readers who have interpreted the trilogy as constituting a single rhetorical strategy, in which all speakers are working towards the same outcome. Gray sees Autokles' intervention as a graphic example of Athenian *parrhesia*, while the very bitterness with which he voices his criticism of Sparta's actions and policies lends all the more force to the generosity of the final speech given to Kallistratos.[58] It is indeed possible to interpret his speech as that of a critical friend, whose address is intended mainly as a contrast and thus prelude to Kallistratos' conciliatory oratory. However, once we take the nature of the audience into account and consider the speeches from their point of view, it is possible to explain the choice of tone and contents of Autokles' speech, and indeed of Autokles himself as a speaker. The speech itself

[56] There is a striking similarity between the part played by Kallias here and that by the unnamed speaker of Lys. 6, who acted as *synegoros* on the prosecution team. See RUBINSTEIN (2000) 140-142 and, in more detail, MARTIN (2009) 137-151.

[57] The widespread negative evaluation of Kallias' speech as conceited and pompous has been prompted in part by the narrator's introduction of him as "the kind of man no less fond of praising himself than of being praised by others" (6, 3, 3). See GRAY (1989) 124. Yet, the frequent self-praise by Athenian defendants in court and occasionally also by prosecutors shows that it must have been regarded as a necessary strategy by orators in certain circumstances, such as the present occasion may have been.

[58] GRAY (1989) 128-131.

can be interpreted as absolutely crucial for the success of the Athenian mission as a whole. As already mentioned, the speakers are not addressing an exclusively Spartan audience, but an audience also numbering representatives sent by Sparta's allies. If we consider the Spartans first, they may have responded favourably to Kallias' speech, despite his allusion to the Sphodrias issue. But as argued earlier, even the most sincere advice from a speaker who is believed to harbour *eunoia* in relation to his audience may still fail to carry conviction, unless the audience can be persuaded that his advice enjoys broad support from the community that he represents. For the Spartans on this occasion, a burning question must have been whether Kallias was merely giving voice to a view prevalent among Lakonophile Athenians, or whether the desire for a treaty was shared by those who were more neutral in their sentiments, let alone those who had been strongly in favour of collaboration with the Thebans in the past. Autokles' speech seems to be aimed in part at persuading them of the latter. By referring explicitly to Sparta's ill-treatment of the Thebans and their occupation of the Kadmeia (6, 3, 9), he seems to identify himself as a man who had himself been sympathetic to the Theban cause. That he personally has now decided to participate in the effort to broker a peace may well have reassured the Spartans in the audience that the mission itself enjoyed Athenian backing that went way beyond a limited Lakonising clique.

Concerns about the level of support that the mission enjoyed in the Athenian *demos* may not have been the only worry that troubled the Spartan listeners – and their allied representatives least of all. There was a historical precedent for such an alignment between the two states, and it was not a happy one from the point of view of either Sparta or Sparta's Peloponnesian allies. The present audience could hardly have forgotten what had happened between 421 and 418,[59] let alone how the Spartans

---

[59] Cf. the Korinthians' approach to officials in Argos after the conclusion of the Peace of Nikias, suggesting anti-Spartan defensive alliances (THUC. 5, 27, 2).

had thrown their weight about in the Peloponnese after the King's Peace, and so the prospect of yet another Athens-Sparta alignment must have given cause for concern. For the Spartans, the concern was likely to have been mainly that the alliance itself might cause further tension in relations between themselves and other Peloponnesian states – which may have been an important reason why they permitted allied representatives to be present at the negotiations. The imperative for the Spartans to keep their allies sweet, and the consequences of their failure to do so, are all too clear from Xenophon's subsequent narrative.

But any such Spartan worries would almost certainly have been dwarfed by those of her allies at the prospect of Athenian military backing of Sparta's policies in the Peloponnese. If we imagine that Kallias' speech had been followed immediately by that of Kallistratos, who ends by asserting that the peace will strengthen both Athens' and Sparta's position in Greece, the result would most likely have been one of alarm. Autokles' speech in fact focusses primarily on Sparta's unacceptable behaviour towards other states, and especially Sparta's policy of waging wars without consulting their allies (6, 3, 7-8). Thus, despite his consistent address to the Spartans in the second person plural, his aim seems first and foremost to be to reassure their allies that there are powerful voices within Athens who are not willing to support a policy of further Spartan oppression. It is also noteworthy that Autokles does not refer explicitly to any specifically *Athenian* grievances: he sets himself up as a man who is concerned with the need to respect the integrity of other Greek states. He alludes only once to Athens' own suffering at the hands of the Spartans, when he says that the Spartans have "installed dekarchies here, and rule by thirty there" (6, 3, 8). The intended effect is probably to create a 'we-feeling' with the allies in the audience: the message seems to be "we know what it's like, and we won't let this happen to you!".

If I am right that Autokles' speech is intended first and foremost to win over Sparta's allies, then that would also explain

Autokles' gruff, if not aggressive, tone. Autokles arguably had to project a credible representation of a political figure who had the courage of his convictions and the will to speak truth to power. If he did not, Sparta's allies would have been left to wonder if Autokles himself and those who shared his opinions would in reality be willing (and able) to restrain the Spartans in any bid for further consolidation of their power over other states in the Peloponnese. A softer and more conciliatory tone towards the Spartans themselves on the critical matter of allied *autonomia* would have done little to reassure them in this respect.

The narrator indicates that, if Autokles' persuasive efforts were aimed mainly at Sparta's allies, he was indeed successful. Although we are told that the reaction was one of dead silence, he "instilled delight in those who felt aggrieved at the Spartans" (6, 3, 10). It is important to note that the articulated participle used here, τοὺς ἀχθομένους, does not imply any emotions of hatred or anger (the verb should not be confused with ἔχθω / ἔχθομαι), nor does it have to refer to those who were declared enemies of the Spartans.[60] Rather, the reference is to Spartan allies with legitimate grievances at Spartan oppression. Thus the narrator gives us to understand that Autokles' message on oppression and freedom had got through to Sparta's allies, and that they believed his sincerity and his commitment. Without his speech, the speech by Kallistratos, ending as it does with its naked and jubilant promise of shared hegemony and increased power of Sparta and Athens, would have been unpalatable.

As mentioned earlier, some modern scholars have noted the narrator's comment that all three speakers were thought to have spoken well. The genitive absolute δοξάντων δὲ τούτων καλῶς εἰπεῖν permits the interpretation that the envoys' combined performance was favourably received not only by the Spartans, but by the composite audience in its entirety. The narrator further states that the Spartans proceeded to ratify the

---

[60] *Pace* DILLERY (1995) 244 and DALFEN (1976) 70.

peace, the terms of which included Spartan withdrawal of their harmosts and a mutual commitment by Athens and Sparta to allied *autonomia* (6, 3, 18). Thus the Athenian mission as a whole has succeeded in achieving the goal imposed on it by the assembly. Moreover, the terms to which the Spartans consent appear, on the surface, to have taken account of some of the criticism voiced by Autokles. If there is any sting in Xenophon's account, it is most likely the narrator's observation (6, 3, 19) that, despite the *autonomia* term, the Spartans subsequently swore to the treaty on behalf of themselves and their allies, whereas the Athenians permitted their allies themselves to swear. This may well be intended to signal to the reader that, in reality, the Spartans were not inclined to mend their ways.

As Xenophon represents the Athenian mission, the arguments presented by the three envoys gain in persuasive force because of who each one is (or is believed to be). Each contribution in turn lends further persuasiveness to the contributions by the two other speakers by complementing them. Thus, in some respects, their combined effect is similar to that which must have been intended by the combination of the three different voices and characters projected in the speech by Herodotos' Alexander.

In his analysis of this trilogy, Schepens resorts to a musical analogy:

> "Although the three Athenian voices pursue, like in a polyphonic musical composition, each in their distinctive pitch, their own way independently from one another, they meet harmoniously at significant points."

On this interpretation, the envoys' combined performance constitutes a parallel to the way some prosecution teams seem to have operated in Athenian public actions, where a similar musical analogy may be applied.[61] One frequently recurring

---

[61] See RUBINSTEIN (2000) 232.

feature seems to have been that each contributor to the prosecution's case plays down his personal link to the formal prosecutor, while emphasising his own motives for becoming involved in the case, as well as his own views on it and on the defendant's guilt.

Often, there seems to have been no clear hierarchical relationship between the main prosecutor and his *synkategoroi*, who tend to represent themselves as *kategoroi* in their own right, just as the three Athenian envoys are represented as addressing their audience independently of one another. Political heavyweights like Demosthenes and Lykourgos are found contributing together to the same cases, adding to the impression that the prosecution's *case*, and not just the prosecutor's person, is endorsed by significant sections of the Athenian political élite. The intention may well have been to convey an impression that the case was the *polis'* case rather than that of a single prosecutor pursuing a personal agenda. At the same time, such a prosecution team may have been more effective in persuading a large dikastic panel which, like the composite audience addressed by the Athenian envoys, was bound to number citizens with different political opinions and sympathies.

Even when envoys addressed audiences consisting entirely of citizens of a single *polis*, they still needed to take into account that their audience would contain individuals with very divergent political outlooks. How a team effort might help to overcome this challenge is illustrated in Xenophon's trilogy in 6, 5, 33-49, in which a composite team, consisting of five named Spartans and representatives of their remaining allies, addressed the Athenian *demos* after the Spartan defeat at Leuktra and the resulting Theban invasion of the Peloponnese. We are told that all the Spartan envoys spoke (6, 5, 33), and that they all said much the same things. A single resumé is given of their speeches in combination, with only one particular point attributed to an individual, but unnamed, Spartan representative. The summary is followed by two speeches in *oratio recta*, delivered by the

Korinthian Kleiteles, and Prokles of Phleious. Prokles' speech has attracted much attention. It is sometimes interpreted as a device with which Xenophon represents Athenian values and the Athenian collective character by relating their positive response to his speech, as well as their subsequent failure to live up to their reputation.[62]

For present purposes, the importance of Xenophon's scene lies in the narrator's comments on the Athenian audience's response to the speeches. They depict a process by which the assembly moves from internal dissent over the merits of the case as presented by the Spartan envoys (6, 5, 36), to more widespread approval following Kleiteles' address (6, 5, 37), and culminating in unanimity in response to the final address by Prokles (6, 5, 49). While the speech given to Kleiteles does not reveal his character at all, but merely represents him as the mouthpiece of the Korinthians (in the first person plural), Prokles' speech allows his own character and opinions to be projected through his oratory. He deploys opinion verbs in the first person singular,[63] and refers to what he himself has heard about the Athenians' reputation in a blatant appeal to their *amour propre* (6, 5, 45). He also takes care to project the collective *ethos* of his own community and the rest of Sparta's allies as trustworthy and motivated primarily by their honourable sense of obligation (6, 5, 44).

Although the narrator does not let on whether Prokles himself was known to the Athenians, the representation of his speech suggests a man who is able to persuade first and foremost through the *ethos* he projects in his speech, and who manages to play his standing as a representative of a relatively insignificant allied state to the advantage of the Peloponnesian team as a whole. Prokles refers to his own and Kleiteles' role with the verb συναγορεύω. This verb often refers to those who

---

[62] E.g. GRAY (1989) 113-118; MARINCOLA (2010) 274-275; BARAGWANATH (2012) 322-329.

[63] οἶμαι (6, 5, 38), ἡγοῦμαι, οἶμαι (6, 5, 39), μοι δοκοῦσι (6, 5, 41), ὁρῶ (6, 5, 45), ὁρῶ (6, 5, 46).

deliver supporting symbouleutic speeches, but it is also used by Xenophon to refer to Sokrates' defence *synegoroi* at his trial, in which sense it is used by the Attic orators, too.[64] Indeed, Prokles' speech shares many of the characteristics associated with the rhetoric of defendants and defence *synegoroi* in the courts.[65] These include appeals to *charis*, the call on the audience to come to the rescue of the main party, the representation of the Lakedaimonians as suppliants, the highlighting of their track record as benefactors alongside the admonition to the audience to remember it, and the high emotional temperature of the speech as a whole. All this is similar to arguments deployed in defence *epilogoi*.[66]

This is not to say that Xenophon necessarily expected his readers to associate Prokles' intervention with the kind of oratory they were familiar with from the courts, let alone that he consciously drew on any particular piece of Attic forensic oratory. In Prokles' speech, the very same arguments and phrases that might make the reader think of the courtroom correspond remarkably well to the instructions issued in the *Rhetorica ad Alexandrum* (34, 2-7) on how to persuade an assembly to come to the rescue of individuals as well as *poleis*. This suggests that Xenophon's representation of his address is unlikely to have contained anything that would have struck the ancient observer as completely out of place in a symbouleutic speech of this type. Rather, my point is that the strategy of the Peloponnesian team, the reported dynamics between the team and their audience and, above all, the way in which Prokles' speech constitutes an effective *epilogos* within the team's combined address are very similar to the strategies of attested defence teams in court.

---

[64] XEN. *Apol.* 22; cf. likewise in a forensic context DEM. 49, 9; AESCHIN. 1, 87; 2, 143; HYP. 3 *Eux.* 11. For the verb used with reference to symbouleutic oratory, see, e.g., THUC. 6, 6, 3; 7, 49, 3; LYS. 12, 25; ISOC. 6, 2; 14, 33; XEN. *Hell.* 3, 5, 16; 5, 2, 20; DEM. 15, 15; 23, 172; 50, 6; AESCHIN. 2, 63 and 123.

[65] For a general discussion, see RUBINSTEIN (2000) 148-172.

[66] Compare, e.g., Prokles' assertion in 6, 5, 40 with that in LYS. 20, 31, and his protestations in 6, 5, 42-43 with LYS. 20, 31-32 and 34; also the argument over returning *charis* in 6, 5, 44 with LYS. 20, 31-32.

Furthermore, Prokles' speech may serve as a reminder that there were in fact very considerable overlaps between dikanic and symbouleutic oratory. In other words, we should not be seduced by Aristotle's classifications into believing that the two genres were entirely compartmentalised.[67]

It is then not altogether surprising if oratorical practice and the strategies adopted by ambassadorial teams corresponded in some respects to those attested for teams operating in forensic contexts. On this comparison Xenophon's representations of the Athenian and Peloponnesian missions make excellent sense. The courtroom parallel should not be pressed too far, however, for there were significant differences between the forensic and symbouleutic stages, in regard to both the setting and the composition of the teams themselves. I shall return these in my final section.

V. Ambassadorial teams in art, life and law

The similarities between oratorical teamwork as represented by Xenophon and the kind of teamwork attested in the Attic Orators may provide some reassurance on the question how far Xenophon was aiming at dramatic realism in his portrayal of ambassadorial teams at work. Yet, if this is the case, we are left to wonder why similar detailed and explicit depictions of team speaking cannot be found in the works of either Herodotos or Thucydides.

One possible explanation which cannot be ruled out *a priori* is that the kind of teamwork that Xenophon represents in his dramatisation of the Athenian and Peloponnesian missions was the exception rather than the rule. He may have chosen to devote so much attention to the interrelated performances by the speakers precisely because they were unusual and therefore

---

[67] Cf. ANDOC. 1, 150, who refers to the task of his *synegoroi* as that of "giving advice" (συμβουλεύειν).

notable. Or, if we believe that the episodes were mostly or entirely invented by Xenophon himself, he may have been inspired by the Homeric precedent of the embassy to Achilleus in the *Iliad*. A further possibility is that team speaking was in fact not unusual, but that both Herodotos and Thucydides have opted deliberately for a more impressionistic representation of ambassadorial practices as part of their literary agendas. Indeed, Xenophon himself may often have chosen to suppress the role of the team as a whole, opting instead for a representation consisting in only a single oration, performed by a single voice and character.

In support of the former explanation, one may note that ambassadorial teams were not always permitted to address their foreign audience *seriatim*, without interruption by other speakers. In his representation of the Akanthian and Apollonian joint embassy to Sparta requesting military intervention, Xenophon gives one speech in *oratio recta* to a single named Akanthian envoy (5, 2, 12-19), which is followed by the Spartans opening the floor to their own citizens and allied representatives. Only after a decision has been made to meet their request do the Akanthians (in the plural) rise to speak again (5, 2, 23). This constitutes an important difference between the forensic and the diplomatic stage, and it is worth noting that two of Xenophon's other accounts of team speaking likewise mention that the envoys' performances were interspersed with interventions by speakers belonging to their audience.[68]

The possibility of interruption by other speakers meant that ambassadorial teams faced a greater need to improvise than forensic teams (especially teams of prosecutors), who would be able to plan in advance a coordinated performance appropriate to the time allocated to them by the waterclock. On the other hand, the need for improvisation does not in itself rule out that the team may still have worked with a common rhetorical strategy: improvisation would also have been required from

[68] XEN. *Hell.* 6, 5, 37; 7, 1, 1.

teams supporting defendants in the courts, since they would not always have a clear idea of precisely what arguments the prosecutor and his team might employ.

The way in which the contributions by foreign envoys were managed as a point on the assembly's agenda may not only have varied from *polis* to *polis*; even within the same community there may have been variations in the way debates were conducted, depending on the occasion and context. Our knowledge of actual practice in the 5th and 4th centuries is extremely limited, even for Athens, especially when it comes to meetings involving representatives of several allied states. When a team of envoys represented their community in an allied congress, the time at their disposal may well have been so limited that it would make most sense for them to assign their presentation to a single speaker. This is particularly relevant when we consider some scenes depicting envoys in action in Thucydides. Two of the set ambassadorial speeches were delivered during formally convened meetings of allied representatives.[69] A third was delivered during a Spartan assembly meeting to which the Spartans had invited representations from "their allies and any other party who claimed to have been unjustly treated by the Athenians" (1, 67, 3).

Yet, two of these episodes can in fact be taken to suggest that Thucydides himself, the characters in his story, and his intended readership were aware not only of the phenomenon of oratorical teamwork, but also of its potential strategic advantages. Both episodes are set in Sparta, both involve a team of Korinthian envoys who are given one speech in *oratio recta* and on both occasions are we told that the Korinthians were the last to speak (1, 67, 5 and 1, 119). On the first occasion, the narrator prefaces the speech by noting that this was a conscious rhetorical tactic: the Korinthians had left the delegates from other communities to bring their Spartan audience into a state

---

[69] THUC. 1, 119-124 and 4, 58-65 (a congress at Gela).

of agitation.[70] This tactic then allows the Korinthians to dispense with all the niceties of a diplomatic *prooimion* and launch straight into a speech which, in terms of its vehement criticism of the Spartan audience and its tone throughout, is not unlike Autokles' speech discussed earlier. It also means that the performance here is one that could easily be carried convincingly by a single speaker.

In a sense, the Korinthians are deploying multiple speakers to their own rhetorical advantage. Only here they appear to have devised their strategy on their own, without consulting the allied representatives whom they use to pave the way for their own address. In a world where composite ambassadorial teams were not at all uncommon, more openly and systematically conceived versions of the Korinthian strategy are highly plausible, aiming at the effect that we are allowed to observe in Xenophon's account of team-based ambassadorial performances at Athens and Sparta. But what should we make of the fact that the Korinthians, on both of these occasions, are referred to as speakers in the plural? It is unfortunately not the case that a speaking verb and corresponding subject in the plural permit the inference that the Korinthian envoys themselves all shared the performance.

Xenophon's account of the Theban mission to Athens in 395 demonstrates precisely how treacherous these plurals can be when they occur in introductory and capping phrases before and after envoys' speeches. We learn that, when the Thebans realised that they would be attacked by the Spartans, "they sent envoys to Athens, who were to speak as follows" (3, 5, 7). The following speech in *oratio recta* ends (3, 5, 16) with the capping phrase "After he had said this, he stopped". Subsequently, we are told, numerous Athenians rose and spoke as *synegoroi* in favour of the proposal.

---

[70] THUC. 1, 67, 5. In 1, 119 we are told that the Korinthians had engaged in systematic lobbying of other communities in advance.

The discrepancy between the plural introductory phrase and the singular in the capping phrase is surprising, and we cannot rule out that it may have been deliberate. If so, it may have been meant to indicate that the Thebans sent out their team with a shared oratorical brief, but that, in the event, the first Theban speaker was so successful that any further speeches were superfluous. Instead, a large number of Athenian participants themselves provided the necessary *synegoriai* – a powerful illustration, then, of the rhetorical efficacy of the case made by the first Theban speaker, of the ringing endorsement by the Athenian *demos* of the Thebans' proposition, and of the Athenian eagerness for war.

Alternatively, the shift from plural to singular was simply due to carelessness on Xenophon's part when he constructed the scene. This seems more plausible, for if Xenophon's aim was to highlight the efficacy of a single speech and speaker, one might have expected him to name the envoy who succeeded so spectacularly in winning over the Athenian assembly. However, the speaker remains unidentified, and his personal voice is entirely absent from the speech assigned to him. All opinion verbs are in the first person plural, with the Theban community as their subject,[71] and only twice is it possible to interpret the first person plural as referring to the envoys themselves as a group, rather than to the Theban collectivity.[72] Like Hekatonymos of Sinope in his first speech, the Theban speaker here is simply the conduit for the argumentation and persuasive effort of his *polis*.

The discrepancy constitutes a warning that speaking verbs in the plural cannot be taken as a safe indication that a speech in *oratio recta* represents the contents of two or more separate speeches rolled into one. But nor does the attribution of a single speech to a team of envoys necessarily mean that we are meant to imagine the speech as being delivered by only one

---

[71] νομίζομεν (3, 5, 8), ἀξιοῦμεν (3, 5, 9), νομίζομεν (3, 5, 15).
[72] λέγομεν at 3, 5, 11 and 15.

speaker who spoke on behalf of all.[73] For there is a general tendency for the historiographers, including Xenophon, to air-brush out the envoys' individual characters from the representations of their oratory.

Sometimes the existence of an embassy is left entirely unmentioned, with the narrator instead representing the diplomatic exchange as a direct encounter between two collective groups.[74] But even when the narrator uses circumstantial participles that allow us to visualise the envoys in action, and even when they themselves are allowed to refer directly to their own position as speakers, their remarks tend to be general and impersonal. They are often restricted to providing information on who had sent them – an important indication, of course, that the envoys were authorised to speak for their community.[75] Their speech may also contain initial observations on the existing relationship between the addressees and envoys' community, with comments on how this affects the envoys' rhetorical position.[76] However, when the envoys are made to refer directly to their own characters (rather than the collective character of their community), their remarks are often little more than ethnic stereotyping.[77]

The sharply delineated personal characters given to the individual envoys discussed in the previous section are exceptions rather than the rule. Apart from Xenophon's Kleiteles, Prokles and his three famous Athenians, the envoys who are given distinct voices and characters of their own tend to be those who are autocratic rulers, men who with some justification could say "L'état, c'est moi". This makes their position very different from envoys given their brief by a collective decision-making

---

[73] As HORNBLOWER remarked (1987) 51, the two named Plataian envoys in THUC. 3, 52, 5-59, 4 hardly spoke in unison, and Thucydides may have 'telescoped' two originally separate speeches.

[74] E.g. THUC. 1, 115, 2; 3, 102, 6; 5, 32, 4-5; XEN. Hell. 5, 2, 1.

[75] HDT. 7, 136, 2; 7, 157, 1; 8, 142, 1; 9, 7A, 1; THUC. 4, 17, 1.

[76] E.g. THUC. 1, 32, 1; 1, 68, 1-2; 1, 73, 1-3.

[77] Cf. the Spartan envoys who comment on their need to speak at un-Lakonic length (THUC. 4, 17, 2-3).

body. The difference is not unlike that which distinguishes a powerful CEO of a modern corporation from an employee in the corporation's PR department. Because of the CEO's personal authority within the corporation, his or her personal values and opinions will contribute directly to the public perception of the *ethos* of the corporation. By contrast, the individual character of a PR officer is of little consequence for the persuasive effect of any statement he or she might issue: what the public is meant to hear is the voice of the corporation and the *ethos* projected is that of the organisation as an entity. In Greek historiography, the voices of elected envoys are for the most part comparable to the latter rather than the former.

It is likely, however, that envoys' symbouleutic oratory may in reality have been much more personal and much more dependent on individual character projection than is normally represented by the historiographers. This is suggested not only by the evidence in the Attic Orators and Xenophon's trilogies, but also by the rhetoric of the one elected envoy whom Thucydides allows to speak with a voice of his own: Hermokrates of Syracuse. Both in his speech at the conference at Gela (4, 59, 1-64, 5) and in his speech to the assembly at Kamarina (6, 76, 1-80, 5), Hermokrates comes across far more as an advisor in his own right than as the representative of his polis. Although he does refer to his brief in both speeches, his frequent use of the first person singular, and his references to his own judgement and opinions are as conspicuous as in Xenophon's trilogies, if not more so. The effect is that his oratory does not convey a particularly strong impression of the Syracusan collective character, but a gripping characterisation of Hermokrates himself as, effectively, the influential CEO of Syracuse.

Furthermore, when he uses the first person plural in his speech at Gela, this is more often the 'we' of the Sicilian Greeks than the Syracusan 'we'. Hermokrates thus sets himself up as an advisor who speaks in the common interest of all Sicilian Greeks. His strategy can be explained by the overall Syracusan objective of creating a united front against an invading enemy, making it particularly important for Hermokrates to allay any fears in his audiences that the Syracusans were in reality planning a power grab.

Arguably, the juxtaposition of Hermokrates' oratory with the later report of his fall from grace does serve as a powerful collective characterisation of the Syracusans – as Hornblower wryly comments, "All this sounds very Athenian".[78] But if we consider the specific occasions, it is Hermokrates' own *ethos* that appears to be decisive in winning over his audience at Gela, while at Kamarina he reportedly fails (6, 88, 1-3). Perhaps significantly, the Kamarinaian equivocal response to his speech and the counter-speech by the Athenian envoy Euphemos is ascribed to their fear of the Syracusans. This Hermokrates evidently has not succeeded in dispelling.

Hermokrates' projection of his own *ethos* is unusual for elected envoys as represented by Thucydides, but this does not permit the inference that it was exceptional for this genre of symbouleutic oratory in real life. The frequent suppression of envoys' individuality may well have been due mainly to the wider literary agendas of the historiographers.

The editing out of the envoys' individual characters permits the reading audience to listen to what appears to be conversations between collectivities. The *ethos* projected in the speeches presented in *oratio recta* is the collective *ethos* of an entire community, very often in ways that correspond closely to the projection of *ethos* in the speeches put in the mouths of individual characters. For example, in Thucydides' speech assigned to a team of Mytilenaians, who are asking for Peloponnesian assistance in their rebellion against the Athenians, the envoys are anxious to demonstrate that their community adheres to a basic code of trust and allegiance between allied states despite its decision to rebel.[79] The thrust of their *prooimion* is strikingly similar to the exiled Alkibiades' justification, in the *epilogos* of

---

[78] HORNBLOWER (2008) 532.
[79] THUC. 3, 9, 1-3.

his speech to the Spartans, of his decision to back the bitterest enemies of his own *polis* (6, 92, 2-5). In both speeches, the demonstration of values – in one case collective, in the other individual – is essential for establishing the trustworthiness of the speeches themselves and of the motives behind them. In the Mytilenaian case, a credible projection of a collective *ethos* is most likely of critical importance. A positive Peloponnesian response is likely to depend on the audience's being persuaded that the envoys' proposition is broadly supported by their community as a whole, and not just by a narrow faction. It may in fact have been the case that several of the envoys spoke in order to prove precisely that point (thus adopting a strategy similar to Xenophon's Athenian envoys in 371);[80] but if so, this does not seem to have been relevant to what Thucydides is aiming to describe.

The impersonal quality of the *ethos* normally projected in envoys' speeches may thus be due mainly to their function as vehicles for collective characterisation. But it may also have served an additional literary purpose. As suggested by Cogan,[81] in cases where the envoys remain nameless and faceless in their orations, the effect is that we, as readers, find ourselves listening to the speeches in the company of the envoys' addressees rather than sitting together with the envoys on their *bema*.

To be sure, a foreign mass audience may well have been in a position to recognise some of the men making up a team of envoys and have responded to them with a preconceived judgement on their individual trustworthiness and authority. This was especially likely to have been the case if a team numbered not only speakers with the standing of *proxenoi* but also one or more celebrities – successful military commanders, famous

---

[80] We are told in 3, 4, 4 that one of the men who had originally disclosed the Mytilenaian plot to the Athenians, but who had now changed his mind, was among the participants on the ambassadorial team sent to Athens to reassure them that they were not intending to secede.

[81] COGAN (1981) 218-222. Note, however, the comments by HORNBLOWER (1987) 50-52 on the two named Plataian envoys in THUC. 3, 52, 5.

actors, trendy philosophers,[82] and renowned orators. All of these are attested frequently as members of ambassadorial teams in the 4th century, and their potential importance for the team's overall performance should not be downplayed. Likewise, an envoy who was previously unknown to his audience may have left a lasting impression because of a spectacular performance – as Xenophon's Prokles did in his first address to the Athenian assembly.

Yet, even when a team featured a number of familiar faces whose individual characters would have been of some rhetorical importance, it is likely that the overriding concern of the foreign audience was the totality of the message they conveyed, in terms of its substance and credibility as a genuine expression of the collective will of the envoys' own community. Thus, Xenophon's blurred representation of the several orations by the five named Spartan envoys at Athens after Leuktra, who "all said much the same thing" (6, 5, 33), may well reflect the way a foreign audience would often have remembered the oratory of an ambassadorial team. That classical Greek audiences responded to ambassadorial teams first and foremost as teams is also suggested by the frequent formula used in Athenian inscriptions recording responses to visiting foreign missions: "On the matters on which the Methymnaians speak" – περὶ ὧν λέγουσιν οἱ δεῖνα.[83] The tendency in classical historiography to let us experience ambassadorial speeches from the point of view of the audience may well have contributed to the conventional

---

[82] The participation by philosophers on ambassadorial teams is especially well attested for the Hellenistic period, but there is at least one 4th-century example, Xenokrates of Chalkedon, who joined the Athenian ambassadors to Antipater after Krannon; see WHITEHEAD (1981) 238-241; HAAKE (2007) 64 n. 222. An earlier example may be Alkidamas of Elaia, whose *Messeniakos* may have been delivered at Sparta during the first half of the 360s, despite a broad scholarly consensus that the speech was merely a rhetorical exercise; see, e.g., MARISS (2002) 20-21 and GRANDJEAN (2003) 65-66.

[83] E.g. *IG* II² 42, 44, 96, etc. The wording of the formula even seems to have crept into DEM. 7, 1 (ὕστερον δέ, περὶ ὧν οἱ πρέσβεις λέγουσι, καὶ ἡμεῖς λέξομεν).

representation of the envoys as speaking with a single, impersonal voice.

The operation of the team collectively and the performances by its individual members look quite different when viewed from the perspective of the envoys' own community. The selection of team members is very unlikely to have been done with a view to maximising the rhetorical potential of the team as a whole, although the potential of individuals to establish a rapport with their non-domestic audiences probably played an important part.[84] When the mission's objectives were potentially contentious, different factions most likely did their utmost to work for the election of team members whose views coincided with their own.[85] The presence of envoys with different political leanings would have been important as a way of ensuring internal 'policing' within the delegation. As Demosthenes comments: on the first of the missions to Makedonia Aischines allegedly owed his election to his avowed hostility to Philip and was chosen as "one of those who was to keep an eye on the rest" (Dem. 19, 12).

No doubt, such considerations would often have informed the composition of ambassadorial teams and made them very different from forensic teams. That did not necessarily present an insurmountable obstacle to rhetorical cooperation and it could even be a strength. As discussed in section iv, the Athenian mission to Sparta in 371 may have been successful precisely because the team appears to have played its internal differences to their collective advantage by combining the projection of very different individual characters and viewpoints with an overall loyalty to the Athenian brief to which they were all ultimately committed.

Nevertheless, it is an important question if effective rhetorical cooperation was generally realistic, especially on a team

---

[84] This is suggested not least by *Rhet. ad Alex.* 24, 3, cited earlier.

[85] The precise methods with which envoys were selected are difficult to reconstruct, even for Athens, where the role of the *boule* in particular, which was emphasised by BRIANT (1968), is disputed.

packed full of men with large egos. Here it is important to bear in mind that Athenian envoys at least had a strong legal incentive to cooperate with fellow team members, however bitter their personal differences. Ambassadorial teams resembled ordinary boards of officials in that individual liability was combined with a certain level of collective liability. The team was debriefed as a team, yet it seems to have been each participant's duty to render account of his own personal performance, as well as of the mission itself. Aischines and Demosthenes provide ample evidence for the importance of debriefing speeches delivered by returning envoys,[86] and the process itself clearly presented a considerable risk to the individual envoys of being shopped by their colleagues.[87] Interestingly, the only specific advice offered to envoys in the *Rhetoric to Alexander* relates directly to the speeches which an envoy might be required to present during his debriefing.[88] The author notes that these, being reports, should contain only a narrative, but spun in such a way that the speaker will persuade his audience not to hold him responsible for the failure of his mission, or to credit him as responsible for the embassy's achievements, if the mission had been a success.

The recognition that an envoy, unlike any other symbouleutic orator, gave advice both as himself and as the mouthpiece of his own community was sometimes explored even in the representations of ambassadorial oratory in the historiographers. We see this in the speech given to the aforementioned Theban envoy to Athens who succeeded in persuading his audience to join the Thebans against the Spartans in 395 despite the Theban call for Athens' destruction ten years earlier. The envoy tackles this by asserting that the proposal had emanated not from his *polis* but from a single man who happened to be present in the congress of Spartan allies. In the context of the

---

[86] E.g. AESCHIN. 2, 47-54, 122; 3, 125; DEM. 19, 5, 18-24.

[87] E.g. the prosecution by Leon of his fellow envoy Timagoras (XEN. *Hell.* 7, 1, 33-38).

[88] *Rhet. ad. Alex.* 30, 2-4.

Hellenica this may seem disingenuous, since the clamour for Athens' destruction is represented as being made by the Thebans and the Korinthians collectively (2, 2, 19). However, the Theban's representation may not have sounded as absurd as is sometimes thought, precisely because an envoy was individually liable for his own words as well as his actions. It was this which made it possible for communities to disown envoys who were perceived as having overstepped the mark.[89] The disowning of an envoy would, it seems, normally require him to be formally punished for his words after debriefing. Thus, the disingenuousness in the Theban representation of the episode arises mainly from the fact that the Thebans had not done so.

Obviously, the most dangerous accusation an envoy potentially faced was that he had sabotaged the mission because of collaboration with hostile states. Thus, even a relatively innocent reluctance to cooperate with the others in working towards the mission's goals might be used against him in support of far more serious allegations.

However much an envoy may have owed his election on a mission to a desire by a particular faction to ensure internal policing of his team, he had nevertheless made a binding personal commitment to ensuring, as far as possible, that the objectives as defined by the assembly and council were indeed met. The accounts of Demosthenes and Aischines show us how such team work might fail due to the over-sized egos of some of the members. Xenophon's accounts, by contrast, show us how they might succeed. The literary conventions in classical historiography do make it difficult to identify how often teams divided up their rhetorical tasks in this way. Yet, there is good reason to believe that team-speaking was, in practice, one of the ways that each team member would be able to support his own argumentation by projecting his personal authority and

---

[89] Compare the Thebans' disowning of their Medism in THUC. 3, 62, 2-4 with reference to the fact that they were ruled by an autocratic government.

knowledge, while the team, at the same time, worked together to strengthen the totality of their case by a shared projection of their city's collective character.

The lack of explicit comment on the practice in the *Rhetoric to Alexander* and Aristotle's *Rhetoric* should not be taken as an indication that it was rare. After all, neither author has much to say on the strategies associated with forensic *synegoria*,[90] yet the evidence for the practice testifies to their important role in real-life litigation.

The evidence does not permit a more precise assessment of the frequency of ambassadorial team speaking as compared with the use of a single spokesman. However, any analysis of the ambassadorial speeches represented in classical Greek historiography has to take into account that each speech may in fact be a distillation of several contributions to what was originally not only a polyphonic but a symphonic performance.

Works cited

BARAGWANATH, E. (2012), "A Noble Alliance: Herodotus, Thucydides, and Xenophon's Procles", in E. FOSTER / D. LATEINER (eds.), *Thucydides and Herodotus* (Oxford), 316-344.
BARON, C.A. (2013), *Timaeus of Tauromenium and Hellenistic Historiography* (Cambridge).
BRIANT, P. (1968), "La boulê et l'élection des ambassadeurs à Athènes au IVe siècle", *REA* 70, 7-31.
BUCKLER, J. / BECK, H. (2008), *Central Greece and the Politics of Power in the Fourth Century B.C.* (Cambridge).
COGAN, M. (1981), *The Human Thing. The Speeches and Principles of Thucydides' History* (Chicago).
DALFEN, J. (1976), "Xenophon als Analytiker und Kritiker politischer Rede (Zu Hell. VI 3, 4-17 und VI 5, 33-48)", *GB* 5, 59-84.

---

[90] Aristotle refers once to what appears to be a *synegoria* in 1374b36-1375a2, while the *Rhet. ad Alex.* devotes 36, 37-41 to advice on how a *synegoros* might justify his participation in the case at hand and counter any suspicion that he was speaking in return for a fee.

DAVIES, J.K. (1971), *Athenian Propertied Families: 600-300 B.C.* (Oxford).

DILLERY, J. (1995), *Xenophon and the History of his Times* (London).

GRANDJEAN, C. (2003), *Les Mésséniens de 370/369 au 1er siècle de notre ère. Monnayages et histoire.* (Athens).

GRAY, V. (1989), *The Character of Xenophon's* Hellenica (London).

HAAKE, M. (2007), *Der Philosoph in der Stadt. Untersuchungen zur öffentlichen Rede über Philosophen und Philosophie in den hellenistischen Poleis* (Munich).

HANSON, V.D. (²1998), *Warfare and Agriculture in Classical Greece* (Berkeley).

HORNBLOWER, S. (1987), *Thucydides* (London).

— (1991), *A Commentary on Thucydides.* Vol. I, *Books I-III* (Oxford).

— (1996), *A Commentary on Thucydides.* Vol. II, *Books IV-V.24* (Oxford).

— (2008), *A Commentary on Thucydides.* Vol. III, *Books 5.25-8.109* (Oxford).

LOW, P. (2007), *Interstate Relations in Classical Greece. Morality and Power* (Cambridge).

MACK, W. (2015), *Proxeny and Polis. Institutional Networks in the Ancient Greek World* (Oxford).

MARINCOLA, J. (2010), "The Rhetoric of History: Allusion, Intertextuality, and Exemplarity in Historiographical Speeches", in D. PAUSCH (ed.), *Stimmen der Geschichte. Funktionen von Reden in der antiken Historiographie* (Berlin), 259-289.

MARTIN, G. (2009), *Divine Talk. Religious Argumentation in Demosthenes* (Oxford).

MARISS, R. (2002), *Alkidamas: Über diejenigen, die schriftliche Reden schreiben, oder über die Sophisten. Eine Sophistenrede aus dem 4. Jahrhundert v. Chr. eingeleitet und kommentiert* (Münster).

MITCHELL, L.G. (1997), *Greeks Bearing Gifts. The Public Use of Private Relationships in the Greek World, 435-323 BC* (Cambridge).

MOGGI, M. (1995), "I *proxenoi* e la guerra nel V secolo a. C.", in E. FRÉZOULS / A. JACQUEMIN (eds.), *Les relations internationales. Actes du Colloque de Strasbourg 15-17 juin 1993* (Paris), 143-159.

MOSLEY, D.J. (1973), *Envoys and Diplomacy in Ancient Greece* (Wiesbaden).

PERLMAN, P.J. (2004), "Crete", in M.H. HANSEN / T.H. NIELSEN (eds.), *An Inventory of Archaic and Classical Poleis* (Oxford), 1144-1195.

PICCIRILLI, L. (2002), *L'invenzione della diplomazia nella Grecia antica* (Rome).

RUBINSTEIN, L. (2000), *Litigation and Cooperation. Supporting Speakers in the Courts of Classical Athens* (Stuttgart).

SCHEPENS, G. (2001), "Three Voices on the History of a Difficult Relationship: Xenophon's Evaluation of Athenian and Spartan Identities in Hellenica VI 3", in A. BARZANÒ *et al.* (eds.), *Identità e valori. Fattori di aggregazione e fattori di crisi nell' esperienza politica antica* (Rome), 81-96.

TUPLIN, C. (1993), *The Failings of Empire. A Reading of Xenophon* Hellenica *2.3.11-7.5.27* (Stuttgart).

WANKEL, H. (ed.) (1976), *Demosthenes. Rede für Ktesiphon über den Kranz.* 2 vols. (Heidelberg).

WHITEHEAD, D. (1981), "Xenokrates the Metic", *RhM* NF 124, 223-244.

WOOTEN, C.W. (1973), "The Ambassador's Speech: A Particularly Hellenistic Genre of Oratory", *QJS* 59, 209-212.

IV

Angelos Chaniotis

HISTORY AS AN ARGUMENT IN HELLENISTIC ORATORY: THE EVIDENCE OF HELLENISTIC DECREES

1. Counting speeches: how much Hellenistic oratory is preserved in inscriptions?[1]

Oratory, as an elaborate, artful, and staged form of oral communication, is doomed by its very oral nature to extinction. Orations are preserved in cultures that possess recording devices – such as our culture –, or when listeners have been trained to take shorthand notes of delivered speeches, or when the speakers themselves record a more or less accurate version of a speech and produce and circulate copies, motivated by vanity, political agenda, the wish to make money, or the ambition to educate future orators. Unless future archaeological discoveries prove otherwise, for Greek and Roman oratory we have to rely on self-promoted, recorded, or (re)constructed speeches as well as on the information provided by teachers of rhetoric and their handbooks.

Unlike the – mainly Athenian – oratory of the 5th and 4th centuries BC, the Latin oratory of the Late Republican period, and the Greek and Latin oratory of the Imperial period

---

[1] All dates, if not otherwise mentioned, are BC. For epigraphic publications I use the abbreviations of the *Supplementum Epigraphicum Graecum*. I am grateful to Henry Heitmann-Gordon (University of Munich) for correcting the English text.

and Late Antiquity, which are well preserved, Hellenistic oratory is notoriously elusive.[2] It might have been instructive to
consider the reasons for this in our encounter, but this cannot
be the task here. Nevertheless, before I turn to my rather narrow subject – the use of history as an argument in Hellenistic
oratory –, it is worth briefly considering what we do have
and how epigraphy can contribute to our understanding of
Hellenistic oratory.

Oratory is a form of direct speech, and the only orations
preserved as direct speech from Alexander to Cleopatra are the
orations that are quoted in the works of the Hellenistic historians,
for instance the famous speech of Agelas in the peace conference in Naupaktos in 217 BC or the speech of the Athenian
statesman Athenion at the beginning of the First Mithridatic
War in 88 BC, presented by Polybius and Poseidonios respectively.[3] Such speeches are not numerous. Although they are the
product of the historians' creative imagination – loosely connected
with what was said, at the best –, they do provide information on
rhetorical techniques, types of arguments, persuasion strategies,
and forms of delivery.[4] I am also convinced that some orations
preserved in Plutarch's *Lives* of Hellenistic statesmen ultimately
derive from Hellenistic historians; but this would be the subject
of a different study.

What about other contemporary, Hellenistic sources, beyond
historiography? As D. Papanikolaou has recently demonstrated,
an 'aretalogy' for Isis from Maroneia (ca. 100 BC)[5] is the only
surviving sophistic encomium to a deity from the Hellenistic

---

[2] See more recently the collection of studies in KREMMYDAS / TEMPEST (2013);
see also WOOTEN (1973); VANDERSPOEL (2007); ERSKINE (2007). See also the
bibliography in notes 4-6.

[3] The speech of Agelaos: POLYB. 5, 104; DEININGER (1973); CHAMPION
(1997). Athenion's speech in POSIDON. *Hist.* fr. 247 ed. THEILER = *FGrH* 87 F
36 § 50-51 = ATH. 5, 212f-213c.

[4] On speeches in Polybius and Hellenistic historiography, see WOOTEN
(1974); SACKS (1986); WIEDEMANN (1990); CHAMPION (2000); USHER (2009);
WIATER (2010).

[5] *I.Thrac.Aeg.* E 205. See PAPANIKOLAOU (2009).

period. Papanikolaou's studies of this text as well as of a decree from Mantineia have made clear that to consider only direct speech for a study of Greek rhetoric would be as deficient an enterprise as to study Greek historiography by ignoring the fragments of Greek historians.[6] Evidence for oral communication is much more abundant than just records of direct speech.

First, we have both in historiographical works and in inscriptions, especially in decrees, abundant evidence for indirect (or reported) speech. For instance, in documents concerning international arbitration the arguments of the parties to the conflict and testimonies of witnesses are sometimes presented in indirect speech.[7] Decrees and *senatus consulta* also commonly summarise the oral presentations of envoys in the council, the assembly, and the senate using expressions such as διελέχθησαν, ἀπελογίσαντο περί, and λόγους ἐποιήσαντο.[8] The lengthier the summary, the more information we get about the rhetorical performance. A good example, to which I will return later because it is directly relevant for my subject, is a well-known inscription from Xanthos concerning an embassy from Kytenion in Doris in 206 BC. It begins with a long summary of the envoy's speech in the assembly, introduced with the verbs ἀπολογίζεσθαι ("to give an account"), διαλέγεσθαι ("to give a lecture or a report"), λέγειν, προσαπολογίζεσθαι ("give an additional account"), and

---

[6] PAPANIKOLAOU (2012). For further epigraphic evidence for Hellenistic oratory see CHANIOTIS (2013a).

[7] See, e.g., arguments introduced with ἐλέγοσαν in the document concerning the delimitation of the sacred land of Delphi in ca. 117 BC: *CID* IV 119 E = ROUSSET (2002), 86 no. 6 B lines 28-33: [ἐλ]έγοσαν ὅτι δεῖ τὸ κρῖμα ἐστηκὸς καὶ κύριον εἶναι, τὸ τότε γεγονός ... The most detailed records are those concerning the arbitration of Rhodes in the territorial dispute between Priene and Samos (new edition: MAGNETTO [2008]; cf. *I.Priene* 37 + 38; AGER [1996] no. 74; MAGNETTO [1997] nos. 3, 44, and 75) and that of Magnesia on the Maeander in the border dispute between Hierapytna and Itanos (*I.Magnesia* 105; *I.Cret.* III iv, 9; AGER [1996] no. 127; MAGNETTO [1997] no. 43). The arguments of parties to the conflict are introduced with the verbs ἀποδείκνυμι, ἐπιδείκνυμι, φάσκω, φημί, δικαιολογέω, and ἐμφανίζω.

[8] E.g. *IG* V 2, 419 line 4; *IG* XII 7, 221 b line 9; *F.Delphes* III 1, 261 line 4; *I.Iasos* 3 lines 2-4; *I.Magnesia* 48 line 6; 61 line 35; *I.Priene* 40.

παραδείκνυσθαι ("to demonstrate"). I quote a short passage, which summarises parts of the envoys' speech, referring to the legend of the hero Aletes ("the Wanderer"):

"Besides, they demonstrated that the colonists, sent out from our land by Chrysaor, the son of Glaukos, the son of Hippolochos, received protection from Aletes, one of the descendants of Herakles; for Aletes, starting from the land of the Dorians, came to their aid when they were being warred upon. Putting an end to the danger by which they were beset, he married the daughter of Aor, the son of Chrysaor."

Also decrees whose *narratio* is introduced with the verbs εἶπεν or εἶπαν summarise the proposal submitted to the assembly. In the Hellenistic period, these narrations are sometimes long and rhetorically elaborate, giving an impression of the content of orations delivered in the assembly. Syncopated orations are a characteristic feature of decrees in the late Hellenistic period, but this phenomenon starts already in the late 4th century BC, providing valuable insights into deliberative oratory.[9]

But in addition to direct and indirect speech, we also have evidence for 'rhetorical events' that took place without leaving any information as to their content. For instance, lists of victors in agonistic festivals include the names of the winner in encomiastic oration,[10] but the only Hellenistic texts of this sort that survive are a speech of the Athenian representative at the Eleutheria of Plataiai, who defended the right of Athens to lead

---

[9] See, e.g., the honorific decree of Athens for Eumenes II and his brothers: *IG* II³ 1323. The best examples are long 'biographical' decrees, such as those for Lykourgos (*IG* II² 457, 513, 3207; LAMBERT [2012] 264-265), and Kallias of Sphettos in Athens (*SEG* XXVIII 60), Diophantos in Chersonesos in Tauris (*IOSPE* I² 352), Protogenes (*IOSPE* I² 32) and Nikeratos in Olbia (*IOSPE* I² 34), Polemaios and Menippos in Kolophon (*SEG* XXXIX 1243 and 1244), Pyrrhakos in Alabanda (HOLLEAUX [1898] 258-266), Moschion in Priene (*I.Priene* 108), Apollonios in Metropolis (*I.Metropolis* 1), and Orthagoras in Araxa (*SEG* XVIII 570). The laudatory fragment *IG* XII 4, 1036 (1st century, Kos) is either part of a 'biographical' decree or of an oration.

[10] E.g. *I.Oropos* 521 (Amphiareia, ca. 85 BC): ἐγκώ[μιο]ν εἰς τ[ὸν θ]εό[ν]; *IG* XII 9, 91 (festival Tamyneia, 1st century): ἐγκώμιον εἰς τὸν Ἀπόλλ[ωνα].

the procession (2nd century),[11] and possibly an encomium for Amphiaraos from Oropos (late 4th century).[12] Innumerable decrees concerning diplomatic relations also use the more or less stereotypical phrase "the envoys delivered the decree and gave a speech in accordance with the decree",[13] without, however, summarising the content of that oration. Similarly, scores of honorific decrees use the stereotypical phrase "may it be resolved that he is praised and crowned".

Just as στεφανῶσαι has a very concrete meaning – the offering of a crown of a specific value –, so does ἐπαινέσαι: at least in some cases, the benefactor was not praised with the laconic phrase "the people praise NN" but with an oration; this may have been more common in the case of posthumous honours. From the Imperial period onwards, we also find a type of decree that offers consolation to the relatives of deceased members of the elite. Again, the short formula "let us offer them consolation"[14] means far more than simply paying a formal visit and saying a few polite words of condolence. As we know both from letters of condolence from Roman Egypt[15] and from consolation decrees from the Roman East,[16] there was a developed genre of consolatory texts, some of which had the form of short rhetorical texts. Whether this genre was as widespread in the Hellenistic period as it was in the Imperial period escapes our knowledge. Finally, when in texts concerning international arbitration we read the phrase "the judges heard the arguments

---

[11] *IG* II² 2778; CHANIOTIS (1988a), 42-48; cf. ROBERTSON (1986). See also note 5 on an encomiastic oration for Isis.
[12] *I.Oropos* 301; cf. the comments in *SEG* XLVII 498.
[13] E.g. *I.Magnesia* 18: [τό τε ψάφισμα ἀ]πέδωκαν [κὴ αὐ]τυὶ διελέ[γησαν ἀκολούθως τοῖς ἐν τῶι ψαφίσμ]ατι γεγραμμένοις; *Syll.*³ 618: τό τε [ψήφ]ισμα ἀπέδωκαγ καὶ αὐτοὶ διελέγησαν ἀκολού[θως τοῖ]ς ἐν τῶ[ι ψη]φίσματι κατακε-χωρισμένοις; cf. *IG* VII 4139: ἐπελθόντες δὲ καὶ αὐτοὶ ἐπὶ τό [τε] συνέδριον καὶ τὸν δῆμον διελέγησαν ἀκολούθως τοῖς ἐν τῶι γραπτῶι κατακεχωρισμένοις; *F.Delphes* III 2, 94: τὸ τε ψάφισμα ἀπέδωκαν ἀμῖν καὶ ἐπελθόντες ἐπὶ τὰν ἐκκλησίαν διελέγησαν ἀκολούθως τοῖς ἐν αὐτῶι κατακεχωρισμέν[ο]ις.
[14] E.g. *IG* IV² 83-84, 86; *IG* XII 7, 53-54, 239, 394, 399-400, 405, 409.
[15] CHAPA (1988).
[16] E.g. STRUBBE (1998).

of the parties to the conflict",[17] this, again, refers to a now elusive 'oral event'; it attests to the delivery of now lost court speeches.

I have presented this long introduction into indirect sources for Hellenistic oratory, often ignored in studies of oratory and persuasion strategies, not only to give an impression of the still largely unexploited epigraphic evidence for oratory and an idea about the kind of sources that I will be using, but also to give a sense of the quantity and diversity of oratory that was produced between the campaigns of Alexander and the Principate of Augustus. Just as many phenomena and practices for which we have isolated attestations in earlier periods increase in frequency from the late 4th century BC onwards and are more widely distributed, rhetorical strategies and types of oration that are mainly attested in Athens and a few big cities likewise become more widespread. This certainly applies to the use of history as an argument. It is not an innovation of Hellenistic oratory; it only becomes more common in the Hellenistic period.

2. History as an argument: why?

Since Thucydides, the belief that people can learn from history serves as a legitimation of the historian's profession. It is not the satisfaction of personal curiosity and pleasure that motivates the historians in their engagement with historical facts and questions, but the conviction that what they discover and describe can be of permanent value – a *ktêma es aei*, in Thucydides' words. In a short book under the title *Geschichte als Argument*, Alexander Demandt discussed how historical traditions were used by statesmen and theoreticians as a medium of persuasion that uses experience in order to appeal to common sense.[18] History – or historical memory – served this purpose as

---

[17] E.g. *I.Cret.* III iv, 9 line 29; *I.Magnesia* 93 line 10.
[18] DEMANDT (1972).

early as the *Iliad.* The myth of Meleagros in Book 9 presented a warning to Achilles about the potential consequences of uncontrolled rage. And much later, in 4th-century oratory the historical experiences of the previous century – the Persian Wars and the Peloponnesian War – played a major part in Athenian oratory, especially in deliberative oratory and in Isocrates' Panhellenic vision.[19] Learning from history is only one of the reasons why history can be used as an argument in rhetorical performances. Legal and moral considerations as well as the emotional impact of historical arguments explain the manifold use of this rhetorical device in negotiations both among individuals and between communities. Let us consider two examples from literary sources of the 5th and 4th centuries: Herodotus and Xenophon.

In 480, just before the beginning of Xerxes' invasion, the tyrant of Syracuse Gelon is said to have negotiated with Athens and Sparta about his participation in the Panhellenic alliance against the Persians. According to Herodotus, Gelon demanded the leadership of the Greek army.[20] When the representative of Sparta, which had a claim on the supreme command, heard this demand, he responded:

> "Agamemnon son of Pelops would truly lament loudly, should he hear that the Spartans were deprived of the command by Gelon and the Syracusans! Do not ever think of this again, that we will give the command to you. If you wish to help Greece, know that you shall be under the command of the Lakedaimonians."

The mere fact that a member of the house of the Pelopids, which had ruled Sparta in legendary times and before the arrival of the Dorians, had led the Greek army against Troy was – at least in Herodotus' eyes – sufficient reason for the Spartans to demand the leadership of the Greek army in the present war against the barbarians. When Gelon's demand was

---

[19] E.g. ALLROGGEN (1972); NOUHAUD (1982); GRETHLEIN (2014).
[20] HDT. 7, 157-162, esp. 159 and 161.

not accepted, the tyrant tried to get the leadership of the fleet, held by the Athenians. The Athenian argumentation was more sophisticated than the Laconic answer of the Spartans:

> "If we, being Athenians, yield the command to the Syracusans, it would be in vain that we possess the largest sea-faring army among the Greeks, we who are the most ancient nation and who alone among the Greeks have never migrated; of all who came to Ilion, as the epic poet Homer says, the best man in ordering and marshalling armies was one of us [Menestheus]."

The Athenians combined a pragmatic argument – they had the largest fleet – with an important element of their identity and self-representation – their autochthony. This argument is culturally determined; it is based on the view that the 'seniority' of a community gives this community precedence over others. The Athenians also used a historical argument: in Homeric times, the best man in marshalling armies was an Athenian.

In Herodotus' narrative, both Spartans and Athenians used historical arguments originating in Homer. The arguments had a rather superficial relation to the conclusion to be drawn. The privilege of military command and the military achievements of a single individual in legendary times (Agamemnon and Menestheus respectively) were projected upon their entire community in the present (Sparta and Athens). This projection is based on the assumption that rights and properties can be inherited. This is not surprising. In Greek culture – and democratic Athens was no exception – not only property titles were inherited but also social prestige, political influence, priestly offices, and privileges. The historical arguments of Athenians and Spartans were based on this mentality. Of course, when we scrutinise these arguments, we recognise discrepancies between argument and conclusion. Agamemnon was a Pelopid, but he was neither a king of Sparta nor of the same 'ethnic' origin as the Spartans. In the late 6th century the Spartans had brought the bones of Agamemnon's son Orestes to Sparta in order to construct a continuity from Achaean times and to legitimise their claim to lead the Peloponnesian League. Menestheus, on the other hand, was described by Homer as experienced in matters related to military tactics on *land*, and not to naval strategy as one would expect, since the issue at hand was the leadership of the fleet.

Now the second example. After the defeat of the Athenians in the Peloponnesian War, the Spartan allies, Corinth and Thebes, were urging the Spartans to destroy Athens. Xenophon presents the argument used by the Spartans to justify their decision not to destroy the city of their enemies:[21]

> "The Lakedaimonians, however, said, that they would not enslave a Greek city which had done great service amid the greatest perils that had befallen Greece."

The Spartans referred to the Athenian contribution to the rescue of Greece more than two generations earlier, during the Persian Wars. Participation in the Persian Wars remained an important element of identity and self-representation of Greek communities for centuries.[22] Here, the argument was not used by the Athenians but by their enemies, who acted upon a moral obligation deriving from the feeling of gratitude. In this case, the historical precedent (the rescue of Greece in the past) has an even more superficial relation with the issue that was negotiated (mercy on the Athenians in the present). But exactly as in the narrative in Herodotus, an achievement in the past, a collective achievement this time, was projected onto the present. The historical argument of the Spartans had an emotional background. It was based on a feeling of gratitude that resulted in moral obligations.

These two examples from non-rhetorical literary sources correspond to the way historical arguments were also used in oratory, both in deliberative oratory and in court speeches. First, the past could give legal support or legitimacy to a claim; second, the past could serve as an exemplum and lend logical

---

[21] XEN. *Hell.* 2, 2, 20.
[22] JUNG (2006).

support to a decision; third, the past underlined a moral responsibility for a decision; and fourth, the commemoration of the past could have an emotional impact. In 4th-century and later oratory, references to the past – references to the history of the Greeks, of a community, or of a family – had these functions: logical or educational, moral, legitimising, and emotional. Historical arguments were used in negotiations within a community and in negotiations between communities; they were used in the assembly, in philosophical discourse, and in the court. But although this usage seems quite banal, and can be observed in our time as well, this does not mean that a historian is not confronted with various questions when studying this phenomenon. In what contexts were historical arguments used and how effective were they? Were historical arguments combined with a more 'pragmatic' argumentation? How were historical traditions manipulated to fit a certain situation? Did this phenomenon remain static throughout Greek history, or can we recognise a development in the use and the acceptance of historical arguments? Were the historical arguments invented ad hoc, by orators, statesmen, and envoys, or were they drawn from a certain stock of arguments belonging to a fixed set of local traditions or to the 'cultural memory' of a community? A study of the Hellenistic material contributes to a better understanding of these issues.

3. History as an argument I: appeal to reason and arousal of emotion

As already mentioned, the *narratio* of Hellenistic decrees, far more detailed than *narrationes* of decrees that antedate the reign of Alexander, sometimes reflects the arguments that were used in the popular assembly. Thus, these narratives provide information on Hellenistic deliberative oratory that can be compared with the information that we find in the works of Hellenistic historians, especially Polybius. The decree proposed by Chremonides in Athens in 267 gives us an impression of discussions before the war against Antigonos Gonatas. Chremonides asked the Athenian popular assembly to ratify a treaty of alliance between Athens, Sparta, and many other Greek communities, which eventually led to the Chremonidean War. Since the preamble contains a rather long justification of this decision, we may reconstruct his strategy of persuasion.[23] The arguments presented by Chremonides are a combination of political pragmatism, subtle propaganda, and historical analogies:

> "The Athenians, the Lakedaimonians, and their respective allies had in the past established a common friendship and alliance with each other and fought together many and fair wars against those who attempted to enslave the cities; with these wars they won fame for themselves and brought freedom to the other Greeks. Now that similar circumstances have afflicted the whole of Greece because of those who attempt to abolish the laws and ancestral constitutions of each city, and king Ptolemy following the policy of his ancestors and of his sister conspicuously shows his zeal for the common freedom of the Greeks, the people of the Athenians have made an alliance with him and the other Greeks and have passed a decree to invite all to follow the same policy ... So that now that a common concord has been established between the Greeks against those who have now committed injustice and broken the treaties with the cities, they may prove eager combatants with king Ptolemy and with each other and in future may save the cities preserving the concord."

---

[23] *IG* II² 687: ἐπειδὴ | πρότερομ μὲν Ἀθηναῖοι καὶ Λακεδαιμόνιοι καὶ οἱ σύμμαχ|οι οἱ ἑκατέρων φιλίαν καὶ συμμαχίαν κοινὴν ποιησάμενο|ι πρὸς ἑαυτοὺς πολλοὺς καὶ καλοὺς ἀγῶνας ἠγωνίσαντο με|τ᾽ ἀλλήλων πρὸς τοὺς καταδουλοῦσθαι τὰς πόλεις ἐπιχειρ|οῦντας, ἐξ ὧν ἑαυτοῖς τε δόξαν ἐκτήσαντο καὶ τοῖς ἄλλ[ο]ις | Ἕλλησιν παρεσκεύασαν τὴν ἐλευθερίαν· καὶ νῦν δὲ κ[α]ιρῶν | καθειλη-φότων ὁμοίως τὴν Ἑλλάδα πᾶσαν διὰ το[ὺς κ]αταλύε|ιν ἐπιχειροῦντας τούς τε νόμους καὶ τὰς πατρίους ἑκάστ|οις πολιτείας ὅ τε βασιλεὺς Πτολεμαῖος ἀκο-λούθως τεῖ τ|ῶν προγόνων καὶ τεῖ τῆς ἀδελφῆς προ[α]ιρέσει φανερός ἐστ|ιν σπουδάζων ὑπὲρ τῆς κοινῆς τ[ῶν] Ἑλλήνων ἐλευθερίας· καὶ | ὁ δῆμος ὁ Ἀθη-ναίων συμμαχίαν ποιησάμενος πρὸς αὐτὸν καὶ | τοὺς λοιποὺς Ἕλληνας ἐψήφι-σται παρακαλεῖν ἐπὶ τὴν αὐτὴ|ν προαίρεσιν· ... ὅπως ἂν οὖν κοινῆς ὁμονοίας γενομ|ένης τοῖς Ἕλλησι πρός τε τοὺς νῦν ἠδικηκότας καὶ παρεσπον|δηκότας τὰς πόλεις πρόθυμοι μετὰ τοῦ βασιλέως Πτολεμαίου | καὶ μετ᾽ ἀλλήλων ὑπάρχωσιν ἀγωνισταὶ καὶ τὸ λοιπὸν μεθ᾽ ὁμον|οίας σώιζωσιν τὰς πόλεις.

Chremonides' main political and pragmatic argument was that the establishment of Macedonian garrisons in central Greece resulted in the subversion of law and the traditional civic institutions. Presenting Antigonos as a threat to freedom and constitution was an accurate representation of reality; the use of words with a strong emotional impact, such as καταδουλοῦσθαι, καταλύειν τούς τε νόμους καὶ τὰς πατρίους ἑκάστοις πολιτείας, ἠδικηκότας and παρεσπονδηκότας aimed at arousing the audience's indignation.[24] But the praise of Ptolemy as a champion of freedom is pure propaganda, and the expectation that joining one monarch in his war against another would free Greece was clearly short-sighted and ignored all historical experience from 307 BC onwards.

The main argument of Chremonides, at least in the recorded summary of his proposal, was a historical exemplum: the subtle assimilation of the Persian invasion with the threat posed by the Macedonian king Antigonos ("... now that similar circumstances have afflicted the whole of Greece"). United Athenians and Spartans had defeated the Persians, winning fame and protecting freedom; united again they will prevail! Glory, justice, and fame were ideas that appealed to the civic values of Greek citizens. Chremonides skilfully combined different strategies of persuasion that appealed to reason, values, and emotions.

This decree permits several observations. First, Chremonides used a combination of political and historical arguments. The historical arguments drew upon a familiar motif of Greek historical consciousness and identity: the wars of Athens and Sparta against the Persians (see note 22). Chremonides *selected* a historical example, not only a familiar one but also one that could easily fit the present situation. There were several obvious or constructed analogies between past and present: Athens and Sparta fought together against the Persians; they should now do the same again. Concord (*homonoia*) was the common denominator and the guarantor of success. The purpose

---

[24] For emotional language in Hellenistic decrees see CHANIOTIS (2013b).

of both wars was the same: the freedom of the Greeks (*eleutheria*). These two analogies were straightforward. A third analogy is implicit and more subtle; the common wars of Athens and Sparta were wars of free Greek communities against a barbarian monarch; similarly, the new war was directed against a monarch. Even though the Macedonian king Antigonos Gonatas was not a barbarian – after all the Macedonian kings were members of the Panhellenic alliance established in Corinth in 337 and renewed by Antigonos' father and grandfather in 302 BC –, his kingdom was foreign to the world of Greek *poleis* and *koina*.

But in order to understand the weight of these historical analogies, we need to consider Antigonid propaganda as well. Chremonides' decree gives us a syncopated version of Chremonides' oration in Athens; but hardly any orator in a free Greek assembly spoke without facing opposition. The Antigonids had followers in Athens and, if their supporters did speak, they probably also used a historical argument: exactly as the Athenians had saved Greece from the barbarians in 490 and 479, Antigonos Gonatas had saved Greece from the barbarians, the Gauls, at the battle of Lysimacheia ten years earlier, in 277 BC. We know how important this victory was for Antigonid propaganda in Greece and how vivid its commemoration remained for many decades. In Athens itself, where Antigonos established a garrison after his victory in the Chremonidean War, Herakleitos, the commander of the garrison, dedicated to Athena Nike a monument "containing memorials of the king's deeds against the barbarians for the salvation of the Greeks" (ca. 250 BC).[25] This monument, probably consisting of painted panels, commemorated Antigonos' victory over the Gauls. Standing in the shadow of the temples of Athena Parthenos and Athena Nike, and borrowing themes of their sculptural decoration, Herakleitos'

---

[25] *IG* II² 677; CHANIOTIS (1988a) 301. Another example of Antigonid commemoration of this victory is the establishment of the festivals Soteria and Paneia in Delos; see CHAMPION (2004-2005).

monument was erected in an ideal setting to convey its message: it was Antigonos Gonatas who had saved the Greeks from the barbarians. In this setting, the victory of the Macedonian king was incorporated into the Greek traditions of victories over the barbarians. Although it postdates the Chremonidean War, it reflects traditional Antigonid propaganda. Exactly as Herakleitos' monument was engaged in a dialogue with the sculptural decoration of the Temple of Athena Nike, that showed the Athenians defending their fatherland from the Persians in Marathon or Plataiai, Chremonides' historical argument a few years earlier had opposed Antigonid propaganda that presented the Macedonian king as the rescuer of Greek freedom. In Chremonides' rhetoric the Persian Wars were not only an exemplum but also an argument counterbalancing Antigonid self-representation.

As already mentioned, Chremonides' historical argument was the result of selection. Selection of one event necessarily means omission of others: the wars of Athens against Sparta and the efforts of Athenians and Spartans to subvert the freedom and the constitutions of other Greek states were conveniently forgotten.

In this case, the historical argument primarily appealed to reason. It is one of the rare instances of the use of history in Hellenistic decrees, with the aim to reach a logical conclusion: the Greeks should learn from their history and unite their forces against those who tried to enslave them. The "similar conditions" mentioned by Chremonides called for similar measures. But although this historical argument appeals to reason, we should not underestimate its emotional power: it appeals to the love of freedom, to pride in past achievements, to indignation against injustice and enslavement, and to concord. By highlighting the concord between Athens and Sparta and recalling the Persian Wars, Chremonides was also implicitly urging his audience to forget the far more common wars between Athens and Sparta. His strategy is very similar to the one we observe in amnesty and reconciliation agreements, that seek to control memory (μὴ μνησικακεῖν) and emotion.[26] We can best understand the impact of this particular historical argument if we place Chremonides' exemplum in its contemporary context. Some time after Chremonides had urged the Greeks to ally themselves with Ptolemy, the defender of "the common freedom of the Greeks", and to preserve concord (*homonoia*), presenting this alliance as the lesson to be learned from the Persian Wars, the same interdependence of freedom and concord was played out in Plataia, the place where the last battle of the Persian Wars had been fought. Our source is a decree of the league of the Greeks that participated in the festival of the Eleutheria, passed after the Chremonidean War (ca. 261-246 BC) but providing information about the instrumentalisation of historical memory before and during the war.[27] On the very battlefield where the concord of the Greeks had prevailed over the enemies of freedom, the decree praises no other than Chremonides' brother: Glaukon, an Athenian in the service of Ptolemy II,

> "had contributed to making more lavish the sacrifice to Zeus Eleutherios and Concord and the contest which the Greeks celebrate on the tomb of the brave men who fought against the barbarians for the freedom of the Greeks."[28]

This is the earliest reference to an altar of Homonoia (*Concord*) that stood next to that of Zeus Eleutherios,[29] serving as a reminder that freedom can be best defended through concord. We do not know if the cult of Homonoia was introduced in Plataia during the Chremonidean War or earlier,[30] but we can be certain that during and after this war the emphasis of the Eleutheria festival

---

[26] CHANIOTIS (2013c).

[27] ÉTIENNE / PIÉRART (1975); *SEG* LXI 352.

[28] Lines 18-24: συνη[ύ]|ξησεν δὲ καὶ τὴν θυσίαν τοῦ Διὸς τ[οῦ] || Ἐλε<υ>θε-ρίου καὶ τῆς Ὁμονοίας καὶ τὸν ἀγῶνα ὃ τιθέασιν οἱ Ἕλληνες ἐπὶ | τοῖς ἀνδράσιν τοῖς ἀγαθοῖς καὶ ἀγω|νισαμένοις πρὸς τοὺς βαρβάρους | ὑπὲρ τῆς τῶν Ἑλλήνων ἐλευθερίας. English translation: AUSTIN (²2006) no. 63 (modified).

[29] THÉRIAULT (1996) 102-122.

[30] WALLACE (2011) proposes to date the introduction of the cult of Homonoia in Boedromion 335 BC, after the destruction of Thebes by Alexander the Great, but this is not supported by any direct evidence.

had shifted from the notion of freedom alone to the combination of concord and freedom. It is interesting to observe that the surviving fragment of a speech delivered by an Athenian representative on the occasion of this festival in the late 2nd century (see note 11), castigates the Spartans for abandoning this concord immediately after the battle of Plataia and not participating in the subsequent wars against the Persians. The result was that Greek cities fell under the rule (*despoteia*) of the Persians.

The striking convergence between the decree of Chremonides (concord defends freedom), the honorific decree for Glaukon (the Persian Wars as exemplum for freedom and concord, joint cult of Zeus Eleutherios and Homonoia), and the oration in Plataia (lack of concord leads to subjugation under foreign rule) shows that historical arguments were effective when they were familiar; when they are continually and consistently used. I will return to this point later.

Before we leave Chremonides' decree, let us compare his arguments with those used on other occasions in Hellenistic oratory. A good parallel is offered by the orations of Chlaineas of Aitolia, an ally of the Romans, and Lykiskos of Akarnania, an ally of the Macedonians, when they attempted to convince the Spartans to become their allies, in 210 BC. Reconstructions of the two speeches are presented by Polybius.[31] Exactly as in 267 BC, the decision to be taken was a decision about an alliance and a war. Chlaineas' aim was to persuade the Spartans to join the anti-Macedonian alliance. To do so, he summarised Greek history from the reign of Philip II to Antigonos Doson, attributing the miseries of Greece to Macedonian policies. The Spartans should, therefore, be the natural enemies of Macedonia. History obliges. But history also encourages. Since the Aitolians had not been defeated by Philip V, Chlaineas continued, the Spartans should be confident that by allying themselves with Aitolia they would be victorious. Chlaineas' historical arguments offered both moral justification and logical encouragement. The Spartans should

[31] POLYB. 9, 28-39.

join the enemies of Macedonia, first because they must hate the Macedonians and, second, because the enemies of Macedonia were strong. A few passages may give an impression of the emotional power of Chlaineas' excursions in history. First, the speaker refers to the actions of Philip II:[32]

> "Having enslaved Olynthos and established an exemplum, he not only took control of the cities in Thrace, but also subjugated the Thessalians because of their fear. Not long after, after he had defeated the Athenians in battle, he responded with magnanimity to this victory, not in order to benefit the Athenians – far from that – but in order to use the benefaction towards them so as to invite the others voluntarily to follow his commands."

He then continued with Antipatros, calling to memory scenes of merciless prosecution, which are very similar to the description of the atrocities of the Thirty by Lysias in his speech *Against Eratosthenes*.[33] The objective of these descriptions is to foment anger:[34]

> "He reached such levels of *hubris* and lawlessness that he appointed hunters of exiles and dispatched them to the cities against those who had opposed the Macedonian royal house or had at all distressed it. Some of them were dragged violently from the sanctuaries or were removed from the altars and were killed with vengeance; and those who escaped were exiled from all of Greece. They could not find refuge anywhere, with one exception: the *ethnos* of the Aitolians."

Moving to more recent events, the orator continually framed his narrative with a variegated palette of emotions: gratitude, hope, fear, envy, and hatred:[35]

> "I return now to the most recent king, Antigonos, so that some of you may not regard the events that he caused without

---

[32] POLYB. 9, 28, 3-4.
[33] LYS. 12, 8-22 and 95-98. See 12, 5: ἀναμνῆσαι; 12, 92: ἀναμνήσας; 12, 94: ἀναμνησθέντες; 12, 95: ἀναμνήσθητε; 12, 96: ἀναμνήσθητε. See BEARZOT (1997) 94-95, 159, 234-235, 238; CHANIOTIS (2013c) 56-59.
[34] POLYB. 9, 29, 3-4.
[35] POLYB. 9, 29, 7; 9, 29, 11-12.

grudge, thinking that you are obliged to feel gratitude towards the Macedonians. ... When he recognised that his rule would not be secure if you were to take over the leadership of the Peloponnesians, and when he saw that Kleomenes was very suitable for this task and that fortune was favouring you splendidly, he arrived with fear and envy not in order to help the Peloponnesians, but in order to deprive you of your hopes and in order to abase your supremacy. Therefore, you are not obliged to feel affection towards the Macedonians for not plundering your city when they captured it, but you should regard them as enemies and hate them, because they have prevented you already many times from becoming the leaders of Greece when you could."

Thereupon, the orator contrasts the behaviour of the Macedonian kings with that of the Aitolians:[36]

"Of all the Greeks, only the Aitolians dared to face Antipatros for the sake of the security of those who suffered unjustly; they alone withstood the attack of Brennos and the barbarians who followed him; they alone came to fight together with you, when they were called upon, in order to re-establish jointly with you ancestral leadership among the Greeks."

Despite its exaggerations and inaccuracies, Chlaineas' speech so impacted on the audience that the next orator, Lykiskos, the envoy of the Akarnanians, had first to wait until silence was restored and the people in the assembly had stopped discussing his speech.[37] In order to counter the impact of Chlaineas' speech, Lykiskos too referred to past events. If Chlaineas' selective version of history aimed to incite anger against the Macedonians, Lykiskos' version aimed to inspire gratitude for Alexander's benefactions to the Greeks and to deflect the anger of the audience away from the Macedonians and towards the Aitolians:[38]

"Again, you have bitterly reproached Alexander for punishing the city of the Thebans, when he believed that he had been

[36] POLYB. 9, 30, 3-4.
[37] POLYB. 9, 32, 1-2.
[38] POLYB. 9, 34, 1-11.

wronged, but you neither mentioned that he avenged the outrages that the Persians had committed on all the Greeks nor that he delivered us all from great evils, by enslaving the barbarians and depriving them of the resources that they used for damaging the Greeks – funding now the Athenians and the ancestors of these (Spartans), now the Thebans, against one another –, nor that he finally made Asia subject to the Greeks. As for his successors, how dare you even mention them? They, indeed, many times benefited some and harmed others, as the circumstances demanded. Others might be justified in feeling resentment against them, but you Aitolians have not the least right to do so, since you have never done any good to anyone, but have done evil to many and at many times. Who invited Antigonos, son of Demetrios, to dissolve the Achaian League? Who swore oaths and made a treaty with Alexander of Epeiros for the enslavement and partition of Akarnania? Was it not you? Who jointly sent out such commanders as you did? These men even dared lay hands on inviolable sanctuaries. Timaios plundered the sanctuary of Poseidon in Tainaron and that of Artemis in Lousoi; Pharykos and Polykriotos pillaged the precinct of Hera in Argos and that of Poseidon in Mantineia. And what about Lattabos and Nikostratos? Did they not violate the sanctity of the Panboiotian festival in peacetime, behaving like Scythians or Gauls? No such deeds were ever committed by Alexander's successors."

Then, Lykiskos cited recent events, asking the Spartans to view with suspicion the Romans and the Aitolians:[39]

"They have already robbed the Akarnanians of Oiniadai and Nasos, and they recently seized the unfortunate city of Antikyra, and together with the Romans they enslaved it. So, the Romans are carrying off the women and children to suffer, of course, what those must suffer who fall into the hands of aliens, while the Aitolians divide the land of the unfortunate people among themselves by lot."

After the presentation of the emotive image of women and children carried off into slavery, and after contrasting the cultural community of the Greeks to the unnatural union of the Aitolians,

[39] POLYB. 9, 39, 2.

who behaved like barbarians, and the Romans, Lykiskos invoked memory and emotion:[40]

"It is good and befitting, men of Lakedaimon, remembering who your ancestors were, placing yourselves on guard against the aggression of the Romans, viewing with suspicion the evil plans of the Aitolians, and, above all, remembering the favours conferred upon you by Antigonos to continue to be haters of wickedness, to refuse the friendship of the Aitolians, and to share the same hopes with the Achaians and the Macedonians."

Lykiskos finished with an appeal to the historical exemplum of the Persian Wars. The Spartans should join the Greeks against the new barbarians, the Romans, exactly as their ancestors did against Xerxes.[41]

Chremonides' oration in the Athenian assembly is lost but the few lines that summarise its content reveal multiple layers of a persuasion strategy that appealed to reason and emotion, were connected with familiar aspects of Greek historical consciousness, and aimed at counterbalancing Antigonid propaganda and the arguments of Antigonos' supporters. Although the main strength of the historical argument lies in its logic – concord protected freedom in the past, concord shall restore freedom in the present –, emotional aspects were very important. The commemoration of past glory strengthened pride, the exemplum supported hope.

Hope is a very peculiar emotion – if we do accept the view that it is an emotion. Usually defined as a positive attitude of the mind, hope is much more closely connected with judgment and appraisal than other emotions; the expectation of a positive outcome in the future is based on past experiences and judgment. When the historical argument is used in order to support hope, its function resembles that of a *historiola* in contemporary magic. A short mythological narrative serves as an exemplum for the desired outcome of the magical prayer.[42]

---

[40] POLYB. 9, 39, 6.
[41] POLYB. 38, 1-39, 5.
[42] On the function of *historiolae* in magic see, e.g., GRAF (1996) 200 and 205.

Exactly as Hephaistos bound his mother and Zeus had Prometheus bound, let the opponent in a trial be bound, states an Aiginetan curse tablet of the late fourth or early 3rd century.[43] Exactly as concord saved freedom in the past, let concord save freedom in the present. Unlike in magic, of course, the success of Chremonides' historical exemplum depended entirely on human agents, on the military abilities of the coalition against Antigonos. The historical argument was convincing, but the hopes that it aroused were not fulfilled. History did not repeat itself. Concord did not save freedom.

Historical arguments such as the one used by Chremonides are occasionally to be found in summaries of deliberative orations in the assembly. A more or less contemporary example is a decree from Miletos. Peithenous, son of Tharsagoras, argued as follows, in order to support his proposal for a treaty of friendship and alliance between Miletos and King Ptolemy II (ca. 262/260):[44]

> "Because the people already in the past chose to have friendship and alliance with Ptolemy, god and rescuer, it occurred that the city came to prosperity and distinction and the people became worthy of many and great good things. For this reason the people honoured him with the greatest and fairest honours. His son, King Ptolemy, having inherited the kingship and renewed the friendship and alliance with the city, shows the greatest zeal for whatever is beneficial to the Milesians. He has granted them additional land, has secured peace for the people, and has been the cause of the other good things for the city."

After this historical account, the orator continues with καὶ νῦμ ("and now"), describing the current state of affairs and explaining

---

[43] *IG* IV² 2, 1012; *SEG* LVII 313.

[44] *I.Milet* I 3, 139C: ἐπειδὴ τοῦ δήμου καὶ πρότερον ἐλ[ο]|μένου τὴμ φιλίαν καὶ τὴν συμμαχίαν τὴμ πρὸς τὸν θεὸν καὶ σωτῆρ[α] | Πτολεμαῖον συνέβη τήν τε πό[λιν] εἰς εὐδαιμονίαν καὶ ἐπιφάνειαν ἐλθεῖν καὶ τ[ὸν] | δῆμον πολλῶγ καὶ μεγάλων ἀγαθῶν ἀξιωθῆναι, δι' ἃς αἰτίας ἐτίμησεν | αὐτὸν ὁ δῆμος ταῖς μεγί-σταις καὶ καλλίσταις τιμαῖς, διαδεξάμενός τε | τὴμ βασιλείαν ὁ υἱὸς αὐτοῦ βασι-λεὺς Πτολεμαῖος καὶ ἀνανεωσάμενος | τήν τε φιλίαν καὶ συμμαχίαν τὴμ πρὸς τὴμ πόλιν, πᾶσαν πεποίηται | σπουδὴν ὑπὲρ τῶν συμφερόντων πᾶσι Μιλησίοις, χώραν τε ἐπιδιδοὺς καὶ | τὴν εἰρήνην παρασκευάζων τῶι δήμωι καὶ τῶν ἄλλων ἀγαθῶν πα|[ρ]αίτιος γινόμενος τῆι πόλει.

why the alliance with Ptolemy II would be beneficial to Miletos. Although this would have been enough as argument, the mention of the benefits that arose from the alliance with Ptolemy I and the moral obligations of the Milesians strengthened the pragmatic justification of the new treaty. We find the same combination of a historical argument that arouses hope, moral arguments that appeal to the feeling of gratitude, and pragmatic arguments as in the decree of Chremonides.

Another, much later example is an Athenian decree concerning the re-organisation of the festival of the Thargelia (129 BC):[45]

> "Since it is a norm of the forefathers and a custom of the Athenian demos and an ancestral tradition to show the greatest care for piety towards the gods and it is for this reason that the Athenians have achieved the fame and the praise of the most glorious deeds both on land and on the sea through many campaigns on land and on board of ships, always beginning all their activities with an homage to Zeus Soter and with the worship of the gods; and since there also exists Apollo Pythios, who is an ancestral god of the Athenians and an interpreter of good things, at the same time a saviour of all the Greeks, the son of Zeus and Leto; and since he has ordered us with oracles to pray to the god who is called 'the god of the forefathers' and to perform the ancestral sacrifices on behalf of the demos of the Athenians annually, offering sacrifices to Apollo as is the ancestral custom of the demos."

The orator, a certain Xeno[--], son of Sopatrides, justified the proposal not only by reference to the divine commands given via oracles and to an ancestral tradition, but also with a historical

---

45 SOKOLOWSKI (1962) no. 14; SEG XXI 469 C: ἐπειδὴ πάτριόν [ἐ]στ[ιν καὶ ἔ]θος τῶι δήμωι τῶι Ἀθηναίων καὶ ὑπὸ τῶν προγόνων π[α]ραδε[δ]ομένον περὶ πλείστου ποεῖσθαι τὴν πρὸς τοὺς θεοὺς [εὐσέβειαν] καὶ διὰ ταῦτα πολλα<ῖ>ς <πεζαῖς> καὶ ἐπὶ ναυσὶ στρατεί<αι>ς τὴν κλε[ιν]οτάτων ἔργων καὶ κατὰ γῆν καὶ κατὰ θάλατταν εὐδοξία[ν] κα̣ὶ̣ [εὐλογίαν κέκτ]ηνται ἀρχόμενοι δι̣ὰ̣ παντὸς ἀπὸ <τοῦ Διὸς τοῦ> Σωτῆρος [τῆς π]ρὸς τοὺς θεοὺς ὁσι̣ότητος̣· ὑπάρχει δὲ καὶ ὁ Ἀπόλλων ὁ Πύθιος ὢν τοῖς Ἀθηναίοις Πατρῶιος καὶ ἐξηγητὴς τῶν ἀγαθῶν, ὁμοίως δὲ καὶ κοινῆι σωτὴρ πάντων τῶν Ἑλλήνων ὁ τῆς Λητοῦς καὶ τοῦ Διὸς [υἱός· τούτ]ο[υ] δὲ διὰ τῶν χρησμῶν προσ[τ]ε[ταχ]ότος αὐτοῖς λ[ι]τ̣αγ[εῦσ]α[ι τὸν] θεὸν τὸν ἐπικαλούμενο{υ}ν Πατρῶιον καὶ ποιουμένους τὰς [πατρί]ου[ς θυσί]-ας ὑπὲρ τοῦ δήμου τοῦ Ἀθηναίων τοῖς τοῦ ἐνιαυτοῦ [καιροῖς τῶι Ἀπ]ό[λ]λωνι [θ]ύοντας ὡς πάτριόν ἐστι τῶι δήμωι.

argument, similar in structure to those we have seen so far. In the past, the Athenians were pious towards the gods; it is for this reason that they were victorious in wars. The conclusion implicitly follows that if they restore their piety, they will be successful in the future. Of course, this historical argument stands or falls depending on whether people believe that what made the Athenians victorious in the past was piety, not the number of their ships, the tactics of the military commanders, the military valour of their soldiers, the strength of their walls, and the money in their treasury. The argument is similar to the one recently used by the then Greek Minister of Culture, Nikos Xydakis: Having the drachma for 200 years, the Greeks achieved great things.[46] It implicitly follows that somehow, by means of magical sympathy, they will achieve great things if they re-introduce their national currency. Before we dismiss such arguments for what they are – pure nonsense –, we need to place them into their context. And the context of the Athenian decree is the increased interest in piety under the influence of the contacts between Greeks and Romans. In one of the earliest documents concerning the relations between Greek cities and Roman authorities, the praetor M. Valerius Messalla justified the grant of inviolability to Teos thus (193 BC):[47]

> "One would surmise that we always pay the greatest attention to piety towards the gods from the fact that we receive the favour of the gods for this reason; but we think that the honour that we pay to the divine has become obvious to all also from many other facts."

Messalla directly linked piety with military success, exactly in the way the Athenian orator did sixty years later. This corresponds

---

[46] http://www.tovima.gr/culture/article/?aid=715204. Interview to the newspaper *Ephemerida ton Syntakton*, June 15, 2015.

[47] SHERK (1969) no. 34 lines 11-17: καὶ ὅτι μὲν διόλου πλεῖστον λόγον ποιούμενοι διατελοῦμεν τῆς πρὸς τοὺς θεοὺς εὐσεβείας, μάλιστ' ἄν τις στοχά-ζοιτο ἐκ τῆς συναντωμένης ἡμεῖν εὐμενείας διὰ ταῦτα παρὰ τοῦ δαιμονίου· οὐ μὴν ἀλλὰ καὶ ἐξ ἄλλων πλειόνων πεπείσμεθα συμφανῆ πᾶσι γεγονέναι τὴν ἡμε-τέραν εἰς τὸ θεῖον προτιμίαν.

to the weight given by Polybius to Roman pious behaviour.[48] The duty to respect the gods was not invented by the Romans. But Polybius' explicit praise of Roman piety suggests that in the 2nd century BC this was regarded by some Greek political leaders and intellectuals as a distinctive feature of the Roman character, as one of the factors that determined Roman policies – as opposed for instance to the notorious lack of piety shown by the Macedonians and the Aitolians –,[49] and was a cause of their success. We observe again that the value of historical arguments is connected with the familiarity of contemporary audiences with historical traditions and with mentalities that are culturally determined.

4. History as an argument II: past services oblige

Apart from deliberative oratory in the assembly and court speeches, a very common type of oration in the Hellenistic period are the orations delivered by envoys in foreign cities, λόγοι πρεσβευτικοί in Polybius' typology.[50] They are quite well represented in the work of Polybius, with speeches such as the aforementioned speeches of Chlaineas and Lykiskos of Akarnania, the speech Eumenes II delivered in Rome in 189 BC, and the oration of the Rhodian Astymedes in Rome in 165 or 164 BC.[51] To judge from the sheer amount of diplomatic missions in Hellenistic Greece, orations by envoys were extremely common, and we should not be surprised if they followed existing models. References to past relations between the negotiating communities appear as a standard feature of these speeches. In

---

[48] On Polybius' appraisal of the piety of the Romans see 6, 56, 6-14. More examples in CHANIOTIS (2015) 93-94.

[49] See, e.g., Polybius' comments on the plundering of sanctuaries by Philip V and the Aitolians: POLYB. 4, 62, 2 (Dion); 4, 67, 3-4 (Dodona); 5, 9-12 (Thermon).

[50] POLYB. 12, 25a, 3; ERSKINE (2007) 274; THORNTON (2013). On orations by envoys see esp. WOOTEN (1973); RUBINSTEIN (2013).

[51] POLYB. 21, 19-21 and 30, 31, 3-18.

most cases we only find vague references to ancestral relations, past services, and traditional friendship. "They renewed (i.e. commemorated) the *philanthropa* [privileged relations of affection based on services and goodwill] that mutually exist from the time of the ancestors on" (ἀνανεωσάμενοι τὰ διὰ προγόνων ὑπάρχοντα πρὸς ἀλλήλους φιλάνθρωπα) is a stereotypical phrase found in many variations.[52] However, in some cases the decrees preserve specific information concerning the content of speeches by envoys.

Among the cases in which concrete historical events are mentioned, the most instructive is the case of the embassy sent by Magnesia on the Maeander to various kings, cities and federal states in 208 BC, requesting the recognition of the inviolability of the city and the elevated status of the local agonistic festival.[53] The Magnesian envoys were accompanied on their journey by an impressive corpus of histories, oracles, poems, and documents documenting local history and demonstrating Magnesia's benefactions to the Greeks in general and to certain cities in particular. From the surviving dossier of documents we can infer that the envoys used different historical arguments in the different cities. Sometimes references to the content of their orations are very vague, e.g. in Antiochia in Persis:[54]

"the Magnesians of Maeander are relatives and friends of our people and have done many and distinguished services to the Greeks, services that contribute to good reputation ... [their envoys] appeared in front of the council and the assembly, delivered a decree of the Magnesians, commemorated the kinship and friendship, and gave a detailed account of the epiphany of

---

[52] E.g. *I.Iasos* 152 lines 31-32; *SEG* XLIX 1114.
[53] *I.Magnesia* 20-65. On the organisation of this embassy see CHANIOTIS (1988) 34-40, and (1999).
[54] *I.Magnesia* 61 lines 11-14: Μάγνητες οἱ ἀπὸ Μαιάνδρου συγγενεῖς ὄντες | καὶ φίλοι τοῦ δήμου καὶ πολλὰς καὶ ἐπιφανεῖς χρεί|ας παρεισχημένο[ι] τοῖς ['Ελλ]ησιν [τῶν εἰς εὐδοξί]|αν ἀνηκουσῶν; lines 32-37: ἐπελθόντες ἐπί τε τὴν βουλὴν καὶ | τὴν ἐκκλησίαν ψήφισμά τε ἀπέδωκαν παρὰ Μαγνή|των καὶ ἀνανε-ωσάμενοι τὴν συγγένειαν καὶ τὴν φιλίαν ἀπελογίσαντο διὰ πλειόνων τήν τε τῆς θεᾶς ἐ|πιφάνειαν καὶ τὰς χρείας ἃς παρέσχηνται Μάγνητες | πολλαῖς τῶν 'Ελλη-νίδων πόλεων.

the goddess and the services that the Magnesians rendered to many of the Greek cities ..."

But in many cases we get precise information. In Kephallenia, e.g., the envoys reminded the audience of the affinity between the mythical founders of the two cities: Magnes and Kephalos, the eponymous heroes, were brothers. In Megalopolis they recalled something more material than that, the fact that they had given the Arcadians 300 Dareikoi for the building of the city walls in 370 BC; the Cretans were reminded of the fact that Magnesia had stopped a war on the island (217 BC), and so on.[55]

We can assume that even the general and vague references to the past such as references to kinship, affinity, friendship, past benefactions and the like (συγγένεια, οἰκειότης, φιλία, εὔνοια, εὐεργεσία) were founded on very specific historical traditions, which were narrated in the speeches of the ambassadors. A good example is provided by the decree of Epidamnos, which gives a more detailed account of the speech of the envoys in that city:[56]

"They sent as envoys and also as theoroi Sosikles, son of Diokles, Aristodamos, son of Diokles, Diotimos, son of Menophilos, who appeared in front of the council and our assembly, handed in the decree, and discoursed with every zeal, presenting the epiphany of Artemis, the (military) assistance that their ancestors offered to the sanctuary in Delphi, when they defeated in a

---

[55] Kephallenia: *I.Magnesia* 52 line 14; Megalopolis: *I.Magnesia* 44 lines 25-29. Crete: *I.Magnesia* 25 lines 8-12.

[56] *I.Magnesia* 46 lines 5-16: ἀφεστά[λκα]ντ[ι] πρεσβευτάς, τ[ο]ὺς δὲ αὐ[τοὺ]ς καὶ θια[ρ]ούς, Σωσικ[λῆ] | Διοκλέος, Ἀρι[σ]τ[όδαμ]ον Διοκλ[έ]ος, Διότιμον Μηνοφί[λου, ο]ἳ ποτελθόντες ποτὶ | τὰν βουλὰν καὶ [τὸν] δᾶμ[ον ἀμῶν τὸ ψά]φισμα ἀπέδωκα[ν καὶ αὐτ]οὶ διελέχθην μετὰ πά|σας φ[ι]λοτιμία[ς] ἐμφανίξ[αντες τάν] τᾶς Ἀρτέμι[δος ἐπιφάν]ειαν καὶ τὰν γεγενημέν[α]ν | βοάθειαν ὑπὸ τ[ῶ]ν π[ρ]ο[γόνων α]ὐτῶν [εἰ]ς τὸ ἱερὸν τὸ ἐν Δελφ[οῖς], νικασάντων μάχαι τοὺς || βαρ[β]άρους το[ὺ]ς ἐπιστ[ρατεύ]σαντας ἐπὶ διαρπαγᾶι τῶ[ν το]ῦ [θ]εοῦ χρημάτων, καὶ τὰν | εὐε[ργ]εσίαν, ἀν [υυ]νε ιελέσαντο εἰς τὸ κοινὸ[ν] τῶν Κρηται-έ[ων] δι[α]λύσαντες τὸν ἐμφύλι[ον] πόλεμον· ἐνεφάνιξαν δὲ καὶ τὰς εἰς τοὺς ἄλλους [Ἕλ]λανας γεγενημένας | εὐε[ρ]γεσίας διά τε τῶν τοῦ θεοῦ χρησμῶν καὶ διὰ τῶ[ν π]οιητᾶν καὶ διὰ τῶν ἱ[σ]|τορ[ι]αγράφων τῶν συγγεγραφότ[ων] τὰς Μαγνήτων πρ[άξ]ει[ς]· παρανέγνωσαν δὲ | καὶ τὰ ψαφίσματ[α] τὰ ὑπάρχοντα αὐτοῖς παρὰ ταῖς πόλ[ε]σιν, ἐν οἷς ἦν καταγε[γραμμ]έ[ε]ναι τιμαί τ[ε] καὶ στέφαν[ο]ι εἰς δόξαν ἀνίχ?γτα <ταῖ> [πό]λ[ε]ι.

battle the barbarians who had campaigned against it in order to plunder the god's property, and the benefaction that they accomplished for the Cretan Koinon, when they ended the civil war with reconciliation. They also presented their benefactions for the other Greeks, documenting (all this) through the god's oracles, the (works of the) poets, the historians, who have written the deeds of the Magnesians. In addition to this, they read the decrees that have been issued for them by the cities, in which honours and crowns are recorded, which contribute to the city's glory."

For many years historians believed that references to kinship cannot be taken at face value – some historians may still believe this. Until 1988 this view might have had some justification. When a document claims that communities believed in antiquity to be of different ethnic origin were in fact *syngeneis* – e.g. the Ionians of Teos and the Dorians of Crete –, one is indeed tempted to regard such a claim as an expression of politeness devoid of any concrete content. However, the publication of an inscription from Xanthos in 1988 provided definite proof that this view is wrong.[57] Who would believe that the Lykians of Xanthos and the inhabitants of the small city of Kytenion in Doris were *syngeneis*? And yet, a dossier of documents dating to the late 3rd century BC proves that a concrete narrative lies behind every such claim – its historicity is another matter. More importantly for our subject, the inscription from Xanthos showed that such a narrative was often an integral part of the πρεσβευτικὸς λόγος delivered by the envoys.

The oration in question was delivered in Xanthos during the assembly on 2 Aoudnaios of the year 206. The arrival of three men from a distant place of which most of the Xanthians had never heard must have caused quite a thrill. Lamprias, Ainetos, and Phegeus had come all the way from Kytenion in Doris,

---

[57] The text: *SEG* XXXVIII 1476: Commentaries: BOUSQUET (1988); CURTY (1995) 183-191 no. 75; JONES (1999) 61-62, 139-143. Here, I summarise the analysis that I have presented in two studies: CHANIOTIS (2009) 249-252, and (2013a).

equipped with two letters of recommendation by the Dorians
and the Aitolians, but also equipped with their eloquence.
Their speech fascinated the Xanthians to such an extent that
the decree voted on by the assembly gives an unusually lengthy
report of their oral presentation, thus providing an interesting
insight into the rhetorical performances in the popular assembly. The three envoys of Kytenion requested financial aid for
the reconstruction of the fortification wall of their city. They
supported this request with a common argument: kinship.[58]
The oral presentation of the envoys is referred to with the terms
apologizesthai ("to give an account") and *dialegesthai* ("to present
a discourse, to give a lecture"). The speech of the envoys included
at least five sections. First, they gave an account of recent events
(lines 10-13):

> "They brought a decree of the Aitolians and a letter of the Dori-
> ans, with which they gave an account (*apologizesthai*) of what
> had befallen their fatherland; they gave a lecture (*dialegesthai*) in
> accordance with what was written in the letter."

Then they presented a mythological narrative treating the birth
of Artemis and Apollo in Lykia and the birth of Asklepios in
Doris (lines 16-20):

> "They said that Leto, the patron/leader of our city, gave birth to
> Artemis and Apollo amongst us; from Apollo and Koronis, the
> daughter of Phlegyas, a descendant of Doros, Asklepios was born,
> in Doris."

From a divine genealogy they then moved to a heroic one
(lines 20-24):

> "Besides their kinship with us, which derives from these gods,
> they gave an additional account (*prosapologizestai*) of the inter-
> twining of kinship which derives from the heroes, putting
> together (*synistasthai*) the genealogy which goes back to Aiolos
> and Doros."

---

[58] Kinship between communities is a subject to which Olivier Curty and
Christopher P. Jones have dedicated profound studies: CURTY (1995), (1999),
and (2005); JONES (1999).

A (presumably long) narrative followed, whose content was the foundation of the Lykian cities (lines 24-30). This narrative is summarised in greater detail, probably because it presented an unknown version of local history:

> "Besides, they demonstrated (*paradeiknysthai*) that the colonists, sent out from our land by Chrysaor, the son of Glaukos, the son of Hippolochos, received protection from Aletes, one of the descendants of Herakles; for Aletes, starting from the land of the Dorians, came to their aid when they were being warred upon. Putting an end to the danger by which they were beset, he married the daughter of Aor, the son of Chrysaor [the Golden Sword]."

The otherwise unattested legend of Aletes and Aor must have been a fascinating adventure and love story, similar to the legend of Leukippos and Leukophryene:[59] a wandering hero with the characteristic name Aletes (the Wanderer), a typical Heraclid, followed his destiny which brought him to Lykia in a crucial moment of its early history. Here, colonists were under attack by some anonymous barbarians. In this moment of despair, Aletes appeared, he defeated the enemies and married the daughter of Aor (the Sword), the only anonymous person in this narrative.

Other historical narratives are alluded to in the phrase "they indicated with many other proofs the goodwill that they had customarily felt for us from ancient times because of the tie of kinship" (lines 30-32). These narratives constituted the 'historical arguments' of the envoys: these 'historical traditions' morally obliged the Xanthians to offer help. First, because they were relatives of the Dorians; second, because the Xanthians themselves had received assistance, when they were in need. The arguments from myth and legend did not appeal to reason but to the feelings of gratitude and affection.

We have already seen that one of the functions of historical arguments is the arousal of gratitude and, consequently, of moral obligations. The Athenians were not the only ones who

---

[59] PARTHENIUS, *Mythogr. Gr.* 2, 1, 5.

used such arguments but they were great experts in this regard. A well-known example, and at the same time a relatively well-preserved fragment of Hellenistic oratory, is preserved in the Amphiktyonic decree that concerns privileges of the association of Dionysiac artists in Athens (118/7 BC):[60]

"… it has occurred that an association of the *technitai* was established for the first time in the city of the Athenians – the people who, becoming the principal cause of all the good things that exist among humans, brought the humans from animal life to civilisation and became the cause of communal life by introducing the tradition of the mysteries; through this the Athenian people counselled the Greeks that interactions with each other and trust are the greatest goods among humans. The Athenians also received from the gods specially for themselves as gifts the laws concerning human relations of friendship, education, and the delivery of grain, but gave the advantage from this gift jointly to the Greeks. Being the first to establish an association of *technitai* and participants in contests, the Athenians created thymelic and scenic contests. Testimony for all this is given by most historians and poets, and truth itself clearly attests to this, reminding that Athens is the mother-city of all dramas and that it invented and developed tragedy and comedy …"

Exactly as the Greeks of today use the invention of democracy in ancient Greece to create the favourable emotional context for requests concerning their present financial misery, the Athenian

---

[60] Lefèvre (2002) 284-285, no. 117: ἐπει[δ]ὴ γεγονέ[ν]αι [τε καὶ συν]ῆχθαι τεχνιτῶν σύνοδον παρ᾽ Ἀθηναίοις συμβέβηκε πρῶτον, ὧν ὁ δῆμος, ἀ‖[πάντων τῶν ἐν ἀνθρ]ώποις ἀγαθῶν ἀρχηγὸς κατασταθε]ίς, ἐγ μὲν τοῦ θηριώδους βίου μετήγαγεν τοὺς ἀνθρώπους εἰς ἡμερότη‖[τα, παραίτιος δ᾽ ἐγε]νήθη τῆς πρὸς ἀλλήλ[ους κοινωνί]ας εἰσαγαγὼν τὴν μυστηρίων παράδοσιν, καὶ διὰ τούτων παρ[α]γγ[‖γείλας τοῖς Ἕλλησιν] ὅτι μ[έγι]στον ἀγαθό[ν ἐστιν ἐ]ν ἀνθρώποις ἡ πρὸς ἑαυτοὺς χρῆσίς τε καὶ πίστις· ἔτι τε τῶν δοθέντων | [ὑπὸ θεῶν περὶ φιλαν-θρώ]πων νόμων [καὶ τῆς π]αιδείας ὁμοίως δὲ καὶ τῆς τοῦ καρποῦ παραδόσεως ἰδίαι μὲν ἐδέξατο | [τὸ δῶρον, κοινὴν δὲ] τὴν ἐξ ἑ[α]υτ<οῦ>(?) εὐχρ[ηστίαν] τοῖς Ἕλλησιν ἀπέδωκεν· πρῶτός τε πάντων, συναγα<γ>ὼν τεχνιτῶν σύνοδον | [καὶ ἀγωνιστῶν, θ]υμελικ[οὺς καὶ σ]κηνικ[οὺ]ς ἀγῶνας ἐποίησεν, οἷς καὶ συμβαίνει μαρτυρεῖν μὲν τοὺς πλείστους τῶν ἱ[στοριαγράφων καὶ] ποιητῶ[ν, αὐτὴν] δὲ καὶ τ[ὴ]ν ἀλήθειαν ἐμφανῶς δεικνύειν, ὑπομιμνήσκουσαν ὅτι μητρόπολίς ἐστι τῶν | [δραμάτων ἁπάντων, τ]ρα[γωιδίαν κ]αὶ κωμωι[δ]ίαν εὑροῦσά τε καὶ αὐξή-σασα.

theatre artists based the request for privileges on the moral obligations deriving from Athens' contribution to culture. The argument of the Kytenians in Xanthos had a similar aim. In the very same way as a legendary Dorian saved your ancestors, you now have the moral obligation to save us. The Kytenian envoys also used another dramatic narrative to appeal to emotion: the narrative of a recent war. It is summarised in the decree of Xanthos and in the letter of the Kytenians:

> "It occurred that in the time when king Antigonos had invaded Phokis [228 BC] parts of the city walls of all the cities had collapsed because of the earthquakes and the younger men had marched to the sanctuary of Apollo in Delphi in order to protect it. When the king arrived in Doris he destroyed the walls of all our cities and burned down our houses."

Even these few lines give us a sense of the dramatic narrative. After earthquakes had destroyed parts of the fortification walls, the enemy exploited this moment of weakness to invade Phokis. The cities of Doris lacked not only the *promachones* of their fortifications, but also the *promachoi*, the young warriors, their usual defenders in such situations. The young men, in accordance with a pattern we find both in real life and in literature, had marched to Delphi, in order to defend it. The defence of the cities of Doris was left to the old men and the women; the enemy prevailed, taking the cities, destroying what had been left of the city walls and burning the houses. Similar narratives in contemporary historiography give us an impression of the possible content of the narrative of the Kytenian envoys.[61] Hellenistic audiences loved these stories, full of suspense, dramatic changes and tragic ironies.

---

[61] Phylarchos' description of the attack of Pyrrhos against Sparta: PLUT. *Pyrrh.* 28, 4-5; Phylarchos' (?) narrative of the sack of Pellene by the Aitolians: PLUT. *Arat.* 31-32; Polybius' narrative of the sack of Abydos: 16, 30-34. See CHANIOTIS (2005a) 198-199, and 208.

It seems, however, that the Kytenian orators, in spite of their preoccupation with these old legends, did not lose their contact with reality. If none of these arguments would work, they could also play a 'political card', implying that they had the support of Ptolemy IV, who was still controlling this part of Asia Minor. What is, however, interesting, is that this support was invested with a historical content. As the Kytenians claimed, Ptolemy's dynasty originated in Herakles, the Dorian hero par excellence (lines 47-49: "for King Ptolemy as a descendant of Herakles, is a relative of the kings who descended from Herakles"; lines 109-110: "for King Ptolemy is our relative on account of his kinship with the kings", i.e. the Argeads). Once again we see in this document the interaction of historical, moral, and pragmatic arguments.

The oration of the Kytenian envoys ended with a dramatic appeal to the distant relatives in Xanthos not to show indifference:

> "They ask us to bring to our memory our kinship to them, which originates in the gods and the heroes, and not to remain indifferent to the fact that the walls of their fatherland have been razed to the ground' (lines 14-17). ... They requested not to look on the elimination of the largest city among the cities of the Metropolis (the Mother-City) with indifference."

The dramatic narratives and the emotional appeal were effective. We may detect the compassion of the assembly in the answer of the Xanthians: "We should respond that all the Xanthians felt the same grief with you (*synachthestai*) for the misfortunes (*akleremata*) which have befallen your city" (lines 42-44).

But despite the emotional impact of the oration and despite the invocation of Ptolemy's name, the allegedly bad financial situation of Xanthos did not allow the Xanthians to give more than a symbolic contribution of 500 drachmas. Still, we should be grateful to the Xanthians, who invested a significant amount to have the 4,500 letters of this inscription inscribed. By doing so and preserving the content of this oration they permit us to come to an important conclusion: even the least plausible claims to historical relations in Greek diplomatic documents were founded in mythological or historical traditions. When these traditions did not already exist, they had to be created. From a decree of Apollonia on the Rhyndakos concerning the relations between this city and Miletos (2nd century) we learn that at least sometimes the historical arguments made by envoys in their orations were carefully scrutinised.[62] The citizens of Apollonia sent an embassy to Miletus to renew their relation to the city they believed was their mother city. They also asked the Milesians to let them participate in the cult of Apollo. The envoys of Apollonia brought with them historiographical works to substantiate their claim that they had been colonists of Miletos:[63]

> "Whereas we sent an embassy to the Milesian people in order to renew the existing kinship between our people and the Milesians, kinship that is founded on the foundation of a colony, the Milesians listened carefully to our envoys, with every goodwill, and after examining (ἐπισκεψάμενοι) the relevant histories and the other documents, they responded that our city has truly (ἐπὶ τῆς ἀληθείας) been a colony of their city. This was achieved by their ancestors, at the time when they sent a military expedition to the region of the Hellespont and Propontis and defeated in war the barbarians who inhabited that land, they founded along with the other Greek cities also our city, Apollo of Didyma being the leader of the expedition."

---

62 *I.Milet* I 3, 155.

63 *I.Milet.* I 3, 155: ἐπεὶ πεμ|φθείσης πρεσβείας πρὸς τὸν δῆμον τὸν Μιλη-σίων περὶ τοῦ ἀνα|νεώσασθαι τὴν ὑπάρχουσαν πρὸς αὐτὸν τῶι δήμωι ἡμῶν | διὰ τὴν ἀποικίαν συγγένειαν Μιλήσιοι διακούσαντες | τῶν πρεσβευτῶν μετὰ πάσης εὐνοίας καὶ ἐπισκεψάμενοι | τὰς περὶ τούτων ἱστορίας καὶ τἆλλα ἔγγραφα ἀπε-κρίθησαν | τὴν πόλιν ἡμῶν ἐπὶ τῆς ἀληθείας γεγενῆσθαι ἄποικον | τῆς ἑαυτῶν πόλεως διαπραξαμένων τῶν προγόνων, | καθ᾽ οὓς καιροὺς ἐκπέμψαντες στρά-τευμα καὶ εἰς τοὺς | [κ]ατὰ τὸν Ἑλλήσποντον καὶ τὴν Προποντίδα τόπους | κρατήσαντες δόρατ(ι) τῶν ἐνοικούντων βαρβάρων κα|τώ(ι)κισαν τάς τε ἄλλας Ἑλληνίδας πόλεις καὶ τὴν ἡμετέραν κα|θηγησαμένου τῆς στρατείας Ἀπόλλωνος Διδυμέως.

The reference to the careful examination of the historical argument by the Milesians confirms the assumption that historical arguments were not mere politeness. Similarly, a king, possibly a Spartokid, who received a Koan embassy that promoted the asylia of the Asklepieion (242 BC), confirmed that the tradition concerning the kinship between his dynasty and Kos was trustworthy:[64] "we accept the asylia and we gladly also accept the kinship, which is true and worthy of you and us" (καὶ τὴν ἀ[συλία]ν δεχ[ό]||μεθα καὶ τὴν συγγένειαν οὖσαν ἀλ[η]θινὴν καὶ [ὑ]||μῶν τε ἀξίαν καὶ ἡμῶν ἡδέως προσ[δε]-δέγμεθα).

Because of the great number of Hellenistic diplomatic undertakings, such as the conclusion of treaties, the recognition of the inviolability of cities (*asylia*), the recognition of the elevated status of agonistic festivals, requests for financial support, requests for the sending of foreign judges, the mutual award of privileges, and so on, we have hundreds of inscriptions that directly mention or indirectly allude to the use of historical arguments. Expressions such as "the Eresians are the friends of our city since old times", or the "Tenians are our relatives and friends and have always been benevolent towards our city" presuppose the presence of historical arguments in orations. An Athenian decree concerning Priene is one example out of many (2nd century).[65] If we only had the first lines ("the Prienians, who are friends and relatives from old times"), we might wonder about the concrete historical content of the envoys' oration. Fortunately, the text continues with concrete information:

> "They always remember all the other benefactions of the Athenian people to them, and above all they remember that the Athenians rebuilt their city after it had been destroyed by Cyrus."

---

[64] RIGSBY (1996) no. 12 lines 22-24.
[65] *I.Priene* 45; new edition: *IG* II³ 1239.

6. History as an argument III: a culturally determined ritual

In 87 BC, during the war against Mithridates VI, Sulla was besieging Athens, then governed by the philosopher Athenion. After a year of siege Athenion sent envoys to Sulla. Their speech is summarised by Plutarch:[66]

> "But after a long time, at last, he sent out two or three of his fellow-revellers to negotiate for peace; when they made no demands which could save the city, but proudly talked about Theseus and Eumolpos and the Persian Wars, Sulla said to them: 'Go away, blessed men, and take these speeches with you; for I was not sent to Athens by the Romans to fulfil love of knowledge, but to subdue rebels'."

The Athenian envoys used a script that was almost four centuries old: "we saved the Greeks from the Amazons, we saved them from the Thracians, we saved them from the Persians".[67] This appeal to the common cultural memory of the Greeks had indeed been effective in the past, if not as the cause of decisions, certainly as their justification; after the Peloponnesian War the Spartans had justified their decision not to destroy Athens in precisely this manner. In negotiations among Greeks, this approach was based on the principle of *do ut des* – we have saved us Greeks, now we deserve to be rescued; it appealed to gratitude and it implied the common ancestry of the Greeks and a shared identity. Persuasion strategies based on gratitude and affection had an impact on decision-making, especially in assemblies. This is why they were used. The historicity of Plutarch's report is therefore irrelevant; no matter whether Athenian envoys *did* use such an approach on that occasion or not, both the literary and the documentary evidence confirm that this was the standard approach. In Plutarch's narrative the Athenian envoys did not realise that a 'script' that worked well in negotiations among Greeks could not possibly have the same

---

[66] PLUT. *Sull.* 13.
[67] CHANIOTIS (2005b).

impact in their negotiations with a Roman general. Other Greeks had learned the lesson and had adjusted their negotiation strategies to Roman values and priorities.[68]

These few lines encapsulate the confrontation of two cultures. On one level Plutarch presents us with the confrontation between the ritualised use of history as an argument in Greek diplomacy on the one hand and the pragmatism of a Roman general, who is not interested in a historical lecture, on the other. But on another level this anecdote of a *ritus interruptus* narrates the failure of communication that was based on the cultural memory of one party, a memory that was totally misunderstood by the other. The oration of the Athenian envoys consisted of the most glorious chapters of Attic history, the best known components of their self-representation. Plutarch simply mentions the names of two heroes (Theseus and Eumolpos) and the Persian Wars, with no further details. He obviously presupposed that his reader (or the reader of his source, possibly Poseidonios) would understand the significance of these names without any explanation. He was certainly right in his assumption. Perhaps not every Athenian would have been in a position to list all of Theseus' adventures, not every Athenian would have known the name of the mythical king who had defended Athens against the Thracian invasion under Eumolpos, and it is doubtful whether many Athenians would have been in a position to place the Persian Wars in an accurate historical context. Nevertheless, Theseus, Eumolpos, and the Persian Wars, in this particular constellation (three victorious wars) and in this particular context (the siege of Athens by a foreign army), conveyed to every Athenian a message that could easily be understood: Athens had often been attacked by foreign armies (the Amazons, the Thracians, the Persians), but it had always prevailed. From Plato's *Menexenos* in the 4th century to Aelius Aristides' *Panathenaic Oration* in the 2nd century AD these three victories, of Theseus over the Amazons, of king

<hr>

[68] CHANIOTIS (2015).

Erechtheus over the Thracians of Eumolpos, and of the Athenians over the Persians, were stereotypically alluded to as the pillars of Athenian self-representation.

Cultural memory is abstract and vague with regard to historical contents, but unequivocal as a means of communication. An event is reduced to a few essential points and becomes a sign that can be activated through the mention of a word or a name. Naturally, cultural memory can serve as communication only among those who share it. For the Athenians, the mention of Theseus, Eumolpos, and the Persian Wars was unequivocal, because these three events were always mentioned in the particular context of the glorification of Athens, as the most important Athenian victories that had saved Greece from invading barbarians. What the Athenians did not take into consideration is the fact that Sulla was not an ordinary recipient of this type of argument: he was just another of the non-Hellenic aggressors; and he was not part of the circle that shared the same cultural memory. Nothing could interest him less than the Athenian contributions to the defence of Greece. More than two centuries earlier Alexander the Great had not destroyed Athens, thus paying his respect precisely to these achievements. Alexander knew and understood the Athenian traditions, Sulla did not.

7. Conclusions

After this presentation of some characteristic cases in which historical arguments were used in Hellenistic orations summarised in decrees, I attempt some general remarks. What we have seen so far, is that historical arguments seem to have been indispensible in political debates and in negotiations, so indispensible that when a relevant historical tradition did not exist, the gap had to be filled with an invented 'tradition'. We have also seen that historical arguments were sometimes only one component of a more sophisticated argumentation, which might include political, legal, economic or military considerations. It is precisely this co-existence of historical with pragmatic arguments that emphatically underlines the firm position of historical traditions in political reasoning. Even when a city had a political argument, it still had to use a historical one as well. The tantalising questions are, of course, why the historical argumentation was indispensible and how effective it might have really been. These two questions cannot be discussed independently.

A first important factor should be seen in the nature of decision-making in Hellenistic communities. All important decisions, including complex diplomatic matters, had to be taken by the popular assembly in all communities that were not ruled by kings. This applies to democratic and oligarchic communities alike, to city-states and confederations. In the majority of the Greek communities, especially in the Hellenistic age, the popular assembly had the right to debate on the political issues at stake.[69] And even in the communities, in which the popular assembly did not have the right of a debate, the debates did take place before the meeting of the assembly, in the market place or at drinking parties. The assembly comprised all the male adult citizens, young and old, educated and not, intelligent and naive, cautious and impulsive. Foreign envoys and the local statesmen who delivered the speeches in the assembly had to deal with a mass that was anything but homogeneous. Different arguments would appeal to different people. For that reason alone arguments of all kinds – historical, pragmatic, legal, and moral – had to be combined. The rules influencing decision-making in assemblies, market places, and drinking parties are by no means identical to those appropriate for the negotiations between sober statesmen. Arguments closely connected with religion and morality, arguments more appealing to sentiment than reason, have good chances to prevail. Aristophanic comedies, speeches in Thucydides, and the works of the Athenian orators reveal a multitude of tricks that smart

[69] GRIEB (2008).

orators used to distract the attention of the audience from the arguments of an opponent. Gossip, oracles, moral lessons, and a great deal of history belonged to the standard repertoire of cunning orators, able to manipulate their audience. Interestingly, among envoys in the Hellenistic period we not only find pragmatic politicians, but also orators, historians, philosophers, actors, dancers, and musicians,[70] and this is suggestive of the nature of the diplomatic activity and persuasion strategies in the assembly.

But this is certainly not the only reason for the use of historical arguments in Hellenistic, as well as in earlier and later deliberative oratory. Another, perhaps more important, reason may be seen in the fact the present draws its legitimacy from the past. This is quite obvious in the case of precedents, e.g. in constitutional history, but also in the legal relations between two states. Legal rights (e.g. privileges, the control of a sanctuary or the claim to a territory) can only be defended by a community if it can provide proof that it had these rights in previous times as well. This was, naturally, very important in territorial conflicts, an area that I cannot treat in this context.[71] For instance, in the conflict between Hierapytna and Itanos on Crete over the possession of a territory near the sanctuary of Zeus Diktaios, the arbitrators, judges from Magnesia on Maeander, summarised in their verdict the legal principles which rendered the claim to a piece of land legitimate:[72]

> "men have proprietary rights over land either because they have received the land themselves from the ancestors, or because they have bought it for money, or because they have won it with spear, or because they have received it from one of the mightier".

These four ways of legal acquisition of property are all directly connected with the past, in other words with history. In order to defend its legal claims, a community has to look to the past

---

[70] CHANIOTIS (1988b).
[71] CHANIOTIS (2004).
[72] I.Cret. III iv, 9. Discussion: CHANIOTIS (2004).

for arguments. *Mutatis mutandis*, this applies to claims of other natures as well. Individuals and communities alike supported claims to prestige and influence, certain honorary privileges and positions that were inherited διὰ γένους, and very often also the claim to receive support for a service that had been done in the past. The principle of reciprocity that determined the relations within communities, between mortals and gods, between cities and monarchs, and between the people and the elite, was also one of the foundations of historical arguments as a persuasion strategy: when one partner of the negotiation requests the reciprocation of past services, he needs to provide the necessary historical narrative and documentation.

The weight of moral arguments, even when combined with pragmatic arguments, can be seen in a story narrated by Xenophon in the Book 6 of his *Hellenica*. After Sparta's defeat at the battle of Leuktra by the Thebans, the Spartans had to ask the support of the Athenians. Their envoys used arguments of political realism, especially pointing to the danger that the new power represented; however, the majority of their arguments were of historical character. The Spartan envoys reminded their audience of the Spartan benefactions to the Athenians – the expulsion of the tyrants in the late 6th century and the fact that they did not destroy Athens after the Peloponnesian War –, thus appealing to their obligation to repay these benefactions. A second group of arguments can be labelled as precedents: the Spartans listed all the previous cases, in which the Athenians had helped them – especially the Third Messenian War – as well as the cases in which Athenians and Spartans had fought together, namely the Persian Wars; of course they did not forget to underline the fact that the present enemies, the Thebans, had taken the Persian side in these wars. The Athenians accepted the Spartan proposal of an alliance. According to Xenophon,

> "the weightiest of the arguments urged by the Lakedaimonians seemed to their hearers to be that at the time when they subdued the Athenians, though the Thebans wanted to destroy

Athens utterly, it was they who had prevented it. Most stress was laid, however, upon the consideration that the Athenians were required by their oaths to come to their assistance."[73]

In the eyes of a conservative and deeply religious historian, the historically founded obligation of the Athenians to repay a benefaction weighed more than any other argument.

So, we have to reach a trivial conclusion: historical arguments in Hellenistic oratory, and more generally, owed their effectiveness to their relation to the very foundations of organised life in ancient Greece: law and moral, social, political, and religious values. They were not more or less effective than law and morality can be in a world of many city-states and confederations opposed to each other, exposed to wars, social and political conflicts, and changes of every kind. History was not the only argument in their political deliberations, but it seems that it could not be absent. In 364 the Thebans attacked and destroyed the neighbouring city of Orchomenos. As Diodorus reports, the Thebans presented their war as an act of revenge for the injustice of the legendary forefathers of the Orchomenians, the Minyans, who had imposed a tribute upon the Thebans:[74]

"So the Thebans, thinking they had a good opportunity (*kairos*, i.e. a civil war in Orchomenos) and having got plausible pretexts (*prophaseis*) for punishing them, took the field against Orchomenos, occupied the city, slew the male inhabitants and sold into slavery the women and children".

A good opportunity was no less necessary for the Theban attack than a plausible moral or legal argument provided by a historical tradition.

The attitude of the Greeks towards law, morality, religion, and historical traditions did not remain unchanged in the course of centuries. The changes, especially the influence of the sophistic movement, certainly affected the way historical arguments

[73] XEN. *Hell.* 6, 5, 35-36.
[74] DIOD. 15, 79.

could be used or were in fact used by individuals and communities. In the Hellenistic period, the specific cultural context of historical arguments is primarily provided by the importance of historical culture: the prolific production of historiographical works; the abundance of commemorative anniversaries; the lectures of itinerant historians.[75] This strong presence of 'history', without precedent in earlier Greek culture, strengthened the already existing trend to endorse pragmatic arguments with historical arguments. One of the fables of Babrius (2nd century AD) very much resembles an ironic comment on the ritualised use of history as an argument – in this case, the presentation of grievances before a declaration of war:

> "Once a wolf saw a lamb that had gone astray from the flock, but instead of rushing upon him to seize him by force, he tried to find a plausible complaint (*enklêma euprosôpon*) by which to justify his hostility. 'Last year, small though you were, you slandered me.' 'How could I last year? It's not yet a year since I was born.' 'Well, then, aren't you cropping this field, which is mine?' 'No, for I've not yet eaten any grass nor have I begun to graze.' 'And haven't you drunk from the fountain which is mine to drink from?' 'No, even yet my mother's breast provides my nourishment'. Thereupon the wolf seized the lamb and while eating him remarked: 'You're not going to rob the wolf of his dinner even though you do find it easy to refute all my charges' (*pasan aitiên*)."[76]

Works cited

AGER, S.L. (1996), *Interstate Arbitrations in the Greek World, 337-90 B.C.* (Berkeley).
ALLROGGEN, D. (1972), *Griechische Geschichte im Urteil der attischen Redner des vierten Jahrhunderts v. Chr.* (Diss. Freiburg Br.).

---

[75] For these phenomena in the Hellenistic period see CHANIOTIS (1988a) and (1991). For similar developments already in fourth-century Athens see LAMBERT (2011).

[76] BABR. *Fab.* 89.

AUSTIN, M.M. (²2006), *The Hellenistic World from Alexander to the Roman Conquest. A Selection of Ancient Sources in Translation* (Cambridge).

BEARZOT, C. (1997), *Lisia e la tradizione su Teramene. Commento storico alle orazioni XII e XIII del* corpus lysiacum (Milan).

BOUSQUET, J. (1988), "La stèle des Kyténiens au Létôon de Xanthos", *REG* 101, 12-53.

CHAMPION, C. (1997), "The Nature of Authoritative Evidence in Polybius and Agelaus' Speech at Naupactus", *TAPA* 127, 111-128.

—— (2000), "Romans as βάρβαροι: Three Polybian Speeches and the Politics of Cultural Indeterminacy", *CPh* 95, 425-444.

—— (2004-2005), "In Defence of Hellas: The Antigonid Soteria and Paneia at Delos and the Aetolian Soteria at Delphi", *AJAH* NS 3/4, 72-88.

CHANIOTIS, A. (1988a), *Historie und Historiker in den griechischen Inschriften. Epigraphische Beiträge zur griechischen Historiographie* (Stuttgart).

—— (1988b), "Als die Diplomaten noch tanzten und sangen: Zu zwei Dekreten kretischer Städte in Mylasa", *ZPE* 71, 154-156.

—— (1991), "Gedenktage der Griechen: Ihre Bedeutung für das Geschichtsbewußtsein griechischer Poleis", in J. ASSMANN (ed.), *Das Fest und das Heilige. Religiöse Kontrapunkte zur Alltagswelt* (Gütersloh), 123-145.

—— (1999), "Empfängerformular und Urkundenfälschung: Bemerkungen zum Urkundendossier von Magnesia am Mäander", in R.G. KHOURY (ed.), *Urkunden und Urkundenformulare im Klassischen Altertum und in den orientalischen Kulturen* (Heidelberg), 51-69.

—— (2004), "Justifying Territorial Claims in Classical and Hellenistic Greece. The Beginnings of International Law", in E.M. HARRIS / L. RUBINSTEIN (eds.), *The Law and the Courts in Ancient Greece* (London), 185-213.

—— (2005a), *War in the Hellenistic World. A Social and Cultural History* (Malden).

—— (2005b), "Ein mißverstandenes Ritual der griechischen Diplomatie: Geschichte als Argument", in C. AMBOS *et al.* (eds.), *Die Welt der Rituale von der Antike bis heute* (Darmstadt), 106–109.

—— (2009), "Travelling Memories in the Hellenistic World", in R. HUNTER / I. RUTHERFORD (eds.), *Wandering Poets in Ancient Greek Culture. Travel, Locality, and Panhellenism* (Cambridge), 249-269.

—— (2013a), "*Paradoxon, Enargeia*, Empathy: Hellenistic Decrees and Hellenistic Oratory", in KREMMYDAS / TEMPEST (2013), 201-216.

—— (2013b), "Emotional Language in Hellenistic Decrees and Hellenistic Histories', in M. MARI / J. THORNTON (eds.), *Parole in movimento. Linguaggio politico e lessico storiografico nel mondo ellenistico* (Pisa), 339-352.

—— (2013c), "Normen stärker als Emotionen? Der kulturhistorische Kontext der griechischen Amnestie", in K. HARTER-UIBOPUU / F. MITTHOF (eds.), *Vergeben und Vergessen? Amnestie in der Antike. Beiträge zum 1. Wiener Kolloquium zur Antiken Rechtsgeschichte, 27.-28.10.2008* (Vienna), 47-70.

—— (2015), "Affective Diplomacy: Emotional Scripts between Greek Communities and Roman Authorities during the Republic", in D. CAIRNS / L. FULKERSON (eds.), *Emotions Between Greece and Rome* (London), 87-103.

CHAPA, J. (1988), *Letters of Condolence in Greek Papyri* (Florence).

CURTY, O. (1995), *Les parentés légendaires entre cités grecques. Catalogue raisonné des inscriptions contenant le terme συγγένεια et analyse critique* (Geneva).

—— (1999), "La parenté légendaire à l'époque hellénistique: Précisions méthodologiques", *Kernos* 12, 167-194.

—— (2005), "Un usage fort controversé: La parenté dans le langage diplomatique de l'époque hellénistique", *AncSoc* 35, 101-117.

DEININGER, J. (1973), "Bemerkungen zur Historizität der Rede des Agelaos 217 v. Chr. (Polyb. 5,104)", *Chiron* 3, 103-108.

DEMANDT, A. (1972), *Geschichte als Argument. Drei Formen politischen Zukunftsdenkens im Altertum* (Konstanz).

ERSKINE, A. (2007), "Rhetoric and Persuasion in the Hellenistic World: Speaking up for the *Polis*", in I. WORTHINGTON (ed.), *A Companion to Greek Rhetoric* (Oxford), 272-285.

ÉTIENNE R. / M. PIÉRART (1975), "Un décret du Koinon des Hellènes à Platées en l'honneur de Glaucon, fils d'Étéoclès, d'Athènes", *BCH* 99, 51-75.

GRAF, F. (1996), *Gottesnähe und Schadenzauber. Die Magie in der griechisch-römischen Antike* (Munich).

GRETHLEIN, J. (2014), "The Value of the Past Challenged: Myth and Ancient History in the Attic Orators", in J. KER / C. PIEPER (eds.), *Valuing the Past in the Greco-Roman World. Proceedings from the Penn Leiden Colloquia on Ancient Values VII* (Leiden), 326-354.

GRIEB, V. (2008), *Hellenistische Demokratie. Politische Organisation und Struktur in freien griechischen Poleis nach Alexander dem Großen* (Stuttgart).

HOLLEAUX, M. (1898), "Décret d'Alabanda", *REG* 11, 258-266.

JONES, C.P. (1999), *Kinship Diplomacy in the Ancient World* (Cambridge, MA).

JUNG, M. (2006), *Marathon und Plataiai. Zwei Perserschlachten als 'Lieux de mémoire' im antiken Griechenland* (Göttingen).

KREMMYDAS, C. / TEMPEST, K. (eds.) (2013), *Hellenistic Oratory. Continuity and Change* (Oxford).

LAMBERT, S.D. (2011), "Some Political Shifts in Lykourgan Athens", in V. AZOULAY / P. ISMARD (eds.), *Clisthène et Lycurgue d'Athènes. Autour du politique dans la cité classique* (Paris), 175-190.

—— (2012) "Inscribing the Past in Fourth-Century Athens", in J. MARINCOLA / L. LLEWELLYN-JONES / C. MACIVER (eds.), *Greek Notions of the Past in the Archaic and Classical Eras. History without Historians* (Edinburgh), 253-275.

LEFÈVRE, F. (2002), *Corpus des inscriptions de Delphes. T. IV, Documents amphictioniques* (Paris).

MAGNETTO, A. (1997), *Gli arbitrati interstatali greci. Introduzione, testo critico, traduzione, commento e indici.* Vol. II, *Dal 337 al 196 a.C.* (Pisa).

—— (2008), *L'arbitrato di Rodi fra Samo e Priene. Edizione critica, commento e indici* (Pisa).

NOUHAUD, M. (1982), *L'utilisation de l'histoire par les orateurs attiques* (Paris).

PAPANIKOLAOU, D. (2009), "The Aretalogy of Isis from Maroneia and the Question of Hellenistic 'Asianism'", *ZPE* 168, 59-70.

—— (2012), "*IG* V.2, 268 (= *SIG*³ 783) as a Monument of Hellenistic Prose", *ZPE* 182, 137-156.

RIGSBY, K.J. (1996), *Asylia. Territorial Inviolability in the Hellenistic World* (Berkeley).

ROBERTSON, N. (1986), "A Point of Precedence at Plataia: The Dispute between Athens and Sparta over Leading the Procession", *Hesperia* 55, 88-102.

ROUSSET, D. (2002), *Le territoire de Delphes et la terre d'Apollon* (Paris).

RUBINSTEIN, L. (2013), "Spoken Words, Written Submissions, and Diplomatic Conventions: The Importance and Impact of Oral Performance in Hellenistic Inter-*polis* Relations", in KREMMYDAS / TEMPEST (2013), 165-199.

SACKS, K. (1986), "Rhetoric and Speeches in Hellenistic Historiography", *Athenaeum* 64, 383-395.

SHERK, R.K. (1969), *Roman Documents from the Greek East. Senatus consulta and epistulae to the Age of Augustus* (Baltimore).

SOKOLOWSKI, F. (1962), *Lois sacrées des cités grecques. Supplément* (Paris).

STRUBBE, J.H.M. (1998), "Epigrams and Consolation Decrees for Deceased Youth", *AC* 67, 45-75.

THÉRIAULT, G. (1996), *Le culte d'Homonoia dans les cités grecques* (Lyon).

THORNTON, J. (2013), "Oratory in Polybius' *Histories*", in KREM-MYDAS / TEMPEST (2013), 21-42.

USHER, S. (2009), "*Oratio recta* and *oratio obliqua* in Polybius", *GRBS* 49, 487-514.

VANDERSPOEL, J. (2007), "Hellenistic Rhetoric in Theory and Practice", in I. WORTHINGTON (ed.), *A Companion to Greek Rhetoric* (Oxford), 124-138.

WALLACE, S. (2011), "The Significance of Plataia for Greek *eleutheria* in the Early Hellenistic Period", in A. ERSKINE / L. LLEWELLYN-JONES (eds.), *Creating a Hellenistic World* (Swansea), 147-176.

WIATER, N. (2010), "Speeches and Historical Narrative in Polybius' *Histories*: Approaching Speeches in Polybius", in D. PAUSCH (ed.), *Stimmen der Geschichte. Funktionen von Reden in der antiken Historiographie* (Berlin), 67-107.

WIEDEMANN, T. (1990), "Rhetoric in Polybius", in H. VERDIN / G. SCHEPENS / E. DE KEYSER (eds.), *Purposes of History. Studies in Greek Historiography from the 4th to the 2nd Centuries B.C.* (Leuven), 289-300.

WOOTEN, C.W. (1973), "The Ambassador's Speech: A Particularly Hellenistic Genre of Oratory", *Quarterly Journal of Speech* 59, 209-212.

—— (1974), "The Speeches in Polybius: An Insight into the Nature of Hellenistic Oratory", *AJPh* 95, 235-251.

DISCUSSION

J.-L. Ferrary: La communication d'Angélos Chaniotis a présenté sous tous ses aspects le rôle complexe attribué à l'histoire dans l'éloquence hellénistique, et montré combien on pouvait tirer parti, en l'absence de discours parvenus jusqu'à nous et compte tenu de la rareté des textes historiographiques (à l'exception de Polybe et du discours d'Athénion chez Posidonius), des considérants des décrets. Du point de vue des rapports entre Grecs et Romains, j'ai particulièrement apprécié son analyse du texte de Plutarque (*Sull.* 13, 5) concernant la réponse de Sylla aux ambassadeurs d'Aristion qui invoquaient Thésée, Eumolpos et les Guerres médiques. Comme souvent, toutefois, l'attitude des Romains restait ambiguë. Après s'être emparé de la cité qu'il traita sans ménagement, Sylla répondit favorablement aux supplications des Athéniens qui étaient restés fidèles aux Romains, avaient fui leur cité et se trouvaient dans son camp, et il déclara qu'il pardonnait "en l'honneur du plus grand nombre", c'est-à-dire des morts, c'est-à-dire de son illustre passé (Plut. *Sull.* 14, 9). La différence entre les deux réponses successives s'explique à la fois par les contextes dans lesquels elles furent données (avant et après la répression de la rébellion), et par l'identité des interlocuteurs (rebelles ou amis fidèles).

A. Chaniotis: Many thanks for this observation. There is a common denominator in the Athenian plea and Sulla's response towards loyal friends: *charis,* the gratitude and benevolence that one deserves for past services. The problem is that the Athenians appealed to *charis*, without noticing that a Roman did not care about their services to the Greeks and would not reward them. The importance of loyalty (*pistis* or *fides*) for the Romans is evident in many contemporary sources that I have discussed in a recent study (Chaniotis [2015]).

P. Ducrey: Nous nous situons ici à l'époque hellénistique. Mais l'évocation d'un passé historique plus ou moins éloigné rappelle le plaidoyer que les Platéens prisonniers des Thébains après la prise de leur ville adressent aux Lacédémoniens, si l'on en croit Thucydide. Ils évoquent en effet pour tenter d'infléchir leurs vainqueurs leur attitude loyale lors des Guerres médiques et de la révolte des hilotes (Thuc. 3, 54, 3-5).

A. Chaniotis: I do not recognise a difference in the use of arguments – very common in Classical historiography and rhetoric –, but there is a difference of cultural contexts. Let me give you three examples of how cultural contexts may affect the use of historical arguments. First, historical experiences, such as the traumatic experiences during the Peloponnesian War and the civil wars that were connected with it, had an impact on values and, consequently, on values to which historical arguments appealed. Second, the growth of historiography and the increased interest in history (e.g. public lectures of historians) had an impact on historical knowledge and on the way historical arguments were used and viewed. Just compare how little local historiography (hardly any) we have in the late 5th century BC, when the Plataeans appealed to the historical past, and how common local histories become from the 3rd century BC on – Jacoby has more than 600 local historians that can be dated to the Hellenistic and Imperial periods. The change in quantity is connected with qualitative changes. The place of history in education, everyday culture, and therefore in rhetoric was different. And thirdly, historiographical styles changed. Exactly as Hellenistic historiography is emotional and filled with vivid narratives, historical arguments in rhetoric are connected with more elaborate narratives and aim at emotional arousal.

L. Pernot: Y a-t-il des degrés de caractère persuasif entre les différentes sortes d'histoire ? Est-ce que les mythes, les traditions locales et la 'grande histoire' étaient utilisés comme arguments au même titre les uns et les autres ou à des titres différents ?

Que savons-nous sur ceux qui pensaient le contraire, à savoir que l'histoire n'est pas un argument ? Dans la littérature grecque classique, certains passages témoignent d'un refus de tirer des leçons de l'histoire, soit en vertu d'une opposition de principe, soit pour des raisons conjoncturelles. Ainsi, Aristophane se moque parfois des références aux Guerres médiques, et le Spartiate Sthénélaïdas, chez Thucydide, rejette les conclusions que les Athéniens veulent en tirer. Il y a aussi le cas de Platon.

A. Chaniotis: There are indeed differences in the way historical arguments were used and received, depending on the historical knowledge and consciousness of the audience. In some cases an orator may just use keywords to invoke events of the past, in other cases long narratives and explanations are needed. There is evidence that historical arguments were scrutinised or rejected. I already mentioned the case of Miletos and Apollonia on the Rhyndakos. In the arbitration of Rhodes between Samos and Priene (*I.Priene* 37), the Rhodian judges rejected a version of history that was presented to them by the Samians, contained in the histories of Milesios, because they discovered that the historical work of Milesios was a forgery.

M. Kraus: Nachdem Sie Ihren Vortrag mit einer Fabel beschlossen haben, sei auf die enge strukturelle Verwandtschaft von Fabeln und historischen Argumenten im rhetorischen Kontext hingewiesen. Beide gehören zur Kategorie der Beispiele. Wie Aristoteles sagt, ist das Beispiel die rhetorische Erscheinungsform des induktiven Arguments, so wie das Enthymem diejenige des deduktiven Beweises (Arist. *Rhet.* 1, 2, 1356b5-6; 12-18; 2, 20, 1393a26-27). Nun gehören aber induktive Beispiele ebenso typischerweise gerade zum deliberativen *genus* wie deduktive Enthymeme zum forensischen (*Rhet.* 1, 9, 1368a29-33). Beispiele (παραδείγματα) wiederum können entweder historisch oder erfunden sein; die erfundenen sind dann entweder Gleichnisse (παραβολαί) oder Fabeln (λόγοι) (*Rhet.* 2, 20, 1393a28-1394a8).

A. Chaniotis: Vielen Dank für diese Beobachtung. In spezifischen Kontexten werden historische *exempla* verwendet. In anderen Fällen, wie in der Fabel von Babrius oder aber im Peloponnesischen Krieg, dient die Vergangenheit als *enklêma*, als Vorwurf, der Handlungen rechtfertigt.

M. Edwards: I note the use of the words "fellow-revellers". Is this important?

A. Chaniotis: The Greek original has *sympotês*. Posidonios, most likely the source for this incident, wanted of course to paint a very negative image of the Athenian supporters of Mithridates; in fragments of his history, Athenion is presented as someone who is not truly an Athenian and a statesman. There may also be a subtext in the reference to drinking, that is, to Dionysiac revelling. Mithridates was known as the New Dionysos and the Dionysiac artists is Athens supported him.

M. Edwards: Perhaps past history was used in this case because the ambassadors to Sulla could see Athens and the Acropolis? Also these were not real ambassadors – so the context is important.

A. Chaniotis: Yes, the geographical context is important. We should not forget that two of the three legends mentioned by the Athenians, the Amazonomachy and the Persian Wars, were parts of the sculptural decoration of the Parthenon and the temple of Athena Nike. The third legend, the attack by the Thracians of Eumolpus and the rescue of Athens through the sacrifice of Erechtheus' daughters may well be the subject of the central scene of the Parthenon frieze, as Joan Connelly has argued.

D. Nelis: The strategy of controlling memory and emotions: there is an element of both sides agreeing to forget certain things for pragmatic reasons, Romans can forget a lack of *fides*?

A. Chaniotis: Memory can be selective, depending on contexts. Ephesos supported Mithridates; it later re-interpreted its policy as the result of fear; and the fact that it was not loyal did not prevent the Romans from keeping Ephesos as capital of the province of Asia. Selective memory is also very important in cases of reconciliation after a civil war, when people have to place the duty to establish concord (*homonoia*) over the duty to take revenge; in order to do this, they have to learn to forget the injustice or the pain that they had suffered. E.g. in Nakone they had to establish artificial families, consisting of members of the two parties and neutral citizens, in order to be able to establish peace; in other words, they had to delete family histories.

M. Edwards: That last remark of yours reminds me of Cleisthenes' reforms and the artificial tribes and phratries.

A. Chaniotis: The amnesty of 404/3 BC in Athens is another characteristic case of a community imposing the duty of *mê mnêsikakein*, the duty to forget the evil things that one had suffered.

M. Edwards: Lysias did not forget.

A. Chaniotis: Also the people of Eresos did not forget their suffering under the tyrants. When the descendants of the tyrants attempted to return to the city, their request was rejected. The relevant decree (*IG* XII 2, 526 + Suppl.) describes all their atrocities in great detail, precisely in order to arouse emotions – indignation and grief – through commemoration.

M. Edwards: You use the term 'Greeks' a great deal.

A. Chaniotis: For the period that I am discussing, that is, after Alexander's conquest, one can do this because of the increased mobility, the foundation of new cities and the re-settlement of populations, the increased number of international festivals, the exchange of diplomatic documents, the use of a shared formulaic language in diplomatic contacts, and consequently increased homogenisation in the Greek world.

M. Edwards: Does this explain why the times of conflict between Athens and Sparta are overlooked?

A. Chaniotis: You raise the important issue of cultural memory in the Hellenistic period. Collective and cultural memory consist of either very early events – foundation legends and early wars against barbarians (the Trojan War, the Persian Wars) – or very late events – events that occurred one or two generations earlier. The Peloponnesian War and other events of the 5th and 4th centuries BC are hardly ever mentioned.

C. Kremmydas: Thank you for your stimulating discussion of Hellenistic decrees as evidence for the actual practice of political oratory. Your discussion of the dossier from Xanthos and the appeal to kinship myth reminds me of Alexander's visit to Mallus in neighbouring Cilicia in 333. He appealed to their foundation by the hero Amphilochus and drew a link to their shared Argive origins. This enabled him to stop the stasis in their community and secure his back before the showdown with Darius. I wonder whether the manipulation of kinship myth and even history in diplomatic discourse might have been rendered easier by the practice of forging pseudo-historical documents attested already in the 4th century.

A. Chaniotis: This is in part an explanation for the production of forged or pseudo-historical documents. Another important reason is *enargeia*, the attempt of historians to make their narrative vivid through the quotation of documents. I suspect that the person who fabricated 'documents' such as the text of the Peace of Callias, the Themistocles' decree, and the Oath of Plataea was the local historian Kleidemos.

L. Pernot: Les documents cités présentent une remarquable homogénéité de style. Ils utilisent le même vocabulaire, les mêmes structures syntaxiques, et ont quelque chose de vaguement isocratique. C'est un style qui rend un son encomiastique autant que délibératif, d'ailleurs. Il reflète probablement une *koinê* stylistique des écoles de rhétorique.

A. Chaniotis: This is an interesting observation, and I am sure that you are right that there is a shared style. Historians, orators, and authors of decrees went through the same schools of rhetoric. Stratokles, the author of the honorific decree for Lykourgos as well as of many other decrees, was also a prominent orator. He was also fully aware of the power of inscriptions. As Stephen Tracy has pointed out, Stratokles had many decrees published on stone. In so doing, he ensured that the inscribers of these documents used blank spaces or line-initial position to give his name visual prominence on the stone.

D. Colomo: My question concerns the point you make in your contribution on the use of mythological narratives as exempla/historical arguments "in order to support hope". Did Hellenistic orators perceive and thus exploit in a different way mythology/'mythological' history on the one hand, and 'real' history on the other?

A. Chaniotis: This is a very interesting question concerning the relation between myth and history and Greek attitudes towards myth. One should avoid generalisations – e.g. the attitudes of intellectuals vary – but if we consider the public course, we may say that the main difference between myths or legends of heroes and what we consider as history is a difference in distance. Legends belong to a far more remote past than historical events and cannot be verified in the same manner as historical events. This affects their use in argumentation; they are more likely to be accepted as exempla than as support of legal claims. But they were nevertheless used for all kinds of purposes. For instance, in the "Lindian anagraphe" (*I.Lindos* 2), a list of dedications to Athena Lindia that aimed to propagate the sanctuary's fame, legendary dedicants (e.g. Herakles and Menelaos) appear alongside historical personalities (e.g. Amasis and Alexander the Great), in the proper chronological sequence.

C. Kremmydas: Could you please clarify the function of *enargeia* in connection with the use of forged, pseudo-historical documents? Do you mean that they were used as inartistic means of proofs, i.e. as witness testimonies, thus introducing an external authority into ambassadorial speeches, or were they used in order to evoke a particular emotional response? Or were these two functions indistinguishable?

A. Chaniotis: Yes, I think that their main function was to provide evidence, to serve as witnesses. E.g. as Plutarch mentions in the *Life of Theseus*, Kleidemos included in his history a forged decree of the Greeks from the time of Theseus. Kleidemos served as secretary of the council. He knew how to formulate a decree.

V

JEAN-LOUIS FERRARY

LES GRECS DEVANT LE SÉNAT ROMAIN

À la fin du IIe siècle av. J.-C., au terme de leur carrière politique, Ménippos et Polémaios de Colophon se virent élever
dans le sanctuaire de Claros deux monuments exceptionnels,
conformément à des décrets dont le texte a été presque intégra-
lement conservé.[1] Après avoir rappelé ses années de formation,
y compris un séjour à Athènes où il suivit l'enseignement des
meilleurs professeurs, le décret en l'honneur de Ménippos commence à faire l'éloge de son activité politique en indiquant
qu'il "alla en ambassade et donna les meilleurs avis en politique
et ne le céda en zèle à aucun des citoyens".[2] Aucune précision
n'est apportée ensuite sur les conseils qu'il donna dans l'Assemblée, mais l'accent est mis sur les ambassades, avec une grada-
tion bien soulignée :

"car nombreuses furent les ambassades qu'il accomplit auprès
des généraux, des questeurs et des Romains passés en Asie, nombreuses aussi celles qu'il fit auprès de la royauté attalide et d'un
grand nombre de cités, mais il a accompli les ambassades les plus
grandes et sur les sujets les plus pressants auprès du Sénat même
des dirigeants".[3]

---

[1] ROBERT (1989). Pour les deux monuments, voir ÉTIENNE / VARÈNE (2004)
93-104 et 135-141.

[2] ROBERT (1989), Ménippos (*SEG* XXXIX 1244), I, 12-14 : πρεσβεύων τε
καὶ συμβουλεύων τὰ κράτιστα καὶ φιλοτιμίας οὐθενὸς λειπόμενος τῶν πολιτῶν.
Trad. J. et L. ROBERT.

[3] ROBERT (1989), Ménippos, I, 14-19 : πολλὰς μὲν γὰρ πρεσβείας τετέλεχε
πρὸς στρατηγοὺς καὶ ταμίας καὶ τοὺς εἰς τὴν Ἀσίαν παραγινομένους Ῥωμαίων,
πολλὰς δὲ εἰς τὴν Ἀτταλικὴν βασιλείαν καὶ πόλεις οὐκ ὀλίγας, μεγίστας δὲ

De fait, Ménippos se rendit cinq fois en ambassade auprès du Sénat, et y obtint des résultats remarquables, qui sont ensuite longuement rappelés et célébrés.[4] On trouve des formulations tout à fait comparables dans le décret en l'honneur de Polémaios :

"(lac.) allant en ambassade et donnant les conseils les plus utiles, ne le cédant en rien pour le zèle. Car il a réalisé de façon satisfaisante des ambassades envers des chefs d'armée (gouverneurs), des questeurs et des cités …, mais les plus belles ambassades et sur les sujets les plus urgents sont celles qu'il fit utilement auprès des gouvernants romains eux-mêmes et du Sénat …".[5]

On se gardera bien entendu de surinterpréter et de généraliser les considérants de ces deux inscriptions, et d'en déduire que l'éloquence délibérative dans le cadre de l'Assemblée avait perdu son importance. Bien qu'elle ne fît pas partie du royaume attalide, une cité comme Colophon avait dû prendre des décisions de la plus grande gravité après la mort d'Attale III : puisqu'elle conserva sa liberté après la création de la province d'Asie bien qu'elle eût été quelque temps au pouvoir d'Aristonicos – Eumène III,[6] il faut admettre que la cité ne se rallia pas volontairement au prétendant, mais qu'elle l'affronta et fut prise de force ou livrée par trahison. Bien que le décret en son honneur n'en parle pas, Ménippos, qui avait déjà participé à des ambassades auprès du roi de Pergame (note 3), fut très vraisemblablement un de ceux qui exprimèrent leur avis à l'Assemblée dans

καὶ περὶ ἀναγκαιοτάτων πρεσβείας τετέλεκε πρὸς αὐτὴν τὴν τῶν ἡγουμένων σύγκλητον.
[4] ROBERT (1989), Ménippos, I, 20 - II, 7. Sur ces ambassades, outre ROBERT (1989), je me permets de renvoyer à FERRARY (1991). Sur les circonstances de la cinquième ambassade, toutefois, je me rallie maintenant à l'interprétation fournie en dernier lieu par SÁNCHEZ (2010).
[5] ROBERT (1989), Polémaios (*SEG* XXXIX 1243), II, 3-16 : πρεσβεύων μὲν καὶ συμβουλεύων τὰ συνφορώτατα, φιλοτιμίας δὲ οὐδεμίας λειπόμενος, ἱκανῶς μὲν γὰρ πρεσβείας τετέλεκεν πρὸς στρατηγοὺς καὶ ταμίας καὶ πόλεις, ἃς πάσας ἐκ τῶν ἰδίων ἀνελείπτως χορηγῶν διῴκησεν, καλλίστας δὲ καὶ περὶ ἀναγκαιοτάτων τετέλεκεν πρεσβείας πρὸς αὐτοὺς τοὺς ἡγουμένους Ῥωμαίους καὶ τὴν σύγκλητον.
[6] FLORUS 1, 35. Cf. ROBERT (1989) 29-31.

ces circonstances exceptionnelles. On ne peut manquer de rapprocher des deux textes de Claros un autre décret, pergaménien cette fois, en l'honneur d'un citoyen qui joua un rôle éminent à l'occasion de la guerre d'Aristonicos, Mènodoros fils de Mètrodoros.[7] Ce texte est de peu antérieur à ceux de Colophon (peut-être de deux décennies), et il met en valeur les deux mêmes aspects de l'activité politique de l'*honorandus* (outre l'exercice de magistratures et de liturgies), à savoir les fonctions de conseil et la participation à des ambassades.[8] Mais à l'opposé des textes clariens, ce sont les premières qui sont l'objet de fort intéressantes précisions, alors qu'aucun détail n'est fourni sur les ambassades. La raison en est simple : particulièrement actif dans les années 133-126, Mènodoros n'eut pas l'occasion d'aller en ambassade à Rome, alors qu'il joua un rôle important de conseil dans diverses instances, à Pergame même et dans le cadre de l'organisation de la province d'Asie.[9] En revanche, c'est après 126 et à l'occasion d'ambassades à Rome que Ménippos et Polémaios se distinguèrent tout particulièrement. Les deux décrets en leur honneur prouvent donc seulement, mais cela est suffisamment intéressant déjà, qu'une cité comme Colophon prit immédiatement conscience de l'importance des ambassades envoyées auprès du Sénat, parce que les décisions adoptées par ce dernier étaient souveraines, et pouvaient même être opposées aux abus des proconsuls d'Asie ou de ceux qui tentaient de les faire intervenir sans raison.

---

[7] WÖRRLE (2000) (*AE* 2000, 1377 ; *SEG* L 1211).

[8] Lignes 11-17 : participation à deux instances délibératives d'une importance exceptionnelle (voir note suivante) ; γενόμενος δὲ καὶ ἐμ πρεσβείαις...

[9] Voir WÖRRLE (2000), en particulier pour l'élection à Pergame, après la mort d'Attale III, de σύνεδροι τῶν ἀρίστων ἀνδρῶν (l. 12), puis la réunion d'un κατὰ τὴν Ῥωμαϊκὴν νομοθεσίαν βουλευτήριον (l. 13). Pour ce dernier, le rapprochement proposé par Wörrle avec le *consilium* convoqué en 167 par Paul-Émile à Amphipolis me paraît convaincant, et je serais tenté d'attribuer l'initiative de cette réunion à M. Perperna qui, après avoir fait prisonnier Aristonicos, organisa à Pergame, sur le modèle de celles d'Amphipolis, des fêtes célébrant sa victoire (*I.Priene* 108, l. 223-230 et 109, l. 91-94).

1. L'activité d'ambassadeur et les catégories de l'art oratoire

Nous venons de voir que les deux verbes *symbouleuein* et *presbeuein* résument en quelque sorte l'activité d'un citoyen constamment dévoué à sa patrie (outre les services qu'il peut rendre plus ponctuellement lorsqu'il exerce des magistratures ou des liturgies).

Le premier de ces verbes servit à caractériser, à côté du judiciaire et de l'épidictique, l'une des trois grandes catégories de l'art oratoire (*symbouleutikon, deliberatiuum* en latin), depuis Aristote au moins jusqu'au compilateur du *Corpus rhetoricum* hermogénien.[10] En revanche, le *logos presbeutikos* n'apparaît d'abord que chez des historiens, Polybe et Diodore, pour désigner l'une des catégories de discours qui apparaissent dans le récit historique, à côté de la harangue politique et de l'exhortation du général avant la bataille.[11] On ne trouve que tardivement la même expression dans un traité sur la rhétorique en général : au IIIe siècle ap. J.-C., et comme une sous-catégorie de discours, dans la *Division des discours épidictiques* de Ménandre le rhéteur. C'est que Ménandre considère en fait le *presbeutikos logos* comme une sorte de variante du *stéphanôtikos logos* accompagnant l'hommage de l'or coronaire, dans le cas d'une cité en détresse qui implore l'aide financière de l'Empereur, et que le *stéphanôtikos logos* lui-même n'est guère qu'une forme abrégée du *basilikos logos*, de l'éloge impérial.[12] On trouve

---

[10] ARIST. *Rhet.* 1, 3, 1358a-1359a. *Préambule à la rhétorique* 15, dans M. PATIL-LON (éd.), *Corpus rhetoricum*, I (daté par M. Patillon du IVe ou Ve siècle de notre ère).

[11] Dans le cadre de sa polémique contre Timée, POLYB. 12, 25a, 3 (δημη-γόριαι, παρακλήσεις, πρεσβευτικοὶ λόγοι) et 25i, 3 (συμβουλευτικοί, παρακλη-τικοί, πρεσβευτικοὶ λόγοι) ; dans une critique de l'excès d'insertion de discours dans le récit historique, DIOD. 20, 1, 1-3 (δημηγόριαι, πρεσβευτικοὶ λόγοι). Dans tous ces textes, il s'agit de caractériser les types de discours qui ont leur place dans l'historiographie, non de présenter une division générale de l'art du discours.

[12] MEN. RHET. 2, 12, 422-423 RUSSELL / WILSON (*stéphanôtikos*) ; 2, 13, 423-424 RUSSELL / WILSON (*presbeutikos* : ἐὰν δὲ ὑπὲρ πόλεως καμνούσης δέῃ πρεσβεῦσαι, ἐρεῖς μὲν καὶ ταῦτα ἃ προείρηται ἐν τῷ στεφανωτικῷ, πανταχοῦ δὲ τὸ τῆς φιλανθρωπίας τοῦ βασιλέως αὐξήσεις).

là le reflet, simultanément, du développement de la rhétorique de l'éloge dans le contexte de la Seconde sophistique, et d'une évolution des rapports entre les cités et le pouvoir central, privilégiant les formes de l'hommage et de la supplique. Il n'y a pas trop à s'étonner que le *presbeutikos logos* n'ait pas bénéficié d'une réflexion approfondie chez les auteurs d'*artes*. Dans les cités démocratiques, l'activité politique se déroulait avant tout au sein de l'Assemblée, par la prise de parole qui était permise à tout citoyen, et en particulier par la proposition d'un décret ou une intervention contraire à une proposition de décret. L'envoi d'ambassadeurs n'était lui-même que la conséquence d'un décret dont ils étaient porteurs, et qui limitait fortement la marge de négociation dont ils pouvaient jouir.[13] L'éloquence délibérative, d'autre part, étant donné la variété des sujets qu'elle était amenée à aborder, se prêtait assez mal aux pratiques de rédaction des traités de rhétorique, dans le domaine en particulier de l'invention et de la disposition. Il ne semble pas non plus qu'elle ait fait l'objet de développements et de progrès comparables à ceux que connut la rhétorique judiciaire à l'époque hellénistique (avec l'apport d'Hermagoras à la théorie de l'état de cause) ou la rhétorique épidictique au temps de la Seconde sophistique.

On notera aussi que les discours des ambassadeurs des cités devant le Sénat ne relevaient pas exclusivement du genre délibératif, et qu'il y avait des cas, assez nombreux, où le Sénat était plutôt approché pour arbitrer un conflit entre deux parties.

---

[13] Ménandre le rhéteur n'omet pas de préciser qu'au terme du *stéphanôtikos* ou du *presbeutikos logos*, l'ambassadeur doit prier l'Empereur de bien vouloir accepter la lecture du texte du décret (respectivement εἶτα ἀξιώσεις ἀναγνωσθῆναι τὸ ψήφισμα, et εἶτα ἀξιώσεις ἐπινεῦσαι αὐτὸν δεχθῆναι τὸ ψήφισμα). Dans les s. c. d'époque républicaine, dans les lettres des magistrats puis de l'Empereur il est fréquemment indiqué que le décret a bien été remis, et que le propos des ambassadeurs était conforme à sa teneur. Il n'y avait d'ailleurs là rien de nouveau, et dans les décrets de la haute époque hellénistique déjà les ambassadeurs sont loués d'avoir parlé conformément aux instructions et à la teneur de la lettre dont ils sont porteurs. Cela n'exclut pas, toutefois, que les discours des ambassadeurs aient conservé une réelle fonction épidictique et même sumbouleutique : voir les justes remarques de RUBINSTEIN (2013).

Il est vrai, et on l'a souvent fait remarquer, que le Sénat renvoyait volontiers l'arbitrage à une cité neutre, qu'il s'agisse d'estimer le montant de dommages et intérêts, ou de trancher un litige frontalier. Mais on n'a pas toujours relevé que les Romains n'avaient pas généralisé la pratique grecque de l'arbitrage international, et que le Sénat imposait en fait une procédure en deux temps caractéristique du procès privé romain, et étrangère à la tradition grecque. La décision sénatoriale correspond à la phase *in iure* qui est de la compétence du préteur : c'est ce dernier qui décide de la recevabilité de la plainte, qui donne un juge ou des arbitres, mais qui définit aussi dans la *formula* les principes selon lesquels le jugement sera rendu ; dans la phase *in iudicio*, le magistrat cède la place au juge/arbitre, mais ce dernier est lié par la *formula* du magistrat. Le Sénat joue le rôle du préteur : si le délit est patent, il peut se contenter de laisser à un arbitre le soin d'estimer la compensation financière qui devra être versée (*arbitrium litis aestimandae*) ;[14] sinon, il confie à l'arbitre le soin de rendre une sentence sur le fond, mais après avoir bien défini les principes dont il devra s'inspirer. Ainsi, en cas de litige territorial, l'arbitre n'est-il pas autorisé à choisir entre les arguments des parties, tentées de remonter parfois jusqu'à des traditions mythiques : le plus souvent, il doit veiller à ce que chaque partie recouvre les territoires dont elle était légitimement propriétaire au moment où elle est entrée dans l'amitié du peuple romain.

Ce n'était pas le seul risque de malentendus entre les Grecs et la puissance hégémonique, et il faut rappeler un certain nombre d'autres spécificités générales qui dérogeaient à la pratique grecque des ambassades. La première est que les ambassadeurs

---

[14] C'est ainsi qu'il faut comprendre les exigences romaines formulées par M. Aemilius Lepidus à Abydos en 200, et qui ne pouvaient que scandaliser Philippe V : voir FERRARY (1988) 47-48. C'est aussi cette procédure qui fut utilisée pour sanctionner la conduite des Athéniens envers Oropos : l'énormité de l'amende infligée par Sicyone eut comme conséquence l'ambassade des scolarques et une réduction de la somme, mais le principe d'un dédommagement accordé à Oropos remontait à la première décision du Sénat, et ne pouvait être remis en cause.

ne parlaient pas devant l'Assemblée, comme dans une cité grecque, mais exclusivement devant le Sénat, c'est-à-dire une audience d'une tout autre nature : Polybe déjà le fit remarquer, en ajoutant que cela pouvait contribuer à donner aux ambassadeurs la fausse impression que les institutions romaines seraient celles d'une pure aristocratie.[15] Il faut ajouter que, même si beaucoup de sénateurs, dès le IIe siècle av. J.-C. en tout cas, devaient pouvoir suivre l'argumentation d'un discours en grec, le sénat exigea pendant assez longtemps la médiation d'un interprète. Nous n'avons aucune raison de mettre en doute l'information selon laquelle Apollonius Molon, ambassadeur des Rhodiens en 81, aurait été le premier à qui cette obligation n'aurait pas été imposée, puisque les trois scholarques envoyés en 155 par Athènes avaient encore dû recourir aux services du sénateur C. Acilius. Encore est-il loin d'être certain que l'honneur fait à Molon (et à travers lui aux Rhodiens qui avaient été contre Mithridate des alliés très précieux) ait ensuite été généralisé immédiatement à toutes les ambassades grecques.[16] Nous ne savons pas comment intervenaient les interprètes, s'ils traduisaient après chaque période oratoire ou s'ils donnaient seulement un résumé après chaque grande partie du discours. En tout cas, il ne fait guère de doute que cette pratique ne permettait guère à la puissance rhétorique des ambassadeurs de donner toute son ampleur. Si les

[15] POLYB. 6, 13, 7-9. Le décret en l'honneur d'Hégésias de Lampsaque fournit un parallèle intéressant : désireux de se prévaloir de la recommandation d'une vieille amie des Romains, les ambassadeurs de Lampsaque se rendirent d'abord à Massalia avant de se présenter devant le Sénat : ils y furent reçus par un organe aristocratique : le Conseil des Six-Cents (*IK* 6-*Lampsakos*, 4, l. 43-46). Pour Cicéron encore, Massalia sera le type même de la bonne aristocratie (*Rep.* 1, 43).

[16] Ambassadeurs athéniens de 155 : GELL. 6, 14, 8 ; MACR. *Sat.* 1, 5, 14. – Apollonius Molon : VAL. MAX. 2, 2, 3. Une autre indication précieuse est fournie par CIC. *Fin.* 5, 89 : *ita, quemadmodum in senatu semper est aliquis qui interpretem postulet, sic isti nobis cum interprete audiendi sunt (Stoici).* Ce dialogue est censé se dérouler en 79, et il ne semble donc pas que le privilège personnel accordé à Molon ait immédiatement entraîné un changement général de la pratique sénatoriale.

philosophes de 155 attirèrent les jeunes Romains au point d'indisposer Caton, ce fut à l'occasion de conférences faites en marge de leur fonction officielle, et non lors de leur audience devant le Sénat.

Le discours prononcé en grec devant le Sénat par Molon est probablement le *Contre les Cauniens* qui fut diffusé et pouvait encore se lire du temps de Strabon.[17] Le cas n'est pas unique : un précédent ambassadeur rhodien, Astymédès, avait publié un texte écrit du discours prononcé lors de son ambassade de 167, et peut-être aussi le second discours qu'il prononça en 164.[18] Il devait cette fois s'agir de textes réélaborés (ne serait-ce que pour faire disparaître toute intervention de l'interprète), et destinés à être diffusés à Rhodes et dans le monde grec en général. Il ne reste pratiquement rien, on le sait, de la production oratoire grecque d'époque hellénistique, mais il est d'autant plus intéressant d'avoir la certitude que furent diffusés un certain nombre de discours prononcés devant le Sénat, ou des textes réélaborant ces discours.

2. Rappeler les services rendus aux Romains sans s'exposer aux risques d'être accusé de *superbia*

Une très intéressante inscription découverte à Samothrace a été publiée en 2003 par K. Clinton, et sa signification pleinement

---

[17] STRAB. 14, 2, 3, 652C. Le titre pourrait aussi convenir, à la rigueur, à un discours prononcé lorsque les Cauniens obtinrent de devenir tributaires des Romains plutôt que des Rhodiens (CIC. *Q Fr.* 1, 1, 33), mais il est beaucoup plus vraisemblable que le discours publié ait été couronné de succès, et que ce soit celui qui fut prononcé en 81 par Molon devant le Sénat *de Rhodiorum praemiis* (CIC. *Brut.* 312).

[18] Polybe ne le précise que pour le premier discours (30, 4, 11), par lequel Astymédès put penser qu'il avait conjuré le risque d'une guerre. Le second est celui qui permit une normalisation des relations entre les deux Républiques, et Polybe en connaissait manifestement très bien le contenu (30, 31). Il me paraît assez vraisemblable que les deux furent publiés, Polybe ne le signalant que pour le premier, parce que c'est celui dont il critiquait l'argumentation et dont il jugeait que l'auteur n'aurait pas dû le diffuser (30, 4, 12-17).

explicitée l'année suivante par M. Wörrle.[19] Sous le règne de Claude, à l'occasion très probablement de la création de la province de Thrace, la cité libre et fédérée de Maronée, dont certains privilèges étaient menacés, envoya à l'Empereur une ambassade qui obtint, en rappelant sa fidélité à Rome et ce qu'elle lui avait coûté pendant la guerre de Mithridate, la pleine restitution de ses droits. À la suite de ce succès, l'Assemblée vota un décret pourvu d'une validité permanente qui lui donnait force de loi, décret qui permettait, en cas de nouvelle menace contre les privilèges de la cité, que tout citoyen qui s'inscrirait par écrit et prêterait serment fût autorisé à partir en ambassade auprès de l'Empereur, sans que quiconque pût faire obstruction à cette initiative. Il s'agit d'une mesure sans parallèle connu, et dont la signification politique est malheureusement obscurcie par le manque total de précisions sur les conditions dans lesquelles l'ambassade envoyée auprès de Claude était partie.[20] Je m'intéresserai seulement ici à l'argumentation développée par ces ambassadeurs :

"alors que nous lui avions envoyé une ambassade et avions montré le soutien de la cité envers le peuple romain et les infortunes qu'a endurées précédemment le peuple de Maronée à cause de son amitié pour les Romains, puisqu'il est devenu ami et allié immédiatement dès l'établissement de leur hégémonie, et qu'après cela il a enduré de voir la destruction de la ville, d'un périmètre de soixante stades, la perte de ses enfants, le pillage, le fait d'être prisonnier et les autres malheurs à leur tour afin qu'aucun des droits des Romains ne soit lésé, en échange de quoi il a été jugé par les décrets du Sénat allié et ami, partie d'un traité sanctionné par des libations, et il a reçu sa liberté et ses lois avec ses autres privilèges, ce qui a été montré par le Sénat au moyen de décrets, par les empereurs au moyen de leurs réponses, – (Claude) a répondu

---

[19] CLINTON (2003) ; WÖRRLE (2004) ; *AE* 2003, 1559 et *SEG* LIII 659, qui tiennent compte de l'article de Wörrle.

[20] C'est pourquoi il ne me paraît pas impossible que M. Wörrle, dans son étude au demeurant remarquable, ait eu tendance à donner une interprétation trop résolument antidémocratique du décret.

qu'il est convenable qu'une telle cité soit ornée d'un remerciement perpétuel…", [21]

argumentation que l'on retrouve résumée dans le décret perpétuel :

"Plaise au Conseil et au peuple de désigner une ambassade qui, arrivée auprès du divin empereur Auguste César, devra le saluer de la part de la cité et, après avoir exprimé sa joie que lui et sa maison aillent bien et que ses affaires et celles du peuple romain marchent au mieux, et avoir mentionné tous les droits de la cité, à lui et au sacré Sénat, devra demander avec toute requête et supplication que nous soient conservés notre liberté, nos lois, notre ville, notre territoire et tous nos privilèges que nos ancêtres et nous-mêmes détenons pour les avoir reçus d'eux, afin que nous, qui avons toujours et constamment conservé notre dévouement et notre fidélité envers les Romains, nous jouissions toujours de leur gratitude pour cela." [22]

Le premier de ces deux textes, en particulier, nous permet de nous faire une idée de la rhétorique d'un ambassadeur grec

[21] Fr. I, l. 5-16 : πρεσβευσάντων ἡμῶν ἐπ'αὐτὸν καὶ δηλωσάντω[ν τὴν] τῆς πόλεως πρὸς τὸν δῆμον τὸν Ῥωμαίων ὑπόστασιν καὶ τὰς τύχας [τὰς πρότε]ρον ἃς ὑπέμεινεν ὁ Μαρωνειτῶν δῆμος διὰ τὴν πρὸς Ῥωμαί[ους φιλί]αν, εὐθέως ἅμα τ<ῆ> τῆς ἡγεμονίας αὐτῶν συστάσει φίλος καὶ σ[ύμμαχος γε]νόμενος καὶ μετὰ ταῦτα ὑπομείνας ἐπιδεῖν κατασκαφὴν μὲ[ν τῆς ἐξήκον]τα σταδίου τὸ περίμετρον πόλεως, τέκνων δὲ ἀπολήας καὶ λε[ηλασίαν κ]αὶ αἰχμαλωσίαν καὶ τὰς ἄλλας τὰς κατὰ μέρος συμφοράς ἵνα μη[δὲν τῶν πρὸς] Ῥωμαίους θραύσῃ δικαίων, ἀνθ' ὧν σύμμαχος μὲν καὶ φίλος ὑπὸ [τῆς συνκλή]του διὰ τῶν δογμάτων καὶ ἐνσύνθηκος καὶ ἔνσπονδος ἐκρίθη, ἐλευθε[ρίαν δὲ καὶ νό]μους μετὰ τῶν ἄλλων φιλανθρώπων ἔλαβε ἃ δεδήλωται ὑπὸ τῆ[ς συνκλή]του διὰ δογμάτων καὶ ὑπὸ τῶν αὐτοκρατόρων διὰ τῶν ἀποκριμάτ[ων, ἀπεκρίνα]το ὡς τὴν τοιαύτην πόλιν ἄξιόν ἐστι αἰωνίῳ χάριτι κεκοσμῆσθαι… (traduction de M. SÈVE dans l'AE).

[22] Fr. II, l. 10-20 : δεδόχθαι τῇ βουλῇ καὶ τῷ δήμῳ ᾑρῆσθαι πρεσβήαν ἥτις ἀφικομένη πρὸς αὐτοκράτορα θεὸν σεβαστὸν Καίσαρα ἀσπάσεταί τε αὐτὸν παρὰ τῆς πόλεως καὶ συνησθεῖσα ἐπὶ τῷ ἐρρῶσθαι αὐτὸν πανοίκιον καὶ τὰ πράγματα αὐτῷ τε καὶ τῷ δήμῳ τῷ Ῥωμαίων κατὰ τὸ κράτιστον χωρεῖν, παραθεμένη τὰ τῆς πόλεως δίκαια πάντα αὐτῷ τε καὶ τῇ ἱερᾷ συνκλήτῳ δεήσεται μετὰ πάσης ἐντεύξεως καὶ ἱκεσίας τήν τε ἐλε[υ]θερίαν ἡμεῖν καὶ τοὺς νόμους καὶ τὴν πόλιν καὶ τὴν χώραν καὶ τἆλλα φιλάνθρωπα πάντα ἃ οἵ τε πρόγονοι ἡμῶν καὶ ἡμεῖς λαβόντες παρ' αὐτῶν ἔσχομεν ταῦθ' ἡμεῖν φυλάξαι, ἵν' οἱ πάντοτε καὶ ἀδιαλείπτως τὴν πρὸς Ῥωμαίους εὔνοιαν καὶ πίστιν φυλάξαντες πάντοτε τῆς ἐξ αὐτῶν διὰ ταῦτα χάριτος ἀπολάωμεν.

dans le cas, particulièrement important, où il s'agit d'obtenir le maintien ou la restitution de privilèges obtenus dans le passé et qui se trouvent menacés. Sur le fond, il s'agit de rappeler que la cité a été favorable à Rome depuis les premiers contacts entre les deux peuples, et que ce dévouement est resté constant comme en témoignent les s. c. et les lettres des Princes. C'est l'argument qui est repris dans le second passage : à la constance de l'*eunoia* et de la *pistis* des Maronitains doit répondre celle de la *charis* des Romains, ainsi que l'avait d'ailleurs reconnu Claude lui-même. Mais ce principe général est accompagné, dans le résumé de l'argumentation qui fut utilisée avec succès auprès de Claude, d'un exemple qui semble avoir été particulièrement développé : l'épisode où Maronée, par fidélité envers les Romains, vit son territoire ravagé, la ville prise de force et une partie de la population réduite en servitude. Aucune précision chronologique n'est fournie, mais cela se produisit sans aucun doute pendant la première guerre de Mithridate.[23] Le discours des ambassadeurs auprès de Claude devait contenir des précisions sur le contexte historique, comme il pouvait faire mention d'autres épisodes des relations entre les deux cités (même s'il dut rester volontairement plus vague sur les premiers rapports entre Rome et Maronée, car l'idée d'une amitié et d'une alliance aussi anciennes que l'établissement de l'hégémonie romaine dans le nord de l'Égée tient plus de la reconstruction que de la réalité historique).[24] Le résumé qu'en fournit

---

[23] C'est ce qu'a bien vu déjà CLINTON (2003) 385-389.

[24] Après avoir été évacuée par Philippe V sur l'ordre des Romains, Maronée, comme Ainos, était repassée sous domination macédonienne lors de la troisième guerre de Macédoine, et refusa d'ouvrir son port à la flotte romaine (LIV. 43, 7, 10). Après Pydna, les deux cités furent demandées au Sénat par Attale, le frère du roi Eumène, et elles lui furent accordées en un premier temps, avant que le Sénat se ravisât et proclamât leur liberté lorsqu'Attale refusa de dénoncer les prétendues ambiguïtés de la politique d'Eumène (POLYB. 30, 3, 3-7). L'authenticité du récit polybien peut être mise en doute sur certains détails, mais non la succession des deux s. c. contradictoires. La thèse d'une amitié et d'une alliance fidèlement préservées par Maronée depuis l'établissement de l'hégémonie romaine apparaît donc pour le moins discutable. C'est ce qui explique que le texte trouvé à Samothrace n'ait pas mis fin, en particulier, à la controverse sur la date du traité

le décret montre en tout cas, me semble-t-il, que l'évocation de l'épisode mithridatique avait reçu un relief tout particulier, et suggère une véritable hypotypose qui redonnait vie à ce moment dramatique de l'histoire de la cité, et visait à susciter la pitié du Prince et du Sénat.[25] L'argumentaire de Maronée censé prendre sous Claude une forme définitive n'est pas sans faire penser au dossier qui fut gravé à Aphrodisias à l'époque sévérienne (après la guerre civile qui assura la victoire de Septime-Sévère, et alors que la confirmation des privilèges de la cité avait revêtu une urgence particulière) : même souci de réunir une collection de sénatus-consultes et de réponses impériales établissant puis confirmant et précisant les privilèges de la cité ; même accent mis sur des périodes où la cité avait donné la preuve incontestable de sa fidélité au pouvoir romain. Dans le cas d'Aphrodisias, il s'agissait en particulier de la résistance opposée à l'armée parthe conduite en 40 par Labienus, mais aussi, encore une fois, de la guerre mithridatique, lorsque la cité avait sans tarder envoyé des renforts militaires à Q. Oppius, en l'assurant du total dévouement du peuple, prêt à périr plutôt que d'abandonner la cause romaine.[26]

Les cités grecques avaient intérêt à faire valoir le souvenir de leur fidélité et (éventuellement) de leur grandeur passée, mais

---

entre Rome et Maronée publié en 1983 (*SEG* XXXV 823) : Clinton (2003) 386 y a vu une confirmation d'une datation en 167, et Wörrle au contraire ([2004] 157 et n. 19) celle d'une datation syllanienne. Cette dernière hypothèse me paraît la plus vraisemblable, et l'on notera que les mots ἐνσύνθηκος καὶ ἔνσπονδος n'apparaissent qu'après le rappel des dommages subis pendant la guerre de Mithridate. Cette note doit beaucoup à une conversation avec A. Chaniotis dans le cadre des *Entretiens*.

[25] Cf. Cic. *Inu.* 1, 107 (dans une liste des *loci* de l'appel à la pitié, *conquestio*) : *quintus per quem omnia ante oculos singillatim incommoda ponuntur, ut uideatur is qui audit uidere et re quoque ipsa, quasi assit, non uerbis solum ad misericordiam ducatur.* Voir aussi *Rhet. Her.* 4, 68 (*demonstratio*). Sur l'importance de l'*énargeia* dans l'éloquence hellénistique, voir Chaniotis (2013).

[26] Reynolds (1982), n° 2 (l. 11-14 : ὅτι πᾶς ὁ δῆμος ἡμῶν σὺν γυναιξὶ καὶ τέκνοις καὶ τῷ παντὶ βίῳ ἐτ{οῖ}μος παραβάλλεσθαι ὑπὲρ Κοίντου καὶ τῶν Ῥωμαίων πραγμάτων καὶ ὅτι χωρὶς τῆς Ῥωμαίων ἡγεμονίας οὐδὲ ζῆν προαιρούμεθα) et 3. Pour l'appartenance de ces deux documents au dossier du 'mur des archives', et la date probable de la gravure de ce dossier, voir les remarques de Bowersock (1984) 50-51.

elles devaient en même temps veiller à ne pas être taxées d'arrogance ou d'orgueil.[27] Pour cela, il était prudent et habile de rappeler les éloges qu'avaient pu leur décerner les Romains eux-mêmes, dans les documents où ils leur avaient décerné récompenses et privilèges : même si ces sénatus-consultes ou ces lettres reprenaient eux-mêmes pour l'essentiel un argumentaire mis en forme par les cités, ils leur avaient donné la sanction des plus hautes autorités romaines, et il ne devait pas paraître outrecuidant de s'en prévaloir.

Rappeler les services rendus aux Romains en se mettant trop en avant exposait en revanche au reproche de *superbia*. Les Étoliens en avaient fait l'expérience, qui avaient cru, même après que leur allié Antiochos eut quitté la Grèce, pouvoir se réclamer du rôle qu'ils avaient joué dans la guerre et la victoire contre Philippe. Les Rhodiens aussi en firent l'expérience lorsqu'ils prétendirent, pendant la troisième guerre de Macédoine, pouvoir amener les deux belligérants à négocier, et éviter une victoire absolue qui ferait des Romains les seuls maîtres du monde. Dans les deux cas, il s'agissait d'alliés qui avaient été récompensés pour les services rendus lors des guerres précédentes, et que les Romains décidèrent de châtier et d'humilier avec d'autant plus de détermination qu'ils les jugeaient coupables d'ingratitude et de perfidie. Les Étoliens, finalement, durent recourir à l'intercession d'ambassadeurs athéniens et rhodiens, et en particulier de l'Athénien Léon : c'est dans ce discours qu'apparaît pour la première fois l'idée que la politique condamnée par les Romains ne devrait être imputée qu'à un nombre restreint d'hommes politiques qui auraient entraîné dans leur sillage les masses populaires et versatiles, et qu'il suffisait d'éliminer cette minorité pour ramener la paix et l'obéissance. C'était là un discours que le Sénat et les magistrats romains étaient volontiers prêts à accepter, et que l'on retrouve assez fréquemment par la

---

[27] On trouve un avertissement de même nature en ce qui concerne l'éloquence judiciaire dans CIC. *Inu.* 1, 22 (à propos de l'exorde) : *beniuolentia quattuor ex locis comparatur, ab nostra, ab aduersariorum, ab iudicum persona, a causa. Ab nostra si de nostris factis et officiis sine arrogantia dicemus...*

suite.[28] Quant aux ambassadeurs rhodiens après Pydna, ils adoptèrent les signes extérieurs du deuil et de la supplication, et dans un premier temps, ils tentèrent de calmer le Sénat en essayant de prouver que leur conduite avait été plutôt moins répréhensible que celle d'autres peuples grecs, tout en prévenant leurs compatriotes de la nécessité d'obéir en tout aux ordres du Sénat ; dans un second temps, ils se contentèrent d'implorer les Romains en soulignant la gravité des mesures qui avaient été prises à leur encontre et en les suppliant de les recevoir de nouveau dans leur amitié.[29] Les analyses polybiennes sont précieuses, mais on ne peut attendre qu'elles aient été objectives alors que lui-même, déporté à Rome, puis entré dans la clientèle des fils de Paul-Émile, se trouvait dans la difficile situation de devoir trouver cohérence et dignité dans ses jugements sur l'hégémonie romaine et sur la politique des Grecs. Même si l'école d'éloquence rhodienne n'avait pas encore atteint son apogée, les ambassadeurs de l'île devaient avoir une bonne formation, et connaître les raffinements de la rhétorique hellénistique dont témoignent, faut de textes grecs de cette époque, la *Rhétorique à Hérennius* et le traité cicéronien *Sur l'invention*, tous deux datables des années 80 av. J.-C. Toute une hiérarchie de lignes de défense avait été définie dans les cas où il était impossible de nier la réalité du fait et même sa qualification : transfert ou rejet de responsabilité, excuse, supplication.[30] C'est dans ce cadre que les ambassadeurs rhodiens affinèrent progressivement leur argumentation.

Un peu plus d'un siècle plus tard, et en dépit de la fidélité exemplaire qu'ils avaient entre temps montrée pendant la guerre de Mithridate, les Rhodiens ne parvinrent pas à prévenir une nouvelle catastrophe, lorsque Cassius persuada Brutus d'éliminer la puissance navale des Rhodiens et des Lyciens, considérés

---

[28] POLYB. 21, 31, 5-16. Cf. THORNTON (2013) 38-39 (cet argument est repris en particulier par Astymédès : 30, 31, 13-15).

[29] POLYB. 30, 4-5 (cf. THORNTON [2013] 21-22) et 30, 31.

[30] Ainsi que le fait remarquer CIC. *Inu.* 1, 24, *in iudicium non uenit (deprecatio), at in senatum aut ante imperatorem et consilium talis causa potest uenire.*

comme favorables aux triumvirs, avant d'affronter ces derniers.
Le récit le plus détaillé est celui d'Appien, manifestement puisé
à bonne source, avec des discours très largement réécrits, mais
qui doivent contenir une part de vérité. Une première ambassade auprès de Cassius aurait été empreinte d'un orgueil et
d'une arrogance qui ne pouvaient que conduire à son échec.
Plus intéressante est une seconde ambassade, confiée au rhéteur
Archélaos qui avait été le professeur d'éloquence de Cassius, et
qui veilla à rappeler, sur un ton plus mesuré, ce que les Romains
devaient aux Rhodiens et ce que Cassius devait à son ancien professeur. Mais le Romain rejeta résolument ces arguments, et
il n'hésita pas à punir durement la ville après s'en être emparé.[31]
Le traitement infligé à Rhodes par Cassius fait penser à celui qui
l'avait été par César à Massalia, pourtant la plus ancienne alliée
de Rome en Occident : la rhétorique pouvait aider à calmer la
colère d'un vainqueur, mais elle n'avait aucun poids lorsque la
guerre faisait encore rage, et que les chefs de guerre romains
n'étaient sensibles qu'au langage de la reddition.

3. Docere dans la rhétorique des ambassadeurs ?

Les analyses qui précèdent ont beaucoup mis l'accent sur le
recours aux émotions, et notamment sur l'appel à la miséri-
corde et à la pitié, et nos sources historiques vont en ce sens,
aimant à présenter les ambassadeurs grecs devant le Sénat dans

---

[31] App. *B Ciu.* 4, 65, 276 - 4, 73, 312. Première ambasse : 66, 280-281 ;
ambassade d'Archélaos : 67, 283 - 70, 299. L'argument tiré des services rendus par
Rome (67, 286 : ἐν Ῥώμῃ δέ, (ἔμαθες) ὅσα ὑμῖν αὐτοῖς καθ᾽ ἑτέρων καὶ Ἀντιόχου
τοῦ μεγάλου συνεμαχήσαμεν, ὧν εἰσὶν ὑπὲρ ἡμῶν ἀνάγραπτοι στῆλαι παρ᾽ ὑμῖν)
est en quelque sorte annulé par Cassius en raison des récompenses que Rhodes a
déjà reçues en échange, et du fait que l'assistance prêtée aux Romains pour aug-
menter leur empire ne serait pas comparable au refus de les secourir alors qu'ils
sont menacés par la tyrannie (70, 295 : σὺ δέ, εἰ μέν ποτε ἡμῖν περικτωμένοις τι
συνεπράξατε, ὧν εὐεργεσίας καὶ μισθοὺς ἀντικεκόμισθέ που, καταλογίζῃ, ὅτι δὲ
ἡμῖν ἐς τὴν ἐλευθερίαν καὶ σωτηρίαν ἀδικουμένοις οὐ συμμαχεῖτε, ἐπιλανθάνῃ).
Le second argument de Cassius est peut-être ce qui explique la curieuse absence de
toute référence à la guerre de Mithridate dans le discours d'Archélaos : Appien en
ce cas manifesterait un biais en faveur du Romain.

une position de suppliants espérant obtenir le pardon de leurs erreurs et de leur légèreté. Il est pourtant bien évident que les choses sont plus complexes, et que, dans bien des cas, les ambassadeurs l'emportèrent aussi *docendo*, et non pas (seulement) *mouendo* (pour reprendre la terminologie cicéronienne du *De oratore*). Telle est en particulier, au milieu du IIe siècle, la conviction de Polybe :

> "lorsqu'un ami fidèle leur rappelle ses droits, ils font généralement tout leur possible pour corriger leurs erreurs",

et encore :

> "jusqu'alors du moins ils attachaient une importance particulière au respect des serments, des traités, et de la loyauté envers leurs alliés... Les Achéens devaient donc, ou bien admettre que le droit ne comptait pour rien aux yeux des Romains, ou bien, s'ils n'osaient pas dire une pareille chose, soutenir leurs droits et ne pas se laisser faire, surtout lorsqu'ils pouvaient opposer aux Romains les raisons les plus solides et les plus honorables."[32]

C'est pourquoi Polybe attribue une grande importance au soin que prirent Philopoemen, puis Lycortas et lui-même (encore après la guerre d'Achaïe) d'instruire (διδάσκειν) les Romains des droits des Achéens, et d'essayer de les convaincre de corriger de mauvaises décisions.[33] Et c'est pourquoi, avec une amère ironie, il écrit que l'ambassade de Callicratès fut la première où l'on prétendit instruire le Sénat de *ses* intérêts en le persuadant d'abaisser ceux qui œuvraient pour le bien public et d'élever ceux qui se rangeaient systématiquement du côté des Romains.[34]

Quelques inscriptions peuvent être versées à ce dossier. Dans un décret des clérouques athéniens de Myrina, et dans un

---

[32] POLYB. 24, 10, 12 ; 24, 13, 3 et 5 (propos prêtés à Philopoemen dans le célèbre parallèle entre sa politique et celle d'Aristainos). Voir FERRARY (1988) 297-299.

[33] POLYB. 24, 8, 3-4 (Lycortas : διδάξῃ) ; 39, 3, 4 (Polybe : διδάσκειν) ; 39, 3, 5 (Philopoemen : διδάσκειν καὶ πείθειν). Voir aussi 22, 11, 6 (διδάξοντας) et 22, 12, 1 (διδασκόντων τὴν σύγκλητον).

[34] POLYB. 24, 10, 3 (διδαχθεῖσα).

contexte malheureusement lacunaire, on trouve les mots διδάξας τὴν σύγκλητον ὡς ἦσαν (lacune).[35] Le décret en l'honneur de Mènodoros de Pergame, dont j'ai déjà parlé, rappelle qu'il fut élu stratège de la cité alors que Manius Aquillius et les dix légats étaient en Asie, et qu'il "montra face à eux, à propos de la cité, son franc-parler, en présentant en faveur de sa patrie une argumentation fondée en droit".[36] Il agit alors en tant que magistrat et non qu'ambassadeur, mais sa conduite était tout à fait dans la ligne prônée par Polybe.

Un peu plus tard, pour revenir aux décrets en l'honneur de Ménippos et Polémaios dont nous sommes partis, il est bien évident que l'obtention de s. c. dont certains désavouèrent l'action du proconsul d'Asie dut exiger un exposé convaincant des droits de la cité. Nous constatons néanmoins l'absence d'un verbe comme διδάσκειν, tandis que l'accent est mis sur l'art qu'eurent les deux Colophoniens de gagner la confiance de grands aristocrates et d'en faire des patrons efficaces de la cité :

"ainsi donc recommandé aux plus grands des Romains à cause de sa valeur en tout, et allant en ambassade en leur nom, et étant jugé digne de confiance, (Ménippos) est devenu illustre dans beaucoup de villes grecques et ayant acquis (les Romains) comme patrons authentiques (véritables) de la ville, il a été extrêmement utile au peuple auprès des gouvernants chez lesquels sont les services les plus nécessaires pour tous les hommes" ;

Polémaios

"obtint audience des chefs romains et, s'étant montré digne de leur amitié, il a procuré le fruit de celle-ci à ses concitoyens, ayant établi des liens de patronat pour sa patrie avec les plus éminents des hommes."[37]

---

[35] *IG* II² 1224, l. 11. Cette inscription est traditionnellement datée des lendemains de Pydna, mais D. Knoepfler vient d'en proposer une nouvelle interprétation, dans le contexte de la guerre d'Achaïe (communication au colloque qui s'est tenu à Athènes en février 2015, en l'honneur de Miltiade Hatzopoulos).

[36] *AE* 2000, 1377 ; *SEG* L 1211, l. 17-21 : μετὰ παρρησίας δικαίως τὸν ὑπὲρ τῆς πατρίδος [προ]σ[αγόμε]νος λόγον.

[37] Ménippos, III, 5-13 : τοιγαροῦν διὰ τὴν ἐμ πᾶσιν ἀρετὴν τοῖς μεγίστοις Ῥωμαίων συσταθεὶς αὐτός τε πρεσβεύων ὑπὲρ αὐτῶν καὶ πίστεως ἀξιούμενος

La *paideia* acquise par les deux hommes, et achevée à Athènes pour Ménippos, à Rhodes pour Polémaios, avait dû leur assurer une formation rhétorique qui leur fut utile dans leurs ambassades. Mais l'accent est mis finalement plus encore sur des qualités morales qui leur gagnèrent la confiance (*pistis*) de grands aristocrates romains et leur permirent d'entrer dans leur amitié (une désignation polie, on le sait, pour des rapports de clientèle). Si, comme il est probable, les textes des deux décrets furent largement inspirés par les *honorandi* eux-mêmes, on admettra qu'ils avaient en effet bien compris des ressorts essentiels du fonctionnement de la vie politique romaine. Ils avaient compris en particulier que l'audience devant le Sénat n'était pas tout, n'était peut-être pas l'essentiel, et qu'elle devait être précédée par une intense activité de lobbying. Ils avaient compris aussi qu'il était essentiel de gagner la confiance de patrons influents, et que la meilleure forme de *beniuolentia* était celle qu'ils pourraient obtenir, plus encore que *a causa* (voir le texte de Cicéron cité note 27), *a persona sua*. Il est vrai qu'il y avait des précédents déjà anciens, que l'on pense à la réponse donnée par le Sénat aux Rhodiens en 167,[38] ou même à celle qui l'avait été aux Achéens en 181.[39]

ἐπίσημος γέγονε παρὰ πολλαῖς τῶν Ἑλληνίδων πόλεων, τῆς τε πόλεως γνησίους αὐτοὺς πεποιηκὼς πάτρωνας χρησιμώτατος παρὰ τοῖς ἡγουμένοις γέγονε τῶι δήμωι παρ᾽ οἷς ἀναγκαιότατι πᾶσιν εἰσὶν ἀνθρώποις χρεῖαι ; Polémaios, II, 24-31 : ἐνέτυχεν μὲν τοῖς ἡγουμένοις Ῥωμαίοις καὶ φανεὶς ἄξιος τῆς ἐκείνων φιλίας τὸν ἀπὸ ταύτης καρπὸν τοῖς πολείταις περιεποίησεν πρὸς τοὺς ἀρίστους ἄνδρας τῆι πατρίδι συνθέμενος πατρωνείας.

[38] POLYB. 30, 4, 9 : "le sens général de la réponse du Sénat était que, sans la considération qu'on avait pour quelques hommes qui étaient les amis des Romains, et en particulier pour (les ambassadeurs Philophron et Astymédès) eux-mêmes, les Rhodiens auraient bel et bien reçu la leçon qu'ils méritaient".

[39] POLYB. 24, 10, 7 : "Callicratès eut droit à une mention spéciale dans la réponse adressée aux ambassadeurs de la Confédération : sans dire un mot de ses collègues, le Sénat déclara qu'il serait bon qu'il y ait des hommes comme lui dans toutes les cités". En règle générale, la réponse du Sénat commençait par quelques mots d'éloge des ambassadeurs, collectivement reconnus comme ἄνδρες καλοὶ κἀγαθοὶ καὶ φίλοι.

Bibliographie

BOWERSOCK, G.W. (1984), compte rendu de REYNOLDS (1982), *Gnomon* 56, 48-53.

CHANIOTIS, A. (2013), *"Paradoxon, Enargeia*, Empathy: Hellenistic Decrees and Hellenistic Oratory", in KREMMYDAS / TEMPEST (2013), 201-216.

CLINTON, K. (2003), "Maroneia and Rome: Two Decrees of Maroneia from Samothrace", *Chiron* 33, 379-417.

ÉTIENNE, R. / VARÈNE, P. (2004), *Sanctuaire de Claros. L'architecture. Les propylées et les monuments de la Voie sacrée* (Paris).

FERRARY, J.-L. (1988), *Philhellénisme et impérialisme. Aspects idéologiques de la conquête romaine du monde hellénistique* (Rome).

—— (1991), "Le statut des cités libres dans l'Empire romain à la lumière des inscriptions de Claros", *CRAI* 135, 557-577.

KREMMYDAS, C. / TEMPEST, K. (2013), *Hellenistic Oratory. Continuity and Change* (Oxford).

REYNOLDS, J. (1982), *Aphrodisias and Rome. Documents from the Excavation of the Theater at Aphrodisias* (Londres).

ROBERT, L. et J. (1989), *Claros I. Décrets hellénistiques*, fascicule 1 (Paris).

RUBINSTEIN, L. (2013), "Spoken Words, Written Submissions, and Diplomatic Conventions: The Importance and Impact of Oral Performance in Hellenistic Inter-*polis* Relations", in KREMMYDAS / TEMPEST (2013), 165-199.

RUSSELL, D.A. / WILSON, N.G. (1981), *Menander Rhetor. Edited with Translation and Commentary* (Oxford).

SÁNCHEZ, P. (2010), "ΕΠΙ ΡΩΜΑΙΚΩΙ ΘΑΝΑΤΩΙ dans le décret pour Ménippos de Colophon : 'pour la mort d'un Romain' ou 'en vue d'un supplice romain' ?", *Chiron* 40, 41-60.

THORNTON, J. (2013), "Oratory in Polybius' *Histories*", in KREMMYDAS / TEMPEST (2013), 21-42.

WÖRRLE, M. (2000), „Pergamon um 133 v. Chr.", *Chiron* 30, 543-576.

—— (2004), „Maroneia im Umbruch: Von der hellenistischen zur kaiserzeitlichen Polis", *Chiron* 34, 149-167.

DISCUSSION

A. Chaniotis: Your rich presentation makes me ask what is peculiar about Greek embassies to the Senate? What was the new challenge that Greek orators had to face? Is it that these embassies concern asymmetrical relations between unequal partners? This is not the case; negotiations between asymmetrical partners are found in earlier periods as well, for instance the relations between Athens and her allies or kings and cities. Also the humiliation that the envoys of subordinate communities have felt is not new. A new quality is provided by the cultural shock that Greek envoys to Rome must have experienced, especially in the first half of the 2ⁿᵈ century BC. We can get an impression of this shock from a decree of Abdera (*I. Thrac.Aeg.* 5, 167 BC) which refers to the 'psychological hardships' of Teian envoys, who in order to help Abdera had to frequent the atria of the houses of senators in Rome, resembling voluntary hostages. The new challenge for Greek envoys and orators was to adopt specific Roman values, especially *fides*, and incorporate them into the rhetorical strategies.

Secondly, an interesting feature in the negotiations with Rome is the selective and inaccurate representation of the past by the Greek cities. E.g. the inscription of Maroneia, which you discussed, claims that the Maronitans became friends and allies of the Romans "immediately upon the establishment of their leadership". In reality, the treaty of alliance of Maroneia with Rome (shortly after 167 BC) was concluded fifty years after the alliance between Rome and Aetolia (212 BC), and thirty years after the Romans had defeated Philip V and had established themselves as a major power in the Greek world. Reading this text, one gets the impression that Maroneia was destroyed because of its loyalty shortly after her alliance with

Rome, and not some eighty years later, during the first Mithridatic War. Similar misrepresentations of the past can be observed in decrees of Aphrodisias and Ephesos from the time of the first Mithridatic War (see my article "Affective Epigraphy: Emotions in Public Inscriptions of the Hellenistic Age", *Mediterraneo Antico* 16.2, 2013, 745-760).

J.-L. Ferrary: Je suis dans l'ensemble tout à fait d'accord avec vos deux remarques et j'en reconnais l'importance. Je me contenterai d'ajouter quelques observations.

1. Le choc éprouvé par certaines ambassades fut d'autant plus fort qu'il était inattendu. C'est le cas, en particulier, des Étoliens qui en 191 viennent se livrer à la *fides* des Romains (Ferrary [1988] 72-81), ou des Rhodiens face au Sénat en 168. Dans les deux cas, les Romains ont laissé se développer des ambiguïtés (sur les obligations de la *fides* ou de l'*amicitia*), parfois même les ont encouragées, jusqu'au moment où ils décident brusquement de les dissiper, pour contraindre leurs interlocuteurs à abandonner toute manifestation de *superbia*. La spécificité des valeurs proprement romaines est donc affirmée avec plus ou moins de fermeté, et cela, au début surtout, n'a pas aidé les Grecs à en prendre conscience.

2. Le caractère sélectif de la représentation que les cités veulent donner de l'histoire de leurs rapports avec le pouvoir romain n'a rien de surprenant, et un discours d'ambassade n'est pas un récit historique. La difficulté pour les cités était de faire accepter par le pouvoir romain ces réécritures partielles du passé, en particulier dans des sénatus-consultes puis des lettres impériales qui confirmaient leurs privilèges ou leur en conféraient de nouveaux en avalisant et résumant les argumentaires présentés par les ambassadeurs.

L. Pernot: On peut parler d'un véritable déficit de théorisation du discours d'ambassade dans la rhétorique grecque, telle que nous la connaissons, puisqu'il faut attendre Ménandre le Rhéteur pour trouver un exposé articulé, encore que *sui generis*, sur cette forme oratoire. Il semble toutefois que Démétrios de Phalère se soit intéressé au sujet : d'après le témoignage de Philodème, il avait défini une catégorie, appelée ἐντευκτικὸς λόγος, qui comprenait des allocutions adressées soit aux masses, soit aux souverains κατὰ πρεσβείαν (Philod. *Rhet*. 1, 222 Sudhaus = Demetr. Phal. fr. 130 Stork / van Ophuijsen / Dorandi).

J.-L. Ferrary: Je vous remercie beaucoup d'avoir attiré mon attention sur ce texte. Je me demande d'ailleurs, quand je le lis avec soin, dans quelle mesure il permet d'attribuer à Démétrios de Phalère autre chose que l'association du σοφιστικός et de l'ἐντευκτικὸς λόγος, par opposition au δημηγορικός et au δικανικός. C'est Philodème, me semble-t-il, qui ajoute qu'il concède le caractère utile (ou nuisible) de l'ἐντευκτικὸς λόγος dans les cas spécifiques de l'allocution adressée aux masses et du discours aux puissants à l'occasion d'une ambassade (τὸν κατὰ πρεσβείαν τοῖς δυνάσταις sc. λόγον). Il n'est pas inintéressant que cet intérêt pour la catégorie du discours des ambassadeurs se trouve au 1er siècle av. J.-C., dans un traité de rhétorique écrit par un philosophe qui a choisi de vivre dans l'entourage d'un noble romain, après être apparu dans les réflexions historiographiques d'un Polybe. Mais il faut toujours être prudent, et se rappeler que Polybe et Philodème sont des survivants dans le grand naufrage de la prose d'époque hellénistique.

M. Edwards: Returning to the cultural shock, I should imagine that Demosthenes and Aeschines faced the same cultural gap on the embassy to Philip.

M. Kraus: Dennoch war die Situation für die Gesandten vor dem Senat eine andere als für Demosthenes und Aischines, die ja darauf gefasst waren, einem autokratischen Potentaten zu begegnen. Die griechischen Gesandten müssen sich, vor allem in der Anfangszeit der diplomatischen Beziehungen zu Rom, vor dem Senat wie Angeklagte vorgekommen sein. Die Prozedur hat doch deutliche Züge eines Gerichtsverfahrens, so dass man sich fragt, ob es noch um deliberative Reden oder nicht vielmehr schon um forensische Verteidigungsreden geht. Man denke auch an die Behandlung karthagischer Gesandtschaften vor dem Senat (vgl. z.B. Liv. 30, 21-23; 42, 23-24; Diod. 32, 1-3; Polyb. 36, 4).

M. Edwards: Is there a source problem when comparing historiography and epigraphy? One of the major problems of forensic oratory is the lack of speeches on both sides of the case, although when we do have both sides of a story (as in the Demosthenes vs Aeschines accounts of the embassy) the versions are irreconcilable.

D. Colomo: As I point out in my own contribution, we have to take into consideration an important difference between papyrological sources and epigraphic ones. On the one hand, in inscriptions we find only positive outputs of embassies, since it would have been humiliating to carve in stones and display negative outcomes. What is going to be carved is in fact shaped by ideological bias and especially by the attempt to preserve a positive image. On the other hand, papyri – for instance minutes of embassy hearings and proceedings of trials – transmit what has been said by the two parties and thus offer a plurality of points of view.

A. Chaniotis: I mentioned earlier the decree of Ephesos: the Ephesians say that they remained loyal against Mithridates, but two years earlier they had killed Romans in the riots.

J.-L. Ferrary: Encore une fois, je suis dans l'ensemble d'accord avec A. Chaniotis. Mais la réécriture de l'histoire par les cités avait ses limites. Le fait de se révolter contre Mithridate après l'avoir soutenu et avoir participé au massacre des *Italici* ne suffit pas aux Éphésiens pour conserver leur liberté lorsque Sylla réorganisa la province romaine d'Asie. Dans l'ensemble, la politique menée par les cités au moment où le pouvoir romain fut véritablement menacé par le roi du Pont détermina les sanctions ou récompenses décidées par Sylla et ratifiées par le Sénat. Mais il y eut des exceptions : Athènes, alliée privilégiée de Rome qui était passée du côté de Mithridate, souffrit d'être assiégée et prise de force, mais ne perdit finalement ni sa liberté ni ses possessions ; Chios, passée à Mithridate mais devenue suspecte au point que ses citoyens étaient en voie d'être déportés lorsqu'ils furent sauvés, garda tous ses privilèges ; Mytilène, restée jusqu'au bout fidèle au roi du Pont, perdit bien sûr les siens, mais recouvra le statut de cité libre dès la fin des années 60 grâce à la faveur dont Théophane jouit auprès de Pompée. Les espoirs des Éphésiens n'étaient donc pas totalement absurdes, et ils avaient quelque raison d'essayer de plaider leur cause.

A. Chaniotis: People write down what someone says, which leads to selection; what is said is filtered so that we get only some of the words spoken.

D. Colomo: I agree with this point. However, reports of embassy hearings and minutes of trials are in any case closer to what was happening in reality.

J.-L. Ferrary: Mieux vaudrait, je crois, distinguer la nature diplomatique des documents indépendamment de leur support (papyrus, pierre ou manuscrit). Il y a des procès-verbaux d'audiences judiciaires, qui peuvent être gravés sur la pierre, par exemple celui d'un procès présidé par Caracalla à Antioche en 216 (*AE* 1947, 182) ; des sénatus-consultes gravés sur la pierre qui résument les arguments des deux parties avant de rendre une sentence définitive ou de désigner un arbitre et de lui indiquer le principe qui devra inspirer sa sentence ; des textes comme les actes des martyrs (chrétiens ou païens) qui ont une vocation apologétique même s'ils peuvent être constitués à partir d'un noyau historique solide. Les proportions peuvent varier selon qu'il s'agit de textes littéraires, papyrologiques ou épigraphiques, mais l'essentiel est de bien distinguer ces catégories.

D. Nelis: Romans allow Greeks to speak Greek to show that *they* are in control, because they know Greek and Latin?

J.-L. Ferrary: Le cas du grec me semble différent de celui d'autres langues, dans la mesure où il devait être parlé, ou du moins compris, par une majorité de sénateurs. Certains de ceux qui demandaient un traducteur devaient le faire parce qu'ils estimaient mal maîtriser cette langue, ou ne pas devoir faire l'effort de prêter aux ambassadeurs grecs une attention plus particulière. Mais à cette explication pratique s'ajoutait une valeur symbolique : le latin était la langue des maîtres, et les interlocuteurs du Sénat devaient en prendre conscience. Que l'on pense à l'usage très symbolique des langues après Pydna : Paul-Émile s'adresse en grec à Persée vaincu, et sans doute aux Grecs auxquels lorsqu'il fait le tour des grands sanctuaires et lieux de mémoire, n'hésitant pas à faire une référence à Homère. Mais à Amphipolis, c'est en latin qu'il donne ses instructions, laissant au préteur qui avait été chargé de la flotte le soin de traduire cette proclamation en grec. On ne pouvait mieux marquer la hiérarchie des langues, et le fait qu'Apollonius Molon ait été dispensé de voir son discours traduit par un interprète est présenté par Valère-Maxime comme un hommage rendu à l'homme, et à la cité fidèle dont il était le porte-parole.

M. Kraus: Da ich unter anderem Lateinische Stilübungen lehre, sei mir die Randbemerkung erlaubt, dass in literarischen Darstellungen einer Rede von Gesandten, die ja als Vertreter und Sprachrohr für ihr ganzes Volk sprechen, in der Form der *oratio obliqua* die Frage, ob die Gesandten sich nun in die von ihnen vertretene Gruppe selbst mit einschliessen, sich auch sprachlich in der Wahl der Pronomina (reflexiv oder nicht-reflexiv) niederschlägt, was Studenten bei Übersetzungen ins Lateinische oft vor Probleme stellt: Wenn es etwa heisst: „Die Gesandten der Helvetier sagten, sie [*sc.* die Helvetier] hätten vor, […] durch die römische Provinz zu ziehen" (vgl. Caes. *Gall.* 1, 7, 3), sagt man dann korrekterweise: *Legati Heluetiorum dixerunt*

se (oder *eos?*) *in animo habere* [...] *iter per provinciam facere* ?
Tatsächlich wählt Caesar in diesem Fall in aller Regel die reflexive
Form, bezieht also die Gesandten mit ein (vgl. z.B. *Gall.* 1, 30, 1;
besonders aufschlussreich aber etwa das Schwanken *Gall.* 1, 37,
1-2: *legati ab Haeduis et a Treueris ueniebant: Haedui questum
quod Harudes, qui nuper in Galliam transportati essent, fines
eorum popularentur: sese ne obsidibus quidem datis pacem Ariouisti
redimere potuisse*).

VI

DANIELA COLOMO

INTERSTATE RELATIONS:
THE PAPYROLOGICAL EVIDENCE*

1. Introduction

1.1. *Presentation of the topic*

My contribution explores the role of deliberative oratory in the interstate relations between the Roman Empire and the province of Egypt during the first three centuries of the common era. I focus on the evidence provided by texts preserved on papyrus, but also include some literary sources.

* I wish to thank for stimulating discussion and advice Lucio Del Corso (Cassino), Giulio Iovine (Naples), Mark de Kreij (Stockholm), Laura Lulli (Rome-L'Aquila), Mario Paganini (Copenhagen), Peter J. Parsons (Oxford), Marco Peralc (Liverpool-Oxford), Reinhold Scholl (Leipzig) and especially Chris Rodriguez (Paris), who has allowed me to consult his unpublished thesis *Les Alexandrins face au juge Trajan. Étude de deux procès des* Acta Alexandrinorum, submitted as a Mémoire de Master 2, Histoire du Droit (Université Paris II) in 2014-2015.
Note that in the quotations from papyri I have normalised the Greek, i.e. I do not reproduce phonetic spellings. For the sections of papyrus texts quoted according to the editions of *APM, CPJ* II, *P.Oxy.*, I reproduce the translations offered in those volumes; for other texts details are given *ad loc.*; other short (not acknowledged) translations are my own. Images of papyri have been reproduced thanks to the courtesy of the Ägyptisches Museum und Papyrussammlung der Staatlichen Museen zu Berlin, the British Library (London), the Biblioteca Medicea Laurenziana (Firenze), the Papyrussammlungen der Justus-Liebig-Universität Gießen.

The very fact that papyrus is a (relatively) perishable writing
material inevitably narrows down the geographical area under
investigation to the Roman province of Egypt: almost only
in the dry Egyptian climate could papyri partially survive,
while they were mostly destroyed by humidity in the rest of the
Empire and even in dampish areas of Egypt itself, like the
Delta.[1] The surviving papyri contain reports of embassy hearings,
copies of speeches of ambassadors, imperial letters and edicts
and a unique group of sub-literary texts, the so-called *Acta
Alexandrinorum*, fictionalised accounts of embassies of the Greek
Alexandrians to the Roman emperor centring on the conflict
between the Greeks and Jews and betraying anti-Roman sentiments. As Kayser acutely observes, the papyrological evidence
concerning embassies is qualitatively different from the epigraphic evidence, which illustrates diplomatic relations for the
other parts of the Roman Empire.[2] An inscription contains
the answer of the Emperor to the plea of an embassy: usually
(and obviously) only the positive answers were published, i.e.
inscribed on stones, since to engrave and display negative outcomes would have been humiliating. By contrast, the papyrological evidence is based on a plurality of documents which,
although often very fragmentary, offer copious information on
the embassies themselves and give voice to different points of
view.

Embassies from Egypt, mainly from the 'capital' Alexandria,[3]
could be sent to Rome to congratulate the Emperor on the

---

[1] Cf. TURNER ([2]1979) 18, 26-27; PARSONS (2007) 41-42.

[2] KAYSER (2003) 439. But note that *P.Oxy.* XLII 3023 seems to provide
papyrological evidence for an audience before an Emperor regarding a non-
Egyptian city, Antioch; similarly *PSI* XI 1222 may refer to a city outside Egypt;
cf. HARKER (2008) 127-130.

[3] However, diplomatic activities concerning other poleis of Egypt are documented: three letters by Gordian III as response to an embassy from Antinoopolis
(HOOGENDIJK / VAN MINNEN [1987]); a letter by Nero to a polis of the Fayoum
(probably Ptolemais Euergetis) and the so-called 6475 (*SB* XII 11012, AD 55);
see HARKER (2008) 208. The 6475 are apparently a group of privileged citizens,
probably descendants of ancient colonists.

occasion of his accession to the throne[4] or of the adoption of an heir – and for these purposes they delivered honorific decrees[5] –, but at the same time they aimed to negotiate political and economic issues of crucial importance, like confirmation of privileges granted by the previous Emperor as well as internal conflicts and disputes. At some stage after the audience the Emperor wrote his reply in the form of a letter to be taken back by the envoys,[6] like the famous letter of Emperor Claudius to the Alexandrians, partially surviving on papyrus (*CPJ* II 153; Pl. 6.1).[7] It seems that on most occasions two different embassies left Alexandria for Rome at the same time: on the one hand, an embassy formed by important members of the Alexandrian aristocracy, extremely proud of their Greek origins and culture; on the other hand, an embassy formed by the representatives of the Jewish community (the so-called Jewish *politeuma*), which since the early Ptolemaic period, after having accomplished a process of deep Hellenisation but remaining faithful to its ancestral religion and customs, played an important role in the political and economic development of Alexandria.[8] Such a 'diplomatic duality' was the concrete expression not just of a diversified ethnic situation of Alexandria, but of a dramatic conflict between the two communities, which were struggling to protect their political, social and economic interests and privileges. From the very early period of interaction and conflict between Rome and Egypt, the two ethnic groups had assumed an opposite stance: while the Greek Alexandrians had tried to

---

[4] OLIVER (1989) 2-4. The embassy documented by *SB* XII 11012 (see n. 3) was sent to Nero to congratulate him on his accession and to deliver an honorific decree.

[5] On the delivery of honorific decrees see *P.Oxy.* XXV 2435v, lines 40-41, 44 (embassy to Augustus in AD 12/13); cf. MEN. RHET. 2, 13 (*Presbeutikos*), 424, 1-2 SPENGEL; RUSSELL-WILSON (1981) 180-181, 337.

[6] See MILLAR ([2]1992) 218; cf. OLIVER (1989) 1-2.

[7] Other examples of imperial letters to the Alexandrians are: *P.Oxy.* XLII 3020, fr. 1, col. i (Augustus); *P.Oxy.* XLII 3022 (Trajan).

[8] Embassies attested in the 1st and 2nd century are listed in KAYSER (2003) 462-464 (envoys attested in the *Acta Alexandrinorum* are also included).

defend their independence, the Jews had offered support to
Rome, in particular to Julius Caesar in the *Bellum Alexandri-*
num and later to Octavian against Mark Antony.[9]
Thus very often the hearing focused on the dispute between
two embassies – Greek Alexandrian envoys on the one hand, a
Jewish delegation on the other – and consisted of an ἀντικατά-
στασις, a confrontation.[10] In other words, the audience became
a legal hearing, a trial that from a juridical standpoint presents
specific features. The procedure followed in those cases was the
so-called *cognitio extra ordinem*, introduced by Augustus for
both civil and criminal cases, in first instance or appeal. According to this procedure, the same magistrate could instruct and
judge a case on the same day, while during the Republican period
the typical procedure, the so-called *per formulas*, consisted of
two distinct phases taking place at different times and admin-
istered by two different officials (the *praetor* held the first phase,
called *in iure,* in which the nature of the case was presented
and instructed; then the judge pronounced the final sentence
in the second phase, called *in iudicio*). In concrete terms, in the
cognitio the plaintiff and the defendant could plead and present
their witnesses to the judging magistrate on the same day.
We can recognise this type of trial in our sources: here the
judging magistrate is the Roman Emperor.[11] Interestingly the
application of this procedure to the diplomatic sphere implies
– at least virtually – a sort of interaction and overlap between
deliberative oratory and forensic oratory.[12]

[9] See HARKER (2008) 214 with references to specific historical sources.
[10] The word is a juridical and rhetorical *terminus technicus*; see *DGE s.v.* 2.
The term is used by Emperor Claudius in his letter to the Alexandrians (*CPJ* II
153, col. iv 75). In addition, the form ἀντικαταστήσομαι occurs in the *Acta
Isidori, CPJ* II 156c, col. ii 22.
[11] A detailed analysis of the *cognitio extra ordinem* from a juridical and historical standpoint is to be found in GAMBETTI (2008) 191-194; cf. MILLAR
([2]1992) 218.
[12] Significantly, Philo of Alexandria, reporting on the Jewish embassy to
Gaius of which he was the leader in his famous *Legatio ad Gaium* (see below),
uses the phrase μεταπεμφθέντες ἀγωνίσασθαι τὸν περὶ πολιτείας ἀγῶνα,
"when we were summoned **to take part in the contention** about our citizenship"

Greek Alexandrian and Jewish ambassadors, thanks to their 'classical' education (παιδεία), were well equipped with the same powerful weapon: rhetoric. Thus it is not surprising that in the embassies of both parties we find professional rhetoricians. Some may be even traced back in the imperial prosopography: for example, Paul of Tyre, who offered his service to the Alexandrians,[13] and Sopater of Antioch, who represented the Jews.[14] As we will see in detail later, envoys not only show the technical competences of the art of persuasion, but are also well informed on the political and economic issues at stake, such as civic rights, tax-exemption and internal conflicts. In this respect they can be compared to the competent orator speaking in an assembly portrayed in Arist. *Rhet.* 1359b.[15]

In what follows I will explore the rhetorical strategies implemented by the Alexandrian embassies to Rome on the basis of documentary sources (mainly copies of minutes of hearings), the subliterary corpus of the *Acta Alexandrinorum*, and the literary works of Philo of Alexandria (*Legatio ad Gaium* and *In Flaccum*) and Josephus (*Antiquitates Judaicae* and *Contra Apionem*).

1.2. Historical background

In 31 BC Egypt ceased to be an independent kingdom and became a Roman province, a conquered territory, governed by

(*Leg.* 349). As GAMBETTI (2009) 215, n. 12 points out, "The verb ἀγωνίσασθαι with the cognitive accusative forms an expression that is regularly found in forensic literature".

[13] *CPJ* II 158a (*Acta Pauli et Antonini*); cf. *CPJ* II 157 (*Acta Hermaisci*) col. i 9-11; HARKER (2008) 86, 125-126.

[14] Cf. *CPJ* II 157, col. i 15-16; KAYSER (2003) 455.

[15] Cf. *CPJ* II 150, col. ii 11-14: the necessity to send suitable (ἐπιτηδείους) individuals as ambassadors is emphasised. In *P.Oxy.* XLII 3020, fr. 1, col. ii 3-7 ambassadors divide between themselves the treatment of the issues at stake before the Emperor according to their respective competences (one speaks on the Egyptian situation, another on the Idioslogos [lit. "privy purse/special account"; Roman official in charge of the imperial property], the third on the situation of the polis); this seems to illustrate 'professional' team-work.

a representative of the Roman emperor, the prefect, who replaced the Ptolemaic king. Accordingly, Alexandria ceased to be the capital of a kingdom, i.e. the centre of power and political life, and became just the main city of a province of the Roman Empire: in spite of its strategic position (which continued to play an important economic role in particular for the export of granary supplies), it was now relegated to a secondary role. Now the Alexandrian citizenship could be bestowed by the Emperor, not any more by local authorities, and from a juridical standpoint was inferior – but prerequisite – to the Roman citizenship.[16] Octavian, aware of Alexandrians' anti-Roman attitude caused by Roman political intrusion under the Ptolemies,[17] tried to present himself as a friend, even pardoning them for having supported his rival Mark Antony in the civil war, and pretended to treat them as allies rather than as subjects. Under the Romans Alexandrian citizens enjoyed tax-privileges consisting in exemption from the poll-tax (the *laographia*, introduced in 24 BC), and some of them even obtained Roman citizenship. However, there were decisive factors that fed the traditional hostility against Rome: Egypt and Alexandria were in fact conquered territory, and as such subject to the abuse of the corrupt Roman administration. The Greek Alexandrians could not rule themselves in autonomy through their town council, the Boule, which had been abolished probably in the 2nd century BC during the reign of Ptolemy VIII after a riot and never reinstated by Augustus.[18] Given that the Boule was an

---

[16] Cf. PLIN. *Ep*.10, 6 and 7.

[17] See KAYSER (2003) 436-437; HARKER (2008) 4.

[18] Basic bibliography on this subject is to be found in HARKER (2008) 5-6. Note that a letter by Augustus to the Alexandrians (*P.Oxy.* XLII 3020, fr. 1, col. i) preserves a form of address to the city that clearly shows that in Alexandria there was no Boule. The Emperor uses the phrase "to the people of the Alexandrians, greetings" (line 3 Ἀλεξανδρείων δήμωι χαίρειν) instead of the formula normally used in official documents to address the Greek cities that had a council, "to the magistrates the council and the people, greetings" (ἄρχουσι βουλῇ δήμῳ, χαίρειν or, in a shorter form without the mention of "the people", ἄρχουσι βουλῇ, χαίρειν).

essential institution of all Greek cities, the lack of it was a major problem for the identity of the Greek Alexandrians, also because it could not be replaced by the Gerousia (the council of the Elders, with 173 members) and the Gymnasium. These two institutions, recognised and maintained by Octavian, although they ended up assuming a political function in order to compensate for the lack of the Boule, had essentially a social and honorific function – the Gerousia fulfilling representative and religious duties,[19] the Gymnasium being in charge of the organisation of the athletic games and largely involved in the education of the younger generations.[20] Moreover, Augustus carried out a drastic military reform, which had dramatic consequences for both the Greek Alexandrians and the Jewish community: he dismantled the Alexandrian garrison. A specific group of Jews, the ones resident in the so-called Delta quarter, were an important part of this garrison. In fact the Delta quarter represents the original Jewish *politeuma*, whose inhabitants, because of their military duties performed from the time of the foundation of Alexandria onwards, had full legal residence rights. The Jews of the Delta quarter formed a group distinct from the Jews that settled in Alexandria at a later stage without obtaining official residence rights. However, with Augustus' military reform, such a distinction faded and the Alexandrian Jews became a single community. Augustus, grateful for their constant support of Rome, recognised the rights they had obtained under the Ptolemies – tax-exemption, access to regular tribunals, lenient forms of punishment applied to Alexandrian citizens *uersus* those reserved for the Egyptians, freedom to observe their customs (ἔθη) and traditional laws

---

[19] Cf. BOWMAN-RATHBONE (1992) 115-118, who ascribe administrative and political function to the Gerousia.

[20] On the Gymnasium in the Roman period, see HABERMANN (2015). In particular, on the role of the Gymnasium in cultural life, see KEHOE (2015) 67-73; cf. CRIBIORE (2001) 34-36, who points out that, in spite of their importance in promoting educational and cultural events, there is no evidence to consider Egyptian gymnasia as *stricto sensu* academic institutions in charge of the systematic organisation of education.

(πάτριοι νόμοι) and the Sabbath, dispensation from the worship of the Emperor.[21] But they did not acquire collective citizenship. After the death of the last ethnarch,[22] Augustus created a Gerousia with a political role (ca. 12 AD).[23] As a community they had the duty to keep the riverbanks clean,[24] a public service that during the Ptolemies was performed by the military and reservists. This public duty that they now had to fulfil as a civic community and the exclusion from the Gymnasium were the two basic differences from the Greek Alexandrians. In any case, although their religion forbade them to participate in the civic cults, there is evidence that some Jews received a Greek education and were members of the Gymnasium as Alexandrian citizens, a fact that gave them the possibility to play an active role in political life.[25] The numerous and wealthy Jewish community of Alexandria was dramatically damaged by the strict scrutiny of tax privileges conducted under Tiberius and Gaius, which ended up not recognising residential rights and thus tax exemption, together with the other rights mentioned above, to the Jews inhabiting areas of Alexandria other than the Delta quarter. A decree issued by the prefect Avilius Flaccus, which implemented Emperor Gaius' *mandata*, declared those Jews "foreigners and aliens" (Gr. ξένοι καὶ ἐπήλυδες; Lat. *peregrini et aduenae*).[26] In the first period of his office, Flaccus had tried

[21] See PHILO *Flacc.* 49-50; *Leg.* 154; *CPJ* II 153, col. vi 82-v 88 with comm. *ad loc.*

[22] Head of the Jewish community of Alexandria, with administrative and juridical duties; see RITTER (2015) 106-107.

[23] PHILO *Flacc.* 74.

[24] JOS. *C. Ap.* 2, 64.

[25] See HARKER (2008) 218-220 on literary and documentary sources; cf. RITTER (2015) 89-100. GAMBETTI (2009) 42, holds a different view, arguing that Alexandrian Jews had no interest in entering the Gymnasium and acquiring full Alexandrian citizenship, because this would have implied active participation in the civic cults against their religious customs.

[26] PHILO *Flacc.* 54; see GAMBETTI (2009) 172-192. According to JOS. *AJ* 14, 187, they possessed documents related to their civic rights in private archives, but could not use them legally because they lacked Roman ratification; cf. GAMBETTI (2009) 232.

to take control of the conflict between Greek Alexandrians and Jews by abolishing the Alexandrian clubs, mobilised by the demagogue Isidorus,[27] and thus apparently siding with the Jews. Later, however, after his administration caused complaints, he allied himself with the Greek Alexandrians led by Isidorus against the Jews in exchange for protection from possible revenge from Gaius because of his 'implications' in the prosecution of members of his family under Tiberius. The conflict escalated in a major bloody riot in AD 38. The explosion of violence was provoked by the presence in the city of Agrippa I, king of Judaea and Gaius' *amicus*, who paraded a flamboyant band of bodyguards. The Greek Alexandrians started a violent attack against the Jews,[28] officially on the ground that they refused to perform the imperial cult proclaimed by Gaius, who planned to install 'sacred' images of himself in temples and in the meeting houses (synagogues) of the Jews. The Jews were confined to the Delta quarter and could be attacked without legal protection if found outside it. A number of synagogues were desecrated through the installation of images of the Emperor and many others were burned. Thirty-eight members of the Jewish Gerousia were publically scourged, tortured, hung and crucified during a Greek festival. Finally the violence was stopped by Roman military intervention.[29]

In September of the same year Flaccus was accused of corruption, arrested and taken to Rome, tried by Gaius early in AD 39, found guilty and condemned to exile and finally executed.

---

[27] On the possible role of Isidorus as Gaius' *amicus* and thus member of the imperial *consilium* on the basis of the evidence provided by *P.Giss.Lit.* 4, 7, see GAMBETTI (2009) 125-127; cf. RODRIGUEZ (2010b) 594. On Isidorus expatriating and member of an embassy to Tiberius in order to complain about Flaccus' alleged anti-Alexandrian policy, see GAMBETTI (2009) 102-104, 109-110.

[28] The conflict between Jews and Greeks is indicated as πόλεμος, "war", in sources of the 1st cent.: *P.Aberd.* 117, fr. 2, line 2; *BKT* IX 115, col. i 7; *CPJ* II 153, line 74; *CPJ* II 158a, col. vi 16-17; *P.Giss.Lit.* 4, 7, col. iii 31-32; *P.Oxy.* XXII 2339, col. i 8-9.

[29] For a full account of the riot see PHILO *Leg.* 120-130; *Flacc.* 29-96; cf. RITTER (2015) 132-140.

After Flaccus' arrest two rival embassies sailed to Rome: the Jewish envoys were guided by Philo of Alexandria, who reported on it in the *Legatio ad Gaium* and also in the *In Flaccum*,[30] while the Greek Alexandrians were led by the famous poet[31] and Homeric scholar Apion.[32] They obtained a proper hearing in Rome only after Gaius' return from Germany (after 31 August, AD 40): according to Philo, the outcome for the Jews was disastrous, although the Emperor apparently did not issue any official final decision.[33] On 24 January, AD 41 Gaius was assassinated; in February the Jews rioted at the breaking of the news and two new embassies were sent by both parties to Rome to congratulate the new Emperor Claudius on the accession. He assumed a more neutral stance than his predecessor concerning the Greek Alexandrians-Jews conflict, as his ruling, the famous letter to the Alexandrians, shows:[34] he ordered them to stop the fighting and decided not to investigate the responsibility for the violence from both sides, restored the legal, social and religious privileges of the Jews abolished by Gaius,[35] but strictly prohibited their entry to the Gymnasium and their participation in the athletic games, i.e. their attempt to obtain full Alexandrian citizenship;[36] finally, he did not comply with the request of the

[30] See RITTER (2015) 140-142.
[31] See *P.Oxy.* LXXIX 5202, *Copy of an Honorific Inscription for the Poetic Victor Apion.*
[32] That Apion was the leader is said by JOS. *AJ* 18, 257-259. On the debate about the date of the departure of the two rival embassies see HARKER (2008) 14. I consider the embassy most likely to have departed in the winter of AD 38/39.
[33] See RITTER (2015) 141.
[34] *CPJ* 153: see here in particular comm. on line 88, regarding the reference to an imperial edict issued before the letter; cf. RITTER (2015) 147-151.
[35] GAMBETTI (2009) 222-225 argues that he could not change Gaius' decision from a legal standpoint, because it was *res iudicata* and in fact he restored rights of residence and tax exemption only to the Jews of the Delta quarter; cf. *ibid.* 215, 247.
[36] Note that this interpretation is based on the text καὶ 'Ιουδαίοις δὲ | ἄντικρυς κελεύω... μηδὲ ἐπισπαίειν (iotacistic spelling for ἐπ-εισ-παίειν) | γυμνασιαρ-χικοῖς ἢ κοσμητικοῖς ἀγῶσι, "and to the Jews, on the other hand, I order... not to intrude themselves into the games presided over by the *gymnasiarchoi* and the *kosmetai*" (col. v 88-93). GAMBETTI (2009) 225-226 offers a different

Greek Alexandrians to re-establish the Boule. At the same time he executed two Alexandrian notables, Isidorus (see above) and Lampon,[37] probably because of wrongdoing and political intrigues under Caligula and/or for their role in the persecution of the Jews in the riots.[38] This execution will make the two notables the prototypes of Alexandrian national heroes, symbol of the heroic resistance against the tyranny of Rome, giving birth to a new literary genre, the *Acta Alexandrinorum*. They will be the models for the Greek Alexandrian ambassadors featuring in the *Acta* under future emperors.

In the following decades the tension between Greeks and Jews continued. Two more Jewish revolts took place in Egypt, in AD 66 and 115-117[39] respectively. In both cases the Romans supported the Greek Alexandrians against the Jews in the first phase, but subsequently tried to stop the continuation of violence from the Greek party. The Emperor Septimius Severus, who visited Egypt in AD 199/200, gave the Alexandrians permission to re-establish the Boule, granting at the same time a city council to all Egyptian metropoleis, a fact that

interpretation of the passage. In particular, at col. v 92 she accepts the alternative reading ἐπισπαίρειν in the sense of "to disturb", instead of ἐπισπαίειν, "to intrude", and argues that Claudius is just warning the Jews not to take revenge for the events of AD 38-41 by disturbing the athletic games, on the assumption that the Jews did not aim to participate in the games and thus to enter the Gymnasium, i.e. to acquire full Alexandrian citizenship; cf. n. 25. I have examined the original papyrus and concluded that ἐπισπαίειν is a more satisfactory reading from a palaeographical standpoint (there is not enough space for a rho after the diphthong alpha-iota). Moreover, the actual meaning of the alternative reading ἐπισπαίρειν in this context is problematic, since the verb is very rare and attested in the sense of "to palpitate, to be in alarm"; cf. *CPJ* II 153, comm. on lines 92-93; Bringmann (2004) 332, n. 47; Harker (2008) 186; Ritter (2015) 145 with n. 42.

[37] Lampon, who prosecuted Flaccus in AD 39, had been involved in lawsuits that caused his bankruptcy and then forced to be a Gymnasiarch by Flaccus; in Rome he was office recorder and took bribes to alter the records. Interestingly Philo (*Flacc.* 20, 131) qualifies him with a rare word taken from Dem. 18, 209, γραμματοκύφων, "porer over records"; see Rodriguez (2010a) 26 with n. 122.

[38] See Philo *Flacc.* 18-21, 135-145; cf. Harker (2008) 15-18.

[39] See *P.Mil.Vogl.* II 47, prefectoral edict ordering the end of violence; Harker (2008) 58-59, 198.

meant the dramatic loss of hegemony for Alexandria. Under him and later under Caracalla Jews were allowed to hold offices and to remain faithful to their faith. The issue of their right to acquire Alexandrian citizenship finally lost relevance when the inhabitants of the Empire were all declared Roman citizens by the *Constitutio Antoniniana* (AD 212). The reign of Caracalla, plagued by explosions of violence and harsh repressions (especially of a riot organised by tradesmen in Alexandria), fed anti-Roman attitudes and contributed to the popularity of the *Acta Alexandrinorum*.[40]

2. Cursory presentation of the sources and methodological remarks

In introducing the topic, I have distinguished two basic types of sources: on the one hand, the sources preserved on papyrus, including documents concerning political and diplomatic relations between Rome and Egypt, and the corpus of the *Acta Alexandrinorum*; on the other hand, literary and historical sources transmitted through the mediaeval and Renaissance manuscripts, *in primis* the works of Philo of Alexandria and Josephus.

First of all I should stress an important feature typical for papyrological sources in general: the extreme fragmentary state of the texts and the chance nature of the papyrus findings through archaeological excavations from the 19th century onwards, which dramatically affect the range of the documents and thus the type and the amount of evidence they provide. As said above, we have a very limited amount of papyri from the area of Alexandria because of the humid natural environment of the Delta: a limited number could survive only because they had been sent or brought to other areas of Egypt. Documents and papyri

---

[40] A detailed account of the Severan period is to be found in HARKER (2008) 130-140.

of the *Acta Alexandrinorum* come from the Egyptian *chora*, from cities like Oxyrhynchus, Hermopolis Magna, and Panopolis, as well as villages of the Arsinoite like Karanis, Tebtunis and Philadelphia.[41]

Moreover, the aftermath of the papyrological discoveries has to be taken into consideration: unfortunately, not all papyri have remained in the public domain, but a great amount of material ended up (and still ends up) in private hands through the black market and still in our time escapes close scholarly investigation. Besides, even public papyri collections around the world contain thousands of still unpublished fragments, many of which have not been precisely classified yet. In addition to this, we have to take into consideration the selection of the material operated by the transmission.

Among the sources preserved on papyrus the so-called *Acta Alexandrinorum* need a brief introduction. These texts, composed by unknown authors at different times,[42] consist of a basic narrative structure framing long sections of dialogue; in other words they follow the format of official minutes (*acta*)[43] of court proceedings recording direct speeches of accuser and defendant. The protagonists are members of the Greek Alexandrian aristocracy and a Roman Emperor. The situation represented is stereotypical and the story features 'stock characters': an embassy of Greek aristocrats travels from Alexandria to Rome to plead to the Emperor their patriotic cause; the Emperor reacts with hostility to their requests and often appears to support their enemies, the Alexandrian Jews, who

---

[41] Cf. HARKER (2008) 2.

[42] On the issue of authorship see LUISELLI (2016) 292-293.

[43] The label *Acta Alexandrinorum* – the official minutes of the Alexandrians – is in fact a 'modern' label inspired by the typical format of these texts. Accordingly, individual texts have been given a 'modern' title containing the genitive of the protagonist(s) of the case: *Acta Isidori, Acta Appiani, Acta Pauli et Antonini, Acta Hermaisci,* etc. HARKER (2008) 7-8 offers a concise and useful survey of modern scholarship. Chris RODRIGUEZ is preparing a comprehensive re-edition of the *Acta Alexandrinorum,* equipped with translation and commentary, to be published as a Supplement of the *JJP.*

are represented as conniving and manipulative. In most cases the official hearing consists of a trial following the *cognitio extra ordinem* procedure. The two parties often exchange insults; often the Emperor, portrayed as a villain, is explicitly accused of being of low birth and having no culture. Finally, some of the Greek Alexandrians are condemned to death and led to execution like heroes and martyrs.[44] But note that *P.Giss. Lit.* 4, 7 should be singled out as the only known case where the Emperor supports the Greek Alexandrians against the Jews (see below).

The basic situation and essential story line are based on historical facts, and thus most protagonists are historical personages. In other words, the authors of these texts must have used official documents kept in public archives or copies of such documents.[45] However, all these texts are the result of a process of manipulation and fictionalisation of the historical data, a fictionalisation implemented through a strong ideological bias of anti-Roman propaganda,[46] so that this type of literature – or better sub-literature – may be classified as 'political pamphlets' that circulated outside official channels.[47] In this respect one has to take into consideration that the literary reworking often took place in the decades following the events 'reported/represented' there and in any case copies were made much later (see below). The complex mixture of history, fiction, ideological bias and rhetorical amplification typical for the *Acta Alexandrinorum* is clearly shown by the following instructive examples. (In what follows for the sake of clarity I briefly summarise the content of individual items.)

---

[44] See HARKER (2008) 1. Because of their similarity with the Christian martyr acts these texts have alternatively been labelled as *Acts of the Pagan Martyrs* (see BAUER [1901] 29-47).

[45] On the taking of minutes, public records and archives see HARKER (2008) 99-112. On the issue of the use and reworking of official documents, see below.

[46] HARKER (2008) 173, 175-176.

[47] On the issue of circulation and transmission, see LUISELLI (2016): in particular, note the possibility that this type of texts could be read and copied as entertainment literature (*ibid.* 304-307).

1. *Acta Isidori* (Pl. 6.2),[48] which is the archetype of the entire corpus of the *Acta Alexandrinorum*,[49] and, from a legal standpoint, the first known example of the *cognitio extra ordinem*,[50] concerns the status of the Alexandrian Jews under Gaius and Claudius, and portrays the famous trial of Isidorus. Isidorus accuses Agrippa I, *amicus* (φίλος) of Emperor Claudius,[51] of impiety (ἀσέβεια) on the basis of the Jewish refusal of the imperial cult. King Agrippa is present at the trial. Claudius accuses Isidorus of having ruined his friends, among whom were Theon and Naevius Macro; he justifies himself by saying that he was following Gaius' orders, and puts himself at his service. The situation degenerates into an open confrontation between Claudius and Isidorus with exchanges of insults.[52] Finally, Isidorus is condemned evidently for *crimen maiestatis*. On the one hand, the historicity of the trial in this form can be doubted, since there is no independent evidence for it and also it is very unlikely that an exchange of insults between the Emperor and the ambassador took place; on the other hand, Isidorus is a historical figure and was executed together with another Alexandrian ambassador, Lampon, probably because of their involvement in political intrigues under Caligula (see above). Moreover, the senators mentioned can be identified with historical figures.[53] The number of historical inaccuracies is not surprising: Isidorus'

---

[48] *CPJ* II 156a-d; RODRIGUEZ (2010a) re-edits the entire text (adding *P.Oxy.* XLII 3021 as part of it) with translation, commentary and historical interpretation.

[49] For this definition see RODRIGUEZ (2010a) 2.

[50] See RODRIGUEZ (2010a) 2.

[51] Φίλος is to be understood in a juridical sense: Agrippa and Claudius had been brought up together (see JOS. *AJ* 18, 165) and their mothers – Berenike and Antonia Minor – were very close friends (*ibid.* 18, 143; 156; 165); cf. RODRIGUEZ (2010a) 19.

[52] I am accepting here a dramatic date of the trial of AD 41, supported by the historical context and prosopographical details. An alternative possibility is AD 52/53: in that case the Jewish King present at the trial should be Agrippa II, son of Agrippa I (since Agrippa I died in AD 44). For a general discussion and a survey of the scholarly debate, see *APM* IV 118-133; HARKER (2008) 23-24; RODRIGUEZ (2010a) 16-21.

[53] See RODRIGUEZ (2010a) 18.

alleged responsibility for the death of Macro is chronologically impossible; similarly the accusation of having ruined Theon[54] is problematic, since in other *Acta Alexandrinorum* Theon appears as ambassador together with Balbillus,[55] and Appian associates him with Isidorus himself and Lampon as the Alexandrian envoys executed by Claudius.[56] Finally, it is not historically proven that Isidorus held the office of gymnasiarch, although this is emphasised in the *Acta*.[57]

2. *Acta Hermaisci* (Pl. 6.3),[58] containing a hearing of two embassies – Jewish and Greek – before Trajan, presumably on an episode of violence,[59] offers a sort of caricature of the Emperor.[60] He is portrayed as prejudiced in favour of the Jews (under the influence of his wife Plotina),[61] and definitely hostile to the Greek Alexandrians.[62] Moreover, the accusation by ambassador Hermaiscus that Trajan's privy council is full of impious Jews, although reflecting the historical presence of the Jewish element in Roman public life,[63] is certainly exaggerated. But the most striking section of this text is the description of a supernatural event: the bust of Serapis brought by the Greek Alexandrians as protection[64] suddenly starts to sweat, provoking agitation among the Roman crowd.

---

[54] *CPJ* II 156b, col. i 13-14; 156a, col. i 19.

[55] He is to be identified with Tiberius Claudius Balbillus, the leader of the embassy sent to Claudius in AD 41, who became prefect of Egypt under Nero; see HARKER (2008) 20.

[56] See *BKT* IX 64 and *CPJ* II 159b, col. iv 5-7; cf. HARKER (2008) 45.

[57] See HARKER (2008) 44 and RODRIGUEZ (2010a) 24-25 with n. 116.

[58] *CPJ* II 157.

[59] It is not possible to specify the historical episode of violence between Greeks and Jews in Alexandria that may have inspired this text.

[60] Cf. *APM* VIII, p. 162.

[61] There is no historical evidence for Plotina's alleged Jewish sympathies; see *APM* VIII, pp. 162-163.

[62] On the contrary Dio Chrysostom in his *Alexandrian Oration* (32, 95) states that Trajan bestowed care (ἐπιμέλεια) upon the Alexandrians with concrete signs, the gift of fountains and monumental gateways.

[63] See *APM* VIII, pp. 168-172.

[64] Because of the fragmentary state of the text we are not told what the Jewish ambassadors brought as counterpart to symbolise the protection of their god:

3. In the *Acta Appiani*[65] the brave gymnasiarch Appian[66] apparently accuses Commodus of illicit speculation in the trade of Egyptian wheat, a fact that may reflect the historical institution of the *Classis Commodiana* for the transportation of corn. In spite of the rhetorical amplification, the insults against the Emperor – dishonest and uneducated, brigand-leader[67] – together with the 'disturbing' scenario – the corpse of another victim of the monstrous tyrant lying on the floor and being seen and addressed by Appian, as he is led to execution – effectively give a 'realistic' glimpse of Commodus' 'reign of terror'. The text clearly shows a high degree of literary elaboration and differs from the minutes of proceedings in the sense that narrative parts are more developed at the expense of direct speeches.

4. A rather interesting case is *P.Giss.Lit.* 4, 7 (Pl. 6.4),[68] which contains references to an embassy to a previous Emperor (Tiberius), a record of the hearing of the Alexandrians and the so-called accusers of the Alexandrians – to be identified with the Jews – before Caligula, and scanty remains of a letter of Caligula to the Alexandrians.[69] The Greek ambassadors, thanks to the defence of their representative Areios, managed to persuade Caligula to issue a ruling in their favour at the end of a trial conducted according to the *cognitio extra ordinem*. Interestingly, from a juridical standpoint we have here an *exceptio peremptoria,* through which plaintiff and defendant change role completely: the plaintiff is accused of being a foreign, not a legal citizen of Alexandria, and of claiming illegally the civic

---

since their religion did not allow the representation of Jahweh, it is likely that instead they carried a scroll of the Torah (see *APM* VIII, col. i 18, comm. at pp. 174-175).

[65] *CPJ* II 159.

[66] Why Appian is condemned to death is unclear because of the fragmentary state of the piece.

[67] τύραννος (*CPJ* II 159b, col. ii 5), σοὶ ... ἔγκειται ... ἀφιλοκαγαθία ἀπαιδία (col. ii 11-13), λήσταρχος (col. iv 8).

[68] See HARKER (2008) 35-37; new interpretation in GAMBETTI (2008) and (2009) 87-136; see also RODRIGUEZ (2010b) 594 and RITTER (2015) 179-181.

[69] Cf. *APM* X (*Acta Athenodori*), fr. 1, col. ii 28-49, preserving remains of an imperial letter by Trajan inserted in the text.

status of Alexandrian resident, in other words of seizing unregistered civic rights,[70] and finally is condemned to death by burning.[71] This text is the only case within the corpus of the *Acta Alexandrinorum* in which the Emperor favours the Greek Alexandrians against their enemies, apparently the Jews. The text may really reflect a historical conflict related to the problems of residential rights and citizenships, although it cannot be taken as an actual copy of a genuine record, in spite of Gambetti's well-constructed arguments.[72] The signs of literary reworking are very clear: it may be the result of the amalgamation of different historical embassies; the chronology of the events is rather unlikely and the names of individuals involved seem to have been made up to fit perfectly the situation (Eulalos, featuring as the leader of the Alexandrians, is clearly a speaking name, while Areios is a homonym of Augustus' tutor).[73] Moreover, we would expect a copy of a genuine document to be almost contemporary with the events reported in it, but the script of this text cannot be earlier than the 2nd/3rd century.

As in the case of *P.Giss.Lit.* 4, 7, the copies of *Acta* are usually much later than the dramatic date: in several *Acta* there are fragments of different versions or *recensiones*, often slightly overlapping, but showing divergences.[74] This fact provides an indisputable proof of the manipulation and fictionalisation of

---

[70] GAMBETTI (2009) 116, 127-128 rightly connects this issue with a document, *BGU* IV 1140 = *CPJ* II 151, from the end of the 1st century BC, a petition of an Alexandrian Jew, Helenos, to the Roman prefect Gaius Turranius, where the definition of his status would determine the exemption from the poll-tax; cf. HARKER (2008) 217-218; RITTER (2015) 86-88, 284-285.

[71] The type of punishment clearly suggests that the claim of illegal residence rights is considered a *crimen maiestatis*; see GAMBETTI (2009) 119-125.

[72] See n. 68. She identifies Gaius' ruling contained in this papyrus with the 'historical' Emperor's *mandatum* that the prefect Flaccus implemented with a decree. In any case, she has certainly the merit to have drawn attention to the historical significance of this text, especially with regard to the plausible identification of the accusers of the Alexandrians with the Jews, although they are not explicitly mentioned in the extant text.

[73] Cf. RODRIGUEZ (2010b) 594.

[74] Cf. LUISELLI (2016) 294-295.

the historical events and characters typical for the genre. The *Acta Isidori* offers an instructive example:[75] the so-called *recensio* C presents a more historical approach to the case, since Isidorus speaks about a concrete juridical and fiscal situation, the poll-tax and the privileges of Greek Alexandrians *versus* Jews and Egyptians (see below).

Usually the *Acta* papyri are not library copies, but rather informally produced exemplars with the aim of sparing writing material, so that some have been copied on the back of papyri previously used for documentary texts (whose legal validity had expired), very often written in rather informal scripts,[76] and containing mistakes and phonetic spellings. They share this feature with copies of 'genuine' documents (see below).

In spite of their disputable historical reliability, it is of crucial importance to examine situations, statements and figures of the *Acta Alexandrinorum*, because they illustrate political 'propaganda', and thus reveal a precise mindset and attitude towards Roman power and the strategies that could be applied to deal with it (at least 'virtually'), and at the same time an 'ideal' representation of ethnic and cultural identity.

Similarly unreliable are the polemical and apologetic writings of Philo of Alexandria and Josephus. Although leader of the Jewish embassy to Gaius in AD 38, in his *Legatio* Philo does not provide an objective, accurate and detailed report.[77] On the contrary, he is affected by his *Weltanschauung* and his ideological bias aiming to discern in the persecution of the Jews the signs of divine intervention.[78] Josephus, who wrote a

---

[75] Cf. HARKER (2008) 39-41.

[76] On bibliological and palaeographical aspects see HARKER (2008) 187-192, 195-196; LUISELLI (2016).

[77] On the genesis, character and textual history of the *Legatio* see HARKER (2008) 10-11, GAMBETTI (2009) 13-17. RITTER (2015) offers a comprehensive *status quaestionis* (pp. 12-20) and general conclusions on Philo's historical reliability (pp. 280-282).

[78] Note that there are discrepancies between the *Legatio ad Gaium* and Philo's other work related to the events of AD 38, *In Flaccum*. These could be due to political reasons related to historical changes, since they were written at two different moments; cf. GAMBETTI (2009) 16, 250-252.

generation later,[79] in spite of his declared intention of reporting documents *uerbatim*,[80] clearly manipulated historical data
and official texts. A very instructive example is his version of
Claudius' ruling in AD 41: he definitely confected a pro-
Jewish attitude by the Emperor (*AJ* 19, 279-285),[81] which can
be proved rather improbable through the comparison with
Claudius' letter to the Alexandrians (*CPJ* II 153).[82]

I would like to say some words on the 'purely' documentary
sources. In principle, one would be inclined to consider them as
absolutely objective and historically reliable. However, we have
to take into account that what we can use today is the result of
a process of selection in the production of copies of originals.
An instructive example is *CPJ* II 153, the papyrus that transmits
Claudius' letter to the Alexandrians. What we have does not
seem to be a *uerbatim* copy of the original letter, but rather an
excerpted version of it, carelessly written[83] on the back[84] of a tax
register belonging to the archive of the tax officer Nemesion,

---

[79] On ideological aspects, the historical reliability and readership of his work
see RITTER (2015) 20-46, 124-125, 130, 280-282.

[80] JOS. *AJ* 14, 188; 266.

[81] See OLIVER (1989) 581-583, App. 4.

[82] HARKER (2008) 26-29; GAMBETTI (2009) 230-235. On the contrary, RITTER
(2015) 140-156, even allowing for exaggerations, considers the edict as historically
reliable and not necessarily in contradiction with Claudius' letter. Moreover, the
possibility that Josephus was using a document forged by a Jew apologist is to be
taken into consideration (cf. *ibid.* 147).

[83] Note that the hand is practised, but there are numerous misspellings. Very
probably the text was composed in Latin and then translated into Greek; see BELL
(1924) 2-4, *CPJ* II 153, introd. pp. 37-38.

[84] Other copies of official documents written on recycled material, in informal
scripts and containing spelling mistakes, are: *SB* XII 11012, the already mentioned letter of Nero to the 6475, written on the back of a school text in a semi-
literary hand with some cursive features; *P.Oxy.* XLII 3022, the above-mentioned
letter to Trajan, written in a crude hand on the back of a badly damaged private
letter. Besides, *P.Oxy.* XXV 2435 is an opistholograph (i.e. a roll written on both
sides for the same purpose) probably copied by a single careless hand, containing
a record of Germanicus' speech to the Alexandrians in AD 19 on the recto
(cf. n. 122), and the minutes of a hearing before Augustus which took place in
AD 12/13 on the verso (cf. n. 5). It is probably a private copy of documents
related to contemporary events, possibly meant for limited circulation as a political
pamphlet.

from the village of Philadelphia in the Arsinoite. For example, the text lists only the Greek Alexandrian ambassadors, omitting the Jewish envoys, although in the text Claudius addresses the Jews directly, a fact that may reveal a particular interest in the Greek Alexandrians and possibly hostility towards the Jews.[85]

Moreover, a rather interesting text is *CPJ* II 150 (= *PSI* X 1160; Pl. 6.5), which preserves a copy of the record of a hearing before an Emperor, precisely the speech of the spokesman of the Alexandrians pleading for the re-establishment of the Boule in the city. For this reason the document is very often referred to in the scholarship as the 'Boule-Papyrus'. Although Musurillo included it in his corpus of the *APM* as the very first item of the collection, I do not consider this papyrus as a fictionalised semi-literary text belonging to the *Acta Alexandrinorum,* but rather the copy of a 'genuine' document (possibly an abbreviated version).[86] The mention of the poll-tax in the text gives us as a *terminus post quem* the year 24/23 BC, which is the first attestation of the *laographia.* A textual element strongly supports the identification of the Emperor with Augustus: the occurrence of the simple Καῖσαρ (col. ii 21), which in official documents is used only for Caesar and Octavian.[87] Some scholars, however, argue for an identification with Gaius or Claudius on the basis of historical considerations.[88]

---

[85] A detailed analysis is to be found in HARKER (2008) 25-26; cf. RODRIGUEZ (2010a) 31, n. 162; for other examples of non-*uerbatim* copies of documents see HARKER (2008) 57-59.

[86] From a bibliological standpoint it is worth noting that it belongs to a *tomos synkollesimos* (lit. volume of pieces glued together, i.e. roll composed by gluing together copies of different official documents) kept in a public archive: the puzzling letters – $\overline{\mu}$ $\overline{\varkappa}$ $\overline{\beta}$ – occurring in the upper margin may represent the number of the *tomos* (roll) and *kollema* (individual glued piece/document), i.e. roll no. 40 and document no. 22. The informal semi-cursive script confirms that it is a copy and not the original, which very probably was written in a formal chancery hand; see MESSERI (1998) 189.

[87] See *CPJ* II 150, comm. *ad loc.*; MONTEVECCHI (1970) 9, n. 1 = MONTE-VECCHI (1998) 87, n. 3; MESSERI (1998) 187-189.

[88] See *APM* I, pp. 84-90; *CPJ* II 150, introd., pp. 26-27; HARKER (2008) 28-30. In particular, those scholars point out the parallels between the plea of the Boule-Papyrus and the responses of Claudius' letter to the Alexandrians.

3. Ambassadors in action

The background of an embassy – i.e. the physical and chronological space in which an embassy hearing takes place – is definitely different from that of an assembly. On the one hand, the assembly is a public event of a democratic form of government and as such takes place in a public space usually according to a predetermined and reliable schedule. On the other hand, the embassy hearing always has a 'private' dimension: it is confined to the Emperor and his restricted entourage, and takes place in a more 'intimate' venue – often imperial gardens[89] –, with location and timing completely depending on the Emperor's agenda and timetable and thus very often unpredictable.[90] 'Genuine' documents and the (semi-)fictional *Acta Alexandrinorum* clearly illustrate this aspect. The restricted audience admitted to the hearing consists of the *consilium* of senators and Emperors' *amici*;[91] *matronae* are sometimes

Note that no palaeographical argument can be decisive to assign the document to the reign of Augustus or that of Gaius or Claudius because the span of time is too short for distinctive changes in the evolution of writing to take place. In any case, even assuming that the copy was made during Gaius' or Claudius' reign, the content does not necessarily refer to those periods, since the papyrus could be a later copy of a document of Augustus' reign (cf. *CPJ* II 150, p. 27); cf. RITTER (2015) 179.

[89] On the custom of receiving embassies in gardens, see MILLAR ([2]1992) 23-24. In *CPJ* II 156a, col. ii 5 = 156b, col. i 1, Isidorus' trial takes place in imperial gardens too, but the name is partially in a lacuna and has been supplied in different ways; see KAYSER (2003) 458, n. 92; HARKER (2008) 23-24; RODRIGUEZ (2010a) 16-17. The Jewish envoys guided by Philo and the Greek Alexandrian ambassadors are received by Caligula in the Gardens of Maecenas and Lamia (cf. below, p. 232). Besides, note that in AD 13 Augustus received an embassy in the Library of temple of Apollo (this temple was one of the traditional meeting places of the Senate; see *P.Oxy.* XXV 2435v, lines 31-32). In *P.Giss.Lit.* 4, 7, col. ii 8 the fact that the ambassadors to Tiberius are welcomed by a *cubicularius* suggests that the venue is a private location; see KAYSER (2003) 457.

[90] In this respect, the enormous difficulties experienced by the Jewish ambassadors in AD 39/40 in obtaining a hearing before the 'crazy' Caligula, vividly recorded by Philo, represent an extreme case; see below.

[91] See *P.Oxy.* XXV 2435v, lines 34-40; *CPJ* II 156a, col. ii 5-7 = 156b, col. i 1-3; *APM* X, fr. 2, col. ii, 61-63. On *consilium* see *APM* X, p. 202-204; MILLAR ([2]1992) 119-122; HARKER (2008) 92-93; GAMBETTI (2009) 126-127 with further bibliography.

present.[92] Members of the imperial entourage could potentially influence the ruling of the Emperor. For example, Philo reports that the rival Alexandrian embassy to Gaius bribed the influent chamberlain Helicon to gain the favour of the Emperor.[93] In the *Acta Hermaisci* Trajan appears under the influence of his wife Plotina.[94]

In this respect the scenario of the *Acta Appiani* represents an anomaly. The author somehow modifies the 'non-public' character of the *cognitio extra ordinem* by constructing a dramatic dimension, pathetically charged, where the condemned Appian, led to execution, calls on the Roman people to come and see what is happening to him: "... he cried out in the middle of Rome: 'Come up, Romans, and see an Alexandrian gymnasiarch and ambassador, one without parallel in history, led to execution!'".[95] In the dynamic of the text his appeal works effectively: immediately the *euocatus*[96] informs the Emperor that the people are complaining about the execution of Appian, so that Commodus gives orders to bring him back.[97]

Any embassy, at the very moment of sailing to Rome, could not even predict where and when exactly a hearing in front of the Emperor could be obtained. For example, the Jewish embassy led by Philo, which sailed to Rome after the arrest of the prefect Flaccus, at the same time as a Greek rival embassy, was greeted very briefly by Caligula at the entrance of Agrippina's Gardens;[98] then the envoys followed the Emperor to Puteoli,[99] where he was spending time in his country houses,

---

[92] *CPJ* II 156a, col. ii 7-8, 156b, col. i 3.

[93] PHILO *Leg.* 172-173; on the contrary, the Jewish envoys prefer to write a letter conveying their message while they are waiting for an audience (*Leg.* 178-179).

[94] See above, n. 61.

[95] *CPJ* II 159b, col. iii 7-11: ... ἀνε|βόησεν [μ]έσης Ῥώμης· συνδράμε|τε, Ῥωμ[α]ῖοι· θεωρήσατε ἕνα ἀπ᾽ αἰῶ|νος ἀπαγόμ[ενο]ν γυμνασίαρχον καὶ | πρεσβευ-τὴν Ἀλεξανδρέων. The translation of *CPJ* has been slightly adapted. The phrase [μ]έσης Ῥώμης (line 8) probably indicates the forum. Cf. p. 239 with n. 139.

[96] Veteran serving as a special officer.

[97] *CPJ* II 159b, col. iii 11-col. iv 2.

[98] PHILO *Leg.* 181.

[99] PHILO *Leg.* 185.

and finally obtained a full hearing, opposite the rival Greek embassy, not before September AD 40 (after Gaius' return from Germany) in Rome, i.e. two years later,[100] in the Gardens of Maecenas and Lamia. There, according to Philo's account in *Legatio ad Gaium*, the Emperor was inspecting his estate and behaved in a very erratic and dismissive way, without paying consistent attention to the negotiations, so that Philo compares the role of the Jewish ambassadors to that of actors mocked in a mime.[101] Even if this may be a caricature of a 'crazy' Emperor, it is easy to imagine to what extent it could be difficult for an embassy to communicate with the Emperor. A hint in this direction is provided by a documentary text: some decades before, around 10 BC, a Greek Alexandrian embassy made the effort to reach Augustus in Gaul to inform him about the city's recent grievances, as mentioned in a letter by the Emperor to the Alexandrians.[102] Similarly, roughly a century later, in AD 98, an Alexandrian embassy must have reached the newly acclaimed Emperor Trajan in Germany, the reply to which is partially surviving in *P.Oxy.* XLII 3022.[103]

At the very beginning of a hearing, before coming to concrete and urgent matters concerning the city, it was of crucial importance for the envoys to gain benevolence and clemency from the Emperor.[104] Thus the attempt of Greek Alexandrians and Jews to present themselves as loyal and devoted subjects appears to be a customary 'diplomatic ritual' and for this reason often resorts to formulaic wording. To begin with, the Emperor

[100] See n. 32. Note that the reason for such a delay could have been Gaius' plan to visit Alexandria and deliver his ruling in person there; see PHILO *Leg.* 172, 250, 338; SUET. *Calig.* 49, 2; cf. the hypothetically planned visit by Augustus to Alexandria possibly (but not necessarily) mentioned in the 'Boule-Papyrus' (see below, n. 166). I should specify that there are different reconstructions of the chronology of the embassies to Gaius; see GAMBETTI (2009) 256-259, 266-267, 269-272.

[101] PHILO *Leg.* 351, 359, 365-366, 368.

[102] *P.Oxy.* XLII 3020, fr. i, col. i; cf. n. 106.

[103] See HARKER (2008) 50-51.

[104] See MEN. RHET. 2, 13, 423, 7-11 SPENGEL; RUSSELL-WILSON (1981) 180-181, 337.

has to be addressed in the appropriate way: Alexandrian ambassadors featuring in documentary sources address Augustus as "Lord",[105] "Caesar, invincible hero";[106] among the envoys of the *Acta,* Areios greets Caligula with the phrase "you are the god of the Universe and the master of the city";[107] Isidorus (or Lampon?), probably with irony, addresses Claudius as "Olympian Caesar".[108] Similarly, the Jewish envoys led by Philo address Gaius as "August Emperor"[109] and "Lord Gaius".[110]

The 'crazy' Caligula, of course, obsessed with the idea of his divine nature, represents an extreme case. Philo critically observes the attitude of the rival envoys and implicitly classifies it as flattery: as the Emperor appears the Greek Alexandrians burst into acclamations, address him with all ritual epithets of the gods, and even use body language through gesticulating and dancing;[111] later they laugh artificially to please the Emperor, who – they think – is trying to be witty.[112] By contrast, the attitude of the Jewish delegation is dignified, respectful and deferential: they simply bow before Gaius.[113]

As subjects, ambassadors present themselves as suppliants before the Emperor. So the *rhetor* Timoxenus before Augustus:

[105] δέσπο[τα, *CPJ* II 150, col. ii 20. This form of address is also used by King Agrippa in the petition to Caligula concerning the desecration of Jewish temples; see PHILO *Leg.* 276, 290; cf. also 171 and DICKEY (2001), esp. 3-5.

[106] Καῖσαρ ἀνίκητε ἥρως, *P.Oxy.* LXII 3020, fr. 1, col. ii 1.

[107] σὺ εἶ ὁ τ[ο]ῦ κόσμου | θεὸς καὶ τῆς πόλεως ἐκράτη[ους, *P.Giss.Lit.* 4, 7, col. ii 35-iii 1.

[108] Ὀλύμπιε Καῖ|[σαρ], *CPJ* II 156b, col. i 25-26 (cf. 17 "my Lord Caesar", κύριέ μου Καῖσαρ). The editors note *ad loc.* that this epithet is very unusual for a Roman Emperor before Hadrian and probably is a mocking allusion to the famous Olympian Pericles (cf. AR. *Ach.* 530, Περικλέης οὐλύμπιος; see *APM* IV, pp. 132-133).

[109] Σεβαστὸς Αὐτοκράτωρ, PHILO *Leg.* 352; cf. 309, 322.

[110] κύριε Γάιε, *Leg.* 356; see DICKEY (2001), esp. 6-7 and cf. here nn. 105, 108.

[111] PHILO *Leg.* 354-355. The body language of the Alexandrians must have included the προσκύνησις (*Leg.* 116), an attitude that Aristotle considers as "barbarian" (*Rhet.* 1361a).

[112] PHILO *Leg.* 361.

[113] PHILO *Leg.* 352.

234   DANIELA COLOMO

"In appearance we are here as your suppliants; but in truth [our city] with full enthusiasm is paying worship to your most sacred [Fortune] …".[114] In the *Acta* Isidorus says to Claudius: "My Lord Caesar, I beseech you to listen to my account of my native city's sufferings".[115]

Roman Emperors, in the same line of diplomatic etiquette, acknowledge the expression of loyalty and assure their benevolence. A rather instructive example is this section of Claudius' letter to the Alexandrians:[116]

"… [subj. twelve Alexandrian ambassadors individually named], your ambassadors, presented me with the decree and spoke at length about the city, directing my attention to your goodwill towards us, which, you may be sure, has long been stored in my memory, since it comes from your natural reverence towards the Emperors, as I know from many instances, and particularly from your devotion to my own family, which we have returned. Of this, to pass over other instances and mention the latest, the best witness is my brother, Germanicus Caesar, who addressed you in the most sincere language."[117]

---

[114] λόγῳ γὰρ **ἡμεῖς** | **[ἱκετε]ύσαντες πάρεσμεν** τὸ δ' ἀληθὲς | [ἡ πόλις] ἁπάσῃ σπουδῇ τὴν σὴν ἱερωτάτην | [τύχην] προσκυνήσασα τυγχάνει, *P.Oxy.* XXV 2435v, lines 58-61. Lines 59-61 contain a clearly corrupted text (το δ αληθος | [.....]απασι α σπουδην την συνιεροτατην | [τυχην] προσκυνησασαν ετυγχανε[ιν]) and therefore I have printed it according to the emended version suggested by the *ed. pr.* in comm.

[115] κύριέ μου Καῖσαρ, τῶν γονά[των σου δέομαι] | ἀκοῦσαί μου τὰ πονοῦν[τα τῇ πατρίδι], *CPJ* II 156a, col. ii 10-11; cf. 156b, col. i 6-8. In addition, note that in *P.Giss.Lit.* 4, 7, col. ii 4-6 S. STEPHENS (*P.Yale* II 107, comm. *ad loc.*, p. 94) has tentatively supplemented ⟨ἱ⟩κεσίοις ("of or for suppliants", in the dative case plural); see GAMBETTI (2009) 106-107 with n. 39.

[116] On the role of εὐσέβεια (piety) in the relationship between Emperor and subjects, see DÖRNER (2014) 242-243.

[117] *CPJ* II 153, col. ii 20-27: … οἱ πρέσβεις ὑμῶν, ἀναδόντες μοι τὸ ψήφισμα πολλὰ περὶ | τῆς πόλεως διεξῆλθον, ὑπαγόμενοί μοι δῆλον πρὸς τὴν εἰς ἡμᾶς | εὔνοιαν, ἣν ἐκ πολλῶν χρόνων, εὖ ἴστε, παρ' ἐμοὶ τεταμιευμένην | εἴχετε, φύσει μὲν εὐσεβεῖς περὶ τοὺς Σεβαστοὺς ὑπάρχοντες, ὡς | ἐκ πολλῶν μοι γέγονε γνώριμον, ἐξαιρέτως δὲ περὶ τὸν ἐμὸν | οἶκον καὶ σπουδάσαντες καὶ σπουδασθέντες, ὧν ἵνα τὸ τελευ|ταῖον εἴπω παρεὶς τὰ ἄλλα μέγιστός ἐστιν μάρτυς οὑμὸς ἀδελφὸς | Γερμανικὸς Καῖσαρ γνησιωτέραις ὑμᾶς φωναῖς προσαγορεύσας. On the interpretation of the passage see ŁUKASZEWICZ (1998). In lines 26-27 Claudius mentions the triumphal welcome given to Germanicus in Alexandria during his

In spite of the use of *topoi* and formulaic language, which can be paralleled in other documents,[118] the mention of his late brother assumes a sort of personal and even emotional nuance. As said above, embassies delivered honorific decrees to Emperors, aiming to express in a concrete way their loyalty as subjects. The Greek Alexandrians were accustomed to offer divine honours, construction of temples dedicated to the imperial cult and nomination of a high priest. An interesting source in this respect is again a section of Claudius' letter to the Alexandrians, where he accepts the statues, but firmly refuses divine prerogatives,[119] following the Roman traditional ideology embraced by Augustus[120] and his successors with the exception of Caligula:[121] "… But the establishment of a high-priest and temples of myself I decline, not wishing to be offensive to my contemporaries and in the belief that temples and the like have been set apart in all ages for the gods alone".[122]

Roughly fifteen years later, Nero reacts with similar attitude in his letter to a Greek polis and the 6475,[123] using the same

visit in AD 19; cf. n. 122 and *Discussion* p. 257. On this occasion Germanicus addressed the Alexandrian crowd in the Greek language; see comm. in *CPJ* 153 on line 27.

[118] Cf. *P.Oxy.* XLII 3022, Trajan's letter to the Alexandrians, similar in tone and formulaic wording; see OLIVER (1989) 136-139, no. 46; HARKER (2008) 50-51.

[119] *CPJ* II 153, col. ii 28-col. iii 51.

[120] On Augustus and imperial cult, see DÖRNER (2014), esp. 19-25, 136-145, 151-180, 202-213, 280-284, 370, 404-429, 461-463.

[121] On Caligula and imperial cult, see DÖRNER (2014), esp. 289-296, 298, 353-356, 360-361, 431-444.

[122] *CPJ* II 153, col. iii 48-51: … ἀρχιερέα δ' ἐμὸν καὶ ναῶν κατασκευὰς | παραιτοῦμαι, οὔτε φορτικὸς τοῖς κατ' ἐμαυτὸν ἀνθρώποις | βουλόμενος εἶναι τὰ ἱερὰ δὲ καὶ τὰ τοιαῦτα μόνοις τοῖς θεοῖς | ἐξαίρετα ὑπὸ τοῦ παντὸς αἰῶνος ἀποδε-δόσθαι κρίν[ω]ν. A very similar formulation is to be found in another letter by Claudius addressed to the Thasians and preserved in an inscription, *IG* XII 8 = *SEG* 39.910 (AD 42), lines 5-7. For other parallels, see OLIVER (1989) 15. On Claudius and imperial cult, see DÖRNER (2014), esp. 219-241, 266-273, 314-318, 444. A comparable attitude towards divine honours is shown by Gaius' father Germanicus, who made a private visit to Egypt and Alexandria in AD 19, where he was proclaimed god and addressed as *imperator*; see *P.Oxy.* XXV 2435r, *SB* I 3924. On the significance of Germanicus' visit, see DÖRNER (2014) 384-389.

[123] *SB* XII 11012, col. i 1-6.

type of formulaic language: "... of the remaining two honours (that you offer), I refused the temple in my honour, because it is just that such an honour is given by men to the gods only".[124] Ethnic and cultural pride is an essential aspect of the way ambassadors 'construct' their image: both Greek Alexandrians and Jews present themselves as members of an élite, definitely separated from the uncivilised Egyptian masses. The Greek Alexandrians define themselves as Hellenes, as a nation (ἔθνος) that embodies a superior culture, re-enacting the Greek traditional bipolarity Hellenes/barbaroi in the dichotomy Greeks/ Egyptians – i.e. allegedly non-Hellenised Egyptians – and/or Greeks/Jews, in spite of the historical fact that the Jews of Egypt were deeply Hellenised.[125] The Alexandrian spokesman of the embassy of the famous 'Boule-Papyrus' tells Augustus that the non-Hellenes – evidently Egyptians and Jews[126] – are uncultured and uneducated (ἄθρεπτοι καὶ ἀνάγωγοι γεγονότες ἄνθρωποι) and risk contaminating (μολύνειν) the Alexandrian *politeuma*.[127] Isidorus ranks the Jews at the same level as the Egyptians: "They are not of the same nature as the Alexandrians, but live rather after the fashion of the Egyptians".[128]

The idealistic reference to their ties with the Greek motherland comes out as 'natural' in the *Acta Athenodori*: Alexandria is ruled by the same laws as Athens, which are the best in the

---

[124] ... ἐ]κ δὲ τῶν ἀπολειπομέ[ν]ων | δύο, τόν τε ναόν μου παρῃτη|σάμην, διὰ τὸ θεοῖς μόνοις ταύτην τὴν τιμὴν ὑπ᾽ ἀν|[θ]ρ[ώ]πων δικαίως ἀπονέ|[με]σθαι [...]. Cf. the detailed analysis by MONTEVECCHI (1970) 11-31 = MONTEVECCHI (1998) 89-109. Note that in line 2 the papyrus has σου (genitive of the personal pronoun of the second person singular), clearly a mechanical mistake that has been corrected with the required form of the pronoun of the first person. On Nero and imperial cult, see DÖRNER (2014), esp. 255-257, 444-454.

[125] It is worth noting that some very fragmentary texts have been included in the category of *dubia uel incerta* of the *Acta Alexandrinorum* by HARKER (2008) 222, 223 on the basis of the occurrence of key words – Hellenism and Alexandria, Greek birth – that may refer to this topos: *P.Harr.* II 173, lines 11-12; *P.Bour.* 7.

[126] But note that in the text the two groups are not explicitly mentioned.

[127] *CPJ* II 150, col. ii 6.

[128] *CPJ* II 156c, col. ii 25-27: οὔκ εἰσιν Ἀλ[εξανδρεῦσιν] | ὁμοιοπαθεῖς, τρόπῳ δὲ Αἰγυπτ[ίων ὁμοῖοι].

world because of their balanced mixture of justice and clemency.[129] Significantly, the ambassador-martyr Appian, in his microsynkrisis[130] between the cruel Commodus and his father Marcus Aurelius, portrays the latter as the ideal Hellenised ruler, a philosopher and thus a noble emperor:[131]

"... Your father, the divine Antoninus, was fit to be emperor. For, look you, first of all he was a philosopher; secondly, he was not avaricious, thirdly, he was good. But you have precisely the opposite qualities; you are tyrannical, dishonest, ignorant!"[132]

The Greek institution that symbolises and at the same time gives concrete reality to their ethnical and cultural status as Hellenes is the Gymnasium, which is largely involved in the education of the younger generations and thus preserves the Greek παιδεία, i.e. the culture of highly educated people, their

---

[129] *APM* X, fr. 1, col. i 12-18: Caesar: "Is it true that the Athenians have the same laws as the Alexandrians?" Athenodorus: "It is; and they are stronger than all other laws, having a happy admixture of clemency." (Καῖσαρ· | τοῖς γὰρ αὐτοῖς νόμοις χρῶ(ν)|ται Ἀθηναῖοι καὶ Ἀλεξα(ν)|δρεῖς; Ἀθηνόδωρος· πάν|[των] γὰρ νόμων ἰσχυρότε|[ροι ὄ]ντες τὴν εὐκρασία(ν) | [τῆς] φιλανθρωπίας ἔχουσι(ν).) The statement is in itself emblematic. At the same time, in the context of the *Acta Athenodori* it has a specific function: it is used as a justification for the fact that the Alexandrians plead their cause – the release of Greek Alexandrians detained in Rome – through an Athenian embassy, probably trying to exploit the favour demonstrated to Athens by Hadrian, the 'philhellene' Emperor. These observations are based on the interpretation of this text according to which the embassy is Athenian and the Emperor involved is Hadrian, which I am accepting here; on different views see *APM* VII, pp. 196-198.

[130] I am using the word σύγκρισις, comparison (Lat. *comparatio*), as a rhetorical *terminus technicus* indicating a specific exercise belonging to the category of the *Progymnasmata*, i.e. the exercises of the first stage of the rhetorical training in the Graeco-Roman world. For other examples of the use of typical progymnasmatic techniques that can be detected in the *Acta Alexandrinorum*, see Index C in *APM, s.v.* progymnasmatic writers (p. 298).

[131] *CPJ* II 159b, col. ii 7-13; the translation of *CPJ* has been slightly adapted.

[132] ... τῷ γὰρ θεῷ | Ἀντωνίνῳ [τ]ῷ π[ατ]ρί σου ἔπρεπε | αὐτοκρατορεύειν. ἄκουε, τὸ μὲν | πρῶτον ἦ[ν] φιλόσοφος, τὸ δεύτερον | ἀφιλάργυρος, τ[ὸ] τρίτον φιλάγαθος· σοὶ | τούτων τὰ ἐναντία ἔγκειται, τυραν|νία ἀφιλοκαγαθία ἀπαιδία. Note that ἀπαιδία (line 13) is an alternative form of ἀπαιδευσία; see *APM* XI, p. 215, comm. on line 13.

humanitas. Expression of this ethnic and cultural pride, which can be summarised in the key word εὐγένεια, nobility of birth/race,[133] emerges in the violent confrontation of several trial scenes of the *Acta*. Paradigmatically Isidorus reacts to Claudius' insult – "son of a (slave) girl-musician" – by proudly stating his status of freeborn man and gymnasiarch of the glorious city of Alexandria, and retaliating with an equally powerful insult, "cast-off son of the Jewess Salome".[134] Similarly in the name of the same values Appian appeals against the Emperor:[135]

Appian: "By your *genius* I am neither mad nor have I lost my sense of shame. I am making an appeal on behalf of my noble rank and my privileges".

The Emperor: "How so?"

Appian: "As one of noble rank and a gymnasiarch".

The Emperor: "Do you suggest that I am not of noble rank?"

Appian: "That I know not; I am merely appealing on behalf of my own nobility and privileges".[136]

This attitude is also reflected in the body language and external appearance of ambassadors described in the *Acta*. Isidorus is

---

133 *CPJ* II 159b, col. iv 15-col. v 8; cf. ARIST. *Rhet.* 1360b. Note that the occurrence in *CPJ* II 159b, col. iii 3 means "*insignia* of noble rank".

134 *CPJ* II 156d, col. iii 7-12: "Claudius Caesar: 'Isidorus, you are really the son of a girl-musician.' Isidorus: 'I am neither a slave nor a girl-musician's son, but gymnasiarch of the glorious city of Alexandria. But you are the cast-off son of the Jewess Salome!'" Κλαύδιος Καῖσαρ· ἀσφαλῶς | [ἐ]κ μουσικῆς εἶ, Ἰσίδωρε. Ἰσίδωρος· | [ἐγ]ὼ μὲν οὔκ εἰμι δοῦλος οὐδὲ μουσικῆς | [υἱ]ός, ἀλλὰ διασήμου πόλεως [Ἀ]λεξαν|[δρ]εί[ας] γυμνασίαρχος. σὺ δὲ ἐκ Σαλώμη[ς] | [τ]ῆς Ἰουδα[ίας] υ]ἱὸς [ἀπό]βλητος. See *APM* IV, pp. 128-130, RODRIGUEZ (2010a) 22-23; RITTER (2015) 155-156. The 'vulgarity' of these insults is comparable to 'Ἰουδαῖος τριωβολεῖος, "a two-penny Jew", uttered by Isidorus against King Agrippa (*CPJ* II 156b, col. i 18; see comm. *ad loc.*; cf. HARKER [2008] 44; RODRIGUEZ [2010a] 10, 39).

135 *CPJ* II 159b, col. iv 13-col. v 8.

136 Ἀππιανός· νὴ τὴν σὴν τύ|χην οὔτε μαίνομαι οὔτε ἀπονενό|ημαι, ἀλλ' ὑπὲρ τῆς ἐμαυτοῦ εὐγε|νείας καὶ τῶν ἐ[μοὶ προσηκόντων] | ἀπαγγέλλω. αὐτ[οκράτωρ· πῶς;] |]Ἀππιανὸς· ὡς εὐγ[ενὴς καὶ γυμνασί]|αρχος. αὐτοκρά-τω[ρ· φῂς οὖν ὅτι ἡμεῖς] | ἀγενεῖς ἐσμεν; [Ἀππιανός· τοῦτο μὲν] | οὐκ ο[ἶ]δα· ἐγὼ [ὑπὲρ τῆς ἐμαυτοῦ] | εὐγενείας καὶ τῶν [ἐμοὶ προσηκόν]|των ἀπαγγέλλω. See MERKELBACH (1994).

being taken away to execution in the robes of a gymnasiarch.[137] The gymnasiarch Appian obtains from Commodus permission to be led to execution with the symbols of his noble office, the headband and the white shoes. The description is detailed and dramatic:[138]

"Appian (then) took his head-band and put it on his head and, putting his white shoes on his feet, he cried out in the middle of Rome: 'Come up, Romans, and see an Alexandrian gymnasiarch and ambassador, one without parallel in history, led to execution!'"[139]

The pride of being a Hellene and of noble birth is intrinsically part of the patriotic attitude, the love for the fatherland (πατρίς)

---

[137] *CPJ* II 156b, col. ii 46-47: ἀπα]|γόμενον ἐν σχ[ήματι γυμνασιαρχικῷ. In respect to body language a rather fragmentary sequence in col. ii 35-37 – [ὁ] | ῥήτωρ τῇ δεξι[ᾷ...] | τὸ ἱμάτιον ἔρρι[ψεν...] | καὶ εἶπεν, κτλ. – is particularly interesting: it seems to suggest a gesture of despair or protest. According to *APM* IV, comm. on lines 35ff, p. 137, perhaps Isidorus' advocate tore his *himation* and threw himself upon the ground before the Emperor, as happens in similar situations found in novels (e.g. CHARITON 5, 2, 4; HELIOD. *Aeth.* 6, 8). Thus the following supplement has been suggested: καὶ τότε ὁ | ῥήτωρ, τῇ δεξιᾷ περιρρη-ξάμενος...] τὸ ἱμάτιον, ἔρρι[ψεν ἑαυτὸν χάμαι] | καὶ εἶπεν, κτλ. Cf. RODRIGUEZ (2010a) 11. However, *CPJ* II 156b, comm. on line 36 questions the presence of a professional *rhetor* assisting Isidorus, since Isidorus plays the role of the prosecutor, unless "[...] we suggest that in the course of the trial he was formally charged with having caused the death of Claudius' friends and was now himself in need of a professional advocate". In other words, the subject of the sentence can be Isidorus, who then would be qualified as a *rhetor*; cf. HARKER (2008) 188 189. Note that MAGNANI's (2009) 150 observation – "Isidoro assume una posizione da retore greco raccogliendo con la destra parte del suo mantello" – does not reflect the actual Greek text.

[138] *CPJ* II 159b, col. iii 5-11.

[139] Ἀππιανὸς λαβὼν τὸ στρόφιον | ἐπὶ τῆς κεφα[λ]ῆς ἔθηκεν, καὶ τὸ | φαικάσ-[ιο]ν ἐπὶ τοὺς πόδας θεὶς ἀνε|βόησεν [μ]έσης Ῥώμης· συνδράμε|τε, Ῥωμ[α]ῖοι· θεωρήσατε ἕνα ἀπ᾽ αἰῶ|νος ἀπαγόμ[ενο]ν γυμνασίαρχον καὶ | πρεσβευτὴν Ἀλε-ξανδρέων. The translation of *CPJ* has been slightly adapted. Cf. p. 231 with n. 95. The phrase in lines 9-10 ἕνα ἀπ᾽ αἰῶ|νος has to be understood in a superlative sense as "unprecedented/without comparison". It occurs in DIO CASS. 63, 20, 5, at the end of the acclamation of the Roman crowd welcoming Nero back from Greece: Ὀλυμπιονῖκα οὐᾶ... ὡς εἰς περιοδονίκης, εἷς ἀπ᾽ αἰῶνος; see *DGE s.v.* εἷς, 2.e. and comm. in *APM*, XI, pp. 216-217, *CJP* II 159b, col. iii 9ff. and cf. HARKER (2008) 193-194. I would like to thank Angelos Chaniotis for his advice on this specific point.

Alexandria. If, on the one hand, this is the noble cause for which ambassadors are ready to accept their martyrdom in the *Acta Alexandrinorum*, on the other hand a documentary source, the famous 'Boule-Papyrus', mentions service to the fatherland (ἡ τῆς πατρίδος ὑπηρεσία) as a fundamental duty to be performed by the citizen of noble rank (εὐγενής) in a more realistic and pragmatic context. In the actual wording the emphasis is on the social control implemented by the community, represented by the Boule, in order to prevent citizens from avoiding such a duty.[140]

The self-assertion of the Greek Alexandrian ambassadors is strictly linked to the demonisation of their Jewish rivals by what seems to be a commonplace: the Jews are labelled as a plague on mankind.[141] Isidorus' statement in the *Acta* – "I accuse them of attempting to stir up the entire world"[142]– recalls the official stance of Claudius in his letter to the Alexandrians, within a threatening warning to the Jews to comply with his order: "If they disobey, I shall proceed against them in every way as fomenting a common plague for the whole world".[143]

In the *Acta* the Jews are defined "impious Jews" (ἀνόσιοι Ἰουδαῖοι),[144] actually a 'documentary' phrase occurring in two official letters concerning the Jewish revolt of AD 115-117.[145]

---

[140] *CPJ* II 150, col. ii 13-14: "… so that no 'one who is suitable' would escape the service to his fatherland" (… μήτε ε[ὔθετός τις] | ὧν φεύγηι τὴν τῆς πατρίδος ὑπηρεσίαν). Interestingly *APM* I, p. 91 comments: "A suggestion that serving on an embassy was already being considered almost as a liturgy", i.e. an undesired financial burden, since they had to undertake to go on the embassy at their own expense (liturgy as a *terminus technicus* indicates a temporary compulsory public service owed to state).

[141] Cf. *Acts of Apostles* 17, 6; 24, 5.

[142] *CPJ* II 156c, col. ii 22-24: ἐγκ[αλῶ αὐτοῖς] | [ὅτι κ]αὶ ὅλην τὴν οἰκουμένην [ἐπιχειροῦσιν] | [ταράσ]σειν.

[143] *CPJ* II 153, 98-100: εἰ δὲ μή, πάντα | τρόπον αὐτοὺς ἐπεξελεύσομαι καθάπερ κοινήν | τινα τῆς οἰκουμένης νόσον ἐξεγείροντας.

[144] *CPJ* II 157, col. iii 42-43 (if, as the editors argue *ad loc.*, this is an official qualification of the Jews after the revolt of AD 115-117, we have a *terminus post quem* for the dating of the composition of the *Acta Hermaisci*); *CPJ* II 158a, col. vi 14 (cf. *ibid.* col. ii 13).

[145] *CPJ* II 438, lines 4 and 443, col. ii 4-5; both documents come from Hermopolis.

The Greek Alexandrians, so inclined to give divine honours to the Roman Emperors, present the Jews as prone to impiety (ἀσέβεια) and thus to betrayal.[146] Philo and his fellow ambassadors, accused of impiety by the 'infamous' Isidorus before Caligula, tactfully try to prove their loyalty to the Emperor in a form of *pietas* compatible with their religious customs:[147] *de facto* they have offered sacrifices on behalf of the Emperor three times, at his accession, when he was very ill and on the occasion of the expedition in Germany. This argument has its strength, although Gaius reacts to it in a dismissive way, stressing the difference between sacrificing to the Emperor as god and sacrificing on behalf of the Emperor.[148]

Interestingly, Jews share the same racial and cultural prejudices as Greek Alexandrians towards the (allegedly non-Hellenised) Egyptians. For example, Philo portrays the Egyptians of Gaius' entourage, led by the 'infamous' Helicon, as "a seed bed of evil in whose souls both the venom and the temper of the native crocodiles and asps were reproduced".[149]

Within the sphere of 'Realpolitik' and economic structures, the (alleged) Greek Alexandrian superiority over both Jews and Egyptians is based on a concrete economic factor: their privileged fiscal status, i.e. the exemption from the *laographia*. This

---

[146] Cf. JOS. *C. Ap.* 2, 65; on the Jews' attitude towards the imperial cult, see RITTER (2015) 45, 169-171, 174-176. The charge of impiety against the Jews seems to occur in the fragmentary *P.Oxy.* XLII 3021, minutes of a hearing of two embassies from the 1st century (the Emperor is not named), col. i 14-16:]ν ἀλλὰ τῆς τῶν θεῶν |]. ἐν τοῖς ἱεροῖς αὐτῶν |] κατεμπατοῦνται, "but ... of the gods ... in their temples ... are trampled ..."; cf. HARKER (2008) 30-31, GAMBETTI (2009) 218-220, 229. Note that RITTER (2015) 142-143, 153, nn. 64 and 65, 287 considers *P.Oxy.* XLII 3021 *tout court* as documentary evidence for an Alexandrian embassy to Claudius.

[147] On Philo's attitude towards imperial cult, see DÖRNER (2014) 353-363.

[148] PHILO *Leg.* 355-357: very likely these sacrifices had been carried out in Jerusalem. This implies that here Philo is referring to the Jewish nation in general, not specifically to the Alexandrian Jews; see RITTER (2015) 105 with n. 103.

[149] PHILO *Leg.* 166: πονηρὰ σπέρματα, κροκοδείλων καὶ ἀσπίδων τῶν ἐγχωρίων ἀναμεμαγμένοι τὸν ἰὸν ὁμοῦ καὶ θυμὸν ἐν ταῖς ψυχαῖς (translation by F.H. COLSON, Loeb edition, vol. X [1962]); cf. *ibid.* 205; see RODRIGUEZ (2010a) 36-37; on the general issue see RITTER (2015) 172-174.

represents a powerful argument in the *Acta Isidori*, in the
confrontation between Isidorus and King Agrippa.[150] Isidorus
says: "[subj. the Jews] are not of the same nature as the
Alexandrians, but live rather after the fashion of the Egyptians.
Are they not on a level with those who pay the poll-tax?".[151]
Here it is worth noting that the alleged fact of the payment of
the poll-tax by the Jews 'naturally' comes out of his mouth in
the form of a rhetorical question. Agrippa promptly replies in
an attempt at resorting to historical evidence: "The Egyptians
had their taxes levied on them by their rulers... But no one has
imposed tributes on the Jews".[152]

As we have seen, the fiscal status is *de facto* determined by the
membership of the Gymnasium: thus this institution has an
essential function at the economic level and, at the same time,
accomplishes a basic cultural function in preserving the Greek
παιδεία. The Greek Alexandrians' preoccupation with protecting their own privileges is particularly visible – historically and
thus rhetorically – in their attempt to reinforce their autonomy
through the re-establishment of the Boule. At the same time,
the Boule, like the Gymnasium – as a basic institution of 'the'
Greek polis – is an essential element of their identity as Hellenes. 'Genuine' documents suggest that this must have been a
core issue in diplomatic activities: as such it can be traced back
to the Augustan period in the above-mentioned 'Boule-Papyrus'.
The ambassador recorded in these minutes manages to provide
a well-crafted application of expediency (τὸ συμφέρον):[153]

> "I submit, then, that the Boule will see to it that none of those
> who are liable to enrolment for the poll-tax diminish the reve-
> nue by being listed in the public records along with the *epheboi*

---

150 *CPJ* II 156c, col. ii 25-30.
151 οὔκ εἰσιν Ἀλ[εξανδρεῦσιν] | ὁμοιοπαθεῖς, τρόπῳ δὲ Αἰγυπτ[ίων ὁμοῖοι.] |
οὔκ εἰσι ἴσοι τοῖς φόρον τελ[οῦσι;
152 [Αἰ]γ[υπτ]ίοις ἔστησαν φόρους [ο]ἱ ἄρχ[οντες] | [..].[.].[...]ν· τούτοις δὲ
οὐδείς. See HARKER (2008) 217; GAMBETTI (2009) 61-62; RODRIGUEZ (2010b)
594-595; RITTER (2015) 88-89, 150, n. 58, 173 with n. 135, 181 n. 153 (occurrence
of the word ὁμοιοπαθεῖς in *Acts of Apostles* 14, 15), 183.
153 ARIST. *Rhet.* 1358b.

for each year; and it will take care that the pure citizen body of Alexandria is not corrupted by men who are uncultured and uneducated.

And if anyone be unreasonably burdened by taxes exacted by the *Idioslogos* or by any other tax-agent who may be oppressing the people, the Boule, in assembly before **your Prefect**, might lend support to the weak and prevent the income that could be preserved **for you** from being plundered by anyone at all, simply through lack of a remedy. Again, if there should be need to send an embassy **to you**, the Boule might elect those who are suitable, so that no one ignoble might make the journey and no one who is capable might avoid this service to his fatherland."[154]

He convincingly presents the function of the Boule of preventing the illegitimate appropriation of citizen rights – by ineligible individuals, clearly Egyptians and Jews – through the membership of the Gymnasium, which means obtaining exemption from the poll-tax at the expense of the Roman treasury. At the same time the Boule would prevent corruption among tax collectors, and would select suitable and dignified ambassadors to be sent to Rome. The *rhetor* is particularly careful to avoid conveying the impression that the Boule would grant independence from Rome, stressing that it would meet before the Roman prefect. His attempt to convey the idea that the Emperor will have the absolute control of the situation can also be observed at the stylistic level: he employs a sort of *polyptoton*, consisting in the repetition of the personal pronoun of the second person

---

[154] *CPJ* II 150, col. ii 1-14: φημὶ γὰρ ταύτην φρ[ο]ντιεῖν ἵνα | μή τι τῶν μελλόντων τινὲς λαογραφεῖσθαι, τοῖς κατ᾽ ἔτος ἐφήβοις | συνεγγραφόμενοι ἐπὶ τὴν δημοσίαν γρα[φήν, τὴν] πρόσοδον | ἐλασσῶσι καὶ τὸ πολίτευμα τῶν Ἀλεξανδρείων ϰα[θ]αρὸν ὑπάρ|χον ἄθρεπτοι καὶ ἀνάγωγοι γεγονότες ἄνθρωποι μολύνωσι· εἰ δέ | τις κατα{βαρ}βαροῖτο παρὰ λόγον πραττόμενος ἢ ὑπὸ Ἰδί[ο]υ | Λόγου ἤ | τινος πράκτορος ἀνθρώπου᾽ς᾽ διασείοντος, συνερχομένη ἡ βου|λὴ **πρὸς τὸν σὸν ἐπίτροπον** συνεπισχύηι τοῖς ἀσθ[ε]νοῦσι, καὶ μὴ | δι᾽ ἐρημίαν βοηθείας **τὰ σοὶ τηρεῖσθαι δυνάμενα** ὑπὸ τῶν τυχόντων | ἀνθρώπων διαφορηθῇ. ἔτι δέ, εἰ δέοιτο **πρεσβείαν πρὸς σὲ** πέμ|πειν, αὕτη προχειρίζηται τοὺς ἐπιτηδείους, καὶ [μήτε ἀσε]|μνός τις ἐκπορεύσηται [μήτε εὔθετός τις] μήτε ε[ὔθετός τις] | ὧν φεύγηι τὴν τῆς πατρίδος ὑπηρεσίαν. The translation of *CPJ* has been slightly adapted. On the reading ϰα[θ]αρὸν (line 5) see PINTAUDI (2011-2012) 159.

singular and the related possessive adjective (printed in bold in the text).

The re-establishment of the Boule is still a 'hot' issue some decades later, in the aftermath of the riots of AD 38-41. A section from Claudius' letter to the Alexandrians reveals that the arguments formulated by those ambassadors are similarly based on expediency:[155]

"About the Boule, what your custom was under the old kings, I cannot say, but that you did not have one under the emperors before me, you are well aware. Since this is a new matter now laid before me for the first time and **it is uncertain whether it will profit the city and my affairs**, I have written to Aemilius Rectus[156] to examine the question and report to me whether the Boule should be established, and, if it should, what form it should take."[157]

From lines 69-70 we may infer that the ambassadors have stressed the utility of the city council both for the Alexandrian subjects and for the Roman rulers. In addition to this, another argument must have been based on alleged historical evidence, the existence of the Boule during the Ptolemaic period.[158]

And what about the rhetorical tactics of Jewish ambassadors? The same document, Claudius' letter, is very instructive in this respect:[159]

"Even now, therefore, **I conjure the Alexandrians** to behave gently and kindly towards the Jews who have inhabited the same city from many years, and not to dishonour any of their customs in their worship of their god, but to allow them to keep their

---

[155] *CPJ* II 153, col. iv 66-72. The translation of *CPJ* has been slightly adapted.
[156] The prefect of Egypt appointed after Caligula's death.
[157] περὶ δὲ τῆς βουλῆς ὅ τι μέν ποτε σύνηθες | ὑμῖν ἐπὶ τῶν ἀρχαίων βασιλέων οὐκ ἔχω λέγειν, ὅτι δὲ ἐπὶ τῶν | πρὸ ἐμοῦ Σεβαστῶν οὐκ εἴχετε σαφῶς οἴδατε. καινοῦ δὴ | πράγματος νῦν πρῶτον καταβαλλομένου ὅπερ **ἄδηλον εἰ συνοί|σει τῇ πόλει καὶ τοῖς ἐμοῖς πράγμασι** ἔγραψα Αἰμιλίωι Ῥήκτωι | διασκέψασθαι καὶ δηλῶσαί μοι εἴτε καὶ συνίστασθαι τὴν ἀρχὴν δεῖ, | τόν τε τρόπον, εἴπερ ἄρα συνάγειν δέοι, καθ' ὃν γενήσεται τοῦτο.
[158] Col. iv 67 ἐπὶ τῶν ἀρχαίων βασιλέων, "under the old kings".
[159] *CPJ* II 153, col. iv 82-col. v 98.

own ways, as they did in the time of the god Augustus and as I too, having heard both sides, have confirmed. **The Jews, on the other hand, I order** not to aim at more than they have previously had and not in future to send two embassies as if they lived in two cities, a thing which has never been done before, **and not to intrude themselves into the games presided over by the *gymnasiarchoi* and the *kosmetai*, since they enjoy what is their own, and in a city which is not their own they possess an abundance of all good things.** Nor are they to bring or invite Jews coming from Syria or Egypt, or I shall be forced to conceive graver suspicions."[160]

From this section we can infer that the Jewish embassy had claimed the recognition of the right to live according to their customs, abolished by Caligula, and supported this claim with historical evidence, namely with the previous confirmation of that right by Augustus. In addition to this, they had very probably claimed political rights: this could be confirmed by Claudius' threatening order to stop any attempt to participate in the athletic games at the Gymnasium, rounded off by the statement that they enjoy many good things in a city "that is not their own".[161] Could they have crafted/confected an argument based on allegedly sound historical evidence to support their claim to

---

[160] διόπερ ἔτι καὶ νῦν **διαμαρτύρομαι ἵνα Ἀλεξανδρεῖς** μὲν | πραέως καὶ φιλανθρώπως προσφέρωνται Ἰουδαίο(ι)ς τοῖς | τὴν αὐτὴν πόλιν ἐκ πολλῶν χρόνων οἰκοῦσι | καὶ μηδὲν τῶν πρὸς θρησκείαν αὐτοῖς νενομισμένων | τοῦ θεοῦ λυμαίνωνται, ἀλλὰ ἐῶσιν αὐτοὺς τοῖς ἔθεσιν | χρῆσθαι οἷς καὶ ἐπὶ τοῦ θεοῦ Σεβαστοῦ, ἅπερ καὶ ἐγὼ | διακούσας ἀμφοτέρων ἐβεβαίωσα. καὶ **Ἰουδαίοις δὲ** | **ἄντικρυς κελεύω** μηδὲν πλείω ὧν πρότερον | ἔσχον περιεργάζεσθαι μηδὲ ὥσπερ ἐν δυσὶ πόλεσιν κα|τοικοῦντας δύο πρεσβείας ἐκπέμπειν τοῦ λοιποῦ, | ὃ μὴ πρότερόν ποτε ἐπράχθη, **μηδὲ ἐπεισπαίειν** | **γυμνασιαρχικοῖς ἢ κοσμη-τικοῖς ἀγῶσι,** | **καρπουμένους** μὲν τὰ οἰκεῖα ἀπολα⟨ύ⟩οντας δὲ | ἐν ἀλλοτρίᾳ πόλει περιουσίας ἀφθόνων ἀγαθῶν, | μηδὲ ἐπάγεσθαι ἢ προσείεσθαι ἀπὸ Συρίας ἢ Αἰγύπ⟨τ⟩ου | καταπλέοντας Ἰουδαίους, ἐξ οὗ μείζονας ὑπονοίας | ἀναγκασθήσομαι λαμβάνειν. Cf. p. 218-219 with n. 36. On the problematic interpretation of the two embassies mentioned in col. v 91, see *CPJ* II 153, comm. on lines 90-91, HARKER (2008) 26; GAMBETTI (2009) 224-225 with n. 38; DÖRNER (2014) 363-364 with n. 1541; RITTER (2015) 146-147.

[161] This claim may be traced in *P.Oxy.* XLII 3021, col. i 12-13:] προόντα τοῖς Ἰουδαίοις |].α νῦν ἐστέρηνται ("... preexisting for the Jews ... now deprived ..."); cf. HARKER (2008) 30-31; GAMBETTI (2009) 218-220.

246 DANIELA COLOMO

political rights? A positive answer may be traced in Josephus' version of Claudius' ruling of AD 41:[162]

"Tiberius Claudius Caesar Augustus Germanicus, of tribunician power, speaks. Having from the first known that **the Jews in Alexandria called Alexandrians were fellow colonisers from the earliest times jointly with the Alexandrians and received equal civic rights from the kings,** as is manifest from <u>the documents in their possession and from the edicts</u>; and that **after Alexandria was made subject of our empire by Augustus their rights were preserved by the prefects** sent from time to time and that these rights have never been disputed; moreover that at the time when Aquila[163] was at Alexandria, on the death of the ethnarch of the Jews, Augustus did not prevent the continued appointment of ethnarchs, desiring that the several subject nations should abide by their own customs and not be compelled to violate the religion of their fathers; and learning that the Alexandrians rose up in insurrection against the Jews in the midst of the time of Gaius Caesar, who through his great folly and madness humiliated the Jews because they refused to transgress the religion of their fathers by addressing him as a god: I desire that none of their rights should be lost to the Jews on account of the madness of Gaius, but their former privileges also be preserved to them; and I enjoin upon both parties to take the greatest precaution to prevent any disturbance arising after the posting of my edict."[164]

---

162 Jos. *AJ* 19, 280-285.
[163] C. Julius Aquila, prefect of Egypt in AD 10/11.
[164] Τιβέριος Κλαύδιος Καῖσαρ Σεβαστὸς Γερμανικὸς (281) δημαρχικῆς ἐξουσίας λέγει. ἐπιγνοὺς ἀνέκαθεν **τοὺς ἐν Ἀλεξανδρείᾳ Ἰουδαίους Ἀλεξανδρεῖς λεγομένους συγκατοικισθέντας τοῖς πρώτοις εὐθὺ καιροῖς Ἀλεξανδρεῦσι καὶ ἴσης πολιτείας παρὰ τῶν βασιλέων τετευχότας,** καθὼς φανερὸν ἐγένετο ἐκ τῶν γραμμάτων (282) τῶν παρ' αὐτοῖς καὶ τῶν διαταγμάτων, καὶ **μετὰ τὸ τῇ ἡμετέρᾳ ἡγεμονίᾳ Ἀλεξάνδρειαν ὑπὸ τοῦ Σεβαστοῦ ὑποταχθῆναι πεφυλάχθαι αὐτοῖς τὰ δίκαια ὑπὸ τῶν πεμφθέντων ἐπάρχων** κατὰ διαφόρους χρόνους μηδεμίαν τε ἀμφισβήτησιν περὶ τούτων γενομένην (283) τῶν δικαίων αὐτοῖς, ἅμα καὶ καθ' ὃν καιρὸν Ἀκύλας ἦν ἐν Ἀλεξανδρείᾳ τελευτήσαντος τοῦ τῶν Ἰουδαίων ἐθνάρχου τὸν Σεβαστὸν μὴ κεκωλυκέναι ἐθνάρχας γίγνεσθαι βουλόμενον ὑποτετάχθαι ἑκάστους ἐμμένοντας τοῖς ἰδίοις ἔθεσιν καὶ μὴ παραβαίνειν ἀναγκαζο(284)μένους τὴν πάτριον θρησκείαν, Ἀλεξανδρεῖς δὲ ἐπαρθῆναι κατὰ τῶν παρ' αὐτοῖς Ἰουδαίων ἐπὶ τῶν Γαΐου Καίσαρος χρόνων τοῦ διὰ τὴν πολλὴν ἀπόνοιαν καὶ παραφροσύνην, ὅτι μὴ παραβῆναι ἠθέλησεν τὸ Ἰουδαίων ἔθνος τὴν πάτριον θρησκείαν καὶ θεὸν

Like their Greek Alexandrian rivals, the Jews may have tried to put forward historical evidence based on their political role under the Ptolemies and the Jewish ancestral role as co-founders of Alexandria, if not the possession of documents and edicts proving these rights mentioned by Josephus.[165] The two documentary sources that we have exploited above to reconstruct the rhetorical strategies of embassies – the 'Boule-Papyrus' and Claudius' letter to the Alexandrians – may also give a glimpse of the answer of the Roman authorities in 'Realpolitik' *uersus* the resort to brute force and thus condemnation to death of the ambassadors in the *Acta Alexandrinorum*. It is particularly interesting to examine in some detail the response to the issue of the re-instatement of the Boule. The 'Boule-Papyrus' records only a laconic reply by Augustus, who vaguely promises to consider the matter: περὶ τούτων διαλήμψο[μαι, "I shall come to a decision", where διαλήμψο[μαι is a 'non-committal' verb.[166] Fortunately, Claudius' reaction was recorded at greater

---

(285) προσαγορεύειν αὐτόν, ταπεινώσαντος αὐτούς· βούλομαι μηδὲν διὰ τὴν Γαΐου παραφροσύνην τῶν δικαίων τῷ Ἰουδαίων ἔθνει παραπεπτωκέναι, φυλάσσεσθαι δ' αὐτοῖς καὶ τὰ πρότερον δικαιώματα ἐμμένουσι τοῖς ἰδίοις ἔθεσιν, ἀμφοτέροις τε διακελεύομαι τοῖς μέρεσι πλείστην ποιήσασθαι πρόνοιαν, ὅπως μηδεμία ταραχὴ γένηται μετὰ τὸ προτεθῆναί μου τὸ διάταγμα. Translation by HARKER (2008) 26-27.

[165] As we have seen above (p. 228), Josephus has manipulated the outcome of Claudius' ruling through his pro-Jewish bias and/or by using a forged document: however, his text can reflect actual political claims that in reality were not fulfilled, as shown by Claudius' letter to the Alexandrians.

[166] I borrow this effective definition from *APM* I, pp. 91-92, comm. on 21ff. In the papyrus (col. ii 22-23), after this phrase there is a lacuna and then the phrase εἰς Ἀλεξάνδρε[ιαν. The *ed. pr.* considers the possibility that Augustus postponed his decision to a planned visit to Alexandria, which never took place and thus suggests the following supplement: περὶ τούτων διαλήμψομαι ἐπειδὰν πρῶτον] | εἰς Ἀλεξάνδρειαν ἐπανέλθω. We know that Augustus visited the East in 20/19 BC and possibly planned a visit to Alexandria: thus the embassy of the 'Boule-Papyrus' could have been sent to the Emperor while he was staying in a town of the East, not necessarily to Rome (cf. *CPJ* II 150, comm. on lines 22-23). However, as pointed out in *APM*, *loc. cit.*, alternative supplements can be considered, e.g. περὶ τούτων διαλήμψομαι καὶ ἀπόκριμα πέμψω] | εἰς Ἀλεξάνδρειαν ..., "I shall come to a decision and will send my (written) answer to Alexandria" or, as recorded in *BL* VI 185, περὶ τούτων διαλήμψο[μαι καὶ τῷ

length: like Augustus, he commits himself to consider the matter, ordering an investigation by the prefect, but at the same time he clearly dismisses the argument based on historical evidence – the existence of the Boule under the Ptolemies – as irrelevant. He brings back the issue to the level of 'contemporary' – i.e. 'Roman' – history, where he finds no traces of the institution of the Boule.[167] Overall, the tone of these imperial responses seems to follow a diplomatic etiquette towards the subjects, confirming their definitely secondary role in the process of decision-making.

Speaking of subjects, it is interesting to detect in the wording of Claudius' letter a different attitude towards the two different groups of subjects, Greek Alexandrians and Alexandrian Jews. Although the order of stopping the violence against each other in the aftermath of the riots of AD 38-41 is drastically imposed on both groups, in addressing the Alexandrians he uses the more 'polite' verb διαμαρτύρομαι ("I conjure"), while the more direct and 'rude' κελεύω ("I order") is reserved for the Jews.[168] Moreover, as we have seen above, the commonplace of the Jews as a plague on mankind echoes in Claudius' threatening admonition to them.

Curiously, even the 'crazy' Caligula is able to follow a sort of diplomatic etiquette, although in a rather clumsy way, in his dismissal of the Jewish ambassadors led by Philo as unworthy people just because of their refusal to recognise his divinity, a dismissal that displays a mixture of contempt and a sort of pity.[169]

ἐπιτρόπῳ] | εἰς Ἀλεξάνδρε[ιαν γράψω ἵνα "I shall come to a decision and will write to the prefect in Alexandria, so that …". Cf. HARKER (2008) 185.

[167] Col. iv 67-68: "but that you did not have one [scil. Boule] under the emperors before me, you are well aware" (ὅτι δὲ ἐπὶ τῶν | πρὸ ἐμοῦ Σεβαστῶν οὐκ εἴχετε σαφῶς οἴδατε).

[168] Cf. CPJ II 153, comm. on col. iv 82. However, we cannot rule out the possibility that the verbal choice goes back to the epitomator of our copy of the letter and is due to a pro-Alexandrian attitude (see above, pp. 244-245).

[169] PHILO Leg. 367: "they seem to me to be people unfortunate rather than wicked and to be foolish in refusing to believe that I have got the nature of a god" (οὐ πονηροὶ μᾶλλον ἢ δυστυχεῖς εἶναί μοι δοκοῦσιν ἄνθρωποι καὶ ἀνόητοι μὴ πιστεύοντες, ὅτι θεοῦ κεκλήρωμαι φύσιν). Interestingly, Philo represents

From the violent verbal confrontation between ambassadors and Emperors of the *Acta Alexandrinorum,* freedom of speech (παρρησία) emerges as a fundamental Greek value.[170] Although it seems very unlikely that such exchanges of insults really took place,[171] one may ask whether outspokenness was tolerated in embassy hearings. I would be inclined to give a positive answer, since there is a piece of evidence provided by a 'genuine' document, not from Egypt this time, but from Syria. It is the well-known Dmeir inscription, containing the (abridged) minutes of a hearing before Caracalla in AD 216,[172] in which one of the two advocates debating the case questions the legitimacy of Caracalla even hearing it, provoking the Emperor's irritated reaction, which finally reduces the advocate to silence.[173] In addition, *PSI* XI 1222, apparently a rhetorical exercise containing a speech by an advocate[174] in defence of a colleague and former ambassador, Didymus, before an unnamed Emperor, mentions the freedom of speech admitted by the Emperor himself.[175]

Gaius' mild reaction as the result of God's merciful intervention: he and his fellows, facing the complete failure of their diplomatic mission, were expecting to be condemned to death by the Emperor (*Leg.* 366).

[170] In the *Acta Athenodori,* in a very fragmentary passage, the poignant word θρασυτολμία, "arrogance", occurs (*APM* X, col. ii 34). On this topic see CROOK (1955) 142-147 and RODRIGUEZ (2010a) 39-40.

[171] Common sense suggests that it is even more unlikely that if uttered they could have been recorded in official minutes. This represents of course a further proof that the *Acta Alexandrinorum* cannot be 'genuine' documents.

[172] *SEG* XVII 759.

[173] See details and bibliography in HARKER (2008) 106. The relevance of this piece of evidence for my argument is not diminished if we interpret the case as a 'rhetorical entertainment' staged by Caracalla, as WILLIAMS (1974) suggests.

[174] This papyrus, found at Oxyrhynchus and written in an informal literary script of the 2nd-3rd century with noticeable cursive features, was classified by the *editor princeps* as a documentary text on the basis of the alleged lack of rhetorical sophistication. HARKER (2008) 129 suggests that it belongs to "a literature similar to the *Acta Alexandrinorum* developed in other cities"; see also KÖRTE (1939) 115-116.

[175] Fr. 1, col. i 22-25: "and when he stood before you in trials where you were acting in the capacity of judge, often he spoke even against your views (lit. against you) and enjoyed the freedom of speech that you allow to all speakers" (... καὶ παρέστη δικάζοντί σοι πολλά|κις καὶ ἐφθέγξατο ἐπὶ σοῦ καὶ ἀπέ|λαυσεν ἧς ἅπασι μεταδίδως τοῖς | λέγουσι πα[ρ]ρησίας ...).

4. Final remarks

I hope to have shown how rhetoric may have shaped the interstate relations between Rome and Egypt, i.e. Alexandria, during the imperial period. The sources that I have exploited are often in a frustratingly fragmentary state and thus I have 'freely' associated, compared and combined pieces and even fragments of evidence which are at first sight rather heterogeneous, although thematically connected. On the one hand, 'genuine' documents from the sphere of 'Realpolitik' have given a glimpse of the 'real' rhetoric, which focuses on concrete issues (the Boule, tax-exemption, eligibility to the Gymnasium). On the other hand, the (semi)-fictional and polemical *Acta Alexandrinorum* have revealed the 'literary' dimension of rhetoric – emotionally and ideologically charged – within a process of ideal self-representation, in other words what could be called the 'rhetorisation' of 'real' rhetoric. Moreover, I have tentatively supplied 'gaps' with information extracted from literary sources, which I have used with caution because of their ideological bias.

I conclude with some provisional remarks. Both in the historical reality and in the fiction of the *Acta Alexandrinorum* rhetoric plays a vital role for both Greek Alexandrians and Jewish ambassadors. *De facto* rhetoric is an essential part of the Greek *paideia*, and *sensu lato* tends to identify with it because it is *par excellence* the way of articulated expression of the *paideia* itself. In the 'Realpolitik' the rhetoric used by Alexandrian embassies intrinsically cannot influence to a considerable extent the decision-making process of the Roman authorities simply because it is the rhetoric of the subjects. However, it is the instrument to defend and protect the Greek identity, its fundamental values and basic cultural institutions together with the economic structure behind it, which grants fiscal privileges. Using the same Greek rhetoric Jewish ambassadors too try to defend their rights and privileges before the Roman rulers, although they cannot identify completely with the Greek *paideia*.

The literary rhetoric of the *Acta Alexandrinorum* constructs a heroic, ideal self-representation of ambassadors *uersus* the tyrannical Roman ruler and as such represents a form of intellectual power and superiority *uersus* the political power. The Roman tyrant is unable to confront and defeat his adversaries with the strength of the argumentation, i.e. at the level of rhetoric. In his lack of *paideia* he can only resort to brute force and order their physical elimination: the Alexandrian ambassadors end up being executed, but by going through the martyrdom they resist and survive at the intellectual level thanks to their rhetorical discourse, which is the medium of their Hellenic *paideia*. It is only at this level that they can obtain an ultimate moral victory over their political oppressor.

Works cited

APM = *The Acts of the Pagan Martyrs. Acta Alexandrinorum*, edited with commentary by H.A. MUSURILLO (Oxford, 1954).

BAUER, A. (1901), "Heidnische Märtyrerakten", *APF* 1, 29-47.

BELL, H.I. (1924), *Jews and Christians in Egypt. The Jewish Troubles in Alexandria and the Athanasian Controversy* (London).

BOWMAN, A. / RATHBONE, D. (1992), "Cities and Administration in Roman Egypt", *JRS* 82, 107-127.

BRINGMANN, K. (2004), "Gymnasion und griechische Bildung im Nahen Osten", in D. KAH / P. SCHOLZ (eds.), *Das hellenistische Gymnasion* (Berlin), 323-333.

CRIBIORE, R. (2001), *Gymnastics of the Mind. Greek Education in Hellenistic and Roman Egypt* (Princeton).

CROOK, J. (1955), *Consilium principis. Imperial Councils and Counsellors from Augustus to Diocletian* (Cambridge).

DICKEY, E. (2001), "Κύριε, δέσποτα, *domine*: Greek Politeness in the Roman Empire", *JHS* 121, 1-11.

DÖRNER, N. (2014), *Feste und Opfer für den Gott Caesar. Kommunikationsprozesse im Rahmen des Kaiserkultes im römischen Ägypten der julisch-claudischen Zeit (30 v. Chr. - 68 n. Chr.)* (Rahden Westf.).

GAMBETTI, S. (2008), "In Defense of a Historical Reading of *P. Yale* II 107 (= *P. Giss.Lit.* 4.7)", *ZPE* 165, 191-208.

—— (2009), *The Alexandrian Riots of 38 C.E. and the Persecution of the Jews. A Historical Reconstruction* (Leiden).

HABERMANN, W. (2015), "Aspekte des römerzeitlichen Gymnasiums in Ägypten", *APF* 61/2, 384-423.

HARKER, A. (2008), *Loyalty and Dissidence in Roman Egypt. The Case of the* Acta Alexandrinorum (Cambridge).

HOOGENDIJK, F.A.J. / VAN MINNEN, P. (1987), "Drei Kaiserbriefe Gordians III. an die Bürger von Antinoopolis: P.Vindob. G 25945", *Tyche* 2, 41-74.

KAYSER, F. (2003), "Les ambassades alexandrines à Rome (Ier-IIe siècle)", *REA* 105, 435-468.

KEHOE, D.P. (2015), "Das kaiserzeitliche Gymnasion, Bildung und Wirtschaft im Römischen Reich", in P. SCHOLZ / D. WIEGANDT (eds.), *Das kaiserzeitliche Gymnasion* (Berlin), 63-96.

KÖRTE, A. (1939), "III. Referate. Literarische Texte mit Ausschluss der christlichen", *APF* 13, 79-132.

LUISELLI, R. (2016), "The Circulation and Transmission of Greek Adespota in Roman Egypt", in G. COLESANTI / L. LULLI (eds.) *Submerged Literature in Ancient Greek Culture*. Vol. 2, *Case Studies* (Berlin), 289-310.

ŁUKASZEWICZ, A. (1998), "Claudius to his Own City of Alexandria (*P.Lond.* VI 1912, 103-104)", *JJP* 28, 71-77.

MAGNANI, A. (2009), *Il processo di Isidoro. Roma e Alessandria nel primo secolo* (Bologna).

MERKELBACH, R. (1994), "Commodus war kein εὐγενής: (Zu den Acta Alexandrinorum XI Musurillo = Pap. Oxy. I 33: Acta Appiani)", *ZPE* 100, 471-472.

MESSERI, G. (1998), in G. CAVALLO *et al.* (eds.), *Scrivere libri e documenti nel mondo antico. Mostra dei papiri della Biblioteca Medicea Laurenziana* (Firenze), 187-189, nr. 113, Tav. CII.

MILLAR, F. (^{2}1992), *The Emperor in the Roman World* (London).

MONTEVECCHI, O. (1970), "Nerone a una polis e ai 6475", *Aegyptus* 50, 5-33 = *Scripta Selecta* (S. DARIS ed.) (Milano, 1998), 83-112.

OLIVER, J.H. (1989), *Greek Constitutions of Early Roman Emperors from Inscriptions and Papyri* (Philadelphia).

PARSONS, P. (2007), *City of the Sharp-Nosed Fish. Greek Papyri Beneath the Egyptian Sand Reveal a Long-Lost World* (London).

PINTAUDI, R. (2011-2012), "Materiali per una riflessione su indirizzi, prescritti e protocolli: Note di lettura e nuove edizioni", *Anal. Pap.* 23-24,143-170.

RITTER, B. (2015), *Judeans in the Greek Cities of the Roman Empire. Rights, Citizenship, and Civil Discord* (Leiden).

RODRIGUEZ, C. (2010a), "Les *Acta Isidori*: Un procès pénal devant l'Empereur Claude", *Revue historique de droit français et étranger* 88, 1-41.

—— (2010b), Review of GAMBETTI (2009), *Revue historique de droit français et étranger* 88, 592-595.

RUSSELL, D.A. / WILSON, N.G. (1981), *Menander Rhetor. Edition with translation and commentary* (Oxford).

TURNER, E.G. (²1979), *Greek Papyri. An Introduction* (Oxford).

WILLIAMS, W. (1974), "Caracalla and the Rhetoricians: A Note on the *cognitio de Goharienis*", *Latomus* 33, 663-667.

DISCUSSION

A. Chaniotis: παρρησία, outspokenness, was one of the virtues for which statesmen were praised in the late Hellenistic and Imperial period. Your analysis of the speeches of the Alexandrian leaders in the imperial court in Rome gives us an instructive demonstration of what the Greeks probably understood under παρρησία.

D. Colomo: Yes, the exchange of insults between Emperor and ambassadors is clearly a literary exaggeration. The word παρρησία is explicitly mentioned only in *PSI* XI 1222, which appears to be a subliterary text, probably a rhetorical exercise, where the (unnamed) Emperor is praised for allowing freedom of speech to every speaker.[1]

M. Edwards: The martyrdom could mean that the stories of ambassadors challenging or swearing at the emperor were not real, but part of the myth behind the martyrdom?

C. Kremmydas: Thank you very much for your well-documented analysis of the papyrological sources. I have a couple of questions relating to Claudius' letter to the Alexandrians. Since *CPJ* II 153 is clearly a copy, what are its possible uses that might explain the need to copy it in the 1st century? Was it being used as a model for letter-writing in the education system?

D. Colomo: We have here a more complicated situation: the papyrus is a private copy of the original document, written in

---

[1] See p. 249.

a careless cursive script on a recycled papyrus roll (the other side was used for a tax register), and containing grammatical and spelling mistakes (which I have corrected in my contribution). To be precise it is an epitomised copy, as shown by the fact that only the Greek ambassadors are individually named, while the Jewish envoys are omitted. This fact may reveal an exclusive interest in Greek Alexandrian history and perhaps even an anti-Jewish ideological bias. In relation to the latter possibility, we cannot rule out that the epitomator may have altered and manipulated the original text. For example, note that Claudius uses on the one hand the more deferential verb διαμαρτύρομαι ("I conjure") in addressing the Greek Alexandrians, on the other the 'rude' κελεύω ("I order") in addressing the Jews:[2] this verbal choice may go back to the epitomator rather than Claudius himself.

On your second question, no, Claudius' letter, in the form in which we have it – a *non uerbatim* epitomised copy –, reveals an interest in politics, precisely in the relations between Alexandria and Rome, and could have been used by some authors of the *Acta Alexandrinorum*. In any case I would exclude a direct use in rhetorical education.

M. Edwards: This reminds me of the mistakes made as a result of phonetic spelling by the copyist of a manuscript of the Attic orators, B (Laurentianus Plut. IV, 11) in Florence.

D. Colomo: With regard to the accuracy of copies, we may consider how copies of official documents were produced (the majority were used in legal cases and in trials, as illustrated by petitions and reports of proceedings). The papyrological evidence points to two types of copies: copies made by professional scribes employed at the state archives, and personal copies made by private individuals, who had access to

---

[2] See p. 248.

those archives.[3] Among these private individuals there must have been not highly educated people, who produced copies with grammatical errors and phonetic spellings.

A. Chaniotis: These texts are interesting for a study of how the composers of texts, orators and historians alike, consciously selected words, in order to arouse emotion – in this case indignation and contempt. I mention, for example, the use of the word ἄνθρωπος in a contemptuous sense, and the use of a vocabulary of impurity (μολύνω), disease (νόσος) and violence. E.g. καταβάρησις is a very rare word, as I happen to know because its only one attestation in an inscription is in Aphrodisias. It is used in the testament of Attalos Adrastos in connection with the violence of the mob (ὀχλικὴ καταβάρησις; *MAMA* VIII 413b).

One also observes the selection of words, such as φροντιεῖν and δι' ἐρημίαν βοηθείας, that remind the emperor of his duty to protect those who have suffered injustice. That a petitioner underscores his helplessness in order to motivate the addressee of his plea is a well attested strategy of persuasion, found not only in petitions but also in magic (e.g. in a curse tablet from Pella, *SEG* XLIII 434: ἐρήμα) and in the Athenian hymn to Demetrios Poliorketes (Athenaios VI 253 D-F: κοὐκ ἔχω μάχεσθαι).

Finally, a small remark on Claudius' response regarding the *Boule* in Alexandria. His refusal to consider what was practised under the Ptolemaic dynasty (ἐπὶ τῶν ἀρχαίων βασιλέων) corresponds to the Roman attitude towards territorial claims in the 2nd century BC. The Roman senate asked arbitrators not to determine what was the original status of a territory but who occupied it at the moment the claimants first concluded a treaty with Rome (S.L. Ager, *Interstate Arbitrations in the Greek*

---

[3] See HARKER (2008) 57-59, 101-102; COLOMO (2015) 114 = COLOMO, D. (2015), "22. Kopie eines Protokolls einer Gerichtsverhandlung", in G. BASTIANINI / N. GONIS / S. RUSSO (eds.), *Charisterion per Revel A. Coles. Trenta testi letterari e documentari dall'Egitto (P.Coles)* (Florence), 109-117.

World [Berkeley, 1996], nos. 120 and 156). Claudius bases his decision on the state of things under his predecessors (ἐπὶ τῶν πρὸ ἐμοῦ Σεβαστῶν), that is, when Egypt became part of the Roman Empire.

D. Colomo: I would like to point out that *P.Oxy.* XXV 2435r, containing a record of Germanicus' speech to the Alexandrians including the crowd's exclamations, appears to be a 'genuine' record on the basis of the content and formulation of the speech, which clearly sounds like an impromptu performance (in some passages he is clearly trying to gain time by referring at length to the hardships of travelling and listing members of his family from whom he is now separated). In particular, the crowd's exclamations recorded as uttered in unison realistically reflect customary popular interruptions 'directed' by cheer-leaders.[4]

L. Pernot: Comme déjà dans les communications de J.-L. Ferrary et de A. Chaniotis, on voit ici que les ambassades sont à la fois délibératives et judiciaires, le judiciaire étant même dominant dans certains cas.

P. Ducrey: Les ambassadeurs d'Alexandrie eurent-ils vraiment à attendre deux ans avant d'être reçus par l'empereur? C'est à peine imaginable!

D. Colomo: Yes, indeed: but in such a long time[5] embassies could certainly try to influence the Emperor and gain his favours through members of his entourage. For example, Philo records that the Alexandrian envoys bribed the powerful and

---

[4] See comm. in *editio princeps* on line 4.

[5] It is worth specifying that there is no agreement among scholars on the precise chronology of the Jewish and Greek Alexandrian embassies to Gaius, since there is not enough evidence to reach any certainty; see GAMBETTI (2009) 256-259, 266-267, 269-272. In any case, what clearly emerges is that the envoys had to wait a very long time.

depraved chamberlain, the Egyptian Helicon, with money and promises of honours, exploiting him as a sort of *proxenos*. This fact caused distress and anxiety among the Jewish envoys.[6]

M. Edwards: The Athenians were kept waiting on their famous embassy to Philip.

D. Colomo: The Jewish envoys guided by Philo actually followed Caligula on a trip to Campania, where he was visiting his various country houses,[7] but all in vain: they obtained the audience much later in the Gardens of Maecenas and Lamia, near Rome. The hearing was extremely humiliating because the Emperor at the same time was inspecting his estate and giving instructions for building renovations, and thus often was not paying attention to what the ambassadors were saying.[8] We know another case in which an embassy had to reach the Emperor far away from Rome: in 10 BC Alexandrian envoys reached Augustus in Gaul (according to *P.Oxy.* XLII 3020, a 'genuine' document).

M. Edwards: The emperor's decisions are affected by a Roman law mentality?

M. Kraus: Bei all diesen Dokumenten eines inneralexandrinischen Konflikts zwischen Juden und Griechen fragt man sich: Wieviel davon ist überhaupt deliberative Rede? Gehören solche Gesandtschaftsadressen noch zum deliberativen Genre oder eher zur forensischen Beredsamkeit oder gar – zumindest in ihren aggressivsten Partien – zur epideiktischen Rede? Wieviel davon ist realistisch, was ist reine Fiktion? Die extreme παρρησία gegenüber den Kaisern scheint in einem merkwürdigen Kontrast zu stehen zu den Auftritten griechischer Gesandter

---

[6] PHILO *Leg.* 172-178.
[7] PHILO *Leg.* 185.
[8] PHILO *Leg.* 351, 365-366; cf. p. 232.

vor dem republikanischen Senat, von denen Jean-Louis Ferrary berichtete. Ferner: Im kaiserzeitlichen Verfahren der *cognitio extra ordinem* agiert der Kaiser oft gewissermassen gleichzeitig als Ankläger und Richter, was die klassische rhetorische Rollenverteilung sprengt.

D. Colomo: In the *Acta Alexandrinorum* certainly forensic rhetoric prevails, because the hearing before the Emperor follows the *cognitio extra ordinem*. The exchange of insults may be classified as epideictic rhetoric, revealing clear traces of progymnasmatic practice in terms of *psogos* and *synkrisis*.[9] However, in the case of the Boule-Papyrus (*PSI* X 1160), a 'genuine' document, we can appreciate the deliberative rhetoric in the speaker's attempt to influence Roman decision-making.

L. Pernot: On pourrait employer à ce propos, comme dénomination plus large que les stricts genres rhétoriques, l'expression 'rhétorique politique'.

M. Kraus: Ich hatte mich das auch schon mehrfach gefragt; die Bezeichnung ist aus moderner Sicht sicherlich griffiger, aber für die antike Perspektive ist der Begriff zu weit; in der *Rhetorik an Alexander* (1, 1421b7) etwa umfassen die πολιτικοὶ λόγοι (im Sinne von „Bürgerreden") alle drei klassischen Redegenera, insofern sie öffentliche Reden im Gegensatz zu privaten Diskussionen betreffen.

Der Rhetor Nikolaos von Myra (5. Jahrhundert) versucht in seinem Progymnasmata-Handbuch als erster, die einzelnen Progymnasmata bestimmten Redegenera (ebenso wie bestimmten Redeteilen) zuzuordnen. Dabei gelingt ihm freilich nur selten eine wirklich eindeutige Zuordnung (Näheres dazu in meinem Beitrag).

---

[9] See p. 237, n. 130.

D. Colomo: The genre of *synkrisis*?

M. Kraus: Die *synkrisis* als Progymnasma ist eng verzahnt mit den Übungen in Lob und Tadel: Jedes *enkomion* und jeder *psogos* enthält eine *synkrisis*, aber umgekehrt auch jede *synkrisis* Elemente von Lob und Tadel. Für Nikolaos gehört sie daher wie Lob und Tadel zwar primär zum epideiktischen Genre, kann aber auch in deliberativer Rede effizient eingesetzt werden (Nicol. *Prog.* 62, 8-15 Felten).

VII

LAURENT PERNOT

LA RHÉTORIQUE DÉLIBÉRATIVE
DE DION DE PRUSE

Nous possédons sous le nom de Dion de Pruse, dit Chrysostome, quatre-vingts ouvrages composés entre les années 70 et 110 ap. J.-C.[1] La plupart de ces ouvrages portent sur des sujets en rapport avec la politique et un quart d'entre eux sont des allocutions adressées à des assemblées de citoyens. Une telle collection est unique dans la littérature grecque conservée pour l'époque du Haut-Empire.[2]

Peut-être, cependant, les chercheurs n'ont-ils pas encore donné à ce corpus tout le relief qu'il mérite du point de vue de l'histoire de la rhétorique. Les études de référence sur la rhétorique délibérative omettent Dion[3] ou le citent en passant.[4] Les études de référence sur Dion, tout en reconnaissant, naturellement, la place importante occupée par les discours politiques dans sa vie et dans son œuvre, ne sont pas consacrés en premier lieu à l'analyse rhétorique de ces discours.[5] Un pas notable fut

---

[1] Sauf mention contraire, nous suivons le texte et la numérotation des discours de l'édition COHOON / CROSBY (1932-1951).

[2] L'œuvre d'Aelius Aristide comprend plusieurs discours adressés à des cités ; dans ses exhortations à la concorde, cet auteur se souvient probablement de Dion. Philostrate mentionne plusieurs fois des discours délibératifs, aujourd'hui perdus : PHILOSTR. VS 1, 24 (529) ; 2, 11 (591), cf. infra, n. 103 ; 2, 33 (628).

[3] BECK (1970).

[4] HARTLICH (1889) 313-315 (le discours 13 comme protreptique) ; KLEK (1919) 37-38 et 152 (les discours Sur la royauté).

[5] Mentionnons ici les études fondamentales de ARNIM (1898) ; DESIDERI (1978) et (1994) ; JONES (1978) ; MILAZZO (2007) ; MOLES (1978) ; NESSELRATH (2009) ; SWAIN (2000).

représenté par les pages que G.A. Kennedy consacra à Dion dans *The Art of Rhetoric in the Roman World* ; car le savant américain y traçait un panorama de l'activité rhétorique de l'auteur, en soulignant son talent en ce domaine.[6] Plus récemment, un recueil relatif à la rhétorique du conseil comporte un chapitre sur les discours *Sur la royauté*.[7] La Collection des Universités de France a publié un volume de discours aux cités (*Or.* 33-36) de grand intérêt pour notre sujet.[8]

La caractérisation qui est tentée ici vise donc à faire mieux connaître un chapitre important de l'histoire de la rhétorique délibérative grecque, mais aussi à discuter la notion de genre délibératif. Dion, en effet, ne fut pas un orateur délibératif au sens strict et technique de ce terme, mais un conseiller et un philosophe, ce qui le conduisit à des prises de position débordant les cadres conceptuels prédéfinis.

1. La rhétorique délibérative en ses avatars

Le concept de rhétorique 'délibérative' renvoie à la tripartition des genres oratoires figurant dans la *Rhétorique* d'Aristote et la *Rhétorique à Alexandre* pseudo-aristotélicienne. Ces deux traités, comme on sait, proposèrent une codification des formes de la parole publique, à la fin de l'époque classique, en prenant pour référence la pratique oratoire de la démocratie athénienne ainsi que des observations théoriques préexistantes.[9] Les systèmes qu'ils présentent l'un et l'autre concordent dans les grandes lignes. Ils isolent les discours délibératifs comme une classe à part, à côté des discours judiciaires et des discours épidictiques, et les qualifient par les termes συμβουλευτικός (Aristote) et δημηγορικός (*Rhétorique à Alexandre*). Ils leur assignent pour but le conseil (συμβουλή, συμβουλεύειν), adressé à une assemblée

---

[6] KENNEDY (1972) 566-581.
[7] SIDEBOTTOM (2006).
[8] BOST-POUDERON (2011a).
[9] Voir PERNOT (2002).

délibérante qu'il s'agit de persuader ou de dissuader en vue du vote final. Ils dressent la liste des principaux sujets (finances, guerre et paix, protection du territoire, commerce extérieur, législation, cultes, régime politique) et des principaux arguments (utilité, mais aussi justice, légalité, beauté morale, facilité, etc.) et donnent des conseils relatifs au plan. Enfin, Aristote note que, devant l'assemblée du peuple, le style élaboré et recherché n'est pas de mise.[10]

Le concept de 'genre délibératif' (συμβουλευτικὸν γένος), inclus dans le système des trois genres oratoires, s'imposa dans la rhétorique grecque et latine après Aristote.[11] À l'époque impériale, il restait en vigueur dans les manuels d'exercices préparatoires[12] et dans les traités des théoriciens,[13] ainsi que dans les déclamations (les 'suasoires', par opposition aux 'controverses' judiciaires).

Mais si l'on cherche dans le corpus de Dion des discours qui correspondent à cette définition, le résultat est décevant. Qui voudrait lire cet auteur muni de la *Rhétorique* d'Aristote et de la *Rhétorique à Alexandre* courrait à l'échec, car il n'a laissé aucune harangue qui corresponde, dans la forme et dans le fond, aux préceptes édictés dans ces traités.

Pour mieux comprendre Dion, il faut donc élargir et repenser la notion de rhétorique délibérative. Plusieurs facteurs invitent à cette démarche.

Aristote admet – fugitivement – que le conseil peut être adressé en particulier, à titre individuel.[14] C'est ouvrir la porte à une définition du genre délibératif qui ne se limite plus aux

---

[10] Voir ARIST. *Rhet.* 1, 3-8 et 3, 12 ; *Rhet. ad Alex.* 1-2 et 29-34.
[11] DIOG. L. 7, 42 (à propos des stoïciens) ; PHILOD. *Rhet.* 1, 212 SUDHAUS ; *Rhet. ad Her.* 1, 2 ; 2, 1 ; CIC. *De or.* 1, 141 ; *Part.* 10 ; etc.
[12] AEL. THEON, *Prog.* 61.
[13] DION. HAL. *Lys.* 16, 2 ; PS.-AEL. ARIST. *Rhet.* 1, 146 ; HERMOG. *Stat.* 1, 25 (34) ; *Id.* 2, 10, 15 (384) ; LONGIN. fr. 49, ligne 80, et fr. 50, § 21 PATILLON / BRISSON ; etc.
[14] ARIST. *Rhet.* 1, 3, 1358b9-10 : καὶ οἱ ἰδίᾳ συμβουλεύοντες καὶ οἱ κοινῇ δημηγοροῦντες ; 2, 18, 1391b8-9 : ἐάν τε πρὸς ἕνα τις τῷ λόγῳ χρώμενος προτρέπῃ ἢ ἀποτρέπῃ. Voir aussi *Rhet. ad Alex.* 1, 2, 1421b14.

discours publics devant une assemblée, mais qui couvre aussi les discours personnels ou privés.

La pratique oratoire, dès l'époque classique, était beaucoup plus souple et variée que la théorie. L'œuvre d'Isocrate en offre un exemple ; car celui-ci, qui avait foi dans le conseil,[15] l'a décliné sous des formes multiples, qui vont au-delà de la définition technique du genre délibératif. Il mêle le conseil et l'éloge, comme dans le *Panégyrique*. Il s'adresse à un unique destinataire, comme dans *À Nicoclès* ou *Philippe*. Il met ses idées dans la bouche d'un tiers (*Plataïque, Archidamos*). Quand il se tourne, ou feint de se tourner, vers les corps constitués d'Athènes, il propose des messages généraux sans chercher à emporter l'adhésion sur une mesure précise (*Sur la paix, Aréopagitique*). Isocrate fit ainsi éclater la structure du débat, en proposant, en sus du débat devant les assemblées, des débats restreints, devant les souverains, et des débats élargis, devant l'opinion.

La théorie rhétorique elle-même trahit une certaine insatisfaction à l'égard de la tripartition des genres rhétoriques. Les spécialistes avaient remarqué qu'il existait des formes oratoires qui entraient difficilement dans les trois genres canoniques : "lorsque nous nous plaignons, que nous consolons, apaisons, excitons, intimidons, encourageons, conseillons, interprétons des énoncés obscurs, racontons, conjurons, remercions, félicitons, reprenons, invectivons, décrivons, recommandons, faisons des rétractations, des vœux, des conjectures et bien d'autres choses".[16] Quintilien, qui dresse cette liste, précise qu'il s'en tient, quant à lui, à la tripartition la plus commune ; mais il n'en a pas moins suggéré que cette tripartition a pu être considérée comme étroite et qu'il faut tenir compte aussi d'autres points de vue.

---

[15] Isoc. *Paneg.* 3 : ἥκω συμβουλεύσων.

[16] Quint. *Inst.* 3, 4, 3 : *cum querimur, consolamur, mitigamus, concitamus, terremus, confirmamus, praecipimus, obscure dicta interpretamur, narramus, deprecamur, gratias agimus, gratulamur, obiurgamus, maledicimus, describimus, mandamus, renuntiamus, optamus, opinamur, plurima alia* (trad. Cousin).

Plus loin, le même Quintilien affirme que l'éloquence délibérative ne se limite pas aux assemblées et à l'administration de l'État, comme l'ont cru la majorité des Grecs ainsi que Cicéron : "Pour moi, la variété des cas me paraît offrir un champ plus vaste, parce que les consultants et les consultations présentent une grande diversité".[17] La délibération, ajoute-t-il, "est le fait d'un groupe ou d'un individu".[18]

Ces réflexions, qui émanent d'un théoricien contemporain de Dion, sont significatives. Derrière l'apparente unanimité autour d'un système consacré par l'École, on voit que des forces de réflexion étaient à l'œuvre pour diversifier et pour nuancer.

Il faut tenir compte, en outre, du passage du temps et de l'évolution des contextes historiques. Comparées à l'Athènes classique, les cités grecques de l'époque impériale, soumises à l'autorité romaine, n'avaient pas le même statut. Elles ne délibéraient pas de façon souveraine et les sujets les plus graves, comme la guerre ou le régime politique, leur étaient interdits. Cela ne signifiait pas que la rhétorique délibérative fût impossible, mais elle était différente et devait se redéployer.

Dion lui-même en atteste, ayant parfaitement observé ce phénomène. Dans un exorde prononcé devant l'assemblée de Pruse, au cours des premières années du IIe siècle, il déclare : "Aujourd'hui, les circonstances sont devenues autres".[19] La phrase est brève, mais suffisante. Nul besoin d'insister, tout le monde comprend à quoi l'orateur se réfère : la conquête romaine a mis fin à l'indépendance des cités grecques, et par conséquent celles-ci ne peuvent plus rivaliser entre elles par les armes. En l'occurrence, Dion vient de citer l'exemple d'Épaminondas, auquel il s'identifie dans la mesure où celui-ci, comme Dion lui-même, avait fait l'objet de critiques de la part de ses concitoyens. Mais Épaminondas fut le bienfaiteur de sa patrie,

---

[17] QUINT. *Inst.* 3, 8, 15 : *nobis maior in re uidetur uarietas ; nam et consultantium et consiliorum plura sunt genera* (trad. COUSIN).
[18] QUINT. *Inst.* 3, 8, 37 : *consultant aut plures aut singuli* (trad. COUSIN).
[19] DIO CHRYS. 43, 4 : νῦν δ' ἕτεροι γεγόνασιν οἱ καιροί (quand aucun nom de traducteur n'est indiqué, la traduction est nôtre).

Thèbes, à laquelle il procura l'hégémonie sur la Grèce. Aujourd'hui, les hommes d'État ont une capacité d'action bien moindre que par le passé.[20] Une trentaine d'années plus tôt, déjà, s'adressant aux Rhodiens, Dion avait souligné le changement d'époque, en des termes qui visaient à la fois l'action et la parole, la vie politique de la cité et les discours publics rythmant cette vie :

"[Vos ancêtres] avaient beaucoup d'autres moyens de faire montre de leur vertu : gouverner autrui, secourir les victimes de l'injustice, gagner des alliés, fonder des cités, vaincre à la guerre. Vous, en revanche, vous n'avez aucune possibilité d'action de ce genre, mais il vous reste, à mon sens, à vous gouverner vous-mêmes, administrer votre cité, décerner les honneurs et les applaudissements différemment de la plupart, délibérer en conseil, rendre la justice, sacrifier aux dieux et célébrer les fêtes : en tout cela, il vous est possible d'apparaître meilleurs que les autres."[21]

Ce passage offre une description synthétique de la politique municipale sous ses aspects moraux, institutionnels et religieux. La rhétorique y est présente ; car l'activité délibérative et judiciaire, à laquelle il est fait référence (καὶ τὸ βουλεύσασθαι καὶ τὸ δικάσαι), passait nécessairement par le discours. Dion estimait donc que la rhétorique délibérative existait toujours, mais qu'elle avait changé, et pas nécessairement en mal. D'autres textes, de Plutarque en particulier, dressent un constat semblable.[22] Le concept de rhétorique délibérative, au sens technique, manifeste ses limites. C'était une invention géniale et de portée universelle, une formalisation du débat politique et une systématisation des critères de l'action ; mais c'était une épure, étroitement liée,

---

[20] Sur la signification d'ensemble du passage, voir SCHMIDT (2013) 383-386.
[21] DIO CHRYS. 31, 161-162 : ἐκείνοις μὲν γὰρ ἐν πολλοῖς ὑπῆρχεν ἑτέροις ἡ τῆς ἀρετῆς ἐπίδειξις, ἐν τῷ προεστάναι τῶν ἄλλων, ἐν τῷ βοηθεῖν τοῖς ἀδικουμένοις, ἐν τῷ συμμάχους κτᾶσθαι, πόλεις οἰκίζειν, νικᾶν πολεμοῦντας, ὑμῖν δὲ τοιοῦτον μὲν οὐθὲν πράττειν ἔνεστιν. καταλείπεται δ', οἶμαι, τὸ ἑαυτῶν προεστάναι καὶ τὴν πόλιν διοικεῖν καὶ τὸ τιμῆσαί τινα καὶ κροταλίσαι μὴ τοῖς πολλοῖς ὁμοίως καὶ τὸ βουλεύσασθαι καὶ τὸ δικάσαι καὶ τὸ τοῖς θεοῖς θῦσαι καὶ τὸ ἄγειν ἑορτήν· ἐν οἷς ἅπασιν ἔστι βελτίους τῶν ἄλλων φαίνεσθαι.
[22] Voir PERNOT (2010).

de surcroît, aux conditions de la démocratie athénienne. Ce concept ne peut pas rendre compte de la richesse et de la variété des situations rhétoriques qui se sont présentées au cours de l'histoire, pas plus que la *Poétique* d'Aristote ne contient toutes les formes prises par l'épopée et le théâtre ou que le système des *genera dicendi* ne résume toutes les variétés du style. Les théories antiques doivent être, pour les lecteurs modernes, une source d'inspiration, non un carcan. C'est pourquoi, sans rejeter, certes, le genre délibératif, il faut l'enrichir, en l'appuyant sur ses points forts : la politique, la délibération, le conseil.

Un tel enrichissement est particulièrement nécessaire dans le cas de Dion ; car celui-ci, tout en connaissant bien la rhétorique, ne se voulut pas un rhéteur professionnel. Esprit original, critique, rebelle, il ne se laissait pas enfermer dans des moules. Sa vie mouvementée, qui fut marquée par l'exil comme par la réussite, ainsi que les multiples facettes de son personnage social – notable, sophiste, philosophe – lui procurèrent des expériences diverses et lui donnèrent un regard surplombant.

2. Une théorie du conseil philosophique

Si Dion n'emploie pas les termes συμβουλευτικός et δημηγορικός, il évoque souvent le "conseil" et le "conseiller" (συμβουλή, συμβουλεύειν, σύμβουλος), et il cite les discours au peuple ou au conseil (βουλή) comme une catégorie bien définie, à côté des discours au tribunal et des conférences d'apparat.[23] Sur la rhétorique du conseil, dont il reconnaissait la spécificité, il s'est plusieurs fois exprimé, dans des ouvrages ou passages d'ouvrages qui n'ont pas tous retenu l'attention des modernes, mais qui composent en vérité un ensemble cohérent et exposent les fondements conceptuels à partir desquels Dion a théorisé sa propre mission.

---

[23] DIO CHRYS. 18, 14 et 17 ; 24, 3 ; 33, 1 ; 69, 3. En mauvaise part : DIO CHRYS. 4, 124. Dion emploie aussi δημηγορεῖν, παραινεῖν, παρακαλεῖν, προτρέπειν.

268   LAURENT PERNOT

Un point de départ est fourni par le bref dialogue *Sur la délibération* (*Or.* 26 : Περὶ τοῦ βουλεύεσθαι). Après avoir cherché à définir le domaine et les conditions de la délibération, dans une optique philosophique,[24] Dion insiste sur l'importance de cette activité. Il est essentiel, dit-il, d'être capable de délibérer sur les affaires, ce qui requiert intelligence et éducation (§ 7), et la délibération débouche sur le discours (§ 7 : λέγειν). Sur la manière de conduire les délibérations, le *Discours eubéen* (*Or.* 7) donne l'exemple de ce qu'il ne faut pas faire. Dion croque une scène d'assemblée, qui a lieu au théâtre, au cours de laquelle s'expriment quatre citoyens (§ 24-63). Or la violence et l'égoïsme y règnent. Les orateurs sont méprisables ou aveuglés, la foule, versatile. Cette satire cruelle vise les démagogues et, sans être dépourvue de parallèles littéraires,[25] elle s'appuie sur des choses vues et comporte des enseignements pour la situation contemporaine.[26] Dion a repris le même thème devant l'assemblée de Tarse, en opposant les mauvais orateurs, qui n'écoutent que leur intérêt personnel, et le "bon conseiller" (τὸν σύμβουλον τὸν ἀγαθόν), véritablement digne de diriger la cité.[27]

Dion critique très sévèrement la rhétorique vulgaire et les sophistes.[28] Il ne veut considérer que la "vraie",[29] la "bonne"[30] rhétorique.

Quelles sont donc les caractéristiques du bon conseiller ? D'abord, il revendique son engagement dans le présent, comme

---

[24] Ce texte présente des ressemblances avec le *Sisyphe* pseudo-platonicien.
[25] P. COLLART, observation à la suite de la communication de MAZON (1943) 87 ; JOUAN (1977) 43 ; SCANNAPIECO (2004) 345-347.
[26] ARNIM (1898) 502 ; JONES (1978) 58-61. RUSSELL (1992) 13 écrit excellemment : "With due allowance made for the large literary element in a speech full of mimesis of Plato and the orators, we can still hear the voice of the preacher directing himself to contemporary evils and propounding solutions which may have a political as well as a moral ring. Dio was a political animal ..."
[27] DIO CHRYS. 34, 28-37.
[28] Par ex. DIO CHRYS. 13, 22 ; 69, 3.
[29] DIO CHRYS. 2, 24 : φιλοσοφίας τε ἅμα καὶ ῥητορικῆς τῆς ἀληθοῦς. Cf. 22, 2 : φιλοσόφους ἐν πολιτείᾳ... ἢ ῥήτορας κατὰ τὴν γενναίαν τε καὶ ἀληθῆ ῥητορικήν.
[30] DIO CHRYS. 22, 5 : λέγω δὲ οὐ ψέγων ῥητορικὴν οὐδὲ ῥήτορας τοὺς ἀγαθούς.

dans la phrase suivante : "Peut-être me méprises-tu et estimes-tu que je bavarde, parce que je ne parle pas de Cyrus et d'Alcibiade, comme font encore aujourd'hui les *sophoi*, mais que je mentionne Néron et ce genre de sujets récents et sans gloire".[31] Entendons que Dion récuse le passéisme en vigueur chez beaucoup d'intellectuels et de sophistes et qu'il veut appartenir résolument à son temps.

Mais, surtout, il se veut philosophe.[32] Sa théorie de l'alliance nécessaire entre rhétorique délibérative et philosophie tient en deux articles. D'une part, le philosophe doit s'engager en politique : une allocution prononcée devant le conseil de Pruse roule sur ce sujet (*Or.* 49). "La tâche du véritable philosophe n'est autre que le gouvernement des hommes."[33] Parce qu'elle consiste à faire le bien (εὐεργετεῖν), cette tâche lui plaît, et de surcroît il y est spécialement préparé (§ 1-3) : car le philosophe exerce l'empire sur lui-même, ce qui est beaucoup plus difficile que de l'exercer sur autrui (§ 8-11). Assurément, il est rare que les philosophes deviennent rois, encore qu'il y en ait des exemples (§ 6). Mais le philosophe a à sa disposition deux autres manières de gouverner : en se faisant le conseiller d'un roi (§ 3-5, 7-8), ou en exerçant une magistrature dans sa propre cité (§ 13-14). Dans l'un et l'autre cas, qu'il s'agisse de s'adresser aux princes ou aux assemblées de citoyens, il va de soi que l'activité philosophique repose sur la parole et que le philosophe doit être orateur. Ce discours offre ainsi une justification théorique à l'alliance entre rhétorique et philosophie.

---

[31] DIO CHRYS. 21, 11 : ἴσως γάρ μου καταφρονεῖς καὶ ἡγῇ με ληρεῖν, ὅτι οὐ περὶ Κύρου καὶ Ἀλκιβιάδου λέγω, ὥσπερ οἱ σοφοὶ ἔτι καὶ νῦν, ἀλλὰ Νέρωνος καὶ τοιούτων πραγμάτων νεωτέρων τε καὶ ἀδόξων [ὧν] μνημονεύω. Le mot ὧν, qui fait difficulté, a été athétisé par Reiske, suivi par von Arnim et de Budé ; Cohoon le conserve.

[32] Cf. NESSELRATH (2009).

[33] DIO CHRYS. 49, 13 : τοῦ γε ὄντως φιλοσόφου τὸ ἔργον οὐχ ἕτερόν ἐστιν ἢ ἀρχὴ ἀνθρώπων. L'engagement politique de Dion a été particulièrement mis en lumière par DESIDERI (1978), qui parle de la philosophie "intesa come servizio sociale" (p. 377) et qui développe les implications idéologiques, sociales et historiques de cette conception. Nous nous concentrons ici sur l'aspect rhétorique des choses.

D'autre part, et réciproquement, si le philosophe doit s'engager en politique, la politique doit être philosophique. Tel est le thème du petit traité *Sur la guerre et la paix* (*Or.* 22), consacré aux rapports entre rhétorique et philosophie.[34] L'auteur dresse une liste de sujets de délibération, en se référant à la Grèce classique et en citant, outre la guerre, les questions d'éducation, de finances, etc. (§ 2-3),[35] puis il oppose deux manières de traiter ces sujets : tandis que les orateurs les examinent à l'occasion de chaque cas particulier, les philosophes prennent de la distance et remontent au principe général, pour être prêts ensuite à faire face à tous les cas particuliers (§ 3-4). La supériorité de la méthode philosophique est patente, et ce sont donc les philosophes qui seront les mieux à même d'être les "conseillers des cités, des peuples ou des rois" (§ 5).[36]

Ces considérations s'appliquent au premier chef à Dion lui-même, qui, en toute occasion, se définit comme un philosophe soucieux de l'intérêt général. Si vous m'avez fait citoyen de votre ville, dit-il par exemple aux Nicomédiens, ce n'est pas que je sois riche et capable de munificence, ni apte à flatter les masses, mais parce que "plus que d'autres, peut-être, j'ai la volonté et la capacité de donner des conseils sur les intérêts communs".[37] "Je vois que ce n'est pas seulement l'éloquence, mais aussi la philosophie qui produit des hommes de bien et des hommes distingués dans notre cité : c'est pourquoi, quant à moi, je n'hésiterai pas à y exhorter les jeunes gens, en privé et en public, quand cela sera opportun."[38] La philosophie est une mission que Dion exerce tant dans des entretiens particuliers qu'au moyen

---

[34] Sur le détail de l'interprétation du discours 22, voir PERNOT (1993) 579, n. 413.

[35] Voir des listes comparables DIO CHRYS. 25, 2 ; 26, 8.

[36] DIO CHRYS. 22, 5 : συμβούλους τῶν πόλεων ἢ τῶν ἐθνῶν ἢ τῶν βασιλέων.

[37] DIO CHRYS. 38, 1 : τὸ συμβουλεύειν ἐμέ τι περὶ τῶν κοινῇ συμφερόντων ἴσως μᾶλλον ἑτέρων καὶ βούλεσθαι καὶ δύνασθαι.

[38] DIO CHRYS. 44, 10 : ὁρῶ δὲ οὐ μόνον ἀπὸ λόγων, ἀλλὰ καὶ ἀπὸ φιλοσοφίας ἄνδρας ἀγαθοὺς καὶ ἀξιολόγους γιγνομένους ἐν τῇ πόλει· ὑπὲρ ὧν ἐγὼ καὶ ἰδίᾳ τοὺς νέους καὶ κοινῇ, ὅταν ᾖ καιρός, οὐκ ὀκνήσω παρακαλεῖν.

de discours publics, emplis d'avertissements et de conseils. Être philosophe implique de parler en public.[39] Ce n'était pas trahir l'esprit de la rhétorique délibérative que de lui donner une dimension philosophique. Isocrate déjà se réclamait de la philosophie dans ses discours de conseil. Aristote indique que toute délibération a pour fin le bonheur,[40] ce qui suppose, de la part de l'orateur, la connaissance des vrais biens. L'alliance entre rhétorique et philosophie était d'autant plus aisée, du point de vue de Dion, que ce dernier ne restreignait pas la philosophie à sa définition spécialisée, mais l'étendait à la sagesse et à la culture. Les bons conseillers sont "les gens honnêtes et cultivés".[41] Ils savent s'adapter aux circonstances.

Les modèles revendiqués par Dion étaient donc les philosophes et les sages : Socrate, Diogène, Nestor ; mais Démosthène n'était pas oublié. Selon une anecdote symbolique, rapportée par Philostrate, Dion, durant son exil, lisait le *Phédon* et le discours *Sur l'ambassade*.[42] Effectivement, dans le corpus de Dion, Démosthène est cité avec faveur pour sa puissance oratoire.[43] Le *Discours rhodien* s'inspire du *Contre Leptine*, et l'on trouve çà et là d'autres allusions et échos démosthéniens.[44]

C'est ainsi que Dion employa sa vie à prodiguer des conseils. Ses lecteurs n'ont pas manqué de relever cet aspect. Ainsi Synésios : "Il entreprit d'admonester les hommes, tant les souverains que les simples particuliers."[45] Photius : "Il eut la réputation d'être habile dans les discours, et particulièrement ceux qui conseillent de discipliner les mœurs" ; "comme je l'ai dit, la plus grande partie des discours de Dion que nous connaissons

---

[39] Dio Chrys. 13, 12 : λέγειν … εἰς τὸ κοινόν.
[40] Arist. *Rhet.* 1, 5-6.
[41] Dio Chrys. 49, 1 : τοῖς ἐπιεικέσιν ἀνθρώποις καὶ πεπαιδευμένοις.
[42] Philostr. *VS* 1, 7 (488).
[43] Dio Chrys. 2, 18-19 ; 18, 11.
[44] Wenkebach (1903) 20-21, 48, 54-87 ; Pernot (2006) 66. Sans être écrasante, cette présence de Démosthène est peut-être plus significative que ne le concède Arnim (1907) 614-615.
[45] Synes. *Dion* 1, 14 : ἐπιθέσθαι δὲ τῷ νουθετεῖν ἀνθρώπους, καὶ μονάρχους καὶ ἰδιώτας.

sont délibératifs".[46] "Philosophe engagé en politique",[47] telle était la conception qu'il se faisait de sa propre utilité. La philosophie n'était pas seulement pour lui un contenu à transmettre, mais une manière de vivre, qu'il mettait en pratique et proposait en exemple. Et il développa une rhétorique à cette fin.

3. Essai de cartographie des discours

Pour passer des fondements théoriques à la mise en pratique, il convient d'essayer de décrire et de classer les discours de Dion qui contiennent des conseils politiques et philosophiques et peuvent être considérés comme délibératifs dans une acception plus ou moins large. La tâche est malaisée : car, document irremplaçable, le corpus de Dion pose de multiples difficultés. Il est étendu (plus de huit cents pages dans l'édition de la Bibliotheca Teubneriana par Guy de Budé) et les ouvrages qui le composent sont de forme et de contenu très divers.[48] La transmission des textes peut avoir comporté des accidents : on a soupçonné des interpolations, des 'conflations' et des mutilations, à tort ou à raison,[49] et reconnu l'insertion d'ouvrages apocryphes.[50] Dion lui-même était conscient des problèmes posés par

---

[46] PHOT. *Bibl.* 209, 165a34-35 : δεξιὸς δὲ περὶ τοὺς λόγους ἔδοξεν εἶναι, καὶ μάλιστα τοὺς ὅσοι ῥυθμίζειν συμβουλεύουσι τὰ ἤθη ; 165b8-10 : ἔστι μὲν οὖν, ὅπερ ἔφην, τὸ πλεῖστον αὐτοῦ τῶν λόγων, οὓς ἡμεῖς ἴσμεν, συμβουλευτικόν.

[47] DIO CHRYS. 48, 14 : φιλόσοφος πολιτείας ἁψάμενος.

[48] DESIDERI (1991b).

[49] Voir par exemple ARNIM (1898) 170-171, 181-204, 414-430, 465-467 ; BUDÉ (1920) ; LEMARCHAND (1926) ; HIGHET (1983). Juste appréciation à cet égard chez ELLIGER (1967) 785. La transmission n'a certainement pas été irréprochable, mais il ne faut pas oublier que Dion ne visait pas à une rigueur méticuleuse ; il fait lui-même état – non sans coquetterie – de ses propres digressions (DIO CHRYS. 7, 128 : τὰς ἐκτροπὰς τῶν λόγων) et de l'allure erratique de ses conférences (DIO CHRYS. 12, 16 : ἐὰν φαίνωμαι πλανώμενος ἐν τοῖς λόγοις), méthode bien commentée par ARNIM (1898) 439-443).

[50] Il est généralement admis que le *Discours corinthien* (*Or.* 37) n'est pas de Dion, mais de Favorinus ; voir AMATO / JULIEN (2005). Nous ne tenons donc pas compte de ce discours. Des doutes pèsent également sur certains discours *Sur la Fortune* (*Or.* 63-65), groupe qui n'est pas important pour notre sujet.

la publication et la circulation de ses œuvres dès son vivant et il s'en est plaint avec humour.[51] Par ailleurs, de nombreuses incertitudes entourent les circonstances de composition et de prononciation. Quelques renseignements sont fournis par les titres que portent les discours dans la tradition manuscrite et par les *testimonia*. Pour le reste, il faut échafauder des hypothèses à partir du contenu des textes eux-mêmes, ce qui est d'autant moins facile que l'auteur est volontiers allusif et ironique. Les savants modernes ont accompli un travail important pour préciser les contextes et les datations, sans pouvoir parvenir pour autant à des conclusions toujours sûres et unanimes.[52] Cette situation est particulièrement dommageable s'agissant de rhétorique délibérative, parce que l'on aurait besoin de connaître dans chaque cas, avec précision, le cadre et les destinataires des conseils prodigués.

Enfin, la pensée de Dion a évolué au cours de sa vie ; il n'a pas toujours eu la même vision des rapports entre rhétorique et philosophie et il a mis l'accent successivement sur des doctrines différentes, du cynisme au platonisme et au stoïcisme.[53] Or, là encore, une reconstitution exacte de toutes les étapes paraît hors de portée. Nous avons perdu une quinzaine d'ouvrages, dont les titres sont connus grâce à Philostrate, à Synésios et à la *Souda*,[54] et ces pertes peuvent fausser les perspectives, notamment à l'égard du fameux problème de la 'conversion' de Dion à la philosophie. Sur ces problèmes, il nous a semblé que nous pouvions nous abstenir de prendre parti ici, car le corpus des discours de conseil de Dion est suffisamment homogène pour autoriser un traitement synthétique. Nous ne cherchons pas à atteindre une précision qui serait illusoire, ou qui à tout le moins nécessiterait dans chaque cas des discussions approfondies. Nous

---

[51] Dio Chrys. 42, 4-5.
[52] En particulier Arnim (1898) ; Jones (1978) ; Desideri (1978) ; Moles (1978) ; Sheppard (1984).
[53] La description des conceptions philosophiques présentes dans l'œuvre de Dion par François (1921) reste utile.
[54] Voir une liste dans Arnim (1893-1896) II, ix-x.

avons également laissé de côté les portions du corpus qui ne relèvent pas, ou qui relèvent moins, de notre sujet, et ceci inclut entre autres des œuvres dans lesquelles Dion, probablement dans des périodes circonscrites de sa vie, a tourné le dos à la rhétorique pour se poser en "philosophe mendiant ennemi de la culture", selon la formule de von Arnim.[55] Compte tenu de ces avertissements préalables, il est possible de décrire les discours de conseil, qui constituent une part notable du corpus total, en les répartissant en trois ensembles principaux. Leur contexte, gradué, va des circonstances précisément politiques et institutionnelles à des occasions plus éthiques et parénétiques.

1) On regroupe sous le nom de *Discours bithyniens* quatorze allocutions prononcées par Dion devant les corps politiques de sa province (*Or*. 38-51). Un premier sous-groupe, consacré au thème de la "concorde" (ὁμόνοια), traite de conflits entre cités ou de dissensions internes à la cité, à propos de Nicomédie, Nicée, Pruse et Apamée (*Or*. 38-41). Dion intervient, devant l'assemblée ou devant le conseil, pour prôner la réconciliation ou pour saluer et consolider une réconciliation advenue.

Les dix discours restants sont des prises de parole effectuées à Pruse, à des époques diverses, sur toutes sortes de sujets (*Or*. 42-51). Les affaires sont embrouillées et les enjeux, malheureusement, ne sont pas toujours clairs. Dion se multiplie devant l'assemblée et le conseil, répond à des propositions d'honneurs et de charges qui lui sont décernées, justifie sa conduite, réagit face aux menaces. Un jour, il tance des émeutiers qui avaient tenté d'incendier sa maison (*Or*. 46). Souvent, il fait allusion au programme de grands travaux qui lui était cher, mais qui lui valut des critiques et des oppositions, dont Pline le Jeune s'est fait l'écho.[56] Un des discours est destiné à introduire le gouverneur de Bithynie devant l'Assemblée de Pruse (*Or*. 48). Les titres de ces allocutions – qu'ils remontent à l'auteur ou à un éditeur

---

[55] ARNIM (1898) 394 : "der culturfeindliche Bettelphilosoph".
[56] PLIN. MIN. *Epist*. 10, 81-82.

bien informé – reflètent la diversité des situations et des intentions. Ils précisent le lieu de prononciation (ἐν τῇ πατρίδι, πρὸς τὴν πατρίδα, ἐν ἐκκλησίᾳ, ἐν βουλῇ), le type rhétorique du discours (διάλεξις, πολιτικός, φιλοφρονητικός, ἀπολογισμός, δημηγορία) ainsi que des renseignements plus circonstanciels sur le contexte. C'est la politique locale au quotidien. Les discours que nous lisons ne représentent qu'une partie des interventions de Dion. Il y en eut d'autres, qui ne furent pas publiées ou n'ont pas été conservées. Il évoque lui-même la quantité des discours qu'il a prononcés à Pruse[57] et résume l'un d'entre eux, que nous ne possédons pas.[58] Pline le Jeune mentionne un discours prononcé par Dion in bule.[59]

2) Dans les Discours aux cités (Or. 31-35), Dion intervient en tant que personnalité extérieure, à Rhodes, à Alexandrie, à Tarse et à Célènes. Il s'adresse au peuple de ces cités, c'est-à-dire probablement aux citoyens réunis en assemblée, formelle ou informelle, sans qu'on puisse déterminer les conditions exactes de ses interventions. Les discours dont le contenu politique est le plus précis sont le Discours rhodien, sur la réutilisation des statues honorifiques, et le second Discours tarsien, sur les querelles avec les cités voisines et les rapports avec les gouverneurs. Les autres discours de ce groupe affichent une portée plus générale et morale, alternant conseils et reproches, à propos de l'attitude des Alexandrins aux spectacles, du comportement des Tarsiens et de la prospérité de Célènes.

3) Les discours Sur la royauté, situés à la place d'honneur, en ouverture du corpus, sont parmi les plus célèbres de Dion (Or. 1-4). Les numéros 1 et 3 sont proprement des discours, comportant une adresse à l'Empereur, probablement Trajan, à la deuxième personne du singulier,[60] tandis que les deux autres se présentent comme des dialogues (Or. 2 : Alexandre et Philippe ;

---

[57] DIO CHRYS. 43, 2 : ἐν τοσούτοις λόγοις οὓς εἴρηκα ἐν ὑμῖν.
[58] DIO CHRYS. 40, 5-6.
[59] PLIN. MIN. Epist, 10, 81, 1. À ces discours perdus, s'ajoute encore la mercuriale à la soldatesque citée par PHILOSTR. VS 1, 7 (488).
[60] DIO CHRYS. 1, 9 ; 3, 2 (ὦ γενναῖε αὐτοκράτορ).

Or. 4 : Alexandre et Diogène). Dion parle en "conseiller du prince"[61] et propose une vision ample et articulée de ce que doivent être le pouvoir monarchique et la personnalité du monarque. La propension de Dion à donner des conseils ne se limite pas à ces trois groupes de discours, mais transparaît également dans le reste de son œuvre. Les ouvrages portant sur des sujets d'éthique, voire de théologie et de cosmologie, visent à une action sur l'auditeur ou le lecteur, tout en se distinguant de la rhétorique délibérative *stricto sensu* en ce qu'ils ne portent pas sur des mesures pratiques et ne sont pas adressés à des assemblées délibérantes. Certains de ces ouvrages ne sont pas sans lien avec les groupes précédents, soit parce qu'ils traitent de philosophie politique et font écho aux discours *Sur la royauté* (*Or.* 5, 6, 25, 62), soit parce qu'ils visent à l'édification d'un nombreux auditoire (*Or.* 12). Il est encore question de la définition du bon roi dans des opuscules à sujet mythologique (*Or.* 53, 56, 57).[62] Le *Charidémos* (*Or.* 30), quant à lui, se rattache au genre de la consolation. Enfin, la lettre *Sur la formation oratoire* (*Or.* 18) rassemble des conseils de lecture et de travail à l'intention d'un homme politique : parmi les tâches oratoires qui attendent son illustre élève, Dion n'a garde d'omettre les discours devant le peuple et au *bouleutêrion*.[63] Par une sorte de continuum, le corpus de Dion est tout entier traversé par le thème du conseil, dont l'auteur s'était fait une spécialité.

4. Quelques caractéristiques de la rhétorique délibérative de Dion de Pruse

Conformément aux principes analysés ci-dessus, Dion prodigua des conseils, dans le domaine politique, en alliant la

---

[61] Tel est le titre du chapitre V du livre de DESIDERI (1978) : "Dione consigliere del principe".

[62] Cf. JOUAN (2001).

[63] DIO CHRYS. 18, 14 : εἴτε ἐν δήμῳ λέγων εἴτε ἐν βουλευτηρίῳ ; 18, 17: καὶ ἐν βουλῇ καὶ ἐν δήμῳ.

philosophie et la rhétorique. C'est pourquoi Philostrate le rangea dans la catégorie des philosophes éloquents et la *Souda* le définit comme σοφιστὴς καὶ φιλόσοφος.[64] Tel était le choix de Dion et il s'y est tenu. Il est remarquable que le *Discours rhodien*, que l'on s'accorde en général[65] à placer tôt dans sa carrière, avant l'exil, comporte déjà des éléments philosophiques, comme une allusion à Musonius Rufus (§ 122) et diverses considérations éthiques. Dion s'intéressait à la philosophie avant son exil, et il est resté rhéteur et sophiste, à beaucoup d'égards, jusqu'à la fin de sa vie. Sous Nerva et Trajan, sa stature d'orateur philosophe était parfaitement campée.

Les conseils de Dion se réfèrent à des valeurs qui les fondent et qui les prolongent. Même quand des mesures précises sont envisagées, le discours traduit la volonté de transposer le débat. L'adresse *Aux Nicomédiens sur la concorde avec les Nicéens* (*Or.* 38) en offre un exemple : les solutions pratiques pour régler la querelle à propos du premier rang et du titre de métropole[66] sont encadrées par des développements visant, d'une part, à établir que la concorde, "d'un point de vue général" (§ 8 : καθόλου), est un bien et qu'elle est de nature divine (§ 10-20) et, d'autre part, à décrire les avantages politiques qu'on est en droit d'en attendre (§ 41-48).

Souvent, le message porte sur une attitude politique et éthique, comme dans le second discours à Tarse (*Or.* 34) ou dans l'exhortation finale du discours 44 (§ 10-12). Tout se passe comme si Dion estompait volontairement les contenus concrets. Dans les discours *Sur la royauté*, on ne peut que supposer l'existence d'allusions à l'actualité,[67] la discussion étant délibérément élevée au niveau des plus hauts principes. C'est

---

[64] PHILOSTR. *VS* 1, 7; *Suda* δ 1240. – Apollonios de Tyane, quant à lui, estimait que la philosophie de Dion était trop soucieuse de plaire et trop rhétorique : voir APOLL. TYAN. *Epist.* 9 ; PHILOSTR. *Vit. Apoll.* 5, 40.

[65] Avec l'exception de SIDEBOTTOM (1992) 414.

[66] Sur ces solutions, voir ROBERT (1977) 6 ; JONES (1978) 86-89. Importante mise au point par FERRARY (2008) 1394-1395.

[67] Voir PERNOT (2013) 50.

cette focalisation sur les valeurs qui a attiré sur Dion le qualificatif de 'prédicateur'.[68] Un terme antique qui conviendrait pour désigner de tels conseils, appuyés sur des axiomes moraux, est celui de 'parénèse'.[69]

Autre particularité : les conseils de Dion sont accompagnés de reproches. Pareille attitude n'était pas recommandée par les théoriciens. Quintilien critique les déclamateurs qui s'opposent à leur auditoire et donnent l'impression de réprimander plutôt que de conseiller.[70] Mais le philosophe n'est pas là pour flatter.[71] Sa rhétorique comporte des remontrances qui peuvent être rudes.[72]

Parmi les nombreux thèmes que Dion développe dans ses discours de conseil, deux méritent d'être rappelés, qui sont récurrents et aident à caractériser sa rhétorique. Ils forment un diptyque, et toutes les études sur Dion les abordent et tentent d'en cerner la complexité. Le premier thème est celui de l'hellénisme, Dion ayant le constant souci de situer les cités auxquelles il s'adresse par rapport aux autres cités grecques et par rapport au présent et au passé de la Grèce. Il affirme, par exemple, que les habitants de Pruse et de Nicée sont de purs Hellènes.[73] Il compare les querelles opposant Tarse à ses voisines avec d'autres exemples de querelles entre cités grecques.[74] Il confronte les Rhodiens aux Athéniens d'hier et d'aujourd'hui.[75] Par-delà le poids des grandes familles, à commencer par la sienne,[76] Dion

---

[68] MARTHA (1865) 292-310 : "prédicateur populaire", "évangéliste", "rôle de sermonnaire païen" ; DESIDERI (1978), chapitre VII : "tecnica della predicazione popolare" ; RUSSELL (1992) 13 : "preacher" (*supra*, n. 26) ; BOST-POUDERON (2009). Cf. SYME (1988) 6 : "He (*scil.* Dio) gave benefactions to his own townsfolk, and sermons or earnest exhortation."

[69] Voir notamment PS.-LIB. *Charact. epist.* 5 (dans l'édition FOERSTER de Libanios, vol. IX), sur la différence entre παραίνεσις et συμβουλή.

[70] QUINT. *Inst.* 3, 8, 69 : *obiurgantibus similiores … quam suadentibus.*

[71] DIO CHRYS. 72, 9 : οὐδέν τι θωπεύσων οὐδένα αὐτῶν οὐδὲ φεισόμενος οὐδενός.

[72] DIO CHRYS. 77/78, 42 : σφοδροτέραν τὴν νουθεσίαν καὶ παρακέλευσιν ποιούμενος. Voir GRANDJEAN (2005) et (2009).

[73] DIO CHRYS. 48, 3 ; 39, 1.

[74] DIO CHRYS. 34, 48-51.

[75] DIO CHRYS. 31.

[76] DIO CHRYS. 44, 3-5.

se préoccupe de la valeur du peuple, se réfère aux idéaux civiques et délivre un message d'identité grecque. Ce sujet s'insère dans l'important mouvement de recherche – qui prend en compte le témoignage de Dion – relatif à l'histoire politique et culturelle des cités dans les provinces d'Asie et de Bithynie à l'époque impériale.[77] Les Grecs trouvaient en face d'eux l'autorité romaine, confrontation qui constitue un second thème – domaine de recherche actuel lui aussi, sur lequel ont porté notamment les *Entretiens* de la Fondation Hardt de 2012.[78] Dans les discours *Sur la royauté*, Dion propose sa vision de l'Empire et donne aux Romains des conseils appuyés sur la sagesse et l'exemple des Grecs. Dans les cités grecques, il rappelle le poids de Rome en usant de formules cinglantes : "Les habitants ... jouissent d'honneur et de puissance auprès des gouverneurs s'ils se conduisent sagement" ;[79] les titres honorifiques "font rire les Romains, qui les appellent ... 'péchés grecs'" ;[80] "rien de ce qui se passe dans les cités n'échappe aux autorités" ;[81] le gouverneur devant faire son entrée dans notre assemblée, "maintenant votre tâche est de ne pas faire mentir l'opinion qu'il a de vous" ;[82] vous vous disputez "pour l'ombre d'un âne, comme on dit" ;[83] votre

[77] Voir notamment BEKKER-NIELSEN (2008) ; BRU / KIRBIHLER / LEBRE-TON (2009) ; DAUDE (2002) ; DESIDERI (2000) et (2002) ; FERNOUX (2004) et (2011) ; GUERBER (2009) ; HELLER (2006) ; LAFOND (2010) ; MADSEN (2009) ; MAREK (2003) ; SALMERI (1999) et (2000) ; VUJČIĆ (2009) ; ZUIDER-HOEK (2008).

[78] SCHUBERT (2013).

[79] DIO CHRYS. 40, 22 : πόλιν οἰκοῦντας οὐ σμικρὰν καὶ πολιτείαν ἐξαίρετον ἔχοντας καὶ παρὰ τοῖς ἡγεμόσι τιμήν τινα καὶ δύναμιν, ἐὰν σωφρονῶσι.

[80] DIO CHRYS. 38, 38 : παρὰ τοῖς Ῥωμαίοις γέλωτα κινεῖ καὶ καλεῖται τὸ ἔτι ὑβριστικώτερον Ἑλληνικὰ ἁμαρτήματα. Nous empruntons à ROBERT (1977) 5 la traduction de ἁμαρτήματα par "péchés".

[81] DIO CHRYS. 46, 14 : οὐ γὰρ λανθάνει τῶν ἐν ταῖς πόλεσιν οὐδὲν τοὺς ἡγεμόνας. Sur le sens à donner ici au mot ἡγεμόνας, voir JONES (1978) 167, n. 23; DESIDERI (1978) 135.

[82] DIO CHRYS. 48, 2 : νῦν οὖν ὑμέτερον ἔργον ἐστὶ μὴ ψεύσασθαι αὐτοῦ τὴν διάνοιαν.

[83] DIO CHRYS. 34, 48 : περὶ ὄνου σκιᾶς, φασί.

conduite est celle "de compagnons d'esclavage se querellant entre eux".[84]

Tendant à se poser en représentant de l'hellénisme face au pouvoir romain et en représentant de Rome devant les auditoires grecs, Dion, en médiateur,[85] construit dans ses discours un modèle subtil de rapport avec Rome et associe, à des degrés variables selon les contextes, l'affirmation de l'identité grecque, la critique contre certaines réalités romaines et l'esprit de coopération avec l'Empire.

Pour transmettre ses leçons, qui pouvaient être difficiles à faire admettre, Dion eut recours à des argumentations riches et variées, parmi lesquelles nous sélectionnons certaines procédures rhétoriques qui constituent sa marque.

La mise en scène de soi est dans le droit fil de la théorie rhétorique, qui souligne l'importance particulière de l'*êthos* de l'orateur dans le genre délibératif : "Le jour sous lequel se montre l'orateur est plus utile pour les délibérations".[86] Dion est allé très loin dans cette direction. Dans les *Discours bithyniens*, il est souvent conduit à parler de lui-même pour se justifier face à des critiques et des accusations.[87] Et d'évoquer avec complaisance ses ancêtres, ses voyages, son rôle dans la cité de Pruse. Il fait état de ses rapports avec l'Empereur et en tire argument pour souligner son propre désintéressement et pour asseoir l'autorité de son propos :

"Je n'ai aucunement réservé cette occasion et la bienveillance du souverain à mes fins personnelles, fût-ce partiellement, par exemple en redressant ma fortune détruite ou en acquérant des charges ou des moyens supplémentaires, et au contraire j'ai

---

[84] DIO CHRYS. 34, 51 : ὁμοδούλων πρὸς ἀλλήλους ἐριζόντων.

[85] BOST-POUDERON (2011b).

[86] ARIST. *Rhet.* 2, 1, 1377b28-30 : τὸ μὲν οὖν ποιόν τινα φαίνεσθαι τὸν λέγοντα χρησιμώτερον εἰς τὰς συμβουλάς ἐστιν (trad. DUFOUR). De même QUINT. *Inst.* 3, 8, 13 : *consilia nemo est qui neget secundum mores dari* ; 3, 8, 48 : *multum refert etiam quae sit persona suadentis.* Sur la mise en scène de soi chez Dion, voir KRAUSE (2003). La théorie prévoit aussi l'appel aux émotions (QUINT. *ibid.* 3, 8, 12) : mais, si Dion manie l'*êthos*, le *pathos*, en revanche, n'est pas son fort.

[87] DIO CHRYS. 43, 45, 47, 50.

tourné vers vous tout ce qui était possible et je n'ai eu d'yeux que pour l'intérêt de la cité."[88]

Le moment privilégié pour parler de soi est l'exorde. Dion connaissait les règles rhétoriques qui s'appliquent à cette partie du discours : le début du *Discours rhodien* est un modèle d'exorde délibératif, destiné à présenter le sujet et à éveiller l'intérêt et la faveur du public.[89] Mais, en ce domaine, Dion créa sa propre manière. Comme le notait déjà Photius, il se fit une spécialité des longues entrées en matière, au point de rendre parfois "la tête plus grosse que le corps".[90] Devant l'assemblée de Pruse comme devant le conseil d'Apamée, il n'hésite pas à exprimer des considérations sur lui-même, ses expériences et ses dispositions.[91] Dans certains discours aux cités et certains discours *Sur la royauté*, l'exorde est développé comme un morceau quasi-indépendant, qui sert à capter l'attention du public, à jouer avec ses attentes et à représenter l'orateur en philosophe, à grand renfort d'anecdotes, de comparaisons et de spirituelles protestations d'incapacité.[92] Dion sort des cadres traditionnels de la rhétorique politique – comme l'avait noté encore Photius, qui parle de style de "conversations" (συνουσίαις)[93] –, pour adopter un ton qui s'apparente au genre sophistique de la prolalie.[94] Conférencier hors pair, Dion sait commencer très loin de son sujet et faire d'apparents détours pour amener l'auditoire au point voulu. Là se déploient les qualités de "douceur"

---

[88] DIO CHRYS. 45, 3 : εἰς οὐδὲν τῶν ἰδίων κατεθέμην τὸν καιρὸν ἐκεῖνον οὐδὲ τὴν τοῦ κρατοῦντος εὔνοιαν οὐδὲ ἀπὸ μέρους, οἷον τὰ τῆς οὐσίας ἐπανορθώσας διεφθαρμένης ἢ προσλαβών τινα ἀρχὴν ἢ δύναμιν, ἀλλ' ἅπαν ὅσον ποτὲ ἦν εἰς ὑμᾶς ἔτρεψα καὶ μόνον εἶδον τὸ τῆς πόλεως.

[89] DIO CHRYS. 31, 1-7.

[90] PHOT. *Bibl.* 209, 165b34-39 : τὸ δ' ἐπὶ μακρότατον ἀποτείνειν τὰ προοίμια ἢ τὰ οἷον προοίμια, οὐκέτι ἀφίησιν αὐτὸν τὸ μὴ οὐχὶ ἀντὶ πολιτικοῦ καὶ συγγραφικοῦ τύπου τὸν ἐπὶ ταῖς συνουσίαις ἀλλάξασθαι παραδεδυκότα, καὶ μείζω τὴν κεφαλὴν τὴν ὡς ἐν λόγῳ τοῦ λοιποῦ σώματος διαπλάττειν.

[91] DIO CHRYS. 40 et 41.

[92] DIO CHRYS. 1, 1-8 ; 32, 1-29 ; 33, 1-30 ; 35, 1-12.

[93] *Loc. cit.*, n. 90.

[94] Sur la prolalie, voir PERNOT (1993) 546-568.

et d'apparente "simplicité" (γλυκύτης, ἀφέλεια) qui lui étaient reconnues. Un autre jeu, qui est constant, consiste à se référer à l'éloge tout en s'en distanciant.[95] Dans la rhétorique délibérative de Dion, le genre épidictique n'est jamais loin. Les auditoires de l'époque impériale attendaient que fussent louées les cités, louée la concorde, loué l'Empereur, et l'orateur le savait. Il leur en donnait acte, de toutes les manières, et refusait fondamentalement de se prêter à leur désir. Pour un ou deux discours très structurés,[96] combien d'allocutions ondoyantes, parées de toutes les grâces ! La culture, l'humour sont omniprésents. Certains passages se distinguent aussi par un style recherché et voyant, comme les séries de questions rhétoriques, avec anaphore, polyptote, parallélisme et antithèse, dans les éloges de la concorde.[97] Le fait que ces passages appartiennent à des discours effectivement prononcés est intéressant pour cerner les goûts du public, qui appréciait la virtuosité oratoire et ne la jugeait pas déplacée dans un discours politique.

Enfin, un dernier trait caractéristique est l'usage des allusions et des faux-semblants. Dans les discours *Sur la royauté*, entreprenant la tâche délicate de conseiller l'Empereur, Dion déploie un luxe de précautions. Résolu à ne pas prononcer un éloge du souverain, il s'en excuse adroitement : "Pour ne pas encourir le grief de flatterie auprès des calomniateurs et pour

[95] PERNOT (1993) 578-591.

[96] Le second *Discours tarsien* (*Or.* 34) offre une annonce du plan (§ 6-7), une récapitulation de la première partie (§ 27), des transitions très nettes (§ 38, 43) ; cf. JONES (1978) 76 : "perhaps the most carefully constructed in the whole collection". Le discours *Aux Nicomédiens sur la concorde avec les Nicéens* (*Or.* 38) se signale par un exorde très progressif, dans lequel l'orateur révèle peu à peu son sujet (§ 3-5, 6) ; le plan est annoncé (§ 8) ; les transitions sont explicites (§ 21, 48).

[97] DIO CHRYS. 39, 3 et suiv. : ποῖον μὲν γὰρ θέαμα κάλλιον πόλεως ὁμοφρονούσης; ποῖον δὲ ἄκουσμα σεμνότερον; ποία μὲν βουλεύεται πόλις ἄμεινον τῆς ἅμα βουλευομένης; ποία δὲ εὐμαρέστερον πράττει τῆς ἅμα πραττούσης; ποία δὲ ἧττον ἀποτυγχάνει τῆς ταὐτὰ βουλευομένης; etc. (la série comporte dix-huit questions au total). – 41, 13 et suiv. : τίνες μὲν γὰρ εὐπρεπέστερον κτῶνται τἀγαθὰ τῶν φίλων συμποριζόντων αὐτοῖς; τίνες δὲ ἀποφεύγουσι τὰ κακὰ ῥᾶον ἢ οἷς ἂν φίλοι συμμαχῶσι; etc.

que toi, de ton côté, tu n'encoures pas celui de vouloir être loué en face, je ferai porter mon discours sur le bon roi".[98] Si je ne te loue pas, c'est pour ton bien... C'est donc en philosophe que Dion s'exprimera, non en panégyriste, tout en en ayant dit assez, cependant, pour que l'Empereur et la cour pensent à appliquer ses propos théoriques à la situation présente et pour que le prince puisse se reconnaître, s'il le souhaite, dans le miroir qui lui est tendu. Dans les discours 2 et 4, le recours au dialogue est une autre tactique, qui permet à Dion de ne pas s'exprimer en son nom propre, mais de s'abriter derrière des personnages qui sont autant de masques.

Dans les discours aux cités, Dion manie l'ironie, par exemple à Célènes (Or. 35), où il feint d'admirer la prospérité de la cité pour faire entendre, a contrario, une leçon morale sur le thème "les biens matériels ne font pas le bonheur". Le faux-semblant sert à faire passer les messages difficiles.[99]

Parfois, l'intention est si bien voilée que le lecteur moderne n'est pas sûr de la saisir. L'exemple le plus pittoresque est fourni par le premier Discours tarsien, dans lequel Dion, reprochant aux habitants leur déchéance morale, les incite à se réformer sur un point, qui est particulièrement grave et déshonorant : il faut cesser de ῥέγκειν ("ronfler", "renifler").[100] Sur ce curieux reproche, toutes sortes d'explications ont été proposées.[101] Certains commentateurs ont envisagé de prendre le mot à la lettre et ont supposé que les gens de Tarse se singularisaient par quelque habitude nasale grossière. D'autres ont cherché un sens détourné. Mais lequel ? Dion reproche-t-il aux Tarsiens leurs mœurs débauchées, le reniflement renvoyant à des comportements bestiaux et sexuels ? Ou bien s'agit-il d'une prononciation

---

[98] DIO CHRYS. 3, 25 : ἵνα δὲ μήτε ἐγὼ κολακείας αἰτίαν ἔχω τοῖς θέλουσι διαβάλλειν μήτε σὺ τοῦ κατ᾽ ὀφθαλμοὺς ἐθέλειν ἐπαινεῖσθαι, ποιήσομαι τοὺς λόγους ὑπὲρ τοῦ χρηστοῦ βασιλέως.

[99] PERNOT (2015) 104-105.

[100] DIO CHRYS. 33, 33.

[101] Présentation de ces explications, avec bibliographie, dans BOST-POUDERON (2011a) 7-9. La discussion se poursuit : cf. KIM (2013).

fautive du grec, manifestant la perte de la pureté hellénique sous l'influence de la composante indigène de la population ? Le verbe ῥέγκειν s'entend-il au sens de "renifler", d'"ahaner", de "baragouiner" ? Selon toute probabilité, la signification du reproche devait être compréhensible en situation. Mais pour nous, aujourd'hui, ce discours soigneusement crypté, "figuré" (ἐσχηματισμένος), garde son mystère.

Les *Discours bithyniens* comportent également des incertitudes, qui ne sont pas seulement dues à notre ignorance du contexte, mais s'expliquent aussi par le fait que Dion parle à mots couverts. Ainsi, il prit deux fois la parole à Pruse pour refuser des honneurs ou des charges qui lui étaient proposés, et ses refus sont si polis qu'on se demande si ce ne sont pas des acceptations. Au début du discours 44 (*Démonstration d'affection à sa patrie qui lui proposait des honneurs*), il décline avec ménagements ce qui lui est offert,[102] mais C.P. Jones a suggéré que l'on pouvait avoir affaire à une apparence de refus, conforme à l'étiquette qui voulait que les bienfaiteurs, y compris les empereurs, affectassent de repousser ou de modérer les honneurs qui leur étaient décernés.[103] Le discours politique grec est un jeu social qui obéit à des règles, et Dion se meut, au milieu des conventions, avec beaucoup de tact et d'habileté. Dans le discours 49 (*Refus d'une magistrature devant le conseil*), il explique longuement, on l'a vu,[104] que les philosophes ont vocation à gouverner (§ 1-14), avant de conclure, de manière inattendue, qu'il doit décliner la charge d'archonte qui lui est proposée ; car il doit quitter Pruse (§ 14-15). Pourquoi ne pas avoir fait état tout de suite de cette impossibilité ? Par courtoisie, certes. Mais on soupçonne que la tirade initiale, sur le rôle des philosophes, n'était pas dépourvue d'arrière-pensées et qu'elle pouvait servir à pousser un autre candidat,

---

[102] ARNIM (1898) 212.
[103] JONES (1978) 105 ; cf. BOWERSOCK (1965) 120. PHILOSTR. *VS* 2, 11 (591) mentionne un discours de Chrestos de Byzance devant l'assemblée des Athéniens visant à dissuader ceux-ci de le proposer pour la chaire de rhétorique.
[104] *Supra*, n. 33.

qui était philosophe, ou à en contrecarrer un autre, qui ne l'était pas.[105]

Fort énigmatique, encore, et controversé, le discours *À Diodoros* (*Or.* 51).[106] Cette courte allocution met en scène plusieurs personnages dont les rôles ne sont pas clairs, à propos d'une élection récemment advenue à Pruse. Après une introduction consacrée à la critique des éloges insincères, Dion adresse au peuple des compliments qui ont toute chance d'être ironiques.

Deux passages des *Discours bithyniens* peuvent être signalés comme représentatifs de la rhétorique délibérative de Dion, dont ils rassemblent les principaux aspects. Figurant dans les discours 40 (*Dans sa patrie, au sujet de la concorde avec Apamée*) et 47 (*Démégorie dans sa patrie*), deux harangues prononcées devant l'assemblée de Pruse, ils portent sur le programme de travaux publics dont Dion avait pris la responsabilité[107]. Ces passages ne sont pas les plus célèbres ni les plus brillants du corpus : témoignages du discours délibératif 'ordinaire', ils attestent du rôle de la rhétorique dans la politique municipale, puisque Dion y fait référence aux discours prononcés par lui-même et par ses adversaires, et ils mettent eux-mêmes en œuvre une adroite rhétorique. Dion y use tantôt du style simple, tantôt du style élevé ; il recourt successivement au récit et à l'argumentation, et variant les tons, se fait tour à tour modeste, flatteur, ironique. Il se défend, contre-attaque, fait des promesses, cherche à persuader : ce qui ne l'empêche nullement de parler en philosophe. Dans le discours 40, il remonte au principe, pour réfléchir sur la fierté de la cité et sur les rapports avec l'autorité romaine. Dans le discours 47, il ne craint pas de se comparer à Zénon et à Aristote. Il va même, renversant les rôles, jusqu'à lancer à l'auditoire une requête spirituelle, et paradoxale pour un orateur délibératif : "Conseillez-moi !"[108]

[105] CUVIGNY (1994) 163-164.
[106] Voir en dernier lieu AMATO (2014) 91-96.
[107] DIO CHRYS. 40, 5-10 ; 47, 18-20.
[108] DIO CHRYS. 47, 18 : συμβουλεύσατέ μοι.

Conclusion

La rhétorique fut, pour Dion, plus qu'un instrument et un moyen d'expression de ses idées : un cadre de pensée et un mode de vie. Le cas de cet auteur influent est intéressant pour la recherche sur la rhétorique délibérative, parce qu'il conduit à réviser les définitions courantes. Chez Dion, les discours politiques se révèlent plus diversifiés et profonds que ne le laisserait croire la théorie rhétorique en usage dans les écoles de l'Antiquité. Ils mettent en jeu le pouvoir – pouvoir de la rhétorique, rhétorique face au pouvoir. Ils sont liés à la philosophie. Ils s'adaptent aux différents contextes et aux différents auditeurs. Ils recourent à de multiples méthodes de persuasion, qui vont des arguments logiques à l'*êthos*, à l'éloge, aux prestiges du style, aux faux-semblants. Pour analyser tous ces aspects, le concept aristotélicien de συμβουλευτικὸν γένος ne suffit pas et doit être élargi.

Telle est la rhétorique délibérative de Dion. Elle pose, pour finir, deux questions, qui seraient la matière d'une autre enquête et qui ne comportent peut-être pas de solution définitive. Du point de vue historique, on souhaiterait savoir si Dion était un cas particulier, ou s'il a existé d'autres sophistes-philosophes et conseillers politiques du même type que lui. S'il y en a eu, comme il est probable, quel était leur nombre ? Par ailleurs, du point de vue de l'efficacité pratique, on voudrait apprécier l'effet des discours de Dion et mesurer jusqu'à quel point sa rhétorique était persuasive. Fut-il écouté ? À Pruse, oui, sans doute. Dans les autres cités, et auprès de l'Empereur, cela est moins sûr.

Bibliographie

AMATO, E. (2014), *Traiani praeceptor. Studi su biografia, cronologia e fortuna di Dione Crisostomo* (Besançon).

AMATO, E. / JULIEN, Y. (2005), *Favorinos d'Arles. Œuvres I, Introduction générale. Témoignages. Discours aux Corinthiens. Sur la Fortune* (Paris).

ARNIM, H. VON (1893-1896), *Dionis Prusaensis quem vocant Chrysostomum quae exstant omnia.* 2 vols. (Berlin).

—— (1898), *Leben und Werke des Dio von Prusa. Mit einer Einleitung: Sophistik, Rhetorik, Philosophie in ihrem Kampf um die Jugendbildung* (Berlin).

—— (1907), compte rendu de E. WENKEBACH, *Quaestiones Dioneae*, *BPhW* 27, 614-616.

BAILEY, C. (2015), "'Honor' in Rhodes: Dio Chrysostom's Thirty-First Oration", *ICS* 40, 45-62.

BECK, I. (1970), *Untersuchungen zur Theorie des Genos symbuleutikon* (diss. Hamburg).

BEKKER-NIELSEN, T. (2008), *Urban Life and Local Politics in Roman Bithynia. The Small World of Dion Chrysostomos* (Aarhus).

BOST-POUDERON, C. (2006), *Dion Chrysostome. Trois discours aux villes (Orr. 33-35)* (Salerne).

—— (2009), "Entre prédication morale, parénèse et politique : les *Discours 31-34* de Dion Chrysostome (ou : la subversion des genres)", in D. VAN MAL-MAEDER / A. BURNIER / L. NÚÑEZ (éds.), *Jeux de voix. Énonciation, intertextualité et intentionnalité dans la littérature antique* (Berne), 225-256.

—— (2011a), *Dion de Pruse dit Dion Chrysostome. Œuvres. Premier discours à Tarse (or. XXXIII). Second discours à Tarse (or. XXXIV). Discours à Célènes de Phrygie (or. XXXV). Discours Borysthénitique (or. XXXVI)* (Paris).

—— (2011b), "Intermédiaires et conciliateurs entre administrés et administration dans les provinces grecques de l'Empire romain : les témoignages de Dion de Pruse, Plutarque et Épictète", in A. GANGLOFF (éd.), *Médiateurs culturels et politiques dans l'Empire romain. Voyages, conflits, identités* (Paris), 93-101.

BOWERSOCK, G.W. (1965), *Augustus and the Greek World* (Oxford).

BRANCACCI, A. (1985), Rhetorike philosophousa. *Dione Crisostomo nella cultura antica e bizantina* (Naples).

BRU, H. / KIRBIHLER, F. / LEBRETON, S. (éds.) (2009), *L'Asie Mineure dans l'Antiquité. Échanges, populations et territoires. Regards actuels sur une péninsule* (Rennes).

BRUNT, P. (1973), "Aspects of the Social Thought of Dio Chrysostom and of the Stoics", *PCPhS* 19, 9-34 = *Studies in Stoicism* (Oxford, 2013), 151-179.

BUDÉ, G. DE (1916-1919), *Dionis Chrysostomi orationes.* 2 vols. (Leipzig).

—— (1920), *Liste d'interpolations du texte de Dion Chrysostome* (Genève).

COHOON, J. W. / CROSBY, H. L. (1932-1951), *Dio Chrysostom* (London).

CUVIGNY, M. (1994), *Dion de Pruse. Discours Bithyniens (Discours 38-51)* (Paris).

DAUDE, C. (2002), "Formes subjectives de la citoyenneté : l'exemple de Dion Chrysostome à Pruse", in S. RATTI (éd.), *Antiquité et citoyenneté* (Besançon), 219-232.

DESIDERI, P. (1978), *Dione di Prusa. Un intellettuale greco nell' impero romano* (Messine).

—— (1991a), "Dione di Prusa fra ellenismo e romanità", in *ANRW* II, 33, 5, 3882-3902.

—— (1991b), "Tipologia e varietà di funzione comunicativa degli scritti dionei", in *ANRW* II, 33, 5, 3903-3959.

—— (1994), "Dion Cocceianus de Pruse dit Chrysostome", in R. GOULET (dir.), *Dictionnaire des philosophes antiques* II (Paris), 841-856.

—— (2000), "City and Country in Dio", in S. SWAIN (2000), 93-107.

—— (2002), "Dimensioni della polis in età alto-imperiale romana", *Prometheus* 28, 139-150.

ELLIGER, W. (1967), *Dion Chrysostomos, Sämtliche Reden. Eingeleitet, übersetzt und erläutert* (Zurich).

FERNOUX, H.-L. (2004), *Notables et élites des cités de Bithynie aux époques hellénistique et romaine (IIIe siècle av. J.-C. - IIIe siècle ap. J.-C.)* (Lyon).

—— (2011), *Le* Demos *et la Cité. Communautés et assemblées populaires en Asie Mineure à l'époque impériale* (Rennes).

FERRARY, J.-L. (2008), "Les apports du dossier des mémoriaux de délégations de Claros dans le fonds Louis Robert", *CRAI*, 1377-1404.

FRANÇOIS, L. (1921), *Essai sur Dion Chrysostome, philosophe et moraliste cynique et stoïcien* (Paris).

GANGLOFF, A. (2006), *Dion Chrysostome et les mythes. Hellénisme, communication et philosophie politique* (Grenoble).

GRANDJEAN, T. (2005), *Le blâme des cités chez Dion de Pruse* (thèse Strasbourg 2, Lille).

—— (2009), "Le blâme des cités chez Apollonios de Tyane et chez Dion de Pruse", in G. ABBAMONTE / L. MILETTI / L. SPINA (éds.), *Discorsi alla prova. Atti del Quinto Colloquio italo-francese, Napoli, 21-23 settembre 2006* (Naples), 139-187.

GUERBER, É. (2009), *Les cités grecques dans l'Empire romain. Les privilèges et les titres des cités de l'Orient hellénophone d'Octave Auguste à Dioclétien* (Rennes).

HARTLICH, P. (1889), "De exhortationum a Graecis Romanisque scriptarum historia et indole", *LSKPh* 11, 209-335.

HELLER, A. (2006), *"Les bêtises des Grecs". Conflits et rivalités entre cités d'Asie et de Bithynie à l'époque romaine (129 a. C. - 235 p. C.)* (Bordeaux).

HIGHET, G. (1983), "Mutilations in the Text of Dio Chrysostom", in R.J. BALL (éd.), *The Classical Papers of Gilbert Highet* (New York), 74-99.

JAZDZEWSKA, K. (2015), "Do not Follow the Athenians! The Example of Athens in Dio Chrysostom's *Orations*", *CPh* 110, 252-268.

JONES, C.P. (1978), *The Roman World of Dio Chrysostom* (Cambridge, MA).

— (2015), "Five Letters Attributed to Dio of Prusa", *CPh* 110, 124-131.

JOUAN, F. (1977), "Les thèmes romanesques dans l'*Euboïcos* de Dion Chrysostome", *REG* 90, 38-46.

— (2001), "Nestor et Dion de Pruse, conseillers des princes", in A. BILLAULT (éd.), Ὀπώρα. *La belle saison de l'hellénisme. Études de littérature antique offertes au Recteur Jacques Bompaire* (Paris), 43-57.

KASPRZYK, D. / VENDRIES, C. (2012), *Spectacles et désordre à Alexandrie. Dion de Pruse, Discours aux Alexandrins* (Rennes).

KENNEDY, G.A. (1972), *The Art of Rhetoric in the Roman World 300 B.C.-A.D. 300* (Princeton).

KIM, L. (2013), "Figures of Silence in Dio Chrysostom's *First Tarsian oration* (Or. 33): aposiopesis, paraleipsis, and huposiôpêsis", *G&R* 60, 32-49.

KINDSTRAND, J.F. (éd.) (1981), *An Index to Dio Chrysostomus*. Compiled by R. KOOLMEISTER and T. TALLMEISTER (Uppsala).

KLEK, J. (1919), *Symbuleutici qui dicitur sermonis historia critica per quattuor saecula continuata* (Kirchhain).

KRAUSE, C. (2003), *Strategie der Selbstinszenierung. Das rhetorische Ich in den Reden Dions von Prusa* (Wiesbaden).

LAFOND, Y. (2010), "L'idéal d'excellence et l'éthique des cités grecques à l'époque de Trajan", in L. CAPDETREY / Y. LAFOND (éds.), *La cité et ses élites. Pratiques et représentation des formes de domination et de contrôle social dans les cités grecques* (Bordeaux), 103-117.

LEMARCHAND, L. (1926), *Dion de Pruse. Les œuvres d'avant l'exil* (Paris).

MADSEN, J.M. (2009), *Eager to be Roman. Greek Response to Roman Rule in Pontus and Bithynia* (Londres).

MAREK, C. (2003), *Pontus et Bithynia. Die römischen Provinzen im Norden Kleinasiens* (Mayence).

MARTHA, C. (1865), *Les moralistes sous l'Empire romain. Philosophes et poètes* (Paris).

MAZON, P. (1943), "Dion de Pruse et la politique agraire de Trajan", *CRAI*, 74 et 85-87.

MILAZZO, A.M. (2007), *Dimensione retorica e realtà politica. Dione di Prusa nelle orazioni III, V, VII, VIII* (Hildesheim).

MOLES, J.L. (1978), "The Career and Conversion of Dio Chrysostom", *JHS* 98, 79-100.

—— (1990), "The Kingship Orations of Dio Chrysostom", in F. CAIRNS (éd.), *Papers of the Leeds International Latin Seminar* VI (Leeds), 297-375.

NESSELRATH, H.-G. (éd.) (2009), *Dion von Prusa. Der Philosoph und sein Bild* (Tübingen).

PERNOT, L. (1993), *La rhétorique de l'éloge dans le monde gréco-romain.* 2 vols. (Paris).

—— (2002), "Aristote et ses devanciers. Pour une archéologie du genre délibératif", *Ktèma* 27, 227-235.

—— (2006), *L'ombre du Tigre. Recherches sur la réception de Démosthène* (Naples).

—— (2010), "Che cosa resta dei nostri discorsi ?", in G. PETRONE / A. CASAMENTO (éds.), *Studia ... in umbra educata. Percorsi della retorica latina in età imperiale* (Palerme), 17-29.

—— (2013), *Alexandre le Grand. Les risques du pouvoir. Textes philosophiques et rhétoriques traduits et commentés* (Paris).

—— (2015), *Epideictic Rhetoric. Questioning the Stakes of Ancient Praise* (Austin).

ROBERT, L. (1977), "La titulature de Nicée et de Nicomédie : la gloire et la haine", *HSPh* 81, 1-39 = *Choix d'écrits* (Paris, 2007), 673-703.

RUSSELL, D.A. (1992), *Dio Chrysostom. Orations VII, XII, and XXXVI* (Cambridge).

SALMERI, G. (1982), *La politica e il potere. Saggio su Dione di Prusa* (Catania).

—— (1999), "La vita politica in Asia Minore sotto l'impero romano nei discorsi di Dione di Prusa", *Studi ellenistici* 12, 211-267.

—— (2000), "Dio, Rome, and the Civic Life of Asia Minor", in SWAIN (2000), 53-92.

SCANNAPIECO, R. (2004), "Tecnica della narrazione e gioco combinatorio nel racconto dell'*Euboico* (D. Chrys., *or.* VII §§ 1-80)", in S.M. MEDAGLIA (éd.), *Miscellanea in ricordo di Angelo Raffaele Sodano* (Naples), 327-368.

SCHMIDT, T. (2013), "L'histoire au service du politique : Épaminondas comme *exemplum* dans les *Discours bithyniens* de Dion Chrysostome", in D. CÔTÉ / P. FLEURY (éds.), *Discours politique et histoire dans l'Antiquité* (Besançon), 379-396.

SCHUBERT, P. (éd.) (2013), *Les Grecs héritiers des Romains. Huit exposés suivis de discussions* (Genève).

SHEPPARD, A.R.R. (1984), "Dio Chrysostom: The Bithynian Years", *AC* 53, 157-173.

SIDEBOTTOM, H. (1992), "The Date of Dio of Prusa's Rhodian and Alexandrian Orations", *Historia* 41, 407-419.

—— (2006), "Dio Chrysostom and the Development of *On Kingship* Literature", in D. SPENCER / E. THEODORAKOPOULOS (éds.), *Advice and its Rhetoric in Greece and Rome* (Bari).

SWAIN, S. (éd.) (2000), *Dio Chrysostom. Politics, Letters, and Philosophy* (Oxford).

SYME, R. (1988), "Greeks Invading the Roman Government", in A.R. BIRLEY (éd.), *Ronald Syme. Roman Papers* IV (Oxford).

TRAPP, M. (1995), "Sense of Place in the Orations of Dio Chrysostom", in D. INNES / H. HINE / C. PELLING (éds.), *Ethics and Rhetoric. Classical Essays for Donald Russell* (Oxford), 163-175.

VEYNE, P. (2005), *L'Empire gréco-romain* (Paris).

VUJČIĆ, N. (2009), "Greek Popular Assemblies in the Imperial Period and the Discourses of Dio of Prusa", *EA* 42, 157-169.

WENKEBACH, E.A. (1903), *Quaestiones Dioneae. De Dionis Chrysostomi studiis rhetoricis capita selecta* (Kirchhain).

WHITMARSH, T. (2001), *Greek Literature and the Roman Empire. The Politics of Imitation* (Oxford).

—— (2004), "Dio Chrysostom", in I.J.F. DE JONG / R. NÜNLIST / A. BOWIE (éds.), *Studies in Ancient Greek Narrative.* Vol. 1, *Narrators, Narratees, and Narratives in Ancient Greek Literature* (Leiden), 451-464.

ZUIDERHOEK, A. (2008), "On the Political Sociology of the Imperial Greek City", *GRBS* 48, 417-445.

DISCUSSION

M. Kraus: Es gibt doch einige wichtige Unterschiede zwischen Dio und der Zweiten Sophistik einerseits und z.B. Libanios und der Dritten Sophistik andererseits. So gewinnt das Thema der hellenischen παιδεία im 4. Jahrhundert auch eine religiöse Dimension im Sinne einer paganen, antichristlichen Haltung. Auch die Haltung zum Kaisertum ist im 1./2. Jahrhundert noch weit unproblematischer und kooperativer als in der Spätantike; das Motiv des ‚guten Monarchen‘ (χρηστὸς βασιλεύς, Dio, *Or.* 3, 25) etwa sucht man später bei Libanios vergeblich. Dio hat in seinen Reden über das Königtum auch noch ein einheitliches Römisches Reich im Auge, während sich im 4. Jahrhundert die westlich-lateinische und die östlich-griechische Reichshälfte bereits deutlich entfremdet haben. Auch der Gegensatz von lateinischer und griechischer Sprache und Kultur spielt bei Dio noch kaum eine Rolle.

L. Pernot: Dion de Pruse et Libanios avaient beaucoup en commun du point de vue de la *paideia* et de la culture rhétorique. Les différences qui les séparent, cependant, sont très grandes. Ils n'avaient pas du tout le même caractère, ni les mêmes choix de vie. Dion se définissait comme philosophe: Libanios, non; Libanios se définissait comme professeur: Dion, non. En outre, les époques dans lesquelles ils ont vécu étaient fort dissemblables, sous le rapport de la politique, de l'état social ou encore de la religion. Dion ne pouvait pas imaginer l'instauration d'un Empire chrétien.

A. Chaniotis: Many thanks for this excellent overview of Dio's deliberative oratory, which gives me the opportunity to make a few remarks on the context of some of Dio's statements. Since

Dio was keen on comparing himself with the great Athenian orators of the Classical period, his interest in the Greek past is very selective. He focuses on Classical Athens, largely ignoring the Hellenistic period. That he paints a very negative image of statesmanship at his time – as compared with that of earlier periods – is not an original trait of his rhetoric. It is found in Plutarch's *Political Precepts*, but also much earlier. A decree of Beroia for the local statesman Harpalos (*I.Beroia* 2, late 2nd century BC), regrets that Harpalos was unable to serve as a general like his grandfathers, but praises him for showing his courage by "courageously (εὐθαρσῶς) accepting the greatest priesthood which involves the largest expenses".

Dio's contempt for contemporary political life is not entirely justified. Greek cities continued having a robust political life. As we can infer from the epigraphic evidence, administration and political leadership could be very demanding tasks in cities of the Imperial period. Dio's exaggerations have been observed in his description of Olbia in the *Borysthenitikos*.[1]

As for his Rhodian oration that deals with the re-use of statue bases and statues, Dio gives the impression that this practice was a Rhodian phenomenon. In reality, the re-use of statues and bases was very widespread. For instance, a poetess in Kos around Dio's time was honoured with the statue of another earlier poetess (*IG* XII 4, 845), and more evidence for the recycling of statues and bases comes from late Hellenistic and Roman Athens.[2]

---

[1] HUPE, J., "Der Dedikantenkreis des Achilleus als ein Gradmesser von Akkulturationsprozessen im kaiserzeitlichen Olbia: Ein Beitrag zur olbischen Onomastik", in F. FLESS / M. TREISTER (eds.), *Bilder und Objekte als Träger kultureller Identität und interkultureller Kommunikation im Schwarzmeergebiet. Kolloquium in Zschortau/Sachsen vom 13.2.-15.2.2003* (Rahden, 2005), 43-52.

[2] SHEAR, J.L., "Reusing Statues, Rewriting Inscriptions, and Bestowing Honours in Roman Athens", in Z. NEWBY / R. LEADER-NEWBY (eds.), *Art and Inscriptions in the Ancient World* (Cambridge, 2007), 221-246; KEESLING, C.M., "Vor klassischem Hintergrund: Zum Phänomen der Wiederverwendung älterer Statuen auf der Athener Akropolis als Ehrenstatuen für Römer", in R. KRUMREICH / C. WITSCHEL (eds.), *Die Akropolis von Athen im Hellenismus und in der römischen Kaiserzeit* (Wiesbaden, 2010), 329-398.

Considering contexts like these, we get a better understanding of Dio's rhetorical strategies.

L. Pernot: Dion réécrit le passé avec une très grande liberté, non seulement l'histoire, mais aussi la mythologie, en fonction des besoins de ses démonstrations. Le point qui lui importe est la leçon morale à tirer dans chaque cas. En particulier, il a tendance à idéaliser Sparte. La liberté dans le choix et le traitement des exemples empruntés au passé est une caractéristique de la rhétorique. Cependant, cela n'empêchait pas Dion de garder les yeux ouverts sur le présent. Dans le passage du *Discours rhodien* qui est cité ci-dessus (p. 266), il dresse un bilan très juste de la situation des cités grecques à l'époque impériale. Sur ce point, il rejoint Plutarque, en cherchant, comme lui, "ce qui reste". Au mot καταλείπεται employé par Dion (31, 162) font écho, chez Plutarque, λείπονται (*Praec. ger. reip.* 805a) et λείπεται (*ibid.* 824d), ainsi que ὑπελείπετο (*Cic.* 4, 7). Les affinités ne manquent pas entre Dion et Plutarque, comme j'ai essayé de le montrer ailleurs.[3]

C. Kremmydas: Thank you for your stimulating analysis of Dio's deliberative rhetoric. I was struck by the remarkable continuity of deliberative *topoi* first attested in the Demosthenic Assembly speeches, especially those relating to the speaker's *ethos*. They seem to be more than mere survivals of a deliberative tradition. And Demosthenes is not just a distant memory; he seems to be a model consciously imitated (you mentioned a few examples of Demosthenic echoes). He sets the bar for assessing the quality of Dio's deliberative rhetoric. But should one not also consider the question of Dio's audience and their knowledge of the Demosthenic model? Unless those listening to (or reading at a later stage) Dio's speeches were well acquainted with Demosthenic oratory, his efforts to set himself up as a

---

[3] In P. Volpe Cacciatore / F. Ferrari (éd.), *Plutarco e la cultura della sua età* (Naples, 2007), 103-121.

worthy continuator of the great classical oratorical model would not have succeeded.

Immediately after the passage quoted above, p. 266 (*Or.* 31, 161-162 and then 163) Dio seems to compliment the Rhodians on the way that they pay attention to their external appearance and this in turn sets them apart from the rest of the world. Unless this is ironical (and I am not persuaded it is not), it seems to suggest that the speaker now places emphasis on the external appearance of the citizens, and this is a feature that does not appear in classical Attic deliberative oratory.

L. Pernot: La question de l'apparence extérieure s'applique aussi à l'orateur: la façon dont il se présente conditionne son efficacité persuasive. Sur cette question importante, Dion donne des renseignements précis et intéressants le concernant. Il se décrit vêtu d'un méchant manteau, portant la barbe et les cheveux longs, arborant la mise d'un Cynique (32, 22; 34, 2; 47, 25). Même après l'exil, Dion, de ce point de vue, se distinguait des autres orateurs. Son aspect extérieur traduisait visuellement le caractère philosophique de sa rhétorique.

M. Edwards: Is Dio reconstructing history, like Andocides in speech 3? Angelos raises important issues about the employment of history in oratory. But the reconstruction of earlier history goes back to Andocides in his *On the Peace with the Spartans*, where he invents (in our terms) Athenian history of the Pentecontaetia period. And what is more, Aeschines repeats this invention in his *On the False Embassy* speech. This is partly, at least, a matter of constructing the audience, who presumably would not know much better than the orator (or they would presumably have shouted him down)? Dio, of course, talks about the present, whereas for Aristotle deliberative oratory is about the future.

M. Kraus: Die theoretische Zuordnung des deliberativen Genres zur Zeitstufe der Zukunft scheint (über Hermogenes) sogar für Libanios noch gegolten zu haben. In den deliberativen Deklamationen der Rhetorenschule, die in der Regel historische Sujets haben, werden die geschichtlichen Fakten oft grob verzerrt. Sie sind keine historischen Quellen und wollen es nicht sein. Inwieweit das auch auf Dios politische Reden ausstrahlt, ist schwer zu sagen. Vergessen wir nicht, dass Dio auch als Historiker schrieb (*Über die Tugenden Alexanders, Getika*). Ich möchte aber gerne noch eine Frage zu Dio als Philosophen anschliessen: Traditionell wird Dio meist als Kyniker und Stoiker angesehen, aber gerade in den zitierten Reden zeigen sich ausserordentlich viele platonisierende Elemente (so etwa der Gedanke des Philosophenkönigtums). Dio las, wie berichtet wird, Platons *Phaidon* ebenso wie Reden des Demosthenes (Philostr. *VS* 488). Sein Stil hatte dementsprechend platonische ebenso wie demosthenische Anklänge (Philostr. *VS* 487). Andererseits beruft er sich auf den Kyniker Diogenes (*Or.* 4). Welcher philosophischen Richtung kann man ihn also am ehesten zurechnen? Oder muss man ihn einfach als Synkretisten betrachten?

J.-L. Ferrary: En ce qui concerne l'influence du stoïcisme sur Dion de Pruse, il faut, je crois, prendre garde à ne pas tomber dans un cercle vicieux. Hans von Arnim, qui se trouve avoir été successivement l'éditeur et le biographe de Dion (1893 et 1898), puis l'éditeur des *Stoicorum veterum fragmenta* (1903-1905), a, dans cette dernière œuvre, abusivement inclus dans les fragments de Chrysippe de nombreux textes qui lui paraissaient d'inspiration vétéro-stoïcienne, et en particulier des textes de Dion. Un recueil limité aux authentiques fragments de Chrysippe et témoignages sur Chrysippe (selon les principes qu'il a lui-même adoptés pour Zénon et Cléanthe) aurait sans doute permis de fonder sur des bases plus sûres le problème du rapport entre Dion et l'Ancien Stoïcisme, qui mériterait d'être repris.

L. Pernot: La question de l'éclectisme philosophique de Dion de Pruse est une question difficile. Il a certainement évolué au

cours de sa vie et mis davantage l'accent tantôt sur une doctrine, tantôt sur une autre. Par ailleurs, les modèles invoqués
n'étaient pas cantonnés à une seule et unique doctrine; pour les
penseurs grecs de l'époque impériale, les Socrate et les Diogène
étaient devenus une sorte de bien commun et l'on pouvait se
réclamer d'eux de plusieurs points de vue différents.

VIII

MANFRED KRAUS

RHETORIK UND MACHT:
THEORIE UND PRAXIS DER DELIBERATIVEN REDE
IN DER DRITTEN SOPHISTIK

LIBANIOS UND APHTHONIOS

1. Einleitung

Nahezu achthundert Jahre liegen zwischen der Zeit der frühen attischen Redner und der Epoche der antiochenischen Sophisten Libanios und Aphthonios im späten 4. Jahrhundert n. Chr. Vieles hat sich über diesen langen Zeitraum hin verändert, auch und gerade im Bereich der Rhetorik. Zwar existiert die Rhetorik als gesellschaftlich relevante Macht auch zu dieser Zeit weiter, ja sie manifestiert sich in fast noch grösserem Umfang und durchdringt Gesellschaft und Alltagsleben mit eher noch grösserer Intensität und Selbstverständlichkeit als je zuvor. Aber ihr Charakter hat sich im Laufe der Jahrhunderte tiefgreifend verändert. Schon in der Zeit eines Quintilian und Tacitus bemerkte man diesen Wandel. Die Rhetorik hatte ihren Schwerpunkt von Agora und Forum und aus den Gerichtssälen verlagert in das Bildungswesen. Sie war von einem Phänomen des öffentlichen Lebens zunehmend zu einem Schulfach, zu einem formalen Bildungsinhalt geworden, zu einem durchaus zentralen Bildungsinhalt freilich. Den Grund dafür suchte und fand man schon früh im Wandel der politischen Verhältnisse.[1]

---

[1] Vgl. die Erklärungsansätze des Maternus bei TAC. *Dial.* 36-41. Ähnliches vertrat auch Quintilian sowohl in der *Institutio Oratoria* als auch sehr wahrscheinlich

Mit dem Übergang des römischen Reiches von der Republik zu einer autokratischen Staatsform, wie immer man diese auch bezeichnen mochte, war – so glaubten kritische Analytiker zu erkennen – notwendig auch ein Verlust an freier Rede, an παρρησία verbunden, jener παρρησία, die einst konstitutiv für das Aufblühen der Rhetorik in den griechischen Stadtstaaten und namentlich in Athen gewesen war. Betroffen davon mussten von den drei klassischen Redegattungen naturgemäss insbesondere die politische Rede und die Gerichtsrede sein. Wichtige politische Entscheidungen wurden zwar auch in dieser Zeit noch im Senat erörtert, doch getroffen wurden sie faktisch vom Herrscher und seinen engsten Beratern. Auch im Gerichtswesen wurde das freie Spiel der Kräfte des alten römischen Formularprozesses schon im Laufe des 3. Jahrhunderts n. Chr. in Zivil- wie Strafverfahren zunehmend verdrängt vom sogenannten Kognitionsprozess vor beamteten, staatlich bestellten Amtsträgern, der im Jahre 342 n. Chr. dann auch formell den Formularprozess endgültig ablöste.[2]

Man sollte freilich vorsichtig sein, die alte These vom Verfall der Beredsamkeit unkritisch zu wiederholen. Wertungen dieser Art sind aus der Sicht der heutigen Forschung kaum am Platz. Angemessener wäre es, statt dessen von einem Wandel der Redekunst zu sprechen. Denn ein solcher hat in jedem Falle stattgefunden. In Griechenland hatte dieser innere Veränderungsprozess der Beredsamkeit schon früher eingesetzt, im Grunde bereits mit der Eroberung Griechenlands durch die Makedonen und der daraus resultierenden Umwandlung der alten Polislandschaft in monarchische Flächenstaaten, endgültig aber mit der Eingliederung Griechenlands in das Römische Reich, durch die äusserlich zwar eine Befreiung der Griechen vom makedonischen Joch erfolgte, faktisch jedoch der autonomen politischen Beredsamkeit im Rahmen der Polis auf Dauer der Boden entzogen war.

in der verlorenen Schrift *De causis corruptae eloquentiae*. Dazu vgl. z.B. BRINK (1989).
    [2] Vgl. KASER / HACKL ([2]1996) 171; 435-436.

Noch weitaus deutlicher mussten diese Veränderungen aber im 4. Jahrhundert n. Chr. fühlbar werden, in dem die griechisch-römische Ökumene sich erneut tiefgreifenden politischen und gesellschaftlichen Veränderungen ausgesetzt sah. Es ist daher mit Recht zu fragen, welche Rolle deliberative Rhetorik und insbesondere griechische deliberative Rhetorik unter den durchaus veränderten Bedingungen des 4. Jahrhunderts überhaupt noch spielen konnte, bzw. in welcher Fom sie in dieser Zeit noch in Erscheinung trat.

Um diese Veränderungen aufzuzeigen, eignet sich schon allein aufgrund der Quellenlage kaum ein Œuvre besser als dasjenige des Libanios, in dem sich die Situation der griechischen Rhetorik in der Spätantike wie in einem Brennspiegel gebündelt darstellt. Es soll daher im Folgenden der Versuch unternommen werden, die Situation der spätantiken griechischen deliberativen Rhetorik am Beispiel der Werke des Libanios und seines Schülers Aphthonios zu skizzieren.

2. ‚Dritte Sophistik'?

Im Titel dieses Beitrags wird für die hier zur Debatte stehende Epoche der in jüngerer Zeit populär gewordene Begriff der ‚Dritten Sophistik' verwendet. Da diese Bezeichnung jedoch nicht unumstritten ist, bedarf es vorab einiger Klärungen. Selbstverständlich entbehrt der Begriff einer Dritten Sophistik, anders als der von Philostrat geprägte der Zweiten Sophistik,[3] der antiken Grundlage. Er ist letztlich eine reine moderne Analogiebildung. Dennoch gibt es gute Gründe, die Epoche des späten 4. Jahrhunderts von der Zweiten Sophistik des 1. bis 3. Jahrhunderts als eigenständige Epoche zu scheiden. Erlebte doch das 4. Jahrhundert mindestens drei grundlegende politisch-soziale Veränderungen, die ihren Einfluss auf die Entwicklung von Bildung und Rhetorik nicht verfehlen

---

[3] PHILOSTR. *VS* 481, 507.

konnten: Erstens die endgültige Entwicklung des Römischen Reiches hin zu einer zentralistischen und hierarchisch strukturierten absoluten Monarchie; zweitens die allmähliche Dissoziation der beiden Reichshälften, der westlich-lateinischen und der östlich-griechischen, die mit den Reformen Diokletians im Jahre 293 einsetzte und mit der definitiven und offiziellen Separation nach dem Tode des Theodosius im Jahre 395 (mithin etwa zur Zeit des Lebensendes des Libanios) ihren Abschluss fand; und schliesslich den Aufstieg des Christentums von einer subversiven, marginalen und verfolgten Sekte zum entscheidenden Machtfaktor, beginnend mit dem Toleranzedikt Konstantins im Jahre 313 und vollendet mit der Erhebung des Christentums zur offiziellen Reichsreligion wiederum durch Theodosius im Jahre 391. Die äusseren Bedingungen sind also für einen Sophisten wie Libanios im 4. Jahrhundert in der Tat durchaus andere als sie es noch im 2. oder 3. Jahrhundert waren.

Angesichts dieser markanten Unterschiede hat als erster Laurent Pernot für diese Epoche zunächst die Bezeichnung ‚Seconde Sophistique bis'[4] und später dann ‚Troisième Sophistique' vorgeschlagen.[5] Darin sind ihm unter anderem Jacques Schamp, Alberto Quiroga Puertas sowie Bernard Schouler und Pierre-Louis Malosse gefolgt[6]. Der Terminus wurde aber auch aufgegriffen z.B. von Bernadette Puech in ihrem bedeutenden Buch über Redner und Sophisten in kaiserzeitlichen Inschriften.[7] Auch der Verfasser selbst hat ihn bereits in früheren Publikationen verwendet.[8]

Andererseits sind gegen die Tauglichkeit des Begriffs gravierende Einwände erhoben worden, so zuletzt insbesondere von Lieve Van Hoof. In einem Aufsatz von 2010 hat diese in

---

[4] PERNOT (1993) vol. I, 14 n. 9.
[5] PERNOT (2000) 271-272; (2006-2007).
[6] SCHAMP (2006); QUIROGA PUERTAS (2007) bes. 41; MALOSSE / SCHOULER (2009); FOWLER / QUIROGA PUERTAS (2014).
[7] PUECH (2002) 7.
[8] Z.B. KRAUS (2011a) 145.

Anlehnung an eine auf die Zweite Sophistik gemünzte Formulierung von P.A. Brunt[9] geradezu von einem „'Bubble' of the 'Third Sophistic'" gesprochen.[10] Van Hoof kritisiert zunächst eine definitorische Unschärfe des Begriffs; er werde von seinen verschiedenen Vertretern in jeweils durchaus unterschiedlicher Weise verwendet; so sei z.b. seine chronologische Eingrenzung keineswegs eindeutig, ebensowenig, ob nur pagane Autoren davon erfasst sein sollen oder auch christliche. In der Tat ist einzuräumen, dass der Ausdruck einer hinreichenden terminologischen Präzision bislang entbehrt und z.b. nicht nur auf die Spätantike, sondern bisweilen auch auf ganz andere Epochen angewendet worden ist, so etwa von Antonis Kaldellis auf die klassizistisch ausgerichtete Epoche der mittelbyzantinischen Komnenenzeit.[11] Schwerer noch wiegt, dass der Terminus einer Dritten Sophistik sogar zuallererst in einem gänzlich anderen Zusammenhang geprägt wurde, nämlich von dem amerikanischen Philosophen Victor J. Vitanza im Sinne einer propagierten postmodernen Wiederbelebung des epistemologischen Relativismus und der korrespondierenden Argumentationsformen gerade der Ersten Sophistik.[12] Ich plädiere daher aus den obengenannten Gründen dafür, eine Dritte Sophistik in bezug auf die Spätantike etwa mit der Epoche Diokletians beginnen zu lassen, die auch sonst in der antiken Literatur eine fühlbare Zäsur darstellt, und die geistige Auseinandersetzung zwischen Christentum und paganer Religion ebenso wie diejenige zwischen griechischer und lateinischer Sprache und Kultur, die beide so in der Zweiten Sophistik (noch) nicht stattfinden, zu definitorischen Kernpunkten des Epochenbegriffs zu machen.[13]

Van Hoof glaubt ausserdem im Begriff einer Dritten Sophistik eine Abwertung der klassizistischen spätantiken Rhetorik als „static, moribund, and no longer engaged or influential in society"

[9] BRUNT (1994).
[10] VAN HOOF (2010); vgl. auch WESTBERG (2010) 18-20.
[11] KALDELLIS (2007) 225-316.
[12] VITANZA (1991).
[13] Ähnlich AMATO (2006) V und PENELLA (2013) 3.

sowie eine übermässige Betonung einer Diskontinuität zur vor-
ausgehenden Epoche zu erkennen, welche die ihrer Meinung
nach gebotene Ausdehnung der erfolgversprechenden Forschungs-
ansätze zur Zweiten Sophistik auf die spätantike Rhetorik
behindere.[14] Demgegenüber seien vielmehr die gesellschaftlich-
politische Funktion der Rhetorik in dieser Zeit und ihre Kontinuität zur Zweiten Sophistik hervorzuheben.

Eine solche Abwertung und ein solches Dekadenzmodell
sind dem Begriff jedoch keineswegs inhärent. Im Gegenteil:
Gerade die kontrastierende Gegenüberstellung mit der Situation
der Zweiten Sophistik schärft den Blick für die Neuentwicklun-
gen und das Andersartige auch der späteren Epoche und erlaubt
so eine angemessenere Betrachtung der spezifischen Eigenheiten
spätantiker Rhetorik. Eher würde womöglich sogar ein übertrie-
bener Kontinuitätsgedanke auf ein Dekadenzmodell führen.
Zudem betont der Begriff in seiner deutlichen Bezugnahme auf
die Zweite Sophistik Kontinuität ja mindestens ebensosehr wie
Diskontinuität. Er behindert folglich auch in keiner Weise die
von Van Hoof geforderte Anwendung des in der Forschung zur
Zweiten Sophistik erarbeiteten methodologischen Instrumenta-
riums auf die Spätantike.

Wenngleich Van Hoof darin durchaus zuzustimmen ist, dass
von einem gesellschaftlichen Bedeutungsverlust der Rhetoren,
wie er bei manchen Autoren wie etwa Simon Swain konstatiert
worden sein mag,[15] gerade in der Spätantike nicht die Rede sein
kann, so verdient dennoch hervorgehoben zu werden, dass die
Rhetorik dieser Epoche sich auch in ihrer klassizistischen Aus-
richtung beileibe nicht als „refuge against contemporary religious,
political, and socio-cultural evolutions",[16] sondern vielmehr, wie
noch zu zeigen sein wird, als hörbare Stimme einer offensiven
politischen Zeitkritik versteht, was man aber erst erkennt, wenn
man den Blick auf die spezifischen Besonderheiten der Epoche

[14] Van Hoof (2010) 212; cf. 224.
[15] Swain (1996) 3-6.
[16] Van Hoof (2010) 212.

richtet. Nicht eskapistische Flucht in die Vergangenheit, sondern Vergewisserung und Behauptung der eigenen griechischen
kulturellen Wurzeln im Angesicht römischer politischer Macht
ist die Intention der Sophisten. Van Hoofs Einschätzung, dass
„studies thus far have suggested that the Second Sophistic saw
the last great flourishing of classical Greek rhetoric with the
'Third Sophistic' representing its death struggle"[17] ist somit
deutlich übertrieben. Versucht doch gerade Pernots Ansatz, tra-
ditionelle Denkmuster von Aufstieg, Blüte und Verfall durch
den Blick auf die positiven Entwicklungen spätantiker Rhetorik
zu überwinden.[18] Ich sehe daher im Begriff einer Dritten Sophistik auch nicht wie Van Hoof eine die Betrachtung verzerrende
Linse,[19] sondern im Gegenteil eine hermeneutische Anregung,
die nutzbar zu machen wäre. – Doch wenden wir uns nun
Libanios selbst zu!

3. Libanios und das *genus deliberatiuum* in der Dritten Sophistik

In der späten 35. Rede (zu datieren nach 388), in der er sich
mahnend an diejenigen unter seinen Schülern wendet, die es
ängstlich vermeiden, in politischen Angelegenheiten das Wort
zu ergreifen, bestimmt Libanios die Aufgabe der politischen Rede
folgendermassen:

> „Mit Rat zu dienen und in Reden das Notwendige vorzu-
> bringen, Schaden abzuwenden, den einen beizupflichten, den
> anderen aber entgegenzutreten, vernünftigen Amtsträgern
> (ἄρχουσι) zu folgen, aber sich mit denen zu streiten, die das

---

[17] VAN HOOF (2010) 224.
[18] Vgl. dazu auch STENGER (2009) 16 mit Anm. 69. In der Etablierung des
Terminus einer ‚Dritten Sophistik' zeige sich nach Stenger gerade „das allmählich
vorhandene Bewußtsein, daß die gegenüber der Kaiserzeit veränderten politischen,
gesellschaftlichen und religiösen Rahmenbedingungen sich auf die Produktion
von Literatur niedergeschlagen haben müssen" (16). Vgl. auch die Einschätzungen
von PENELLA (2013) 2-5 und CRIBIORE (2013) 36-37.
[19] VAN HOOF (2010) 224.

Nützliche nicht sehen, der Stimme der Macht (ταῖς ἀπὸ τοῦ θρόνου φωναῖς) die Stimme der Vernunft (τοῦ βουλεύειν) entgegenzusetzen, in der Rede mehr Furcht zu erregen als selbst zu fürchten".[20]

Libanios ist sich also der hergebrachten Aufgaben deliberativer Rede sehr genau bewusst und wiederholt ihre klassischen Beschreibungen bis in die Terminologie hinein. Doch bricht seine Beschreibung in der zweiten Hälfte in markanter Weise um, und ein bemerkenswerter Unterschied zur Situation des Redners in der alten Polis tut sich auf: Sind die „Amtsträger" (ἄρχοντες) zunächst noch ganz neutral bezeichnet, so geht es jedoch nunmehr darum, ob man ihnen „folgen" (ἀκολουθῆσαι) solle oder nicht, worin bereits ein hierarchisches Element angedeutet ist, ehe schliesslich ganz offen von der Stimme der Macht (wörtlich: des ‚Thrones', sprich Amtssitzes) die Rede ist, der der Redner nur die Stimme des vernünftigen Rates entgegenzusetzen hat.

Das hier angesprochene Machtgefälle ist evident. Hier reden nicht mehr Gleiche mit Gleichen, sondern (zumindest äusserlich) Machtlose zu Mächtigen. Rhetorik wird in einem solchen Umfeld zur stärksten, wenn nicht einzigen Waffe der Machtlosen. Wer nicht selbst die Macht hat, Dinge zu entscheiden oder zu bestimmen, kann nur hoffen, mit den Mitteln der Persuasion auf die Mächtigen einzuwirken, um deren Entscheidungen zu beeinflussen. „Ich habe keine Macht", schreibt Libanios schon im Jahre 361 an den *comes Orientis* Modestos, „aber ich schäme mich dessen keineswegs; mir genügt der Gesang, wie der Nachtigall".[21] Der deliberativen Rede fällt somit eine durchaus veränderte Aufgabe zu; sie wird im vollen

---

[20] LIB. *Or.* 35, 3: γνώμῃ λειτουργῆσαι καὶ λόγοις εἰσηγήσασθαι τὸ δέον, κωλῦσαι τὰ βλαβερά, τοῖς μὲν συνειπεῖν, τοῖς δὲ ἀπαντῆσαι, ἀκολουθῆσαι μὲν εὖ φρονοῦσιν ἄρχουσι, μαχέσασθαι δὲ τὸ λυσιτελοῦν οὐχ ὁρῶσιν, ἀντιστῆσαι ταῖς ἀπὸ τοῦ θρόνου φωναῖς τὰς ἀπὸ τοῦ βουλεύειν, τὸ φοβεῖν μᾶλλον ἢ δεδιέναι ἐκ ῥητορείας ἔχειν.
[21] LIB. *Ep.* 617: νῦν δέ εἰμι ἀσθενής, αἰσχύνομαι δὲ οὐδαμῶς, ἀλλ' ἀρκεῖ μοι τὸ ᾄδειν, ὥσπερ τῇ ἀηδόνι. Vgl. CRIBIORE (2007) 18.

Sinne des Wortes zur Beratungsrede, wie es schon der lateinische Terminus der *suasoria* andeutet. Das Verhältnis des Redners zur Macht definiert sich neu. Mag es in den Stadtsenaten (Kurien) der Poleis des griechischen Ostens durchaus noch Gelegenheit zu offener Beratung und Debatte quasi auf horizontaler Ebene gegeben haben, wie Libanios sie am Anfang der Passage anzudeuten scheint (obwohl auch diese Gremien sich im 4. Jahrhundert immer mehr zu reinen Kasten von Leiturgiepflichtigen entwickelten, denen man sich tunlichst zu entziehen suchte[22]), so wird daneben die sozusagen vertikale Funktion der politischen Rede in der Auseinandersetzung mit den mächtigen Amtsträgern des Reiches immer wichtiger. Es geht nicht mehr so sehr um die Erringung oder Sicherung eigener Macht, sondern um die Eindämmung und Kontrolle, gegebenenfalls auch um die Lenkung oder Nutzung der Macht anderer. Im selben Sinne hat sich auch Pierre-Louis Malosse in seinem letzten, postum erschienenen Beitrag zu Libanios geäussert: „Libanius sees it as the orator's duty to speak up to those in power".[23]

Dazu bedarf der Redner freilich zuvörderst einer gesicherten eigenen Position. Besass Libanios politische Macht? In einem vordergründigen Sinne zunächst durchaus. Stammte er doch sowohl väterlicher- wie mütterlicherseits aus Kurialenfamilien, die die Geschicke seiner Vaterstadt seit mehreren Generationen mitbestimmt hatten.[24] Doch war, wie bereits angedeutet, einerseits der Kurialenstand zu seiner Zeit bereits zu einer reinen finanziellen Bürde herabgesunken, und zum anderen hätte er ihm in der ‚vertikalen' Auseinandersetzung mit Amtsträgern der Zentralgewalt kaum eine ausreichende Machtgrundlage geboten. Dennoch hätte Libanios nach dem Wunsch seines

---

[22] Vgl. LIB. *Or.* 35, 6 ff.; vgl. LIEBESCHUETZ (1972) 103: "The councillors spend money and give advice, but there is no pretext that they govern the city. They advise the governors, but the governors make the decisions"; PACK (1951) 176: "*honores* […] transformed into *munera*".

[23] MALOSSE (2014) 88.

[24] Vgl. PACK (1951) 178-182; WINTJES (2005) 43-62.

freilich früh verstorbenen Vaters und seiner nächsten Verwandten wohl diesen Weg gehen sollen.[25] Er selbst wollte es anders. Um den lästigen Pflichten eines Kurialen zu entgehen, öffentliche Bauprojekte, Tempel, Götterfeste, Spiele oder Wohlfahrtseinrichtungen finanzieren oder Steuern einheben zu müssen, gab es mehrere Möglichkeiten: sich freizukaufen, eine höherrangige Position in der Hauptstadt zu erlangen, in das Heer einzutreten, oder Immunität zu erreichen durch Erringung einer sozial angesehenen beruflichen Position wie Arzt, Grammatiker oder Rhetor.[26] Libanios ging den letzteren Weg und begab sich nach einer Grundausbildung in der Heimatstadt zum weiteren Rhetorikstudium nach Athen.[27]

Weitere Stationen führten ihn als Rhetoriklehrer in die Hauptstadt Konstantinopel, dann nach Nikaia, Nikomedia und wieder zurück nach Konstantinopel,[28] ehe er endlich auf einigen Umwegen im Jahre 354 nach Antiochia zurückkehren durfte, um dort als Nachfolger des Zenobios die offizielle Rhetorenstelle der Stadt zu bekleiden.[29]

Als weit wichtiger als diese durchaus prestigeträchtige Stelle erwies sich jedoch für ihn, dass er während der Aufenthalte in der Hauptstadt und in der Nähe des Kaiserhofes wichtige persönliche Beziehungen hatte knüpfen können. So hatte er unter anderem in Konstantinopel und Nikomedia die ihm später höchst nützliche Bekanntschaft des jungen Rhetorikschülers und nachmaligen Kaisers Julian machen können. Als offizieller Rhetoriklehrer und Sophist Antiochias konnte er später dieses Netzwerk an Beziehungen durch die grosse Zahl seiner Schüler, von denen es einige zu sehr einflussreichen Positionen in Regierung und Verwaltung brachten, noch wesentlich erweitern und verdichten. Hinzu kam der Rückhalt durch weitreichende familiäre Verflechtungen mit den höheren Schichten

---

[25] LIB. *Or.* 1, 6 und 13; vgl. PACK (1951) 178-179.
[26] Vgl. LIB. *Or.* 48, 7; vgl. DRECOLL (1997) 43-77, bes. 74-77.
[27] WINTJES (2005) 66-76.
[28] WINTJES (2005) 77-97.
[29] WINTJES (2005) 99-117.

Antiochias. Allein dieses immense Netzwerk an persönlichen Beziehungen und seine stupende rhetorische Fähigkeit, auf dieser Klaviatur virtuos zu spielen, erlaubte es ihm, weit mehr als seine äussere Position als Sophist, ohne Angst um Gut, Leib und Leben haben zu müssen, selbstbewusst gegenüber mächtigen Amtsträgern des Reiches im Sinne des oben genannten „speaking up to those in power" auftreten zu können. Man hat ihn deshalb auch einen ‚Überlebenskünstler' genannt.[30] Dieser ganz besonderen Position ist es wohl zu verdanken, dass Libanios immer wieder auch und gerade in Krisensituationen als Fürsprecher seiner Heimatstadt oder einzelner Personen öffentlich das Wort ergreifen konnte.

Neben dieser Rückversicherung durch persönliche Beziehungen und Freundschaften war es für eine öffentliche Persönlichkeit wie Libanios aber nicht minder wichtig, in der Formulierung seiner politisch relevanten Reden entsprechendes taktisches Geschick zu beweisen. Es musste wohl abgewogen sein, wann eine freie Sprache geführt werden konnte und wann man sich vorsichtig ausdrücken musste. Offene Kritik an Amtsträgern war oft erst nach deren Tod oder mindestens Absetzung vorstellbar. In einzelnen Fällen mögen Reden des Libanios mit besonders drastisch ausfallenden Passagen auch nicht für den öffentlichen Vortrag, sondern für die Lektüre innerhalb ausgewählter Kreise bestimmt gewesen sein.[31]

Raffaella Cribiore stellt immerhin fest, sämtliche erhaltenen Reden des Libanios gehörten gattungsmässig „in the deliberative or epideictic categories", und verzeichnet einen erheblichen Teil seiner Reden als „political orations" bzw. „speeches on public issues".[32] Das Beispiel des Libanios zeigt also, dass deliberative Rede auch unter den veränderten Bedingungen des 4. Jahrhunderts noch möglich sein konnte, dass sie jedoch weniger im horizontalen Meinungsaustausch zwischen gleichberechtigten

[30] WINTJES (2005) 218.
[31] Vgl. z.B. LIB. *Or.* 42. PETIT (1956) 488-489.
[32] CRIBIORE (2013) 35; 18-19; ebenso MALOSSE (2014) 83-92.

Mitgliedern eines politischen Gremiums stattfand, sondern häufiger im ‚vertikalen' Versuch der Einflussnahme auf Entscheidungen von Amtsträgern, ferner dass diese Möglichkeit nicht mehr unbedingt einem jeden offenstand, sondern allenfalls demjenigen, der durch persönliche Absicherungen und rhetorisches Geschick die oft drastischen drohenden Folgen eines politischen Fehltrittes zu umgehen verstand. Die Dunkelziffer an Akteuren, die weniger Überlebensgeschick bewiesen als Libanios, dürfte hoch sein.

4. Theorie und pädagogische Praxis der deliberativen Rede in der Spätantike

Im Vergleich zu den solcherart veränderten äusseren Bedingungen für deliberative Rede blieben deren theoretische Grundlagen hingegen erstaunlich konstant. Libanios selbst hat keine theoretische Schrift zur Rhetorik hinterlassen. Wir müssen daher davon ausgehen, dass die kanonischen Schriften der Epoche der Zweiten Sophistik weiterhin ihre Gültigkeit hatten.[33] Es ist hinlänglich oft betont worden, dass in der Praxis der Spätantike das epideiktische *genus* zunehmendes Gewicht gewann, und was dazu zu sagen war, ist von Laurent Pernot längst gesagt.[34] Bemerkenswerterweise aber haben gerade in den Schriften des *Corpus Hermogenianum*, die wir auch für die Spätantike wohl heranziehen dürfen, das judiziale und das deliberative *genus* ihren Platz mehr als behauptet. So bietet die spätestens aus dem 3. Jahrhundert stammende pseudohermogenianische Schrift *De inuentione* (Περὶ εὑρέσεως) Anweisungen zur *inuentio* für die ersten drei Bauelemente (*prooemium, narratio, argumentatio*) sowohl von Gerichtsreden als auch von politischen Reden. Ja sogar die genuine Hermogenische Schrift zur Statuslehre (Περὶ στάσεων) kennt unter den verschiedenen

---

[33] Cf. CRIBIORE (2014) 75.
[34] PERNOT (1993); (2000); (2015).

status als Unterart des *status qualitatis* (ποιότης) zumindest auch die στάσις πραγματική, die sich auf die Zeitstufe der Zukunft beziehe,[35] was sie nach der bekannten Einteilung des Aristoteles[36] ebenso als dem deliberativen *genus* zugeordnet erweist wie die ihr zugewiesenen *capita finalia* des Gesetzmässigen, Gerechten, Nützlichen, Möglichen und Glaubhaften.[37] Diese Persistenz des deliberativen und judizialen *genus* erklärt sich daraus, dass diese Lehrwerke, wie auch aus der Wahl ihrer Beispiele klar ersichtlich, in erster Linie als Anweisungen für die Abfassung von Deklamationen gedacht waren, und Deklamationen gab es ausschliesslich in diesen beiden *genera* (als Controversien und Suasorien), nicht jedoch im *genus demonstratiuum*. Im Übungsprogramm der Schule des Libanios wurden also deliberative und judiziale Reden ganz selbstverständlich geübt. Die von ihm erhaltenen Deklamationen belegen dies (s.u. Abschnitt 6). Man darf daraus schliessen, dass auch die theoretischen Grundlagen des judizialen und deliberativen Redegenus in den Schulen der Spätantike in jedem Fall bekannt waren und vermittelt wurden.

Dieser Befund bestätigt sich auch für den Bereich der auf die Deklamation hinführenden vorbereitenden Übungen, der Progymnasmata. Noch im 5. Jahrhundert weist der Rhetor Nikolaos von Myra in seinem Progymnasmata-Handbuch die einzelnen Übungen auch den drei Redegenera zu. Dabei gehören seiner Ansicht nach eindeutig zum deliberativen *genus* die Übungen Fabel, Chrie, Gnome und Thesis.[38] Lob und Tadel seien zwar primär dem panegyrischen *genus* zugeordnet, seien

---

[35] HERMOG. *Stat.* 38, 3-8 RABE: πραγματικὴ γάρ ἐστιν ἀμφισβήτησις περὶ πράγματος μέλλοντος, εἰ δεῖ γενέσθαι τόδε τι ἢ μὴ γενέσθαι, δοῦναι ἢ μὴ δοῦναι, οἷον βουλεύονται Ἀθηναῖοι, εἰ χρὴ θάπτειν τοὺς ἐν Μαραθῶνι πεσόντας τῶν βαρβάρων („der pragmatische Status ist eine Meinungsverschiedenheit bezüglich einer zukünftigen Handlung, ob sie ausgeführt werden soll oder nicht, ob etwas gewährt werden soll oder nicht, wie z.B. wenn die Athener darüber beraten, ob man die bei Marathon gefallenen Barbaren bestatten solle“).
[36] ARIST. *Rhet.* 1, 3, 1358b2-8.
[37] HERMOG. *Stat.* 76, 3-79, 16 RABE; vgl. SCHOULER (1984) 181.
[38] NICOL. *Prog.* 8, 14-15; 23, 11-12; 28, 13-14; 76, 6-7 FELTEN.

aber ebenso wie der Vergleich auch als Bestandteile deliberativer Reden einsetzbar.[39] Erzählung, Ethopoiie und Ekphrasis
bereiteten gar gleichermassen auf alle drei *genera* vor,[40] und
selbst die primär zur Gerichtsrede gehörende Gesetzesbeurteilung zeige in der Form des Gesetzesantrags deutliche Beziehungen zur deliberativen Rede.[41]

Weder Theorie noch Übungsformen der deliberativen Rede
sind also der spätantiken Rhetorenschule fremd. Das bestätigen
auch die vor allem von Raffaella Cribiore untersuchten Papyrus-
funde mit Schülerübungen.[42] Cribiore hat auch das Lehrcurri-
culum der Schule des Libanios in seinen Grundzügen rekon-
struiert.[43] Das Programm bestand zunächst weitgehend in der
Lektüre eines Kanons beispielhafter Texte (am Anfang vor allem
Homer, Platon und Demosthenes) und in der Abfassung und
Korrektur schriftlicher Stilübungen. Die eintönige Repetitivität
des Programms gab dabei offenbar häufiger Anlass zu Unmut.[44]
Auch Reden bedeutender Redner der jüngeren Zeit wie etwa
Aelius Aristides wurden als Vorbilder laut vorgelesen. Daneben
konnten die Schüler aber auch gelegentlich Zeugen von öffentlich vorgetragenen Prunkdeklamationen ihres Lehrers werden,
die zumindest teilweise ebenfalls dem deliberativen *genus* ent-
stammten (s.u. Abschnitt 6).

Das Bewusstsein davon, dass die im Übungsprogramm ein-
studierten Regeln prinzipiell auch in der Praxis anwendbar
waren, zeigt eine Passage in einem Brief des Libanios an Kaiser
Julian:

> „Wenn wir denn in unseren Scheingefechten in den Dekla-
> mationswettbewerben genau wissen, wie man zu Perikles,
> Kimon und Miltiades zu sprechen hätte, dann wäre es doch

---

[39] NICOL. *Prog.* 48, 5-10; 62, 8-15 FELTEN.
[40] NICOL. *Prog.* 15, 12-15; 66, 16-67, 2; 70, 7-15 FELTEN.
[41] NICOL. *Prog.* 79, 1-5 FELTEN.
[42] CRIBIORE (1996), mit Tafeln; (2001).
[43] CRIBIORE (2007); (2014).
[44] Cf. LIB. *Or.* 34, 15; *Or.* 35, 16 und 21.

ungeheuerlich, wenn wir diese Vorschriften im wahren Leben ausser acht liessen."[45]

Auffällig ist aber immerhin, dass Libanios dem Kaiser gegenüber hier nicht davon spricht, dass man *wie* Perikles, Kimon oder Miltiades, sondern wie man *zu* diesen athenischen Machthabern zu sprechen habe. In diesem Detail deutet sich die gewandelte Auffassung von deliberativer Rede denn doch an. Denn die Stelle steht in dem Zusammenhang, dass Libanios nun, nach der Ernennung Julians zum Caesar, es nicht mehr wage, die alte παρρησία der Jugendfreundschaft weiter walten zu lassen.

5. Die Progymnasmata des Libanios und Aphthonios als politisch-kulturelles Bekenntnis

Das rhetorische Trainingsprogramm in der Schule des Libanios begann, wie erwähnt, mit den Anfängerübungen der Progymnasmata. Diese dienten zwar primär der Einübung rhetorisch-kompositioneller Grundtechniken. Doch konnten diese Techniken nicht inhaltsleer unterrichtet werden, sondern mussten stets jeweils an konkreten Beispielen eingeübt werden. Diese Beispiele aber hatten selbst bei noch so fiktiven oder entlegenen Sujets wegen ihres mit der Materie der Rhetorik gegebenen Bezugs zum menschlichen Handeln unweigerlich ethische oder politische Relevanz. Gerade diese moralisch erzieherische Komponente der antiken Progymnasmata ist jüngst von Craig Gibson in aller Deutlichkeit unterstrichen worden.[46]

Man hat beobachtet, dass die Sujets solcher Übungen sich bisweilen in einer deutlichen Distanz zur realen Welt befanden: „L'enseignement rhétorique a choisi de rester à l'écart de

---

[45] Lib. *Ep.* 369, 4: δεινὸν γάρ, εἰ σκιαμαχοῦντες μὲν ἐν ταῖς τῶν ἀγώνων μελέταις εἰσόμεθα, πῶς Περικλεῖ καὶ Κίμωνι καὶ Μιλτιάδῃ διαλεκτέον, ἐπὶ δὲ τῆς ἀληθείας παροψόμεθα τὸν νόμον.

[46] GIBSON (2014); vgl. dazu schon KRAUS (2011a); (2011b).

la réalité contemporaine, pour se contenter de maintenir l'héritage culturel des siècles précédents", schreibt Laurent Pernot.[47] Schon den Griechen der Zweiten Sophistik hatte die affirmative Hinwendung zu einer rhetorisch konstruierten kulturellen Konzeption von klassischem Griechentum als Vergewisserung und Behauptung ihrer Existenz als kultureller Nation angesichts der politischen Übermacht Roms gedient.[48] Die Diskrepanz dieses Idealbilds gegenüber der zeitgenössischen Lebenswelt hatte sich zum 4. Jahrhundert hin aber noch weiter vergrössert. Das lag freilich weniger an einer Verschiebung dieses Idealbilds, das über mehrere Jahrhunderte hin praktisch konstant blieb, sondern an den schon beschriebenen Veränderungen in der realen Welt. Zentralisierung und Hierarchisierung der politischen Macht, Dissoziation und Entfremdung von griechischer und römischer Oikumene und zunehmende Christianisierung sind die entscheidenden Stichworte. Demgegenüber waren die Themen der Rhetorenschule geprägt von einem bewussten Bekenntnis zu Partikularismus und Demokratie, zu griechischer Kultur und Bildung (παιδεία) und zu paganer Religiosität.

Sind viele Stücke der unter dem Namen des Libanios überlieferten Progymnasmata-Sammlung, wie Bernard Schouler gezeigt hat, durchgängig geprägt von paganer Mythologie und von einer geradezu delphischen Moralität des Masses und der Besonnenheit,[49] so wird der Kontrast zur Lebenswelt im politischen Bereich vollends deutlich.

Ein bestimmtes politisches Element in den Progymnasmata des Libanios und seines Schülers Aphthonios ist dabei besonders augenfällig, nämlich die strikte Opposition gegen jede Form der Tyrannei.[50] Bei Libanios richtet sich das vierte Musterbeispiel für einen Gemeinplatz gegen einen Tyrannen.[51] Bei

[47] PERNOT (2000) 139.
[48] Cf. BOWIE (1970); SWAIN (1996) 87-89; GOLDHILL (2001).
[49] SCHOULER (1984) 71-75.
[50] Vgl. KRAUS (2013) 124-127.
[51] LIB. *Loc.* 4; GIBSON (2008) 178-187.

Aphthonios ist dies gar das einzige Beispiel.[52] Dabei gibt es zwischen beiden Versionen so viele Übereinstimmungen, dass die Version des Aphthonios gar als eine verkürzte Version derjenigen des Libanios erscheinen könnte. Hierbei ist in beiden Versionen die Herrschaft des Tyrannen in beständigem Kontrast zu einem am Athen der klassischen Periode orientierten demokratischen System beschrieben. Freiheit (ἐλευθερία), Demokratie (δημοκρατία), Verfassung (πολιτεία) und Gesetz (νόμος) sind die Leitworte dieses Gegenmodells. Was den Tyrannen dabei im Besonderen kennzeichnet, ist seine grundsätzliche Verachtung der Gesetze.[53] Besonders signifikant ist aber, dass sich bei Libanios daneben auch das Pendant eines *locus communis* zum Lobe eines Tyrannenmörders findet, während andere Autoren wie Aphthonios oder Nikolaos die Möglichkeit eines positiven *locus communis* sogar ausdrücklich ablehnen.[54] Gerade das Beispiel des Tyrannenmörders, der Freiheit und Demokratie verteidigt und das Gesetz wiederherstellt, unterstreicht nachdrücklich die Bedeutung des Tyrannenthemas bei Libanios, das auch in seinen Deklamationen häufig wiederkehrt.[55] Da weder bei Libanios noch bei Aphthonios dem Tyrannen die Figur eines vernünftigen und weisen Monarchen gegenübergestellt wird, kann man diese scharfe Verurteilung der Tyrannis durchaus auch als Kritik an der Monarchie als solcher lesen, insbesondere weil sich bei beiden Autoren auch jeweils eine Individualisierung dieses allgemeinen *locus communis* in Form einer Invektive gegen König Philipp von Makedonien findet,[56] dem namentlich Libanios freilich den Titel eines βασιλεύς prinzipiell verweigert und ihm statt dessen nur den Namen eines τύραννος zubilligt.

---

[52] APHTH. *Prog.* 7, 3-11; PATILLON (2008) 127-131.
[53] Cf. LIB. *Loc.* 4, 4 und 10; GIBSON (2008) 178-179; 182-183; APHTH. *Prog.* 7, 3 und 6; PATILLON (2008) 127, 129.
[54] APHTH. *Prog.* 7, 1; PATILLON (2008) 126; NICOL. *Prog.* 37-38 FELTEN.
[55] Vgl. PENELLA (2014) 126.
[56] LIB. *Vit.* 5; GIBSON (2008) 292-289; APHTH. *Prog.* 9, 4-9; PATILLON (2008) 138-140.

Im selben Sinne unterstreichen bei Libanios ein Lob des
Demosthenes und eine Invektive gegen Aischines und eine
Synkrisis beider Redner indirekt den Preis der athenischen
Demokratie gegenüber der tyrannischen makedonischen Monarchie ebenso wie den der Unabhängigkeit der Polis gegenüber
dem Zentralismus der Monarchie.[57]
In all diesen Stücken ist es stets die Oberhoheit des Gesetzes
und des Rechtsstaates, die als politisches Ideal aufscheint. Dieses
Ideal wird auch besonders deutlich in dem Beispiel des Aphthonios für einen Gesetzesantrag.[58] Dort bezieht der Redner unmiss-
verständlich Stellung gegen ein Gesetz, das die Tötung eines auf
frischer Tat ertappten Ehebrechers durch den betrogenen Ehe-
mann im Sinne der Selbstjustiz erlauben würde. Wiederholt
unterstreicht der Sprecher demgegenüber, dass es ausschliesslich
dem Gesetz und den Richtern zukomme, Gerechtigkeit zu üben.
Wer waren denn nun die Tyrannen, gegen die Libanios und
Aphthonios so klar Stellung bezogen? Man muss dabei nicht
unbedingt sofort an die römischen Kaiser selbst denken,
obwohl Libanios mit manchen davon durchaus seine Schwie-
rigkeiten hatte. Doch gab es auch die kleineren Tyrannen der
Reichsverwaltung. Es lag nämlich die besondere Situation vor,
dass in Antiochia als einer der vier bedeutendsten Städte des
Reiches gleich zwei Reichsbeamte verschiedener hierarchischer
Ebenen ihren Amtssitz hatten: zum einen der höherrangige,
für die gesamte östliche Reichsdiözese verantwortliche *comes
Orientis*, zum Anderen der niederrangigere, für die Provinz
Syrien zuständige *consularis Syriae*.[59] In beiden Amtspositionen
gab es häufige Wechsel,[60] und mit den Inhabern beider Ämter
hatte Libanios oft genug Kämpfe auszufechten. Für Libanios

---

[57] LIB. *Enc.* 5; *Vit.* 4; *Comp.* 3; GIBSON (2008) 236-245; 288-295; 334-343.
[58] APHTH. *Prog.* 14, 3-15; PATILLON (2008) 158-162.
[59] Vgl. LIEBESCHUETZ (1972) 110-114; CABOURET (2002); (2004); BRAD-
BURY (2004) 16-18; MALOSSE (2014) 88. MALOSSE (2014) 88, Anm. 22 verweist
darauf, dass Libanios in seinen Reden meist darauf verzichtet, die jeweilige Stellung eines Amtsträgers ausdrücklich anzugeben.
[60] Listen der *comites Orientis* und *consulares Syriae* in JONES / MARTINDALE /
MORRIS (1971) 1082-1083; 1105-1106.

stand seine Heimatstadt stets im Vordergrund, und obwohl er
sich selbst dieser Verpflichtung entzogen hatte, wurde er nicht
müde, gegen das politische Desinteresse seiner Landsleute zu
kämpfen und die Flucht gerade der Söhne aus höheren Kreisen
aus der kurialen Verantwortung anzuprangern.[61]
Schliesslich muss auch noch einmal daran erinnert werden,
dass die progymnasmatischen Musterbeispiele bei Libanios und
Aphthonios sämtlich von paganer Geisteshaltung zeugen. Dies
war in einer Stadt wie Antiochia zu dieser Zeit nicht selbstverständlich. Zur Zeit von Libanios und Aphthonios war Antiochia bereits schätzungsweise zu 80% christianisiert und Sitz
eines der wichtigsten christlichen Patriarchate des Ostens, das
nur hinter Rom und Alexandria zurückstand. Obwohl er auch
Schüler christlichen Glaubens hatte, blieb Libanios aber Zeit
seines Lebens dem alten Glauben treu. Seine Schule blieb eine
veritable Bastion heidnisch-hellenischer Tradition inmitten einer
mehrheitlich christlichen Stadt.[62]
Auch Aphthonios blieb, wie sein Lehrer, dem alten Glauben
treu. Das zeigt sich vor allem in seinem Musterbeispiel für das
Progymnasma der Ekphrasis, wofür er als Sujet das berühmte
Heiligtum des Serapis auf der Akropolis von Alexandria wählt.
Dieser Tempel, das bedeutendste Monument paganer Kultur
in Alexandria, wurde im Jahre 391 oder 392[63] von einem
christlichen Mob auf Anstiftung des Patriarchen Theophilos
und mindestens mit stillschweigender Duldung des Kaisers
Theodosius in Brand gesteckt und völlig zerstört.[64] Einige hal-
ten das Zerstörungsjahr daher für den *terminus ante quem* der
Ekphrasis des Aphthonios. Es ist jedoch wohl eher damit zu
rechnen, dass es vielmehr einen *terminus post quem* darstellt

---

[61] Vgl. z.B. LIB. *Or.* 38.
[62] SANDWELL (2007) 154-160 plädiert hingegen eher für eine religiös neutrale
Haltung des Libanios im Bereich des öffentlichen Lebens.
[63] Cf. HAHN (2006).
[64] Cf. EUNAP. *VS* 472; SOZOM. *Hist. eccl.* 7, 15; MACMULLEN (1984) 99.
Zum archäologischen Befund vgl. MCKENZIE / GIBSON / REYES (2004); MCKEN-
ZIE (2007) 188-209.

und dass Aphthonios das Sujet bewusst gewählt hat als eine Geste des Protests gegen die barbarische Zerstörung des Heiligtums samt seiner Dependance der alexandrinischen Bibliothek durch die Christen. So passt dieses Stück des Aphthonios in der Tendenz sehr gut zu dem nur wenige Jahre zuvor von Libanios an Theodosius gerichteten Appell für die Erhaltung der heidnischen Kultstätten in Antiochia, der ebendies Heiligtum noch als unzerstört voraussetzt,[65] ja es könnte womöglich sogar direkt darauf Bezug nehmen.

So verstanden, werden selbst die Progymnasmatasammlungen des Libanios und Aphthonios zu einem Fanal gegen autoritären Zentralismus einerseits und aufstrebendes Christentum andererseits und zu einem Bekenntnis zur Tradition der klassischen paganen hellenischen Kultur und somit zu einem unüberhörbaren politischen Statement, das gerade durch seine Bildungswirkung durch den Einsatz in der Rhetorenschule eine nicht zu unterschätzende Macht entfalten konnte.

6. Deklamationen aus dem *genus deliberatiuum*

Es war bereits davon die Rede, dass im Bereich der vollständigen Übungsreden, der Deklamationen, das *genus deliberatiuum* neben dem *genus iudiciale* eine wichtige Rolle spielte. Allerdings sind die Deklamationen des Libanios bisher nur unzureichend untersucht worden. War doch, wie Robert Penella konstatiert, die allgemeine Einschätzung: „Why go to them when we have Libanius' orations on real-life themes and his letters, both filled with a wealth of contemporary political, social, prosopographical and cultural information?"[66] Zudem ist auch in diesem Corpus, wie schon bei den Progymnasmata, sehr vieles dem Verdacht der Unechtheit ausgesetzt.[67]

---

[65] LIB. *Or.* 30, bes. § 44. Zur Datierung vgl. WIEMER (1995b).
[66] PENELLA (2014) 107.
[67] Zu Echtheitsfragen vgl. FOERSTER / MÜNSCHER (1925) und zuletzt NAJOCK (2007).

Es ist ferner nicht immer leicht, innerhalb der Deklamationen des Libanios deliberative klar von gerichtlichen Reden zu scheiden. Mischformen sind zahlreich. So kreuzen sich häufig (deliberative) Gesetzesanträge mit (judizialen) Anklage- oder Verteidigungsreden, wobei auch wieder, wie in den Progymnasmata des Aphthonios, oft Gesetze über Ehebruch eine Rolle spielen.[68] Schwer einzuordnen sind auch die häufigen Selbstdenunziationen und Anträge auf ein Todesurteil gegen den Antragsteller selbst, da oft nicht klar ist, ob sie sich an die Volksversammlung oder ein Richtergremium richten.

Die Sujets sind, abgesehen von reinen Charaktertypendeklamationen, dem Mythos oder zentralen Epochen der griechischen Geschichte entnommen, wobei besonders wiederum Episoden um Demosthenes und seinen Kampf gegen Philipp von Makedonien im Vordergrund stehen.

Die einzige wirklich eindeutig dem *genus deliberatiuum* zuzuordnende Deklamation ist leider nur in Fragmenten erhalten, so dass ihre Struktur nicht mehr klar zu erkennen ist. Nur Proömium und *narratio* sind noch fassbar.[69] Diese entsprechen, wie der Gewährsmann Johannes Doxapatres andeutet, ganz den Anleitungen aus Ps.-Hermogenes, *De inuentione*. Die Ausgangssituation bildet die Annahme, die Thebaner hätten den Dichter Pindar zur Strafe für seinen Lobpreis Athens in einem Dithyrambos als „Stütze Griechenlands (Ἑλλάδος ἔρεισμα)" in den Perserkriegen[70] zu Tode gesteinigt (von Wilamowitz als „alberne Fiktion" der Rhetorenschule bezeichnet[71]). Daraufhin beantragt ein anonymer Athener in der Volksversammlung, einen Straffeldzug gegen Theben zu führen. Die Frage eines Kriegsbeschlusses durch die Volksversammlung ist ein klassisches deliberatives Thema. Ein weiteres Mal stehen auch Athen und seine Sonderstellung im klassischen Griechenland im Mittelpunkt. Die Argumentation ist nicht mehr vollständig zu

---

[68] Z.B. LIB. *Decl.* 25, 38, 39, 40.
[69] LIB. fr. 49, in *Opera* XI (1922) 637-641.
[70] PIND. fr. 76 SNELL-MAEHLER.
[71] WILAMOWITZ-MOELLENDORFF (1922) 273, n. 1.

rekonstruieren. Immerhin ist erkennbar, dass den Thebanern unterstellt wird, aus Neid auf Athen gehandelt zu haben. Es wird behauptet, Pindar sei gar nicht mehr wirklich Thebaner gewesen, sondern habe Athen zu seiner Wahlheimat gemacht; nur dadurch sei er kultiviert genug geworden, um den Göttern gegenüber Pietät zu zeigen und sich als Dichter auszuzeichnen. Auch mit dem Mittel der Pathoserregung wird gearbeitet: Es wird Mitleid mit dem Schicksal Pindars erregt und Hass auf die Thebaner geschürt. An die Stelle des Dankes an den lebenden Dichter müsse nun die Rache für den Toten treten.

In die Kategorie der ebenfalls dem *genus* der deliberativen Rede zugehörenden und in Libanios' eigener Zeit nicht unwichtigen Gesandtschaftsreden reihen sich die Deklamationen 3 und 4 ein, die Robert Penella jüngst eingehender untersucht hat.[72] Auch Bernard Schouler weist sie aufgrund der obwaltenden στάσις πραγματική dem deliberativen *genus* zu.[73] Das Sujet sind die beiden Gesandtschaftsreden des Menelaos und Odysseus in Troja nach *Ilias* 3, 212-224 zum Zwecke der Forderung der Auslieferung Helenas und der Abwendung des Trojanischen Krieges. Hier sind die Strukturen deutlich erkennbar. Penella zeigt, dass die *argumentatio* beider Reden typischerweise (wie in deliberativen Progymnasmata einstudiert) der Beantwortung einer Serie von *hypophorai*, also Einwänden der Gegenseite, folgt, wobei Odysseus die weit grössere Zahl von sieben *hypophorai* erhält, Menelaos hingegen nur zwei. Dies dient der demonstrativen Hauptabsicht der beiden Reden, den unterschiedlichen Stil beider Redner, den einfachen lakonischen des Menelaos und den grossartigen, ausschweifenden des Odysseus, kontrastiv zu charakterisieren. Ist doch auch die Odysseus-Rede weit umfangreicher als die des Menelaos. An Argumenten finden sich unter anderem das Recht auf der Seite des Menelaos gegenüber der Hybris des

---

[72] PENELLA (2011).

[73] SCHOULER (1984) 202: "Ce discours d'ambassade relève du genre de l'apparat, mais du point de vue de la logique il s'agit d'une suasoire. La position est donc pragmatique et les topiques attendus sont les critères de l'action".

Paris-Alexandros (δίκαιον), der Bruch des Gastrechts durch
Paris (νόμιμον), die höhere Annehmlichkeit des Friedens
gegenüber dem Krieg (ἡδύ), der Hinweis auf die Risiken des
Krieges (συμφέρον) oder die Drohung mit der Überlegenheit
des griechischen Heeres (ἀναγκαῖον), alles schulmässige deliberative Argumentationstopoi. Wie aus Homer bekannt, bleiben
beide Reden trotz stringenter Argumentation erfolglos. Ebenfalls in den trojanischen Sagenkreis und im weiteren Sinne
zum Bereich der Gesandtschaftsreden gehört Deklamation 5,
eine Antwort des Achill auf die Überredungsversuche des
Odysseus in der berühmten Gesandtschaft des 11. Buches der
Ilias. Argumentativ geht es im Wesentlichen um die Zurück-
weisung der einzelnen Versöhnungsangebote Agamemnons
(u.a. Ehrengeschenke, Hochzeit mit seiner Tochter, Rückgabe
der Briseis). Dabei wird gezeigt, dass die einzelnen Angebote
die Beleidigung der Ehre Achills eher noch steigern, nicht
mildern.

In den Deklamationen zu historischen Themen geht es häufig um die Forderung Philipps an Athen, ihm Demosthenes
auszuliefern,[74] oder um Vorgänge im Umfeld der Perserkriege[75]
oder des Peloponnesischen Krieges,[76] also eben jene Sujets, die
auch aus der Zweiten Sophistik als Standardthemen hinlänglich
bekannt sind, wobei generell der direkte Einfluss von Deklamationen älterer Redner aus der Zweiten Sophistik offenbar
relativ hoch zu veranschlagen ist.

Festzuhalten bleibt, dass der Aufbau deliberativer Deklamationen bei Libanios in der Regel dem typischen Strukturschema
deliberativer Progymnasmata höherer Ordnung wie der Thesis
oder des Gesetzesantrags folgt (Abarbeitung von Gegenargu-
menten in *hypophorai*).

---

[74] LIB. *Decl.* 19-22.
[75] LIB. *Decl.* 9-11.
[76] LIB. *Decl.* 13.

7. Libanios' politische Reden

Aufgrund seiner herausragenden Stellung als offizieller Sophist
Antiochias und seiner persönlichen Beziehungen zu einflussreichen Persönlichkeiten kam Libanios zwangsläufig häufiger
in die Situation, sich im Sinne seiner Vaterstadt verwenden zu
müssen, was er im Interesse seiner eigenen Selbsteinschätzung
auch nicht ungerne tat. Hatte er unter dem christlichen Kaiser
Constantius eher schwierige Zeiten erlebt und sich vielfach mit
ihm missgünstigen Reichsbeamten in Antiochia herumschlagen
müssen, so schien sich mit der Erhebung seines ehemaligen
Schülers und Freundes Julian zum Kaiser im Jahre 361 erst-
mals die Chance einer direkten Einflussnahme auf das Kaiser-
haus zu bieten.[77] Versuchte er zunächst durch Briefe nach
Konstantinopel und durch Freunde in der Hauptstadt auf den
Kaiser einzuwirken (er konnte ja nicht wissen, ob er nicht etwa
durch sein letztlich erreichtes Arrangement mit Constantius
beim neuen Kaiser kompromittiert war),[78] so schien sich die
Situation zu seinen Gunsten zu wenden, als Julian im Jahre
262 persönlich nach Antiochia kam und dort für längere Zeit
seine Residenz nahm. War eine erste Begegnung mit dem Kaiser zwar nicht ganz nach Wunsch verlaufen,[79] und musste
Libanios zunächst auch noch vorsichtig agieren, da einige Höf-
linge offenbar gegen ihn intrigierten, so wurde er doch bald zu
einem der engsten Berater des Kaisers. Besass doch andererseits auch der Kaiser in seinem alten Lehrer und Freund aus
Jugendtagen einen unschätzbaren politischen Verbündeten in
einer ihm aufgrund ihres christlichen Gepräges eher feindselig
gesinnten Stadt, so dass man fast von einer glücklichen Symbiose
sprechen kann.

Libanios konnte sich denn auch tatsächlich in der Folgezeit
erfolgreich für mehrere Verwandte und Freunde in Antiochia

---

[77] Zum Verhältnis von Libanios zu Julian vgl. WIEMER (1995a).
[78] Vgl. WINTJES (2005) 125.
[79] Vgl. WINTJES (2005) 126-127.

beim Kaiser einsetzen. Auf die Probe gestellt wurde seine Rolle als Vermittler zwischen Stadt und Kaiser jedoch, als es im Jahre 362, mitten in den Vorbereitungen des Kaisers für seinen Persienfeldzug, durch eine ungewöhnliche Trockenheitsperiode und die Überbelegung der Stadt mit Militär zu einer Anspannung der Versorgungssituation kam. Als Lebensmittelhortungen durch Ratsmitglieder die Getreidepreise in die Höhe trieben, reagierte der Kaiser mit einem Höchstpreisedikt, um der Teuerung Einhalt zu gebieten,[80] das aber keine Wirkung hatte. Vielmehr verschlechterte sich die Versorgungslage weiter, was Julian vornehmlich der antiochenischen Kurie anlastete, wogegen die Kurie sich ihrerseits staatliche Eingriffe verbat. So eskalierte die Situation dahingehend, dass die Popularität des im christlichen Antiochia ohnehin nie sonderlich beliebten Kaisers vollends auf den Nullpunkt sank und in der Stadt Spottverse auf Julian kursierten, worüber nun der Kaiser seinerseits verärgert war und darauf mit der noch vor seiner Abreise in den Osten veröffentlichten Satire *Misopogon* reagierte.

In dieser verfahrenen Situation wandte man sich offenbar an Libanios mit der Bitte um Vermittlung. Libanios verfasste denn auch in seiner 15. Rede eine förmliche Gesandtschafts- und Bittrede an den schon abgereisten Kaiser, die allen Kunstregeln der ‚vertikalen' Variante des deliberativen *genus* entspricht, um den Kaiser wieder gnädig zu stimmen. Doch kam er nie dazu, diese Rede vor dem Kaiser tatsächlich vorzutragen,[81] und dessen früher Tod im Perserfeldzug verhinderte das Weitere. So bleibt ungeklärt, ob es Libanios letztlich gelungen wäre, den Kaiser umzustimmen. Dennoch stellt die Versorgungskrise der Jahre 362/363 nach Jorit Wintjes einen ersten Höhepunkt in der politischen Tätigkeit des Libanios dar, indem er zum wichtigsten politischen Ansprechpartner für die Vertreter seiner Heimatstadt wurde. „Eine erfolgreiche Besänftigung des Kaisers und dessen Rückkehr nach Antiochia auf Drängen seines

---

[80] Cf. LIB. *Or.* 18, 195; WINTJES (2005) 129-130.
[81] LIB. *Or.* 17, 37.

Freundes Libanius hätte die Stellung des letzteren in der Stadt sicherlich weiter gestärkt und in eine noch prominentere Position befördert."[82] Vergleichen wir damit eine ganz ähnliche Situation in einer späteren Lebensphase. Als es im Jahre 382 erneut zu einer Hungersnot in Antiochia kam und der verantwortliche Beamte, der *comes Orientis* Philagrios, ein persönlicher Freund des Libanios, mit harten Strafmassnahmen gegen die Zunft der Bäcker reagierte, intervenierte Libanios erneut mit einer spontanen Rede im Sinne des Bäckerstandes, was ihm den Ruf als Wohltäter nicht nur der Bäcker, sondern seiner ganzen Heimatstadt eintrug.[83] Wiederum war es neben der Fähigkeit des Sophisten zum glänzenden spontanen Auftritt[84] die persönliche Beziehung zu einem Amsträger, die ihn zum Retter der Stadt werden liess, als der er sich selbst stilisierte.[85]

Eine weitere Gelegenheit, sein Geschick als mutiger Verhandler, Ratgeber und Vermittler zu beweisen, ergab sich für ihn, als er, nunmehr gegenüber dem christlichen Kaiser Theodosius, in der 30. Rede Stellung nahm für die Erhaltung der heidnischen Kultstätten im griechischen Osten. Geauer Anlass und Datierung der Rede sind (bis auf den *terminus ante quem* 391) umstritten. Doch ist die Rede wiederum schulmässig geliedert in ein *exordium* mit *captatio beneuolentiae* (Verweis auf seine früheren guten Ratschläge an den Adressaten), eine *narratio* der Geschichte des Umgangs mit heidnischen Kultstätten seit Konstantin und der empörenden Rechtsbrüche der Christen in jüngster Zeit, einen *argumentatio*-Teil, in dem wiederum systematisch die vier Hauptargumente der Tempelzerstörer eines nach dem anderen entkräftet werden, kulminierend in der pathosgeladenen Schilderung der jüngsten Zerstörung eines besonders herrlichen Tempels, und schliesslich eine *peroratio* mit Hinweis auf die sonstige tolerante Haltung des Kaisers

---

[82] WINTJES (2005) 130.
[83] WINTJES (2005) 203-204.
[84] Cf. NORMAN (1965) 205.
[85] LIB. *Or.* 1, 208-210.

Nichtchristen gegenüber. Auch in dieser Rede verbinden sich, wie Heinz-Günther Nesselrath festgestellt hat, Elemente der symbuleutischen Rede (Libanios als Ratgeber des Kaisers) und der Gerichtsrede (Verteidigung der Nichtchristen gegen christliche Anschuldigungen).[86]

Die grösste Herausforderung in dieser Hinsicht stellten für Libanios aber zweifellos die sogenannten Statuenunruhen des Jahres 387 dar,[87] als in Antiochia ein kaiserliches Edikt, das höhere Steuerabgaben einforderte, zunächst noch geregelte Proteste seitens der Kurialen, dann aber eine ausser Kontrolle geratende Wutreaktion des Strassenmobs auslöste, die in der Schändung und Zerstörung von Bildnissen der Kaiserfamilie kulminierte. Auf den Bericht von diesen Ereignissen hin entsandte Theodosius zwei Sonderermittler, Flavius Caesarius und Ellebichus, nach Antiochia. Libanios wurde von diesen beiden nicht etwa ebenfalls verhört, sondern als Berater zu den Verhören hinzugezogen, was seine mittlerweile erreichte Ausnahmestellung innerhalb Antiochias beleuchtet. Möglicherweise auch auf seine Fürsprache hin empfahlen die beiden dem Kaiser letztlich unerwartete Milde, woraufhin Libanios beiden Dankadressen widmete.[88]

Libanios konnte es sich nun in den achtziger und neunziger Jahren auch erlauben, den in Antiochia residierenden Reichsbeamten Ratschläge zu erteilen. So richtete er 384 an den *comes Orientis* Ikarios eine deutliche Warnung, sich mit den Anhängern seines Vorgängers Proklos einzulassen und empfahl ihm strenges Vorgehen gegen Parteilichkeit und Korruption, aber Zurückhaltung in der Anwendung von Gewalt.[89] Man hat diese Rede geradezu ein Handbuch für Provinzgouverneure genannt.[90] Um so harscher fiel jedoch im folgenden Jahr seine Kritik an Ikarios aus, als er feststellen musste, dass dieser keinen seiner

[86] Nesselrath (2011) 32.
[87] Vgl. Lib. *Or.* 19-23; vgl. Malosse (2014) 85.
[88] Lib. *Or.* 21 und 22.
[89] Lib. *Or.* 26 (384).
[90] Malosse (2014) 88: "handbook for governors".

Ratschläge befolgt hatte.[91] Ähnliche wohlgemeinte Ratschläge richtete er auch an den *comes Orientis* Timokrates.[92] Vergleichbare Scheinprozessreden wie gegen Ikarios, zum Teil in sehr scharfer Form, verfasste er in diesen Jahren auch gegen eine Reihe weiterer hoher Verwaltungsbeamter des Reiches.[93] Auch sonst mischte er sich immer mehr in die Politik seiner Heimatstadt ein, nahm unter anderem Stellung gegen unmenschliche Haftbedingungen, gegen Zwangsarbeit oder gegen illegale private Sicherheitsdienste.[94]

All dies konnte er aber nur wagen aufgrund seines weitverzweigten Netzwerks persönlicher Beziehungen, das ihn vor Bestrafung und Rache durch die Betroffenen schützte und ihm eine flexible Reaktion auf plötzliche politische Veränderungen erlaubte. Dieses Netzwerk wird vor allem deutlich in der Unzahl seiner erhaltenen Briefe.[95] Über die Briefe fast mehr noch als durch seine Reden war es ihm möglich, zugunsten von Freunden und Landsleuten an höherer Stelle zu intervenieren, ihnen gewünschte Stellen zu verschaffen oder hochgestellten Persönlichkeiten Ratschläge zu erteilen. So verlagert sich das deliberative *genus* bei Libanios zumindest zum Teil von den Reden in die Briefe.

8. Zusammenfassung

In dem weitverzweigten Œuvre des Libanios und in Teilen auch in demjenigen seines Schülers Aphthonios hat sich zeigen lassen, dass die Gattung der deliberativen Rede auch in der Periode der sogenannten Dritten Sophistik durchaus nicht

---

[91] LIB. *Or.* 27 und 28 (385).

[92] LIB. *Or.* 41 (nach 382).

[93] Cf. LIB. *Or.* 33 (Gegen Tisamenos, 386); 56 (Gegen Lukianos, 388); 57 (Gegen Severos, 389/90); 54 (Gegen Eustathios, 389); 46 (Gegen Florentios, 393); vgl. dazu WINTJES (2005) 210; 219-225; CASELLA (2010); CRIBIORE (2013) 78-79; MALOSSE (2014) 89-90.

[94] LIB. *Or.* 45 (386); 50 (385); 47 (391); vgl. MALOSSE (2014) 86-87.

[95] Cf. BRADBURY (2004); (2014); SANDWELL (2009).

fehlt. Ihre theoretischen Grundlagen sind nach wie vor präsent. In Progymnasmata und Deklamationen wird sie weiterhin intensiv eingeübt. Es wurde aber auch deutlich, dass sie im Bereich des öffentlichen Lebens aufgrund der veränderten politischen und gesellschaftlichen Bedingungen ihren Charakter merklich gewandelt hat; sie wird von der echten buleutischen Ratsrede des demokratischen Politikers zur symbuleutischen Beratungsrede des erfahrenen Sachkenners. Ebenfalls konnte gezeigt werden, dass die Sophisten des 4. Jahrhunderts, oder zumindest die bedeutendsten unter ihnen, zu denen Libanios zweifelsohne zu zählen ist, sich keineswegs aus der praktischen Tagespolitik in die Theorie der Schulstube zurückgezogen haben, sondern sich aktiv in der einen oder anderen Weise in die gesellschaftlichen Diskussionen und die Politik in ihrer unmittelbaren Umgebung, aber auch auf höherer Ebene einmischen. Schliesslich ergab sich aber auch, dass die unabdingbare Voraussetzung für solche aktive Einmischung in dieser Zeit die Erringung einer in gewisser Weise unangreifbaren sozialen Position und die Ausbildung eines engmaschigen persönlichen sozialen Netzwerks ist, das den Redner vor unliebsamen Reaktionen seitens der Mächtigen zu schützen geeignet ist.

Literaturverzeichnis

Amato, E. (2006), "Avant-Propos", in E. Amato / A. Roduit / M. Steinrück (Hrsg.), *Approches de la Troisième Sophistique. Hommages à Jacques Schamp* (Bruxelles), V-VIII.

Bowie, E.L. (1970), "Greeks and their Past in the Second Sophistic", *Past and Present* 46, 3-41, nachgedr. in M.I. Finley (Hrsg.), *Studies in Ancient Society* (London 1974), 166-209.

Bradbury, S. (2004a), *Selected Letters of Libanius from the Age of Constantius and Julian* (Liverpool).

—— (2004b), "Libanius' Letters as Evidence for Travel and Epistolary Networks among Greek Elites in the Fourth Century", in L. Ellis / F.L. Kidner (Hrsg.), *Travel, Communication, and Geography in Late Antiquity* (Burlington), 73-80.

—— (2014), "Libanius' Networks", in Van Hoof (2014), 220-240.

BRINK, C.O. (1989), "Quintilian's *De causis corruptae eloquentiae* and Tacitus' *Dialogus de oratoribus*", *CQ* 39, 472-503.

BRUNT, P.A. (1994), "The Bubble of the Second Sophistic", *BICS* 39, 25-52.

CABOURET, B. (2002), "Le gouverneur au temps de Libanios : Image et réalité", *Pallas* 60, 191-204.

—— (2004), "Pouvoir municipal, pouvoir impérial au IVᵉ siècle", in B. CABOURET / P.L. GATIER / C. SALIOU (Hrsg.), *Antioche de Syrie. Histoire, images et traces de la ville antique. Actes du colloque de Lyon (octobre 2001)* (Lyon), 117-142.

CASELLA, M. (2010), *Storie di ordinaria corruzione. Libanio, orazioni LVI, LVII, XLVI* (Messina).

CRIBIORE, R. (1996), *Writing, Teachers, and Students in Graeco-Roman Egypt* (Atlanta).

—— (2001), *Gymnastics of the Mind. Greek Education in Hellenistic and Roman Egypt* (Princeton).

—— (2007), *The School of Libanius in Late Antique Antioch* (Princeton).

—— (2013), *Libanius the Sophist. Rhetoric, Reality, and Religion in the Fourth Century* (Ithaca).

—— (2014), "The Rhetorical Context: Traditions and Opportunities", in VAN HOOF (2014), 59-78.

DRECOLL, C. (1997), *Die Liturgien im Römischen Kaiserreich des 3. und 4. Jh. n. Chr. Untersuchung über Zugang, Inhalt und wirtschaftliche Bedeutung der öffentlichen Zwangsdienste in Ägypten und anderen Provinzen* (Stuttgart).

FELTEN, J. (Hrsg.) (1913), *Nicolai Progymnasmata* (Leipzig).

FOERSTER, R. (Hrsg.) (1922), *Libanii Opera*. Vol. XI, *Epistulae 840-1544 una cum pseudepigraphis et Basilii cum Libanio commercio epistolico, Fragmenta* (Leipzig).

FOERSTER, R. / MÜNSCHER, K. (1925), „Libanios", in *RE* XII.2 (Stuttgart), 2485-2551.

FOWLER, R.C. / QUIROGA PUERTAS, A.J. (2014), "A Prolegomena to the Third Sophistic", in R.C. FOWLER (Hrsg.), *Plato in the Third Sophistic* (Berlin), 1-30.

GIBSON, C.A. (Hrsg.) (2008), *Libanius's* Progymnasmata. *Model Exercises in Greek Prose Composition and Rhetoric*. Trans. with an introd. and notes (Atlanta).

—— (2014), "Better Living through Prose Composition? Moral and Compositional Pedagogy in Ancient Greek and Roman Progymnasmata", *Rhetorica* 32, 1-30.

GOLDHILL, S. (Hrsg.) (2001), *Being Greek under Rome. Cultural Identity, the Second Sophistic and the Development of Empire* (Cambridge).

HAHN, J. (2006), „*Vetustus error extinctus est*: Wann wurde das Sarapeion von Alexandria zerstört?", *Historia* 55, 368-383.

VAN HOOF, L. (2010), "Greek Rhetoric and the Later Roman Empire: The Bubble of the 'Third Sophistic'", *AntTard* 18, 211-224.

—— (Hrsg.) (2014), *Libanius. A Critical Introduction* (Cambridge).

JONES, A.H.M. / MARTINDALE, J.R. / MORRIS, J. (1971), *The Prosopography of the Later Roman Empire*. Vol. I, *A.D. 260-395* (Cambridge).

KALDELLIS, A. (2007), *Hellenism in Byzantium. The Transformations of Greek Identity and the Reception of the Classical Tradition* (Cambridge).

KASER, M. / HACKL, K. (²1996), *Das römische Zivilprozessrecht* (München).

KRAUS, M. (2011a), "Les conceptions politiques et culturelles dans les progymnasmata de Libanios et Aphthonios", in O. LAGACHERIE / P.-L. MALOSSE (Hrsg.), *Libanios, le premier humaniste. Études en hommage à Bernard Schouler (Actes du colloque de Montpellier 18-20 mars 2010)* (Alessandria), 141-150.

—— (2011b), "Rhetoric, Classicism, and Democracy: The Conveyance of Moral and Political Values in Late Antique Rhetorical Education", in T. VAN HAAFTEN *et al.* (Hrsg.), *Bending Opinion. Essays on Persuasion in the Public Domain* (Leiden), 49-60.

—— (2013), "Rhetoric or Law? The Role of Law in Late Ancient Greek Rhetorical Exercises", in A.J. QUIROGA PUERTAS (Hrsg.), *The Purpose of Rhetoric in Late Antiquity. From Performance to Exegesis* (Tübingen), 123-137.

LIEBESCHUETZ, J.H.W.G. (1972), *Antioch. City and Imperial Administration in the Later Roman Empire* (Oxford).

MACMULLEN, R. (1984), *Christianizing the Roman Empire (A.D. 100-400)* (New Haven 1984).

MALOSSE, P.-L. (2014), "Libanius' *Orations*", in VAN HOOF (2014), 81-106.

MALOSSE, P.-L. / SCHOULER, B. (2009), "La Troisième Sophistique : Qu'est-ce que la Troisième Sophistique?", *Lalies* 29, 161-224.

MCKENZIE, J.S. (2007), *The Architecture of Alexandria and Egypt (c. 300 BC to AD 700)* (New Haven).

MCKENZIE, J.S. / GIBSON, S. / REYES, A.T. (2004), "Reconstructing the Serapeum in Alexandria from the Archaeological Evidence", *JRS* 94, 73-121.

NAJOCK, D. (2007), „Unechtes und Zweifelhaftes unter den Deklamationen des Libanios – Die statistische Evidenz", in M. GRÜNBART (Hrsg.), *Theatron – Rhetorische Kultur in Spätantike und*

330   MANFRED KRAUS

Mittelalter = *Rhetorical Culture in Late Antiquity and the Middle Ages* (Berlin), 305-355.

NESSELRATH, H.-G. *et al.* (Hrsg.) (2011), *Für Religionsfreiheit, Recht und Toleranz. Libanios' Rede für den Erhalt der heidnischen Tempel* (Tübingen).

NORMAN, A.F. (Hrsg.) (1965), *Libanius' Autobiography. Oration I* (Oxford).

PACK, R. (1951), "*Curiales* in the Correspondence of Libanius", *TAPA* 82, 176-192.

PATILLON, M. (Hrsg. u. Übers.) (2008), *Corpus Rhetoricum. Anonyme, Préambule à la rhétorique; Aphthonios, Progymnasmata; en annexe: Pseudo-Hermogène, Progymnasmata* (Paris).

PENELLA, R.J. (2011), "Menelaus, Odysseus, and the Limits of Eloquence in Libanius, *Declamations* 3 and 4", in O. LAGACHERIE / P.-L. MALOSSE (Hrsg.), *Libanios, le premier humaniste. Études en hommage à Bernard Schouler. Actes du colloque de Montpellier 18-20 mars 2010* (Alessandria), 93-105.

—— (2013), "Prologue", in A.J. QUIROGA PUERTAS (Hrsg.), *The Purpose of Rhetoric in Late Antiquity. From Performance to Exegesis* (Tübingen), 1-7.

—— (2014), "Libanius' *Declamations*", in VAN HOOF (2014), 107-127.

PERNOT, L. (1993), *La rhétorique de l'éloge dans le monde gréco-romain.* 2 vols. (Paris).

—— (2000), *La rhétorique dans l'antiquité* (Paris).

—— (2006-2007), "Seconda Sofistica e Tarda Antichità", *Koinonia* 30-31, 7-18.

—— (2015), *Epideictic Rhetoric. Questioning the Stakes of Ancient Praise* (Austin).

PETIT, P. (1956), "Recherches sur la publication et la diffusion des discours de Libanius", *Historia* 5, 479-509.

PUECH, B. (2002), *Orateurs et sophistes grecs dans les inscriptions d'époque impériale* (Paris).

QUIROGA PUERTAS, A.J. (2007), "From 'Sophistopolis' to 'Episcopolis': The Case for a Third Sophistic", *JLARC* 1, 31-42.

SANDWELL, I. (2007), *Religious Identity in Late Antiquity. Greeks, Jews and Christians in Antioch* (Cambridge).

—— (2009), "Libanius' Social Networks: Understanding the Social Structure of the Later Roman Empire", in I. MALKIN / C. CONSTANTAKOPOULOU / K. PANAGOPOULOU (Hrsg.), *Greek and Roman Networks in the Mediterranean* (London), 129-143.

SCHAMP, J. (2006), "Sophistes à l'ambon: Esquisses pour la Troisième Sophistique comme paysage littéraire", in E. AMATO / A. RODUIT /

M. Steinrück (Hrsg.), *Approches de la Troisième Sophistique. Hommages à Jacques Schamp* (Bruxelles), 286-338.

Schouler, B. (1984), *La tradition hellénique chez Libanios.* 2 vols. (Paris).

Stenger, J. (2009), *Hellenische Identität in der Spätantike. Pagane Autoren und ihr Unbehagen an der eigenen Zeit* (Berlin).

Swain, S. (1996), *Hellenism and Empire. Language, Classicism, and Power in the Greek World AD 50-250* (Oxford).

Vitanza, V.J. (1991), "'Some More' Notes: Toward a 'Third' Sophistic", *Argumentation* 5, 117-139.

Westberg, D. (2010), *Celebrating with Words. Studies in the Rhetorical Works of the Gaza School* (Diss. Uppsala).

Wiemer, H.-U. (1995a), *Libanios und Julian. Studien zum Verhältnis von Rhetorik und Politik im vierten Jahrhundert n. Chr.* (München).

—— (1995b), „Die Rangstellung des Sophisten Libanios unter den Kaisern Julian, Valens und Theodosius. Mit einem Anhang über Abfassung und Verbreitung von Libanios' Rede Für die Tempel (Or. 30)", *Chiron* 25, 89-130.

Wilamowitz-Moellendorff, U. von (1922), *Pindaros* (Berlin).

Wintjes, J. (2005), *Das Leben des Libanius* (Rahden).

DISCUSSION

L. Pernot: Quand j'ai lancé l'expression 'Troisième sophistique', en 1993, dans *La rhétorique de l'éloge dans le monde gréco-romain* (p. 14, n. 9), je n'imaginais pas qu'elle susciterait les recherches et les discussions qu'elle a soulevées et qu'elle soulève aujourd'hui encore. N'ayant pas fait d'enquête bibliographique particulière avant d'employer cette expression, je n'exclus d'ailleurs pas qu'elle ait pu être utilisée par d'autres avant moi.[1]

Ce que je voulais dire, c'est que la sophistique ne s'est pas arrêtée brutalement, un beau jour des années 230 ap. J.-C., à cause de la publication des *Vies des sophistes* de Philostrate. Il a existé dans la seconde moitié du IIIe siècle (cf. Callinicos de Pétra, Ménandros le Rhéteur), puis au IVe siècle, et encore au-delà, des sophistes qui présentaient des caractéristiques comparables à celles des sophistes décrits par Philostrate. L'expression 'Troisième sophistique' vise donc à insister sur la continuité de la sophistique après Philostrate ; mais elle vise aussi à reconnaître les changements intervenus, et c'est pourquoi 'Troisième' succède à 'Seconde'. Ces changements se sont produits notamment en matière religieuse (à cause de l'officialisation du christianisme) et en matière politique (à cause de la séparation croissante entre la partie orientale et la partie occidentale de l'Empire).

Puis, l'expression que j'avais lancée m'a échappé, et elle a été employée pour désigner toute la littérature de l'Antiquité tardive, ou même la littérature et la civilisation. Cet

---

[1] Ainsi, elle figure dans l'article de VITANZA (1991) 117-139, cité par M. Kraus. Je ne connaissais pas cet article quand je préparais mon livre paru en 1993. Sous la plume de V. J. Vitanza, "'Third' Sophistic" ne se réfère pas à la littérature grecque, mais vise un contexte différent, celui du postmodernisme contemporain.

élargissement est comparable à l'élargissement de l'expression
'Seconde sophistique', qui a parfois été appliquée aux roman-
ciers, aux apologistes, voire à toute la culture et à l'esprit du
Haut-Empire.
    Je suis entièrement d'accord avec la présentation de M. Kraus
et je suis heureux que lui et moi partagions le même avis.
Sa démonstration met en valeur les points d'ancrage de la
'Troisième sophistique' : la rhétorique, la déclamation, les *progymnasmata*, ainsi que les notions de réseau, d'influence, de
'persuasion verticale', tous éléments comparables avec ceux que
connaissaient les sophistes de Philostrate, mais dans un monde
qui par ailleurs était en train de changer.

    M. Kraus: Ich kann mich dem nur voll und ganz anschlies-
sen. Auch der eigene Beitrag von Laurent Pernot beleuchtet
sehr schön die Kontinuität von der ‚Zweiten' zur ‚Dritten'
Sophistik. Ich sehe Vergleichspunkte etwa in der Verbindung
von Philosophie und Rhetorik, die schon (freilich in anderem
Sinne) bei Isokrates angelegt ist, in der Zweiten Sophistik bei
Dio von Prusa, aber auch z.B. Favorinus begegnet, besonders
aber für die Spätphase typisch wird (Sopater, Themistios,
Himerios, Syrianos, Synesios), am geringsten vielleicht tatsächlich bei Libanios; ferner in einer Ausweitung des Begriffs der
deliberativen Rede in Richtung auf eine Verknüpfung mit
demonstrativen Elementen und auf die Funktion des Redners
als Ratgeber (σύμβουλος), wobei bei Dio die Beratung von
Herrschern (Trajan) im Vergleich zu Libanios noch eher die
Ausnahme neben der Beratung von Volksversammlungen,
Städten oder Provinzen darstellt. Vergessen sei auch nicht, dass
auch die Redner der Zweiten Sophistik (v.a. Aelius Aristides)
im Schulprogramm der spätantiken Sophisten neben den klassischen Rednern als Vorbilder herangezogen werden. Unterschiede sehe ich wie gesagt in der Auseinandersetzung zwischen
Heidentum und Christentum (das die Zweite Sophistik prä-
gende Thema von Hellenentum und griechischer Identität
gewinnt im 4. Jahrhundert eine starke religiöse Komponente,

indem ‚Hellenen' geradezu zur Bezeichnung für Heiden wird), in der gewandelten Haltung zu Rom und zur Monarchie (von wohlwollender Kooperation, Vermittlungsabsicht und dem Glauben an den „guten Herrscher" hin zu deutlicher antimonarchischer Kritik), in der Auseinandersetzung zwischen griechischer und lateinischer Sprache und Kultur als Folge der Dissoziation der Reichshälften, die ein eigenständiges griechisch dominiertes Teilreich schafft. Bezeichnenderweise kam Theodosius I., der letzte gesamtrömische Kaiser, der das Christentum faktisch zur Staatsreligion erhob, aus Spanien, regierte aber im wesentlichen im Osten.

J.-L. Ferrary: Parmi les facteurs qui peuvent expliquer la spécificité d'une 'troisième sophistique', quel rôle donnez-vous à l'essor, dans la partie hellénophone de l'Empire, d'un enseignement du latin et du droit romain lié à l'importance croissante d'une fonction publique impériale ?

M. Kraus: Genau mit diesem Thema, speziell aus der Perspektive des Libanios, habe ich mich vor kurzem eingehender beschäftigt.[2] Besonders für die griechischen Rhetoren der Spätantike wird das Studium des Römischen Rechts und der lateinischen Sprache (merkwürdigerweise daneben auch der Kurzschrift) als alternatives Sprungbrett zu Wohlstand und politischer Karriere zunehmend zu einer ernsthaften und heftig befehdeten Konkurrenz. Libanios beklagt sich bitter über die Abwanderung etlicher seiner Schüler nach Berytos oder Rom zum Zwecke des Rechtsstudiums und verteidigt demgegenüber die Überlegenheit der griechischen rhetorischen Bildung. Die in seinen rhetorischen Übungen zugrundegelegten (fiktiven) Gesetze haben hingegen klar griechischen Charakter und sind an einer typischen griechischen Polisverfassung nach dem Vorbild Athens orientiert. Ich erkenne darin die Absicht einer Affirmation der Superiorität der griechischen Kultur und

---

[2] Vgl. meinen Aufsatz KRAUS (2013) 123-137.

rhetorischen *paideia* über die römische, eines Beharrens auf der entscheidenden Funktion der Rhetoren im Bereich der Jurisdiktion (erst ab 460 wurde für advokatische Tätigkeit auch eine juristische Qualifikation verlangt!) und einer Abwehrhaltung gegenüber dem Römischen Recht. Schliesslich blieben in der täglichen Rechtspraxis der griechischen *poleis* des Ostens auch nach der *Constitutio Antoniniana* 212 lokale griechische Gesetze, sofern sie dem Römischen Recht nicht widersprachen, weiterhin in Gültigkeit. Gerade diese Auseinandersetzung zwischen griechischer und römischer Tradition erscheint mir sehr typisch für die ‚Dritte Sophistik‘. Zumindest sprachlich hat das Griechische am Ende sogar gesiegt: Seit 535 wurden die Novellen zum *Codex Iustinianus* auch in Griechisch veröffentlicht, und spätestens ab dem 7. Jahrhundert, als die Kenntnis des Lateinischen endgültig schwand, wurde in Byzanz das *Corpus Iuris Civilis* nur noch in griechischen Übersetzungen benutzt. Es wurde zu einem griechischen Gesetzeswerk auf römischer Grundlage.

D. Colomo: You mention suspicion of the authenticity of some declamations and progymnasmata in the Libanius corpus. Could you indicate your opinion on this issue?

M. Kraus: Die Sachlage ist hier ziemlich kompliziert. Die Diskussion darüber dauert seit Richard Foersters und Karl Münschers *RE*-Artikel zu Libanios (in Pauly-Wissowa Bd. 12 [Stuttgart, 1925], 2485-2551, hier 2509-2522) an, mit variierenden Ergebnissen. Dass in beide Corpora Unechtes eingedrungen ist, scheint unabweisbar, das Ausmass aber ist höchst umstritten. Was die Deklamationen angeht, hat Dietmar Najock (2007) durch sprach- und stilstatistische Analysen zu klareren Ergebnissen zu kommen versucht. Den aktuellsten Forschungsstand hierzu bietet Robert Penellas Beitrag zu den Deklamationen in Lieve Van Hoofs Companion zu Libanios (2014) 110-112 und Tafel 3, 323-330. Demnach wären von den 51 Deklamationen nur 33 echt, 10 fragwürdig und 8 sicher unecht. Bei den

Progymnasmata liegt die Hauptschwierigkeit darin, dass das libanianische Corpus zahlreiche Dubletten mit zwei anderen Progymnasmata-Corpora, nämlich Pseudo-Nikolaos und Severus aufweist, die somit auch als Quellen einzelner Stücke in Frage kommen. Die Meinungen reichen hier von optimistischster Einschätzung bis zu völligem Agnostizismus. Die konziseste Dokumentation des gegenwärtigen Forschungsstandes findet sich bei Craig Gibson in seiner Übersetzung (2008) XXIII-XXV und in seinem Beitrag zu Van Hoof (2014) 130-131. Sicher scheint z.b., dass etwa das einzige Beipiel einer Gesetzesbeurteilung aufgrund seines biblischen Themas nicht von Libanios stammen kann. Persönlich neige ich zu einer vermittelnden Position, ziehe aber in Analysen grundsätzlich nur unbestritten authentische Stücke heran.

C. Kremmydas: Thank you very much indeed for your stimulating paper. I was particularly interested in your discussion of the way in which Libanius (and Aphthonius) uses the diachronically popular *topos* of the tyrannicides. I managed to do a quick *TLG* search and it turns out that there are only three attestations of Harmodius and Aristogeiton, the famous Athenian tyrannicides, in the corpus of Libanius: two in declamations (*Decl.* 1, 71; 22, 11) and one in an oration (12, 11, addressed to the Emperor Julian). Meanwhile, τυραννοκτόνος and its verbal forms are attested thirty times in declamations. Why do you think he avoids referring to the famous Athenian tyrannicides, preferring the generic term τυραννοκτόνος instead? And how can we account for the reference to Harmodius and Aristogeiton in an oration addressed to Julian?

M. Kraus: Tyrannen und Tyrannenmörder gehörten, neben Piraten, Kriegshelden, geschändeten Jungfrauen, Ehebrechern, knausrigen Vätern und enterbten Söhnen zum traditionellen Standardrepertoire der gerichtlichen Schuldeklamation – jedoch stets als typische Figuren ohne individuelle Namen, da sich nach Donald Russells klassischer Formulierung (*Greek Declamation*

[Cambridge, 1983], 22-39) die verhandelten komplizierten Rechtsfälle sämtlich in einem fiktiven ‚Sophistopolis' abspielten (etwa: Wenn die Gattin eines Tyrannen den Tyrannen tötet, ist sie dann als Tyrannenmörderin zu ehren oder als Gattenmörderin zu verurteilen?). Das erklärt das häufige Vorkommen des generischen Begriffs τυραννοκτόνος in den Deklamationen. Um historische Tyrannenmörder geht es nicht. Die Tyrannenkritik als solche aber bleibt. An allen von Ihnen genannten Stellen hingegen hat die Erwähnung von Harmodios und Aristogeiton jeweils nur eine beiläufige Nebenfunktion. In Deklamation 1, 71 (*Apologia Socratis*) bezieht sie sich auf das athenische Dekret, keine Sklaven jemals mehr mit diesen Namen zu benennen, als Beispiel für im alten Athen ausgesprochene Verbote, und dient daher wohl eher dem Zweck, athenisches Lokalkolorit zu erzeugen. Interessanter ist wegen des Freiheitsthemas der Fall in Deklamation 22, 11 (*De ara misericordiae*), wo dem von Philipps Häschern abgeführten Demosthenes nicht mehr gestattet wird, einen letzten Blick auf die Statuen der Tyrannenmörder zu werfen; ähnlich auch in der (wohl unechten) Apologie des Demosthenes (*Decl.* 23, 45 und 71). In der Rede an Kaiser Julian wiederum (*Or.* 12, 11) geht es darum, das Julian soeben verliehene Konsulat als ein immaterielles Denkmal zu preisen, das anders als eherne Denkmäler wie etwa das der athenischen Tyrannenmörder nicht Verwitterung und Verfall ausgesetzt sei, so dass die Erwähnung dieses Denkmals hier eher geradezu der Erhöhung des Kaisers dient und keinesfalls Anstoss erregen konnte. Übrigens kommen Harmodios und Aristogeiton noch in einer weiteren Rede vor, nämlich in dem einzigartigen Stück der fiktiv an Aelius Aristides adressierten Rede *Für die Tänzer* (Or. 64, 83), freilich nur in einer langen Liste von Männern, die trotz des Zusehens bei Tanzdarbietungen nicht verweichlicht seien.

M. Edwards: Following on from Christos' point about tyrants, it is interesting to me that the resistance to tyrants (however much this was dissociated from monarchs like the

Roman Emperor) continued to be a central topic in rhetorical education down to Libanius. Many tyrannical regimes, past and present, would have censored this kind of teaching – and the young emperor would be exposed to anti-monarchical sentiments. It is perhaps fine that the Persian Wars were a topic, because resistance to Persia could be paralleled with Roman resistance to the Parthians. But praise of Demosthenes (notably absent, of course, from Aristotle, the tutor of Alexander) and the fight for freedom might have seemed more problematic to some emperors?

M. Kraus: Themen aus dem Umkreis des Demosthenes waren in Deklamationen wegen ihres Bezugs zum klassischen Athen seit jeher besonders beliebt. Ihre politischen Implikationen konnten aber kaum verborgen bleiben, zumal nicht zu leugnen ist, dass die Progymnasmata und Deklamationen der Rhetorenschule neben der kompositorischen Schulung auch eine wichtige politisch-ethische Erziehungswirkung hatten, wie zuletzt Craig Gibson in seinem Aufsatz in *Rhetorica* 2014 zu Recht unterstrichen hat (Gibson [2014]). Entweder war die Welt der Rhetorenschule so weit von der realen Welt der Zeit entfernt, dass ein Zusammenhang gar nicht mehr empfunden wurde (es bleibt ja in jedem Fall eine Kritik in der Form des λόγος ἐσχηματισμένος), oder es gab damals tatsächlich ein erstaunliches Ausmass an politischer Toleranz seitens der Mächtigen.

L. Pernot: Le tyran est aussi un problème philosophique.

M. Kraus: Das ist sicherlich richtig. Im Gegensatz zu Kaiser Julian war Libanios allerdings an philosophischen Problemen wenig interessiert. Julians intensive platonische Studien haben in den Gesprächen der beiden kaum eine Rolle gespielt, werden jedenfalls von Libanios nicht erwähnt.

M. Edwards: Plato and censorship?

M. Kraus: Wahrscheinlich war Platon toleranter als heutige Ansichten über ihn oft glauben machen wollen. Gedanken wie der des Vorrangs von Recht und Gesetz vor dem Willen eines Machthabers oder der Unantastbarkeit eines Heiligtums wurden jedenfalls in den Rhetorenschulen implizit im Zuge der Rhetorikausbildung vermittelt. Libanios trug derartige Gedanken aber auch aus der Schulstube hinaus in die Öffentlichkeit, indem er in politischen Reden freimütig Kaisern und Reichsbeamten gegenüber Unrecht benannte und anklagte und die mutwillige Zerstörung heidnischer Heiligtümer anprangerte. Denn Heiligtümer und Redekunst gehörten für ihn als Symbole hellenischer Kultur zusammen; wer die einen zerstörte, zerstörte auch die andere (*Or.* 62, 8). Dabei unterrichtete Libanios sehr wohl auch christliche Schüler. Antiochia war zu seiner Zeit eine überwiegend christliche Metropole von grosser Bedeutung. Andererseits urteilten antiochenische Richter, da des Lateinischen oft unkundig, weiterhin nach den lokalen griechischen Gesetzen, was Libanios nur unterstützen konnte. Sein unermüdliches Eintreten für die griechische Redekunst und Bildung sollte sich letztlich in ihrem lebendigen Fortbestand in Byzanz sogar erfüllen.

M. Edwards: Could you say something about the rhetorical curriculum in the East and West?

M. Kraus: Dass die Ausbildung in Rhetorik in Ost und West in den Grundzügen ähnlich aussah, ist anzunehmen, waren doch die theoretischen Grundlagen mehr oder weniger die gleichen. Während wir aber durch Philostrat und Eunapios über die institutionellen Strukturen der höheren Studien im griechischen Osten ziemlich gut informiert sind und in den Schriften des *Corpus Hermogenianum* und von Menander Rhetor massive Zuwächse an rhetorischer Theorie beobachten, erfahren wir über die Praxis im lateinischen Westen zwischen dem 2. und 4. Jahrhundert (abgesehen von einigen gallischen und nordafrikanischen Bildungszentren) nur wenig. Es scheint, als wäre in dieser Periode die griechische Rhetorik zu übermächtig und tonangebend gewesen. Wer aus dem lateinischen Bereich Rhetorik studieren wollte und auf sich hielt, ging damals nach Griechenland, vor allem nach Athen. Erst ab der Mitte des 4. Jahrhunderts, als die Kenntnis des Griechischen im Westen abnahm, hören wir wieder von bedeutenderen lateinischen Rhetoriklehrern (Aelius Donatus, Marius Victorinus). Auch in der rhetorischen Praxis gibt es abgesehen von den Panegyrici Latini in dieser Zeit aus dem lateinischen Bereich recht wenig, vor allem nichts zur deliberativen Rhetorik.

M.S. Celentano: Agostino e Ambrogio?

M. Kraus: Was von Ambrosius und Augustinus erhalten ist, sind Predigten und Trauerreden, also exegetische, paränetische oder demonstrative Stücke, aber keine deliberativen Reden. Selbstverständlich ist Augustinus mit dem 4. Buch von *De doctrina Christiana* auch als Rhetoriktheoretiker von Bedeutung, allerdings in deutlicher Abgrenzung von den Traditionen der heidnischen Antike. Leider fehlen uns für die spätantike Periode auch gänzlich die Zeugnisse für Deklamationen in lateinischer Sprache, in denen man deliberative Stücke erwarten könnte. Mit den pseudo-quintilianeischen *Declamationes maiores* und *minores* ebenso wie mit Calpurnius Flaccus kommen wir nicht über das 2. Jahrhundert n. Chr. hinaus.

Verglichen mit den beachtlichen Theoriefortschritten bei Hermogenes und Menander bieten die in den Rhetores Latini Minores zusammengefassten lateinischen Theoretiker der späteren Antike entweder (wie bei Iulius Victor) nur blasse Exzerpte aus Cicero und Quintilian oder (wie bei Sulpicius Victor) Importe aus dem griechischen Bereich. Auch Priscian muss im späten 5. Jahrhundert Pseudo-Hermogenes übersetzen, um den Lateinern die Progymnasmata nahezubringen. Während in der Periode der Zweiten Sophistik im lateinischen Westen noch fast jeder Gebildete Griechisch sprach, galt dies nach dem Auseinanderdriften der beiden Reichshälften seit Errichtung des

tetrarchischen Systems durch Diokletian 293 für das 4. Jahrhundert nicht mehr im selben Masse (vgl. etwa Augustinus).
Nunmehr waren es umgekehrt eher die Griechen des Ostens,
die noch der Amtssprache Latein mächtig waren oder gar in
dieser Sprache schrieben (Claudian, Ammianus Marcellinus).
Auch hierin liegt ein bedeutsamer Unterschied zwischen ‚Zwei-
ter' und ‚Dritter' Sophistik.

M. Edwards: Would you like to end by saying something
more about the importance of Aphthonius?

M. Kraus: Aphthonios ist natürlich insbesondere bedeutend
aufgrund der immensen Wirkung seines Werkes in Byzanz und
in der Neuzeit, die weitaus grösser war als die seines Lehrers
Libanios. Für die eigene Zeit ist er aber wichtig als Parallele
und Ergänzung zu den schulorientierten Werkteilen des Libanios.
Die Musterbeispiele seiner Progymnasmata, die oft gekürzte
oder erweiterte Varianten zu ähnlichen Themen bei Libanios
darstellen, können in der bei Libanios so komplizierten Echt-
heitsdebatte mitunter wertvolle Hilfe bieten. Inhaltlich scheinen mir von Bedeutung vor allem seine starke Betonung von
Gesetz und Rechtsstaatlichkeit (besonders etwa am Beispiel der
Behandlung des Ehebrechers in der Gesetzesbeurteilung) und
seine dezidiert pagane Position (etwa in der Beschreibung
des zerstörten alexandrinischen Sarapisheiligtums). Nach dem
Zeugnis der Suda schrieb Aphthonios auch Deklamationen,
die leider verloren sind. Auch hier würde man gerne etwaige
Parallelen zu Libanios untersuchen können. Leider gibt es von
ihm keine erhaltenen Reden, nicht einmal Titel, so dass er für
unser Thema der deliberativen Rede nur indirekt über die delibe-
rativ ausgerichteten Progymnasmata herangezogen werden kann.

Maria Silvana Celentano

GIOVANNI CRISOSTOMO, *SULLE STATUE* 2: OMELIA E/O ORAZIONE POLITICA?

Gli *Entretiens Hardt* 2015 "La rhétorique du pouvoir. Une exploration de l'art oratoire délibératif grec", ideati e coordinati da Mike Edwards, si sono incentrati su molteplici tematiche tutte connesse con teoria e prassi dell'oratoria politica greca dalle origini all'età tardoantica.

In questa ampia ma ben definita cornice la presenza dell'intervento conclusivo degli *Entretiens* potrebbe suscitare una qualche perplessità nel lettore, già a partire dal titolo volutamente ambiguo: "Giovanni Crisostomo, *Sulle statue* 2: omelia e/o orazione politica?".

Insomma sarebbe del tutto naturale che qualcuno si chiedesse se un'omelia (= cioè una conversazione di un pastore con i suoi fedeli o meglio una predicazione con finalità etico-didascalica in occasione di celebrazioni religiose) possa avere il tenore di riflessione politica o possa addirittura sostanziare in sé un'ipotesi, un progetto di realizzazione politica da esaminare, discutere, valutare.

Soprattutto nel caso di Giovanni, denominato Crisostomo per la sua perfetta eloquenza: sacerdote e vescovo molto amato dai suoi fedeli (un po' meno da alcuni potenti, da lui redarguiti più volte pubblicamente, i quali ne decretarono l'esilio e la conseguente prematura morte), e infine santo molto venerato ancora oggi. Quindi non un uomo impegnato attivamente nella vita politica della città, ma un pastore dedito alla cura delle anime. E a questo le sue omelie contribuivano di sicuro.

Ma è anche vero che un sacerdote e soprattutto un vescovo non solo devono condividere pienamente la vita dei fedeli loro affidati, ma, all'occasione, devono anche saper interagire nel contesto civile con sovrani e governanti in nome e per conto di quegli stessi fedeli. E questo è anche un contesto politico. Peraltro Giovanni, da buon cristiano, crede in un disegno provvidenziale che, in momenti storici determinati, attribuisce a singoli uomini quei ruoli e quelle responsabilità pubbliche che vanno esercitati con equità e giustizia. Al buon operato dei governanti deve corrispondere la fiducia e il rispetto da parte di chi è sottoposto a questa o a quella autorità.

Ma, se è vero che tutti i cittadini sono tenuti all'osservanza delle medesime leggi civili, i cristiani hanno tuttavia obblighi maggiori dei non cristiani, dovendo contemperare il rispetto per le autorità terrene e i doveri verso Dio, osservare le leggi e mettere in pratica i dettami religiosi.

C'è da aggiungere che qui si fa riferimento ad una delle omelie *Ad populum Antiochenum de statuis*, che sono storicamente molto rilevanti e che costituiscono nel loro insieme uno degli esempi più significativi dell'eloquenza di Giovanni Crisostomo.[1] Tenute tra il febbraio e la primavera del 387, in coincidenza

---

[1] Sulle eccellenti qualità oratorie di Giovanni Crisostomo la tradizione aneddotica conserva la testimonianza del suo celeberrimo maestro Libanio: essendogli stato chiesto in punto di morte chi avrebbe voluto come suo successore sulla cattedra di retorica, rispose: "Giovanni, se solo i Cristiani non me l'avessero rubato!" (SOZOM. *Hist. eccl.* 8, 2). Per un riesame complessivo e analitico del *corpus* "Sulle statue" rinvio soprattutto a VAN DE PAVERD (1991), che delinea un insieme organico e sistematico di 22 omelie (XXI ss.), nel più ampio quadro delle settimane quaresimali ad Antiochia. Molta attenzione, e da più punti di vista, ha dedicato al *De statuis* A. J. QUIROGA PUERTAS, con interessanti contributi che datano dal 2007. Sulla retorica tardoantica mi limito a rinviare a MURPHY (1974); KENNEDY (1980) e (1983); ma vd. anche CAMERON (2002); CRIBIORE (2007) e (2013). Sulla cosiddetta Terza Sofistica, denominazione ormai consueta per indicare non solo la teorizzazione e produzione retorica dei secc. IV-VI, ma in senso più lato anche tutte le coeve espressioni intellettuali di ambito filosofico, storico, letterario, connotate da continui confronti e spesso felici interferenze tra cultura classica, pagana e cultura cristiana, oltre a PERNOT (1993) spec. 14 e n. 9; (2000) spec. 254 e 271; e (2006) 42, rinvio a SCHAMP (2006); MALOSSE / SCHOULER (2009); QUIROGA PUERTAS (2010).

anche con il tempo di Quaresima, tali omelie sono strettamente collegate alla cosiddetta rivolta delle statue, scoppiata all'indomani di una nuova, gravosa tassazione imperiale.[2] Il sacerdote opera in circostanze eccezionali: immediatamente dopo i violenti disordini, culminati nella mutilazione e l'abbattimento di alcune statue della famiglia imperiale. Il suo compito è anzitutto quello di consolare e incoraggiare i fedeli letteralmente atterriti dagli accadimenti; ma anche quello di ristabilire una relazione virtuosa tra il potere imperiale e la popolazione antiochena, supplendo anche in qualche misura alla contemporanea assenza del vescovo Flaviano, che il 7 marzo parte in ambasceria a Costantinopoli, appunto per ottenere dall'imperatore Teodosio il perdono per Antiochia.

A questo punto credo di avere brevemente indicato elementi sufficienti sulla base dei quali proporre una prospettiva d'indagine mirata a verificare se e quali aspetti di oratoria deliberativa presentino le omelie *Sulle statue*. E soprattutto quali novità comunicative introducano nell'oratoria pubblica. E ancora: la tipologia complessiva di comunicazione instaurata nel *De statuis* può trovare oggi un qualche esito? E quale?

Mi permetto di aggiungere che queste coordinate di analisi, non mi risultano finora esplorate, pur in presenza di una più che nutrita bibliografia su quest'opera, aggiornata anche di recente o di molto recente.

Di particolare interesse appare l'omelia 2, la prima ad essere tenuta dopo la rivolta: pur priva della cronaca dei fatti,[3] ci restituisce nel modo più partecipe e realistico il clima di sbigottimento, terrore, inerzia che di solito caratterizza una situazione individuale o collettiva conseguente ad un trauma e nella

---

[2] Sugli eventi del 387, sulla realtà antiochena tardoantica si vedano, tra gli altri; FESTUGIÈRE (1959); DOWNEY (1961) e (1963); LIEBESCHUETZ (1972); CRACCO RUGGINI (1986) e (1989); HUNTER (1989); CAMERON (1991) e (1995); FRENCH (1998); SANDWELL / HUSKINSON (2001); AMATO / RODUIT / STEINRÜCK (2006); SANDWELL (2007); NIGRO (2009); ZINCONE (2009).

[3] Il primo riferimento 'storico' alla rivolta delle statue si trova nell'omelia 3, tenuta il 7 marzo, giorno della partenza di Flaviano per Costantinopoli.

fattispecie consente di monitorare i differenti livelli comunicativi e argomentativi messi in atto da Giovanni, prima di tutto per stabilire un effettivo contatto verbale con i suoi fedeli subito dopo lo shock della ribellione e delle immediate, gravissime sanzioni attuate dalle autorità; per portarli poi gradualmente a prendere coscienza di quanto è avvenuto, e ad individuare le responsabilità per i fatti accaduti; e infine per delineare un possibile scenario futuro. Il tutto attraverso il consueto cammino catechetico di ammaestramento, coniugando la sapienza biblica con la visione provvidenziale della volontà di Dio, instaurando paralleli e comparazioni con figure sapienziali e profetiche, ma anche con immagini tratte dal mondo naturale (vegetale e animale) soprattutto agricolo, articolando i pensieri in blocchi simmetrici, sottolineando con enfasi e pathos i contenuti etici più importanti.[4]

L'omelia ha una struttura bipartita: ad una prima sezione incentrata sulla situazione critica in cui versa la città, sulla condivisione della paura che ne deriva e sull'appello a Dio per aiuto, conforto e perdono, fa seguito una sezione di poco più ampia, che costituisce il vero e proprio ammaestramento del giorno ispirato a Paolo, *Tim.* 1, 6, 17, in cui si esortano i cristiani a non essere orgogliosi nel tempo presente, a non aspirare al lusso e alla ricchezza improduttiva.

In questa omelia si possono cogliere in tutta evidenza nuove dinamiche comunicative tra nuovi soggetti: il potere centrale, il popolo e la chiesa nelle persone del vescovo o, come in questo caso specifico, del sacerdote che assume il ruolo di intermediario. In particolare si apprezza il costante coinvolgimento emotivo degli ascoltatori, così come l'argomentazione analogica che si realizza in immagini giustapposte a forte impatto patetico e che richiama alcune tecniche del discorso figurato: il sacerdote-oratore, impegnato a mediare tra più interlocutori, riesce ad

---

[4] Propongo in questa sede una versione aggiornata del testo che ho presentato agli *Entretiens Hardt* 2015. Alcune impressioni di lettura dell'omelia *De statuis* 2 erano state anticipate in CELENTANO (2015).

ottenere la fiducia dei fedeli, denunciando l'eccesso delle sanzioni già applicate in città dalle autorità preposte e auspicando l'assenza di più dure e definitive punizioni future per volere imperiale, ma al tempo stesso ribadisce la necessità che gli Antiocheni ammettano la responsabilità del crimine (abbattimento delle statue = lesa maestà), e tornino al rispetto dell'autorità imperiale pienamente legittimata.

La bellezza del dettato di Giovanni Crisostomo sembra restituire pressoché intatti tutti gli elementi della comunicazione orale, del colloquio diretto tra pastore e fedeli: emozioni, ammonimenti, esortazioni, ragionamenti articolati si susseguono, si alternano, si richiamano a distanza; il lessico e le immagini evocano parimenti tradizioni poetiche classiche e scritturali. La limpida scansione delle differenti parti del discorso fa quasi intuire il gesto, il tono della voce, l'intensità dell'espressione del volto che le accompagnavano. O almeno consente di ipotizzarli, applicando i dettami performativi elaborati dalla lunga tradizione retorica classica in cui Crisostomo si è formato alle nuove esigenze della sua catechesi omiletica.[5]

Omelia 2 – Didascalia

Λεχθεῖσα ἐν 'Αντιοχείᾳ ἐν τῇ παλαιᾷ λεγομένῃ ἐκκλησίᾳ, ὄντος αὐτοῦ πρεσβυτέρου, περὶ τῆς συμβάσης συμφορᾶς ἐν τῇ πόλει, ἐπὶ τῇ ἀταξίᾳ τῆς καταστροφῆς τῶν ἀνδριάντων τοῦ Θεοδοσίου τοῦ εὐσεβοῦς βασιλέως τοῦ μεγάλου· καὶ εἰς τὸ ῥητὸν τοῦ 'Αποστόλου, Τοῖς πλουσίοις παράγγελλε ἐν τῷ νῦν αἰῶνι μὴ ὑψηλοφρονεῖν· καὶ κατὰ πλεονεξίας (Paul. *Tim.* 1, 6, 17).[6]

---

[5] Le principali caratteristiche che distinguono un discorso destinato alla declamazione da un discorso destinato alla lettura restano fondamentalmente quelle sintetizzate da Aristotele in *Rhet.* 3, 12, per cui rinvio, tra gli altri, a CELENTANO (2001): la peculiare oralità di destinazione dell'omelia 2 di Giovanni Crisostomo può essere per così dire valorizzata e compresa al meglio proprio sulla scorta delle riflessioni aristoteliche.

[6] "Pronunciata ad Antiochia nella chiesa detta 'antica', quando egli era sacerdote, riguardo alla disgrazia accaduta in città, per il disordine del rovesciamento delle statue di Teodosio, il grande re religioso; e sul detto dell'Apostolo: 'Ai ricchi annuncia di non essere orgogliosi nel tempo presente; e contro l'avarizia'".

348   MARIA SILVANA CELENTANO

La prima parte della didascalia ci informa sinteticamente:
a. del luogo dove l'omelia 2 è stata tenuta (ἐν ᾽Αντιοχείᾳ ἐν τῇ
παλαιᾷ λεγομένῃ ἐκκλησίᾳ, ad Antiochia nella chiesa denomi-
nata "antica"); **b.** del fatto che Giovanni Crisostomo era già
sacerdote (ὄντος αὐτοῦ πρεσβυτέρου: la sua ordinazione risale
al 386 e costituisce quindi un *terminus post quem* per la data-
zione dell'omelia); e soprattutto **c.** delle circostanze eccezionali
in cui ha luogo l'omelia medesima: cioè all'indomani dei disordini in città e della distruzione delle immagini imperiali (περὶ
τῆς συμβάσης συμφορᾶς ἐν τῇ πόλει, ἐπὶ τῇ ἀταξίᾳ τῆς καταστροφῆς τῶν ἀνδριάντων τοῦ Θεοδοσίου τοῦ εὐσεβοῦς βασιλέως τοῦ μεγάλου)[7] e in contemporanea con la severa e indi-
scriminata repressione conseguente agli atti vandalici e criminali
(esecuzioni capitali, torture, prigionia). Infatti la protesta, che
in origine doveva mirare ad ottenere un alleggerimento della
tassa medesima o almeno un rinvio, si è trasformata in una
rivolta, soprattutto ad opera di facinorosi infiltrati tra la folla
dei manifestanti.[8] Il danneggiamento, la distruzione delle statue imperiali peraltro si configura come crimine gravissimo di

---

[7] I drammatici eventi del 387 ci sono noti in dettaglio, e in tutt'altra prospettiva, anche da Libanio (vd. spec. *Or.* 19-23, ma cf. anche *Or.* 1, 252-253),
che aggiunge pure il riferimento specifico ai familiari di Teodosio le cui statue
sono state oltraggiate (*Or.* 20, 10; 22, 8). Ulteriori notizie sulla rivolta si leggono
in SOZOM. *Hist. eccl.* 7, 23 (GCS 50: 336-337); THEODOR. *Hist. eccl.* 5, 20
(GCS 44: 315-317); ZOS. 4, 41 (CSHB 20: 223-224). Sulla nuova tassazione
considerata di importo comunque esorbitante e certamente non alla portata della
media dei cittadini di Antiochia, oltre a Giovanni Crisostomo (*Stat.* 5, 3 e 8, 4),
si vedano ancora Libanio (*Or.* 22, 4), Sozomeno e Teodoreto (*locc. citt.*). Per
quanto concerne le diverse o concorrenti motivazioni di tale nuova tassa cf.
BROWNING (1952) 14; PETIT (1955) 234-245; DEPEYROT (1996) 20-23; KING
(1961) 50-65. Le differenti prospettive comunicative e culturali di Libanio e
Crisostomo in relazione alla rivolta del 387 sono analizzate in QUIROGA PUERTAS
(2008); ma cf. anche FRENCH (1998).
[8] Cf. LIB. *Or.* 19, 28; 20, 3. Sono menzionati stranieri di dubbia fama
cacciati dalle loro città, le *claques* dei teatri tra cui si annidano malintenzionati
ecc. Cf. PETIT (1955) 245; BROTTIER (1993) 627 n. 49; FRENCH (1998) 469 ss.
Sul ruolo crescente delle *claques* vd. BROWNING (1952) 13-20; ma di parere
contrario VAN DE PAVERD (1991) 31-33. A stranieri e avventurieri accenna anche
Giovanni Crisostomo in *Stat.* 3, 1. Peraltro sia Libanio (*Or.* 19, 7, 29; cf. 1, 252),
sia Giovanni Crisostomo (*Stat.* 2, 1) parlano rispettivamente di κακὸς/πονηρὸς

lesa maestà, vista la funzione altamente simbolico-cultuale che le immagini dell'imperatore svolgevano, anche e soprattutto in assenza della sua persona.[9] Ma scorrendo il testo dell'omelia medesima, si può riscontrare fin dalle prime parole come gli eventi drammatici della rivolta non abbiano ancora avuto termine; ma anzi come ci si trovi invece nel vivo della vicenda, cosicché gli scenari più dolorosi e nefasti per Antiochia siano ormai tutti possibili, compreso l'annientamento totale degli abitanti e delle strutture cittadine.

Omelia 2

L'*incipit* drammatico del discorso caratterizzato da frasi secche e antitetiche, che esclude la possibilità che il consueto ammaestramento catechetico possa avere luogo in un momento così grave come quello presente, entra subito nel vivo dell'argomento, senza preamboli inutili e sottolinea che ogni parola a questo punto della situazione in realtà è inopportuna, inefficace: la sofferenza non ha bisogno di parole, semmai di lamenti; di preghiere non di pubblici discorsi; e a volte non ha cura, senza un aiuto potente:

> 2, 1, 33 τί εἴπω καὶ τί λαλήσω; δακρύων ὁ παρὼν καιρός, οὐχὶ ῥημάτων· θρήνων, οὐχὶ λόγων· εὐχῆς, οὐ δημηγορίας· τοιοῦτον τῶν τετολμημένων τὸ μέγεθος, οὕτως ἀνίατον τὸ ἕλκος, οὕτω μέγα τὸ τραῦμα, καὶ πάσης ἰατρείας μεῖζον, καὶ τῆς ἄνωθεν δεόμενον βοηθείας.[10]

δαίμων e di διάβολος come vero responsabile della rivolta, servendosi di singoli uomini per attuare il suo piano.

[9] Del resto il culto delle immagini imperiali sarà abolito solo successivamente da Teodosio II nel 425 (*Cod. Theod.* 15, 4, 1); cf. BROTTIER (1993) 620 e n. 9.

[10] "Che dire? Di che parlare? Quello presente è tempo di lacrime, non di parole; di lamenti, non di discorsi; di preghiera, non di discorsi al popolo; tanta e tale è la gravità di quanto si è osato, così insanabile la piaga, così grande la ferita, resistente ad ogni medicina e bisognosa d'aiuto dall'alto."

La successiva menzione esemplare di Giobbe che sta in silenzio accoccolato nell'immondizia privato di ogni suo affetto, di ogni suo bene – 2, 1, 33 ὁ Ἰὼβ ἅπαντα ἀποβαλών, ἐπὶ τῆς κοπρίας ἐκάθητο (cf. *Iob* 2, 12) –, stabilisce una similarità (Giobbe = Antiochia) che si protrarrà a più riprese nell'omelia e che consente di aggiungere un altro elemento nel discorso: sollievo al dolore può essere la condivisione delle sofferenze con persone amiche. E a Giobbe i suoi amici hanno manifestato il loro condolersi con gesti rituali (lamentazioni ad alta voce, cenere sul capo, vesti stracciate: *ibid.* οἱ φίλοι παρεγένοντο, καὶ ἰδόντες αὐτὸν πόρρωθεν, τὰ ἱμάτια διέρρηξαν, καὶ σποδὸν κατεπάσαντο, καὶ μέγα ἀνῴμωξαν, cf. *Iob* 2, 13). Ma ad Antiochia finora non è toccata nemmeno questa consolazione. Le città nei dintorni non si sono affrettate a mandare loro rappresentanti per condividere dolore con gli Antiocheni (per la repressione in parte già avvenuta) e terrore (per l'ulteriore inasprimento della repressione medesima). E invece sarebbe stato necessario:

ibid. νῦν τοῦτο τὰς πόλεις ἁπάσας τὰς κύκλῳ ποιῆσαι ἐχρῆν, καὶ πρὸς τὴν πόλιν τὴν ἡμετέραν ἐλθεῖν, καὶ θρηνῆσαι τὰ γεγενημένα μετὰ συμπαθείας ἁπάσης.[11]

Giobbe era nell'immondizia e Antiochia ora è presa in trappola:[12] il tutto è opera del diavolo che un tempo ha fatto scempio delle greggi, degli armenti, di tutti i beni di Giobbe il Giusto, e che ora ha causato gesti folli in tutta la città:

ibid. ἐκεῖνος ἐπὶ τῆς κοπρίας ἐκάθητο τότε, αὕτη ἐν μεγάλῃ παγίδι κάθηται νῦν. Καθάπερ γὰρ τότε ὁ διάβολος εἰς τὰ ποίμνια καὶ τὰ βουκόλια, καὶ πᾶσαν ὠρχήσατο τοῦ δικαίου τὴν οὐσίαν· οὕτω νῦν εἰς τὴν πόλιν ἅπασαν ἐβάκχευσεν.[13]

[11] "Adesso c'era bisogno che tutte le città circostanti facessero questo e venissero presso la nostra città e lamentassero i fatti accaduti con piena compartecipazione al dolore".

[12] L'immagine della trappola ritorna poco dopo: Antiochia stessa è vissuta come una trappola dai cittadini che ne vorrebbero fuggire per salvarsi la vita: 2, 1, 35 πάντες ὥσπερ παγίδα φεύγουσιν.

[13] "Quello giaceva nell'immondizia allora, questa giace in una grande trappola ora. Come, infatti, allora il diavolo si accanì contro le greggi e gli armenti e

In ogni caso, pur ammettendo che tutto sia opera nefasta del diavolo – a suo tempo per Giobbe e adesso per Antiochia – resta il fatto che Dio ha permesso che tutto ciò accadesse. Nel caso di Giobbe perché l'eccellenza luminosa di un uomo giusto emergesse chiaramente; nel caso di Antiochia perché la gravità degli eventi e soprattutto le conseguenze immediate degli stessi potesse rendere più consapevoli i cittadini riguardo ai loro comportamenti:

> *ibid.* ἀλλ' ὁ Θεὸς καὶ τότε καὶ νῦν συνεχώρησε τότε μέν, ἵνα τὸν δίκαιον λαμπρότερον ποιήσῃ τῷ μεγέθει τῶν πειρασμῶν, νῦν δέ, ἵνα ἡμᾶς σωφρονεστέρους ἐργάσηται τῇ τῆς θλίψεως ταύτης ὑπερβολῇ.[14]

In buona sostanza è qui espressa una visione provvidenziale degli eventi: Dio non ha fermato la rivolta per far sì che gli Antiocheni si ravvedessero, tornassero ad avere nei governanti la consueta fiducia che li ha sempre contraddistinti.

Dopo questa premessa-proemio generale, Giovanni, preso atto che al pari degli amici di Giobbe anche lui e i suoi fedeli hanno osservato il silenzio rituale per sette giorni dopo i disordini violenti, chiede formalmente di poter parlare, di esternare in pubblico il comune compianto per gli eventi drammatici e luttuosi appena avvenuti:

> 2, 1, 34 δότε μοι θρηνῆσαι τὰ παρόντα. Ἐσιγήσαμεν ἡμέρας ἑπτά, καθάπερ οἱ φίλοι τοῦ Ἰώβ· δότε μοι στόμα διᾶραι σήμερον, καὶ τὴν κοινὴν ταύτην ὀδύρασθαι συμφοράν.[15]

Per riassumere in uno schema quanto fin qui illustrato:

---

contro tutti i beni del giusto, così ora ha dato libero sfogo alla follia in tutta la città." Sulle responsabilità della rivolta che ricadono soprattutto su altri, piuttosto che sui cittadini di Antiochia, cf. *supra* n. 7.

[14] "Ma Dio sia allora sia ora lo ha permesso: allora per rendere più luminoso il giusto attraverso la grandezza delle tentazioni, ora per rendere noi più saggi con l'eccessivo peso di questa oppressione."

[15] "Concedetemi di lamentare i fatti presenti. Siamo stati zitti per sette giorni, come gli amici di Giobbe. Concedetemi di aprire la bocca oggi e di compiangere questa comune disgrazia."

Introduzione diretta e tipicamente orale con duplice domanda ripetuta (2, 1, 33 τί εἴπω καὶ τί λαλήσω;) e con immediato inserimento dei motivi fondanti nella parte proemiale dell'omelia: 1) constatazione dell'orrore presente, disperazione che trova unica salvezza nell'aiuto di Dio; 2) richiamo analogico 'spontaneo' all'esempio di Giobbe, privato di ogni suo bene, di ogni affetto e persino della dignità (giaceva nell'immondizia), e nonostante ciò, nonostante la sofferenza fisica, spirituale ed emotiva, paziente nel sopportare la propria sorte, senza conoscerne le motivazioni, lo stato (se temporaneo o definitivo), affidando tutto se stesso come sempre alla volontà di Dio: unico suo sollievo l'accorrere di amici che lo hanno compatito, compianto e hanno esternato a voce alta e con gesti rituali la loro partecipazione al suo dolore; ad Antiochia invece nessuna delle città vicine è accorsa a esternare ritualmente la compartecipazione al dolore presente; 3) ipotesi sul responsabile delle disgrazie di Giobbe e della presente disgrazia della città (= il diavolo); 4) suggerimento ai fedeli di domandarsi perché si è data una tale analogia tra quanto accaduto un tempo a Giobbe e quanto è appena accaduto ad Antiochia e ai suoi cittadini; 4a) esplicitazione delle ragioni per cui Dio ha permesso che tutto ciò avvenisse in entrambi i casi; 5) cambio di tonalità di dizione e, per così dire, nuovo proemio dell'omelia (2, 1, 34), sempre analogico: al pari degli amici di Giobbe, per sette giorni la comunità dei fedeli e Giovanni hanno osservato il silenzio, ma ora sia concesso a lui di esprimere a nome di tutti e a viva voce il compianto.

Continuiamo a delineare struttura e contenuti dell'omelia:

(2, 1, 34) *Narratio*-prima parte effettiva dell'omelia:

1. nuova premessa iniziale, in forma interrogativa, per riprendere il controllo dell'uditorio: τίς ἡμῖν ἐβάσκηνεν, ἀγαπητοί; τίς ἡμῖν ἐφθόνησε; πόθεν ἡ τοσαύτη γέγονε μεταβολή,[16] e prima

---

[16] "Chi ci guardò con malanimo, carissimi? Chi ci invidiò? Da dove nasce questo stravolgimento?"

affermazione che nulla in precedenza era più splendido della città di Antiochia, e ora nulla appare più degno di pietà: οὐδὲν τῆς πόλεως τῆς ἡμετέρας σεμνότερον ἦν· οὐδὲν γέγονε ἐλεεινότερον νῦν. L'attenzione si focalizza più a fondo sulla città, sul popolo di Antiochia, attraverso una comparazione dal mondo animale: il popolo appare simile a un mite cavallo domestico che improvvisamente si ribella, si sottrae alle mani di chi lo governa, come il popolo si è ribellato al volere dell'imperatore:

> *ibid.* δῆμος εὔτακτος οὕτω καὶ ἥμερος, καὶ καθάπερ ἵππος χειροήθης καὶ τιθασσός, ἀεὶ ταῖς τῶν ἀρχόντων εἴκων χερσίν, ἐξαίφνης τοσοῦτον ἡμῖν ἀπεσκίρτησε νῦν, ὡς τοσαῦτα ἐργάσασθαι κακά, ἃ μηδὲ εἰπεῖν θέμις;[17]

2. dichiarazione che il dolore, il compianto per le condizioni miserevoli in cui giace la città è motivato non tanto dalla minaccia di ritorsioni in qualche misura attese, previste, ma piuttosto dalla gravità eccessiva del folle comportamento dei cittadini di Antiochia:

> *ibid.* ὀδύρομαι καὶ θρηνῶ νῦν, οὐ διὰ τὸ μέγεθος τῆς προσδοκωμένης ἀπειλῆς, ἀλλὰ διὰ τὴν ὑπερβολὴν τῆς γεγενημένης μανίας.[18]

Infatti anche se l'imperatore non fosse adirato, fortemente in collera, né decretasse punizioni e vendetta, in Antiochia non potrebbe esserci nemmeno la coscienza della follia perpetrata.

E' questo il primo passo perché il sacerdote possa guidare i suoi fedeli a rivivere le azioni compiute da alcuni (l'abbattimento delle statue imperiali), a prenderne coscienza nel momento in cui stanno vivendo la terribile repressione della rivolta e l'applicazione sbrigativa della giustizia sommaria.

Ha inizio insomma una sorta di pratica comunicativa e psicologica del superamento dello stato di shock conseguente ad

---

[17] "Il popolo così ben ordinato e mite, e come un cavallo addomesticato e mansueto, che cede sempre alle mani dei governanti, all'improvviso ora ha recalcitrato contro di noi, tanto da compiere mali di tale gravità che neppure è lecito dire."
[18] "Piango e mi lamento ora, non per la gravità della minaccia attesa, ma per l'eccesso della follia avvenuta."

un forte trauma, a cui deve accompagnarsi l'assunzione di responsabilità individuali nella rivolta da parte dei singoli; e da parte di tutta la cittadinanza, di tutta la comunità l'accettazione del fatto che l'inerzia, il non essere intervenuti a fermare chi distruggeva con violenza, non esclude dalla compartecipazione alla colpa, anzi si configura come correità.

Si comincia quindi a intravvedere nell'omelia il profilo del cosiddetto discorso di consenso condiviso – come è talora denominato oggi – nel quale l'oratore non è esterno all'assemblea a cui si rivolge: ne è parte integrante. D'altra parte l'omelia, come indica il nome stesso, è una conversazione, insomma un discorso informale o poco formale, un tipo di predicazione in cui la semplicità delle forme espressive sostanzia l'approfondita e pragmatica riflessione, condivisa tra sacerdote e fedeli, di tipo morale, etico e politico-sociale: insomma su temi e problemi di vita quotidiana, individuale e associata, e sulle possibili scelte che possono essere esercitate in merito. L'ammaestramento dei fedeli (quotidiano o limitato ai giorni festivi) non si fonda sull'autorevolezza del sacerdote che da sola garantirebbe la bontà dell'ammaestramento medesimo, ma piuttosto sulla funzione del sacerdote-pastore quale guida esperta e coinvolgente per recepire ed applicare la parola di Dio.

Dopo questo primo accenno nel merito delle conseguenze della rivolta – un'azione inammissibile di lesa maestà che equivale a una vera e propria sfida all'imperatore a sanzionare il misfatto con i primi durisimi provvedimenti punitivi – è tratteggiata una collettiva presa di coscienza dell'atto criminoso compiuto, pure se inconsulto, accompagnata da un vivo sentimento di vergogna: ma le condizioni miserevoli della città sono sotto gli occhi di tutti e il naturale sfogo doloroso che nasce da questa desolazione rende pressoché impossibile procedere come di consueto all'ammaestramento catechetico. In una drammatica, enfatica immagine, Giovanni Crisostomo descrive con precisione la fisiopatologia tipica del blocco emotivo-psicologico di cui è vittima: rappresenta se stesso mentre riesce a stento ad aprire bocca e labbra, a muovere la lingua, ad emettere parole.

Anzi lo scoraggiamento quasi lo paralizza, gli fa inghiottire la lingua, trattenere le parole:

ibid. διακόπτεταί μοι τῆς διδασκαλίας ὁ λόγος τῷ θρήνῳ· μόλις ἰσχύω διᾶραι στόμα, καὶ ἀνοῖξαι χείλη, καὶ κινῆσαι γλῶτταν, καὶ ῥήματα προέσθαι· οὕτω καθάπερ χαλινὸς ὁ τῆς ἀθυμίας ὄγκος ἀποστρέφει μου τὴν γλῶτταν, καὶ τῶν ῥημάτων ἐπιλαμβάνεται.[19]

A questo punto si rinnova il rimpianto e il dolore per lo stato felice della città nel passato e per l'infelicità del presente: "niente prima era più felice della nostra città, niente ora è diventato più triste" (2, 1, 34-35 οὐδὲν τῆς πόλεως τῆς ἡμετέρας πρότερον μακαριώτερον ἦν, οὐδὲν ἀτερπέστερον γέγονε νῦν).

E altre immagini, altre comparazioni analogiche concorrono ad enfatizzare il lamento doloroso del presente di Antiochia e l'elogio del suo felice passato:[20]

2, 1, 35 καθάπερ μέλιτται κηρίον βομβοῦσαι, οὕτω τὴν ἀγορὰν περιίπταντο καθ' ἑκάστην ἡμέραν οἱ τὴν πόλιν οἰκοῦντες, καὶ πάντες ἡμᾶς ἐπὶ τῷ πλήθει τούτῳ πρότερον ἐμακάριζον. Ἀλλ' ἰδοὺ νῦν τὸ κηρίον τοῦτο γέγονεν ἔρημον· καθάπερ γὰρ τὰς μελίττας ἐκείνας καπνός, οὕτω τὰς μελίττας ταύτας φόβος ἀπήλασε.[21]

[19] "Il discorso di ammaestramento è interrotto dal lamento; a stento riesco ad aprire la bocca, a schiudere le labbra, e a muovere la lingua, emettere parole; così, come un morso il peso dello scoraggiamento mi fa tornare indietro la lingua, trattiene le parole."
[20] Sulle *laudes urbium* tardoantiche, con dettagliato riferimento all'*Antiochikos* di Libanio (= *Or.* 11) e ai tradizionali *topoi* epidittici da lui impiegati, vd. la messa a punto di PELLIZZARI (2011) e l'ulteriore bibliografia ivi citata. Una interessante disamina dell'Antiochia elogiata da Libanio – città ideale da ogni punto di vista – anche in correlazione con le vicende storiche più significative che dall'età ellenistica alla tarda anitichità hanno variamente trasformato la realtà di Antiochia medesima, si legge in FRANCESIO (2004). Sulla lettura 'retorica' della topografia di Antiochia da parte di Libanio e Giovanni Crisostomo, in cui l'intreccio di parole e immagini trasforma il paesaggio urbano e aiuta a sostenere ora la prospettiva pagana degli spazi pubblici ora quella cristiana, vd. QUIROGA PUERTAS (2015).
[21] "Come le api che ronzano intorno al favo, così quelli che abitavano la città si aggiravano intorno alla piazza ogni giorno, e tutti prima ci dicevano felici per questa moltitudine. Ma ecco ora questo favo è diventato deserto; come il fumo allontanò quelle api, così la paura allontanò queste api."

La contrapposizione tra passato felice e presente miserevole si amplia di fatto in una nuova similitudine di più consistente struttura e articolazione, tratta ancora dal mondo animale, dopo quella del popolo antiocheno accostato all'immagine di un cavallo mansueto che si ribella inopinatamente (vd. *supra* p. 353): come le api abitualmente si aggirano ronzando intorno al favo, la gente numerosa che si trovava in città si aggirava per la piazza ogni giorno, e tutti prima apprezzavano questa moltitudine di persone.

L'immagine ricorda in qualche modo la comparazione proemiale (2, 1, 33) tra gli amici di Giobbe (vicini al Giusto) e gli abitanti delle città circostanti Antiochia (indifferenti al destino degli Antiocheni), ma vi è aggiunto un elemento metaforico in più: oltre ai cittadini, assimilati alle api, anche la città ha ora una sua immagine propria: il favo.

Ulteriore amplificazione dell'immagine della città in passato privilegiata e nel presente degna d'oblio, del lamento più specificamente in linea con i procedimenti catechetici cristiani è l'accostamento del compianto di Antiochia con le *Lamentazioni* su Gerusalemme:[22]

2, 1, 35 μᾶλλον δὲ καὶ ὃ περὶ τῆς Ἱερουσαλὴμ θρηνῶν ὁ προφήτης ἔλεγε, τοῦτο καὶ ἡμεῖς εἰς καιρὸν ἐροῦμεν νῦν· Ἐγενήθη ἡμῖν ἡ πόλις, ὡς τερέβινθος ἀποβεβληκυῖα τὰ φύλλα, καὶ ὡς παράδεισος ὕδωρ μὴ ἔχων (*Is.* 1, 30). Καθάπερ γὰρ παράδεισος τῆς ἀρδείας ἐπιλιπούσης, ἔρημα τῶν φύλλων καὶ γυμνὰ τῶν καρπῶν τὰ δένδρα δείκνυσιν, οὕτω δὴ καὶ ἡ πόλις ἡμῶν γέγονε νῦν· τῆς γὰρ ἄνωθεν βοηθείας ἐγκαταλιπούσης αὐτήν, ἔστηκεν ἔρημος, γυμνὴ τῶν οἰκητόρων γενομένη σχεδὸν ἁπάντων. **Οὐδὲν πατρίδος γλυκύτερον, ἀλλ' οὐδὲν πικρότερον νῦν γέγονε·** πάντες τὴν ἐνεγκοῦσαν ὥσπερ παγίδα φεύγουσιν, ὥσπερ βάραθρον ἐγκαταλιμπάνουσιν, ὥσπερ πυρᾶς ἀποπηδῶσι· καὶ καθάπερ οἰκίας ἁπτομένης οὐχ οἱ τὴν οἰκίαν οἰκοῦντες μόνον, ἀλλὰ καὶ πάντες οἱ πλησίον μετὰ πολλῆς ἀποπηδῶσι τῆς σπουδῆς, γυμνὸν τὸ σῶμα διασῶσαι σπουδάζοντες οὕτω δὴ καὶ νῦν τῆς βασιλικῆς ὀργῆς καθάπερ πυρᾶς τινος ἄνωθεν ἥξειν προσδοκωμένης, πρὶν ἐπ' αὐτοὺς ὁδῷ βαδίζον ἔλθῃ τὸ πῦρ, ἕκαστος ἐπείγεται προεξελθεῖν, καὶ γυμνὸν διασῶσαι τὸ σῶμα.[23]

---

[22] Su questo aspetto vd. BROTTIER (1993) 621 e nn. 11-13.

[23] "Ancor di più ciò che il profeta diceva lamentando Gerusalemme, e questo anche noi ora diremo per l'occasione: *La città è diventata per noi come un terebinto*

Si notino le frasi ricorrenti a scandire singole porzioni di testo ("niente prima era più felice della nostra città, niente ora è diventato più triste"; "nulla era più dolce della patria, nulla è diventato ora più amaro"), a correlarle in sequenza tra loro, quasi un adattamento, un parallelo della distribuzione strofica in composizioni poetiche o delle ricorrenze formulari epiche nel mondo greco, o anche dell'andamento ritmico della narrazione biblica. Una notazione particolare merita l'esame del variato lessico che sottolinea l'ansia, l'angoscia, il timore, la sofferenza ecc., anche in relazione alle *Lamentazioni* su Gerusalemme.[24]

Il forte contrasto tra il presente malinconico, fonte di inerzia e scoraggiamento, e lo stato di invidiabile libertà in cui fino a pochi giorni prima versava Antiochia è sottolineato anche nella sezione successiva dell'omelia – di nuovo attraverso comparazioni analogiche e antitetiche – e culmina nell'immagine degli Antiocheni del tutto annichiliti: anche il loro sguardo non è più limpido; non riesce più a vedere uno spiraglio di luce:

2, 2, 36 τῶν ἡμετέρων ὀφθαλμῶν τῷ τεθολῶσθαι τῆς ἀθυμίας τῷ νέφει, μὴ δυναμένων καθαρῷ μηδὲ μετὰ τῆς αὐτῆς διαθέσεως τὸ παρὰ τῶν ἀκτίνων δέχεσθαι φῶς.[25]

In particolare l'immagine della nube dello scoraggiamento è funzionale a richiamare alla memoria un passo dal *Libro di Amos* e di offrirne il relativo commento esplicativo attualizzante:

che ha perso le foglie, come un giardino senza acqua. Come il giardino, quando è mancata l'irrigazione, mostra gli alberi privi di foglie e spogli di frutti, così è diventata ora anche *la nostra città;* infatti, *dopo che anche l'aiuto dall'alto l'ha abbandonata, è rimasta deserta, quasi spoglia di tutti gli abitanti.* Nulla era più dolce della patria, nulla è diventato ora più amaro; tutti fuggono lei che la tiene come in trappola, la abbandonano come un baratro, sfuggono come dal fuoco; e come quando la casa si incendia, non solo quelli che la abitano, ma anche tutti i vicini fuggono a precipizio, affrettandosi a salvare il nudo corpo, così appunto anche ora, quando è atteso che l'ira del re venga dall'alto come un incendio prima che il fuoco procedendo verso di loro li raggiunga, ciascuno si affretta ad uscire e a salvare il nudo corpo."

[24] Cf. BROTTIER (1993) 629 ss. e note.

[25] "Poiché i nostri occhi sono stati intorbiditi dalla nube dello scoraggiamento, non potendo con chiarezza e con la stessa disposizione di prima ricevere la luce che viene dai raggi del sole."

ibid. τοῦτό ἐστιν ὃ πάλαι ὁ προφήτης ἐθρήνει λέγων· *Δύσεται αὐτοῖς ὁ ἥλιος μεσημβρίας, καὶ συσκοτάσει ἡ ἡμέρα (Am.* 8, 9).
Τοῦτο δὲ ἔλεγεν, οὐχ ὡς τοῦ ἄστρου κρυπτομένου, οὐδὲ ὡς τῆς ἡμέρας ἀφανιζομένης, ἀλλ᾽ ὡς τῶν ἀθυμούντων οὐδὲ ἐν μεσημ-βρίᾳ δυναμένων ὁρᾶν τὸ φῶς διὰ τὸν ἀπὸ τῆς ὀδύνης ζόφον· ὃ δὴ καὶ νῦν γέγονε· καὶ ὅπουπερ ἂν ἴδῃ τις, κἂν εἰς τὸ ἔδαφος, κἂν εἰς τοὺς τοίχους, κἂν εἰς τοὺς κίονας τῆς πόλεως, κἂν εἰς τοὺς πλησίον, νύκτα ὁρᾶν δοκεῖ καὶ ζόφον βαθύν· οὕτω πάντα πολλῆς γέμει τῆς κατηφείας.[26]

Data la situazione non resta che il compianto, il lamento rituale sulla disgrazia avvenuta, anche facendo ricorso di nuovo ad un riferimento analogico biblico:

ibid. εὔκαιρον νῦν εἰπεῖν· *Ἀποστείλατε πρὸς τὰς θρηνούσας, καὶ ἐλθέτωσαν, καὶ πρὸς τὰς σοφάς, καὶ φθεγξάσθωσαν (Ier.* 8, 9, 17). Ῥεέτωσαν οἱ ὀφθαλμοὶ ὑμῶν ὕδωρ, καὶ τὰ βλέφαρα ὑμῶν καταγέτω δάκρυα· οἱ βουνοί, λάβετε κοπετόν, καὶ τὰ ὄρη, θρῆνον. Καλέσωμεν τὴν κτίσιν ἅπασαν εἰς συμπάθειαν τῶν ἡμετέρων κακῶν, οἱ βουνοί, λάβετε κοπετόν, καὶ τὰ ὄρη, θρῆνον. Καλέσω-μεν τὴν κτίσιν ἅπασαν εἰς συμπάθειαν τῶν ἡμετέρων κακῶν.[27]

Alla citazione di Geremia segue una considerazione pragmatica e politica, per così dire, per scongiurare il declassamento di Antiochia, la perdita dello *status* metropolitano. L'offesa gravis-sima arrecata a Teodosio, al più potente degli uomini sulla terra, può essere sanata solo implorando l'aiuto di Dio, del Re che è al di sopra di tutto e di tutti e senza la cui benevolenza non esiste perdono per alcuno:

[26] "Questo è ciò che lamentava il profeta (*scil.* Amos) dicendo: *tramonterà per quelli il sole di mezzogiorno e il giorno diventerà scuro*. Questo diceva, non perché l'astro si copriva, né perché il giorno scompariva, ma perché quelli che erano scoraggiati non potevano vedere la luce neppure a mezzogiorno a causa dell'oscu-rità del dolore; e ciò accade anche ora. E ovunque uno guardi, o verso il suolo, o verso le mura, o verso le colonne della città, verso i vicini, gli sembra di vedere sempre la notte e una profonda oscurità; così tutto è pieno di molta tristezza."
[27] "Ora è opportuno dire: 'convocate le donne che intonano lamenti e ven-gano, e quelle più esperte ed emettano alti lamenti. I vostri occhi facciano scorrere il pianto e le vostre palpebre facciano scendere le lacrime. Colli, fate lutto! e mon-tagne, fate lamenti! Chiamiamo tutto il creato a partecipare alle nostre disgrazie'."

ibid. πόλις οὕτω μεγάλη καὶ τῶν ὑπὸ τὴν ἕω κειμένων ἡ κεφαλή, ἐκ μέσης ἀναρπασθῆναι κινδυνεύει τῆς οἰκουμένης· νῦν ἡ πολύπαις ἄπαις ἐξαίφνης γεγένηται, καὶ ὁ βοηθήσων οὐδείς. Οὐ γάρ ἐστιν ὁ ὑβρισθεὶς ὁμότιμόν τινα ἔχων ἐπὶ τῆς γῆς· βασιλεὺς γάρ ἐστι κορυφὴ καὶ κεφαλὴ τῶν ἐπὶ τῆς γῆς ἀνθρώπων ἁπάντων. Διὰ τοῦτο δὴ πρὸς τὸν ἄνω καταφεύγωμεν βασιλέα· ἐκεῖνον καλέσωμεν εἰς βοήθειαν· εἰ μὴ τῆς ἄνωθεν ἀπολαύσοιμεν εὐνοίας, οὐδεμία λείπεται τοῖς γεγενημένοις παραμυθία.[28]

Dopo queste considerazioni Giovanni afferma che avrebbe voluto smettere di parlare perché coloro che hanno l'animo oppresso dal dolore non sono capaci né di proporre né di ascoltare discorsi ampi, estesi.

E come all'inizio dell'omelia ha ben descritto tutta la fisiopatologia della sofferenza che si manifesta il lui e che gli blocca la fonazione, gli impedisce di articolare suoni, emettere parole,[29] così ora aggiunge che, come in natura accade che una nuvola possa nascondere i raggi del sole e impedirne la vista e la percezione del loro calore, così su di lui e su chi lo ascolta grava una densa nube di scoraggiamento che impedisce l'instaurarsi di qualunque comunicazione: persiste il blocco emotivo che fa concentrare tutta l'attenzione su ciò che è fonte di dolore e potrà esserlo ancora di più, piuttosto che dire o ascoltare qualcosa che dia speranza e sollievo:

2, 3, 36-37 ἐβουλόμην ἐνταῦθα καταλῦσαι τὸν λόγον· οὐ γὰρ ἐθέλουσι τῶν ὀδυνωμένων αἱ ψυχαὶ μακροὺς ἀποτείνειν λόγους· ἀλλ' ὥσπερ νεφέλη τις πυκνὴ γενομένη, καὶ τὴν ἡλιακὴν ἀκτῖνα ὑπεκδραμοῦσα, ἀποστρέφει τὴν αὐγὴν πᾶσαν εἰς τοὐπίσω· οὕτω

---

[28] "Una città così grande e capitale dell'Oriente, rischia di essere tolta dal centro del mondo; ora la ricca di figli è diventata all'improvviso priva di figli e non c'è nessuno che la aiuterà. Non c'è alcun offeso che abbia la stessa pari dignità; il re infatti è il culmine e il primo tra tutti gli uomini della terra. Per questo ci rivolgiamo al re che sta in alto; chiamiamo quello in aiuto; se non guadagneremo la benevolenza dall'alto, non rimane nessun perdono per i fatti commessi." Antiochia è appunto la μητρόπολις, la città-madre d'Oriente che, in conseguenza della rivolta del 387, sarà privata di questo titolo prestigioso e dell'eccellenza politica, economica, culturale che esso comportava. Il titolo e il prestigio saranno attribuiti a Laodicea: vd. CRACCO RUGGINI (1986) 274.

[29] Cf. *supra* p. 355 e n.19 *ad* 2, 1, 34.

δὴ καὶ ἀθυμίας νέφος, ἐπειδὰν στῇ πρὸ τῆς ψυχῆς τῆς ἡμετέρας, οὐκ ἀφίησιν εὔκολον γενέσθαι τὴν τοῦ λόγου διάβασιν, ἀλλ᾿ ἀποπνίγει καὶ συνέχει μετὰ πολλῆς τῆς ἀνάγκης ἔνδον αὐτόν. Καὶ τοῦτο οὐκ ἐπὶ τῶν λεγόντων, ἀλλὰ καὶ ἐπὶ τῶν ἀκουόντων γίνεται. Ὥσπερ γὰρ ἀπὸ τῆς τοῦ λέγοντος ψυχῆς οὐκ ἀφίησιν αὐτὸν ἐκπηδῆσαι μετ᾿ εὐκολίας, οὕτως οὐδὲ εἰς τὴν τῶν ἀκουόντων διάνοιαν ἐμπεσεῖν συγχωρεῖ μετὰ τῆς οἰκείας δυνάμεως.[30]

Subito dopo, però nasce spontaneo il collegamento analogico con lo stato di prostrazione un tempo provato dagli Ebrei, schiavi in Egitto, che impediva loro di dare ascolto a Mosè che parlava della futura salvezza (*Ex.* 6, 9). Il richiamo biblico, unito all'osservazione che anche in natura le condizioni atmosferiche sono repentinamente mutevoli e il sole può tornare presto a splendere, consente opportunamente a Giovanni di recedere dal proposito di considerare finito il discorso. Anzi gli fa trovare più forza nell'esortare i fedeli a dargli ascolto ancora una volta, a nutrire speranza, ad affidarsi a Dio e ad essere consapevoli del fatto che il cristiano, rispetto ad altri, ha una salvaguardia in più, ha maggiore probabilità di salvezza proprio in virtù della sua fede e della benevolenza di Dio nei suoi confronti:

2, 3, 37 ἠβουλόμην μὲν οὖν καὶ αὐτὸς ἐνταῦθα καταλῦσαι τὰ εἰρημένα· ἀλλ᾿ ἐννοήσας ὅτι οὐκ ἀντιφράττει μόνον νεφέλης φύσις τὴν εἰς τὸ πρόσω φορὰν τῆς ἀκτῖνος, ἀλλὰ καὶ τοὐναντίον αὐτὴ πάσχει πολλάκις· ἐπειδὰν γὰρ ὁ ἥλιος θερμότερος προσπεσὼν διηνεκῶς τρίβῃ τὸ νέφος, μέσον τε αὐτὸ διέρρηξε πολλάκις, καὶ ἀθρόον ἐκλάμψας φαιδρὸς ταῖς τῶν ὁρώντων προσέπεσεν ὄψεσι· τοῦτο καὶ αὐτὸς προσδοκῶ ποιήσειν σήμερον, καὶ τοῦ λόγου συνεχῶς ὁμιλοῦντος ὑμῶν ταῖς ψυχαῖς, καὶ ἐπὶ πλεῖον ἐνδιατρίβοντος, ῥαγήσεσθαι ἐλπίζω τῆς ἀθυμίας τὸ νέφος, καὶ καταλάμψειν

---

[30] "Avrei voluto finire questo discorso: le anime di coloro che sono afflitti non desiderano stendere grandi discorsi; ma come una nuvola che è diventata fitta e corre sotto il raggio del sole, volge indietro tutto lo splendore, così la nebbia dello scoraggiamento, dopo che si è collocata davanti alla nostra anima, non lascia che il passaggio del discorso sia agevole, ma lo soffoca e lo trattiene dentro con molta forza. E questo accade non solo a chi parla, ma anche a chi ascolta. Come infatti non permette che quello balzi fuori dall'anima di chi parla con agilità, così non consente che penetri nella mente di chi ascolta con l'efficacia che gli è propria."

ὑμῶν τὴν διάνοιαν τῇ εἰωθυίᾳ πάλιν διδασκαλίᾳ. Ἀλλ' ἐπίδοτέ μοι τὴν ψυχὴν τὴν ὑμετέραν, ἐπίδοτέ μοι τὴν ἀκοὴν μικρόν· ἀπο-τινάξασθε τὴν ἀθυμίαν· ἐπὶ τὸ πρότερον ἔθος ἐπανέλθωμεν, καὶ ὥσπερ εἰώθαμεν ἀεὶ μετ' εὐθυμίας ἐνταῦθα παραγίνεσθαι, οὕτω καὶ νῦν ποιῶμεν, τὸ πᾶν ἐπὶ τὸν Θεὸν ῥίψαντες. Τοῦτο καὶ πρὸς αὐτὴν ἡμῖν τῆς συμφορᾶς συμβαλεῖται τὴν λύσιν.[31]

A questo punto dalla folla dei fedeli deve essere scoppiato in modo spontaneo e liberatorio un applauso di ammirazione e parimenti di gratitudine, fenomeno comune sia in spazi citta-dini destinati a discorsi pubblici, spettacoli teatrali e assimilati, sia nelle chiese. Giovanni rimprovera i fedeli e li richiama appunto al rispetto per il luogo in cui si trovano e per la finalità per cui sono riuniti.[32] E cerca anche di spiegare che l'elogio,

[31] "Avrei dunque voluto anch'io finire qui il discorso; però sapendo che la natura della nebbia non solo ostacola il passaggio del raggio, ma spesso subisce anch'essa il contrario: quando, infatti, il sole più caldo sopraggiunto consuma continuamente la nebbia, spesso la squarcia nel mezzo e mandando bagliori insieme incontra splendente lo sguardo di chi vede; io stesso ho speranza di fare questo oggi e mentre il discorso penetra senza sosta nelle vostre anime e di più vi indugia, spero che si spezzerà la nebbia dello scoraggiamento e che la vostra mente risplenderà di nuovo grazie al consueto insegnamento. Ma prestatemi attenzione, datemi un po' d'ascolto; scrollate di dosso lo scoraggiamento; tor-niamo alle abitudini di prima e come eravamo soliti venire qui sempre di buon animo, così facciamo anche ora, affidando tutto (il dolore) a Dio. Ciò contri-buirà per noi alla liberazione stessa dalla disgrazia."

[32] Sull'influenza negativa della diffusa spettacolarizzazione di ogni tipo e occasione di discorso in età tardoantica, del diffondersi di sperimentazioni per-formative adatte ai nuovi gusti delle classi colte, con conseguente progressiva perdita delle competenze di ricezione/ascolto da parte del pubblico comune, esi-stono molte testimonianze, a cominciare dallo stesso Crisostomo che anche in altre omelie denuncia appunto questa propensione del pubblico per il chiacchie-riccio da teatro o da circo anche in circostanze inappropriate come appunto la catechesi. Ma anche alcuni vescovi sembravano indulgere a ottimizzare più lo stile e la declamazione che non i contenuti dei loro discorsi (cf. GREG. NAZ. *Or.* 2, 47). AMBROGIO (*Off.* 1, 18, 72-73; 19, 84) e GEROLAMO (*Ep.* 22) parlano di un nuovo tipo umano che pervadeva gli ambienti filosofici e religiosi: l'*aner thea-trikos*. Insomma un uso inopportuno delle risorse retoriche, non più strettamente determinate e armonizzate in base ai contenuti da proporre, ma utilizzate per stupire in mille modi il pubblico, confondere l'avversario in un dibattito ecc. Su questa realtà tardoantica rinvio soprattutto a PETIT (1955) 126-136; FESTUGIÈRE (1959) 113; e più di recente a CRIBIORE (2007) 229 e QUIROGA PUERTAS (2013b) VIII; (2013c); (2015).

l'apprezzamento vero del sacerdote si realizza qualora i fedeli dimostrino con i fatti che hanno recepito quanto è stato loro indicato per la pratica quotidiana, per il miglioramento di sé, per l'adempimento vero dei precetti cristiani. E nel caso presente, se non si sforzeranno di correggersi l'un l'altro, il crimine commesso da uno solo porterà un danno comune e non tollerabile per la città intera:

2, 4, 38 οὐκ ἔστι θέατρον ἡ ἐκκλησία, ἵνα πρὸς τέρψιν ἀκούωμεν· ὠφεληθέντας ἐντεῦθεν ἀπιέναι χρή, κερδάναντάς τι πλέον καὶ μέγα, οὕτως ἀναχωρεῖν δεῖ· ἐπεὶ μάτην καὶ εἰκῇ παραγινόμεθα, εἰ πρὸς καιρὸν ψυχαγωγηθέντες οὕτως ἀναχωροίημεν, ἔρημοι καὶ κενοὶ τῆς ἀπὸ τῶν λεγομένων ὠφελείας γενόμενοι. Τί μοι τῶν κρότων ὄφελος τούτων; τί δὲ τῶν ἐπαίνων καὶ τῶν θορύβων; Ἔπαινος ἐμὸς τὸ διὰ τῶν ἔργων ὑμᾶς ἐπιδεῖξαι τὰ λεγόμενα ἅπαντα· τότε ἐγὼ ζηλωτὸς καὶ μακάριος, οὐχ ὅταν ἀποδέχησθε, ἀλλ᾽ ὅταν ποιῆτε μετὰ προθυμίας ἁπάσης, ἅπερ ἂν ἀκούσητε παρ᾽ ἡμῶν. Ἕκαστος τὸν πλησίον διορθούσθω· Οἰκοδομεῖτε γὰρ εἰς τὸν ἕνα, φησίν (Paul. Thess. 1, 5, 11)· ἂν γὰρ μὴ τοῦτο ποιῶμεν, ἡ παρ᾽ ἑκάστου γινομένη πλημμέλεια κοινήν τινα καὶ ἀφόρητον οἴσει τὴν βλάβην τῇ πόλει.[33]

---

[33] "La chiesa non è un teatro, dove ascoltare per diletto; bisogna uscire da qui edificati, avendo tratto un guadagno più grande e più consistente: così bisogna andare via; quando veniamo invano e per caso, se andiamo via attratti solo per un breve momento, siamo privi e carenti dell'utilità di ciò che è stato detto. Qual è l'utilità per me di questi applausi? Qual è l'utilità di queste lodi e di questi strepiti? La mia lode è che voi dimostriate con i fatti tutte le cose dette. Allora io sarò beato e felice, non qualora voi accettiate, ma qualora mettiate in pratica con grande ardore ciò che avete ascoltato da noi. 'Ciascuno corregga il vicino: edificatevi l'un l'altro', dice (S. Paolo); se infatti non facciamo questo, il delitto commesso da ciascuno porterà un danno comune e insopportabile alla città." Sull'apprezzamento, per così dire a scena aperta, del sacerdote-oratore e su altri aspetti delle dinamiche comunicative che si instaurano con il pubblico vd. STUIBER (1954) e RONCORONI (1980). Cf. anche WALLACE (1997) 99 n. 6 e 158 (ad n. 6). Su alcune strategie oratorie di Giovanni e sugli ambiti in cui la sua predicazione si realizza, vd. MAYER (1997) e (1998); BROTTIER (2004); MAXWELL (2006) 51-54. Sulla topica antinomia tra lo spazio assembleare della chiesa e del teatro in Giovanni Crisostomo (cf. e.g. Act. hom. 10, 4 PG 60, 90; Ioan. hom. 1, 4 PG 59, 28) vd. LUGARESI (2008) 780 ss., a cui rinvio, più in generale, per un dettagliato inquadramento dei complessi e conflittuali rapporti tra Chiesa e teatro nel sec. IV: la persistente ostilità e conseguente condanna ecclesiatica di tutti gli spettacoli ludici non impediva che vi accorressero – e in gran numero naturalmente! – anche i cristiani.

E poi ricorda loro che, pur non avendo compiuto atti malvagi,
essi provano il timore di chi ha osato farlo e temono comunque
che la collera dell'imperatore raggiunga tutti; e nessuna difesa è
sufficiente: non basta dire che non si era presenti, che non si
sono condivisi i crimini.

Semmai è probabile che si subisca una pena anche maggiore
dei colpevoli perché ci si è tenuti distanti dai luoghi della
rivolta, non si è cercato di impedirla, non si è cercato di trattenere i facinorosi, non si è corso alcun rischio a difesa dell'onore
del re. Non è un merito non aver partecipato ai fatti; è un
demerito non averne fermato lo svolgimento e dunque si sarà
accusati per questo:

ibid. ἰδού, μηδὲν συνειδότες τοῖς γεγενημένοις τῶν τετολμη-
κότων οὐκ ἔλαττον δεδοίκαμεν, καὶ φρίττομεν, μὴ πάντας ὁ τοῦ
βασιλέως θυμὸς καταλάβῃ· καὶ οὐκ ἀρκεῖ εἰς ἀπολογίαν ἡμῖν τὸ
λέγειν· Οὐ παρήμην, οὐ συνῄδειν, οὐκ ἐκοινώνησα τῶν γεγενη-
μένων. Δι' αὐτὸ μὲν οὖν τοῦτο κολάζου, φησί, καὶ δίδου δίκην
τὴν ἐσχάτην, ὅτι μὴ παρῆς, μηδὲ ἐκώλυες, μηδὲ τοὺς ἀκοσμοῦντας κατεῖχες, μηδὲ ἐκινδύνευες ὑπὲρ τῆς εἰς τὸν βασιλέα τιμῆς.
Οὐ μετέσχες τῶν τετολμημένων; ἐπαινῶ τοῦτο καὶ ἀποδέχομαι·
ἀλλ' οὐδὲ ἐπέσχες τὰ γινόμενα· τοῦτο κατηγορίας ἄξιον.[34]

A conforto di questa argomentazione giurisprudenziale, se ne
aggiunge un'altra derivata dai *Vangeli* (*Mt.* 25, 24):

2, 4, 38-39 ταῦτα καὶ παρὰ τοῦ Θεοῦ τὰ ῥήματα ἀκουσόμεθα,
ὅταν σιγῇ φέρωμεν τὰς εἰς αὐτὸν ὕβρεις καὶ παροινίας γενομέ-
νας· ἐπεὶ καὶ ὁ τὸ τάλαντον ἐκεῖνο καταχώσας οὐχ ὑπὲρ τῶν
καθ' ἑαυτὸν ἐνεκαλεῖτο τότε (ὁλόκληρον γὰρ τὴν παρακατα-
θήκην ἀπέδωκεν), ἀλλ' ὅτι αὐτὴν οὐκ ἐπλεόνασεν, ὅτι ἑτέρους
οὐκ ἐπαίδευσεν, ὅτι τὸ ἀργύριον τοῖς τραπεζίταις οὐ κατέβαλε,
τουτέστιν, οὐ παρήνεσεν, οὐ συνεβούλευσεν, οὐκ ἐπετίμησεν, οὐ

---

[34] "Ecco, pur non essendo a conoscenza dei fatti temiamo non meno di
coloro che hanno osato compierli, e abbiamo il terrore che la collera del re col-
pisca tutti; e non giova a noi dire a nostra difesa: 'non ero presente, non ne ero
al corrente, non condividevo le azioni'. Perciò dunque paga questo e, dice, paga
la più grande pena, perché non eri presente, non lo impedivi, né trattenevi
coloro che operavano male, né correvi rischi per l'onore verso il re. Non partecipasti alle imprese? Lodo questo e lo accetto; ma neppure fermasti le azioni: e ciò
è già meritevole di accusa."

διώρθωσε τοὺς πλησίον ἀκοσμοῦντας τῶν πονηρῶν· διὰ τοῦτο χωρὶς συγγνώμης ἁπάσης εἰς τὰς ἀφορήτους ἐπέμπετο κολάσεις ἐκείνας.[35]

La parabola del talento conclude di fatto la prima parte dell'omelia. Giovanni aggiunge che comunque ha nutrito la massima fiducia che, seppure finora non è accaduto, da adesso in poi i fedeli si sforzeranno di correggere chi sbaglia, di porre attenzione a che Dio non sia offeso. Poiché quanto è avvenuto è più che bastevole a convincere anche i più insensibili circa i pericoli dell'inosservanza dei precetti cristiani e spingerli a cercare la salvezza.

Il passaggio dalla prima alla seconda parte del discorso avviene: 1) attraverso il rimprovero diretto per i fatti accaduti, nel corso dei quali il popolo non ha fermato i responsabili della rivolta = la pusillanime inerzia di tutti nel frenare, fermare i tumulti è paragonata all'inerzia di chi, nella parabola del talento, ha saputo solo conservare il talento che gli era stato affidato, ma non metterlo a frutto; 2) attraverso la presentazione di sé come figura autorevole e degna di fiducia: Giovanni rivendica il merito di avere consigliato un atteggiamento più mite e prudente, ma il consiglio è stato disatteso. Il risultato è la rovina generalizzata che ne è derivata e che tutti vedono distintamente. Ma da ora in poi i fedeli, resi consapevoli degli errori commessi e rianimati dalle parole e dalle esortazioni del sacerdote potranno tornare ad agire da buoni cristiani, con fiducia e speranza.

Dopodiché, come se si trattasse di una delle tante, abituali occasioni di ammaestramento dottrinario, Giovanni passa a commentare il passo paolino sul tema della ricchezza e sul vizio

---

[35] "Ascolteremo anche queste parole dal Signore quando in silenzio sopporteremo le offese e gli oltraggi fatti a lui; poiché anche colui che ha seppellito il suo talento non era accusato per le sue azioni (infatti aveva restituito integro il deposito), ma perché non l'aveva accresciuto, perché non aveva educato gli altri, perché non aveva affidato il denaro ai banchieri, ovvero non ammonì, non consigliò, non rimproverò, non corresse dalle azioni malvagie i suoi prossimi che vivevano disordinatamente; per questo egli era mandato in quegli insopportabili castighi senza alcun perdono."

morale dell'avarizia e avidità che può spingere ad azioni dissennate, che costituisce propriamente la lettura del giorno: dall'analisi delle conseguenze dopo i disordini contro la pur gravosa tassa imposta da Teodosio nasce la riflessione etica sulla ricchezza, un bene strumentale, di cui si ha un possesso comunque temporaneo e spesso confuso con una proprietà inalienabile, un bene che resta inerte se lo si custodisce gelosamente invece di trasformarlo in benefici per sé e per altri:

ἀλλ' ὅτι μέν, εἰ καὶ μὴ πρότερον, νῦν γοῦν ταύτην ἐργάσεσθε τὴν διόρθωσιν, καὶ τὸν Θεὸν ὑβριζόμενον οὐ περιόψεσθε, σφόδρα πεπίστευκα. Ἱκανὰ γὰρ τὰ συμβεβηκότα, εἰ καὶ μηδεὶς ὁ παραινῶν ἦν, καὶ τοὺς σφόδρα ἀναισθήτως διακειμένους πεῖσαι λοιπὸν τῆς οἰκείας ἐπιλαβέσθαι σωτηρίας. Ἡμῖν δὲ ὥρα λοιπὸν τὴν εἰωθυῖαν ὑμῖν ἀπὸ τοῦ Παύλου παραθεῖναι τράπεζαν, τὴν σήμερον ἀναγνωσθεῖσαν ῥῆσιν προχειρισαμένους, καὶ εἰς μέσον καταθεμένους ἅπασι. Τί ποτ' οὖν ἐστι τὸ σήμερον ἀναγνωσθέν; *Τοῖς πλουσίοις ἐν τῷ νῦν αἰῶνι παράγγελλε μὴ ὑψηλοφρονεῖν· καὶ κατὰ πλεονεξίας* (Paul. *Tim.* 1, 6, 17).[36]

Ma la vera ricchezza è altro e la seconda parte dell'omelia (2, 5-9), con l'aiuto di S. Paolo e di illustri modelli scritturali, chiarisce perfettamente qual è per il cristiano la vera ricchezza, o meglio la ricchezza vera.

La ricchezza materiale, il valore ad essa generalmente attribuito, la paura di essere privati di questo vanto e le conseguenze nefaste che ne possono derivare sul piano etico e su quello civile, politico: ecco il tema-guida sviluppato pragmaticamente lungo tutta l'omelia, in forme distinte e complementari nelle due parti in cui essa si articola.

---

[36] "E ho avuto molta fiducia che, se anche non è avvenuto prima, ora dunque esercitiate questa correzione e non permettiate che Dio sia offeso. Infatti le cose accadute sono sufficienti, anche se non c'era nessuno che ammoniva, a convincere coloro che sono stati molto insensibili a cogliere per il resto la propria salvezza. Ci resta solo di approntare per voi la consueta mensa (allestita) dall'apostolo Paolo, offrendovi la lettura di oggi e proponendola a tutti. Che cosa è stato letto oggi? 'Ammonisci i ricchi a non essere orgogliosi nel tempo presente; e contro l'avarizia'."

Bibliografia

AMATO, E. / RODUIT, A. / STEINRÜCK, M. (edd.) (2006), *Approches de la Troisième Sophistique. Hommages à Jacques Schamp* (Bruxelles).

BROTTIER, L. (1993), "L'image d'Antioche dans les homélies *Sur les statues* de Jean Chrysostome", *REG* 106 , 619-635.

—— (2004), "Jean Chrysostome, un pasteur face à des *demi-chrétiens*", in B. CABOURET / P.-L. GATIER / C. SALIOU (edd.), *Antioche de Syrie. Histoire, images et traces de la ville antique* (Parigi), 439-457.

BROWNING, R. (1952), "The Riot of A.D. 387 in Antioch: The Role of the Theatrical Clacques in the Later Empire", *JRS* 42, 13-20.

CAMERON, A. (1991), *Christianity and the Rhetoric of Empire. The development of Christian Discourse* (Berkeley).

—— (1995), *Il tardo impero romano*, trad. italiana (Milano).

—— (2002), "The 'Long' Late Antiquity: A Late Twentieth-century Model", in T.P. WISEMAN (ed.) *Classics in Progress. Essays on Ancient Greece and Rome* (Oxford).

CELENTANO, M.S. (2001), "Tradurre e interpretare i classici: A proposito di Aristotele, *rhet.* 3.12", *SemRom* 4, 127-142.

—— (2015), "L'arte della mediazione in una tempestosa Quaresima: Giovanni Crisostomo", *De statuis* 2, in M.S. CELENTANO / P. CHIRON / P. MACK (edd.), *Rhetorical Arguments. Essays in Honour of Lucia Calboli Montefusco* (Hildesheim), 273-285.

CRACCO RUGGINI, L. (1986), "Poteri in gara per la salvezza di città ribelli: Il caso di Antiochia (387 d. C.)", in Hestíasis. *Studi di tarda antichità offerti a S. Calderone* (Messina) I, 265-290.

—— (1989) "La città imperiale", in A. MOMIGLIANO / A. SCHIAVONE (edd.), *Storia di Roma. 4, Caratteri e morfologie* (Torino), 201-266.

CRIBIORE, R. (2007), *The School of Libanius in Late Antique Antioch* (Princeton).

—— (2013), *Libanius the Sophist. Rhetoric, Reality, and Religion in the Fourth Century* (Ithaca).

DEPEYROT, G. (1996), *Crisis e inflación entre la Antigüedad y la Edad Media* (Barcelona).

DOWNEY, G. (1961), *A History of Antioch in Syria, from Seleucus to the Arab Conquest* (Princeton).

—— (1963), *Ancient Antioch* (Princeton).

FESTUGIÈRE, A.-J. (1959), *Antioche païenne et chrétienne. Libanius, Chrysostome et les moines de Syrie* (Parigi).

FRANCESIO, M. (2004), *L'idea di città in Libanio* (Stuttgart).

FRENCH, D.R. (1998), "Rhetoric and the Rebellion of A.D. 387 in Antioch", *Historia* 47, 468-484.

HUNTER, D.G. (1989), "Preaching and Propaganda in Fourth century Antioch: John Chrysostom's *Homilies on the Statues*, in D.G. HUNTER (ed.), *Preaching in the Patristic Age. Studies in Honor of Walter J. Burghardt* (New York), 119-138.

KENNEDY, G.A. (1980), *Classical Rhetoric and its Christian and Secular Tradition from Ancient to Modern Times* (Londra).

—— (1983), *Greek Rhetoric under Christian Emperors* (Princeton).

KING, N.Q. (1961), *The Emperor Theodosius and the Establishment of Christianity* (Londra).

LIEBESCHUETZ, J.H.W.G. (1972), *Antioch, City and Imperial Administration in the Later Roman Empire* (Oxford).

LUGARESI, L. (2008), *Il teatro di Dio. Il problema degli spettacoli nel cristianesimo antico (II-IV secolo)* (Brescia).

MALOSSE, P.L. / SCHOULER, B. (2009), "La Troisième Sophistique : Qu'est-ce que la Troisième Sophistique?", *Lalies* 29, 161-224.

MAXWELL, J.L. (2006), *Christianization and Communication in Late Antiquity. John Chrysostom and his Congregation in Antioch* (Cambridge).

MAYER, W. (1997), "The Dynamics of Liturgical Space. Aspects of Interaction between John Chrysostom and His Audience", *Ephemerides Liturgicae* 111, 104-115.

—— (1998), "John Chrysostom: Extraordinary preacher, ordinary audience", in M.B. CUNNINGHAM / P. ALLEN (edd.), *Preacher and Audience. Studies in Early Christian and Byzantine Homiletics* (Leiden), 105-137.

MURPHY, J.J. (1974), *Rhetoric in the Middle Ages. A History of Rhetorical Theory from Saint Augustine to the Renaissance* (Berkeley).

NIGRO, G. (2009), "Antiochia nella seconda metà del IV secolo: Giovanni Crisostomo fra cristiani, pagani ed eretici", *Annali di storia dell' esegesi* 26, 81-98.

VAN DE PAVERD, F. (1991), *St. John Chrysostom, the Homilies on the Statues. An Introduction* (Roma).

PELLIZZARI, A. (2011), "Tra retorica, letteratura ed epigrafia: Esempi di *laudes urbium* tardoantiche", *Historikà* 1, 23-144.

PETIT, P. (1955), *Libanius et la vie municipale à Antioche au IVe siècle après J.-C.* (Parigi).

QUIROGA PUERTAS, A.J. (2007a), *La retórica de Libanio y de Juan Crisóstomo en la Revuelta de las estatuas* (Salerno).

—— (2007b), "Elementos hagiográficos en las *Homilías de las estatuas* de Juan Crisóstomo", *Collectanea Christiana Orientalia* 4, 169-187.

—— (2008), "Deflecting Attention and Shaping Reality with Rhetoric (the Case of the Riot of the Statues of A.D. 387 in Antioch)", *Nova Tellus* 26, 135-153.

—— (2010),"La Tercera Sofística en el marco teórico de la historiografía sobre la Antigüedad Tardía y el Postmodernismo", *Talia dixit* 5, 75-90.

—— (ed.) (2011), ἱερὰ καὶ λόγοι. *Estudios de literatura y de religión en la Antigüedad Tardía* (Zaragoza).

—— (2013a), "*Vir sanctus dicendi peritus*: Rhetorical Delivery in Early Christian Rhetoric", in F. MESTRE / P. GÓMEZ (edd.), *Three Centuries of Greek Culture under the Roman Empire*. Homo Romanus Graeca Oratione (Barcelona), 347-356.

—— (ed.) (2013b), *The Purpose of Rhetoric in Late Antiquity. From Performance to Exegesis* (Tübingen).

—— (2013c), "Libanius' *Horror Silentii*", in QUIROGA PUERTAS (2013b), 223-244.

—— (2015), "The Palimpsestic City: Fourth Century A.D. Antioch Through Spatial Rhetoric", *SMSR* 81 (=AA. VV., *Retorica, scuola, religioni ad Antiochia (IV-V sec. d.C.)*, 105-117.

RONCORONI, A. (1980), "Origine della retorica cristiana dell'applauso", in AA.VV., *Studi in onore di Ferrante Rittatore Vonwiller*. Parte 2 (Como), 411-423.

SANDWELL, I. (2007), *Religious Identity in Late Antiquity. Greeks, Jews and Christians in Antioch* (Cambridge).

SANDWELL, I. / HUSKINSON, J. (edd.) (2004), *Culture and Society in Later Roman Antioch. Papers from a Colloquium, London, 15th December 2001* (Oxford).

SCHAMP, J. (2006), *Sophistes à l'ambon. Esquisses pour la Troisième Sophistique comme paysage littéraire*, in AMATO / RODUIT / STEINRÜCK (2006), 286-338.

STUIBER, A. (1954), "Beifall", in *RAC* 2, 98-102.

WALLACE, R.W. (1997), "Poet, public, and 'Theatrocracy'. Audience Performance in Classical Athens", in E. EDMUNDS / R.W. WALLACE (edd.), *Poet, Public, and Performance in Ancient Greece* (Baltimore), 97-111.

ZINCONE, S. (2009), "Religione e società, città e campagna nell'ambiente antiocheno di Giovanni Crisostomo", *Annali di storia dell' esegesi* 26, 65-79.

DISCUSSION

L. Pernot: À en juger d'après les extraits reproduits, ce discours très travaillé est un beau morceau de rhétorique. On y reconnaît d'abord des caractéristiques du style asianiste, comme le staccato (2, 1, 33 τί εἴπω κτέ. 2, 1, 34 διακόπτεταί μοι κτέ.) ou le jeu sur les mots (2, 2, 36 πολύπαις ἄπαις), ainsi que des *topoi* (la douleur qui rend muet l'orateur, le contraste entre le passé et le présent). Ceci rappelle les préceptes de Ménandros le Rhéteur sur la monodie et se situe dans la tradition des déplorations d'Aelius Aristide sur Smyrne et de Libanios sur Nicomédie. Puis, dans la deuxième partie, avec l'intervention de la Bible, le registre stylistique change. L'éloquence chrétienne transcende la rhétorique païenne. Significatif est le refus de πρὸς καιρὸν ψυχαγωγηθέντες en 2, 4, 38. Il marque un rejet simultané de la rhétorique des orateurs (le καιρός à la manière de Démosthène) et des philosophes (la ψυχαγωγία au sens du *Phèdre*).

C. Kremmydas: Thank you very much for your refreshing analysis of John Chrysostom's oratory. I was struck by the remarkable continuity in terms of rhetorical strategies and oratorical style within the *genus deliberatiuum*. The classical oratorical tradition as well as the biblical texts are both sources of inspiration. I singled out the passage at 2, 4, 38 where he repudiates the theatrical culture as recalling the Mytilenean debate in Thucydides book 3 and Cleon's condemnation of the fact that contemporary assembly debates in Athens had turned into spectacles. This later became a *topos* of censure of the audience and in other speeches of John Chrysostom the theatre is explicitly associated with the devil. But this same passage is also remarkable in terms of the similarity of the way in which he promotes his own *ethos* to what we saw in Demosthenes. Of course, John is also looking back to the *ethos* of Paul as a pastor/advisor. But do you think that any echoes of classical paradigms might be conscious imitations or simply a natural result of his rhetorical training?

M.S. Celentano: Anzitutto ringrazio Christos di constatare la "remarkable continuity in terms of rhetorical strategies and oratorical style within the *genus deliberatiuum*" e pertanto di condividere la mia lettura dell'omelia 2 del *De statuis* in una prospettiva anche politica, piuttosto che soltanto didascalico-epidittica, come comunemente avviene. E grazie a Laurent Pernot per avere messo in evidenza nell'omelia l'impiego nutrito e variato di tratti stilistici molto significativi e di frequente riconducibili ad un consolidato repertorio tecnico, soprattutto epidittico.

Entrambi i colleghi nell'omelia: *a*) colgono un qualche debito di Giovanni Crisostomo nei confronti dell'oratoria 'classica' – a partire dall'eccellenza ateniese di IV secolo a.C. e soprattutto a partire da Demostene, consacrato da una lunga tradizione retorica come campione di quella eccellenza –; *b*) rilevano alcuni specifici adattamenti al contesto cristiano e religioso di stilemi e/o moduli espressivi codificati di tempo in tempo nella prassi oratoria, divenuti poi oggetto di insegnamento-apprendimento nelle scuole di retorica, e infine raccolti in modo sistematico nei manuali tecnici.

In merito a quest'ultimo ambito: di certo alcuni stilemi di tipo patetico presenti nell'omelia riportano più direttamente all'epidittica e quindi è del tutto naturale riferirsi alla precettistica di Menandro retore. Così come certamente è ben sedimentata in Giovanni e adattata a se stesso, ai suoi discorsi, la conoscenza profonda della tradizione oratoria greca, dei modelli esemplari nella varie epoche, ivi compresi anche alcuni a lui contemporanei. E per di più è ben testimoniata la sua capacità di scegliere i registri elocutivi e performativi di volta in volta più adatti nel discorso. Quindi può essere ragionevole che talora il lettore di Giovanni Crisostomo si trovi a richiamare alla memoria l'*ethos* oratorio di Demostene o i suoi tratti espressivi più significativi. Senza contare che, com'è noto, Demostene costituiva un modello didattico di eccellenza nelle scuole orientali di retorica.

Dopo questa premessa vorrei però chiarire più in dettaglio alcuni altri elementi.

(Pernot) Quanto alla notazione "dans la deuxième partie, avec l'intervention de la Bible, le registre stylistique change. L'éloquence chrétienne transcende la rhétorique païenne", va precisato che riferimenti ispirati alla Bibbia, e relativi registri narrativi, sono presenti fin dalla prima parte dell'omelia: basti pensare alla descrizione iniziale di Giobbe, tratteggiato al culmine delle sue disgrazie (2, 1, 34) che prefigura lo stato miserevole in cui versa la città di Antiochia nel momento in cui l'omelia è tenuta. Mentre la seconda parte, dedicata alla lettura del giorno – un'epistola di S. Paolo – e relativa catechesi su uno specifico luogo (*Tim.* 1, 6, 17) ha inizio a 2, 5, 39. A partire da 2, 1, 35 moduli espressivi classici e biblici si alternano anche nella ripetuta esternazione del dolore per le presenti sventure di Antiochia accompagnata dal rimpianto di un felice passato. Ben prima dell'inizio della seconda parte.

Ma certamente è doveroso il richiamo ai *topoi* epidittici dell'elogio (funebre) delle città (L. Pernot menziona i precetti di Menandro, ma anche il compianto di Elio Aristide su Smirne e di Libanio su Nicomedia, "les préceptes de Ménandre le Rhéteur sur la monodie et ... les déplorations d'Aelius Aristide sur Smyrne et de Libanios sur Nicomédie").

Da parte mia ricorderei soprattutto i *topoi* relativi alla città assediata.

Più che allo stile, in particolare ad uno stile 'asiano', all'uso enfatico e protratto a) dell'appello al pubblico (= vd. *staccato* nelle interrogative in 2, 1, 33 e 34), nonché b) dell'*energeia* per rappresentare i dettagli dell'emozione dell'oratore farei invece riferimento ad una organica caratterizzazione orale del discorso, con i dovuti adattamenti, mette felicemente in pratica le regole aristoteliche sul discorso (Arist. *Rhet.* 3, 12, 1413b3 ss.) secondo che sia destinato alla lettura o piuttosto all'ascolto. Insomma l'omelia costituisce un esempio discorsivo del tutto nuovo: non tanto 1) per l'utilizzo abituale o invece innovativo di strumenti retorico-stilistici tradizionali, e 2) neanche per la contestualizzazione di elementi biblici e semitici in un impianto di tipo didascalico e informativo (= omelia), ma soprattutto e più ampiamente, per il fatto che tutti questi elementi nel loro insieme sono applicati ad una comunicazione questa sì in parte tradizionale e in parte necessariamente innovativa. Non a caso nel mio testo ho precisato che l'omelia presenta i tratti del cosiddetto discorso di consenso condiviso, nel quale l'oratore non è esterno all'assemblea a cui si rivolge: ne è parte integrante.

Riguardo a 2, 4, 38:

Suggestiva l'ipotesi di una lapidaria e densa allusione = rifiuto simultaneo delle pratiche retoriche di oratori e filosofi. Ma non c'è spazio in questa occasione per parlarne distesamente.

(Kremmydas) Anche in questo caso è molto suggestivo il richiamo alla spettacolarità dei discorsi assembleari in Tucidide (3, 38, 3 ss.) e al conseguente comportamento del pubblico: i cittadini diventano "spettatori delle parole e ascoltatori dei fatti" (§ 4) dando maggiore fiducia a quanto viene detto da altri – e in modo nuovo e seducente – piuttosto che alla propria esperienza autoptica.

E ancora più suggestivo di ulteriori riflessioni perché effettivamente Giovanni in questo luogo dell'omelia non sta trattando del diffuso successo che hanno gli spettacoli in Antiochia (ahimè anche presso i cristiani!) o delle aspettative inappropriate dei fedeli per *performances* di tipo teatrale (sulla persistete ostilità e conseguente condanna ecclesiastica di tutti gli spettacoli in età tardoantica si veda quanto ho scritto nel mio testo definitivo p. 362 e n. 33). Egli sta reagendo agli applausi per così dire a scena aperta che gli sono appena stati rivolti. A questa approvazione spontanea ed entusiastica, ma anche teatrale, spettacolare egli risponde ricordando a tutti i presenti quali sono i rispettivi ruoli nella presente circostanza e quali di conseguenza devono essere i comportamenti e le aspettative di chi parla (il sacerdote-oratore) e di chi ascolta (i fedeli).

Quindi: 1) sì, Giovanni fa trasparire ripetutamente il proprio *ethos* oratorio; 2) di certo la scuola di Libanio e la parallela formazione religiosa costituiscono un raro e completo curriculum oratorio fra tradizione e innovazione; 3) ma non necessariamente S. Paolo è l'unico modello di riferimento di Giovanni.

M. Kraus: Eine Zwischenbemerkung: Wenn Johannes Chrysostomos sagt: οὐκ ἔστι θέατρον ἡ ἐκκλησία (*De statuis* 2, 4, 38), dann sollten wir das auf keinen Fall metaphorisch verstehen (etwa im Sinne: „Kirche ist kein Theater"), sondern wir sollten im Auge behalten, dass *théatron* seit der Spätantike auch und vor allem eine Zusammenkunft von Gelehrten und Intellektuellen zum Zweck des Gedankenaustauschs über Literarisches meint, also eben den Ort, an dem professionelle Rhetoren und Sophisten vor Publikum wettkampfmässig ihre Prunkdeklamationen vortrugen.[1] Hier buhlten diese „Konzertredner", wie Ludwig Radermacher die Schaudeklamatoren der Zeit treffend genannt hat (übrigens ohne dass das Zitat für ihn irgendwie beleghaft zu sichern wäre), um den Applaus des Publikums und sparten dabei nicht mit brillanten Schaueffekten. Was Johannes also meint, ist: Dies hier ist kein wohlfeiles Spiel, kein *l'art pour l'art*; hier geht es um Ernst, mit möglicherweise einschneidenden Folgen (spektakuläre Schiffbrüche der an die Kunstwelt von Klassenzimmer und Konzertbühne gewöhnten Schulrhetoren der Spätantike im realen Ernstfall sind bezeugt). Zudem hat ja auch das Wort ἐκκλησία in dem Zitat einen signifikanten Bedeutungswandel vollzogen: von der Volksversammlung zur Kirche (faktisch ist es ja eine Versammlung in einer Kirche – laut der Didaskalie ἐν τῇ παλαιᾷ λεγομένῃ ἐκκλησίᾳ –, zu der Johannes in der Homilie spricht). Hätte man denselben Satz im 4. Jahrhundert v. Chr. also noch verstanden als „die Volksversammlung ist kein Theaterrund",

---

[1] Vgl. GRÜNBART, M. (Hrsg.), *Theatron. Rhetorische Kultur in Spätantike und Mittelalter = Rhetorical Culture in Late Antiquity and the Middle Ages* (Berlin, 2007), VII.

so im 4. Jahrhundert n. Chr. vermutlich als „die Kirche ist keine Deklamationsbühne". Übrigens hat auch Libanios, was Johannes verschweigt, in derselben Sache das Wort ergriffen (*Or.* 19).[2] Nur waren weder Libanios noch Johannes Mitglieder der nach Konstantinopel entsandten Delegation, deren Anführer und Sprecher vielmehr Bischof Flavianus war (vgl. Johannes, *De statuis* 21). Dieser war aber längst vor den Reden der beiden abgereist, konnte ihre Argumente also für seine Mission gar nicht verwerten. Allenfalls konnten die in Antiochia anwesenden Sonderermittler des Kaisers, Flavius Caesarius und Ellebichus, durch Boten den Inhalt der Reden in die Hauptstadt gemeldet haben. Jedenfalls dankt Libanios alsbald den beiden für ihre Vermittlung (*Or.* 21 und 22) und dem Kaiser für die erwiesene Milde (*Or.* 20, bes. § 1).

A. Chaniotis: This oration is very impressive as regards its persuasion strategy and its structure. In the first part of his oration, John uses expressions and images that insinuate the lack of agency, and consequently the lack of responsibility, on the side of the Antiochenes. The incidents are characterised with metaphors of illness (e.g. *aniaton elkos*) and frenzy (*bakcheuein, mania*) and attributed to the evil eye and devil's actions. In this first part, John also uses expressions that highlight inability (*ti eipô, ti alêso?*) – his inability to speak – and lack of control due to excessive emotion (cf. the vocabulary of emotion: *thrênos, dakry, odyresthai*). The orator concludes the first part by saying that this is where he originally intended to stop his oration; and by saying this he draws the attention of his audience to the entirely different tone of the second part of his speech, which no longer is dominated by the lack of agency but by the importance of responsibility. He invites his audience to regain agency and responsibility by reminding it that it is not the passive audience of a theatrical performance. An interesting aspect is

---

[2] Vgl. STENGER, J., *Hellenische Identität in der Spätantike. Pagane Autoren und ihr Unbehagen an der eigenen Zeit* (Berlin, 2009), 243-244; vgl. auch *Or.* 23.

John's broad definition of responsibility, which includes inertia. This definition is paralleled by pagan religious texts that condemn the individual who knows of or observes the commitment of a crime or a sacrilege and remains inactive; e.g. we encounter this in the cult regulation of an association in Philadelpheia (*Tituli Asiae Minoris* V 3, 1539, 1st century BC) and in a 'confession inscription' from Kollyda (*SEG* LVII 1185, AD 197). By constructing this contrast between the first and second part, John aims to transform the listeners from a passive audience to active agents, conscious of their responsibility to change their situation.

M. Kraus: Wenn Johannes Chrysostomos die Verteidigungstaktik einschlägt, die Verantwortung für das Delikt der Statuenschändung von den Bürgern Antiochias auf einen ganz anderen Schuldigen (nämlich den gegen die Stadt wütenden Teufel, den διάβολος) abzuwälzen, so handelt es sich aus schulrhetorischer Sicht um das in der Statuslehre als μετάστασις oder *remotio criminis* bekannte Verfahren.[3] Was sich hier abspielt, ist also klassische Rhetorenschule, freilich in charakteristisch christlichem Gewand. Johannes plädiert gewissermassen auf einen speziellen Fall von ,Befehlsnotstand'.

M. Edwards: This excellent discussion adds to our *Entretiens'* new 'rhetoric': the mixed genres of the speech, the context, John's use of history and classical rhetorical methods. Thank you all.

---

[3] Cf. *Rhet. Her.* 1, 25; Cic. *Inu.*1, 15; 2, 86-91; Quint. *Inst.* 7, 4, 13-14; Victorin. *Gramm.*, p. 191, 26-43; 285, 23-286, 15 Halm; Sulp. Vict. *Inst. or.* 54, p. 347, 14-25 Halm; Iul. Vict. *Rhet.* 3, 8, p. 381, 23-31 Halm = p. 13 Giomini / Celentano; Fortun. *Rhet.* 1, 15, p. 93, 11-19 Halm = p. 89 Calboli Montefusco; Hermog. *Stat.* 2, p. 39, 6-9 Rabe; 6, p. 72, 7; 75, 11-21 Rabe; Aquila *De figuris* 16, p. 23, 10-24, 14 Elice = Hermag. I B 16b Matthes = Hermag. Mai. T 40 Woerther; Sopat. Rhet. *In Hermog. stat. comm.*, p. 174, 16-26 Walz = Hermag. III 10 Matthes = Hermag. Min. T 13 Woerther; zu weiteren Belegstellen siehe die Übersicht bei Woerther, F. (Hrsg.), *Hermagoras. Fragments et témoignages* (Paris, 2012), 194-195.

INDEX

A. Auteurs et textes anciens

Acta Alexandrinorum (APM): 210-
211, 213, 219-224, 226-227, 229-
230, 236, 247, 249-251, 255, 259.
I, p. 84-90: 229.
I, p. 91: 240.
I, p. 91-92: 247.
IV, p. 118-133: 223.
IV, p. 128-130: 238.
IV, p. 132-133: 233.
IV, p. 137: 239.
VII, p. 196-198: 237.
VIII, p. 162-163: 224.
VIII, p. 168-172: 224.
VIII, i 18, p. 174-175: 225.
X, col. ii 34: 249.
X, fr. 1, i 12-18: 237.
X, fr. 1, i 28-49: 225.
X, fr. ii 61-63: 230.
X, p. 202-204: 230.
XI, p. 215: 237.
XI, p. 216-217: 239.
Acta Appiani: 221, 225, 231.
Acta Athenodori: 225, 236-237, 249.
Acta Hermaisci: 213, 221, 224, 231,
240, pl. 6.3.
Acta Isidori: 212, 221, 223-224, 227,
242.
Acta Pauli et Antonini: 213, 221.
Aeschines: 31, 64, 71, 100, 125, 204-
205.
1 (*In Timarchum*):
1, 71: 101.
1, 87: 112.
2 (*In Ctesiphontem*): 78, 91.
2, 21-22: 90.
2, 25-33: 93.
2, 34: 30.
2, 47-54: 124.
2, 63: 112.
2, 79: 80.
2, 101-107: 90.
2, 109-112: 93.
2, 113-117: 93.
2, 122: 124.
2, 123: 112.
2, 141: 86-87.
2, 143: 112.
3 (*De falsa legatione*): 72, 74, 91,
295.
3, 119-122: 93.
3, 125: 124.
3, 137: 80.
3, 138: 87.
3, 138-139: 85.
3, 173: 50.
3, 242: 80.
3, 258: 87.
Alcidamas: 39.
Ambrosius Mediolanensis: 340.
De officiis:
1, 18, 72-73: 361.
1, 19, 84: 361.
Ammianus Marcellinus: 341.
Anaximenes: 36, 42, 49, 71, 76. V.
aussi Ps.-Aristoteles, *Rhetorica ad
Alexandrum*.

Andocides: 19-23, 30, 37, 39, 48.
De mysteriis 1, 150: 113.
De pace: 20, 72, 91, 295.
3, 1-12: 20.
3, 3: 87.
3, 3-12: 20.
3, 13-16: 21.
3, 17-19: 21.
3, 17-23: 21.
3, 24-32: 21.
3, 28: 21.
3, 28-32: 21.
3, 33-41: 21.
3, 37-39: 21.
De reditu: 22-23.
2, 5: 22.
2, 10-16: 22.
2, 12: 22.
2, 18: 22.
2, 19: 22.
2, 20-21: 22.
2, 22: 22.
2, 24: 22.
2, 26: 22.
Fr. 3 Blass: 19, 23.
Antiphon: 16-17, 24, 30, 37, 39.
Or.:
1, 14-20: 18.
5: 38.
Fr. 25-33 Thalheim: 17.
Fr. 49 Thalheim = Suda s.v. Σαμοθράκη: 18-19, 37-38.
Fr. 49-56 Thalheim: 17.
Fr. 50 Thalheim = Demetrius,
Eloc. 53: 18-19, 37-38.
Fr. 51 Thalheim = Priscianus, 18,
280: 18.
Fr. 52 Thalheim = Harpocration
s.v. ἐκλογεῖς: 19.
Aphareus: 28.
Aphthonius: 299, 301, 313-319,
326-327, 336, 341.
Prog.:
7, 1: 315.

7, 3-11: 315.
7, 3: 315.
7, 6: 315.
9, 4-9: 315.
14, 3-15: 316.
Apollodorus Atheniensis, Chronicon:
79.
Apollonius Tyanensis, Epist. 9: 277.
Appianus, B Ciu. 4, 65, 276 - 4, 73,
312: 197.
Aquila, De figuris 16, p. 23, 10-24,
14 Elice = Hermagoras 1 B 16b
Matthes = Hermagoras Maior T
40 Woerther: 375.
Aristides, Aelius: 261, 333, 369, 371.
Panathen.: 164.
Ps.-Aristides, Aelius, Rhetor. 1, 146:
263.
Aristophanes: 166, 177.
Ach. 530: 233.
Aristoteles: 36, 38, 71, 338.
Ath. Pol. 42, 5: 50.
Poet.: 267.
Rhet.: 32, 35, 42, 80, 89, 113,
262-263, 295.
1, 1, 1-10, 1354a-b: 42.
1, 1, 10, 1354b22-25: 15.
1, 1, 1354b22-35: 35.
1, 2, 1356a: 41, 45.
1, 2, 1356a2: 76.
1, 2, 1356b5-6: 177.
1, 2, 1356b12-18: 177.
1, 3, 1358a-1359a: 186.
1, 3, 1358b: 242.
1, 3, 1358b2-8: 311.
1, 3, 1358b9-10: 263.
1, 3, 2-3, 1358b: 15-16, 37,
242.
1, 3, 5, 1358b20-25: 21, 28.
1, 3, 5, 1358b22: 45.
1, 3-8, 1358a-1365b: 263.
1, 4, 1359b: 213.
1, 4, 3, 1359a38-39: 28.
1, 4, 7, 1359b19-23: 81.

1, 5, 1-5, 1360b: 238.
1, 5, 6-9, 1361a: 233.
1, 5-6, 1360b-1363b: 271.
1, 6, 1, 1362a18-20: 45.
1, 8, 2, 1365b25: 45.
1, 9, 1368a29-33: 177.
1, 14, 3, 1374b36-1375a2: 126.
2, 1, 1-4, 1377b20-31: 82.
2, 1, 1377b28-30: 280.
2, 1, 1378a: 42, 44.
2, 1, 5, 1378a6-9: 82.
2, 5, 1382a21-22: 25.
2, 12-17, 1388b31-1391b6: 76.
2, 18, 1391b8-9: 263.
2, 20, 1393a26-27: 177.
2, 20, 1393a28-1394a8: 177.
2, 21, 1394a-1395b: 49.
3, 7, 6, 1408a25-30: 81.
3, 12, 1413b: 263, 347, 371.
3, 14, 12, 1415b7: 20.
3, 16, 11, 1417b11-13: 19.
3, 17, 5, 1418a1: 21.
3, 17, 10, 1418a27: 22-23.
Ps.-Aristoteles, *Rhetorica ad Alexandrum*: 35-36, 42, 89, 126, 262-263.
1, 1421b7: 45, 259.
1, 2, 1421b14: 263.
1-2, 1421b7-1425b35: 263.
2, 2, 1423a23-29: 81.
4, 1426b22: 35.
10, 1-2, 1430a23-35: 83.
11, 1-6: 49.
14, 1431b9-19: 76.
24, 3, 1435a15-18: 84, 123.
29-34, 1436a33-1440b4: 263.
29-36, 1436a33-1445a29: 35.
29, 6-7, 1436b15-28: 85.
29, 6-23, 1436b15-1437b5: 82.
30, 2-4, 1438a6-22: 124.
34, 2-7, 1439b18-1440a3: 112.

35, 17-18, 1441b19-20: 42.
35, 18, 1441b20-23: 42.
Ep. 16-17, 1421b4: 42.
Athenaeus:
5, 212f-213c = Posidonius, Fr. 247 Theiler = *FrGrH* 87 F 36: 130, 175, 178.
6, 253d-f: 256.
Augustinus: 341.
Doctr. christ. 4: 340.

Babrius, *Fab.* 89: 170, 178.

Caecilius Calactinus: 39.
Caesar, v. aussi Index C *s.v.* César:
Bell. Alex.: 212.
Gall.:
1, 7, 3: 207-208.
1, 30, 1: 208.
1, 37, 1-2: 208.
Callinicus Petraeus, *REG* 123, 2010, p. 86-90: 332.
Calpurnius Flaccus: 340.
Chariton 5, 2, 4: 239.
Chrysippus: 296.
Cicero: 78, 265, 340.
Brut. 312: 190.
De or. 1, 141: 263.
Fin. 5, 89: 189.
Inu.:
1, 15: 375.
1, 22: 195, 200.
1, 24: 196.
1, 107: 194.
2, 86-91: 375.
Part. 10: 263.
Q Fr. 1, 1, 33: 190.
Rep. 1, 43: 189.
Claudianus: 341.
Cleanthes: 296.
Cleidemos: 180, 182.
Codex Iustinianus: 335.
Codex Theodosianus 15, 4, 1: 349.

Constitutio Antoniniana: 220, 335.
Corpus iuris ciuilis: 335.
Critias: 16.

Demetrius Phalereus:
  De elocutione 53 = Antiphon, fr.
  50 Thalheim: 18.
  Fr. 130 Stork / van Ophuijsen /
  Dorandi = Philod. *Rhet.* 1,
  222 Sudhaus: 204.
Demosthenes: 29-32, 36-38, 80,
  100, 110, 125, 204-205, 271,
  294-296, 321, 338, 369-371.
  1 (*Olynth.* 1):
  1, 8: 91.
  1, 14-16: 58.
  1, 16: 58.
  1, 17-20: 58.
  1-6: 50.
  2 (*Olynth.* 2):
  2, 3-4: 59.
  2, 5-10: 59.
  2, 12: 91.
  2, 14-20: 59.
  2, 27-30: 59.
  2, 30-31: 59.
  3 (*Olynth.* 3):
  3, 1: 48.
  3, 3: 59.
  3, 10-13: 60.
  3, 11: 61.
  3, 14-15: 60.
  3, 16: 60.
  3, 18: 48, 60.
  3, 19-20: 60.
  3, 21-27: 60-61.
  3, 22: 48.
  3, 24: 60.
  3, 24-27: 61.
  3, 34: 61.
  3, 36: 52.
  4 (*Phil.* 1): 55.
  4, 1: 50, 52, 56.

4, 5-6: 57.
4, 10-11: 57.
4, 17: 57.
4, 30: 58.
4, 41: 44.
4, 51: 56-57.
5 (*Pac.*):
5, 1: 48, 62.
5, 2: 62.
5, 3: 52.
5, 4: 48, 52, 63, 74.
5, 4-12: 62, 65.
5, 5: 63, 65.
5, 9: 62.
5, 11-12: 63-64.
6 (*Phil.* 2): 65.
6, 4: 65.
6, 5: 65.
6, 6: 44.
6, 8: 44.
6, 9-11: 65.
6, 19-26: 91.
6, 20-25: 65.
6, 30: 65.
6, 31-34: 65.
7 (*Hal.*): 30, 50.
7, 1: 91, 122.
7, 19: 91.
7, 19-20: 99.
7, 20-23: 91, 99.
8 (*Chers.*): 66.
8, 23: 66.
8, 35-37: 66.
8, 38: 66.
8, 67-76: 66.
8, 68: 58.
8, 73: 58.
8-10: 50.
9 (*Phil.* 3): 66.
9, 2: 48, 67.
9, 3: 67.
9, 7: 67.
9, 36-37: 67.

9, 42-46: 67.
9, 49-50: 67.
9, 53: 67.
9, 59-64: 67.
9, 65: 67.
9, 72: 91.
9, 74: 52.
9, 77: 67.
10 (*Phil.* 4): 30, 66.
10, 1-5: 67.
10, 7: 67.
10, 11: 66.
10, 35-36: 67.
10, 46: 52.
10, 46-47: 67.
10, 57: 67.
10, 68: 67.
10, 70-76: 67-68.
11 (*In epist. Phil.*): 30.
12 (*Phil. epist.*): 30.
13 (*Contr.*): 30, 50.
13, 29: 60.
14 (*De symm.*): 51-52.
14, 1: 51.
14, 2: 52.
14, 12: 86.
14, 15: 57.
14, 24 ss.: 52-53.
14-16: 50.
15 (*De Rhodiorum lib.*): 55.
15, 1: 54, 57.
15, 6: 54.
15, 7: 54.
15, 9: 54.
15, 15: 54, 86, 112.
15, 16: 54.
15, 21: 54.
15, 22: 91.
15, 32: 48.
16 (*Pro Megalopol.*):
16, 1-3: 53.
16, 2: 48.
16, 3: 53.

17 (*De foedere cum Alexandro*):
30, 50.
17, 16-17: 91.
17, 19: 91.
18 (*De corona*): 69, 72, 74-75,
78, 91.
18, 4: 75.
18, 18: 51.
18, 27: 44.
18, 60: 51.
18, 129-131: 23.
18, 143: 46.
18, 209: 219.
18, 298: 63.
19 (*De falsa legatione*): 72, 74, 78,
91, 271.
19, 5: 124.
19, 11: 80.
19, 12: 123.
19, 18-24: 124.
19, 113: 62.
19, 127: 63.
19, 277-279: 19.
19, 304: 80.
20 (*Adu. Leptinem*): 4, 50, 271.
20, 73: 91.
21 (*In Midiam*), 154: 50.
22 (*Adu. Androt.*): 50.
23 (*In Aristocr.*):
23, 172: 112.
23, 196: 61.
23, 198: 61.
23, 207: 61.
23, 209: 61.
47 (*In Euerg. et Mnesib.*): 50.
49 (*Contra Timotheum*), 9: 112.
50 (*Contra Polyclem*):
50, 5: 91.
50, 6: 112.
51 (*De corona trierarchiae*): 50.
60 (*Epitaphius*), 4-5: 52.
Exord.: 30, 78.
4: 48.

8, 2: 48.
44, 1: 48.
Olynth.: 26, 58-61.
Phil.: 26, 41-78.
Dinarchus: 31-32, 39.
1, 12-13: 91.
1, 16: 91.
1, 18-20: 91.
1, 28: 91.
1, 80-82: 91.
4, 1: 63.
4, 3: 63.
4, 11: 63.
4, 13: 63.
4, 26: 63.
4, 29: 63.
4, 45: 63.
4, 93: 63.
4, 98: 63.
4, 103: 63.
6, 6: 63.
6, 22: 63.
Dio Cass. 63, 20, 5: 239.
Dio Chrysostomus: 261-297, 333.
De uirtutibus Alexandri: 296.
Getica: 296.
Or.:
1-4 (*De regno*): 275, 277, 279.
1, 1-8: 281.
1, 9: 275.
2: 283.
2, 18-19: 271.
2, 24: 268.
3, 2: 275.
3, 25: 283, 292.
4: 276, 283, 296.
4, 124: 267.
5 (*De regno*): 276.
6 (*De tyrannide*): 276.
7 (*Venator*): 9.
7, 24-63: 268.
7, 128: 272.
12 (*De dei cognitione*): 276.

12, 16: 272.
13 (*De exilio*):
13, 12: 271.
13, 22: 268.
18 (*De dicendi exercitatione*):
276.
18, 11: 271.
18, 14: 267, 276.
18, 17: 267, 276.
21 (*De pulchritudine*), 11: 269.
22 (*De pace et bello*): 270.
22, 5: 268, 270.
24 (*De felicitate*), 3: 267.
25 (*De genio*): 276.
25, 2: 270.
26 (*De consultatione*), 7: 268.
26, 8: 270.
30 (*Charidemus*): 276.
31-35: 275.
31 (*Rhodiaca*): 278, 293-294.
31, 1-7: 281.
31, 122: 277.
31, 161-162: 266, 295.
31, 162: 294.
31, 163: 295.
32 (*Ad Alexandrinos*):
32, 1-29: 281.
32, 22: 295.
32, 95: 224.
33-36: 262.
33 (*Tarsica prior*):
33, 1: 267.
33, 1-30: 281.
33, 33: 283.
34 (*Tarsica altera*): 277, 282.
34, 2: 295.
34, 28-37: 268.
34, 48: 279.
34, 48-51: 278.
34, 51: 280.
35 (*Celaenis Phrygiae*): 283.
35, 1-12: 281.
36 (*Borysthenitica*): 293.

37 (*Corinthiaca*): 272.
38-51: 274-275.
38 (*Ad Nicomedienses*): 277.
38, 1: 270.
38, 8: 277.
38, 10-20: 277.
38, 38: 279.
38, 41-48: 277.
39 (*Ad Nicaeenses*):
39, 1: 278.
39, 3 ss.: 282.
40-41: 281.
40 (*De concordia cum Apamensibus*): 285.
40, 5-6: 275.
40, 5-10: 285.
40, 22: 279.
41 (*Ad Apamenses*), 13 ss.: 282.
42 (*De regno et tyrannide*), 4-5: 273.
43 (*Politica*): 280.
43, 2: 275.
43, 4: 265.
44 (*Gratitudo*): 284.
44, 3-5: 278.
44, 10: 270.
44, 10-12: 277.
45 (*Defensio*): 280.
45, 3: 281.
46 (*De tumultu*), 14: 279.
47 (*Concio*): 280, 285.
47, 18-20: 285.
47, 25: 295.
48 (*In concione*): 274.
48, 2: 279.
48, 3: 278.
48, 14: 272.
49 (*Recusatio magistratus*): 269, 284.
49, 1: 271.
49, 13: 269.
50 (*De administratione*): 280.
51 (*Ad Diodorum*): 285.

53 (*De Homero*): 276.
56 (*De regno*): 276.
57 (*Nestor*): 276.
62 (*De regno et tyrannide*): 276.
63-65 (*De fortuna*): 272.
69 (*De uirtute*), 3: 267-268.
72 (*De habitu*), 9: 278.
77/78 (*De inuidia*), 42: 278.
Diodorus Siculus:
15, 38, 3: 101.
15, 79: 169.
20, 1, 1-3: 186.
32, 1-3: 205.
Diogenes Laertius 7, 42: 263.
Dionysius Halicarnassensis: 39.
Din.:
2: 32.
10: 32.
11: 32.
Isoc. 2: 26.
Lys.:
1: 24.
3: 24.
14: 26.
16, 2: 263.
31-33: 24.
Donatus, Aelius: 340.
Duris: 79.

Eunapius: 339.
Vit. soph. 472: 317.

Favorinus: 333.
Florus 1, 35: 184.
Fortunatus, *Rhet.* 1, 15, p. 93, 11-19 Halm = p. 89 Calboli Montefusco: 375.

Gellius, Aulus 6, 14, 8: 189.
Gorgias: 39.
Gregorius Nazianzenus, *Or.* 2, 47: 361.

Harpocration:
  s.v. Ἀλκέτας: 29.
  s.v. ἐκλογεῖς: 19.
  s.v. Ἐπικράτης: 29.
  s.v. πέπλος: 29.
Hegesippus: 30, 50.
Heliodorus, *Aeth.* 6, 8: 239.
Hermagoras: 187.
  1 B 16b Matthes = Aquila, *De figu-*
    ris 16, p. 23, 10-24, 14 Elice =
    Hermagoras Maior T 40 Woer-
    ther: 375.
  III 10 Matthes = Sopater, *In*
    Hermog. Stat. comm., p. 174,
    16-26 Walz = Hermagoras
    Minor T 13 Woerther: 375.
Hermogenes: 295, 339-340.
  De ideis:
    2, 10, 15, p. 384 Rabe: 263.
    2, 11, p. 400 Rabe: 17.
    2, 11, p. 402 Rabe: 16.
    2, 11, p. 403 Rabe: 20.
  De inuentione: 310, 319.
  De statibus:
    1, 25 (34 Rabe): 263.
    2, p. 39, 6-9 Rabe: 375.
    6, p. 72, 7 Rabe: 375.
    38, 3-8 Rabe: 311.
    75, 11-21 Rabe: 375.
    76, 3-79, 16 Rabe: 311.
Herodotus: 42, 92, 109, 113-114,
  136-137.
  1, 30: 101.
  1, 69, 1-3: 98.
  5, 92: 81.
  6, 49: 80.
  7, 136, 2: 118.
  7, 157, 1: 118.
  7, 157-162: 135.
  8, 136: 87, 96-97.
  8, 140: 96-98.
  8, 141: 99.
  8, 142, 1: 118.
  8, 142, 4-5: 99.

8, 143: 98.
9, 7A, 1: 118.
Hieronymus, *Ep.* 22: 361.
Himerius: 333.
Homerus: 207.
  Il.: 114, 136-137.
    3, 212-224: 320-321.
    9: 135.
    9, 443: 1.
    11: 321.
Hyperides: 31, 38.
  1 *Dem.*, col. 8: 91.
  1, fr. 3, col. 15, l. 2: 63.
  1, fr. 8, col. 34, l. 9: 63.
  1, fr. 8, col. 35, l. 25: 63.
  1, fr. 9, col. 39, l. 25:
  1, fr. 9, col. 40, l. 1: 63.
  1, fr. 62, col. 25, l. 25: 63.
  3, *Eux.* 11: 112.
  3, *Eux.* 24-25: 91.
  3, *Eux.* 39, l. 25: 63.
  Epitaph., col. 5, l. 2: 63.

Ioannes Chrysostomus: 343-375.
  Act. apost. hom. 10, 4 *PG* 60, 90:
    362.
  Ioan. hom. 1, 4 *PG* 59, 28: 362.
  Stat.: 343-375.
    2, 1: 348.
    2, 1, 33: 349-350, 352, 356,
      369, 371.
    2, 1, 34: 352-355, 369, 371.
    2, 1, 35: 350.
    2, 2, 35: 355-357, 371.
    2, 2, 36: 357-359, 369.
    2, 3, 36-37: 359-361.
    2, 4, 38: 362-363, 369, 372-
      373.
    2, 4, 38-39: 363.
    2, 5-9: 365.
    2, 5, 39: 371.
    3, 1: 348.
    5, 3: 348.
    8, 4: 348.

21: 374.
Iosephus, Flavius: 220.
AJ: 213.
  14, 187: 216.
  14, 188: 228.
  14, 266: 228.
  18, 143: 223.
  18, 156: 223.
  18, 165: 223.
  18, 257-259: 218.
  19, 279-285: 228.
  19, 280-285: 246-247.
Ap.: 213.
  2, 64: 216.
  2, 65: 241.
Isaeus: 28-29, 32, 39.
  12: 29.
  Fr. XXVII: 29.
Isocrates: 36-38, 99, 271, 333.
  4 (*Paneg.*): 26-28, 264.
    3: 264.
    21-132: 26.
    53: 27.
    133-169: 27-28.
  5 (*Phil.*): 264.
  6 (*Archid.*), 2: 112, 264.
  7 (*Areopag.*): 264.
  8 (*De pace*): 264.
  12 (*Ad Nic.*): 264.
  14 (*Plat.*), 33: 112, 264.
  15 (*Antid.*), 278: 45.
  19 (*Aeginet.*): 38.
Iulianus, imperator, v. aussi Index C
  s.v. Julien, Empereur.
  Misopogon: 323.
Iulius Victor: 340.
  Rhet. 3, 8, p. 381, 23-31 Halm = p.
    13 Giomini / Celentano: 375.

Lesbonax: 39.
Libanius: 64, 292, 296, 301-302,
  305-341, 369, 371.
  Decl.:
    1, 71: 336-337.

3-4: 320.
5: 321.
9-11: 321.
13: 321.
19-22: 321.
22, 11: 336-337.
23, 45: 337.
23, 71: 337.
25: 319.
38: 319.
39: 319.
40: 319.
Ep.:
  369, 4: 312-313.
  617: 306.
Loc.:
  4: 314.
  4, 4: 315.
  4, 10: 315.
Or.:
  1, 6: 308.
  1, 13: 308.
  1, 208-210: 324.
  1, 252: 348.
  1, 252-253: 348.
  11: 355.
  12, 11: 336-337.
  15: 323.
  17, 37: 323.
  18, 195: 323.
  19-23: 325.
  19: 374.
  19, 7: 348.
  19, 28: 348.
  19, 29: 348.
  20, 1: 374.
  20, 3: 348.
  20, 10: 348.
  21-22: 325, 374.
  22, 4: 348.
  22, 8: 348.
  23: 374.
  26: 325.
  27-28: 326.

30: 318, 324-325.
30, 44: 318.
33: 326.
34, 15: 312.
35, 3: 305-306.
35, 6 ss.: 307.
35, 16: 312.
35, 21: 312.
38: 317.
41: 326.
42: 309.
45: 326.
46: 326.
47: 326.
48, 7: 308.
50: 326.
54: 326.
56: 326.
57: 326.
62, 8: 339.
64, 83: 337.
Prog.:
  Comp. 3: 316.
  Enc. 5: 316.
Vit.:
  4: 316.
  5: 315.
Fr. 49: 319.
Ps.-Libanius, *Characteres epistolici* 5: 278.
Livius, Titus:
  30, 21-23: 205.
  42, 23-24: 205.
  43, 7, 10: 193.
Longinus:
  Fr. 49, l. 80 Patillon-Brisson: 263.
  Fr. 50, l. 21 Patillon-Brisson: 263.
Lycurgus: 31, 39.
Lysias: 24-26, 32, 179.
  2, 3: 52.
  2, 6: 52.
  2, 17: 52.
  6: 105.

12, 5: 145.
12, 8-22: 145.
12, 25: 112.
12, 92: 145.
12, 95-98: 145.
20, 31-32: 112.
20, 34: 112.
34: 24-26.
34, 6: 25.
34, 7-9: 25.
Fr. XLVI Carey = XLIV FI: 26.
Fr. CXI Carey = CV FI: 26.

Macrobius, *Sat.* 1, 5, 14: 189.
Menander Rhetor: 203-204, 332, 339-340, 369-371.
  2, 12, 422-423 (*stephanôtikos*): 186-187.
  2, 13, 423-424 (*presbeutikos*): 186-187.
  2, 13, 423, 7-11: 232.
  2, 13, 424, 1-2: 211.
Musonius Rufus: 277.

Nicolaus Rhetor, *Progymnasmata*: 259-260.
  8, 14-15 Felten: 311.
  15, 12-15 Felten: 312.
  23, 11-12 Felten: 311.
  28, 13-14 Felten: 311.
  37-38 Felten: 315.
  48, 5-10 Felten: 312.
  62, 8-15 Felten: 260, 312.
  66, 16-67, 2 Felten: 312.
  70, 7-15 Felten: 312.
  76, 6-7 Felten: 311.

Parthenius, *Mythogr. Gr.* 2, 1, 5: 157.
Philo Alexandrinus: 220.
  Flacc.: 213, 218, 227.
  18-21: 219.
  20, 131: 219.

29-96: 217.
49-50: 216.
54: 216.
74: 216.
135-145: 219.
Leg.: 218, 227.
116: 233.
120-130: 217.
154: 216.
166: 241.
171: 233.
172: 232.
172-173: 231.
172-178: 258.
178-179: 231.
181: 231.
185: 231, 258.
205: 241.
250: 232.
276: 233.
290: 233.
309: 233.
322: 233.
338: 232.
349: 212-213.
351: 232, 258.
352: 233.
354-355: 233.
355-357: 241.
356: 233.
359: 232.
361: 233.
365-366: 232, 258.
366: 249.
367: 248.
368: 232.
Philochorus, *FGrH* 328 F 149a: 19, 101.
Philodemus, *Rhet.*:
1, 212 Sudhaus: 263.
1, 222 Sudhaus = Demetr. Phal. fr. 130: 204.
Philostratus: 273.

Ap. 5, 40: 277.
VS: 332-333.
481: 301.
487: 296.
488: 271, 275, 277, 296.
507: 301.
529: 261.
565: 20.
591: 261, 284.
628: 261.
Photius, *Bibl.*:
61, p. 20a: 31.
209, p. 165a34-35: 271-272.
209, p. 165b8-10: 271-272.
209, p. 165b34-39: 281.
262, p. 488b: 24.
263, p. 490a: 28.
264, p. 490a: 31.
266, p. 496a: 31.
268, p. 496b: 31.
Pindarus: 320.
Fr. 76 SM: 319.
Plato: 36, 177, 338-339.
Menex.: 164.
Phaed.: 271, 296, 369.
Sis.: 268.
Plinius Minor:
Epist.:
10, 6-7: 214.
10, 81-82: 274.
10, 81, 1: 275.
Plutarchus:
Apophthegmata Laconica 221E: 86.
Arat. 31-32: 159.
De laude ipsius: 74.
Dem.:
8: 30.
11: 30.
Mor. 350b = *P.Oxy.* XLVII 3360: 31.
Praecepta ger. reip.: 293.
805a: 294.
824d: 294.

Pyrrh. 28, 4-5: 159.
Sull.:
    13: 163-165.
    13, 5: 175.
    14, 9: 175.
Them. 32: 22-23.
Thes.: 182.
Ps.-Plutarchus: 38.
  Aesch.:
    840e: 31.
    850a: 31.
  Andoc. 835a: 19.
  Antiph. 834a-b: 19.
  Cic. 4, 7: 294.
  Din. 850c: 32.
  Hyp.: 848e: 31.
  Isocr.:
    839c: 28.
    839f: 28.
  Lys.:
    836a: 26.
    836b: 24.
Polybius: 138, 175, 199, 204.
  4, 62, 2: 152.
  4, 67, 3-4: 152.
  5, 9-12: 152.
  5, 104: 130.
  6, 13, 7-9: 189.
  6, 56, 6-14: 152.
  9, 28-39: 73, 144.
  9, 28, 3-4: 145.
  9, 29, 3-4: 145.
  9, 29, 7: 145.
  9, 29, 10-12: 145.
  9, 30, 3-4: 146.
  9, 32, 1-2: 146.
  9, 34, 1-11: 146.
  9, 39, 2: 147.
  9, 39, 6: 148.
  12, 25a3: 152.
  12, 25a3-i3: 79, 186.
  16, 30-34: 159.
  21, 19-21: 152.

21, 31, 5-16: 196.
22, 11, 6: 198.
22, 12, 1: 198.
24, 8, 3-4: 198.
24, 10, 3: 198.
24, 10, 7: 200.
24, 10, 12: 198.
24, 13, 3: 198.
24, 13, 5: 198.
30, 3, 3-7: 193.
30, 4-5: 196.
30, 4, 9: 200.
30, 4, 11: 190.
30, 4, 12-17: 190.
30, 31: 190, 196.
30, 31, 3-18: 152.
30, 31, 13-15: 196.
36, 4: 205.
38, 1-39, 5: 148.
39, 3, 4: 198.
39, 3, 5: 198.
Posidonius, Fr. 247 Theiler = *FGrH*
  87 F 36, *ap.* Athen. 5, 212f-213c:
  130, 175, 178.
Priscianus: 340.
  18, 280 = Antiphon, fr. 51 Thal-
    heim: 18.

Quintilianus: 40, 299-300, 340.
  Inst. or.:
    3, 4, 3: 264.
    3, 8, 12: 280.
    3, 8, 13: 280.
    3, 8, 15: 265.
    3, 8, 22-25: 28.
    3, 8, 37: 265.
    3, 8, 48: 280.
    3, 8, 69: 278.
    7, 4, 13-14: 375.
Ps.-Quintilianus: 340.

Rhetorica ad C. Herennium: 196.
  1, 2: 263.

1, 25: 375.
2, 1: 263.
4, 68: 194.

Sopater: 333.
In Hermog. Stat. comm., p. 174,
16-26 Walz = Hermagoras III
10 Matthes = Hermagoras
Minor T 13 Woerther: 375.
Sozomenus, *Hist. eccl.*:
7, 15: 317.
7, 23: 348.
8, 2: 344.
Strabo 14, 2, 3, 652C: 190.
Suda: 273, 341.
δ 1240: 277.
λ 825: 31.
σ 79: 18.
Suetonius, *Calig.* 49, 2: 232.
Sulpicius Victor: 340.
Inst. or. 54, p. 347, 14-25 Halm:
375.
Synesius: 273, 333.
Dion 1, 14: 271.
Syrianus: 333.

Tacitus: 299.
Dial. 36-41: 299.
Testamentum Nouum:
Matth. 25, 24: 363.
Act.:
14, 15: 242.
17, 6: 240.
24, 5: 240.
1 Thess. 5, 11: 362.
1 Tim. 6, 17: 346-347, 365, 371.
Testamentum Vetus:
Ex. 6, 9: 360.
Iob:
2, 12: 350.
2, 13: 350.
Is. 1, 30: 356.
Ier. 8, 9, 17: 358.

Am. 8, 9: 357-358.
Themistius: 333.
Theodoretus, *Hist. eccl.* 5, 20: 348.
Theon, Aelius, *Prog.*: 71.
61: 263.
Theophrastus, *Characteres*: 75.
Theopompus, *FGrH* 115 F 88: 87.
Thucydides: 21, 24, 28, 37, 42, 48,
72, 74-75, 77, 92, 113-114, 134,
166, 177.
1: 73.
1, 32, 1: 118.
1, 67, 3: 115.
1, 67, 5: 115-116.
1, 68, 1-2: 118.
1, 73, 1-3: 118.
1, 95, 3: 80.
1, 115, 2: 118.
1, 119-124: 115-116.
2, 36: 52.
2, 60, 1: 47.
2, 60, 5: 47.
2, 61, 2: 47.
2, 85, 5: 85.
3: 369.
3, 4, 4: 121.
3, 9, 1-3: 120.
3, 38, 1: 45.
3, 38, 2-7: 47.
3, 38, 3 ss.: 372.
3, 38, 7: 52.
3, 40: 45.
3, 44, 4: 45.
3, 47, 5: 45.
3, 52, 5-59, 4: 118.
3, 52, 5: 121.
3, 54, 3-5: 176.
3, 56, 3: 45.
3, 59, 3: 45.
3, 62, 2-4: 125.
3, 102, 6: 118.
4, 17, 1: 118.
4, 17, 2-3: 118.

4, 58-65: 115.
4, 59, 1-64, 5: 119.
5, 27, 2: 106.
5, 32, 4-5: 118.
5, 59, 5: 87.
5, 76, 3: 87.
6, 6, 3: 112.
6, 9-23: 45.
6, 16, 1: 47.
6, 16, 3-6: 47.
6, 76, 1-80, 5: 119.
6, 88, 1-3: 120.
6, 92, 2-5: 121.
7, 49, 3: 112.
8, 64, 1-2: 81.
8, 68, 1: 16-18.

Valerius Maximus 2, 2, 3: 189, 207.
Victorinus, Marius: 340.
  Gramm.:
    P. 191, 26-43 Halm: 375.
    P. 285, 23-286, 15 Halm: 375.

Xenophon: 77, 92-113.
  Anab.: 77.
    5, 4, 1-4: 87.
    5, 5, 7-24: 94.
    5, 5, 20: 95.
    5, 5, 22: 95.
    5, 5, 22-23: 95.
    5, 5, 24: 95.
    5, 6, 1-14: 95.
    5, 6, 3-10: 96.
  Apol. Socratis 22: 112.
  Hell.: 93.
    2, 1, 6-7: 99.
    2, 2, 19: 125.
    2, 2, 20: 137.
    3, 1, 8: 80.
    3, 5, 7: 116.
    3, 5, 8-9: 117.

3, 5, 11: 117.
3, 5, 15: 117.
3, 5, 16: 112, 116.
5, 2, 1: 118.
5, 2, 11-23: 94.
5, 2, 12-19: 114.
5, 2, 20: 112.
5, 2, 23: 114.
5, 4, 20-21: 104.
5, 4, 34: 104.
6: 76.
6, 1, 4: 87.
6, 3, 2-17: 100-102.
6, 3, 2-19: 94.
6, 3, 3: 101, 105.
6, 3, 4: 87.
6, 3, 7-8: 107.
6, 3, 8: 107.
6, 3, 9: 106.
6, 3, 10: 108.
6, 3, 18: 103, 109.
6, 3, 19: 109.
6, 4, 19: 94.
6, 5, 33: 122.
6, 5, 33-48: 94, 100.
6, 5, 33-49: 110-112.
6, 5, 35-36: 168-169.
6, 5, 37: 114.
6, 5, 37-48: 89.
7, 1, 1: 114.
7, 1, 1-11: 89.
7, 1, 1-14: 94.
7, 1, 33-38: 124.
7, 4, 39-40: 80.
  Mem.:
    3, 10, 1-8: 93.

Zenobius: 308.
Zenon: 285, 296.
Zosimus 4, 41: 348.

B. Inscriptions et papyrus

Inscriptions:
Année épigraphique (AE):
39, 910 = *IG* XII 8: 235.
1947, 182: 206.
2000, 1377: 185, 199.
2003, 1559: 190-194.
Corpus des inscriptions de Delphes (CID) IV 119 E: 131.
Επιγραφές κάτω Μακεδονίας.
Τεύχος Α, Επιγραφές Βέροιας *(I.Beroia)* 2: 293.
Επιγραφές της Θράκης του Αιγαίου. Μεταξύ των ποταμών Νέστου και Έβρου *(I.Thrac. Aeg.):*
5: 202.
E 205: 130.
Οι επιγραφές του Ωρωπού *(I.Oropos)* (Petrakos):
301: 133.
521: 132.
Fouilles de Delphes. III, Épigraphie *(FD):*
1, 261, l. 4: 131.
2, 94: 133.
Inschriften griechischer Städte aus Kleinasien (IK):
6-*Lampsakos:*
4, l. 43-46: 189.
28, 1-*Iasos:*
3, l. 2-4: 131.
152, l. 31-32: 153.
63, 1-*Metropolis* 1: 132.
Inschriften von Magnesia am Maeander (I.Magnesia) (Kern):
18: 133.
20-65: 153.
25, l. 8-12: 154.
44, l. 25-29: 154.
46, l. 5-16: 154.
48, l. 6: 131.

52, l. 14: 154.
61, l. 11-14: 153.
61, l. 32-37: 153.
61, l. 35: 131.
93, l. 10: 134.
105: 131.
Inschriften von Priene (I.Priene) (Hiller von Gaertringen):
37: 131, 177.
38: 131.
40: 131.
45: 162.
108: 132.
108, 223-230: 185.
109, 91-94: 185.
Inscriptiones antiquae orae septentrionalis Ponti Euxini Graecae et Latinae (IOSPE):
I² 32: 132.
I² 34: 132.
I² 352: 132.
Inscriptiones Creticae (I.Cret.) (Guarducci):
III iv, 9: 131, 167.
III iv, 9, l. 29: 134.
Inscriptiones Graecae (IG):
II² 42: 122.
II² 44: 122.
II² 96: 122.
II² 457: 132.
II² 513: 132.
II² 677: 141.
II² 687: 139.
II² 1224, l. 11: 199.
II² 2778: 133.
II² 3207: 132.
II³ 1239: 162.
II³ 1323: 132.
IV² 2, 1012: 149.
IV² 83-84: 133.
IV² 86: 133.

V 2, 419, l. 4: 131.
VII 4139: 133.
XII 2, 526 + Suppl.: 179.
XII 4, 845: 293.
XII 4, 1036: 132.
XII 7, 53-54: 133.
XII 7, 221b, l. 9: 131.
XII 7, 239: 133.
XII 7, 394: 133.
XII 7, 399-400: 133.
XII 7, 405: 133.
XII 7, 409: 133.
XII 8 = SEG 39, 910: 235.
XII 9, 91: 132.
Lindos. Fouilles et recherches. T. 2,
    Inscriptions (I.Lindos) 2: 182.
Milet. Ergebnisse der Ausgrabungen
    und Untersuchungen seit dem
    Jahre 1899. 1, Heft 3, Das Del-
    phinion (Milet 1, 3):
    139C: 149.
    155: 161.
Monumenta Asiae Minoris Anti-
    qua (MAMA) VIII 413b: 256.
Supplementum epigraphicum Grae-
    cum (SEG):
    XVII 759: 249.
    XVIII 570: 132.
    XXI 469 C: 150.
    XXVIII 60: 132.
    XXXV 823: 193-194.
    XXXVIII 1476: 155-160.
    XXXIX 1243: 132, 184, 199-
        200.
    XXXIX 1244: 132, 183-184,
        199.
    XLIII 434: 256.
    XLVII 498: 133.
    XLIX 1114: 153.
    L 1211: 185.
    L 1211, l. 17-21: 199.
    LIII 659: 190-194.
    LVII 313: 149.
    LVII 1185: 375.
    LXI 352: 143.
Sylloge inscriptionum Graecarum.
    3a ed. (Syll.³) (Dittenberger)
    618: 133.
Tituli Asiae Minoris (TAM) V 3,
    1539: 375.

Papyrus:
    Berliner griechische Urkunden
        (BGU) IV 1140 = CPJ II 151:
        226.
    Berliner Klassikertexte (BKT):
        IX 64: 224.
        IX 115, col. i 7: 217.
    Corpus papyrorum Judaicarum
        (CPJ):
        II 150 = PSI X 1160 (Boule-
            Papyrus): 229-230, 232,
            236, 240, 242, 247, 259,
            pl. 6.5.
        II 150, col. ii 1-14: 242-243.
        II 150, col. ii 6: 236.
        II 150, col. ii 11-14: 213.
        II 150, col. ii 13-14: 240.
        II 150, col. ii 20: 233.
        II 150, col. ii 21: 229.
        II 151 = BGU IV 1140: 226.
        II 153: 21, 218-219, 228,
            254-255, pl. 6.1a-b.
        II 153, col. ii 20-27: 234-235.
        II 153, col. ii 22-23: 247.
        II 153, col. ii 28-iii 48-51: 235.
        II 153, col. iv 66-72: 244.
        II 153, col. iv 67-68: 248.
        II 153, col. iv 75: 212.
        II 153, col. iv 82-v 98: 244-
            245, 248.
        II 153, col. vi 82-v88: 216.
        II 153, l. 74: 217.
        II 153, l. 90-91: 245.
        II 153, l. 98-100: 240.
        II 156a-d: 223.

II 156a, col. i 19: 224.
II 156a, col. ii 5 = 156b, col. i 1: 230.
II 156a, col. ii 5-7 = 156b, col. i 1-3: 230.
II 156a, col. ii 7-8: 231.
II 156a, col. ii 10-11: 234.
II 156b, col. i 1 = 156a, col. ii 5: 230.
II 156b, col. i 1-3 = 156a, col. ii 5-7: 230.
II 156b, col. i 3: 230.
II 156b, col. i 6-8: 234.
II 156b, col. i 13-14: 224.
II 156b, col. i 18: 238.
II 156b, col. i 25-26: 233.
II 156b, col. ii 35-37: 239.
II 156b, col. ii 46-47: 239.
II 156c, col. ii 22: 212, pl. 6.2.
II 156c, col. ii 22-24: 240.
II 156c, col. ii 25-30: 242.
II 156d, col. ii 25-27: 236.
II 156d, col. iii 7-12: 238.
II 157: 224, pl. 6.3a-b.
II 157, col. i 9-11: 213.
II 157, col. i 15-16: 213.
II 157, col. iii 42-43: 240.
II 158a: 213.
II 158a, col. ii 13: 240.
II 158a, col. vi 14: 240.
II 158a, col. vi 16-17: 217.
II 159b: 225.
II 159b, col. ii 5: 225.
II 159b, col. ii 7-13: 237.
II 159b, col. iii 3: 238.
II 159b, col. iii 5-11: 239.
II 159b, col. iii 7-11: 231.
II 159b, col. iii 9 ss.: 239.
II 159b, col. iii 11-iv 2: 231.
II 159b, col. iv 5-7: 224.
II 159b, col. iv 13-v 8: 238.
II 159b, col. iv 15-v 8: 238.
II 438, l. 4: 240.

II 443, col. ii 4-5: 240.
P.Aberd. 117, fr. 2, l. 2: 217.
P.Bour. 7: 236.
P.Giss.Lit. 4, 7: 217, 222, 225-226, pl. 6.4.
Col. ii 4-6: 234.
Col. ii 8: 230.
Col. ii 35-iii 1: 233.
Col. iii 31-32: 217.
P.Harr. II 173, l. 11-12: 236.
P.Mil.Vogl. II 47: 219.
P.Oxy. XXII 2339, col. ii 8-9: 217.
P.Oxy. XXV 2435: 228.
P.Oxy. XXV 2435r: 235, 257.
P.Oxy. XXV 2435v, l. 31-32: 230.
P.Oxy. XXV 2435v, l. 34-40: 230.
P.Oxy. XXV 2435v, l. 40-41, 44: 211.
P.Oxy. XXV 2435v, l. 58-61: 234.
P.Oxy. XLII 3020: 258.
P.Oxy. XLII 3020, fr. 1, col. i: 211, 214, 232.
P.Oxy. XLII 3020, fr. 1, col. ii 1: 233.
P.Oxy. XLII 3020, fr. 1, col. ii 3-7: 213.
P.Oxy. XLII 3021: 223, 241.
P.Oxy. XLII 3021, col. i 12-13: 245.
P.Oxy. XLII 3021, col. i 14-16: 241.
P.Oxy. XLII 3022: 211, 228, 232, 235.
P.Oxy. XLII 3023: 210.
P.Oxy. XLVII 3360: 31.
P.Oxy. LXXIX 5202: 218.
P.Yale II 107: 234.
Papiri greci e latini, Società Italiana per la ricerca dei papiri greci e latini in Egitto (PSI):

X 1160 = *CPJ* II 150 (Boule-
Papyrus): 229-230, 232,
236, 240, 242, 247, 259,
pl. 6.5.
col. ii 6: 236.
col. ii 20: 233.
XI 1222: 210, 249, 254.

Fr. 1, col. i 22-25: 249.
*Sammelbuch Griechischer Urkun-
den aus Ägypten (SB)*:
I 3924: 235.
XII 11012: 210-211, 228.
XII 11012, col. i 1-6: 235-236.

C. Noms de lieux, de personnes et de divinités

Abdère: 202.
Acarnanie, Acarnaniens: 146-147.
Achaïe, Achéens: 198-200.
Achille: 114, 135, 321.
Acilius, Caius: 189.
Aemilius Rectus: 244.
Agamemnon: 135-136, 321.
Agélas: 130.
Agrippa Ier de Judée: 217, 223, 233, 238, 242.
Ainétos: 155.
Alcibiade: 45, 47, 121, 269.
Alétès: 132, 157.
Alexandre Ier de Macédoine: 65.
Alexandre d'Épire: 80, 147.
Alexandre, fils d'Amyntas: 96-100, 109.
Alexandre le Grand: 130, 134, 138, 143, 146, 165, 179-180, 182, 275-276.
Alexandrie, Alexandrins: 39, 209-260, 275, 317.
  Sérapeum: 317, 341.
Amasis: 182.
Amazones: 163-164, 178.
Amphiaraos: 133.
Amphilochus: 180.
Amphipolis: 185, 207.
Antigone Doson: 144.
Antigone Gonatas: 139-142, 145, 147-149.
Antioche: 153, 206, 308-309, 316-318, 322-325, 339, 344-345,

347-353, 355-359, 371-372, 374-375.
Antiochos: 195.
Antipater: 145-146.
Aor: 132, 157.
Apamée: 274, 281.
Aphrodisias: 194, 203, 256.
Apion: 218.
Apollon: 150, 156, 159, 161.
Apollonie sur le Rhyndakos: 161, 177.
Appien, gymnasiarque: 224-225, 231, 237-239.
Aquila, C. Julius: 246.
Arcadiens: 53, 154.
Archélaos, rhéteur: 197.
Argos, Argiens: 21, 25, 87, 106.
Aristide: 60-61.
Aristion: 175.
Aristomédès: 67.
Aristonicos: 184-185, 193.
Arius (Areios): 225-226, 233.
Artémis: 147, 154, 156.
Arthmios de Zéleia: 67, 87.
Asclépios: 156.
Asie: 147, 179, 183-185, 199, 205, 279.
Asie Mineure: 22, 160.
Astymédès: 152, 190, 196, 200.
Athéna Lindia: 182.
Athènes, Athéniens: 24-27, 29, 32, 36, 38-39, 46, 50, 53-54, 58-61, 63-68, 72-73, 80-82, 85, 87,

89-91, 94-111, 113, 115-118, 120-125, 132, 134-137, 139-142, 144-145, 147, 150-151, 157-159, 162-165, 168-169, 175, 177-180, 183, 188-189, 199-200, 202, 206, 236-237, 258, 264-265, 278, 284, 293, 300, 308, 315, 319-321, 334, 337-338, 340, 369.
Acropole: 293.
Parthénon: 141, 178.
Temple d'Athéna Niké: 141-142, 178.
Athénion: 130, 163, 175, 178.
Attale III de Pergame: 184-185, 193.
Auguste, empereur, Octavien: 134, 212, 214-216, 228-230, 232-233, 235-236, 245, 247-248, 258.
Autoclès: 101-102, 105-109, 116.
Avilius Flaccus: 216-217, 219, 226, 231.

Balbillus: 224.
Béroia: 293.
Berytos: 334.
Bithynie: 274, 279.
Briséis: 321.
Brutus: 196.
Byzance, v. Constantinople.

Cadmée: 106.
Caesarius, Flavius: 325, 374.
Caligula: 212, 216-219, 223, 225-227, 229-233, 235, 241, 244-246, 248-249, 257-258.
Callias: 87, 101-107, 180.
Callicratès: 198, 200.
Callistratos: 101-103, 105, 107.
Caracalla: 206, 220, 249.
Cassandre de Macédoine: 32.
Cassius: 196-197.
Caton le Censeur: 190.
Célènes: 275, 283.
Céphallénie: 154.

Céphalos: 154.
César: 197, 229, 233-234, 237. V. aussi Index A s.v. Caesar.
Chabrias: 61.
Chalcis: 29.
Chios: 206.
Chlénéas d'Étolie: 144-146, 152.
Chrémonidès: 139-144, 148-150.
Chrysaor: 137, 157.
Cimon: 60, 312-313.
Claros: 183, 185.
Claude, empereur: 191-194, 211-212, 218-219, 223-224, 228-230, 233-235, 238-241, 244-248, 254-257.
Cleidemos: 180, 182.
Cléon: 45, 47, 52, 369.
Cléopâtre de Macédoine: 80, 130.
Clisthène: 179.
Clitélès: 111, 118.
Colophon, Colophoniens: 183-185, 199.
Commode: 225, 231, 237, 239.
Constantin: 302, 324.
Constantinople: 308, 322, 335, 339, 341, 345.
Constantius: 322.
Corinthe, Corinthiens: 21, 73, 106, 111, 115-116, 125, 137, 141.
Cos: 162, 293.
Crète, Crétois: 154-155, 167.
Ctésiphon: 80, 91.
Cyrus: 162, 269.
Cyténion, Cyténiens: 131, 155-156, 159-160.

Darius: 180.
Delphes: 93, 131, 154, 159.
Déméter: 101, 104.
Démétrius Poliorcète: 256.
Démocharès: 30.
Didyme, avocat: 249.
Dioclétien: 302-303, 341.
Diogène: 271, 276, 296-297.

Doride: 131, 155-156, 159.
Doriens: 132, 135, 155-157.
Égypte, Égyptiens: 133, 209-211, 213-215, 219-220, 224, 227, 236, 241-246, 249-250, 257, 360.
Éleusis, sanctuaire: 103-104.
Ellebichus: 325, 374.
Épaminondas: 265.
Éphèse, Éphésiens: 179, 203, 205-206.
Épidamnos: 154.
Érechthée: 165, 178.
Érèse, Érésiens: 162, 179.
Étéonicos: 99.
Étolie, Étoliens: 144-148, 152, 156, 159, 195, 202-203.
Eulalos: 226.
Eumène II de Pergame: 132, 152.
Eumène III de Pergame, v. Aristonicos.
Eumolpos: 163-165, 175, 178.
Euphrée: 67.

Flavianus, évêque: 345, 374.

Gaius, v. Caligula.
Gaule: 141, 147.
Gélon, tyran de Syracuse: 135.
Germanicus: 228, 234-235, 246, 257.
Glaucon: 143-144.

Hadrien: 233, 237.
Harmodius et Aristogiton: 336-337.
Harpale: 293.
Hécatonymos: 95-96.
Hélène: 320.
Hélicon: 231, 241, 258.
Héphaistos: 149.
Héraclès: 132, 157, 160, 182.
Héraclitos d'Athènes: 141-142.
Hermaiscus: 224.

Hermocratès de Syracuse: 119-120.
Hérode Atticus: 20.
Hiérapytna: 131, 167.
Homonoia: 143-144.

Icarios, *comes Orientis*: 325-326.
Iphicrate: 61.
Isidorus, notable d'Alexandrie: 217, 219, 223-224, 227, 230, 233-234, 236, 238-242.
Isis: 130, 133.
Itanos: 131, 167.

Jérusalem: 356-357.
Job: 350-352, 356, 371.
Juifs: 210-213, 215-229, 232, 236, 240-248, 255, 360.
Julien, empereur: 308, 312-313, 322-323, 336-338. V. aussi Index A *s.v.* Iulianus, imperator.

Korylas, roi de Paphlagonie: 96.

Labienus: 194.
Lampon, notable d'Alexandrie: 219, 223-224, 233.
Lamprias: 155.
Léon, ambassadeur athénien: 195.
Leucippe: 157.
Leucophryène: 157.
Leuctres: 94, 110, 122.
Lycie, Lyciens: 155-157, 196.
Lycortas: 198.
Lycurgue: 110, 181.
Lykiskos d'Acharnanie: 144, 146-148, 152.
Lysandre: 99.
Lysimacheia: 141.

Macédoine, Macédoniens: 91, 93, 96, 123, 144-146, 152, 300.
Macron: 223-224.
Magnès: 154.

Magnésie du Méandre: 131, 153-155, 167.
Mallus: 180.
Manius Aquillius: 199.
Mantinée, Mantinéens: 25, 131, 147.
Marathon: 142.
Marc Antoine: 212, 214.
Marc Aurèle: 237.
Mardonios: 96-99.
Maronée: 130, 191, 193-194, 202.
Massalia: 189, 197.
Megalopolis: 154.
Méléagre: 135.
Ménélas: 182, 320.
Menesthée: 136.
Ménippos de Colophon: 183-185, 199-200.
Ménodoros: 185, 199.
Messalla, M. Valerius: 151.
Messéniens: 65.
Milésios: 177.
Milet, Milésiens: 149-150, 161, 177.
Miltiade: 60-61, 312-313.
Minyens: 169.
Mithridate: 130, 163, 178-179, 189, 191, 193-194, 196-197, 203, 205-206.
Modestos, *comes Orientis*: 306.
Moïse: 360.
Molon, Apollonius: 189-190, 207.
Myrina: 198.
Mytilène, Mytiléniens: 120-121, 206.

Nakone: 179.
Naupacte: 130.
Némésion: 228.
Néron: 210-211, 224, 228, 235-236, 239, 269.
Nerva: 277.
Nestor: 271.
Nicée: 274, 278, 308.
Nicias: 26, 45, 60.

Nicomédie, Nicomédiens: 270, 274, 308, 369, 371.

Olbia: 293.
Oppius, Quintus: 194.
Orchomène: 169.
Oreste: 136.
Oropos: 133, 188.

Paphlagonie, Paphlagoniens: 95.
Pâris: 321.
Paul de Tyr: 213.
Paul-Émile: 185, 196, 207.
Peithenous, fils de Tharsagoras: 149.
Pélopides: 135-136.
Péloponnèse: 93, 100-101, 104, 106-108, 110-113, 120-121.
Pergame: 184-185, 199.
Périclès: 40, 47, 60, 312-313.
Perse, Perses: 22, 27, 37, 135, 140, 142, 144, 147, 163-165, 168, 338.
Phégeus: 155.
Philagrius, *comes Orientis*: 324.
Philippe II de Macédoine: 50-51, 55, 57-60, 62, 64-67, 80, 90, 99, 123, 144-145, 258, 275, 315, 319, 321, 337.
Philippe V de Macédoine: 144, 152, 188, 193, 195, 202, 204.
Philocrate: 55, 63.
Philopoemen: 198.
Phocide: 159.
Phocion: 73.
Phocos: 73.
Platées, Platéens: 132, 142-144, 176, 180.
Plotina: 224, 231.
Polémaios de Colophon: 183-185, 199-200.
Pompée: 206.
Priène: 131-132, 162, 177.
Proclès de Phlionte: 111-113, 118, 122.

Prométhée: 149.
Pruse: 265, 269, 274-275, 278, 280-281, 284-286.
Ptolémée Ier: 150.
Ptolémée II: 139-140, 143, 149-150.
Ptolémée IV: 160.
Ptolémée VIII: 214.
Pydna: 193, 196, 199, 207.
Python de Byzance: 99.

Rhodes, Rhodiens: 54, 131, 152, 177, 189-190, 195-197, 200, 203, 266, 275, 278, 295.
Rome, Empire romain: 152, 185, 191, 193-194, 196-197, 202-204, 206, 209-215, 217-221, 231-232, 237, 243, 247, 250, 254-258, 261, 279-280, 292, 300, 302, 314, 317, 334.

Samos, Samiens: 18-19, 37, 131, 177.
Samothrace: 190, 193.
Septime-Sévère: 194, 219.
Sinope, Sinopéens: 94-96, 99, 117.
Smyrne: 369, 371.
Socrate: 271, 297.
Sopater d'Antioche: 213.
Sparte, Spartiates, Lacédémoniens: 19-22, 25, 51, 53, 80, 84, 87, 98-112, 114-116, 118, 121-124, 135-137, 139-142, 144, 147-148, 159, 163, 168, 180.
Sphodrias: 104, 106.
Sthénélaïdas: 177.
Stratoclès: 181.
Sylla: 163, 165, 175, 178.

Syracuse: 119-120.
Syrie: 245, 249.

Tarse, Tarsiens: 268, 275, 277-278, 283.
Téniens: 162.
Téos: 151, 155, 202.
Thèbes, Thébains: 51, 85-87, 94, 101-102, 104, 106, 110, 116-117, 124-125, 137, 143, 146-147, 168-169, 176, 266, 319-320.
Thémistocle: 60-61, 180.
Théodose: 302, 317-318, 324-325, 334, 345, 347-348, 358, 365.
Théon: 223-224.
Théophane: 206.
Théophile d'Alexandrie: 317.
Thésée: 163-165, 182.
Thrace, Thraces: 145, 163-165, 178.
Tibère: 216-217, 225, 230.
Timocrates, *comes Orientis*: 326.
Timothée, stratège: 61, 66.
Timoxenus, rhéteur: 233.
Trajan: 224-225, 228, 231-232, 235, 275, 277, 333.
Triptolème: 104.
Troie: 135, 320.

Ulysse: 320-321.

Xanthe: 131, 155-157, 159-160, 180.
Xerxès: 135, 148.

Zeus: 149-150.
Zeus Dyctaios: 167.
Zeus Éleuthère: 143-144.

D. Index thématique

Ambassade, ambassadeur: 22, 37, 79-128, 131-133, 138, 146, 152-157, 159-164, 166-168, 183-208, 210-213, 217-219, 221, 223-227, 229-251, 254-258.
amitié: 188, 191, 193, 196, 199-200.

Assemblée: 41-78, 131-132, 138-139, 141, 146, 148-149, 152-156, 160, 163, 166-167, 183-184, 187, 189, 191, 263-265, 268-269, 274-276, 281, 285.

Bienveillance: 232, 234.
boule: 214-215, 219, 229, 240, 242-244, 247-248, 250, 256.

Canon des orateurs attiques: 15-40.
chrétienne (rhétorique) et classicisme: 347, 369-370, 375.
christianisme: 302-303, 318, 333-334.
cité: 22, 44, 51-53, 55-57, 59-61, 66-68, 72, 187-189, 191, 194-195, 203, 205-206, 262, 265-266, 268-269, 274-275, 278-279, 282-283, 285, 294, 300.
citoyenneté: 29, 212, 214, 216, 218-220, 226.
cognitio extra ordinem: 212, 222-223, 225, 231, 259.
collectif (discours): 47, 74, 79-128.
concorde: 261, 274, 277, 282.
confrontation: 212, 223, 238, 242, 249, 279.
conseil: 261-297, 307, 311, 327, 333.
consensus: 354, 372.
contexte historique: 265.
convenance: 21-22, 26-28.
crainte: 21, 25.
critique: 48-49, 57-58, 60, 62, 66-67, 69, 73, 78, 265, 268, 274, 280, 285.
culte impérial: 217, 223, 235-236, 241.

Déclamation: 263, 311-312, 315, 318-327, 335-338, 340-341.
décret: 129-182, 183-185, 187, 189, 191-192, 194, 198-200, 202-203, 205, 211, 216, 226, 234-235.

délibératif, délibération: 15-40, 80, 184, 186-187, 205, 209, 212, 257-260, 261-297, 299-341, 345, 369-370.
démégorique (discours): 26, 31, 35-36, 79-80, 262, 267, 275.
démocratie: 19, 22-23, 187, 262, 267.
déploration: 351-353, 356, 358, 371.
didascalique (discours): 343, 347-348, 370, 372.
discours d'ambassade: 31, 37, 74, 320-321, 323.
docere: 197-200.
documents
    originaux: 227-228, 230, 242, 249, 250.
    copies *verbatim*: 228-229, 255.

Éloge: 48-49, 133, 140, 143, 150, 152, 183, 186-187, 195, 264, 282, 285-286, 355, 361, 371.
émeute: 214, 217-220, 244, 248.
émotions: 135, 137-138, 140, 142-143, 145, 148, 158-160, 176, 178-179, 182, 197, 203, 280.
empereur: 186-187, 191, 275, 280, 282-283, 286.
épidictique: 15, 26, 31, 37, 186-187, 262, 282, 355, 370-371.
ethnarque: 216, 246.
ethos: 41-76, 79-128, 280, 286, 294, 369-370, 373.
exemples historiques, *paradeigmata*: 20-21, 49, 60, 129-182.
exorde: 265, 281-282.

Faux-semblant: 282-283, 286.
flatterie: 282.

Genres rhétoriques: 262-264.
Gérousie: 215-217.
gnome: 49.

guerre: 81, 94, 98, 102, 107, 117, 217.
gymnasiarque: 218-219, 224-225, 231, 238-239, 245.

Hellénisme: 278, 280.
histoire: 205, 319, 324.
historiographie: 93, 100, 119, 122, 125-126, 130-131, 159, 161, 170, 175-176.
homélie: 343-354, 357, 359, 364, 370-372.
humour: 273, 282.

Idioslogos: 213, 243.
impiété: 223, 241.
individu: 265.
interprète: 189-190, 207.
ironie: 283.

Judiciaire (discours): 15-18, 23-24, 26, 28-29, 31-32, 37-39, 186-187, 195, 206.
justice: 21-22, 26-28, 237.

Langage formulaire: 212, 232, 235-236.
laographia: 214, 229, 241.
liberté de parole: 199, 249, 254, 258.
liturgie: 240.
logographie: 17, 33, 37.
logos
    basilikos: 186.
    presbeutikos: 79-80, 186-187.
    stephanôtikos: 186-187.
    symbouleutikos: 79-82, 85, 88, 92, 94, 96, 112-113, 119-120, 124, 186, 262-263, 267, 272, 286, 325, 327.

Médiation: 323, 334.
méta-rhétorique: 48, 51-52, 57-60, 65-68.

municipale (politique): 266, 285.
mythe: 135, 148, 154, 156-157, 176, 180-181, 314, 319.

Naissance noble: 238-240.

Obligation morale: 137-138, 150, 157, 159.
opportunité: 22, 26, 28.
oralité et écriture: 36, 347, 352, 371-372, 374.
oratio recta: 95, 97, 100, 110, 114-117, 120.

Paganisme: 333.
paideia: 250-251.
parénèse: 278.
parler de soi: 48, 51-53, 55-62, 65-66, 68, 74, 280-281.
pathos: 22-23, 320, 324, 346, 370.
persuasion (discours): 213, 256.
philosophie: 261-297.
politeuma: 211, 215, 236.
politique: 183, 195-196, 205, 255, 261-297, 326-327, 343, 370.
possibilité: 26-28.
pouvoir: 168, 187, 194, 203, 205, 214, 227, 251, 276, 280, 286, 299, 305-307, 314, 318, 345-346.
prédicateur: 278.
préfet: 214, 216, 224, 226, 231, 243, 246, 248.
présentation de soi: 45-49, 56, 62, 64, 69, 72-73.
procès: 188, 206, 212, 222-223, 225, 238, 249, 255.
progymnasmata: 311, 313-321, 327, 333, 335-336, 338, 340-341.
prolalie: 281.
proxenos: 85-87, 97, 101, 103-104, 121.

Recensio: 226-227.

récit: 18-19, 22-23.
référence à soi: 47-48, 57, 62, 65-66, 68.
refus: 282, 284.
relations interétatiques: 133, 151-153, 161, 167, 209-260.
relations personnelles: 308-309, 322, 326.
reproche: 195, 275, 278, 283-284.
réseau social: 308-309, 326-327.
responsabilité collective: 124.
Révolte des statues: 345, 348-349, 351, 353-354, 363-364, 375.
révoltes juives: 219, 240.
rhétorique: *passim*.

Seconde sophistique: 187, 292, 301-304, 310, 314, 321, 333, 340-341.
Sénat romain: 183-208.
sophistique: 281.

stratégie rhétorique: 88-93, 99, 105, 114.
style: 263, 267, 281-282, 285-286.
sujets de la rhétorique délibérative: 261, 263, 265, 270, 274, 276, 296.
superbia: 190, 195, 203.
synagogue: 217.
synegoros: 89-90, 105, 112-113, 116, 126.
synkrisis: 259-260.

Topos: 48, 51-53, 58-59, 62, 355, 369, 371.
traité: 139, 147, 149-150, 162.
transition: 282.
transmission des textes des discours: 221, 272-273.
Troisième sophistique: 292, 299-341.
tyran, tyrannie: 314-316, 336-338.

TABLE DES ILLUSTRATIONS

Pl. 0.1. *La Rhétorique d'Aristote en françois*, Paris, Denis Thierry, 1675. Deuxième édition, revue et corrigée, de la traduction de François Cassandre. Exemplaire du dramaturge Jean Racine, avec signature (sur le titre) et notes autographes. © Fondation Martin Bodmer, Cologny.

Pl. 6.1a. Letter of Emperor Claudius to the Alexandrians: *CPJ* II 153 (*P.Lond.* 1912; 29 × 116.5 cm [W x H]). © British Library Board (pap. inv. 2248).

Pl. 6.1b. Letter of Emperor Claudius to the Alexandrians: *CPJ* II 153 (*P.Lond.* 1912). Detail: column v. © British Library Board (pap. inv. 2248).

Pl. 6.2. *Acta Isidori: CPJ* II 156c (14 × 19.5 cm [W x H]). © Staatliche Museen zu Berlin – Ägyptisches Museum und Papyrussammlung, P 8877 V.

Fig. 6.3a. *Acta Hermaisci: CPJ* II 157 (15.8 × 53.9 cm [W × H]). © British Library Board (pap. inv. 2436).

Fig. 6.3b. *Acta Hermaisci: CPJ* II 157. Detail: column iii. © British Library Board (pap. inv. 2436).

Fig. 6.4. Record of the hearing of two embassies (Greek Alexandrian and Jewish) in front of Caligula: *P.Giss.Lit.* 4.7, fr. A (21.5 × 28.5 cm [W × H]). © Papyrussammlungen der Justus-Liebig-Universität Gießen (P. B.U.G. Inv. 308), Fr. A.

Fig. 6.5. The "Boule-Papyrus": *CPJ* II 153 (*PSI* X 1160). Firenze, Biblioteca Medicea Laurenziana, Ms. 18108 (16.5 × 23 cm [W × H]). Reproduced by permission of the Ministero delle Attività Culturali e del Turismo (MiBACT). Further reproduction in any form is strictly forbidden.

LA
RHETORIQUE
D'ARISTOTE
EN FRANCOIS.

TRADVCTION NOVVELLE.

Racine

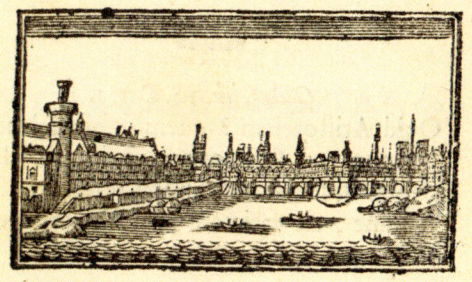

A PARIS,

Chez DENYS THIERRY, ruë S. Jacques,
à l'Enfeigne de la Ville de Paris.

M. DC. LXXV.

AVEC PRIVILEGE DV ROY.

Pl. 0.1

Pl. 6.1a

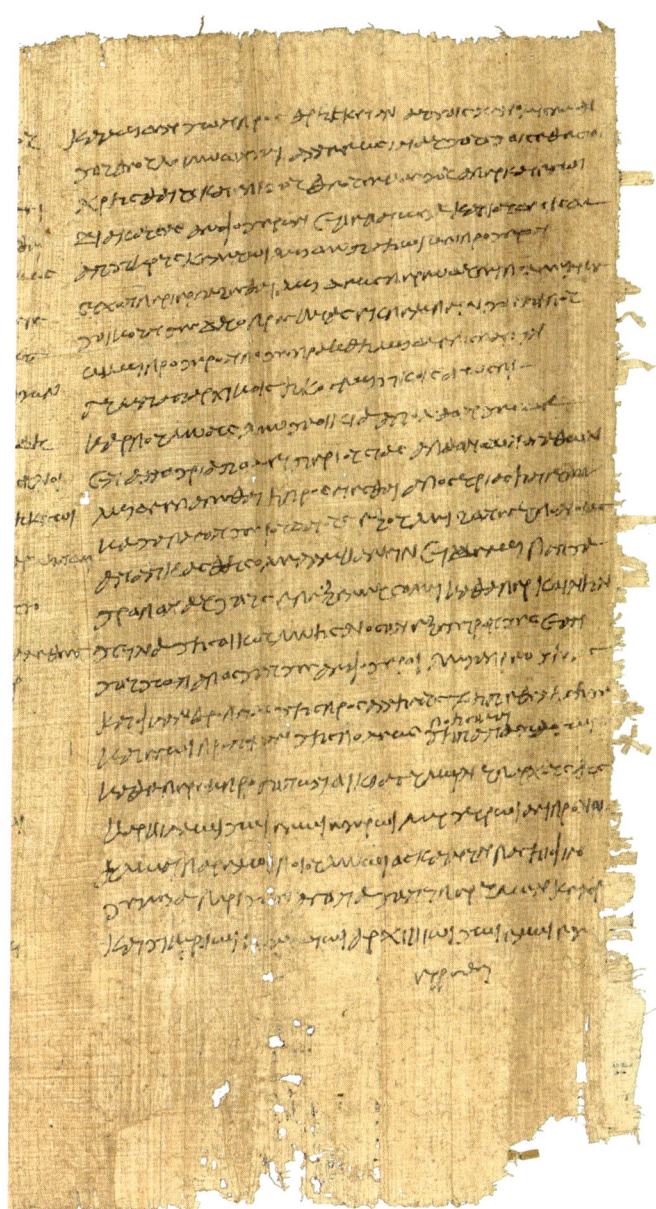

Pl. 6.1b

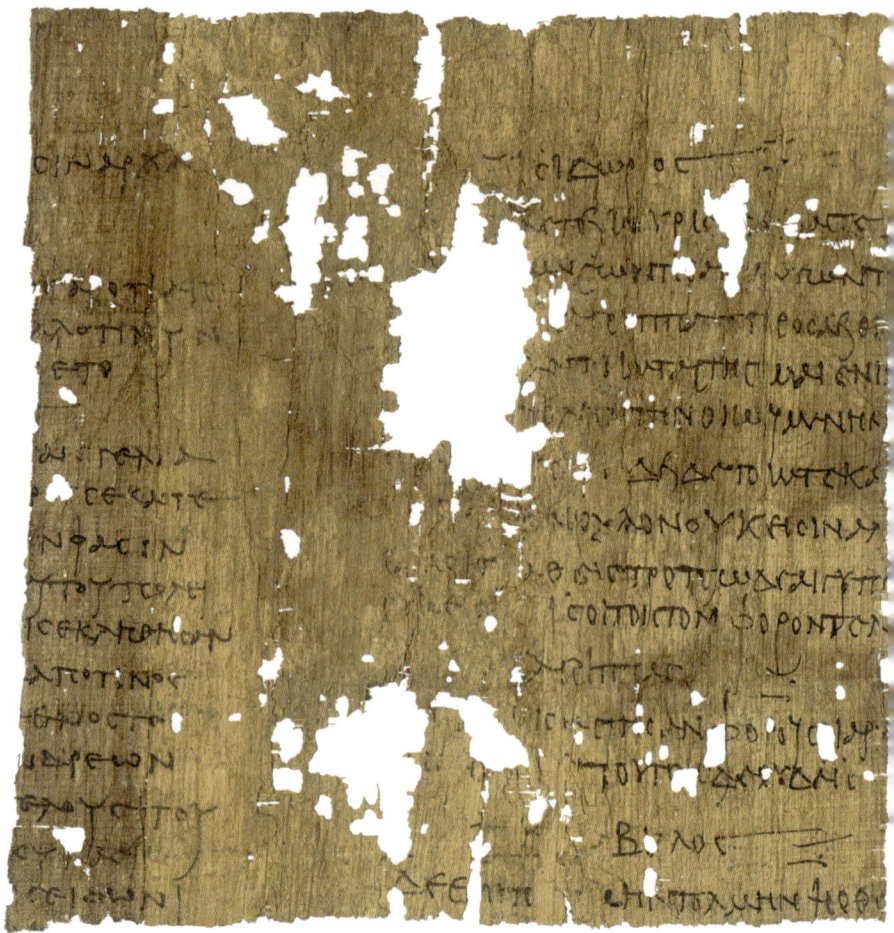

Pl. 6.2

Pl. 6.3a

Pl. 6.3b

Pl. 6.4

Pl. 6.5